Industrial Relations

Industrial Relations in Context

General Editors: Paul Edwards, Richard Hyman and Keith Sisson

INDUSTRIAL RELATIONS

Theory and Practice in Britain

Edited by
PAUL EDWARDS

BLACKWELL
Business

Copyright © Blackwell Publishers Ltd, 1995

First published 1995
Reprinted 1996

Blackwell Publishers Ltd
108 Cowley Road
Oxford OX4 1JF
UK

Blackwell Publishers Inc.
238 Main Street
Cambridge, Massachusetts 02142
USA

British Library Cataloguing in Publication Data

A CIP catalogue record for this book is available from the British Library.

Library of Congress Cataloging in Publication Data

Industrial relations: theory and practice in Britain / edited by Paul Edwards.
    p.   cm.
    'A completely revised version of Industrial relations in Britain'–Foreword.
    Includes bibliographical references and index.
    ISBN 0–631–19166–6
    1. Industrial relations – Great Britain.   I. Edwards, P. K. (Paul K.)
    II. Industrial relations in Britain.   III. Series: Human
resource management (Cambridge, Mass.)
    HD8391.I478 1995
    331'. 0941–dc20   94–38016
                                             CIP
    ISBN 0–631–19166–6

Typeset in 11 on 13pt Plantin
by Best-set Typesetter Ltd., Hong Kong
Printed in Great Britain by Hartnolls Limited, Bodmin, Cornwall

This book is printed on acid-free paper.

Contents

Figures and Tables

Figures

Tables

Contributors

Stephen Bach: Lecturer in Industrial Relations, School of Industrial and Business Studies, University of Warwick.

William Brown: Professor of Industrial Relations, University of Cambridge.

Trevor Colling: Senior Research Fellow, de Montfort University Business School.

Colin Crouch: Professor of Comparative Social Institutions, European University Institute, Florence, and Fellow, Trinity College, Oxford.

Linda Dickens: Professor of Industrial Relations, School of Industrial and Business Studies, University of Warwick.

Paul Edwards: Professor of Industrial Relations and Deputy Director, Industrial Relations Research Unit, University of Warwick.

Anthony Ferner: Principal Research Fellow, Industrial Relations Research Unit, University of Warwick.

John Geary: Lecturer, Graduate School of Business, University College, Dublin.

Mark Hall: Senior Research Fellow, Industrial Relations Research Unit, University of Warwick.

Richard Hyman: Professor of Industrial Relations, School of Industrial and Business Studies, University of Warwick.

Ewart Keep: Senior Research Fellow, Industrial Relations Research Unit, University of Warwick.

Ian Kessler: Research Fellow, Templeton College, Oxford.

Sonia Liff: Lecturer, School of Industrial and Business Studies, University of Warwick.

Paul Marginson: Senior Lecturer in Industrial Relations, School of Industrial and Business Studies, University of Warwick.

Peter Nolan: Montague Burton Professor of Industrial Relations, School of Business and Economic Studies, University of Leeds.

Kathy O'Donnell: Senior Lecturer in Economics, School of Business and Economic Studies, University of Leeds.

John Purcell: Fellow in Human Resource Management, Templeton College, Oxford.

Helen Rainbird: Professor of Social Sciences, Nene College, Northampton.

Jill Rubery: Senior Lecturer, Manchester School of Management.

Richard Scase: Professor of Sociology, University of Kent at Canterbury.

Keith Sisson: Professor of Industrial Relations and Director, Industrial Relations Research Unit, University of Warwick.

Michael Terry: Reader in Industrial Relations, School of Industrial and Business Studies, University of Warwick.

Jeremy Waddington: Senior Research Fellow, Industrial Relations Research Unit, University of Warwick.

Janet Walsh: Lecturer in Industrial Relations, School of Business and Economic Studies, University of Leeds.

Colin Whitston: Lecturer, Department of Human Resource Management and Industrial Relations, University of Keele.

David Winchester: Senior Lecturer in Industrial Relations, School of Industrial and Business Studies, University of Warwick.

Foreword

This book is a completely revised version of *Industrial Relations in Britain*, the text with which George Bain launched the 'Industrial Relations in Context' series. Since then, there have been six other volumes: *Labour Law in Britain* (1986), edited by Roy Lewis; *Employment in Britain* (1988), edited by Duncan Gallie; *Personnel Management in Britain* (1989), plus the extensively revised and enlarged *Personnel Management* (1994), both edited by Keith Sisson; and two European volumes, *Industrial Relations in the New Europe* (1992), and *New Frontiers in European Industrial Relations* (1994), both edited by Anthony Ferner and Richard Hyman.

Each volume comprises original essays, by acknowledged experts, that bring together theoretical and empirical knowledge and understanding. Each emphasizes analysis and explanation as well as description. And each volume is welded into a coherent whole by its editor.

The series is intended for students taking postgraduate, undergraduate and diploma courses in universities and colleges in industrial relations and human resource management as well as students of industrial sociology, labour economics, labour law, and business studies. Though the volumes are analytical and comprehensive, and though the apparatus of bullet points and questions for further discussion is avoided, they are also relevant to those in adult education and to practitioners in management and trade unions. They are written clearly and they summarize and synthesize an array of evidence and argument. They avoid undue simplification and they aim to deepen understanding of complex and often controversial topics.

As explained in the Preface, the present volume aims to continue many of the strengths of its predecessor. In particular, that volume, as well as selling in large numbers for more than a decade, served to take stock of several questions of theory and practice. One index of this is the degree to which it is, unusually for a text, cited in research publications as an authoritative analytical statement. Though much has changed in the world of industrial relations, the book has dated more slowly than many. We hope that the present volume helps to maintain this tradition.

Anthony Ferner
Richard Hyman
Keith Sisson

Preface

This book is the successor to *Industrial Relations in Britain*, edited by George Bain and published in 1983. It is a descendant rather than simply a second edition. This is signalled in the change of title.

In terms of continuity, it aims to retain the qualities of the original: comprehensiveness, and an authoritative blend of description and analysis. One feature calls for particular emphasis at present. Universities are now accustomed to the evaluation and ranking of their research activity, a process unheard of in 1983. It is currently widely rumoured that articles in refereed journals will be given particular weight, with textbooks and other forms of output being given less value. There are certain textbooks, in all social science disciplines, which merely offer potted summaries of others' work and in which the author's own views, if indeed there are any, are hard to discern. *Industrial Relations in Britain*, and the five successor volumes in the Industrial Relations in Context series, eschew this easy path. Each chapter aims to synthesize an array of material within an original argument. Successful work of this kind calls for deep knowledge of a field, the analytical ability to stand back from the detail and generate a satisfying overview, and the presentational skills to convey the information clearly. These attributes are at least as valuable as those needed for the writing of specialist journal articles. In the case of *Industrial Relations in Britain*, several chapters are frequently cited in research publications, thus indexing their role in developing explanation, and not merely summarizing the work of others. The present book hopes to continue this mode of analysis.

The original volume was conceived as mainly a Warwick product. This approach has been continued. The list of contributors reflects a heavy reliance on the industrial relations teaching and research community at Warwick. Other contributors have strong links with the University. In some other cases, experts from other institutions have been asked to contribute their specialized knowledge of their subject fields.

Yet this book also differs from its predecessor. Most obviously, it analyses the massive changes in the world of industrial relations since 1983. In some cases, chapters on established themes, such as trade unions and strikes, have been retained, though all are completely new and several have new authors. In other cases, major new issues such as the rise of individualism, the effects of privatization, and the links between industrial relations and productivity, have come to the fore.

In some respects, new developments integrate the volume more than its predecessor: a theme of most chapters is the nature of change, together with the reasons for it and the extent to which it marks a qualitative shift from the past. This development has also meant, however, an overlap of themes. It is less easy than it once was to have largely free-standing chapters. Every effort has been made to eliminate repetition, but there is necessarily some reiteration as separate chapters need to address common themes such as the rise of market-based approaches to labour management. I hope that the overlap is constructive, in pointing to linkages between different topics.

One role of the final chapter is to draw together these linkages. In doing this, the place of each chapter should be underlined. Though common themes are addressed, and though the authors share some broad perspectives, there are naturally differences of emphasis and interpretation. Each chapter is written by an expert, whose arguments speak for themselves. No attempt has been made to impose complete uniformity. The final chapter represents one particular interpretation of events which would not necessarily be shared by all contributors.

A final aspect of development, which reflects the ways in which chapter authors have interpreted their task and of which the editor can claim little credit, is the analytical depth of many of the contributions. Industrial relations used to be chastised for its lack of theory (always somewhat unfairly, for analysis was often present but it was not expressed in the formal equations that represent Theory for economists, or the abstract jargon that performs the same function for sociologists). We know much more, analytically and not just descriptively, than we used to about the behaviour of management, the role of the state, the sources of discrimination and disadvantage in the labour market, the links between firms and markets, and the day-to-day regulation of work. Several chapters provide analytical treatments of such issues which will be of value to students of industrial relations in any country. But in all cases they illustrate these points by reference to the British experience. The book is less a summary of the institutions of industrial relations in Britain in the mid-1990s than an analysis of the nature of the field with reference to this particular case. The title, *Industrial Relations: Theory and Practice in Britain*, is intended to reflect this aspect.

In other respects, there is more diversity than in 1983. The boundaries of the field of industrial relations are less clear-cut than they used to be. There is also a growing wish to address debates in related disciplines. Whereas the first volume did not need to ask what industrial relations was, this is no longer the case. Hence the first chapter considers the nature and development of the subject. It tries to indicate what is distinctive while recognizing that industrial relations is less separate from other fields than it was. As with the interpretation of events in chapter 20, the analytical view of the coherence of a subject called industrial relations may not be shared by all contributors.

In the real world, moreover, the linkages between industrial relations and economic change and corporate policy are increasingly apparent. This issue is addressed in several chapters, notably those on management and collective bargaining (chapters 4 and 5), which demonstrate how behaviour in industrial relations is shaped by business strategy and structure. But the inclusion of a separate chapter on the economic context (chapter 3) particularly reflects the importance of viewing industrial relations in a broader perspective than used to be the case, a point made explicitly by its authors.

A final element of continuity and change is the number of acronyms in the field and the frequency with which they change. The glossary lists some of the most common abbreviations, and each chapter explains its own specific terms. One feature is worth highlighting for the reader new to the subject. Information on industrial relations is published not only in books and academic journals but also in reports and specialist publications by organizations referred to by acronyms. These are particularly important for studying contemporary developments in a rapidly changing field. The publications of two independent organizations, Incomes Data Services (IDS) and Industrial Relations Services (see IRRR), are cited frequently throughout the book. As indicated in the glossary, each produces several types of report; these are available in most university and college libraries as well as the larger public libraries. Other research bodies include the Institute of Employment Studies (IES), based at the University of Sussex; the London School of Economics (LSE), notably its Centre for Economic Performance; and the source of the present book, the Industrial Relations Research Unit at Warwick. Bodies such as ACAS and the EOC also produce significant reports. Other sources of information include the press, particularly the *Financial Times*, and for statistical information on the labour market, the Employment Department's *Gazette*. Articles in practitioner journals, notably *Personnel Management*, often address contemporary issues in an analytical way. The main academic journals are the *British Journal of Industrial Relations* and the *Industrial Relations Journal*, but other journals also include relevant articles. These other journals include *Work, Employment and Society* (from a sociological viewpoint, often examining work experience and the 'labour process'), the *Industrial Law Journal*, and the *Human Resource Management Journal*.

Returning to this volume, a major feature of continuity is the support necessary to complete such a project. I am grateful to many colleagues in the Industrial Relations Research Unit for guidance on the overall shape of the book as well as on specific features of it, and to Norma Griffiths who acted as secretary to the whole project. I am also very grateful to the contributors, who have produced their material to deadlines despite, in many cases, numerous other demands on their time. Several, notably John Geary and Keith Sisson, have also helped with the overall shape of the volume.

Finally, George Bain established the model not only for this book but for its companion volumes in the Industrial Relations in Context series. Everyone associated with the series owes a great debt to him. I also have a more personal debt in that George was Director of the Industrial Relations Research Unit when, having failed to obtain a number of academic jobs, I applied, with some trepidation, to join it in 1977. As well as being willing to hire me, George offered me every encouragement to pursue my research interests, even when they did not follow his own preferences. I owe to him nothing less than the opportunity to develop an academic career. I hope that the present volume does not depart too far from his exacting standards.

Paul Edwards

Common Abbreviations

ACAS	Advisory, Conciliation and Arbitration Service
AEEU	Amalgamated Engineering and Electrical Union (merger of AEU and EETPU)
AEU/AUEW	Amalgamated Engineering Union, previously Amalgamated Union of Engineering Workers (*see* AEEU)
ASTMS	Association of Scientific, Technical and Managerial Staff (*see* MSF)
CBI	Confederation of British Industry
CCT	Compulsory competitive tendering
COHSE	Confederation of Health Service Employees (*see* Unison)
Donovan	Royal Commission on Trade Unions and Employers' Associations, chaired by Lord Donovan, 1965–8
EA	Employment Act (of various years)
EAT	Employment Appeal Tribunal
ED	Employment Department (previously Department of Employment (DE) and other similar titles)
EEF	Engineering Employers' Federation
EETPU	Electrical, Electronic, Telecommunications and Plumbing Union (*see* AEEU)
EO	Equal opportunities
EOC	Equal Opportunities Commission
ET	Employment Training
GMB	General, Municipal and Boilermakers' Union
HRM	Human resource management

IDS	Incomes Data Services (the pay research body which produces series entitled *Focus*, *Study* and *Report*)
ILO	International Labour Organization
IPM	Institute of Personnel Management (now Institute of Personnel and Development, IPD)
IR Act	Industrial Relations Act 1971
IRRR	*Industrial Relations Review and Report* (a bimonthly publication by Industrial Relations Services, now known as *Employment Trends*; each issue also contains the *Pay and Benefits Bulletin* and the *Industrial Relations Legal Information Bulletin*)
ITB	Industrial Training Board
JIT	Just in time
LFS	Labour Force Survey
LRD	Labour Research Department
MNC	Multinational corporation
MSC	*see* TA
MSF	Manufacturing, Science, Finance (the white-collar trade union, formed by merger of ASTMS and TASS)
NALGO	National and Local Government Officers' Association (*see* Unison)
NEDO	National Economic Development Office
NES	New Earnings Survey
NUPE	National Union of Public Employees (*see* Unison)
NVQ	National Vocational Qualification
OECD	Organization for Economic Cooperation and Development
PRP	Performance related pay
QC	Quality circle
TA	Training Agency (formerly Manpower Services Commission)
TASS	Technical, Administrative and Supervisory Staffs section (*see* MSF)
TECs	Training and Enterprise Councils
TGWU	Transport and General Workers' Union
TQM	Total quality management
TUC	Trades Union Congress
UCATT	Union of Construction, Allied Trades and Technicians

Unison	The public sector union, formed in 1993 through amalgamation of COHSE, NALGO and NUPE
VET	Vocational education and training
WIRS	Workplace Industrial Relations Surveys (WIRS1, 2 and 3, conducted in 1980, 1984 and 1990)

PART I

Introduction

1

The Employment Relationship

Paul Edwards

'People are our most important asset', say many large companies; politicians and commentators stress the role of a skilled and committed workforce in Britain's competitiveness. As with all hackneyed phrases, there is an important truth in such statements. Global competition is intensifying, technology is widely available, and a country such as Britain has few natural resources on which to depend. The organization of work is thus central, particularly the large part of the work of the economy performed through paid employment. Industrial relations studies the relationship between employer and employee in paid employment: the ways in which employees are rewarded, motivated, trained and disciplined, together with the influence on these processes of the major institutions involved, namely, managements, trade unions and the state.

The central parts of this chapter lay out an analytical approach to the subject. But intellectual approaches do not exist in a vacuum. Some features of the employment relationship have received much more attention than others, and in practice 'industrial relations' has meant a subset of possible issues. It thus helps to begin by outlining why these issues have been the focus and how they have been approached. Finally, the structure of the book is explained.

Focus and Development of the Subject

What is industrial relations?

Until the end of the 1970s, industrial relations was an evident issue of national importance. The militant shop steward was a popular figure in the press. The 'winter of discontent' of 1978–9 became a powerful image in the then Conservative opposition's election campaign of 1979. As well as overt conflict, more fundamental aspects of the British industrial relations system attracted attention. They included wage inflation and the level of labour productivity, which was often attributed to restrictive practices on the shopfloor. Trade unions were significant institutions, influential not only at the workplace but also in national political debates. Reasons for studying the subject thus seemed obvious: how serious were strikes, what did shop stewards really do, what went on inside unions, and how might the relations between unions and managements best be handled?

During the 1980s, a series of economic, political and legal changes produced dramatic changes in the contours of British industrial relations. The number of strikes fell to levels not seen since the 1930s, and trade unions lost membership and influence. Basic assumptions about the regulation of the employment relationship altered substantially. Collective bargaining between managements and unions, which had been the officially approved method since a Royal Commission of 1894, no longer received government support. Managements, which during the 1970s had favoured institutional reform and the formalization of the position of the shop steward, now often ignored stewards; some consciously turned their backs on what they saw as a rule-bound and proceduralist approach in favour of teamwork, quality circles, and direct communication with the shopfloor.

A first task for a text is to review and account for the extent of change. This book does this in three ways. First, specific indicators such as strikes and union membership are examined. Second, underlying processes are addressed. A key theme is that many of the basic assumptions and approaches governing industrial relations display important continuities with the past. Finally, there are substantial parts of the labour force which have barely been touched by the 'new industrial relations', and they have to be taken into account when the balance sheet of change and continuity is drawn up.

The second rationale concerns the meaning of the term 'industrial relations' (IR). The term can imply a focus solely on the collective relationships between managements and unions, together with a bias towards industry in the sense of manufacturing and away from the service sector. If the field were being defined from scratch, a term such as 'employment relations' might be preferable (Sisson 1991). But 'industrial relations' has become established, and there is no reason to abandon it once its remit is properly understood.

A standard text defines IR as the 'study of the rules governing employment' (Clegg 1979: 1). This does not limit the subject to the collective relations between managements and trade unions, for a rule can derive from other sources, and there are rules governing non-union groups; nor does it restrict analysis to one sector, for it covers all forms of paid employment. A rule is a social institution involving two or more parties which may have its basis in law, a written collective agreement, an unwritten agreement, a unilateral decree or merely an understanding that has the force of custom. In non-union settings, as much as in union ones, rules determine rates of pay, hours of work, job descriptions and many other aspects of employment. The subject is thus about the ways in which the employment relationship is regulated. To regulate means to control, to adapt or adjust continuously or to adjust by rule. Regulation is here conceived in this broad manner.

The rules of employment are shaped by their legal, political, economic, social and historical context: legal because the law defines certain rules, for example on the fairness of dismissal; political because the approaches to industrial relations of political parties can plainly differ, with some differences being reflected in legislation and others indirectly (for example differing beliefs in the value of incomes policies or intervention in industrial disputes); economic because the state of the economy affects the bargaining power of workers and managements; social because norms in society as a whole affect behaviour (for example, British workers differ markedly from their counterparts in other countries in their views about social inequality, and this affects their behaviour within the workplace); and historical (since the legacy of the past shapes current developments, a point which applies particularly strongly in Britain). A proper understanding of the employment relationship thus needs to be multi-disciplinary.

Less obviously, the various elements of this context do not exert direct effects on behaviour. Consider the law, for example. Some laws can simply be ignored. Others give the parties rights which they have to choose whether to exercise. Thus employers have the right to seek injunctions against unions over the conduct of industrial action, but the use of this right depends on a calculation of the costs and benefits, notably whether the short-term gain in relation to a particular dispute outweighs the long-term effect on the continuing relationship with the union (Evans 1987). Other laws depend on a complaint to be implemented. British laws on unfair dismissal and on sex discrimination generally require an aggrieved party to enter a complaint, a process shaped by knowledge of legal rights, the power to pursue a case and many other factors. Finally, there may be alternatives to the law. An employer may be more dissuaded from dismissing a worker by the bargaining power of a union than by legal rights. Understanding the role of law in industrial relations calls not just for analysis of statute and case law but also for a consideration of the interaction between law and other processes of regulation. Industrial relations is more than just a field of inquiry in which separate academic disciplines apply their own approaches. The test of the relevance of a discipline is whether the use of it informs understanding of the employment relationship rather than merely taking industrial relations phenomena to address debates within the discipline.

Development of the subject

The academic analysis of industrial relations dates back to a series of studies by Sidney and Beatrice Webb during the late nineteenth and early twentieth centuries. The Webbs introduced one of the subject's key terms, collective bargaining. A collective bargain is an agreement between an employer, or a group of employers, and the representatives of a group of workers, which prescribes certain rules. These rules may be substantive (the level of wages to be paid, holiday entitlements, and so on) or procedural (for example, what is to be done if there is a dispute between the parties). Collective bargaining was distinguished from unilateral regulation (by employer or union) and from the statutory determination of the terms and conditions of employment.

In many countries, statutory regulation is particularly important. There are two aspects of this: the direct setting of the rules of work through the law, and an indirect effect through the legal enforceability of collective agreements. The former means that certain issues are taken out of the realm of collective bargaining. The effect of the latter is to give a clear standing to the collective agreement. This encourages the settling of significant substantive issues through such agreements, which often operate at the level of a whole industry or even nationally (Ferner and Hyman 1992). In Britain, by contrast, there developed the tradition of voluntarism, discussed in chapter 2. Not only did this exclude the state from any direct role in creating the rules of the employment relationship, but it also saw the collective agreement as no more than a 'gentleman's agreement'. It was not legally binding, and focused on procedural rather than substantive issues.

If the exclusion of statutory regulation reflects the voluntarist tradition, the neglect of unilateral regulation is less easily explained. That by unions has certainly been of declining importance. The Webbs were thinking of the regulation of apprenticeship and many other aspects of work practised by traditional craft unions, but the development of mass production increasingly limited such job controls to small sectors of employment.

Employer unilateralism has been much more important. For only a very few years has union membership in Britain exceeded 50 per cent, so most employees do not participate in collective bargaining. With the benefit of hindsight, several factors explain the focus on collective bargaining. First, the problem of regulation was assumed to refer to only some employees. For example, managers and workers in small firms were not felt to represent distinct issues. Second, some institutions operated alongside collective bargaining. In particular, as discussed in chapter 18, wages councils, which covered at their peak almost 20 per cent of the workforce, were legally empowered to set terms and conditions for the low-paid in ways analogous to bargaining; a common assumption was that the councils would evolve into genuine collective bargaining. Third, since the end of the nineteenth century it was public policy to promote collective bargaining as the desired means of resolving disputes. Collective bargaining thus seemed to be the core institution of British industrial relations.

A small academic community analysing bargaining and related issues followed the lead of the Webbs and began to grow in the 1950s (see Bain and Clegg 1974). But industrial relations did not emerge as a subject of public concern until the 1960s. In 1965 a Royal Commission, usually called the Donovan Commission after its chairman, was established to investigate the state of labour–management relations. Donovan brought into focus a series of concerns and analytical approaches to them. The concerns were the level of unofficial strikes, the role of the shop steward, and the extent of wage drift (that is, the growth of wages outside increases agreed by formal agreements). These concerns reflected the belief that the 'formal system' of collective bargaining was out of tune with reality. Agreements often set no more than minimum standards, and the effective determination of the rules of employment took place informally.

Analysis focused on the ways in which the 'system' could be reformed in order to resolve these issues. The Commission favoured the voluntary action of employers and unions, as opposed to compulsion by the state. Since it was employers who were in the first instance responsible for the rules of employment, the burden of reform was placed primarily on their shoulders. The Donovan prescription was to regularize 'disorder' on the shopfloor by introducing formal procedures for resolving disputes, by recognizing the position of the shop steward, and by developing comprehensive bargaining arrangements at the level of the company. During the 1970s much of the analytical debate considered how far reform had been achieved; if it had, what were its costs and benefits to the parties to the employment relationship; and whether it had promoted the wider aim of improving the performance of the economy.

This focus on the institutions of collective bargaining was challenged by a series of developments. First, it became increasingly clear that the Donovan agenda applied only to part of the economy, namely, those private sector firms which were unionized and which were large enough for proceduralization to be relevant. Most attention was addressed to the public sector, where a series of disputes throughout the 1970s made the state of its industrial relations a debating point for the first time. But there were also large parts of the private sector which lay outside the reform agenda, reflected in growing concerns about the failure of existing institutions to improve the relative position of the low-paid, most of whom were not covered by collective bargaining. Most of the low-paid are women; this fact was long-recognized, but it gained particular significance with the emergence of feminism. The adequacy of collective bargaining as a means of pursuing women's interests was increasingly questioned, as indeed was the broader assumption that it was possible to study the employment relationship without explicit attention to gender issues.

Second, several other developments were impinging on collective bargaining. Governments of both major parties, faced with growing problems of economic management, tried to shape the regulation of the employment relationship directly, through new labour laws, and indirectly, notably through incomes policies. Part of this new strand of regulation could involve cooperation between governments, unions and employers' associations at national level, a set of relations often analysed through the concept of corporatism (Crouch 1977; see chapter 8 below).

Third, there was growing recognition of a need to deepen analysis of collective bargaining empirically and analytically. A key empirical factor was managerial policy. Though the structure of collective bargaining explained a great deal about such things as trade union behaviour, this structure was itself shaped by the policies of employers (Clegg 1976). More generally still, key decisions affecting labour, for example on investment and plant location, were made outside collective bargaining, and it was necessary to explore firms' business structures and strategies (Purcell 1983). Analytically, bargaining relationships came to be seen as a reflection of a more fundamental set of power relations (Hyman 1989: ch. 2): 'industrial relations' was an institutionalized expression of the conflict between capital and labour. These two concerns were combined in a new analysis, often from outside IR as traditionally defined, of the 'labour process'. This highlighted the fact that the worker's wage buys only the capacity to work, with this capacity being translated into actual labour within the process of production. Collective bargaining was only part of a much wider set of relationships. Central to these was managerial strategy of labour control (Friedman 1977).

In short, a focus on collective bargaining no longer captured the key issues of the regulation of the employment relationship. This fact became increasingly evident during the 1980s and 1990s, in all three of the aspects identified above. Under the first head of the appropriateness of a collective bargaining model, so-called atypical forms of employment, such as temporary, casual and above all part-time work, grew in importance. Many of the workers concerned were not covered by collective bargaining; more fundamentally, there was the question of the relevance of a model based on permanent employment to a group without permanent ties. In the second area, the operation of political forces, a series of Conservative governments aimed to dismantle institutions that were felt to interfere with the free working of the labour market. Employers also moved away from institutional reform towards the reassertion of managerial authority. This could involve a simple authoritarian style, or a use of 'human resource management' techniques, or a range of intermediate positions. But the common feature was the distrust of proceduralism and collectivism. Finally, at shopfloor level, the issues shifted from worker resistance towards the reimposition of managerial control and the effects of this on the degree of workers' subordination. As this book demonstrates, research has addressed all these issues. What analytical tools have been available to guide it?

The Nature of the Employment Relationship

This section considers the basic nature of the employment relationship. One of the best-known debates revolves around three 'frames of reference', which are still often presented in textbooks, sometimes as self-contained approaches from which the reader can apparently choose at will. They are presented briefly before a more adequate view is then outlined, first by considering the nature of rules and then by sketching some analytical themes. Finally some issues of research method are indicated.

Frames of reference

The origin of the debate on frames of reference was a distinction made by Fox (1966) between unitary and pluralist approaches. The unitary view is that there is an identity of interest between employer and employee. Any conflict that may occur is then seen as 'the result of misunderstanding or mischief; in other words, as pathological' (Crouch 1982: 18). Pluralists see conflict as inevitable because, to cite Clegg (1979: 1) again, various organizations participate in determining the rules of employment, these have their own bases of authority, and 'whenever there are separate sources of authority there is the risk of conflict'. Pluralism underlay the views of the Donovan Commission, in particular as they affected the approach of management: instead of a unitary denial that there was any rational basis for conflict, managers should recognize the inevitability of disputes and seek means to regulate them. In Flanders' (1970: 172) oft-quoted dictum, 'the paradox, whose truth managements have found it so difficult to accept, is that they can only regain control by sharing it'.

The third, radical, approach developed as a critique, or in the significant case of Fox (1974) an auto-critique, of pluralism (see also Goldthorpe 1977; Hyman 1978). Pluralists assumed, first, that reform could be in the interests of all, thus neglecting major differences of interest between workers and managers, and, second, that institutional tinkering could meet the goals of a reformist management, thus failing to acknowledge that 'disorder' ran much deeper than a weakness of institutions.

These approaches should not be seen as self-contained perspectives. Consider the unitary view. To assume that all conflict is pathological is plainly an unsatisfactory view of organizational life. Yet the view made two key points. First, surveys have found that managers, and indeed many workers, tend to see their firms in unitary terms; for example, when asked whether a firm is like a football team or whether employers and workers are on opposite sides, majorities of workers often choose the former. Similarly, overt disputation is relatively rare. Second, at the analytical level there are areas of shared interest: if workers and managers were totally opposed to each other, workplace relations would simply break down. In short, a unitary view does not describe organizational reality, but there are features of it which any serious analysis of industrial relations has to recognize.

As for the pluralist and radical views, there may at one time have been clear distinctions. Differences certainly remain, but the debate has moved on. British pluralism proved to be flexible. Clegg (1979) responded to radicalism in a measured way, arguing that pluralism could embrace many of the radicals' points and that for many practical purposes there was nothing to choose between the perspectives. This contrasts with the situation in the United States where conventional writers (Kochan 1982) simply dismissed the radical critique (Hyman 1982). Though this difference is hard to explain, one reason is surely the openness of British pluralism. In particular, the stress on the inevitability of conflict at the point of production was compatible with a pluralist view. In his pluralist phase Fox (1966: 14) had noted that 'co-operation needs to be engineered'; that is, securing workers' consent is an active and uncertain process. Flanders (1964: 243–4) had earlier drawn on the important work of Baldamus (1961) to argue that bargaining was a continuous and uncertain process. When radicals began to speak of the indeterminacy of the labour contract and the centrality of conflict and its management, they were pushing on an open door. What, then, is meant by such concepts?

Rules and the negotiation of order

It is useful to begin with the nature of rules. Rules do not have to be clearly enunciated, and many of the most important ones are not. A long series of shopfloor studies (summarized in Edwards 1988,

1994) has revealed that effective expectations about how work is to be performed often arise from informal understandings. For example, a worker new to an establishment may discover that a supervisor permits workers to leave early at the end of a shift. She may then learn that this concession is granted only when work is slack or when a strict manager is absent, and that it is not wise to advertise it too widely. She may even find that this local understanding counts for nothing if managers decide to enforce the formal rules. Whether or not action is in fact taken will depend on a variety of factors: the formal rules and procedures of the firm (does it have a system of warnings and appeals?); the presence of a union (can a representative make out a case for clemency on the grounds of inexperience or that the relevant practice had become taken for granted?); and the role of the law (can it be argued that the dismissal was unfair because the practice had been implicitly tolerated, or because the firm had not followed its own procedures?).

This example shows that 'the rules' are many and varied, that different types of rule may apply to any given situation, and that rules have to be interpreted in action for them to have any practical meaning. The status of a rule also varies. A loose understanding may indicate normally accepted practice. But it may have little force. When understandings attain rather more acceptance and legitimacy they may be termed custom and practice rules. As the classic study of the subject (Brown 1973) shows, managements may unwittingly allow one-off concessions to grow into established expectations. Where workers have the power to insist that the expectations are honoured, a custom and practice rule is born. A later study showed that managers, too, generate custom and practice rules (Armstrong and Goodman 1979). In one case, a written rule in a collective agreement requiring that workers be given notice if they were to be laid off was successfully ignored by managers who pointed out that workers who stood on their rights would be entitled to only their low basic rate of pay, whereas if they went home early they could 'get a lift with the housework'. Finally, why does not custom and practice continue to grow by a process of accretion? One important answer is that managements crack down on activities which get out of hand. They may do so on a piecemeal basis or, as in efforts to regain control during the 1980s, as part of a general campaign such as the 'Blue Book' of new working practices introduced in the then British Leyland in 1980 (Willman and Winch 1985: 132–41). Rules are variable and negotiable.

The point is particularly significant in Britain. The lack of legal enforceability of contracts, combined with the preferences among managements and unions for informality, means that settling issues through unwritten understandings has played a particularly large part in the way in which the rules of employment are generated and sustained.

Why is the making of rules so difficult? A key reason is that the labour contract is indeterminate. In a commercial contract, a product or service is supplied for a price. In the labour contract, the worker sells an ability to work, which is translated into actual labour only during the course of the working day. Expectations about standards of performance have to be built up during the process of production. A rule is a complex social institution, not just a few sentences in a rule book. It can comprise beliefs, ideologies and taken-for-granted assumptions as well as formal provisions of rights and obligations. As noted above, the actual operation of legal rights in the workplace depends on the power, knowledge and organization of the parties as well as on the statute book.

Perspectives on rules

Three levels of analysis may be distinguished within the emerging analytical approach. The *first level* concerns the immediate balance of cooperation and conflict. Radicals and labour process writers, for example, allegedly saw everything in terms of conflict and managerial efforts to control workers more completely. Yet no serious discussion would deny that there can be shared interests (for example, workers may develop new abilities when advanced technology is introduced as well as benefit from the employment security of working for a successful firm), while also recognizing potential lines of tension (the technology may place new demands on workers and reduce the scope for informal control of the pacing and timing of work effort). The point is not whether employers and workers have interests that are shared or that conflict. It is how these dimensions of the employment relationship are organized: how far does new technology, for example, promote both the shared interest of working for an advanced company and possibly conflicting interests around the work practices that it may entail?

Second, the broader policies underlying workplace relations received attention. To continue with the example of new technology, what does it mean to say that it entails certain work practices? Are these inherent in the technology or, as many writers began to argue, the product of managerial choice? Although at the level of the individual workplace certain developments may seem inevitable, seen more broadly they may themselves reflect choice. There are two aspects of analysis here.

The first considered the various approaches to labour regulation that managers might pursue, with the concept of managerial strategy being intensively debated. From a relatively orthodox position, Purcell and Sisson (1983) identified a set of 'styles'. The way in which analysis was moving on from the Donovan agenda is illustrated by their inclusion of two styles which lay outside the reformist model. These were an authoritarian non-union approach and a 'sophisticated paternalist' style, the latter generally involving a refusal to recognize unions and the intensive fostering of a sense of commitment to the company. From a labour process approach, Friedman (1977) introduced the distinction between the strategies of responsible autonomy and direct control. These strategies can be seen as underlying the more concrete styles identified by Purcell and Sisson. For Friedman, managements faced the problem of securing workers' cooperation while controlling them so that they would continue to accept the authority of management and to work as directed. The two strategies represented approaches based on one or the other approach to the problem. Though Friedman sometimes presented the strategies as polar opposites, it is preferable to see them as elements which can be combined in various ways. Thus an employer may introduce quality circles to try to release workers' creativity while also asserting 'direct control' over issues such as absenteeism and time-keeping.

The analytical task is to show how the various strands of labour management are connected. For example, a major theme to emerge in Britain concerned the lack of deliberate linkages and the absence of a coherent approach implied by the term 'strategy'. A theoretical perspective on this was provided by Hyman (1987), who argued that, because firms pursue the contradictory objectives of consent and control and because, moreover, they are operating in an unpredictable external environment, strategies must be routes to partial failure. That is, a strategy is not a neat package producing clear outcomes but necessarily contains several competing elements and has to be constantly reinterpreted as new results emerge and as the world changes. Management, in short, is a continuous, active and uncertain process.

The second aspect of analysis concerned the environment of labour management policies. The links between the regulation of labour and business structure and strategy received considerable attention. How far are different approaches to labour the product of different product market circumstances? For example, does a competitive situation promote certain approaches and retard others? Attention was also directed not at variations between firms but at the overall environment in which they operated. How far is the labour policy of British firms shaped by the macroeconomic circumstances of the country and by generic features of its operation, notably the education and training of the workforce?

The *third level of analysis* concerns the fundamental nature of the employment relationship. Many texts note that conflict and cooperation are both important, but they tend to stop at this point. This raises the question of whether conflict is any more than an occasional accident and whether it is more basic than cooperation? The key point about the indeterminacy of the labour contract and strategies of labour control is that managers and workers are locked into a relationship that is contradictory and antagonistic. It is contradictory not in the sense of logical incompatibility but because managements have to pursue the objectives of control and releasing creativity, both of which are inherent in the relationship with workers and which call for different approaches. The relationship is antagonistic because managerial strategies are about the deployment of workers' labour power in ways which permit the generation of a surplus. Workers are the only people who produce a surplus in the production process but, unlike the independent artisan, they do not determine how their labour power is deployed to meet the objective.

There is thus a relation of 'structured antagonism' between employer and worker (Edwards 1986). This term is used to stress that the antagonism is built into the basis of the relationship, even though on a day-to-day level cooperation is also important. It is important to distinguish this idea from the more usual one of a conflict of interest. The latter has the problem of implying that the real or fundamental interests of capital and labour are opposed, and hence that any form of participation scheme is simply a new way of bending workers to capital's demands. The fact that workers have several interests confounds this idea. A structured antagonism is a basic aspect of the employment relationship which shapes how day-to-day relations are handled but is not something which feeds directly into the interests of the parties. Firms have to find ways to continue to extract a surplus, and if they do not then both they and their workers will suffer. Balancing the needs of controlling workers and securing commitment rests ultimately on ensuring that a surplus continues to be generated. It may well be in workers' interests that it is indeed generated, but this should not disguise the fact that they are exploited.

The contemporary significance is simply that much workplace change is presented as though it cuts through old relations of conflict to promote total unity. Yet any unity has to be actively created, and it cannot be total because of the structural conditions in which employers and workers find themselves.

Methods of inquiry

What methods have been used to pursue this agenda? A feature of many older texts, and indeed some more recent ones, which readers educated in other disciplines may find surprising, is the detailed account of institutions and of how bargaining is carried out. There is little self-conscious discussion of methodology or of exactly how information is gathered. This reflects the way in which they are written: they draw on the author's personal knowledge of the operation of procedures, which is generally backed up by statistics on wages or strikes and the results of official inquiries. Over the past ten or fifteen years, analysis has become less institutionally focused and more conscious of the nature of the research base. Two developments stand out.

First, a series of surveys has been conducted. The best-known are the three Workplace Industrial Relations Surveys of 1980, 1984 and 1990 whose results are discussed extensively in the following chapters. These cover the great majority of establishments in Great Britain; they provide a mass of information about institutional arrangements such as the presence and role of trade unions and also about employment practice more generally. The surveys provide a more accurate description of what has been happening on the ground than is available in any other country.

Second, case study work has explored the processes underlying the patterns described by surveys. Case studies have developed in three main ways. First, their theoretical orientation has developed in the light of interests in the labour process and management strategy. Second, particular attention has been given to the effects of change on workers, thus developing the point that the rules of employment are not just about the activities of managements and trade unions. Third, some researchers have used case studies in more than one location, in order to explore variations in behaviour and thus to deepen the explanations offered. IR research combines survey and case study methods, as well as using established methods such as analysis of official statistics. The following chapters draw on these methods in varying degrees and where relevant they highlight gaps in knowledge as well as differences in interpretation.

Models of Change

Given this basic view of the employment relationship, how can the evolution of rules be characterized? Is it a matter of pointing to complexity and variety or are there some identifiable lines of development?

A logic of flexibility?

A basic distinction is whether firms internalize or externalize the regulation of employment. Internalization refers to what Flanders (1974) called managerial relations and also to the ideas of hierarchy associated with Williamson (1975). The basic point is that there are benefits, in terms of control and predictability, of managing key relationships inside the firm. Rather than have to deal with an array of separate subcontractors, it may be preferable to bring the relevant operations within the firm and to employ workers directly. The story of the rise of the large multi-divisional firm was told in terms of the benefits of hierarchy. During the 1980s, however, many firms throughout Europe and North America became interested in flexibility. As noted above, 'atypical' employment grew, reflecting a move towards the externalization of relations. These moves in the employment field paralleled more general business tendencies towards a concentration on a firm's core activities.

A particular debate during the 1980s concerned the 'flexible firm'. It focused on the idea that firms sought flexibility by separating a core of activities that were managed internally from a periphery that was externalized. As shown in chapter 4, research has repeatedly shown that few firms make this sharp distinction and that the use of atypical employment often involves specific contingencies and not a clear-cut strategy (Pollert 1991; Hunter et al. 1993). But there are several broader aspects about the balance of internal and external relations which are addressed. Many legal initiatives were aimed to 'make labour markets work'; that is, to make decisions on employment and pay levels reflect market pressures and not internal bureaucratic preferences. Commercialization within and privatization of the public sector moved in similar directions. Within firms already in the private sector two trends were heavily discussed: a decentralization of pay bargaining, which was supposed to allow individual business units to relate pay to their own specific market circumstances; and a move away from ideas of formal hierarchies towards individualized payment systems.

It is, in short, not a matter of a sharp distinction between the internal and the external but of the ways in which external pressures are incorporated within organizations. This issue appears throughout this book. For example, chapter 4 considers management policy on flexibility. Chapter 5 looks at the key issue of pay bargaining: how far has decentralization really gone, and how far has it reduced the role of control mechanisms within the firm? The chapters on the state and on privatization pursue the question of 'marketization', while those on training and on low pay explore the consequences of market-led solutions and the growth of precarious forms of employment.

Strategic choice?

Perhaps the best-known model claiming to explain such developments is that of strategic choice, which originates in the United States (Kochan et al. 1986). Its analytical core is that decisions on industrial relations are made at the levels of the whole enterprise, the collective agreement, and the workplace, and that actors have a degree of choice over the approach that they take. Actions are strategic to the extent that they tie together the three levels and that they involve concerted actions aimed at a significant goal. A key feature of the application of the model concerns change. In North America, the system of industrial relations has been 'transformed'. The established system was bureaucratic and legalistic. A typical unionized firm would have a range of narrowly specified jobs, and workers were expected to carry out instructions from above. Relations with unions were adversarial. Collective agreements were long and detailed, specifying the rights of the parties and prescribing arbitration as the route to resolve disputes. This rigid system was challenged by non-union firms which developed new systems of labour management stressing a broad sense of commitment in place of the formal language of rights and duties. Choice becomes important in the exact response to these challenges. In the airline industry, for example, some firms opted for a high-commitment approach, linked to a 'quality' approach to competition, while others preferred a low-cost and strongly anti-union style (Cappelli 1985).

This account gives a clear picture of the old system. Just what it is being transformed into is perhaps less clear. A strand which has been particularly stressed is the use of new forms of employee involvement and participation such as team working, quality circles and briefing groups. For many commentators, this constituted, in Walton's (1985) words, a move from control to commitment. But Kochan et al. also stressed, first, the limited degree to which even firms seeking new ways of regulating work had really achieved an integrated approach and, second, that an alternative model based on managerial domination and simple union avoidance strategies was observable. In later work these authors have argued that a full-blown 'commitment' model is very rare and have acknowledged the costs and tensions of transformation, notably the decline in real wages that has been an outstanding feature of the American economy since the mid-1970s (Katz 1990; Kochan and Dyer 1992).

Much of the present book considers the empirical issue of how far there has been a transformation of British industrial relations. The concluding chapter attempts an overall evaluation. The present aim is to outline how the analytical framework of strategic choice is employed.

At the most general level, there can be little dispute with a model which posits interaction between the leading parties and change in the nature of the relationship over time. But beyond this it is not clear how the framework directly explains phenomena. As Chaykowski and Verma (1992: 3) note, it was derived 'inductively' from the American case; that is, it emerged from the empirical analysis and was designed more to organize the analysis than to explain why certain trends were taking place. It is, as Kochan et al. stress, simply an adaptation of a systems model (Dunlop 1958) to allow for change. Such a model does little more than list the parties to industrial relations and their interactions. It gives no flavour of the relations of conflict and dependence which tie the parties together. Indeed, it is scarcely populated by people at all, its actors being disembodied managements and unions (with workers and the state not really figuring as active participants).

This weakness is particularly evident in the treatment of management. Managers are portrayed as responding to external events by choosing how to change the conduct of industrial relations. There are two problems. First, it is as though there are clearly marked routes from which managers select. A growing number of studies, several of them discussed in following chapters, reveal the complexities, tensions and uncertainties of choice. Managements have to develop policies in the face of uncertain information, and how they do so is shaped by the strength of particular groupings. For example, a study of the well-known confectionery firm Cadbury's, in particular its Bournville site, showed that change was a complex and conflict-laden activity (Smith et al. 1990). Second, the fact that a labour strategy involves the regulation and control of workers tends to be forgotten. As Hyman (1987) stresses, a military strategy is a way of dealing with an actual or potential enemy. Within industrial relations, strategy has sometimes been seen as no more than a linked set of policies, with the fact that these are driven by the need to regulate the contradictory relationship of the labour process being forgotten.

The results of this weakness of the strategic choice model are clear in its picture of change in the United States. The 'old' system is seen as static and as broadly accepted by all. This neglects managerial dissatisfactions with it. The decline of trade unions, a key indicator of the move from the old system, began not in the 1980s but in the mid-1950s, and there were several cases where managements tried to impose new working practices, notably at the end of the 1950s. As for the move to the new system, the costs to workers (in terms of job losses, declining real earnings and, according to some accounts, an intensification of work effort) receive little attention. Strategic choice is industrial relations with much of the politics removed.

These problems highlight several themes running through the present book. First, as indicated above, there has in Britain been extensive debate about managerial strategy. Following Friedman (1977, 1990), it is useful to distinguish strategy and policy. Strategy refers to the two basic ways in which managements can relate to workers, namely, through control and regulation or through promoting creativity. A policy combines specific instruments, some of which may come from one strand and some from the other. For example, firms have been found to seek creativity through such things as quality circles while at the same time tightening control in areas such as attendance and the use of disciplinary sanctions. The analytical need is not to go over the various frameworks for categorizing strategy but to consider how in practice different elements have been combined, drawing on the insights about the contradictory and uncertain nature of managerial behaviour referred to above. For example, chapters 4, 10 and 16 consider managerial change policies. They do not propose a leap from one discrete type to another but identify the concrete dynamics of change and consider their causes and consequences. This leads to the second point: 'old' and 'new' styles of labour management may have much in common, as chapter 12 in particular stresses. Third, the effects of change on the day-to-day regulation of work needs to be addressed. This is taken up in the chapter just mentioned, and also in chapter 10 on the public sector, and in chapter 7 (which considers how far the leading route through which workers have negotiated changed work practices, namely, representation through shop stewards, has been affected by new managerial initiatives).

There is a final problem with the strategic choice approach. It says very little about the role of the state. This is perhaps understandable in a North American context, though even there the role of the state in establishing and regulating the traditional system is an important issue: state sponsorship of the proceduralized system was a major reason for the containment of shopfloor protest (Burawoy 1985). In other countries the state's role has been even more obvious, such as the legally prescribed system of works councils in Germany. In Britain, there have been three main phases in the state's approach to industrial relations: traditional abstention up to the 1960s; 'corporatist' experiments in the 1970s, as discussed in chapter 8; and the free market liberalism of the 1980s and 1990s.

The policies of the state form one key element of a national regime of labour regulation; that is, the means through which the interests of capital, labour and the state are organized and represented. A regime has important consequences for economic performance. In the German case, Streeck (1992) has argued that a network of institutions promoted a high-quality route to competitiveness; for example, the state, employers and unions participate in the design and operation of the system of training. This contrasts with the more market-driven approach in Britain, where issues like training have increasingly been left to the wishes of the individual employer, as chapter 17 explains.

A key theme of this book, therefore, is the character of the British regime. The following section explains this focus in more detail.

Approach and Plan of the Book

Texts on industrial relations reflect the analytical developments discussed above. The traditional method was to concentrate on the main institutions and trends, with any explanation being inductive. More recent books pursue theoretical debates on management strategy and the labour process with rather little empirical information being provided. This book tries to steer a course between these extremes. It aims to describe the key trends in British industrial relations. But it is also analytical: each chapter provides a strong argument, and issues such as the coherence of strategy and the balance between externalization and internalization run through the book as a whole.

Within this broad approach the book reflects the developments in the subject discussed above. Though any employment relationship can be analysed in terms of its regulation, and though there are many aspects of this process which might command attention, in practice IR has focused on some aspects of some relationships. Thus it began with a strong focus on collective bargaining, from which it has developed into new areas. There is no clear line demarcating it from related subjects such as industrial sociology and organizational behaviour.

The following selection of topics reflects three criteria. First, there must be sufficient research material. One of the most obvious exclusions concerns managers. Though the management role in regulating work is a central focus, the regulation of managers' own work is not addressed in any detail. This is simply a result of the rarity of studies adopting what may be called an industrial relations approach to managerial work. Second, other volumes in this series discuss certain topics in depth, such as labour law (Lewis 1986) and the nature of the employment relationship and the labour market (Gallie 1988). The volumes on Europe (Ferner and Hyman 1992; Hyman and Ferner 1994) set Britain in the context of developments in other countries. More comment is needed on the text on personnel management (Sisson 1994), for it covers some topics also included here.

A degree of overlap is inevitable. Indeed, as discussed above, the distinction between industrial relations and personnel management is much less clear than it used to be. That said, only five of the chapters in the present volume have direct counterparts in the personnel management text. And the books take different, complementary, approaches. A personnel text needs to explore issues from the point of view of the practising or potential manager. This is not to say that Sisson's text is managerialist; on the contrary, its specific strength is its critical analysis, as opposed to description and prescription. But it is analysis informed by the needs of the reflective, thinking, manager. The present volume takes a broader approach. For example, instead of a detailed chapter on performance pay (PRP), the present discussion of this issue (in chapter 11) places it in the context of debates about individualism and collectivism. For most readers of an IR text, this is most pertinent, but for those also needing a close analysis of PRP systems in their own right the personnel text can be consulted.

Any similarity reflects the third criterion, namely, the need to cover what would be considered to be the leading issues within industrial relations as the subject has evolved. Some issues, such as the structure of trade unions, are long established; others, like the links between industrial relations and economic performance, received growing attention during the 1980s; yet others, for example privatization, were entirely new. The present selection of topics tries to reflect key areas of current debate.

The remaining two chapters in this introductory part set out respectively the historical and economic context. But they do more than merely provide background. Chapter 2 stresses the important historical legacies which continue to shape the British approach to employment regulation. Chapter 3 considers major trends in the labour market, such as the decline of manufacturing and the growth of part-time work, to assess how far the pattern of employment is moving towards the high-skill, high-commitment model implied in accounts of the new industrial relations.

The chapters in part II explore the activities of the main parties to employment regulation, namely, employers, unions and the state. Those on management tackle such issues as managerial strategy, and externalization versus internalization. Those on unions consider how far the changes of the 1980s and 1990s have affected the membership levels and activities of unions. Chapter 6 focuses on unions as institutions, and chapter 7 gives special attention to the changing role of the shop steward, who traditionally played a major role in British industrial relations. The three chapters on the state consider the state as: manager of the economy, including issues such as corporatism; legislator, considering the changing nature and effects of labour law; and employer of a substantial proportion of the workforce, examining the effects of commercialization.

Part III addresses some of the processes of change. Its first two chapters consider directly the work relationship: how far do innovations such as merit pay mean that it is now run on individualized lines (chapter 11); and what is happening at the level of the work task itself (chapter 12)? Both chapters explore the combination of 'old' and 'new' methods in the emerging pattern of work relations. Chapter 13 turns to the outcomes of such developments in relation to productivity: how far has any improvement in productivity been due to change in industrial relations, and what sort of change has been the most important? Chapter 14 examines how far patterns of conflict have changed.

The following five chapters focus on a range of issues in the organization of work. Chapter 15 shows how discrimination continues to disadvantage women and ethnic minorities. Chapter 16 examines the effects of the privatization of public enterprises on the conduct of industrial relations within them; it thus complements the analyses of commercialization in chapter 10 and of work practices in chapter 12. Market-led solutions also feature strongly in chapter 17, which analyses the key issue of training. Chapters 18 and 19 turn to groups neglected as much by the new industrial relations as by the collective bargaining model, examining respectively the low-paid and the situation in small firms.

The book thus sets out to provide a comprehensive analysis of the major issues of industrial relations in Britain. In particular, it tries to blend a synthesis of empirical materials with analysis and argument so as to provide the reader with an understanding of the significance of the processes being discussed.

References

Armstrong, P. J. 1989: Management, Labour Process and Agency. *Work, Employment and Society*, 3, 3, 307–22.
Armstrong, P. J. and Goodman, J. F. B. 1979: Managerial and Supervisory Custom and Practice. *Industrial Relations Journal*, 10, 3, 12–24.
Bain, G. S. and Clegg, H. A. 1974: A Strategy for Industrial Relations

Research in Great Britain. *British Journal of Industrial Relations*, 12, 1, 91–113.

Baldamus, W. 1961: *Efficiency and Effort*. London: Tavistock.

Brown, W. 1973: *Piecework Bargaining*. London: Heinemann.

Burawoy, M. 1985: *The Politics of Production*. London: Verso.

Cappelli, P. 1985: Competitive Pressures and Labor Relations in the Airline Industry. *Industrial Relations*, 22, 3, 316–38.

Chaykowski, R. P. and Verma, A. 1992. *Industrial Relations in Canadian Industry*. Toronto: Dryden.

Clegg, H. A. 1976: *Trade Unionism under Collective Bargaining*. Oxford: Blackwell.

Clegg, H. A. 1979: *The Changing System of Industrial Relations in Great Britain*. Oxford: Blackwell.

Crouch, C. 1977: *Class Conflict and the Industrial Relations Crisis*. London: Heinemann.

Crouch, C. 1982: *Trade Unions*. London: Fontana.

Dunlop, J. T. 1958: *Industrial Relations Systems*. New York: Holt.

Edwards, P. K. 1986: *Conflict at Work*. Oxford: Blackwell.

Edwards, P. K. 1988: Patterns of Conflict and Accommodation. In D. Gallie (ed.), *Employment in Britain*. Oxford: Blackwell.

Edwards, P. K. 1994: Discipline and the Creation of Order. In K. Sisson (ed.), *Personnel Management*, 2nd edn. Oxford: Blackwell.

Evans, S. 1987: The Use of Injunctions in Industrial Disputes, May 1984–April 1987. *British Journal of Industrial Relations*, 25, 3, 419–35.

Ferner, A. and Hyman, R. (eds) 1992: *Industrial Relations in the New Europe*. Oxford: Blackwell.

Flanders, A. 1964: *The Fawley Productivity Agreements*. London: Faber and Faber.

Flanders, A. 1970: *Management and Unions*. London: Faber and Faber.

Flanders, A. 1974: The Tradition of Voluntarism. *British Journal of Industrial Relations*, 12, 3, 352–70.

Fox, A. 1966: *Industrial Sociology and Industrial Relations*. London: HMSO.

Fox, A. 1974: *Beyond Contract*. London: Faber and Faber.

Friedman, A. L. 1977: *Industry and Labour*. London: Macmillan.

Friedman, A. L. 1990: Managerial Strategies, Activities, Techniques, and Technologies. In D. Knights and H. Willmott (eds), *Labour Process Theory*. Basingstoke: Macmillan.

Gallie, D. (ed.) 1988: *Employment in Britain*. Oxford: Blackwell.

Goldthorpe, J. H. 1977: Industrial Relations in Great Britain. In T. Clarke and L. Clements (eds), *Trade Unionism under Capitalism*. London: Fontana.

Hunter, L., McGregor, A., MacInnes, J. and Sproull, A. 1993: The 'Flexible Firm'. *British Journal of Industrial Relations*, 31, 3, 383–408.

Hyman, R. 1978: Pluralism, Procedural Consensus and Collective Bargaining. *British Journal of Industrial Relations*, 16, 1, 16–40. (Reprinted as

Ch. 3 in R. Hyman, *The Political Economy of Industrial Relations.* Basingstoke: Macmillan.)

Hyman, R. 1980: Trade Unions, Control and Resistance. In G. Esland and G. Salaman (eds), *The Politics of Work and Occupations.* Milton Keynes: Open University Press. (Reprinted as ch. 2 in R. Hyman, *The Political Economy of Industrial Relations.* Basingstoke: Macmillan.)

Hyman, R. 1982: Contribution to Review Symposium on Collective Bargaining and Industrial Relations by T. A. Kochan. *Industrial Relations,* 21, 1, 73–122.

Hyman, R. 1987: Strategy or Structure. *Work, Employment and Society,* 1, 1, 25–56.

Hyman, R. 1989: *The Political Economy of Industrial Relations.* Basingstoke: Macmillan.

Hyman, R. and Ferner, A. (eds) 1994: *New Frontiers of European Industrial Relations.* Oxford: Blackwell.

Katz, H. C. 1990: The Restructuring of Work and Industrial Relations in the US. In M. Ambrosini et al., *Transforming US Industrial Relations.* Milan: FrancoAngeli.

Kochan, T. A. 1982: Contribution to Review Symposium on Collective Bargaining and Industrial Relations by T. A. Kochan. *Industrial Relations,* 21, 1, 73–122.

Kochan, T. A. and Dyer, L. 1992: Managing Transformational Change. Paper to Ninth World Congress of the International Industrial Relations Association, Sydney.

Kochan, T. A., Katz, H. C. and McKersie, R. B. 1986: *The Transformation of American Industrial Relations.* New York: Basic.

Lewis, R. (ed.) 1986: *Labour Law in Britain.* Oxford: Blackwell.

Pollert, A. (ed.) 1991: *Farewell to Flexibility?* Oxford: Blackwell.

Purcell, J. 1983: The Management of Industrial Relations in the Modern Corporation. *British Journal of Industrial Relations,* 21, 1, 1–16.

Purcell, J. and Sisson, K. 1983: Strategies and Practice in the Management of Industrial Relations. In G. S. Bain (ed.), *Industrial Relations in Britain.* Oxford: Blackwell.

Sisson, K. 1991: Industrial Relations. *Employee Relations,* 13, 6, 3–10.

Sisson, K. (ed.) 1994: *Personnel Management,* 2nd edn. Oxford: Blackwell.

Smith, C., Child, J. and Rowlinson, M. 1990: *Reshaping Work.* Cambridge: Cambridge University Press.

Streeck, W. 1992: *Social Institutions and Economic Performance.* London: Sage.

Walton, R. E. 1985: From Control to Commitment in the Workplace. *Harvard Business Review,* 53, 2, 77–84.

Williamson, O. E. 1975: *Markets and Hierarchies.* New York: Free Press.

Willman, P. and Winch, G. 1985: *Innovation and Management Control.* Cambridge: Cambridge University Press.

2

The Historical Evolution of British Industrial Relations

Richard Hyman

Until recently, any text on British industrial relations would emphasize at the outset the importance of history. Sidney and Beatrice Webb (1894) commenced their analysis of trade unionism, a century ago, with a classic narrative which traced unions' development from the seventeenth century; most of their successors displayed similar concerns. The first forerunner of the present book, *The System of Industrial Relations in Great Britain* (Flanders and Clegg 1954), which appeared forty years ago, opened with a chapter by an eminent social historian. The members of the 'Oxford School' who led the consolidation of industrial relations as an academic subject in the 1960s were as accomplished in the study of the past as of the present.

At the time, the reasons for an historical focus seemed self-evident. Most of the institutions of British industrial relations had evolved incrementally over decades or even centuries – most obviously trade unions, described by one writer (Turner 1962: 14) as 'historical deposits and repositories of history'. As in so many areas of British public affairs, appeals to precedent and tradition figured prominently in the conduct of industrial relations. Union representatives at workplace level conventionally employed the rhetoric of 'custom and practice' – meaning informal rules, conventional arrangements, or merely behaviour which had become tolerated over time – in order to justify their own claims or resist those of management (Brown 1972). The fact that institutions and practices had seemingly persisted for so long was often regarded as a decisive argument against change.

'The traditions of all dead generations weigh like a nightmare on the brain of the living': most academic writers, until a dozen years ago, emphasized the strength of inertia in British industrial relations. They insisted that the functioning of institutions is shaped by the inheritance of beliefs and relationships which frame their context. There were no simple panaceas for the perceived problems of industrial relations: German works councils, Swedish centralized bargaining or American legalism might be effective on their home ground, but could not readily be transplanted into so different a cultural setting. Change could not be achieved – or only at immense cost – if it was imposed 'against the historical grain' (Fox 1985: xii–xiii). The experience of the 1971 Industrial Relations Act – a fiasco in its attempts to erect novel regulations and procedures – seemed to offer solid confirmation (Weekes et al. 1975).

Writing in the 1990s, the historical inheritance must evidently be reappraised. The Conservative government in office since 1979 has presided over the most radical changes in British industrial relations since the industrial revolution. Has it succeeded in eradicating the constraints of the past, or have traditional assumptions and arrangements proved more persistent than is usually assumed today? The authors who follow will provide evidence on which to base an answer to this question. This chapter, meanwhile, has two purposes: to outline the historical background to the developments of the 1980s and 1990s; and to highlight a number of important long-term continuities whose fate is relevant to any assessment of recent experience. The discussion will cover in turn the role of the state, of employers and of trade unions, exploring how each contributed to the evolution of a system of industrial relations so different from those in almost every other country. A key contention is that the popular view of trade unions as the primary cause of Britain's economic weakness is misconceived. The character and practices of British unions were very largely shaped by national political traditions and by the structure and priorities of employers. The adversarial nature of British industrial relations reflects distinctive features of society which were evident long before the rise of trade unionism and which remain apparent despite the recent weakening of union membership and influence.

The State in Industrial Relations: The Tradition of Voluntarism

In the early formative period of British industrial relations, governments and the law were serious obstacles to the growth of collective regulation of employment. This was reflected not only in the oppressive content of statute law (most notably the Combination Acts of 1799 and 1800, partially repealed a quarter of a century later) but more fundamentally in the individualist free-market presuppositions of the common law. The latter underwrote the rights of property, and as a corollary the sanctity of individual contracts. Attempts by workers to organize collectively, to submit joint demands to their employers, or to unite in strike action all fell foul of the prohibition of 'restraint of trade'; those committing such acts risked conviction on the serious charge of conspiracy. While there is debate about how rigorously and systematically the legal restrictions were enforced, there exists a lengthy record of fines, imprisonment and even penal deportation suffered by nineteenth-century trade unionists.

The method by which trade unions and collective bargaining were eventually legalized was not, as in many countries, by establishing a positive right to organize, to negotiate and to strike, but by defining an area of industrial relations 'immunities' where the effect of the common law was inhibited. As Wedderburn has emphasized (1980: 69), 'in strict juridical terms, there does not exist in Britain any "right" to organise or any "right" to strike'. The key legislative initiatives – the Trade Union Act of 1871, the Conspiracy and Protection of Property Act of 1875 and the Trade Disputes Act of 1906 – were designed to remove the specifically legal obstacles to collective action. But while workers were thus free to organize collectively, the employer was equally free to dismiss a worker for joining a union; while unions were entitled to bargain collectively, employers were equally at liberty to refuse to negotiate; and while a union could lawfully call a strike 'in contemplation or furtherance of a trade dispute', striking workers were in breach of their contracts of employment and might therefore be dismissed (or even sued individually for damages). This is in marked contrast to many other national labour law regimes, which oblige employers to respect workers' right to unionize, to bargain 'in good faith' with representative unions, and to impose no penalty (beyond withholding pay) on those who legally strike.

Why British trade unions, for the most part, found so ambiguous a framework of rights acceptable is discussed in more detail below. Two particular consequences deserve emphasis at this point. The first, particularly important in the context of strike law, is that a relatively technical redefinition of the scope of trade union immunities (whether by new enactment or by judicial creativity) could substantially alter the boundaries of legitimate action. The second, more diffuse, is that the interrelationships of workers, employers and unions became treated in public policy as a largely private arena of social behaviour. Moreover, the traditional disjuncture between industrial relations and the law has meant that the very notion of a collective contract, of central importance in many other nations, does not exist in Britain: collective agreements have always been 'binding in honour only', of legal relevance only to the extent that their terms might be explicitly or implicitly incorporated into the individual employment contracts of those covered. Likewise, trade unions have not traditionally possessed the status of agents of their members.

It is plausible to explain the tradition of legal 'abstentionism' by reference to distant history. Successful resistance to royal power in the seventeenth century involved the assertion of the rights of the individual against the state. This in turn encouraged the entrenchment of market individualism as the dominant principle of the British political economy: an ideology which both underwrote the rights of property and gave legitimacy to notions of plebeian independence (Fox 1985). The outcome was a society in which consciousness of class distinction and division was particularly acute, but in which opposing interests were normally reconciled through compromise and accommodation. This was the matrix in which industrial relations evolved: marked by an adversarial tradition in which it was natural to speak of the 'two sides' of industry (the continental vocabulary of 'social partners' is almost incomprehensible in English), yet which generated 'rules of the game' facilitating voluntary agreement. Workers, unions and employers (who typically behaved pragmatically once unions gained too much support to be easily repressed or excluded) drew on dispositions inherited from the past in order to regulate their mutual relationships.

The absence of statutory regulation, a condition known as voluntarism or collective laissez faire (see chapters 8 and 9), was long celebrated as an index of maturity and sophistication. The Royal Commission on Labour in 1894 concluded its lengthy deliberations by insisting that strong organizations of workers and employers, and voluntary agreement between the two parties, offered the most stable and desirable basis for regulating employment. For almost a century thereafter, a major policy commitment of governments of every political complexion was to encourage the institutions and processes of collective self-regulation.

This is not to say that the law and the state had no direct impact in industrial relations. As Flanders (1974) has demonstrated, even fervent supporters of voluntarism tended to apply the principle selectively. But while legislation on individual employment conditions has always been part of the British system, the rights provided have in general been far weaker than in most other European countries (making the more ironical the government's passionate commitment in the 1980s and 1990s to deregulation). Traditionally, most individual employment law covered either segments of the labour market not adequately regulated by collective bargaining, or issues (such as health and safety) with a clear-cut public interest. More systematic legal regulation which can be found in many other national jurisdictions – minimum wages, maximum working hours, protection against dismissal – was considered undesirable by most of those who shaped British developments.

When governments assumed an industrial relations role, this was most often restricted to providing assistance to collective bargainers. The Labour Department set up within the Board of Trade in 1893 was designed primarily to provide statistical information, the better to inform the decisions of employers and unions. This essentially advisory and auxiliary status was sustained after the creation of a separate Ministry of Labour in 1917. A touchstone was the question of intervention in industrial disputes. An Act of 1898 established a governmental conciliation service (since 1974 institutionally separated within the Advisory Conciliation and Arbitration Service); but its role depends totally on the readiness of the conflicting parties to accept its mediation, and even voluntary conciliation is offered only when any company- or industry-specific procedures for dispute resolution have been exhausted. In major conflicts, governments may appoint a Court of Inquiry, but without power to arbitrate. More radical intervention is possible under the Emergency Powers Act of 1920; but even in the case of 'national emergencies' a government cannot – as in some other countries – impose a 'cooling-off' period, order strikers back to work, or impose a settlement.

Finally, the treatment of public employees is noteworthy. At the end of the nineteenth century the government accepted the principle that the conditions of its own employees should not be inferior to those established by collective bargaining for analogous workers in the private sector. Until the Whitley Reports in 1917, public-sector unions faced serious problems in gaining recognition and establishing negotiating procedures; but thereafter the legitimacy of union organization was confirmed, and was indeed explicitly underwritten in the nationalization legislation which extended the scope of the public sector after 1945. The period after the Second World War also saw the elaboration of the principle of 'fair comparisons' between pay and working conditions in public and private sectors, with institutionalized arrangements ensuring that the terms of agreements in the latter were transferred to analogous workers in the former. Although (with very minor exceptions) the right of public employees to strike has never been subject to special restrictions, such arrangements helped sustain relative industrial peace. In general, then, the government as employer tended to follow 'good practice' in the private sector; only in recent times has it embraced a more active and initiating role.

Employers: The Tradition of Unscientific Management

Karl Marx saw the nineteenth-century British employer as progenitor of 'modern industry', a form of production in which the worker was subjected to the new organizational disciplines of the factory system, with a detailed subdivision of tasks and sophisticated technology eliminating all traditional skills. This view was consistent with the arguments of many contemporary British commentators on the 'industrial revolution'; and certainly there was evidence to support such a perspective. Many of the new factory entrepreneurs imposed the 'barrack-like discipline' of which Marx wrote; some of the leading coal-owners were notorious for their autocratic treatment of labour; the railways were managed on military lines; and so on.

Nevertheless, such contexts were not the main influence on the development of industrial relations. The rise of British industry was not primarily based on large-scale factory production; the slogan 'workshop of the world' reflected the reality of a multiplicity of small-scale producers. The metal-working trades which figured so prominently in the success of Victorian capitalism manufactured an immense variety of commodities, often tailored to the specific requirements of individual customers. Vertical integration was low; complex products were often the outcome of a lengthy chain of supplier–contractor relationships (a feature which was later to distinguish the British motor industry from most of its foreign competitors).

In short, the very notion of an industrial revolution is misleading. Technological innovation was intermittent and uneven: new machinery was often expensive, unreliable and inflexible (Samuel 1977). To cope with fluctuating and diversified product markets, employers in much of British industry relied heavily on the expertise and versatility of a labour force whose skills pre-dated capitalist manufacturing (Littler 1982). Some firms might possess a formal hierarchy of managers, supervisors and chargehands; but more commonly the employer depended on the largely autonomous self-regulation of work teams, sustained either by systems of payment by results (the 'internal sub-contract') or by workers' acceptance of the obligation to perform 'a fair day's work'. A classic instance is the case of cotton-spinning: the introduction of the 'self-acting' mule in the first half of the century was regarded by Marx (and other contemporaries) as a means of enforcing unqualified managerial control; but mule-spinning soon became established as a craft-type occupation exercising a high degree of autonomous job control (Lazonick 1990).

The system of 'unscientific management' was attractive to small employers in uncertain markets – and even in the heyday of British capitalism's global dominance, the small workshop rather than the large factory was the primary locus of production. The costs of supervisory and technical staff – and of fixed capital – could be kept to a minimum, their functions performed by a skilled manual workforce which could be hired and fired with scant notice. 'Craft control', as Lazonick (1990: 113) has argued, 'was consistent with, and perhaps even fundamental to, British industrial success.' However, only some industries, notably engineering and printing, had clear craft traditions involving the control of the work process by craft workers and associated controls of entry to the trade. Others had similar practices, though without any craft control in the strict sense, cotton being the key example. Many others, notably new mass production and chemicals sectors, had no such traditions (Glucksmann 1990). There are thus two key qualifications to Lazonick's account. First, the role of crafts in engineering did not prevent all change: work was rationalized. But the process was limited and uneven, and was dependent on traditional ideas of management. Second, in other sectors the failure to rationalize was due not to any externally imposed craft rules but to employers' own preferences. To experiment with alternative systems of work organization and labour control could be rationally viewed as an unnecessary risk for companies which were already achieving acceptable levels of profit.

It is only relatively recently that this system has been widely regarded as a source of stagnation and an explanation of eventual competitive decline, in the face of economic rivals with far more elaborate managerial systems and far more sophisticated methods of organization and control. In a global economy where strategic innovation came to count for more than pragmatic adaptation, the traditional strengths of British industrial organization became increasingly regarded as weaknesses. Very often, labour was made the scapegoat for the newly perceived deficiencies. Workers' natural response to labour market insecurity was to regard change suspiciously, to protect inherited job territories, and hence to defend traditional demarcations in the organization of work. In the twentieth century such job controls were commonly denounced as 'restrictive practices', as employee-imposed constraints on managerial initiative. It is, however, far more appropriate to regard them as the heritage of a traditional relationship between management and labour, in which decisions on product range, marketing, technology and corporate structure all helped shape employers' approaches to the organization of work (Hyman and Elger 1981; Elbaum and Lazonick 1986). In this sense, any transformation of the management–labour relations from which employers had historically benefited required much more far-reaching changes within management itself: one reason for the problematic nature of the rationalization processes attempted in the recent past.

This traditional basis of the management of work within the enterprise had important implications for the evolution of industrial relations in its conventional sense. Employers were anxious to assert the right to the unfettered control over their own capital. This was the meaning of the term 'laissez faire': the historic demand of the new entrepreneurial class for the removal of pre-capitalist state restrictions on economic activity. Most employers had no desire – and saw no need – for government intervention in the nineteenth-century labour market. 'Collective laissez faire' thus suited their perceived self-interest. By the same token, many employers considered trade union organization a challenge to their right to dispose of their own property without interference; hence the long record of conflict over the right to union membership. But, as the Victorian era proceeded, employers became increasingly reconciled to the existence of unionism, and some indeed came to appreciate collective regulation of the labour market as a means of taking wage costs out of competition.

Most employers were reluctant, however, to concede a formal role for trade union representation within their own establishments; the characteristic means to 'neutralize the workplace from trade union activity' (Sisson 1987: 13) was to agree to meet union representatives only in the context of multi-employer collective bargaining. Such collective regulation developed initially at district level, but after the turn of the century also nationally, primarily over rates of pay. What most employers continued to resist was collective bargaining over questions of work organization, a subject which fell squarely within the protected territory of 'managerial prerogatives'. Employers and their associations were prepared to go to the lengths of enforcing protracted lock-outs in response to trade union challenges, real or imagined, to their 'right to manage'. 'The Federated Employers, while disavowing any intention of interfering with the proper functions of the Trade Unions, will admit no interference with the management of their businesses': with this formula began the terms of settlement imposed by the engineering companies at the end of the lock-out of 1897–98. Yet the elusive boundary between management rights and trade union functions was in practice untenable, not least because – as already argued – employers so often lacked both the will and the competence to 'manage their businesses' without at least the tacit agreement of their workforce (whether unionized or not).

The familiar managerial dilemma of sustaining control while retaining consent was resolved in Britain – in the absence of the formal machinery of employee workplace representation which emerged in most continental countries – by covert and ad hoc accommodation (Tolliday and Zeitlin 1991). There is a direct historical linkage from the social regulation of the Victorian workplace to the pattern described by the Donovan Commission (1968: 12) as 'two systems of industrial relations. The one is the formal system embodied in the official institutions. The other is the informal system created by the actual behaviour of trade unions and employers' associations, of managers, shop stewards and workers.' While employers refused to undertake formal and coordinated negotiation with trade unions over issues which trespassed on their 'right to manage', in reality the day-to-day exigencies of production in most unionized environments required a constant process of give-and-take between first-line supervisors, individual workers and their workplace union representatives. Shopfloor bargaining, as Flanders argued (1970: 169), was 'largely informal, largely fragmented and largely autonomous'. Employers traditionally preferred matters this way, in the fond belief that concessions not explicitly admitted could more readily be withdrawn if circumstances altered. The uncertain progress of voluntary industrial relations 'reform' from the 1960s onwards showed that even informal social arrangements could acquire the resilience of officially consecrated institutions. This helps explain the more traumatic and conflictual implementation of change in the 1970s and 1980s.

Trade Unions: The Tradition of Free Collective Bargaining

British trade unions originated as local societies of skilled workers (and were regarded by some historians as direct successors of the medieval craft guilds). In many cases their functions were only marginally related to industrial relations as the term is usually understood: the typical craft association operated as a social club, a local labour exchange, and an insurance society (providing 'friendly benefits' in the case of death, injury, unemployment, or loss of tools). In terms of regulating employment conditions, their usual concern was to ensure that masters respected customary rates of pay, job demarcations and ratios of apprentices to adult workers. If price levels and technologies remained stable, and employers (whose own roots were often within the craft tradition) observed the proprieties, there was no occasion for collective bargaining. Indeed the Webbs – who coined the term 'collective bargaining' at the end of the nineteenth century – referred to the practice of the early craft societies as 'the method of mutual insurance': workers would simply refuse employment with masters who flouted the standard conditions of the trade, and would be supported by union funds until they found acceptable work elsewhere. The corollary of this method – unilateral regulation, as Flanders later called it – was that the need for formal organizational structures was minimal. The early unions operated on the basis of what the Webbs termed 'primitive democracy', with lay officers who often served only for a limited period of time, and with policy decisions based on collective discussion by the whole membership.

Craft unions were forced to adapt over time as technologies altered, employers became larger and more assertive, and sharp occupational segmentation within the labour market became blurred. From the middle of the nineteenth century, local societies began to form national amalgamations; after the turn of the century, unions of cognate trades began to merge; subsequently, most craft unions opened their membership to include non-craft occupations. Increased size and scope, and the development of formal collective bargaining, led to the growth of more elaborate organizational structures and the creation of a hierarchy of full-time officials. Nevertheless, the process of bureaucratization was relatively limited: there were few officers per member, lay representatives and officials retained important functions, and the traditions of rank-and-file democracy remained powerful.

The coverage of trade unionism extended progressively from the 1860s, as phases of successful recruitment spread to new sectors and occupations. Stable unionism became established in the large-scale Victorian industries with no significant basis in craft production: mining, textiles, railways. Two waves of expansion around the turn of the century – in 1888–90 and 1910–20 – laid the basis for the giant modern general unions. The unionization of public-sector and white-collar workers – to a large extent, within separate organizations – followed thereafter. Lacking the craft societies' traditional unilateral control within specialist labour markets, these newer unions were from the outset concerned to develop collective bargaining relationships with employers. In many cases they were also more centralized and authoritarian – one writer (Turner 1962) has described them as 'popular bossdoms'. Yet non-craft unions often modelled their governance on the craft societies, and incorporated their own traditions of decentralized initiative. The Transport and General Workers' Union (TGWU), for example, was the product of a series of amalgamations involving a hundred or more separate organizations, notably dockers' unions in individual ports with a strong commitment to local democracy.

The long historical evolution of British trade unionism explains three distinctive features which deserve emphasis. They are: structural complexity and fragmentation; an ambiguous orientation to political action; and the potent moral value attached to the principle of 'free collective bargaining'.

Britain is notable for the number of competing trade unions. In the 1890s, when official statistics were first compiled, there were well over a thousand, with an average membership of little over a thousand. As discussed in chapter 6, only since the Second World War has the number fallen rapidly, largely through amalgamation; but several hundred still survive. The great majority of unions have always been tiny, with a handful of large organizations accounting for the bulk of trade union membership (for several decades, the largest dozen have contained over 60 per cent of aggregate membership). The formation by merger of a small group of numerically dominant unions, while in some respects reducing structural complexity, has in other respects intensified it. In the early decades of the twentieth century, the familiar distinction between craft, industrial and general unionism had some foundation in reality; but amalgamation has increasingly made multi-industry and multi-occupational unionism the norm; most workers could in principle join any of a number of cross-cutting organizations.

It is common to stress that Britain is one of the few countries in which a single central confederation exists, encompassing the great majority of unionized workers (even though only a minority of unions). This contrasts with the situation in most other nations, where rival confederations embrace opposing political or ideological principles, or where manual, white-collar and professional unions are affiliated to separate central bodies. The monopoly position of the Trades Union Congress (TUC) is indeed distinctive in this respect. No less significant, however, are its limited role and status. Founded in 1868 as an annual 'parliament of labour', it was not until the 1920s that the TUC acquired its own organizational apparatus. Affiliated unions have always been parsimonious in the resources which they vote to the central body, and even more restrictive in the powers that they are willing to cede to it. In recent decades it has acted as an adjudicator in organizational disputes between member unions; a channel of communication with government, and with its counterpart on the employers' side, the Confederation of British Industry (CBI); and a 'think-tank' for trade unions collectively. But the majority of influential unions have been consistently reluctant to allow it to launch policy initiatives on their behalf, to intervene in collective bargaining, or to engage in 'neo-corporatist' centralized negotiations on continental lines which might result in commitments on behalf of the movement as a whole (see chapter 8).

The latter reservation reflects a more general ambivalence towards politics and the law. One important reason why British unions accepted a system of labour law based on immunities rather than positive rights was their experience of the incomprehension and hostility of judges and the courts: the anti-collectivist bias of the legal system was such that even seemingly supportive legislation might be construed to their detriment. Laissez faire was in this respect as resonant a slogan for trade unionists as for early British capitalists. There was also a powerful opinion that what the law bestowed, the law could take away; and that rights and benefits guaranteed by legislation would deter workers from unionizing. For this very reason, many union leaders were critical of the 1909 legislation establishing Trade Boards (later Wages Councils) to prescribe minimum pay in badly organized sectors; as discussed in chapter 18, hostility towards legislative 'interference' continued to the 1970s.

As late as 1966 the TUC, in its evidence to the Donovan Commission, articulated the traditional suspicion of legal regulation:

> no state, however benevolent, can perform the function of trade unions in enabling workpeople themselves to decide how their interests can best be safeguarded. It is where trade unions are not competent, and recognise that they are not competent, to perform a function, that they welcome the state playing a role in at least enforcing minimum standards, but in Britain this role is recognised as the second best alternative.

The preferred alternative was the consolidation of unions' own bargaining strength in order to negotiate acceptable standards with employers through 'free collective bargaining'. A good example is the question of the regulation of working time. Towards the end of the nineteenth century, a legally enforced eight-hour day was a prominent demand of many socialists. The objective was endorsed by many 'new unionists' organizing lower-skilled workers whose bargaining power was uncertain. It was fervently opposed by more established union leaders, who insisted that legislation would conflict with bargaining autonomy. While the TUC was persuaded to declare in principle for the statutory regulation of hours, in practice the views of the advocates of piecemeal collective bargaining prevailed. In certain industries – notably coal-mining – unions campaigned successfully for the statutory regulation of working time, but the comprehensive enforcement of maximum hours was never seriously pursued.

In more recent times, the commitment to 'free collective bargaining' has had two important implications. The first has been a generally hostile attitude to government attempts to control the level of pay settlements (a theme considered further below). The second has been a widespread suspicion of forms of employee participation in management decision-making which have long been institutionalized in many other European countries. The recommendations of the Bullock Committee, in 1977, for legislation to introduce worker representatives on company boards, was as strongly opposed by some trade unionists as by employer organizations (Elliott 1978). 'There is an essential need to preserve trade union independence', one union leader had written at an earlier stage of the industrial democracy debate. 'The unions must not be directly involved in controlling industry' (Scanlon 1968: 7).

There is an apparent paradox in the political stance of British trade unions. They have always been strongly committed to the autonomy of their negotiations on behalf of their specific membership constituencies, but have also long employed the language of socialist class politics, regarding the Labour Party as a partner in an integrated labour movement. But rhetoric and practice – declamatory appeals to a general working-class interest, day-to-day preoccupation with the bread-and-butter concerns of much narrower sectoral and occupational groups – have traditionally diverged. For British unions, unlike those elsewhere in Europe, the state was not a major focus of concern once the basic legal framework of the 1870s had been achieved; the democratization of the franchise, an issue which encouraged unions elsewhere to politically oriented militancy, was achieved incrementally and relatively consensually over many decades; British socialism was non-existent in the key mid-Victorian years when union organization was consolidated.

Superficially, the end of the nineteenth century brought a new alignment between trade unionism and socialist politics. But whereas in much of Europe modern union organization emerged as an offshoot of social democracy, in Britain the relationship was reversed. In the 1890s, the aggressive stance of some leading employers together with a series of hostile judicial decisions persuaded many orthodox trade unionists of the need for a more active political strategy. The outcome was the foundation in 1900 of what would soon become the Labour party; but this stemmed from a decision within the TUC that the representation of workers' interests in parliament should be 'hived off' to a separate (and, it was initially assumed, subsidiary) body, allowing the unions to concentrate on their primary function in collective bargaining.

The relationship between party and unions has been described as a 'contentious alliance' (Minkin 1991). For most of the twentieth century, however, a relatively consensual demarcation of functions existed. Most major unions are affiliated to the Labour party (though the TUC itself is not), contribute the bulk of its funds and hold the majority of votes at its conference; but they have rarely attempted to interfere with the autonomy of the parliamentary leadership in determining general party policy. Conversely, the party has traditionally refrained from taking policy initiatives which impinge on the trade union role in regulating employment matters through collective bargaining. The more recent strains in the relationship have largely reflected the growing artificiality of any demarcation between the spheres of 'politics' and 'industrial relations'. It is the same erosion of traditional boundaries which has put the whole traditional system of industrial relations in Britain under increasing stress.

Pressures for Change

The doctrine of laissez faire prescribed and presupposed a clear separation between the economy and the state. Governments should protect the integrity of contracts, and sustain whatever force was needed to guarantee the security of British capital at home and overseas, but had no other role in the marketplace. As has been seen, the traditional institutions of industrial relations were cast within the mould of these assumptions.

Developments in the twentieth century made 'collective laissez faire' increasingly anomalous. Two world wars, and high levels of peacetime military expenditure, gave the state a central economic role. Keynesian notions of macroeconomic management, encouraged by the experience of crisis and mass unemployment between the wars, established economic policy as a legitimate concern of government. The nationalization of specific industrial sectors, and the growth of public services, made the state an increasingly important employer (directly or indirectly responsible for almost a third of the labour force by the late 1970s).

In this changed context three key issues – inflation, public expenditure and productivity – made industrial relations increasingly a focus of political attention. Post-war governments of both parties were committed to the goal of full employment, but were concerned that workers' increased labour market strength would result in inflationary wage movements. Already during the Second World War this was perceived as a potential problem, and there were calls for government regulation of wages; but the Ministry of Labour (headed during the coalition government by Ernest Bevin, leader of the TGWU) insisted on sustaining the principle of 'voluntaryism' (Bullock 1967), relying on the self-restraint of union negotiators together with temporary provision for compulsory arbitration in the case of disputes. Faced with a serious economic crisis, the post-war Labour government in 1948 introduced a policy of wage restraint – which received the backing of the TUC and had no compulsory legal foundations. After a Conservative government attempted to influence pay determination in the early 1960s, its Labour successor elected in 1964 made a prices and incomes policy central to its economic strategy. Initially voluntary, the policy was given statutory backing in 1966, despite objections from the TUC. New governments elected in 1970 and in 1974 first abandoned their predecessors' incomes policies, then introduced their own measures of wage restraint when faced with severe economic difficulties.

In the main, governments in their intermittent pursuit of wage restraint policies attempted to avoid too frontal a challenge to 'free collective bargaining'. Labour governments in particular were anxious to win trade union cooperation, and in 1964 attempted to institutionalize this by creating the National Board for Prices and Incomes with trade union (and employer) members. The TUC was likewise represented on the National Economic Development Council (created by the Conservatives in 1962), having acquired over previous decades the right to appoint nominees on a multiplicity of less important quasi-governmental bodies. As discussed in chapter 8, however, continental-style tripartite macroeconomic bargaining was only superficially imitated in Britain. Firstly, the TUC lacked control over its affiliates, as did most individual unions over their local negotiators; formal agreement to a pay norm gave no guarantee that it would be respected in practice. Secondly, the voluntarist tradition still shaped union attitudes. The majority, in 1964, were prepared to endorse what Labour leaders called the 'planned growth of incomes'; wage restraint was quite a different matter, from time to time tolerated rather than approved when a Labour government faced overwhelming economic difficulties. The proactive agreement on a set of demands which might be bargained against collective union self-regulation in pay negotiations – what in other countries is often known as 'political exchange' – has never been feasible in Britain.

Government concern with the general level of pay settlements has been even stronger in the case of public employees. The principle that the state should follow the trends in collective bargaining in the private sector (the principle often known as 'fair comparisons') came under growing strain as public employment and expenditure expanded, and as pressures for fiscal economy mounted. Most exercises in incomes policy were regarded by public-sector unions – usually correctly – as bearing particularly rigorously on their own members, since the government could exert more direct influence over their negotiations. After 1970, controls over public expenditure levels also impinged directly on the resources available for pay increases. The dual impact of these constraints was to make public employment – for the most part traditionally a haven of peaceful industrial relations – into a major arena of conflict.

Preoccupations with productivity crystallized a variety of criticisms which were regularly voiced in the post-war decades, and which identified the declining competitiveness of British industry with the established industrial relations arrangements. Three themes were prominent in a catalogue of complaints: strikes, trade union power and restrictive practices.

Traditionally, all main parties to industrial relations assumed that conflict between employers and workers was inevitable from time to time, but could best be contained by allowing the two sides to reach their own settlements rather than attempting to impose peace from outside. This argument, regarded as self-evident by industrial relations pluralists, was one of the conclusions of the 1894 Royal Commission: strong organization on both sides of industry might occasionally give rise to major confrontations, but in the long run it would bring more regular and peaceable relationships. This view was at least partially vindicated by subsequent experience: apart from periods of great social and economic turbulence – notably the years around the First World War, which began with the 'labour unrest' of 1910–13 and culminated in the 1926 General Strike – industrial conflict in Britain was relatively contained, in terms both of the volume of strike activity and of its usually low-key nature. The decades around the Second World War were indeed notable for the complete absence of official industry-wide stoppages.

The development of 'two systems' of industrial relations was, however, particularly marked in the case of strikes. In the period when national trade unions virtually abandoned the strike weapon, the number of small, local, usually 'unofficial' disputes increased considerably. The process began in the 1930s as unemployment declined, trade union membership increased, and workplace bargaining by shop stewards became more common, and was only partially inhibited by wartime conditions. Much of the early growth of strike activity was in coal-mining (mainly involving disputes about piece rates and working conditions); but from the end of the 1950s, strike-proneness in manufacturing industry increased rapidly; the total number of officially recorded strikes reached almost four thousand in 1970 (see chapter 14).

The most common reaction to these trends – particularly among Conservative politicians and the press – held workers and trade unions exclusively responsible. The system of legal immunities meant, it was argued, that trade unions were 'above the law'. The prevalence of the closed shop – an agreement or practice that only union members would be employed at a particular workplace – was held to give unions unjustifiable power over individual workers. Many alleged that 'politically motivated' union leaders or shop stewards were able to apply this power to sinister ends. Industrial militancy, it was suggested, was sabotaging British economic performance and thus explained the deteriorating position in world markets.

Such arguments were a major reason for the appointment in 1965 of the Donovan Royal Commission. Its analysis, however, differed considerably from more strident opinions: British industrial relations were indeed marked by 'anarchy and disorder', but this stemmed primarily from institutional deficiencies for which all parties shared responsibility. Employers had failed, or refused, to maintain the collective solidarity necessary to make industry-wide agreements effective; but in the main they had been equally unwilling or unable to admit the reality of shopfloor collective bargaining and to plan and coordinate this. Unions for their part were too weak rather than too strong, doing little to advise or assist, let alone control, their workplace representatives. Shopfloor bargainers were often 'striving to bring some order into a chaotic situation'; but the uncoordinated and opportunistic manner in which decisions on pay and conditions, hiring and firing, and the organization of work were taken led inevitably to conflict.

The Donovan Report also addressed the issue of 'restrictive practices'. The popular argument was that workers or their unions gratuitously enforced a variety of archaic or artificial restrictions which prevented employers from introducing new technologies, reorganizing work more efficiently, or increasing the pace of production. The Donovan view was that the sources of poor productivity were more complex. Sheer managerial incompetence was one cause. More generally, workers often responded rationally to situational imperatives which were not of their making. Job protection was inevitably a powerful motive when employment was insecure. Those whose basic rates of pay were low had every incentive to spin out the work so as to increase their earnings through overtime (a distinctive feature of much manual employment in Britain). Cooperation in productivity improvements could be expected only if workers had reason to believe that these would work to their benefit rather than their disadvantage; and only management could provide such guarantees – as had been offered in the case of some much commended 'productivity agreements' in the 1960s, notably at Esso's Fawley refinery (Flanders 1964).

The 1970s: The Failure of Reform?

The Donovan recommendations placed the responsibility firmly upon management to develop a system of industrial relations more attuned to the realities of work and employment in the 1960s. At the same time, government itself should take a more active role in encouraging reform. The National Board for Prices and Incomes was already giving systematic attention in its reports to productivity questions. Following the Donovan recommendations, a permanent Commission on Industrial Relations was also established. These initiatives helped accelerate an already apparent trend by many companies to reorganize their handling of industrial relations: drawing up more systematic negotiation and disputes procedures, formalizing the status of shop stewards, introducing new arrangements for discipline and dismissals, rationalizing payment systems, and harmonizing employment conditions in different establishments.

One body of opinion within the Donovan Commission had doubted whether a purely voluntary reform strategy would prove adequate, and the Report was widely criticized on this score. The Labour government which had appointed the Commission proposed legislation in 1969 which, while largely consistent with the Donovan recommendations, included more coercive elements; but faced with the resistance of most trade unions and many of its own back-benchers it retreated (Jenkins 1970). The Conservative government elected in 1970 was committed to a far more interventionist approach. Its Industrial Relations Act imposed elaborate regulations on trade unions (whose internal procedures had hitherto been scarcely affected by the law); severely restricted strike immunities; and made unions liable to heavy penalties if judged responsible for a variety of 'unfair industrial practices'.

The 1971 Act was a failure; but the legalism which it introduced was to persist. As well as its obviously anti-union elements the Act had established a new concept of unfair dismissal and provided (limited) legal remedies. A procedure for unions to claim recognition from employers was also created. The legislation of the new Labour government (Trade Union and Labour Relations Act 1974, Employment Protection Act 1975) sustained and extended these rights – largely because the TUC, virtually without debate, had changed its views considerably from the strict 'voluntarist' line which it had expounded to the Donovan Commission. Together with other pieces of legislation enacted in the 1960s and 1970s (notably those concerning sex and race discrimination), and in the context of the external jurisdiction stemming from accession to the European Community in 1973, the traditional idea of 'legal abstentionism' no longer matched reality.

On other counts, the attractions of 'free collective bargaining' were waning by the 1970s. Many critics of Donovan had argued that the Commission had overestimated the possibility of consensual change. Shopfloor workers may not have been the prime authors of the 'informal system' of decentralized workplace negotiation, but to an important extent those with sufficient collective strength were its beneficiaries, able to combine a high degree of job control with opportunities to raise earnings regularly through piecework bargaining. With levels of unemployment rising through much of the 1970s, the incentive to resist rationalization measures (often involving job cuts) was increased. If some companies did succeed in introducing reform by agreement, others faced resistance. Confronted by rapidly intensifying competitive pressures, employers – including a growing number of multinationals accustomed to very different overseas industrial relations institutions – were in many cases losing patience.

Within unions themselves there were also more critics than in the past of 'free collective bargaining'. In particular, the influence of feminism within some unions brought growing awareness that collective bargaining had traditionally been oriented to a white, male workforce employed full-time in relatively secure occupations. This was the population in which union organization was strongest and among which the coverage of collective bargaining was most extensive; and the whole agenda of union–employer negotiations, it was argued, was orientated to their particular interests. There were calls for an agenda which met the problems and wishes of the growing proportion of the labour force that did not fit the traditional stereotypes, and for types of action going beyond the exclusive reliance on collective bargaining.

Such arguments had particular resonance in public-sector unions, with a high proportion of female, part-time, low-paid members, and without the 'industrial muscle' of many traditional sections of unionized workers. Here too, though, there were pockets of workers with greater capacity to take disruptive collective action; and feelings of grievance reduced customary inhibitions against militancy. The Donovan analysis of the deficiencies of British industrial relations and the consequential proposals for reform had focused almost exclusively on private industry. The pressures already provoking public-sector conflict were ignored; but they were to become increasingly obvious – as already noted – in the 1970s, culminating at the end of the decade in the so-called 'winter of discontent'.

The End of History?

This chapter has surveyed the emergence, the long and seemingly robust consolidation, and the eventual erosion of a system of industrial relations which differed radically from other national models. British exceptionalism rested on the interlocking and mutually reinforcing features of (relative) state abstention, unscientific management, and business unionism.

The stability of the system depended, above all else, on the international viability of the British economy. Its character was set in the golden age of British capitalism. Competitiveness was already under threat by the end of the nineteenth century; but victory in two world wars provided interludes of temporary respite. By the 1970s, however, the evidence of sustained relative decline was undeniable; and this is one reason why, by the time of the fateful general election of 1979, defenders of the existing system of industrial relations were far fewer than a decade earlier. Yet there was little consensus on what might replace it. Had voluntary reform proved inadequate because a more fundamental shift in the balance of power between employers on the one hand, unions and workers on the other, was essential? Or was the problem more deep-rooted, in a structure of relationships profoundly resistant to change? Would the malady linger on, even under a very different regime?

The chapters which follow, documenting the balance of change and continuity in the key areas of industrial relations since the 1970s, offer the basis for an informed assessment. Most readers are likely to judge that the heritage of the past still exerts a profound influence on contemporary employment relationships in Britain.

References

Brown, W. A. 1972: A Consideration of 'Custom and Practice', *British Journal of Industrial Relations*, 10, 1, 42–61.

Bullock, A. 1967: *Life and Times of Ernest Bevin: Volume II, Minister of Labour*. London: Heinemann.

Donovan Commission 1968: Royal Commission on Trade Unions and Employers' Associations, *Report*. London: HMSO.

Elbaum, B. and Lazonick, W. (eds) 1986: *The Decline of the British Economy*. Oxford: Clarendon.

Elliott, J. 1978: *Conflict or Cooperation?* London: Kogan Page.

Flanders, A. 1964: *The Fawley Productivity Agreements*. London: Faber.

Flanders, A. 1970: *Management and Unions*. London: Faber.

Flanders, A. 1974: The Tradition of Voluntarism. *British Journal of Industrial Relations*, 12, 3, 352–70.

Flanders, A. and Clegg, H. A. (eds) 1954: *The System of Industrial Relations in Great Britain*. Oxford: Blackwell.

Fox, A. 1985: *History and Heritage*. London: Allen and Unwin.

Glucksmann, M. 1990: *Women Assemble*. London: Routledge.

Hyman, R. and Elger, T. 1981: Job Controls, the Employers' Offensive and Alternative Strategies, *Capital and Class*, 15, 115–49.

Jenkins, P. 1970: *The Battle of Downing Street*. London: Charles Knight.

Lazonick, W. 1990: *Competitive Advantage on the Shop Floor*. Cambridge, Mass.: Harvard University Press.

Littler, C. 1982: *The Development of the Labour Process in Capitalist Societies.* London: Heinemann.

Minkin, L. 1991: *The Contentious Alliance: Trade Unions and the Labour Party.* Edinburgh: Edinburgh University Press.

Samuel, R. 1977: The Workshop of the World: Steam Power and Hand Technology in Mid-Victorian Britain, *History Workshop*, 3, 6–72.

Scanlon, H. 1968: *The Way Forward for Workers' Control.* Nottingham: Institute for Workers' Control.

Sisson, K. 1987: *The Management of Collective Bargaining.* Oxford: Blackwell.

Tolliday, S. and Zeitlin, J. (eds.) 1991: *The Power to Manage? Employers and Industrial Relations in Comparative-Historical Perspective.* London: Routledge.

Turner, H. A. 1962: *Trade Union Growth, Structure and Policy.* London: Allen & Unwin.

Webb, S. and Webb, B. 1894: *History of Trade Unionism.* London: Longman.

Wedderburn, K. W. 1980: *The Worker and the Law.* Harmondsworth: Penguin.

Weekes, B. C., Mellish, M., Dickens, L. and Lloyd, J. 1975: *Industrial Relations and the Limits of the Law.* Oxford: Blackwell.

3

The Structure of the Economy and Labour Market

Peter Nolan and Janet Walsh

It is commonplace to argue that the study of industrial relations should be properly contextualized, and that behaviour and institutions in the workplace should be investigated against the backdrop of a broader set of socio-economic processes. Nevertheless, all too often the employment relationship is disconnected from these wider dynamics and treated as a relatively autonomous 'subsystem'. The aim of this chapter is to unravel some of the relevant linkages by exploring the interface between the economy and industrial relations. Focusing on the period since 1945, it examines the evolution of Britain's economy and labour markets against the backdrop of wider shifts and transformations in the international division of labour. In terms of its relationship to the rest of the book, this chapter explores some of the wider contextual factors underlying the historical account of the evolving British system in chapter 2. It shares with chapter 5 a concern with economic theories of the employment relationship, and with chapter 13 a focus on the links between industrial relations processes and economic performance. In setting out the economic context in which industrial relations actors have operated, it also addresses the extent of the choice open to these actors and thus introduces the themes of managerial and state behaviour and of the balance of change and continuity in industrial relations which are pursued throughout the book.

The analysis is in five parts. The first examines the relationship between academic industrial relations and economics and the second highlights key changes in the labour market, while the third is concerned with broader economic developments and the significance of the forces of internationalization. The fourth section engages with the restructuring literature and examines the contention that Britain's deindustrialization is the product of a set of rigid institutions (such as trade unions) and misguided policies which have locked firms into a 'Fordist' time warp. The final section highlights some of the critical connections between the structure of the economy and the character of labour markets and industrial relations in Britain.

The Academic Legacy

The underdeveloped treatment of economic issues within academic industrial relations is a concern of long standing. Serious warnings were issued by three leading commentators at the time of the publication of the Donovan Report. Reviewing the Report for the *Economic Journal*, Turner (1969: 7) complained that its authors had failed to ground their analysis of the sources of workplace disorder – the main concern of the Royal Commission – in terms of the critically important economic issues of the time:

> The section of the Donovan Report on collective bargaining (which has been considered its major theoretical contribution to contemporary discussions of industrial relations) thus seems only to demonstrate that the Commission knew little about economics, was rather underinformed on both the actual organization and development of wage determination, and largely ignored the connection between the institutional organization of the labour market and economic trends and policy.

Similarly, Crossley (1968: 297–8) argued that the Report substituted description for analysis and too readily assumed that the developments in workplace bargaining which it had highlighted were irreversible. Such deficiencies, he opined, resulted from the Report's 'historicist' method and the fact that the study of industrial relations had become isolated 'from the other social sciences, especially economics'.

Still more telling was Reid's (1968: 306) argument that the Commission's 'inadequate appreciation' of economic issues had prevented it from grasping 'the fact . . . that in the post-war conditions of the British economy no-one worried too much about disorderly pay structures'. The relatively buoyant context, in his view, had encouraged patterns of behaviour in the workplace that were inimical to the more orderly relationships sought by the Commission. The basic cause of inefficient work practices was not the conflict between 'the formal and informal systems', as alleged by the Donovan Commission, but the character and effects of prevailing economic incentives.

Reid, unfortunately, did not elaborate his case or specify the conceptual elements of an adequate treatment of the dynamic relationships between structure and strategy, and subsequently his important insights were neglected. Why did employers fail to upgrade their products and processes, and what were the effects of trade union and management bargaining relationships on investment behaviour and competitiveness? To what extent were inefficient producers kept afloat by the existence of a relatively cheap, disposable and segmented workforce? These are but some of the questions that might have been addressed, and they are explored more fully in the final section of this chapter. Here it is important to highlight some of the immediate implications of the academic division of labour, identified by Turner, Crossley and Reid, for the study of economics and industrial relations.

Prominent among these was the unwelcome compartmentalization of the study of the institutions of job regulation and the study of their economic consequences. The Donovan Report helped cement this division. It took for granted that industrial performance had been seriously impaired by industrial relations, and argued for a programme of extensive institutional reforms to help promote industrial competitiveness. But, as discussed elsewhere (Nolan 1993), at no point did it attempt to unravel the nature of the causal connections: the linkages were assumed rather than demonstrated, thought to be too obvious to warrant further investigation.

In the decade or so after Donovan, concern about the condition of domestic industry increased, and many commentators linked Britain's faltering performance to industrial relations difficulties, particularly union 'obstructionism'. Most economists, trained to believe that collective institutions such as trade unions are a potent source of inefficiency, required little persuasion on this matter. Accordingly, when Hayek (1980) alleged that unions were 'the prime source of unemployment', and the main reason for 'the decline of the British economy in general', he was expressing the conventional view among economists. He was also speaking in a vacuum, for this crucial terrain of analysis had been largely vacated by researchers in industrial relations.

Latterly there has been some blurring of the demarcation line between economics and industrial relations (see chapter 13), but the legacy of years of fragmented debate remains. As noted above, it is reflected in the industrial relations literature by the continuing influence of the notion of the 'subsystem', and by the lack of research directly investigating the interplay of economic and social relations in the workplace. It is also to be seen in the underdevelopment of important branches of economic theory, for example the analysis of internal organization, as acknowledged recently by Stiglitz (1991: 15):

> Most economists have traditionally relegated the study of organizations to business schools, or worse still, to sociologists. The general attitude seemed to be that while it might be important for managers, or the firm's Personnel officers, to know something about organizations, the subject was not worthy of Economic Science . . . The behaviour of the firm could be described completely without knowledge of those details.

Arguing a similar case in the first edition of this book, Nolan (1983: 299–300) observed that the neo-classical theory of the firm

> abstracts from basic problems in industrial relations and work organisation by reducing the labour process to a set of technical relations, as summarised by the production function . . . Since workers' co-operation is assured through the act of exchange, technical efficiency can simply be assumed. The problem of how to get work out of the worker does not even arise.

While these points remain pertinent to the basic textbook treatment of production, the emergence in the past decade of new research on the economics of organization has gone some way towards rectifying these deficiencies. Especially notable in this respect are the connected literatures on transactions costs, agency and governance. Have these new theoretical currents removed the barriers to an integrated treatment of production, industrial relations and economic restructuring?

Its claims notwithstanding, the new economics of organization remains resistant to the logic of a historically grounded, materialist analysis of production and industrial relations. Issues of power and conflict, in particular, are slighted by an overriding preoccupation with the conditions of efficient exchange, whether internal or external to the organization. To be sure, the concept of efficiency has been broadened to encompass the costs of transactions, including those associated with the management and control of labour power. But, in common with other unitarist perspectives on work relations outlined in chapter 1, transactions costs theory sees limitless opportunities for mutually beneficial exchanges. The employment relationship is thus treated as but one example in which all parties are said to gain from the pervasiveness in contemporary economies of authority structures and hierarchical modes of work organization (for criticism, see Bowles 1985; Bowles and Gintis 1993; Nolan 1992; Marginson 1993). Alternative conceptions, emphasizing the exploitative nature of capitalist production and the dominance in economic transactions of the forces of power over efficiency, are accordingly judged irrelevant (Williamson, 1980, 1993). The perspective developed below, and elsewhere in this book (notably chapter 12), recognizes the salience of power dynamics in the labour market and employment relations and hence does not presume that observed outcomes are necessarily efficient.

The Labour Market

Few tasks have proved more intractable in the study of industrial relations than that of unravelling the connections between changes in the employment relationship and the wider labour market context. A necessary starting point is the changing structure of the labour market.

The critical developments in employment since 1945 include a decisive shift, in broad sectoral terms, away from agriculture, primary industries and manufacturing towards services, and a corresponding movement from manual to non-manual occupations. Part-time employment has expanded at the expense of full-time employment, and there has been a revolution in the sexual composition of employment, with female participation rates continuing to increase so that by the early 1990s women constituted half of the paid labour force. In the first three decades after 1945, employment restructuring took place against the backdrop of rising employment (falling unemployment); thereafter the context was one of rising unemployment. Some of the trends described below, for example the growth of service sector employment, have been evident in many advanced economies. Others, notably the collapse of full-time employment, are far more pronounced in Britain and reflect the country's particular history and insertion into the international economy.

Employment restructuring

The changes in UK employment structure by broad sector since 1946 are described in figure 3.1. It shows that the process of employ-

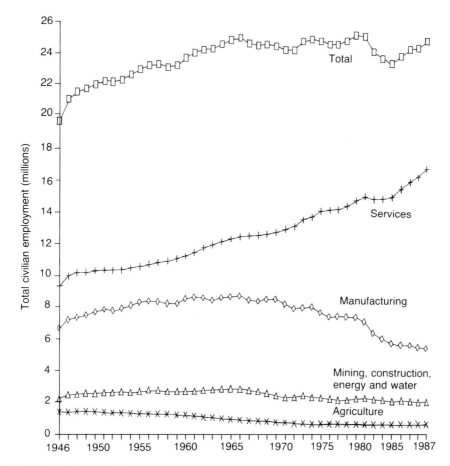

Source: *Employment Gazette*

Figure 3.1 UK employment by sector, 1946–1987 (millions): total civilian employment (employees in employment plus self-employed, including employers).

ment decline in agriculture and primary industries has been of long standing, that manufacturing began to decline in the mid-1960s, and that service sector employment has been growing, both in absolute terms and as a percentage of total civilian employment, since the mid-1950s. The share of manufacturing employment has fallen in many advanced economies – Japan is the striking exception – but the magnitude of decline in Britain has been especially pronounced at 41 per cent since 1960.

In terms of the balance between 'standard' and 'non-standard' employment, there has been a dramatic movement from the former to the latter. Standard employment refers to full-time dependent jobs; non-standard to part-time, temporary and self-employed workers. Reliable information for temporary and self-employment exists for the 1980s. The data show that, as a proportion of total employment, temporary employment has remained more or less constant at between 5 and 6 per cent (Casey 1991), though this figure conceals a substantial increase in the incidence of short, fixed-term contracts in the public sector (Millward et al. 1992). The number of self-employed workers rose sharply by 4 percentage points between 1979 and 1984, from 7.3 to 11.2 per cent, and has since settled at around the 12 per cent level. Most striking of all is the dramatic shift in the relative importance of part-time and full-time employment.

Figure 3.2 charts the movements in aggregate employment and the changing balance between full-time and part-time work since the

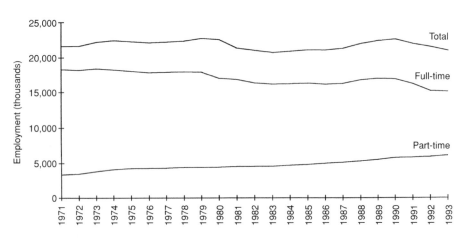

Source: *Employment Gazette*

Figure 3.2 Full-time and part-time employment in the UK

early 1970s. The level of aggregate employment has changed very little, cyclical variations notwithstanding, but whereas in 1971 only one in six employees worked part-time, by 1993 the ratio was almost one in three. In the late 1970s there were 18 million full-time employees, but that figure has shrunk to below 15 million, and with almost 2 million standard jobs lost since 1989 the trend appears to be accelerating. The collapse of full-time work has been most keenly felt by male workers in manual occupations, notably in manufacturing, and in the coal, shipbuilding, steel and dock industries which have been decimated since the late 1960s under the twin pressures of international restructuring and government rationalization and privatization policies.

By contrast, the rapid expansion of part-time employment has been driven by the growth of services. The number of employees engaged in the provision of services exceeds 15 million, which represents a net addition since 1979 of 2 million jobs. This growth has been concentrated in the private sector, particularly in banking, finance and insurance, retail, and hotel and catering. Predominantly filled by women, these jobs are often poorly paid, unstable, and commonly fail to attract such benefits as redundancy and sick pay (see chapter 18). The public sector, with approximately 6 million workers, has retained its share of employment, but, as in the private sector, part-time, non-manual, female employment accounts for an increasing share of the total. Casey (1991) thus estimates that over one-third of the overall growth in non-standard jobs between 1983 and 1987 occurred in the public sector, with particularly high growth rates in education, health and public administration.

Approximately 1.5 million part-time jobs have been created since 1979, lifting the total to around 6 million, yet this expansion has not been sufficient to offset the decline of full-time jobs. Indeed, the overall net loss of jobs is greater than the aggregate figures suggest. For, as Casey (1991) has noted, 70 per cent of all part-time workers have 'small' jobs involving fewer than 16 hours, and many work as little as 8 hours per week. Hence if the number of new part-time jobs is converted into full-time equivalents, the jobs deficit since 1979 is probably closer to 2.5 than 1.5 million.

With the number of part-time women workers approaching 5 million – approximately half of all female employees – it is relevant to ask whether the growth of part-time working is a product of women's preferences. A recent Department of Employment survey argues that this is the case (Naylor and Purdie 1992), but there are good reasons for remaining sceptical. Two points are relevant in this context. First, among the factors which may have served to limit women's choices in respect of paid employment is the availability of child care facilities. By the standards of many advanced economies, public provision in Britain is extremely limited: hence many women may 'choose' to work part-time because this is the only way to combine domestic and paid labour in the face of such shortcomings. Second, from the demand side, there is evidence of a growing preference on the part of employers for part-time workers, with recent examples of major companies (such as Burton and Wool-worths) in the retail sector converting their existing full-time jobs into part-time slots. Such practices, as argued below, should be seen as a response by employers to prevailing legal, political and economic incentives to reduce labour costs by degrading wages, rights and conditions.

Internalization and internal labour markets

The election of Mrs Thatcher's first government in 1979 represented an important turning point in the evolution of Britain's labour markets. It signalled the emergence of a new policy agenda, which included measures to free market forces, restrict trade unions, and enhance the power of management over workers in the labour process. And for the first time since 1945, the principle (if not the practice) of maintaining full employment was abandoned for other policy objectives, in particular monetary and fiscal restraint.

These important developments notwithstanding, it would be too simplistic to argue that the policy shift after 1979 was wholly responsible for the character of emerging trends thereafter. The Thatcher governments' hostile stance towards labour reflected a broader shift in the character of production politics in the advanced economies, the impetus for which can be traced to the accumulating contradictions of the post-war expansionary years which culminated in a generalized productivity slowdown and profits squeeze in the mid-1960s.

Yet to recognize the significance of these broader dynamics is not to gainsay the force of the changes unleashed on the British workforce. Established systems of collective bargaining and labour regulation at industry, enterprise and workplace level were challenged, frequently diluted, and sometimes dismantled altogether as employers sought to exploit gaps in the labour contract in pursuit of cost economies in production. Job security was threatened in virtually all areas of employment, particularly in manufacturing where to date more than three million workers have lost their jobs. The vast majority had worked full-time, had been trade union members, and had settled their pay and conditions through collective bargaining. Often employed in large, multi-establishment enterprises, these workers had variously gained rights to training, overtime working, annual pay increases, and a measure of autonomy within the labour process. Conditions differed within and between industries, of course, but for thousands of skilled and semi-skilled workers the 1960s and 1970s were years of significant material advance (Bélanger and Evans 1988; Lyddon 1994).

Characterized by contemporary observers as a period of developing chaos in the workplace, this period is perhaps better seen in retrospect as a time of formative change. As noted in chapter 2, in many organizations the arrangements governing access to jobs, work allocation, remuneration and promotion were in the process of being reordered and systematized through the elaboration of enterprise-specific job, pay and promotion structures, commonly referred to as 'internal labour markets'. The changes were often negotiated, sometimes imposed by management, but whatever their immediate source the elaboration of more formal rules and procedures at workplace level entailed a redefinition of the boundaries between the organization and the external labour market.

The research literature on the origins, incidence and significance of internal labour markets highlights these contradictory pressures. American writers have tended to emphasize the dominant and strategic role of management, arguing that such systems were spearheaded by firms such as IBM and Kodak in the early decades of the twentieth century in order to forestall the spread of unionism (Jacoby 1985). In Britain, they were firmly embedded in areas of the public sector such as the Civil Service and Post Office before 1945, but elsewhere their presence and effects have been patchy. One possible explanation for this uneven pattern of development is the persistence of craft union practices, which helped sustain patterns of intra-occupational mobility between firms. Another is the lack of strategic management in many parts of British industry.

Evidence for the 1960s confirms this picture of tentative and piecemeal advances in the scope and coherence of internal structures. In finance, chemicals and oil refining, where large international firms dominated production and service provision, 'strategies of internalisation' were very much in evidence 'especially during the first three decades of post-war full employment' (Gospel 1992: 165). Elsewhere the process of change was more protracted. A major study of engineering firms in Glasgow and the West Midlands, spanning the period 1959–66, highlighted the continuing salience of management prerogative in matters of recruitment, work allocation and promotion, while concluding that the 'internal labour markets in the plants studied, and in the engineering industry generally, [had] not . . . reached a very advanced and formal stage of development' (Mackay et al. 1971: 321).

Efforts by management to systematize and formalize the arrangements governing the deployment and remuneration of labour power intensified in the 1970s, however, particularly in medium and large scale manufacturing establishments where work study methods, job evaluation and single-employer bargaining, either at company or establishment level, became the norm. The impact of these and related innovations was probably most visible in the arena of pay determination. Studies (such as Nolan and Brown 1983) discussed in detail in chapter 5 showed that firms continued to find benefits in preserving a stable internal wage structure, often with trade union support, in the face of shifting conditions in the external labour market.

While it remains an open question as to whether these practices served to dilute or enhance management prerogative, it is clear that many employers had come to regard internalization as a form of 'best' practice: indeed so much so that, by the mid-1980s, half the employed workforce was covered by an internal labour market of one sort or another (Siebert and Addison 1991). Yet no sooner had the principles of internalization become established than the tide turned again. The compelling equation which linked internal labour markets with increased employee commitment and greater production and transactions cost efficiency came under siege from New Right theorists committed to the law of contract, deregulation and employment flexibility. Their arguments did not take root immediately, nor did they necessarily inform the practice of all, or even the most important, employers. But neither can they be dismissed as having been inconsequential. Casualized employment increased steadily throughout the 1980s and effectively reversed previous trends towards more secure employment forms.

Arguably, the most potent challenge to internalization came from the government itself. As discussed in chapters 10 and 16, its policies, directly and indirectly, served to promote fragmentation and casualization in the privatized industries (gas, electricity, water, steel, airways and the docks), in the remaining nationalized industries (coal, railways, the BBC and the post office), and in the resource-constrained local authorities and health and education services where the use of fixed-term and part-time contracts proliferated. Compulsory competitive tendering, moreover, forced many work groups to accept real and relative pay cuts and more intensive work routines in order to remain viable in the face of low-wage competition from private-sector firms. In the civil service, once a major source of secure, lifetime employment, the transformation of employment conditions has been dramatic, as illustrated by Lovering's (1990: 14) account of the Admiralty dockyard in Devonport:

> formerly part of the civil service, staff were automatically eligible for promotion up a career ladder by virtue of seniority and mobile grades had the chance of promotion to other Admiralty sites in the UK or beyond. The contraction of the yard, together with privatisation, has meant that both sets of ladders have been severed. Few of Plymouth's new employers offer major internal labour markets, most are small firms.

Yet it would be misleading to suggest that the disintegration and compression of job structures have been all-embracing trends. Various countervailing pressures, for example the labour market shortages that resurfaced in the late 1980s, exposed the hazards for employers of assuming a position of unlimited dependency on the external labour market. In retail, for example, the larger companies (such as Asda, Sainsbury and Tesco) sought to free themselves from developing labour shortages by elaborating new training schemes and more favourable pay and promotion opportunities. Such initiatives, according to Lovering, produced a new type of 'truncated' internal labour market, typically characterized by fewer job slots and opportunities for promotion and limited to a single establishment and locality. As in the past, such jobs remain highly segmented by gender: thus in the banks and building societies it is common for women to pass through the clerical hierarchy to the position of assistant branch manager, but rarely to advance further (see chapter 15).

Segmentation and flexibility

Attempts to account for, rather than simply document, the direction and timing of shifts in the boundaries between internal and external labour markets are surprisingly underdeveloped. In part this is because of the enduring legacy of the competitive model in economics, which treats phenomena such as internal labour markets as aberrations from the 'natural order' of the market. Nevertheless, two perspectives have gained particular prominence in recent years: the transactions costs and segmentation theories.

The transactions costs framework, popularized by Williamson (1975), argues that internalization is an efficient response to the pervasiveness of market failure in modern, complex economies. It emphasizes, in particular, the difficulties that employers face in writing, monitoring and enforcing efficient (that is, cost minimizing) contracts of employment in an uncertain environment, characterized by imperfect competition, asymmetries of information, and opportunism – that is, self-seeking behaviour with guile. Employers, the argument runs, will internalize key labour market functions (for example, the allocation and pricing of labour services) when the costs of market-mediated transactions exceed those of maintaining appropriate internal personnel and administrative systems.

Rejecting the standard textbook treatment of the wage–labour relationship, Williamson argues that the contract of employment is rarely complete in the sense of specifying the precise nature, quantity and quality of work to be performed, especially in the distant future. These issues are open for negotiation and interpretation after the labour contract has been concluded. Hence the possibility of opportunistic behaviour (for example, effort restrictions, lapses in quality, or embezzlement) cannot be ruled out in the life of a contract. The hazards, moreover, will be greatly increased if asset-specific investments, such as on-the-job training, are involved. For in such circumstances the employment relationship is effectively transformed into a bilateral monopoly situation, with each party able to impose costs on the other.

Arguing that internalization provides employers with 'access to a distinctive inventory of incentive and control techniques', Williamson provides a plausible case as to why so many firms were eventually moved to elaborate internal labour markets. Long-term 'relational' contracts are said to offer transactions costs efficiency outcomes that are superior to spot market (or 'arm's length') contractual forms. The key issue for management is to organize jobs 'in a way that best promotes cooperative adaptions to changing market and technological conditions' (Williamson 1975: 69).

But this account of the efficiency gains allegedly accruing from internal labour markets neglects the social dynamics of trust and cooperation (see Edwards 1990; Jacoby 1990). Williamson's claim that such structures are effective in eliciting employees' 'consummate as distinct from perfunctory cooperation' is not empirically substantiated, but rests on an assumed link between deferred earnings, job tenure and employee commitment. Trust for Williamson is, as Jacoby notes, 'an add-on': the complex interplay between trust, status and cooperation is not explored 'because his operating assumption . . . remains that of pervasive opportunism' (Jacoby 1990: 334).

Williamson is also less successful in accounting for subsequent 'turning points'. Why have the 'obligational' or 'long-term' employment relationships associated with strategies of internalization been replaced in many areas of work by 'spot market' or 'arm's length' commercial or employment contracts? References to the diminishing hazards of opportunism, perhaps because of advances in technology, improved information and monitoring systems, or the growth of transferable skills, fail to convince (see Nolan 1992). Is the alternative, segmentation framework free from such difficulties?

Interest in the causes and dimensions of labour market segmentation in Britain dates back to the mid-nineteenth century, when the political economists Cairnes and Mill first examined the origins and determinants of labour market inequalities. Both writers emphasized the significance of 'pre-market' factors, such as education and class background. Their concerns have continued to influence contemporary analysis and debate, but increasingly attention has shifted towards 'in-market' segmentation processes, with the strategies of employers, the state and organized labour moving centre stage.

As with the analysis of internal labour markets, contributions from researchers in the United States have tended to give causal primacy to employers. Their 'divide and rule' strategies towards labour, the argument runs, have opened up major differences in the employment patterns, pay and conditions of different groups of workers (Gordon et al. 1982). In Britain, more emphasis had been given to the role of organized labour as a force for inequality (for example, Rubery 1978), but latterly – perhaps in recognition of the changing balance of power in British industry – the focus of analysis has switched to the strategies of management.

Pertinent in this context is the influential model of the 'flexible firm', popularized by Atkinson (1984). The phenomenon of labour market segmentation – the progressive compartmentalization of the labour force into 'good' and 'bad' jobs – was already deeply entrenched in Britain prior to 1979, but Atkinson claimed it took new forms in the 1980s and was underpinned by a new dynamic. Employers allegedly pursued more systematic labour force differentiation strategies in pursuit of cost savings and flexibility gains. The result was a new duality of privileged 'core' workers on the one hand, and a larger mass of 'peripheral' employees on the other.

Core workers, according to Atkinson, are employed full-time, have relatively high status, and possess rare skills. The core labour force includes managerial and professional staff, technicians, and a growing number of 'multi-skilled' employees working with the latest microelectronic computerized production systems. By developing such a core, employers are said to achieve 'functional' flexibility – that is, minimum friction in the movement of employers within and between different functional tasks. Peripheral workers have fewer specific skills and can be more easily replaced through the labour market. The corollary is that their numbers can be varied at short notice, thereby affording employers greater 'numerical' and 'financial' flexibility. Atkinson presented his model as a description of emergent trends in some organizations, yet there is also a strong implication that it is prefigurative of future dominant trends. What does the empirical record show?

First, the evidence contradicts the idea that employers are adopting more systematic human resource management policies. Hakim (1990), on the basis of the 1987 Employers' Labour Utilization Survey, concluded that a minority of employers (35 per cent) claimed to be pursuing a coherent employment strategy. Out of the total of 877 employers surveyed, only 11 per cent said that they sought to compartmentalize their employees into core and periphery segments. The majority admitted to having an 'opportunistic' approach to human resource management, and the latest case study research confirms this finding (Hunter et al. 1994).

Second, Hakim's findings are corroborated by a recent study of the changing character of tasks and skills in manufacturing, the main focus of Atkinson's model of the flexible firm. Cross (1988) revealed that, despite widespread reports of changing working practices throughout industry, multi-skilling is rare. He surveyed the working practices of 236 major manufacturing sites and found that while there had been some erosion of traditional boundaries between production and maintenance work, there had been no comparable progress in the breaking down of divisions among craft workers.

Engineering and electrical work remained distinct activities undertaken by different craft groups.

More broadly the case study and survey findings contradict the view that work patterns have been revolutionized by advanced microelectronic technologies. The evidence, as reviewed by Elger (1990), suggests that change has been uneven and piecemeal: most studies report that technical changes have been assimilated into pre-existing patterns of occupational segregation. Furthermore, by international standards the diffusion of new technologies and new work patterns has been slow. In 1987, only 16 per cent of manual workers in manufacturing worked directly on processes utilizing microelectronics. Elsewhere, in office work and the banks, for example, automation has advanced swiftly, but in other areas of clerical work the pace of change has been slow. Elger concludes that greater flexibility at work in Britain has been dominated by labour intensification and the horizontal enlargement of tasks, rather than moves to deepen skills. (The flexibility model is discussed further in chapter 4, while chapter 12 pursues the ways in which the work process has been restructured.)

Although much of the recent literature has emphasized the objectives and policies of employers, the pattern of labour market segmentation in Britain has been shaped in important ways by the changing fortunes of trade unions and the character of state policy. As discussed above, recent moves by employers to erode the effects and truncate the span of internal labour markets have not been taken in a vacuum. The erosion since 1979 of union membership and influence, and the policies and laws of the state, have helped construct an environment in which the retreat by many employers from employment policies that were once judged 'best practice' has come to be considered unexceptional. Accordingly, for millions of employees increasing inequality, reduced job security, and poverty wages have been the most telling expressions of the state's deregulation and privatization policies and employers' quest for increased flexibility in production.

Yet to point to the crucial interplay of state, management and trade union policies in the formation of labour market segments and the perpetuation of inequalities is not to explain their character, or account for the timing of the changes in approach. For that task, it is necessary to reintegrate agency and structure, to place the actors of the industrial relations system in context. The next section attempts this by situating the foregoing discussion of the labour market in terms of wider economic developments in Britain, with the aim of exposing some of the longer-term influences and constraints at play in the post-war period.

Britain and the International Division of Labour

Britain emerged from the Second World War as the leading industrial nation in Europe, yet by the early 1960s the domestic economy was manifestly under-performing across a range of critical indicators. The symptoms of relative weakness were most apparent in manufacturing, and were such that the focus of analysis and debate shifted in the mid-1970s from the problems of relative to absolute decline: to the haunting spectre of 'deindustrialization' (for example, Singh 1976; Blackaby 1978).

To some extent these fears receded in the 1980s as a new mood of optimism, founded on claims about the revival of industry's fortunes, was struck by the government and some academic commentators (for example, Maynard 1988). But the accumulating evidence of enduring structural weaknesses suggested a different reality. Britain's role in the international division of labour had been consolidated, not transformed, during the Thatcher years. With its manufacturing capacity and employment greatly depleted, Britain emerged from the 1980s as a relatively low-skill, low-productivity economy forced to compete in international markets on the basis of low labour costs.

Deindustrialization

The decline of manufacturing employment is not a uniquely British phenomenon. Table 3.1 describes the changing pattern of manufacturing employment since 1960 in five leading industrial economies. It shows that the share of manufacturing employment has fallen in all cases, except for Japan, but also highlights the fact that the rate of decline has been more pronounced here than elsewhere. Since 1979, for example, employment has shrunk from a little over 7 million to 4 million; and since 1960 it has almost halved. By contrast, in Germany roughly a third of all civilian employees continue to work in manufacturing. Japan has a smaller share at around a quarter of the workforce, but it has increased as a proportion of total employment since 1960.

Table 3.1 Employment in manufacturing as a percentage of civilian employment, 1960–1990

| | *1960* | *1974* | *1980* | *1990* | *Percentage change* | |
					1980–1990	*1960–1990*
USA	26.4	24.2	22.1	18.0	−19	−32
Japan	21.3	27.2	24.7	24.1	−2	+13
Germany	34.3	35.8	33.9	31.5	−7	−8
France	27.3	28.3	25.8	21.3	−17	−22
UK	38.4	34.6	30.2	22.5	−25	−41

Source: OECD 1991.

The sharp contraction of employment in British manufacturing may of course be a symptom of success rather than failure, the product of a history of rapid productivity growth. If productivity grows faster than output, then the level of employment must eventually fall. Such an account would be misleading for the British economy, however, which has achieved quite modest advances in productivity and particularly so in comparison with Germany and Japan. The central problem has been Britain's poor record of manufacturing output growth, which has remained more or less static since the early 1970s. Between 1979 and 1981 it fell by a staggering 20 per cent; thereafter the recovery of output merely served to re-establish the levels achieved in previous peak years – for example in 1974, which was not surpassed until 1989.

Britain's peculiar trajectory has been characterized by some writers as a process of 'negative' deindustrialization. According to Rowthorn and Wells (1987), 'a dynamic manufacturing sector may be shedding labour, yet at the same time, contributing to the creation of employment in the economy as steady increases in industrial production lay the material foundation for a prosperous and expanding service sector'. This is the case of 'positive' deindustrialization. But Britain's experience has been different: manufacturing output and employment changes have been conditioned by internal weaknesses (lack of investment and competitiveness) and by adverse shifts in the pattern of demand. On the one hand, the pattern of domestic demand has shifted in favour of commodities produced overseas; on the other hand, as table 3.2 shows, manufacturers located in Britain have experienced increasing difficulties in maintaining their share of international markets.

Table 3.2 Shares of world trade in manufactures (per cent)

	1960	1970	1979	1990
France	9.6	8.7	10.5	9.7
Germany	19.3	19.8	20.9	20.2
Japan	6.9	11.7	13.7	15.9
UK	16.5	10.8	9.1	8.6
USA	21.6	18.6	16.0	16.0

Source: Crafts 1991.

Table 3.3 Technology and production shares in UK manufacturing output, 1971–1986

	1971	1979	1980	1986	Increase (% pa) 1971–9	1980–6
High-tech	11.9	11.4	12.5	16.0	−0.5	4.2
Mid-tech	29.2	30.8	29.2	29.9	0.7	0.6
Low-tech	58.9	57.8	58.3	53.8	−0.2	−1.3

Source: Buxton and Clokie 1992.

Britain became a net importer of manufactures, for the first time in its history, in 1983. Part of the explanation for this adverse development is to be found in the structure of industry located in Britain. Table 3.3 describes this structure in terms of technological mix, and shows that domestic production is overwhelmingly centred on low- and mid-technology-intensive activities. Nevertheless, care is required in interpreting the table, for it is consistent with several competing views about the nature and direction of structural change.

Most obviously, it shows that the share of production in high-technology industries has been rising since 1980, a result which is certainly in line with the view that industry has been experiencing a process of renewal and upgrading. But an alternative reading of the evidence would be that the low-tech, 'mature' industries (clothing, footwear, textiles etc.) suffered particularly badly during the severe contraction of manufacturing in the first half of the 1980s (Walsh 1991). In any case, as Driver and Dunne (1992) point out, an 'increased shift towards high-tech production does not say anything about the relative quality of the commodities that are produced'.

The evidence for the 1960s and 1970s, as summarized by Stout (1978), highlights quality as a major factor in Britain's deteriorating trade performance, and the relevant indices on 'value per ton' of British manufacturing exports in the 1980s suggest little improvement. In 1987, Britain's share of world exports of high-tech products, at 6.5 per cent, was down from its 1979 level (Archibugi and Michie 1995). Germany's share, at 13 per cent, was double that of Britain's, yet the relative proportion of its industries in the high-tech category is broadly comparable to that of Britain's. What seems to have been happening is that firms in Britain have been importing higher value added products, while exporting goods with a lower value added content; and this is true not only for the high-tech sector but across the spectrum. Recent evidence for the relatively 'low-tech' food processing industry, for example, shows that when international productivity comparisons are adjusted for product quality, Britain's relative position, particularly with respect to Germany, is far worse than is suggested by the crude comparative data on output per employee hour (Mason et al. 1994).

Wages and productivity

As early as the 1960s, Britain had become a centre for relatively cheap labour. This is revealed by the data in table 3.4 on total labour costs, which are derived by summing total hourly earnings and social charges (national insurance, holiday and sick pay). It places the UK well down the international league table. After the Second World War Britain was a relatively high wage economy, but by 1970, only

Table 3.4 Labour costs in manufacturing

	1960[a]	1970[a]	1980[a]	1986[a]	1992[b]
USA	296	250	126	161	16.17
Japan	30	57	80	129	16.16
France	94	105	121	122	16.88
Germany	98	144	165	173	25.94
UK	100	100	100	100	14.69
Spain					13.39
Sweden					24.23

[a] Labour costs are compared at current market exchange rates, with UK set at 100;
[b] Total hourly compensation in US$.

Sources: Ray 1972, 1987; Turner and van 't dack 1993.

Japan of the leading capitalist countries had lower labour costs than Britain. Since then Britain has fallen behind Japan, and even further behind the other countries, such that Britain is more commonly grouped within Europe with Spain, rather than France, Italy and West Germany.

The final column compares total hourly labour costs in absolute terms (US dollars) and confirms Britain's relatively lowly position, as indicated in the first four columns. The final column also points to a significant narrowing of the differential between the United States and Japan, and a growing gap between the United States and the high labour cost European countries (Germany and Sweden), a result which is perhaps suggestive of a two-tier structure between the more and less regulated economies (Nolan 1994a).

The low cost of labour in Britain is one issue, but how productively is that labour utilized? Productivity, it should be stressed, is notoriously difficult to measure, and comparisons across time, different industries and national frontiers are fraught with difficulties (see chapter 13). Nevertheless the evidence – whatever its shortcomings – does reveal a substantial and enduring shortfall in productivity levels in Britain as compared to the United States, Japan and the leading West European countries.

The differential with the United States opened up early on in the twentieth century, and, while the extent of the gap varies significantly across industries, it is estimated to be as high as 100 per cent on average (Crafts and Broadberry 1990). The gap with workers in Europe developed much later, in the 1950s and 1960s, as other countries achieved much higher productivity growth rates following the reconstruction of their industries after 1945. By the 1970s, as table 3.5 reveals, this pattern had become entrenched.

Table 3.5   Output per employee hour and unit costs in manufacturing

	1960	1973	1979	1988
USA	242	220	226	207
Japan		125		175
France	81	113	142	126
Germany	105	133	162	137
UK	100	100	100	100

Source: Crafts 1991.

A decade of poor, often negative annual rates of productivity growth in the 1970s was followed by more rapid advances in the 1980s. The apparent improvement was widely attributed to the Thatcher governments' policies, and was thought to be indicative of a new sustainable high-growth trajectory (for example, Crafts 1988). Compared with the record of the 1970s, there was indeed an improvement, but the argument about government policies is unconvincing: productivity rises for the economy as a whole, including services and primary industries, were quite modest, rising annually by only 2.3 per cent between 1979 and 1988, which is broadly in line with international experience. Moreover, as one recent commentator noted: 'if the Thatcher revolution boosted productivity by bashing unions, cutting taxes and privatizing nationalized industries, why were the effects limited to manufacturing?' (Gordon 1992: 425).

But even the record for manufacturing looks less impressive when judged against Britain's own experience in the 1960s. According to one study (Darby and Wren-Lewis 1988), productivity growth in the 1980s returned to the trend established in the 1960s: it was the performance of the 1970s that was out of step. And, as table 3.5 shows, the gains in the 1980s were insufficient to close the gap with other leading economies. The result, as far as cost competitiveness is concerned, is to leave industries in Britain at a substantial disadvantage. Unit labour costs – total labour costs divided by the productivity of labour – are relatively high despite Britain's low labour costs.

Internationalization

The evidence considered thus far suggests that Britain is inserted into the world economy as a specialist producer, among the advanced nations, of relatively low value added, labour-intensive commodities. Patterns of international trade and divisions of labour within and between nation states traditionally were thought to reflect the operation of the 'law of comparative advantage'. Each country or region, on this view, would specialize in the production of those goods and services in which it had a cost advantage, as determined by its endowments of factor inputs (natural resources, land, labour and capital).

But the realities of trade and capital flows suggest that the determinants of the international division of labour are more complex. A growing proportion of world trade takes place between advanced economies with similar factor endowments, and between the sub-sidiaries of multinational corporations (MNCs): developments which are incompatible with the traditional, static approach. Indeed, a crucial distinguishing feature of the contemporary capitalist economy is the extent to which production itself has been 'set free' from specific national and regional resource constraints. The growth of world trade, international portfolio investments, and the growing significance of MNCs are thus three interconnected aspects of the internationalization of capital, a process in which Britain has been a prime mover.

As a home for MNCs which invest abroad, Britain is second only to the United States, while its stock of foreign investment is ex-ceeded only by the United States and Canada. The relevant figures are set out in table 3.6. It shows, on the one hand, that the ratio of the stock of outward to inward investment, at 1.6 for the UK, is not out of line with the rest of Europe. On the other hand, in terms of magnitude, the UK alone accounts for half of Europe's total stock of outward direct investment.

Since the 1960s the rate of outward investment has consistently exceeded the rate of inward investment – sometimes, as in the early 1980s, by a ratio of 5 to 1. British based MNCs, to an extent which differentiates them from their German, American and Japanese counterparts, have preferred to source international markets from production facilities located abroad. Hence the scale of international

Table 3.6   Inward and outward foreign direct investment (FDI), 1989 (stocks in billions of dollars)

	Inward FDI		Outward FDI		
	Stock	% of world total	Stock	% of world total	Outward/ inward
USA	374	27	376	27	1.0
Japan	28	2	156	11	5.6
France	51	4	75	5	1.5
Germany	74	5	122	9	1.6
UK	135	10	213	16	1.6
EC[a]	249	22	370	32	1.5

[a] Excludes intra-EC FDI.

Source: United Nations 1992.

production by UK MNCs 'has been more than twice as great as their exports' (Dicken 1993). Before the 1980s, outward investment was concentrated in manufacturing, especially in low-tech industries such as textiles, food, drink and tobacco, but in the 1980s growing investment in services (banking, finance and insurance) and the extractive industries (oil and gas) have cut back the share of manufacturing to a third.

Inward investment in the three decades after 1945 was dominated by US MNCs. Their investments were concentrated in manufacturing, particularly technology-intensive sectors such as chemicals, mechanical and instrument engineering, and electrical and electronic engineering. But for several reasons this pattern has begun to change: aggregate US foreign direct investment has declined; US direct investment in services has grown at the expense of manufacturing; and Britain's status as the preferred location within Europe for US technology-intensive (and other) affiliates has been eroded. The evidence points to a significant reorganization of US MNCs in Europe, with Germany in particular emerging as the favoured site for capital, technology, and skill-intensive production.

Such trends have been reinforced by newer sources of inward direct investment, for example from Japanese MNCs, which have also favoured (financial and commercial) services. Japanese manufacturing plants, for example Nissan, have attracted considerable academic and media attention, yet they account for only a small proportion of total inward investment. In 1988, for example, there were 55 Japanese-owned factories in the UK with 18,000 employees, barely a quarter of one per cent of total manufacturing employment.

Assessments of the impact of MNCs on the British economy have yielded conflicting results. Dunning (1985) claims they have had a positive 'transformative' effect. Capital has been directed to efficient production locations overseas, while 'foreign multinationals have generally benefited the UK's industrial restructuring in as much as they . . . tend to favour growth sectors which are skill and technology intensive'. Other researchers, for example Fine and Harris (1985) and Auerbach (1989), argue that the presence of MNCs in Britain has been neither positive nor benign.

Focusing on the 'feedback' effects of outward investment, for example technology transfers and the formation of backward linkages in the production chain, Fine and Harris (1985) note that direct investment from Britain was until recently heavily skewed towards low-technology, low-skill 'colonial' production, which thrived on low wages and exploitative conditions. Such activities did have important feedback effects, but of a wholly negative kind, in that they served 'to direct the British economy towards more labour intensive low-wage production' (1985: 112). Furthermore, as Auerbach notes, when British MNCs have been active in more dynamic sectors of the world economy, the expected positive feedback effects into domestic technological capabilities and export opportunities have failed to emerge, though chemicals is a notable exception.

Inward investment, in contrast, has produced positive feedbacks, particularly in the form of export opportunities, for American and latterly Japanese and German MNCs. Such exports, as noted above, have tended to have a high value added content, and have been imported into Britain in preference to domestically sourced production. The car industry is a particularly striking case. 'In 1973 US MNCs in Britain had net exports of 200,000 cars, [but] by 1984 they had net imports of 350,000 as British production was cut back and redirected to the assembly and export of kits' (Cantwell 1988: 44). During the following decade 'the local content of Ford's UK cars fell from 88 per cent to 22 per cent, and those of Vauxhall from 98 per cent to 22 per cent'. These developments were reflected in the loss of 150,000 jobs, the erosion of production and research and development facilities, and a spectacular decline in Britain's share of European exports from 22 per cent in 1963 to 6 per cent in 1983.

Yet the British car industry, which as Cantwell notes 'is now regarded as a low wage, low productivity location for European production', is scarcely unique. The redirection overseas of technology-intensive production and jobs has been common across manufacturing, including chemicals. ICI, for example, employs more people outside the UK than within it, and increased its share of overseas employment sharply between 1979 and 1986, from 40 per cent to 54 per cent. In the same period, the UK's top 40 manufacturing companies cut their home-based workforces by 25 per cent (415,000 jobs), while expanding their overseas employment by 15 per cent (Labour Research 1987). Such figures are indicative of the way in which MNCs are able to denude local, regional and national communities, and run contrary to the conventional view of late that Britain's deregulated labour markets and abundant supplies of relatively low-cost, insecure labour have boosted investment in plant, people and technology.

Nor does the evidence suggest that the impact of inward invest-ment is any more positive. If anything, research on specific regional and local economies supports the argument that 'the complex of MNC operations appear almost uniquely designed to exploit as well as to create a relatively declining industrial base characterized by low wage and low-intensity production' (Fine and Harris, 1985: 113). According to Knell 'the bias towards relatively low value added production activities has tended to reflect inherited weak-nesses in the local labour force' (Knell, 1993: 57). His examina-tion of the labour utilization policies of two high-profile inward investors in West Yorkshire revealed that investment in people was limited – despite their managements' espousal of positive human resource management – and that the poaching of skilled and managerial labour power from other firms was the chief means through which these companies gained access to higher 'quality' employees.

Knell's findings are consistent with previous studies. Young et al. (1987) compared the composition of employment in foreign-owned affiliates with that of indigenous companies in the electrical engin-eering, mechanical and chemical industries, and found that the former employed a higher proportion of unskilled manual workers. Similarly, Peck and Stone (1991) examined the recruitment policies of 105 inward investors in the north-east, and found that they employed a far higher proportion of lower-skilled operatives and assembly workers than their indigenous counterparts. Peck and Stone, like Knell, noted that the affiliates were inclined to 'poach' skilled and managerial labour from other established companies, and concluded that 'one of the factors hindering the development of indigenous enterprise in the region is a comparative disadvantage experienced by local firms in the market for key skills' (cited in Knell 1993).

It is difficult to determine from this evidence whether the pro-duction and labour utilization policies of inward investors have been tailored to accommodate existing structural constraints (for example, the lack of skilled labour), or whether such constraints are in large part the product of waves of inward and outward investment. Probably, as Knell implies, these should not be viewed as alternative logics, but rather treated as a set of mutually reinforcing and self-perpetuating conditions. Either way, there is little support for Dunning's claim that MNCs in Britain have had a positive 'transformative' effect.

'Fordism' and 'Flexible Specialization'

Although the British economy has been at the forefront of the processes of internationalization, the debate about Britain's changing relative position in the world economy continues to focus almost exclusively on domestic forces: the role of government policy, the impact of trade unions, the City of London, and so on. It is as though the forces conditioning Britain's insertion into the international division of labour are wholly internal. One such account, which has been particularly influential in recent years, claims that manufacturing firms in Britain have failed to adapt to the 'new competition' and embrace the flexible manufacturing systems which have been successfully spearheaded elsewhere: in Emilia-Romagna in Italy, Baden-Württemberg in (West) Germany, and Sakaki in Japan (Best 1990). We examine this model of 'flexible specialization' briefly, because it provides a particularly sharp contrast with our own argument, which stresses the interplay of domestic and international forces in reproducing in Britain a pattern of low wages, low productivity, low skills and low investment. (The nature of this pattern is examined throughout this book, notably in the chapters on management policy, training, and low pay).

According to Hirst and Zeitlin, two leading proponents of this thesis, 'Britain has failed to anticipate or participate fully in a revolution in manufacturing organization, the shift from mass production to flexible specialization' (1989: 168). Instead, British producers have remained wedded to the outmoded principles of mass production – often referred to as the 'Fordist' system – at a time when structural shifts in the marketplace and developments in technology favoured other routes to competitive advantage.

Underpinning their perspective is a theory of historical contingency, which holds that paths of industrial development are determined by the interplay of the strategies of key actors at critical conjunctures. Mass production took hold in the early years of the twentieth century in the United States and Britain, and was guided by the actions of influential industrialists, such as Henry Ford in the United States, who recognized the merits of a competitive strategy founded on product and process standardization. Ford drew upon the experience of firms such as Swift and Armour in the meat-processing industry, which had pioneered moving assembly line techniques, to produce an integrated technical and social system which reduced complex, skilled work to a set of unskilled routine tasks. The early successes of his River Rouge plant in Detroit helped galvanize a broader shift towards mass production.

The present period is characterized as a second turning point in the development of manufacturing (Piore and Sabel 1984). The principles of craft production, rudely displaced by Ford and his contemporaries, are re-emerging in some, as yet still localized, regions of the world economy, and allegedly are proving superior to the techniques of mass production. Britain and the United States, in particular, are said to be losing out to the thriving industrial districts in Italy, Japan and Germany, which have succeeded in reconfiguring their industries to take advantage of the more fluid market conditions which characterize the present era. Key developments include the decentralization of production operations into 'interdependent networks of small and medium-sized firms subcontracting to one another', and the metamorphosis of large MNCs 'into looser federations of operating units' (Hirst and Zeitlin 1989: 169). At the same time, new technologies have been harnessed by firms to reap the benefits of economies of scope through the production of small batches of specialized, high value added commodities targeted at specific market niches.

These developments were allegedly precipitated by the crisis of mass production, the immediate cause of which was the saturation of mass markets in the late 1960s, and the failure of the diversification and conglomeration strategies which dominated corporate restructuring in the 1970s (Piore and Sabel 1984). Flexible specialization reverses the principles of mass production, and, according to Hirst and Zeitlin, 'involves the combination of general purpose capital equipment and skilled labour to produce a wide and changing range of semi-customized goods'. In Britain, the argument runs, flexible specialization has been blocked by the interplay of powerful vested interests, management ineptitude and government myopia. Trades unions have sought to defend established practices and demarcation lines, built around the mass production system; employers have lacked critical marketing, engineering, and people management skills, and have misdirected investment funds; while successive governments have slavishly sought to create large firms, in pursuit of economies of scale, to service the mass markets which are said to have been in decline since the mid-1960s.

A positive feature of this line of analysis is that it challenges established economic histories which contend that British industry has been in decline for a century or more. Hirst and Zeitlin rightly argue that such a perspective is a 'convenient myth to hide the recent and widespread failure of our manufacturing sector'. But their argument fails to convince in several crucial respects.

First, their characterization of state industrial policy is far too crude. The explicit encouragement of mergers to promote 'national champions' was a feature of policy in the 1960s, but the approach of governments tended to be half-hearted and subject to significant reversals as competition policy considerations periodically dominated (see Nolan and O'Donnell 1991; Walsh 1991). Second, as O'Donnell (1993) points out, the case study findings adduced by Best, Hirst, Zeitlin and others to justify their claims about the superior performance of the industrial districts of Italy is contradicted by recent national survey evidence (see Rey 1989). Particularly questionable is the image of thriving networks of small, craft-based, vertically specialized 'high-tech' firms. Firms are small, to be sure, but workers often receive sweatshop wages, have limited training, and are engaged in routine work which is carried out under conditions of fierce horizontal competition with other firms in the region. Third, their claim that British industry has been locked into a Fordist time warp since mass production first took hold in the 1930s does not fit well with the historical record. Recognition of the domestic economy's partial and very late conversion to such principles has prompted some commentators to speak of a system of 'flawed' Fordism in Britain, while others reject the empirical and analytical force of such taxonomies altogether (see Nolan 1994b).

Finally, and crucially in the present context, Hirst and Zeitlin's discussion of the determining role of domestic institutional rigidities in the decline of British manufacturing is too narrow. Their account, which is similar in structure to classic Keynesianism, proceeds on the assumption that the British economy is a coherent, autonomous entity which can be regulated by governments regardless of international developments: hence their total neglect of the growing salience of MNCs. The approach pursued above, by contrast, emphasizes the interplay of internal and external forces. It does not deny the significance of historically forged social and economic institutions in Britain, but is concerned to examine that significance in the context of an increasingly internationalized economy.

Industrial Relations and the British Economy

Previous sections have identified some of the salient characteristics of the economy, labour market institutions and employment structure, and changes in them since 1945. This final section attempts to draw out some implications for the analysis of the changing character and context of industrial relations.

A striking feature of much of the contemporary literature on industrial relations and the British economy is its one-sided character. Reflecting the entrenched view that industrial performance in Britain has been seriously impaired by a legacy of adversarial industrial relations, the arrow of causation is typically pointed in one direction only, and often with an exclusive emphasis on the damage allegedly inflicted on the economy by sectional and obstructive trade unions. Of course, industrial relations institutions and processes have been important in shaping the performance of industry and the economy more generally. But the relationship is neither unidirectional nor straightforward. Behaviour and institutions in the workplace have been inscribed in important ways by the developing weaknesses of the post-war British economy and its changing international position. An adequate treatment would thus attempt to grasp this interplay of forces rather than specify the problem as a simple linear relationship between dependent and independent variables.

Britain's economy had not been ravaged during the Second World War, nor was it subject to wholesale reconstruction in the aftermath. But by the early 1960s the weaknesses of domestic production and industrial organization were only too obvious. Many contemporary commentators, the Donovan Commission included, took the view that the deteriorating competitiveness of manufacturing industry stemmed in large part from the conduct of workplace industrial relations. Yet few observers sought to relate that conduct to the prevailing structure of economic incentives and constraints. Reid (1968) was one important exception, as noted above, but his analysis was more successful in highlighting the problem than motivating a new research agenda.

That research agenda might have included an attempt to unravel the connections between the pattern of inward and outward foreign investment, the skewing of production towards labour-intensive, low value added work, and the limited and often contradictory industrial and labour market policies of the state. It might have considered whether or not there was a relationship between the availability of a comparatively low wage, under-trained and disposable workforce and management's evident failure to invest adequately in plant, people and technology. It might also usefully have served to check the developing obsession in the media, academia and policymaking circles with the so-called British worker and wages problem, perhaps by drawing appropriate lessons from systematic comparative research.

Instead, demarcation lines between the different social sciences hardened and the study of the processes of job regulation became disconnected from a wider concern with the evolution of the capitalist economy in Britain. Correspondingly, the treatment of industrial relations in studies of economic performance has tended to be rudimentary at best, and more often totally misleading (cf. Nichols 1986). What new insights can be gained from reconnecting these intrinsically related fields of study?

Crucially, there is an opportunity to recast the long-standing debate about the sources of weakness in production and place it on a firmer conceptual footing. The existing literature, which has been dominated by economists, takes as its point of departure a theory of the economy which abstracts from the politics of production and regards conflict in the workplace as perverse. Worker passivity is not only thought to be the norm, it is also judged desirable for production efficiency. Yet this need not be the case. Indeed, as discussed above, in the post-war period employers were able to draw upon a relatively low cost, segmented and disposable labour force – and one, moreover, that was far more accommodating to change than is often implied – yet still emerge in international markets as high cost producers. The problem was that investment and productivity did not advance in British industry at the same rate as in many other developed economies. Is it not possible that high wage, high productivity growth strategies were inhibited by the perpetuation of a permissive legal and labour market context, which yielded over many decades a relatively cheap source of labour power available to be harnessed by employers to outmoded business practices?

Reid noted that sloppy management controls in the workplace were a by-product of the buoyant macroeconomic context of the 1950s and 1960s. But what this argument failed to recognize was the powerful presence in many branches of industry of high 'exit' barriers to inefficient firms. The low costs of employment, the ease with which management could dispose of labour in the event of deteriorating trading conditions, and the enduring traditions of management prerogative in many industries, provided relief for those companies that sought to compete on the basis of outmoded techniques and effort-intensive systems of work organization. The incentive to upgrade was simply not powerful enough.

Nor was the situation aided by the substantial flows of inward and outward investment. For in the same way that cheap labour, and the absence of significant legal constraints on employers in respect of hiring and firing, trade union recognition and collective bargaining, helped to accommodate production inefficiencies among indigenous companies, so too did this configuration of incentives encourage inward investors to direct their comparatively low-skill, low value added production activities to Britain.

Turning to areas of debate dominated by industrial relations specialists, there is arguably much to be gained from investing current studies of management practice – a topic which has dominated the recent literature in much the same way that the analysis of trade unions dominated the 1960s and 1970s – with a stronger economic content. Consider, for example, the widely discussed training gap in Britain, which many claim has resulted in the perpetuation of significant labour quality deficiencies at all levels of industry. Early discussions of this problem highlighted supply side weaknesses, but of late attention has switched to the demand. Why is it that so many employers in Britain fail to invest in people?

A perspective which gives proper attention to the evolving economic structure in Britain, to the predominance of competitive strategies based on low value added, low quality and effort-intensive production systems, and properly situates current management practices in terms of wider shifts and transformations in the international division of labour, can offer penetrating new insights into the limits of the British version of human resource management. There is no need to resort to crude voluntaristic arguments about the myopia of management or the shortcomings of governments dominated by rigid ideologies. The conditioning effects of structural relations over management behaviour remains an underdeveloped field of inquiry and has not been greatly assisted by the current penchant for models of strategic choice (see chapter 1).

These brief observations provide only a flavour of the sort of expanded research programme that might flow from a more integrated approach combining the analytical strengths and research methods of a number of disciplines. As indicated above, this book endeavours to pursue at least some of this agenda. For example, chapters 4 and 5 combine economists' and industrial relations perspectives on management and pay determination; and chapter 8 explores the nature of state intervention, drawing on theories of corporatism. The challenge ahead is to promote an integrated analysis that frees the study of industrial relations and economic restructuring from the pernicious dogmas of the past.

References

Archibugi, D. and Michie, J. 1995: Science and Technology, R & D and Innovation. In J. Michie (ed.), forthcoming, *Economic and Industrial Performance in Europe*. Aldershot: Edward Elgar.

Atkinson, J. 1984: Manpower Strategies for Flexible Organisations. *Personnel Management*, August, 28–31.

Auerbach, P. 1989: Multinationals and the British Economy. In F. Green (ed.), *The Restructuring of the UK Economy*. Brighton: Harvester Wheatsheaf.

Bélanger, J. and Evans, S. 1988: Job Controls and Shop Steward Leadership among Semi-skilled Engineering Workers. In M. Terry and P. K. Edwards (eds), *Shopfloor Politics and Job Controls: The Post-War Engineering Industry*. Oxford: Blackwell.

Best, M. 1990: *The New Competition*. Cambridge: Polity.

Blackaby, F. (ed.) 1978: *De-industrialisation*. London: Heinemann.

Bowles, S. 1985: The Production Process in a Competitive Economy: Walrasian, Neo-Hobbesian and Marxian Models. *American Economic Review*, 75, 1, 16–36.

Bowles, S. and Gintis, H. 1993: The Revenge of Homo Economicus: Contested Exchange and the Revival of Political Economy. *Journal of Economic Perspectives*, 7, 1, 83–102.

Buxton, T. and Clokie, S. 1992: Technology and Structural Change. In C. Driver and P. Dunne (eds), *Structural Change and Economic Growth*. Cambridge: Cambridge University Press.

Cantwell, J. 1988: The Reorganization of European Industries after Integration: Selected Evidence on the Role of Multinational Enterprise Activities. *Journal of Common Market Studies*, 25, 2, 127–151.

Casey, B. 1991: Survey Evidence on Trends in 'Non-standard' Employment. In A. Pollert (ed.), *Farewell to Flexibility?* Oxford: Blackwell.

Crafts, N. 1988: The Assessment: British Economic Growth over the Long Run. *Oxford Review of Economic Policy*, 4, 1, i–xxi.

Crafts, N. 1991: Reversing Relative Economic Decline? The 1980s in Historical Perspective, *Oxford Review of Economic Policy*, 7, 3, 81–98.

Crafts, N. and Broadberry, S. 1990: Explaining Anglo-American Productivity Differences in the Mid-twentieth Century. *Oxford Review of Economics and Statistics*, 52, 4, 375–402.

Cross, M. 1988: Changing Work Practices in UK Manufacturing, 1981–1988. *Industrial Relations Review and Report*, 415, 2–10.

Crossley, J. R. 1968: The Donovan Report: A Case Study in the Poverty of Historicism. *British Journal of Industrial Relations*. 6, 3, 296–302.

Darby, J. and Wren-Lewis, S. 1988: Trends in Manufacturing Labour Productivity. *National Institute of Economic and Social Research Discussion Paper*, 145.

Dicken, P. 1993: *Global Shift: The Internationalisation of Economic Activity*, 2nd edn. London: Paul Chapman.

Donovan Commission 1968: Royal Commission on Trade Unions and Employers' Associations. *Report*. Cmnd. 3623. London: HMSO.

Driver, C. and Dunne, P. (eds) 1992: *Structural Change and Economic Growth*. Cambridge: Cambridge University Press.

Dunning, J. 1985: Multinational Enterprise and Industrial Restructuring in the UK. *Lloyds Bank Review*, October, 1–19.

Edwards, P. K. 1990: The Politics of Conflict and Consent: How the Labor Contract Really Works. *Journal of Economic Behavior and Organization*, 13, 1, 41–61.

Elger, T. 1990: Technological Innovation and Work Reorganisation in British Manufacturing in the 1980s: Continuity, Intensification or Transformation? *Work, Employment and Society*, Special Issue, May, 67–102.

Fine, B. and Harris, L. 1985: *Peculiarities of the British Economy*. London: Lawrence & Wishart.

Gordon, D., Edwards, R. and Reich, M. 1982: *Segmented Work: Divided Workers*. Cambridge: Cambridge University Press.

Gordon, R. 1992: Discussion Note on N. Crafts. 'Productivity Growth Reconsidered'. *Economic Policy*, 15, 4, 414–25.

Gospel, H. 1992: *Markets, Firms and the Management of Labour in Modern Britain*. Cambridge: Cambridge University Press.

Green, F. (ed.) 1989: *The Restructuring of the UK Economy*. Brighton: Harvester Wheatsheaf.

Green, F. 1992: Recent Trends in British Trade Union Density. *British Journal of Industrial Relations*, 30, 3, 445–58.

Hakim, C. 1990: Core and Periphery in Employers' Workforce Strategies: Evidence from the 1987 ELU Survey. *Work, Employment and Society*, 4, 2, 157–88.

Hayek, F. 1980: *Unemployment and the Unions*. London Institute of Economic Affairs.

Hirst, P. and Zeitlin, J. 1989: Flexible Specialisation and the Competitive Failure of UK Manufacturing. *Political Quarterly*, 60, 2, 164–78.

Hunter, L., McGregor, A., MacInnes, J. and Sproull, A. 1994: The 'Flexible Firm': Strategy and Segmentation. *British Journal of Industrial Relations*, 31, 3, 383–407.

Jacoby, S. 1985: *Employing Bureaucracy: Managers, Unions and the Transformation of Work in American Industry, 1900–1945*. New York: Columbia University Press.

Jacoby, S. 1990: The New Institutionalism: What Can It Learn from the Old? *Industrial Relations*, 29, 2, 315–42.

Jessop, B., Bonnett, K., Bromley, S. and Ling, T. 1987: Popular Capitalism, Flexible Accumulation and Left Strategy. *New Left Review*, 195, 104–22.

Knell, J. 1993: Transnational Corporations and the Dynamics of Human Capital Formation: Evidence from West Yorkshire. *Human Resource Management Journal*, 3, 4, 48–59.

Labour Research 1987: UK Firms Seek Rosier Climes. *Labour Research*, 76, 5, 13–14.

Lovering, J. 1990: A Perfunctory Sort of Post-Fordism: Economic Restructuring and Labour Market Segmentation in Britain in the 1980s. *Work, Employment and Society*, Special Issue, May, 9–28.

Lyddon, D. 1994: The Car Industry: 1945–1979. Mimeo, Centre for Industrial Relations, University of Keele.

Mackay, D., Boddy, D., Brack, J., Diack, J. and Jones, N. 1971: *Labour Markets under Different Employment Conditions*. London: Allen & Unwin.

Marginson, P. 1993: Coercion and Co-operation in the Employment Relationship. In J. McCahery, S. Picciotto and C. Scott (eds), *Corporate Control and Accountability*. Oxford: Clarendon.

Mason, G., van Ark, B. and Wagner, K. 1994: Productivity, Product Quality and Workforce Skills: Food Processing in Four European Countries. *National Institute Economic Review*, 147, 62–83.

Maynard, G. 1988: *The Economy Under Mrs Thatcher*. Oxford: Blackwell.

Millward, N., Stevens, M., Smart, D. and Hawes, W. R. 1992: *Workplace Industrial Relations in Transition*. Aldershot: Dartmouth.

Naylor, M. and Purdie, E. 1992: Results of the 1991 Labour Force Survey. *Employment Gazette*, 100, 4, 153–83.

Nichols, T. 1986: *The British Worker Question: A New Look at Workers and Productivity in Manufacturing*. London: Routledge & Kegan Paul.

Nolan, P. 1983: The Firm and Labour Market Behaviour. In G. S. Bain (ed.), *Industrial Relations in Britain*. Oxford: Blackwell.

Nolan, P. 1989: The Productivity Miracle? In F. Green (ed.), *The Restructuring of the UK Economy*. Brighton: Harvester Wheatsheaf.

Nolan, P. 1992: Securing Human Resources: Employer Strategies and the Labour Market. In E. Thorne (ed.), *The Challenge of the Economic Environment*. Milton Keynes: Open University Press.

Nolan, P. 1993: The Past Strikes Back: Industrial Relations and UK Competitiveness. *University of Leeds Review*, 36, 195–210.

Nolan, P. 1994a: Labour Market Institutions, Industrial Restructuring and Unemployment in Europe. In J. Michie and J. Grieve Smith (eds), *Unemployment in Europe*. New York: Academic Press.

Nolan, P. 1994b: Fordism and Post-Fordism. In P. Arestis and M. Sawyer (eds), *The Elgar Companion to Radical Political Economy*. Aldershot: Edward Elgar.

Nolan, P. and Brown, W. 1983: Competition and Workplace Wage Determination. *Oxford Bulletin of Economics and Statistics*, 45, 3, 269–87.

Nolan, P. and O'Donnell, K. 1991: Flexible Specialisation and UK Manufacturing Weakness. *Political Quarterly*, 62, 1, 106–24.

O'Donnell, K. 1993: New Competition: A Review Article. *International Review of Applied Economics*, 7, 1, 109–17.

OECD 1991: *Historical Statistics 1960–1990*. Paris: OECD.

Peck, J. and Stone, I. 1991: *New Inward Investment in the Northern Region Labour Market*. Newcastle Economic Research Unit, Newcastle upon Tyne Polytechnic.

Piore, M. and Sabel, C. 1984: *The Second Industrial Divide: Possibilities for Prosperity*. New York: Basic Books.

Porter, M. 1990: *The Competitive Advantage of Nations*. London: Macmillan.

Ray, G. 1972: Labour Costs and International Competitiveness. *National Institute Economic Review*, 61, 53–8.

Ray, G. 1987: Labour Costs in Manufacturing. *National Institute Economic Review*, 120, 71–4.

Reid, G. 1968: Economic Comment on the Donovan Report. *British Journal of Industrial Relations*, 6, 3, 303–15.

Rey, G. 1989: Small Firms: A Profile of Their Evolution, 1981–85. In E. Goodman (ed.), *Small Firms and Industrial Districts in Italy*. London: Routledge.

Rowthorn, R. and Wells, J. 1987: *De-industrialization and Foreign Trade*. Cambridge: Cambridge University Press.

Rubery, J. 1978: Structured Labour Markets, Worker Organisation and Low Pay. *Cambridge Journal of Economics*, 1, 1, 17–36.

Siebert, W. and Addison, J. 1991: Internal Labour Markets: Causes and Consequences. *Oxford Review of Economic Policy*, 7, 1, 76–92.

Singh, A. 1976: UK Industry and the World Economy: A Case of Deindustrialisation. *Cambridge Journal of Economics*, 1, 2, 113–36.

Stiglitz, J. 1991: Symposium on Organizations and Economics. *Journal of Economic Perspectives*, 5, 2, 15–24.

Stout, D. 1978: Deindustrialisation and Industrial Policy. In F. Blackaby (ed.), *Deindustrialisation*. London: Heinemann.

Turner, H. A. 1969: The Donovan Report. *Economic Journal*, 79, 1, 1–10.

Turner, P. and van 't dack, J. 1993: Measuring International Price and

Costs Competitiveness. *Bank for International Settlements Economic Papers*, 39. Basle.

United Nations 1992: *World Investment Report.* New York: UN.

Walsh, J. 1991: The Performance of UK Textiles and Clothing: Recent Controversies and Evidence. *International Review of Applied Economics*, 5, 3, 277–309.

Wells, J. 1989: Uneven Development and De-industrialisation in the UK since 1979. In F. Green (ed.), *The Restructuring of the UK Economy.* Brighton: Harvester Wheatsheaf.

Williamson, O. E. 1975: *Markets and Hierarchies.* New York: Free Press.

Williamson, O. E. 1980: The Organization of Work. *Journal of Economic Behavior and Organization*, 1, 1, 5–22.

Williamson, O. E. 1993: Contested Exchange versus the Governance of Contractual Relations. *Journal of Economic Perspectives*, 7, 1, 103–8.

Young, S., Hood, N. and Hamill, J. 1987: *Foreign Multinationals and the British Economy.* London: Croom Helm.

PART II

The Parties to Industrial Relations

4
Management: Systems, Structures and Strategy

Keith Sisson and Paul Marginson

Many people do not distinguish between 'management' and 'employer'; some commentators even use the terms interchangeably. Strictly speaking, however, management and employer are not the same. Whereas the employer is 'a fiction endowed with personality by the law' (Wedderburn 1971: 41) – that is, a legally registered corporation – management can be a resource, a process or a group of people who are also employees (Harbison and Myers 1959). Managers are unlike other employees, however, in one respect which is critically important for industrial relations. They have authority invested in them by the board of directors, or its equivalent, to run the organization in conformity with its stated objectives; they therefore have responsibility for managing the relationship with employees in general (Armstrong 1987). It is as a group of people with this particular responsibility that the term 'management' is used throughout the chapter.

In recent years there has been a dramatic change in the treatment of management in the industrial relations literature. Until the 1980s most commentators paid no more than perfunctory attention to it. Indeed, in the first *System of Industrial Relations in Britain* (Flanders and Clegg 1954), management was not given a separate chapter; management's role in industrial relations was largely subsumed in a chapter on employers' organizations, with details of its practice being scattered throughout the book. This reflected the view that, compared to trade unions and the state, management was a relatively unproblematic, if not necessarily unimportant, industrial relations actor; it seemed to have settled for a particular way of doing things and to be more concerned with maintaining the status quo than with changing it. Since the beginning of the 1980s the role of management appears to have changed significantly and there has been a considerable increase in both the empirical and theoretical attention it has received as a result. Instead of largely responding to government and trade unions, management has been taking more initiatives, leading some commentators to suggest that management is now the critical actor in industrial relations.

This chapter is concerned with three key issues to have emerged as a result of the increasing activity of and growing attention paid to management in industrial relations. The first is management's role in industrial relations. Three main models of how it is conceived are identified and considered: the *systems actor*, the *strategic actor* and the *agent of capital*. The second key issue is the variety of management industrial relations practice. Why is there so much diversity, above all in Britain, and how can sense be made of it? The third is the overall strategy of British management. This chapter considers whether or not a paradigm shift is taking place and, if so, whether this takes the form of a more people-centred approach associated with human resource management (HRM) or a reassertion of management prerogative over the employment relationship. Each of these issues is considered in turn. The final section looks at some of the major industrial relations challenges that British management is likely to face in the foreseeable future.

Models of Management

There are two reasons for opening our account with a consideration of the different ways in which the role of management in industrial relations has been conceived. First, an appreciation of the different models, albeit only in outline, will be helpful in putting into context our interpretation of recent developments in later sections. Second, the fact that there are different models, and that each one has strengths and weaknesses, serves to underline the complexity of the issues which have to be taken into account.

A systems actor

The first, and dominant, model of management's role is firmly rooted within the industrial relations tradition. It is most clearly expressed in Dunlop's (1958) *Industrial Relations Systems*. Management is seen as only one of a number of actors working within a system of institutions, processes and rules which, in turn, are shaped by technology and markets. Other actors in the system, notably the state and trade unions, are seen as having equal, if not greater, influence on the development of the system. It is the policies and approaches of the state and trade unions, for example, which are seen as largely shaping the structure of collective bargaining. Managements react to the pressures that come from the other two and have to work with the constraints that the subsequent compromises entail. For the most part, however, they do not do this under duress. The assumption is that managements share the same interests – or 'ideology' in Dunlop's own word – as the state and trade unions in having a relatively stable framework of the 'rule of law' within which it can get on with the job of managing its affairs as efficiently as possible.

A different version of the systems model, which remains highly influential in continental Europe, is the 'societal approach' (Maurice and Sellier 1979). In this case the emphasis is on relationships within the context of the wider society rather than Dunlop's system of institutions, processes and rules. Especially important is the complex process of interaction between the parties which is deemed to be shaped by the pattern of industrialization. Thus the different approach of managements in France and Germany towards training is explained in terms of the occupational stratification within workplaces in the two countries as well as the different status accorded to education as opposed to training in the wider society. In France there is a greater reliance on non-manual employees and education carries the higher status, whereas in Germany there is a higher proportion of manual employees and the qualifications from training are held in high regard. In short, management's behaviour cannot simply be explained in terms of technology or markets; it can only be fully understood in terms of management's specific institutional and historical experience as *systems actors*.

A major weakness of the model is that industrial relations issues can be prioritized and treated outside the broader context of management's business and production priorities. Two important consequences follow. One is that the role of management in industrial relations tends to be accorded less attention than it deserves. Even its motivation in working within the industrial relations 'system' has not been properly explored. The reasons why managements in different countries and industries behave in different ways are reduced to the deterministic forces of technology or 'society'. The active role of managers is neglected; it is only recently, for example, that the logic of multi-employer bargaining has begun to be understood (see, for example, Sisson 1987; Gospel 1992). The second, and more critical, consequence is that the model has considerable problems in accounting for change and, in particular, change that is driven by management. This helps to explain why the model has attracted particular criticism in Britain and the USA; the 'system' of industrial relations is less institutionalized and/or centralized than it is in many continental European countries and, throughout the 1980s and early 1990s, the pace of management-driven change appears to have been much greater. The two points come together in relation to the workplace; as noted in chapter 1, managements affect the conduct of work in many ways, and yet the systems approach neglects this shaping of the effort bargain.

A strategic actor

The second model has largely developed out of the first, though it has also been influenced by the wider recognition accorded to the importance of strategy and strategic choice in social behaviour (Crowe 1989). Put simply, rather than being regarded as members of an interlocking system working to its own internal logic, the parties to industrial relations – management, trade unions and governments – have come to be seen as 'agents' who shape the environment in which they operate as well as being influenced by it. By implication, the environment does not determine behaviour; the parties – and, above all, the management of the large companies that are so important in shaping the framework of industrial relations – have some discretion or choice in deciding what courses of action or strategies they are going to follow.

The approach's focus on the purposive behaviour of the parties, rather than on the outcome of some form of autonomous system working to its own internal logic, has been a positive step. The problem, however, has been to apply the model in a form that is generalizable. For example, there have been several attempts to develop categories or types of management approach which assume strategic choice. In the first edition of this volume one of us suggested that it was possible to identify four types – 'traditional', 'consultative', 'constitutional' and 'sophisticated paternalist' – along with a dominant ad hoc or pragmatic group (Purcell and Sisson

1983). Statistical analysis of the WIRS establishment data (Deaton 1985) and CLIRS company level data (Purcell 1987) offered some confirmation for the pragmatism and 'ad hoccery' of the majority. They could find little evidence for the four particular types, however. Further elaboration of management styles can be found in chapter 11.

The most explicit use of the strategic choice approach is to be found in the work of Kochan and his colleagues in the United States (Kochan et al. 1986) where it is almost elevated to the status of a theory (see also Poole 1986). Management is seen as a *strategic actor* in two particular senses: its actions are held to be critical not only in determining the main changes taking place in industrial relations, but also in reflecting the choice of business strategies pursued. Thus US management, faced with intensifying international competition, is said to be confronted with the choice of pursuing a strategy either of quality or low cost. Both routes involve making radical changes in existing industrial relations arrangements and, in particular, in the provisions for collective bargaining of the so-called 'New Deal' system which dates back to the 1930s. Although a descriptive and analytical account, there is also a very clear prescriptive message. Successful managements are ones which have chosen the quality route, developed people-centred policies to match, and involved trade unions in their making and administration.

In this particular case, there are a number of highly questionable assumptions. One is that strategy formulation is a straightforward process. To the contrary, as business theorists increasingly recognize, strategy is a most problematic concept (see, for example, the review in Whittington 1993). At best, strategies, understood as sense of a direction, emerge as a result of a series of decisions made by people at many levels in the organization; they involve continual reassessments and readjustments of position. Depending on the particular ways in which management runs the organization, strategies, in the sense of a set of medium- and long-term plans, may not emerge at all – there may simply be a series of vague statements or even financial ratios. In these circumstances, it may not be feasible to expect the detailed integration of personnel policies and practices implied in the prescription of Kochan and his colleagues, let alone the fundamental shift in attitudes and behaviours entailed, for example, in managing culture or task participation.

A second, and in many ways the most critical, assumption which has come under scrutiny (see, for example, Storey and Sisson 1989;

Guest 1991) is that managers have the degree of choice with which they are credited. Clearly, managers, especially those who run large private-sector companies, have enormous resources at their disposal and a significant measure of control over large numbers of employees. Yet, the evidence suggests, they still may not be willing or able to shape their environment in ways which may seem logical to the analyst. Significantly, faced with the evidence that far fewer US managements seem capable of moving up-market into quality products and of introducing the associated changes in industrial relations than he hoped for, Kochan has subsequently recognized that:

> the 'strategic' human resource management models of the 1980s were too limited . . . because they depended so heavily on the values, strategies and support of top executives . . . While we see [these] as necessary conditions, we do not see them as sufficient to support the transformational process. A model capable of achieving sustained and transformational change will, therefore, need to incorporate more active roles of other stakeholders in the employment relationship, including government, employees and union representatives as well as line managers. (Kochan and Dyer 1993: 1)

The key point that many proponents of the strategic choice model neglect is that choices are not made in a vacuum. The notion of strategic choice implies, at the very least, circumstances over which even chief executives do not have total control. The structures within which this choice is exercised are profoundly important: they can support or hinder the development of particular approaches. Different configurations of corporate governance structures, patterns of employer association, and networks among producers and suppliers, combine together with industrial relations arrangements to increase or reduce management's ability to choose between quality and low-cost strategies (see, for example, the review in Goodhart 1994; see also Albert 1991; Streeck 1992; Lane 1994).

An agent of capital

The third model comes from outside the industrial relations tradition. It appears in both neo-classical economics and radical theories of capitalist production (see the discussion in Gospel and Palmer 1993: 37). Whereas in neo-classical economics the implications tend to be implicit – an example would be much of the personnel management literature in the prescriptive tradition – in radical theories they are usually very explicit. Basically, this model sees management as an agent which is obliged by the 'laws' of the market to treat the workforce as a factor of production. Like the other factors of production, management must have primary regard to its costs. This does not necessarily mean that management will always be driven to minimize wages; the main concern, as will be explained below, is with unit labour costs. The model none the less implies that the efficiency with which human resources are used will be of overriding concern. It is therefore extended to 'not-for-profit' organizations such as publicly-owned services and voluntary organizations, even though ownership relations are very different from the typical capitalist enterprise with its shareholders.

There have also been significant developments in recent years which have gone a long way to dealing with what was the main weakness of the model, namely its difficulty in dealing with the diversity of management behaviour allowing for similar technology and markets. Thus, writers in the radical tradition have recognized that management has to find ways and means of legitimating its authority in the eyes of the workforce in order to get them to do the job that it wants. This is why management is usually willing to introduce a 'rule of law': the policies, practices and procedures of selection, training and development, appraisal, pay systems and pay structures, which supplement or replace the direct control by individual managers and the technical controls of machines and processes of operations. This is also why, rather than decide the 'rule of law' unilaterally, management often gives workers a say in making and administering it. This may involve individual employees or, as has happened in virtually every industrial society, the trade unions which have grown up to represent their interests. Hence collective bargaining. Writers in the radical tradition have also differentiated between management approaches in which the primary emphasis is securing effort from the workforce through detailed supervision and strict discipline – what Friedman (1977) terms a regime of 'direct control' – and those which emphasize management's need to tap the creativity of the workforce and elicit productivity through yielding a measure of discretion to employees over the organization and performance of work – a regime of 'responsible autonomy'.

By implication, however, a regime of 'responsible autonomy' is contingent on a particular set of market circumstances; it is not an end in itself, as often appears to be the case in the hands of those who tend to the systems actor approach. Thus the agent of capital model of management has sought to explain many of the recent initiatives being undertaken by management in terms of a reassertion of 'direct control'. One of the clearest statements is that of Burawoy (1985). Contrary to the impression usually given, to paraphrase his argument, developments associated with HRM do not replace the supervisory, technical and bureaucratic controls under traditional work regimes of so-called 'Fordist' or 'Taylorist' systems. Many of these controls are as much in evidence as ever they were. Indeed, there is evidence of their more intensive use in the form of 'just-in-time' systems and their like (see chapter 12). The problem is that many of the bureaucratic controls which developed in the wake of 'Fordism' and 'Taylorism', says Burawoy (1985: 263), and which include industrial relations systems, have 'established constraints on the deployment of capital, whether by tying wages to profits or by creating internal labour markets, collective bargaining and grievance machinery which hamstrung management's domination of the workplace'. Such constraints are no longer acceptable under conditions of increasing global competition, which explains why many managements are supporting the deregulation of the labour market and rolling back the influence of trade unions.

Economic thinking, too, is recognizing the scope for variation in management behaviour. Efficiency wage theorists, for example, have noted that management may pay higher wages than competitors, as Henry Ford did in the USA in 1914, or provide superior welfare conditions, as Quaker families did at the turn of the century in Britain, in order to generate higher productivity. Likewise, proponents of the 'new institutional economics' have recognized that many of the industrial relations arrangements which their neoclassical colleagues have seen as impediments to the 'proper' working of the labour market, such as systems of job evaluation, life-long employment, procedures for consultation and negotiation, and compulsory training provisions, can bring significant benefits in terms of economic efficiency (see, for example, Doeringer and Piore 1971; Williamson 1985).

Conclusions

Each of the models offers valuable insights, but is not sufficient in itself. The complexity of the issues that have to be taken in to account in understanding management's role is considerable. Management is a critical actor and efficiency is fundamental to its actions. Institutions contribute to and shape this search for efficiency, however. It must also never be forgotten that management is a group of people; management cannot be abstracted from the wider contexts in which they operate. These contexts, as the next section points out, are extremely diverse. The result is that management practice is also characterized by great complexity and variety.

A Variety of Practice

At first sight, the variety of management's industrial relations practice seems to be almost infinite. Managements seem to differ not only in their approach to trade unions but also in the ways in which they recruit, develop, motivate and reward employees. Such variety is not quite as random as it appears, however. Two considerations are especially important in making sense of it. One is the complex of institutions, processes and rules which make up the national industrial relations system; these serve to facilitate or preclude particular practices. The other is such variables as the size and ownership of the management's organization, and the business strategies, structures and styles that management pursues. Each of these propositions is developed here to aid understanding of the exceptional diversity of British managements' industrial relations practice.

A voluntary system

A comparison between Britain and other European Union (EU) member states illustrates the importance of the national industrial relations system. In other EU member states the great majority of managements belong to employers' organizations and follow the terms and conditions of the multi-employer agreements which they negotiate with trade unions covering entire sectors, either at national or regional level, such as metal-working, chemicals, construction and so on (Ferner and Hyman 1992). Such agreements can be extremely detailed, covering, for example, employment security, training and development, the method of payment, the use of industrial engineering techniques and subcontracting, as well as rates of pay, the working week, holidays and so on. Even though there are considerable supplementary negotiations in individual workplaces, there tends to be considerable uniformity so far as the general pattern is concerned.

In Britain, by contrast, with the exception of industries charac-terized by a large number of highly competitive firms such as electri-cal contracting or printing, multi-employer bargaining has never played such a key role in setting standards; the main emphasis has been on procedures and in particular the procedures for resolving disputes. Moreover, in the 1980s British managements appear to have finally set their backs on multi-employer bargaining as the main means of setting conditions as well as pay. By 1990 only about 20 per cent of establishments in manufacturing and 10 per cent in services were in membership of employers' organizations; member-ship was highest in engineering (32 per cent), textiles (32 per cent) and construction (75 per cent) (Millward et al. 1992: 45). In some industries, notably engineering, there are currently no multi-employer agreements in place. Fewer than one-third of manage-ments in the private sector reported that sectoral multi-employer agreements were the most important levels in setting pay; the establishment or the company was typically the level at which, if they recognized trade unions, they engaged in collective bargaining. A growing majority, however, as the next section will show, did not recognize trade unions and did not negotiate collective agreements with them. In most workplaces, in other words, it is management which determines the terms and conditions of employment in the light of its own particular circumstances.

In the public sector, major programmes of privatization and com-mercialism are having a similar effect. The once dominant Whitley system of national multi-employer bargaining is under threat in the public services with the break-up of the civil service into executive agencies, the development of trusts in the National Health Service and the opting out of schools in education (see chapter 10). A key implication is that the traditional role of government in the public sector in setting management standards for others to follow has effectively been abandoned.

A second and related consideration is the legal framework. In most other countries, legal regulation plays an extremely important role in helping to bring about a measure of uniformity. Multi-employer agreements enjoy considerable legal status: they are legally enforceable contracts and codes; they can also be extended across an entire sector. Moreover, legislation and labour codes requiring managements to introduce a framework of rights and obligations, together with statutory provisions for participation and involve-ment, such as works councils, are the norm. Also many countries, including France and Germany, have highly regulated systems of training.

In Britain, because of the voluntary tradition discussed in chapters 2 and 9, managements have been relatively free to develop their own approaches to industrial relations. Multi-employer agreements, for example, along with collective agreements in general, have never enjoyed the legal status they have in most other countries; they remain 'gentlemen's agreements' binding in honour only. Provisions for the extension of collective agreements to workplaces in the same sector, never comprehensive, have been repealed altogether. Legislation and labour codes requiring managements to introduce a framework of rights and obligations, together with statutory provisions for participation and involvement, such as works councils, are also noticeable by their absence. Britain is also generally regarded as having a voluntary system of training; responsibility for education, until recently, has been in the hands of local authorities and independent examination boards, and the assumption during much of the twentieth century has been that vocational training was a matter for management and employees (see chapter 17).

British management, it must be emphasized, has not simply been a passive victim of the 'voluntarist' system. To the contrary, it was management who were primarily responsible for building collective bargaining on procedural rules rather than a code of substantive rules in force for a specified period. It was management who, at critical points in their relationships with trade unions, opposed the development of the contractual system found in other countries. It was not that they were incapable of showing solidarity in particular on procedural matters; the highly successful lock-outs in the engineering industry in 1898 and 1922 over the issue of managerial prerogative were evidence of that. In these and other cases, the stance reflected the view that management had more to lose than gain from a fully contractual system.

A similarly instrumental approach helps to account for the decline of multi-employer bargaining. In a first phase, in the period following the Second World War, management allowed themselves to be drawn into workplace bargaining with shop stewards in order to maintain production. In a second, in the late 1960s and early 1970s, they found it necessary to move further away from multi-employer bargaining in order to reconstruct their workplace industrial relations. In a third phase, in the 1980s, they came to see that they would be stronger and the trade unions weaker if the focus was shifted from the national to the local level. In each phase the role of large companies and in particular large highly diversified companies with interests in a number of sectors has been especially important: they have been to the fore in promoting organization-based employment systems tailored to their special needs (Marginson and Sisson 1994).

Key variables

If industrial relations surveys have cast doubts about the ideal-type approach to understanding management, they have none the less opened other fruitful lines of inquiry. These are our focus here. Much management practice, the survey evidence suggests, is not entirely random and differs in some predictable ways according to several key variables. These include the size of the organization, its ownership, and the business strategies, structures and styles that managements pursue.

Size   As the three WIRS (Daniel and Millward 1984; Millward and Stevens 1986; Millward et al. 1992) have so clearly demonstrated, the size of workplace in particular is positively related with a wide range of industrial relations phenomena. These include whether or not the workplace has specialist personnel managers, belongs to employers' organizations, recognizes trade unions, uses a wide range of involvement and participation methods, practises job evaluation, and has profit sharing.

Size is also a key factor in many of the changes taking place in British industrial relations. During the 1980s, as table 4.1 shows in the case of manufacturing, there was a significant reduction in the size of workplaces in Britain. Much of the decline in trade union membership and the scope of collective bargaining, for example, reflects closure and redundancy in the larger workplaces in manufacturing.

Why is size so important in management industrial relations practice? Other things being equal, the larger the organization, the more complex the management task. The more complex the management task, the greater the need for rules and procedures to achieve consistency of behaviour on the part of individual managers. The greater the need for rules and procedures, the greater the need for workers and workers' representatives to accept their legitimacy. Significantly, a recognition of the importance of size of organization in industrial

Table 4.1   Establishment size in manufacturing industries in the United Kingdom, 1951–1990

	1951	*1979*	*1990*
Per cent of employees working in establishments with:			
1–49 employees	11.4	13.5	19.8
50–99 employees	10.4	6.8	9.3
100–199 employees	13.1	9.5	11.3
200–499 employees	20.7	16.1	18.6
500–999 employees	13.6	13.2	13.4
1,000–1,499 employees	7.2	8.0	5.9
1,500 and more employees	23.6	32.9	21.7
	100.0	100.0	100.0

Source: For 1951 the data are from *Census of Production for 1951: Summary Tables*. London: HMSO, 1956, pt. 1, table 4; for 1979 the data are from Business Statistics Office, *Business Monitor Report on the Census of Production, 1979: Summary Tables*, PA 1002, London: HMSO, 1982, table 6; and for 1990 from ibid. 1990, London: HMSO, 1992.

relations is one of the considerations in the adoption of more de-volved forms of management structures, such as the strategic busi-ness units discussed later.

Ownership   Size is also closely related to our second structural vari-able, which is ownership. The significance of the owner/manager for industrial relations is dealt with in detail in chapter 19. It is sufficient to note here that:

> Typically, the views of owner/managers on labour relations showed little evidence of pre-planning and stressed that as long as workers were working there was no problem. This was associated with wide-spread evidence, in all but the largest firms, of a unitary view of industrial relation, both in its classic form stressing the autonomy of organizational needs, and in a more personalized form, stressing the owner/manager's 'self-creation' of the firm coupled with very positive evaluations of their own reasonableness. The notions of communi-cation and the management of labour are not on the whole formulated as 'problematic' and in need of pre-planning unless they actually become a problem. (Scott et al. 1989: 91)

In the circumstances, as will be shown later, it is not surprising that owner/managers feel little need for rules and procedures. They are also the group most resentful of the presence of trade unions, which are seen as an external influence which threatens the family atmosphere that the owner/manager believes he or she has created.

Until recently, as chapters 10 and 16 describe in more detail, public ownership was also a significant factor in management practice. This is because, at a peak in the early 1980s, some seven million people, or more than one quarter of the working population, were employed in the public sector. As in the case of size, it was possible to list a range of industrial relations phenomena strongly associated with public ownership. These included the recognition of trade unions, which was virtually universal, even among managers up to director level, and the structure of collective bargaining, which was extremely centralized. Especially important was the widespread acceptance that the public sector should be the 'good' or 'model' employer whose management should set standards for others to follow. Though disappearing, strong elements remain. Many aspects of practice in, for example, local authorities and the health service, including pensions and grading structures, reflect this. But increasing diversity of practice is evident: there have been considerable differences in approach to compulsory competitive tendering between Labour and Conservative controlled local authorities, which reflect contrasting commitments to the principle of the 'good employer' (Colling 1993).

A third major difference, noted in chapter 3, is between British and overseas-owned companies. Britain is the 'home' of a large number of international companies; of the 100 largest companies operating in the EC in 1991, 39 were British and two more were Anglo-Dutch (Marginson and Sisson 1994). The country is also 'host' to an equally large number of foreign-owned companies, such as Ford, IBM, Nestlé and Nissan. Following a survey of 176 large companies with 1,000 or more employees, Marginson and his colleagues found that, although there was little difference in approach to trade unions and collective bargaining, there were significant differences in a range of other aspects.

> Overseas-owned companies were distinctive in their approaches to employee development, communication and involvement. As compared with UK-owned companies, they tended to have relatively high levels of expenditure on employee training; they used a wider range of methods of employee communication; they were more likely to use upwards and two-way forms of communication; they were more likely

to provide information on investment plans to employees; and they were less likely to utilize forms of financial participation.

Overseas-owned companies were also distinctive in their policies towards managerial employees. Overseas-owned multinationals were more likely to move managerial staff between countries, to use a common job grading scheme for senior managers (such as Hay-MSL) across their world-wide operations, and to have a separate head office department responsible for the training and development of managers in their subsidiaries overseas, than were UK-owned multinationals. (Marginson et al. 1993: 13–14)

Furthermore, overseas-owned companies accorded personnel a higher profile in their management structures. Thus they were twice as likely to have a personnel director on the main board in Britain as their British-owned counterparts. They were also more likely to have a corporate personnel policy committee comprised of senior managers from a range of functions and to hold meetings of personnel managers from different locations. The overall conclusion was that the influence of the personnel function over budgetary and strategic decisions was greater in overseas-owned than in British-owned enterprises.

These findings can be related to fundamental differences in systems of corporate governance. Especially important is the exposure to hostile take-over and a concentration on short-run financial performance characteristic of the 'outsider' system, and protection from hostile take-over and concentration on longer-run performance associated with 'insider' systems. The 'outsider' system, Franks and Mayer (1992) have suggested, is exemplified by the Anglo-American mode, and the 'insider' system by arrangements in France, Germany and the Nordic countries. Arguably, these features of 'insider' systems encourage owners to display a greater degree of commitment to the assets that they own than is the case in 'outsider' systems. Thus, under 'insider' systems employees are more likely to be regarded as enduring assets who form a potential source of competitive advantage, and to be associated with an employee development approach to labour management. In turn, employees and other stakeholders are also encouraged to make longer-term commitments to the company. This is especially so in countries, such as Germany, where employees or their representatives have considerable rights as stakeholders. Under 'outsider' systems, by contrast, employees are more likely to be regarded as disposable liabilities and to be associated with a cost minimization approach to labour management. As such, employee management is more likely to be of strategic concern to companies based in 'insider' systems, and therefore to be the subject of centrally determined approaches and policies. Companies based in 'outsider' systems are more likely to see employee management as solely a matter for the operating units (see Marginson and Sisson 1994).

Strategies, structures and styles   As table 4.2 suggests, although the bulk of employees work in small organizations, comparatively speaking, Britain has a very significant number of large companies. In the case of these large organizations, three significant axes of differentiation are evident: diversification, divisionalization and strategic style. Diversification concerns whether companies are involved in related activities, and the associated degree of integration between different activities, or in unrelated activities; or whether they are spatially diversified but undertake the same kind of activity in many different locations. Divisionalization relates to internal structure, which can be primarily territorial (that is, segmented according to regions or districts) or business-based (that is, segmented into product or service divisions). Strategic style concerns the level at which strategic business decisions are taken (business unit, division, national subsidiary or corporate headquarters); the role of corporate headquarters in business development (planning, reviewing, monitoring); and the degree to which the headquarters stresses 'numbers-

Table 4.2   Size distribution of European enterprises

	UK	*France*	*Germany*	*Italy*	*Spain*
Number of enterprises each with 1,000+ employees	3,024	873	2,449	479	351
Number of enterprises each with 1,000+ employees and two subsidiaries in the then 12 EC member states	332	117	257	32	13
Number of enterprises among the largest 100 EC-based international companies operating in the then EC	48	20	21	5	–

Source: Sisson et al. 1992.

driven' rather than 'issue-driven' planning (Goold and Campbell 1987; see also McKinsey and Co. Inc. 1988).

Differences along these three axes generate differences in the extent to which companies are centralized or decentralized in their overall management approach, with consequent implications for their industrial relations policies. For example, where there is a high degree of integration in production or service provision, as in the cases of automobile manufacturers (Ford, General Motors (Vauxhall), Peugeot-Talbot and Rover), management will tend towards a centralized approach. This is also likely where the organization is carrying out the same activity in different locations, because of gains to be made in standardized operating procedures and/or common purchasing. Here the main clearing banks (Barclays, Lloyds, National Westminster and Midland) and multiple retailers (such as Sainsbury and Tesco) would be examples. A decentralized approach is more likely where different kinds of business activity, which are not closely related, are being undertaken in different locations. The extreme case would be that of the diversified conglomerate or industrial holding companies such as Lonrho or BTR (Marginson et al. 1988; Marginson et al. 1993).

Variations in the size of corporate personnel function, for example, are only partially accounted for by the employment size of companies (Marginson et al. 1993: 5). The largest corporate personnel functions tend to be found among single business enterprises and among strategic planners, whereas conglomerates and financial controllers tend to have small numbers of specialist staff or no corporate function at all. Similarly, it is no coincidence that it is the single business enterprises, such as the automobile manufacturers, clearing banks and multiple retailers, which have multi-establishment bargaining or pay determination, whereas it is the conglomerates which are more likely to have decentralized arrangements.

Overall, the conventional wisdom is that management should devolve operational and financial responsibility to the lowest possible unit so that business-level managements are in a position to determine their own costs. In many cases, however, the organization structures that management are seeking to introduce are at odds with the realities of industrial relations. Business-level managers cannot be given total autonomy for fear of establishing embarrassing precedents. The result, as Brown and his colleagues suggest in the following chapter, is that much decentralization is an illusion. Things may 'happen' at local level, but are not necessarily decided there. In the case of pay, a range of coordination mechanisms, such as meetings, 'mock' negotiations and 'instructions' can be found even in the most decentralized companies (Storey and Sisson 1993); strict budgetary controls are also exercised over pay by the corporate finance function (see Marginson et al. 1993). Issues such as the working week or trade union recognition may be the subject of a 'taboo' in that managers at local level must not make concessions on them.

Conclusions

Management industrial relations practice in Britain is characterized by immense variety. In the absence of a detailed framework of multi-employer agreements or legal regulations, this reflects the fact that British management have had considerable scope to exercise choice in what they do. Such practice is not entirely random, however. Much of it can be related to specific structural features. Of the many involved, it has been argued that size, ownership, and the business strategies, structures and styles of the management's organization are especially important in shaping, but not determining, practice. Not everything can be related to structural features in this way, however. Moreover, in a rapidly changing environment management have to respond, and the ways in which they do so are likely to be highly pragmatic. This is above all true of the overall approach of British management, and is the subject of the next section.

A Paradigm Shift?

There are a number of common themes in the debate over whether a fundamental shift is taking place in British management's approach to industrial relations. These provide the starting point for the discussion here. The attention then shifts to the two main interpretations of what is going on – the 'soft' and the 'hard' versions – and to the survey and case study evidence for them. The overall conclusion is that, while there is considerably more evidence for the 'hard' than for the 'soft' version, most British managements are being nowhere as 'strategic' as many commentators have claimed. Rapid changes in products, markets and competitive conditions have placed a premium on management's ability to adapt production. But the implications for industrial relations are rarely clear-cut. Two detailed illustrations are given of the reality of decision-making in industrial relations and an attempt made to relate this to the wider context in which managers have to manage.

The primacy of business conditions

A number of common themes continually appear and reappear in the debate. The first, which harks back to the model of management as a strategic actor, is that management's approach to industrial relations is increasingly business-led. Management, it is argued, faced with ever-intensifying competition in an increasingly global economy, is having to rethink the sources of competitive advantage. One of these is people, and the way in which they are managed. Senior line managers in particular can no longer afford to allow specialist personnel or industrial relations managers simply to maintain a 'system' for its own sake. The key decisions in industrial relations must have regard to the business strategy and must be taken by line managers.

A second theme is an emphasis on flexibility: management, it is argued, needs to develop the capacity to respond more quickly to business conditions. This is reflected in developments as diverse as: the introduction of devolved organizational structures, such as the quasi-autonomous units, divisions and agencies touched on above; the emergence of new forms of cooperation between employers whereby resources are pooled on a particular business project, as is the case with joint ventures and strategic alliances; the growth of outsourcing; the integration of design and production through re-engineering which is radically reducing lead times for new products; and new production arrangements such as cellular manufacturing, flexible manufacturing systems and team working.

The impact of these developments on the organization of work, working practices and industrial relations is equally diverse. Different forms of labour flexibility have been sought by managements. One is numerical. In this case managements are supposedly questioning the logic of so-called standard forms of employment and increasing the amount of subcontracting as well as temporary and part-time working. A second is time flexibility. In this case managements are said to be finding basic hours arrangements increasingly unsatisfactory and replacing them with 'minimum–maximum' hours contracts, which predefine the range of hours to be worked within the day or week, and 'annual hours' agreements, which guarantee annual salaries in return for the freedom to vary the number of hours worked in a given period within the scope of the standard working hours of the year as a whole. A third is functional or task flexibility. Rather than the certainty of specialization, it is argued, managements are looking for greater interchangeability between tasks and jobs. Finally, there is financial flexibility. In this case managements are reported to be turning their backs on the 'rate-for-the-job' concept which has dominated in the past, in favour of arrangements which depend on individual performance and profit-sharing (for examples of this type of analysis, see Atkinson 1984; see also Brewster and Connock 1985).

The third theme relates to arrangements for managing the employment relationship. Management is no longer supposed to see collective bargaining with trade unions as the bedrock of the system as it did in the 1950s, 1960s and 1970s and is putting more emphasis on the direct relationship with individual employees. This, together with the emphasis on the links with business strategy and the role of line managers, makes up the essence of HRM approach, about which there has been so much debate (see, for example, the reviews in Blyton and Turnbull 1992; Storey 1992). The following quotation from the 1992 White Paper, *People, Jobs and Opportunity*, gives a strong flavour of the kind of thinking involved, even if its descriptive accuracy is open to question:

> There is new recognition of the role and importance of the individual employee. Traditional patterns of industrial relations, based on collective bargaining and collective agreements, seem increasingly inappropriate and are in decline.
> . . .
> Many employers are replacing outdated personnel practice with new policies for human resource management, which put the emphasis on developing the talents and capacities of each individual employee. Many are also looking to communicate directly with their employees rather than through the medium of a trade union or a formal works council. There is a growing trend to individually negotiated reward packages which reflect the individual's personal skills, experience, efforts and performance. Employees in turn have higher expectations of their employer. They are increasingly aware of the contribution they are making – as individuals – to the business for which they work. They want to know how it is performing and to contribute to its development. They increasingly expect to influence their own development and to be rewarded for their achievement and initiative.
> . . .

They also want the opportunity to influence, in some cases to negotiate, their own terms and conditions of employment, rather than leaving them to the outcome of some distant negotiations between employers and trade unions. (Employment Department 1992)

'Soft' and 'hard' versions

There are two main interpretations of what is going on. The 'soft' version 'traces its roots to the human-relations school: it emphasizes communication, motivation and leadership' (Storey 1989: 8). Essentially, it sees management, faced with ever-intensifying competition in an increasingly global economy, not only rethinking the sources of competitive advantage but also realizing that they cannot compete head-on solely in terms of cost with their competitors in Eastern Europe and the Far East, let alone the Third World. This means switching from mass production to 'flexible specialization'; that is, the provision of high quality semi-customized goods and services tailored for niche markets (see chapter 3). This, in turn, means getting much closer to the customer to establish his or her desires, the introduction of 'total quality management' (TQM) designed to achieve continuous improvement in product and service quality, as well as reductions in cost, and the adoption of a range of people-centred policies aimed at the development of a highly committed and adaptable workforce willing and able to learn new skills and take on new tasks. The approach is variously described as that of the 'empowered organization', the 'learning organization' and the 'open company', as well as HRM (see Sisson 1994).

The 'hard' version shares key elements of the analysis, and the prescriptions of the 'soft' version. Managements, it is accepted, are under pressure to rethink their approach to managing people. They are seeking a better fit between their human resource strategies and business strategies. They are transforming their practice. The 'hard' version differs fundamentally, however, in its interpretation of the direction that this transformation is taking. Few British companies, especially given the corporate governance arrangements discussed above, appear to be able to compete on the basis of quality and to make the necessary investments in human capital that the 'soft' version entails. If there is a paradigm shift, it is certainly not in the direction of the people-centred approach of the 'soft' version. Instead, the emphasis is on the 'quantitative, calculative and business-strategic aspects of managing the headcounts resource in as "rational" a way as for any other economic factor' (Storey 1989: 8), which takes us back to the model of management as an 'agent of capital'. Cost reduction is the order of the day and management is bent, in Burawoy's words (1985: 263), on 'domination of the workplace', which means deregulation of the labour market and rolling back the influence of trade unions. Hence the stress on 'individualism' at the expense of 'collectivism'.

In practice, it is not always easy to distinguish between the 'hard' and 'soft' versions. Not only are there many common themes, but also shared assumptions. Thus, although there are some formulations of the 'soft' version which see a role for trade unions and collective bargaining (see, for example, Kochan et al. 1986; Jones 1991), most are silent on the issue or assume that the organization is non-union. Second, as Keenoy and Anthony (1992) have powerfully argued, the language, metaphors and symbols that have come to be associated with the 'soft' version, and that are increasingly finding their way into the everyday vocabulary of managers, can be used to put a very different gloss on what is really happening – for example: total quality management (doing more with less), lean production (mean production), right sizing (redundancy), emphasizing the individual (undermining trade unions). Third, the dividing line between the 'soft' and 'hard' versions of HRM is very fine in any event. Faced with ever-increasing demands of competition, many managers see themselves engaged in the delicate exercise of simultaneously cutting costs and manufacturing yet greater consent.

The ability of some managements to follow the 'soft' version may also depend on other managements being obliged to adopt the 'hard'. The managements of many small and medium-sized companies which are in a subcontracting relationship with larger companies may well find themselves in the latter position (see chapter 19). This is above all true if the management of the larger company decides that it is going to base this relationship purely on lowest costs or, in the case of the public sector, is obliged by legislation to do so.

A review of the evidence

So much for the theory. In a recent review of the survey and case study evidence, one of us (Sisson 1994) has pointed out that, outside of a small number of mostly foreign-owned 'greenfield' workplaces (Clark and Winchester 1994), there are very few examples of the 'soft' version. At first sight, there has been what Storey (1992: 28) has referred to as the 'remarkable take-up by large British companies of initiatives which are in the style of "human resource management" model'. Yet many of the initiatives, as Storey's study confirms, rarely seem to add up to an integrated approach. There are major inconsistencies – an emphasis on team working, for example, and yet an insistence on having individual performance pay; the different forms of participation and involvement being seen as alternatives rather than complementary; 'human resource' and 'industrial relations' departments being kept separate. Key practices such as single status and guarantees of employment security are also very often noticeable by their absence. Those managements introducing even some of the practices are also the exception. Above all, WIRS3 confirms, these practices are rare in the non-union workplaces which now account for the majority of employees (Millward et al. 1992).

The interpretation to be put on some of these developments is also open to question. Although the implications for personnel are profound, devolved forms of management may be the result of the accountancy-driven logic of reducing costs by the delayering of ranks of managers. As Clark and Winchester (1994) argue, decentralization can also be seen as a form of derecognition in that it denies trade union representatives the platform to raise company or sector issues. Similarly, in some cases the take-up of practices, such as individual performance pay and direct communications, has more to do with an assertion of management control *vis-à-vis* trade unions and collective bargaining than it does with the adoption of HRM. Significantly, there is a growing body of evidence in the case of individual performance pay that British management is not introducing genuinely individual contracts which set out the mutual obligations and expectations in the way that the White Paper quoted above suggests; they are for the most part issuing standardized packages in the guise of personal contracts effectively requiring individuals to do what they are told (Evans and Hudson 1993; see also Mather 1990; Kessler 1994).

This brings us to the 'hard' version. Certainly much of what is going on, however it is labelled, is better understood in terms of 'hard' rather than the 'soft' version. Above all, this is true of developments in many small and medium-sized non-union enterprises which have been under the most severe financial pressures during the recession of the early 1990s. The bulk of the evidence (ACAS 1992, 1993; Millward et al. 1992: 364–5; Citizens' Advice Bureaux 1993) suggests that the model of Bleak House is more appropriate than HRM. It is not just that there is a lack of employment security; pay levels are set unilaterally by managements, differentials are wider and lower-paid employees more common. A sizeable number of companies have no procedures for raising grievances or health and safety issues and do little to communicate with or involve their employees. There are, in other words, no mechanisms for employees to 'voice' their views. Significantly, too, although strikes are unheard of, forms of so-called 'unorganized conflict' are much in evidence. Employee turnover is as high as in union workplaces, and safety, measured by a higher rate of accidents than in union workplaces, is a major concern. Dismissals other than those arising from redundancy were nearly twice as frequent per employee as in the union sector. Claims to industrial tribunals for unfair dismissal and other alleged mistreatment were no less common than in union workplaces.

As for large mainstream organizations, there is very considerable evidence of a shift from 'collectivism' to 'individualism' in management's approach. Not only can many of the changes considered above, such as performance pay, best be understood in these terms; there has also been an increase in derecognition in recent years. Almost one in five of companies with more than 1,000 employees reported that recognition for negotiating purposes had been partially or wholly withdrawn on their established sites (Marginson et al. 1993: 56). The incidence of individual forms of communication was also higher among large companies which recognized unions than among those which did not, suggesting that managements may be engaged in a battle for 'hearts and minds' in the former.

Not all the evidence points in the same direction, however. Derecognition remains relatively rare, especially compared to the situation in the United States. There is some evidence to suggest, moreover, that the collective bargaining agenda may be changing. Admittedly, the WIRS survey found little or no change (Millward et al. 1992: 249–55), but other surveys (IRRR 1992: 7–8) and case studies have identified a number of new aspects on the agenda. Agreements on skills-based pay, for example, have emerged from major restructuring exercises and the drive for improved performance. Similarly, many managers at local level find that they need the cooperation of shop stewards and local trade union representatives in handling contracting out or the introduction of team working, whatever may be the views of senior managers (Colling and Geary 1992; and chapter 12).

The realities of industrial relations decision-making

Although, on balance, there is more evidence to support the 'hard' rather than the 'soft' version of events, it is a moot point whether anything as dramatic as a paradigm shift is taking place. Much of the evidence sits very uneasily with the model of management as a *strategic actor*, discussed at beginning of this chapter. Certainly, business conditions are the main referent and flexibility, defined as management being able to do what it wants, is at a premium. Yet the notion of managers making strategic choices from a menu of options seems far removed from reality. They are taking advantage of the political context to assert their control, but their use of it, and their response to business conditions, remains largely ad hoc and pragmatic.

Two examples will help to illustrate the reality of decision-making in industrial relations. The first involves the 'core–periphery' model suggesting that British management was breaking up the labour force into 'increasingly peripheral, and therefore numerically flexible groups of workers clustered around a numerically stable core which will conduct the firm's key, firm specific activities' (Atkinson 1984: 29). At first sight, the model, which became *de facto* a key element in government policy, seems to enjoy considerable empirical support (see, for example, the increases in the number of self-employed and in the number of part-time workers reported in Casey 1991). Closer inspection, however, suggests that these changes were primarily to be explained in terms of shifts in industrial structure, a reduction in the average size of establishments, and regional distribution of employment, rather than the development of a more strategic approach to employment matters. Thus, a survey of nearly 1,000 establishments selected because they used peripheral labour revealed that no more than one in nine reported a manpower strategy which is consistent with the model (McGregor and Sproull 1991: 79). Most employed peripheral workers for 'traditional' reasons, such as matching manning levels to demand peaks, rather than 'new' reasons associated with the model, for example that peripheral workers were cheaper or enjoyed fewer rights; they were also clustered in industries which already made considerable use of such forms of employment.

A number of follow-up case studies (Hunter and McInnes 1991) in the companies offer further insights. Business concerns were the critical factor in management decision-making, but this led to a predominantly pragmatic approach rather than one driven by deliberate manpower strategy. Traditional ways of doing things were the order of the day. Only when problems occurred did managers consider other possibilities. It was very rare, for example, for even large companies to have an ideal view about manpower strategy; the main concern of the centre was monitoring and control; detailed decisions about the forms of contract were left to individual units. It was also rare for companies to undertake detailed cost comparisons between different types of worker. The perceptions of what would work or would not work were far more important:

> decisions over labour use were rarely part of a coherent and articulate employment strategy, coordinated by a powerful personnel function which could identify and respond to changing labour market conditions. Instead the use of different forms of labour had usually built up in an ad hoc and pragmatic manner as general and line management responded to what they saw as the needs of the business. (Hunter and McInnes 1991: 49)

This is not to argue that moves towards more precarious forms of work have not occurred. As Procter et al. (1994) point out, in a 'defence' of the flexible firm model, there has been a growth in such employment, and this can occur without there being a deliberate strategy on the part of firms. Yet this is precisely the point. Firms have not deployed strategic choice in a clear-cut manner. Instead, there has been drift and a stress on the uncertainties of the market in place of internal labour markets. In these conditions, it is unlikely that 'flexibility' plays much part in any integrated policy of human resource management.

Our second example involves relations between management and trade unions. A major finding of Storey's case studies referred to above was that there were very few instances of even a hidden agenda to withdraw recognition from trade unions. The exception were managers themselves, who were being withdrawn from collective bargaining arrangements in those organizations, such as British Rail, where they had previously been covered. An important consideration here was the relatively underdeveloped nature of the human resource function and the tendency for it to be preoccupied with management grades. Equally, however, there were only one or two cases, such as Ford and Rover, where management had accepted the need to build a new working relationship with trade unions. Even where relations were conflictual – Storey quotes the example of Lucas and Jaguar – management did not seem to see it as a priority to rectify this state of affairs. An attitude of neglect was sufficiently evident to be interpreted as if management wanted trade unions to wither on the vine. Yet even this, says Storey (1992: 259), was to 'attribute rather more order than was observable in practice'.

In fact, most of the managements were operating dual arrangements. That is to say, HRM initiatives were being run side-by-side – sometimes by separate management departments – with traditional, mainly adversarial, stances towards trade unions. It was as if management wanted to signal to the trade unions that things had to change, but also at the same time to keep its options open just in case trade unions became stronger again. Even this 'dualism' was not entirely deliberate, however; there was considerable friction between 'HR' and 'IR' managers in some cases and a wide divergence of views among managers generally about the role of trade unions and the place of collective bargaining. Storey's overall conclusion is worth quoting in full.

> Across the variety of approaches, one startling fact stood out: while the old-style industrial relations 'fire fighting' was disavowed, there was hardly an instance where anything approaching a 'strategic' stance towards unions and industrial relations could be readily discerned as having taken its place. It would appear that identifying clear managerial policies towards trade unions and collective bargaining is as difficult to do now, if not indeed more difficult, than it was 20–30 years ago when the lack of policy on such matters was frequently berated. (1992: 258–9)

Taking these two illustrations together, it seems that the managements of many large organizations are similar to the owner/managers discussed earlier in not having a strategic approach to industrial relations. There is no simple explanation for this. Management approaches to industrial relations need to be placed within the context of companies' business priorities. Thus industrial relations policy is contingent, and as Purcell and Ahlstrand (1994: 42–7) argue, subordinate to considerations of business strategy, restructuring and production reorganization, which in turn are driven by such competitive imperatives as cost reduction or quality standards. But it is not just that industrial relations is a second-order issue to business strategy: as we have seen, integrated approaches to employee management are less evident among British-owned companies than among their foreign-owned counterparts.

In addressing this difference, recent analysis focuses on two related themes. One is the historical experience of British management in managing labour, discussed in chapter 2. Thus British managements' failure to rationalize the production process, and, within that, the management of labour, is deeply embedded in a preference for ad hoc methods and in the weakness of managerial education and training. As Aldcroft (1992: 122) notes, one key weakness of shopfloor management in Britain was a lack of training and technical competence. The other theme is the impact of the corporate governance arrangements briefly discussed in the previous section. In the absence of an overarching legal system of employment rights, it can be argued, these generate a substantial premium on 'behaviours and investments which have an immediate payback . . . a consequential effect is to discourage, and even to penalise, actions which are geared to a long term horizon' (Storey and Sisson 1993: 76). In these circumstances, it is very difficult to develop experience even of the individual activities, such as appraisal, that are taken for granted in the standard prescriptive texts, let alone any learning of the importance that an integrated set of policies can make. Likewise, it is very difficult to build up positive long-term relationships with trade unions. The significance of these missing links in developing a strategic approach, and the time it takes to put them in place, emerges in Whipp's summing up of a number of key points about Jaguar's experience in the 1980s:

> The first relates to the huge efforts required merely to 'catch-up' with the conventional personnel practices of other companies in the 1980s. Overcoming the inherited problems of the UK engineering sector with regard to the management of people took virtually a decade. Second, it is noticeable how HRM techniques were not developed to fit the company's strategy. Rather, Jaguar in the 1980s developed its capacity to think strategically and use HRM concepts and practices, in parallel. It is the need to mobilize such a range of conditioning work and supportive secondary mechanism which stand out. Nonetheless, by the end of the 1980s, even a company such as Jaguar – held up to be the epitome of the HRM approach – found it hugely difficult to make such an approach count in terms of competitive performance. (Whipp 1992: 46)

An emphasis on the need for a strategic approach lies at the heart of many of the prescriptions for the reform of British industrial relations, ranging from the Donovan recommendations in respect of collective bargaining in the 1960s to the advocacy of HRM in the 1990s. It has been rarely recognized, however, that a strategic approach sits very uneasily with the reality of management decision-making in a context in which business considerations are impacting ever more sharply on industrial relations practice and the institutional context serves to emphasize short-run returns.

Challenges Ahead?

Looking to the future, there are already signs that British management is likely to face a number of major challenges to the way in which it has conducted industrial relations in recent years. One will be to achieve the high levels of commitment on the part of individual employees which many commentators see as critical to performance and competitiveness. It seems increasingly difficult for many organizations to deliver any of the reciprocal obligations that have traditionally been associated with so-called 'high-trust' relationships. This is above all true of the employment security which German and Japanese experience suggests is critical in winning cooperation in introducing effective and efficient change. The overriding pressure which many managements feel under to make redundancies has rendered the notion of employment security a virtually meaningless concept in all but a handful of cases. Critically, too, relatively few organizations seem to be able to maintain the prospect of a career for managers themselves. The talk is of *employability* which, roughly translated, means the provision of training and development opportunities that will make it possible for employees to move on to alternative employment in other organizations (see, for example, Godswen 1994). It is a moot point whether many organizations will have the resources, let alone the motivation, to turn the rhetoric into practice. Moreover, if most large organizations are favouring *employability* rather than *employment security*, it is not immediately obvious where the future employment opportunities will be.

A second challenge, which is closely connected, is the considerable growth taking place in outsourcing and subcontracting generally. Managements, in other words, are shifting the emphasis from control though the employment relationship to control through the market. Externalizing the problems associated with managing the employment relationship does not mean, however, that the problems disappear. Issues such as performance and quality, and training and development, remain fundamentally important (see Gilbert 1994). How to handle them seems clear enough. The organization is advised to develop a close working relationship with suppliers and to help them to introduce the appropriate systems to ensure that they are able to resolve them (Kanter 1988: 133–40). In a few cases, such as the automotive sector, producers are doing just that. But, more generally, if the organization itself has little or no experience of these systems, it is very difficult to see how they will be able to help the subcontractors to develop them. Who, in this event, takes responsibility for training or health and safety is a matter for considerable concern.

The third challenge depends on the political context. It is the prospect of having to deal with new forms of collective representation. An immediate source of pressure to introduce such representation is the EU. The lack of provision for collective representation in non-union workplaces has already been highlighted as a major issue by the European Court in judgements relating to transfer of undertakings and collective redundancies legislation. There is also likely to be a directive providing for the introduction of European works councils in large multinational companies (see Gold and Hall 1994). Such a directive, despite the opt-out secured by the British government from the social policy provisions of the Maastricht Treaty in 1991, is likely to affect a significant number of British-owned multinationals as well as those MNCs with their headquarters in other EU member states which have significant numbers of employees in Britain. Furthermore, in the event of a change in government in Britain, there is the strong likelihood of domestic legislation providing for trade union recognition or some form of employee-based representation arrangements such as works councils. How British management deals with these developments – as threats whose impact is to be minimized, or as an opportunity to build more constructive collective relationships with their workforces – is likely to be an important influence on industrial relations for many years to come.

References

ACAS 1992: *Annual Report*. London: Advisory, Conciliation and Arbitration Service.

ACAS 1993: *Annual Report*. London: Advisory, Conciliation and Arbitration Service.

Albert, M. 1991: *Capitalism contre Capitalisme*. Paris: Editions du Seuil.

Aldcroft, D. H. 1992: *Education, Training and Economic Performance, 1944–1990*. Manchester: Manchester University Press.

Armstrong, P. 1987: Engineers, Management and Trust. *Work, Employment and Society*, 1, 4, 421–40.

Atkinson, J. 1984: Manpower Strategies for Flexible Organisations. *Personnel Management*, August, 28–31.

Blyton, P. and Turnbull, P. (eds) 1992: *Reassessing Human Resource Management*. London: Sage.

Brewster, C. and Connock, S. 1985: *Industrial Relations: Cost-Effective Strategies*. London: Hutchinson.

Burawoy, M. 1985: *The Politics of Production: Factory Regimes under Capitalism and Socialism*. London: Verso.

Casey, B. 1991: Survey Evidence on Trends in Non-Standard Employment. In A. Pollert (ed.), *Farewell to Flexibility?* Oxford: Blackwell.

Citizens' Advice Bureaux 1993: *Job Insecurity*. London: Social Policy Section, Citizens' Advice Bureaux.

Clark, J. and Winchester, D. 1994: Management and Trade Unions. In K. Sisson (ed.), *Personnel Management: A Comprehensive Guide to Theory and Practice in Britain*. Oxford: Blackwell.

Colling, T. 1993: Contracting Public Services: The Management of Compulsory Competitive Tendering in Two County Councils. *Human Resource Management Journal*, 3, 4, 1–15.

Colling, T. and Geary, J. 1992: Trade Unions and the Management of Change in the Workplace. Paper presented at the IREC Conference, Changing Systems of Workplace Representation in Europe, Dublin, 5–6 November, 1992. Mimeo.

Crowe, G. 1989: The Use of the Concept of 'Strategy' in Recent Sociological Literature. *Sociology*, 23, 1, 1–24.

Daniel, W. W. and Millward, N. 1983: *Workplace Industrial Relations in Britain*. London: Heinemann.

Deaton, D. 1985: Management Style and Large-Scale Survey Evidence. *Industrial Relations Journal*, 16, 2, 67–71.

Doeringer, P. and Piore, M. 1971: *Internal Labour Markets and Manpower Analysis*. Lexington, Mass.: D. C. Heath.

Dunlop, J. T. 1958: *Industrial Relations Systems*. New York: Holt.

Employment Department 1992: *People, Jobs and Opportunity*. Cm 1810. London: HMSO.

Evans, S. and Hudson, M. 1993: *Standardised Packages Individually Wrapped? A Study of the Introduction of Personal Contracts in the Port Transport and Electricity Supply Industries*. Warwick Papers in Industrial Relations, 44. Coventry: Industrial Relations Research Unit.

Ferner, A. and Hyman, R. (eds) 1992: *Industrial Relations in the New Europe*. Oxford: Blackwell.

Flanders, A. and Clegg, H. A. 1954: *The System of Industrial Relations in*

Great Britain. Oxford: Blackwell.

Franks, J. and Mayer, C. 1992: Corporate Control: A Synthesis of International Evidence. Unpublished Paper, London Business School and University of Warwick, November.

Friedman, A. L. 1977: *Industry and Labour. Class Struggle at Work and Monopoly Capitalism.* London: Macmillan.

Gilbert, R. 1994: An Employer's View. *Employment Relations 2000*: Proceedings of a Conference to Launch the Centre for International Employment Relations Research. Warwick Papers in Industrial Relations, 50. Coventry: Industrial Relations Research Unit.

Godswen, M. 1994: VIP Treatment. *Involvement.* Spring/May, 10–15.

Gold, M. and Hall, M. 1994: Statutory European Works Councils: The Final Countdown? *Industrial Relations Journal*, 25, 3, 177–86.

Goodhart, D. 1994: *The Reshaping of the German Social Market.* London: Institute for Public Policy Research.

Goold, M. and Campbell, A. 1987: *Strategies and Styles. The Role of the Centre in Managing Diversified Corporations.* Oxford: Blackwell.

Gospel, H. 1992: *Markets, Firms, and the Management of Labour in Modern Britain.* Cambridge: Cambridge University Press.

Gospel, H. and Palmer, G. 1993: *British Industrial Relations*, 2nd edn. London: Routledge.

Guest, D. 1991: Personnel Management: The End of Orthodoxy? *British Journal of Industrial Relations*, 29, 2, 149–75.

Harbison, F. H. and Myers, C. A. 1959: *Management in Industrial Societies.* New York: McGraw-Hill.

Hunter, L. C. and McInnes, J. 1991: *Employer Use Strategies – Case Studies.* Department of Employment Research Paper, 87. Sheffield: Employment Department.

IRRR 1992: Single Union Deals in Perspective. *Industrial Relations Review and Report*, 523, November, 6–15.

Jones, G. 1991: *Quality of Working Life and Total Quality Management.* Work Research Unit, Occasional Paper No. 50. London: Advisory, Conciliation and Arbitration Service.

Kanter, R. M. 1988: *When Giants Learn to Dance.* London: Unwin Paperbacks.

Keenoy, T. and Anthony, P. 1992: HRM: Metaphor, Meaning and Morality. In P. Blyton and P. Turnbull (eds), *Reassessing Human Resource Management.* London: Sage.

Kessler, I. 1994: Performance Pay. In K. Sisson (ed.), *Personnel Management: A Comprehensive Guide to Theory and Practice in Britain.* Oxford: Blackwell.

Kochan, T. A. and Dyer, L. 1993: Managing Transformational Change: The Role of Human Resource Professionals. Proceedings of the Conference of the International Industrial Relations Association, Sydney, 1992. Geneva: International Industrial Relations Association.

Kochan, T. A., Katz, H. C. and McKersie, R. B. 1986: *The Transformation of American Industrial Relations*. New York: Basic Books.

Lane, C. 1994: Industrial Order and the Transformation of Industrial Relations: Britain, Germany and France Compared. In R. Hyman and A. Ferner (eds), *New Frontiers in European Industrial Relations*. Oxford: Blackwell.

McGregor, A. and Sproull, A. 1991: *Employer Use Strategies: Analysis of a National Survey*. Department of Employment Research Paper, 83. Sheffield: Employment Department.

McKinsey and Co. Inc. 1988: *Strengthening Competitiveness in UK Electronics*. London: NEDO.

Marginson, P. and Sisson, K. 1994: The Structure of Capital in Europe: The Emerging Euro-Company and its Implications for Industrial Relations. In R. Hyman and A. Ferner (eds), *New Frontiers in European Industrial Relations*. Oxford: Blackwell.

Marginson, P., Edwards, P. K., Martin, R., Purcell, J. and Sisson, K. 1988: *Beyond the Workplace. The Management of Industrial Relations in Large Enterprises*. Oxford: Blackwell.

Marginson, P., Edwards, P. K., Armstrong, P. and Purcell, J. with Nancy Hubbard 1993: *The Control of Industrial Relations in Large Companies: An Initial Analysis of the Second Company Level Industrial Relations Survey*. Warwick Papers in Industrial Relations, 45. Coventry: Industrial Relations Research Unit.

Mather, G. 1990: *Promoting Greater Use of Employment Contracts*. London: Institute of Economic Affairs.

Maurice, M. and Sellier, F. 1979: A Societal Analysis of Industrial Relations: A Comparison between France and West Germany. *British Journal of Industrial Relations*, 17, 3, 322–36.

Millward, N. and Stevens, M. 1986: *British Workplace Industrial Relations 1980–1984*. Aldershot: Gower.

Millward, N., Stevens, M., Smart, D. and Hawes, W. R. 1992: *Workplace Industrial Relations in Transition*. Aldershot: Gower.

National Economic Development Office / Manpower Services Commission 1987: *People, The Key to Success*. London: NEDO.

Poole, M. 1986: *Industrial Relations: Origins and Patterns of National Diversity*. London: Routledge.

Procter, S. J., Rowlinson, M., McArdle, L., Hassard, J. and Forrester, P. 1994: Flexibility, Politics and Strategy: In Defence of the Model of the Flexible Firm. *Work, Employment and Society*, 8, 2, 221–42.

Purcell, J. 1987: Mapping Management Styles in Employee Relations. *Journal of Management Studies*, 24, 5, 533–48.

Purcell, J. and Sisson, K. 1983: Strategies and Practice in the Management of Industrial Relations. In G. S. Bain (ed.), *Industrial Relations in Britain*. Oxford: Blackwell.

Purcell, J. and Ahlstrand, B. 1994: *Human Resource Management in the*

Multi-Divisional Company. Oxford: Oxford University Press.

Purcell, J. Marginson, P., Edwards, P. K. and Sisson, K. 1987: The Industrial Relations Practices of Multi-Plant Foreign Owned Firms. *Industrial Relations Journal,* 18, 2, 130–7.

Scott, M., Roberts, I., Holroyd, G. and Sawbridge, D. 1989: Management and Industrial Relations in Small Firms. Department of Employment Research Paper, 70. London: HMSO.

Sewell, G. and Wilkinson, B. 1992: Empowerment or Emasculation? Shopfloor Surveillance in a Total Quality Organisation. In P. Blyton and P. Turnbull (eds), *Reassessing Human Resource Management.* London: Sage.

Sisson, K. 1987: *The Management of Collective Bargaining: An International Comparison.* Oxford: Blackwell.

Sisson, K. 1994: Paradigms, Practice and Prospects. In K. Sisson (ed.), *Personnel Management: A Comprehensive Guide to Theory and Practice in Britain.* Oxford: Blackwell.

Sisson, K., Waddington, J. and Whitston, C. 1992: *The Structure of Capital in the European Community: The Size of Companies and the Implications for Industrial Relations.* Warwick Papers in Industrial Relations, 38. Coventry: Industrial Relations Research Unit.

Storey, J. (ed.) 1989: *New Perspectives on Human Resource Management.* London: Routledge.

Storey, J. 1992: *Developments in the Management of Human Resources.* Oxford: Blackwell.

Storey, J. and Sisson, K. 1989: The Limits to Transformation: Human Resource Management in the British Context. *Industrial Relations Journal,* 21, 1, 60–5.

Storey, J. and Sisson, K. 1993: *Managing Human Resources and Industrial Relations.* Milton Keynes: Open University Press.

Streeck, W. 1992: *Social Institutions and Economic Performance: Studies of Industrial Relations in Advanced Industrial Countries.* London: Sage.

Wedderburn, K. K. (Lord) 1971: *The Worker and the Law,* 2nd edn. Harmondsworth: Penguin.

Whipp, R. 1992: Human Resource Management, Competition and Strategy. In P. Blyton and P. Turnbull (eds), *Reassessing Human Resource Management.* London: Sage.

Whittington, R. 1993: *What is Strategy and Does it Matter?* London: Routledge.

Williamson, O. E. 1985: *The Economic Institutions of Capitalism: Firms, Markets, Relational Contracting.* New York: Free Press.

5

Management: Pay Determination and Collective Bargaining

William Brown, Paul Marginson and Janet Walsh

The management of pay, and of bargaining over pay, are of fundamental importance to the conduct of industrial relations. The employment relationship is formed around the payment of labour;
payment is the most conspicuous focus of collective concern for
labour. This chapter discusses the strategies adopted by employers
in pay bargaining in Britain. But pay is also the price of labour, and
as such is subject to market forces encompassing far wider terrains
than those of any single employer. How far does this constrain the
employer's discretion? Is it a delusion to consider employers to have
any more influence over pay than the adding of cosmetic touches as
they transmit immutable market messages?

The answer to this question about how pay *is* determined has
direct implications for recent British official views about how pay
ought to be determined. Since the beginning of the 1980s, the
government has noted with approval 'a new recognition of the role
and importance of the individual employee. Traditional patterns of
industrial relations, based on collective bargaining and collective
agreements, seem increasingly inappropriate and are in decline'
(Employment Department 1992: 11). Other 'valuable and healthy
developments' include a widening of skill differentials, new forms
of performance and incentive pay and, 'even where collective
bargaining persists, pay determination has become increasingly de-
centralised to local level; there are now much greater regional variations in pay within organisations where previously employees were
paid at the same rate regardless of differences in labour market
conditions' (ibid.: 36). This policy commitment to liberating competitive forces in the labour market, we shall argue, depends upon

theoretical assumptions which fatally neglect the reality of employer strategy.

We introduce the question of employer discretion with an overview of the explanations developed by economists for inter-firm wage differences. This is necessary if we are to challenge the implicit denial by conventional economic theory that employers have a distinct role. We then introduce our own perspective by drawing attention to the differing ways in which employers try to secure productive effort from their workforces, including the ways in which pay is used within the firm as a device for raising labour productivity. This leads on to a discussion of the impact of trade unions through collective bargaining and to the employer's choice of the structure within which pay is fixed. We describe the substantial way in which the bargaining structure of the British private sector has changed recently. Of growing significance has been the decision to manage pay without trade unions. The chapter ends with a more speculative discussion of employer pay strategies at the national and international level.

The Dispersion of Pay

A central question, and the subject of long-standing controversy among economists, is why workers performing similar jobs in the same labour market are commonly paid differing rates by different employers. The starting point for the orthodox economic analysis of pay is the work of Hicks (1932) in his application of marginalist economic theory to the labour market. Wages, he argued, are determined by the interaction of the forces of labour supply and labour demand in a competitive labour market with the result that, at the equilibrium wage for a particular occupational group, no firm will wish to hire any more workers. Moreover, because the equilibrium wage is assumed to be equivalent to the contribution to revenue of the last (or marginal) worker employed in each firm, the competitive process by which such a wage is determined serves also to secure an efficient allocation of labour between different firms. Consequently, wage differentials between firms for a given type of labour will not be sustainable for long. Any firm paying above the competitive wage will make a loss and will eventually be driven out of business. Any firm paying below the competitive wage will find itself unable to recruit and retain its workforce.

An important departure from the competitive model of wage determination which has received substantial attention from economists is the effect of trade unions on wages. Hicks portrayed unions as monopoly suppliers of labour able to raise wages above their competitive level. In an otherwise competitive economy the consequence of unions' effect on wage levels will be that employment will contract in the unionized sector, and the displaced workers will eventually find employment in non-union firms which will lower their wage offers in the face of excess labour supply. There is the implication that, in aggregate, output and income will fall because the allocative efficiency of the competitive labour market has been impaired. But introducing the effects of unionism does not, by itself, assist an explanation of inter-employer wage differences.

The question of inter-firm wage dispersion is important because, contrary to the expectations implied by the competitive model of wage determination, empirical studies have repeatedly found that this pay dispersion is substantial and sustained. Within the same local labour market – that is, where there are no spatial barriers to labour mobility – it is normal to find a range of earnings across firms for workers in similar occupational categories at a given point in time. The magnitude of inter-plant pay differentials is substantial. For example, a study of engineering firms in Glasgow and Birmingham in 1966 found inter-plant coefficients of variation (CVs) of average pay ranging from 16 to 23 per cent for different occupations (Mackay et al. 1971).

Substantial local, intra-occupational, inter-firm wage dispersions have been identified in the United States (for example, Lester 1952; Rees and Schultz 1970) and in Australia (Brown et al. 1980), as well as in the UK (for example, Robinson 1968). It is notable that there is a surprising similarity in the extent of dispersion in the different countries for which this has been investigated even though they have very different labour laws and institutions. A comparison of the labour markets of Chicago, Coventry and Adelaide found the inter-plant CVs of, for example, fork-lift truck drivers to be, respectively, 15, 13 and 11 per cent (Brown et al. 1980).

Additional evidence of the distinctive role played by the firm in pay determination comes from studies, not of pay levels, but of pay changes. The pay rises achieved by individual workers in a given year are commonly more in line with pay rises received by other occupations within the same firm than with those received by other individuals in the same occupation in other firms in the same labour market. This was demonstrated, for instance, by Nolan and Brown (1983) in an examination of the pay in West Midlands engineering firms over the course of the 1970s. Engineering workers' pay rises appeared to be determined more strongly by the competitive circumstances confronting their employers in their product market than by those confronting them as individuals from a particular occupational group in their local labour market. Their pay rises owed far more to whom they worked for than to what skill they had. Evidence from a more industrially diverse Australian sample suggested that this dominance of the firm-specific effects was a feature of manufacturing industry rather than of industries with more fluid labour markets such as building or retailing. Within manufacturing it was particularly strong for larger firms in more monopolistic industries (Brown et al. 1984).

Findings of this sort led the authors of the early American studies to question the competitive model of wage determination. Lester (1952) concluded that wage setting in local labour markets was characterized by a substantial 'range of indeterminacy' within which employers could select a stable point consistent with their chosen style of labour management, largely untroubled by short-term fluctuations in the labour market. This range of indeterminacy has been estimated to be of the order of 20 per cent of average earnings in one recent British study (Blanchflower et al. 1990).

Evidence on inter-firm wage dispersion also draws attention to the extent to which employers deliberately seek to shelter their workforces from the effects of the external labour market. A clear reflection of this was the creation of so-called 'internal labour market' structures. These are coherent wage and career structures internal to the firm by means of which employers use organizational rather than market relationships to motivate labour. They are characterized by ports of entry at lower job grades, by on-the-job training, by internal promotion, and by seniority systems in which pay and job security are related to length of service (Doeringer and Piore 1971). We shall return to other implications of internal labour markets later in the chapter.

It is not only the unruliness of pay dispersion that poses problems for conventional labour market theory. There are also empirical regularities which have so far eluded market-related explanation. An outstanding example is the observed relationship between firm size and pay levels. Evidence from several countries shows that occupational earnings tend to increase with the size of establishment and, in the case of multi-plant enterprises, with the size of the parent company (Weiss and Landau 1984; Thomson and Sanjines 1990). The sources of these size effects have been the subject of considerable speculation, and are likely to be connected with other size-dependent aspects of labour management (Marginson 1984).

Economic Explanations of Pay Dispersion

Economists have responded to the challenge posed by the findings on pay dispersion with several different approaches (Groshen 1991). Three of these approaches remain within the orthodox framework of competitive equilibrium. One approach suggests that labour may be *'sorted by ability'*, so that differences in earnings reflect different productive capacities of workers, either innate or acquired. But while such considerations may account for earnings differentials between individual workers, they do not thereby explain differences between firms. Another approach seeks to explain wage dispersion by the *absence of perfect information* to workers about job opportunities so that their job search is costly. Hence workers may take a job at a wage rate less than that prevailing elsewhere, thereby giving rise to a range of wages for similar jobs at any one time. But, again, random variations in search behaviour or wage offers cannot account for the persistence of inter-firm pay differentials.

An approach that has the great attraction of suggesting firm-specific effects is that there may be *'compensating differentials'* of non-wage factors. It is argued that the wages that are paid do not fully reflect employees' net compensation because they leave out a range of other factors which affect the return to employment. Positive factors include such things as fringe benefits and good working conditions, whereas negative factors cover dirty or dangerous working conditions and unsocial hours. This theory suggests that, once these compensating differentials have been taken into account, returns to employment should be similar across all firms in the labour market. Unfortunately for the theory, however, evidence from a variety of studies finds that wages tend to be positively, not negatively, correlated with the provision of fringe benefits and good working conditions (Mackay et al. 1971; Brown 1980; Freeman 1989). To them that hath, more is given.

These approaches to pay dispersion do not explain why particular employers might choose to pitch their wage offers higher or lower in the range of indeterminacy than others. They are cast as passive recipients of labour market conditions (Nolan and Brown 1983). This weakness is addressed by two approaches which have attracted considerable attention in recent years: 'insider–outsider' models and 'efficiency wage' models.

The central presupposition of *'insider–outsider' models* is that firms enjoy a degree of product market power, and hence possess the ability to extract an economic rent from consumers over and above the costs of producing goods and services. Workers can obtain a share of this rent if they are able to deploy bargaining power. Such power is said to derive either from the possession of firm-specific skills (which are therefore costly for the firm to replace) or from union organization (which enables workers to exercise monopoly power over the supply of labour). Wages are consequently determined by two sets of influences: 'outsider', reflecting the interaction of supply and demand in the labour market, and 'insider', reflecting the relative bargaining power of the employer and workers within the firm. Providing the forces shaping the 'insider' influences can be shown to be firm-specific, then an explanation can be developed of the employer effect on wages (Lindbeck and Snower 1986; Carruth and Oswald 1989).

Empirical evidence provides some support for 'insider–outsider' models expressed in terms of worker bargaining power. Analysis of the 1984 Workplace Industrial Relations Survey (Blanchflower et al. 1990), for example, found, first, that the presence of a pre-entry closed shop is associated with relatively high manual earnings and, second, that the ability of skilled workers to extract a rent appears to be less dependent on trade union organization than is the case for semi-skilled or unskilled workers. But how far the sources of 'insider' bargaining power depend upon union organization rather than employer circumstances was questioned by Stewart (1990). He was able to demonstrate that, providing firms possess a degree of product market power, semi-skilled workers in non-union plants are as likely to benefit from a wage mark-up above competitive levels as their counterparts in unionized plants.

This suggests that it may be fruitful to consider Slichter's notion of the firm's 'ability to pay' (Slichter 1950). According to this, those firms which possess a degree of product market power are more likely to pay above competitive wage levels because of their 'super-normal' profits. Given the usual economic assumption of profit maximization, however, conventional theory does not explain why employers should choose to pay over the competitive rate, unless coerced by union pressure. The fifth approach offers an explanation.

'Efficiency wage' theories share the central proposition that workers' productivity will, in part, be determined by the level of wages (Akerlof 1984; Akerlof and Yellen 1986). The payment of a wage in excess of competitive levels can, by eliciting extra productivity from workers, result in increments to output from which the revenue offsets the extra wage costs incurred. From this perspective, pay is an important element in securing productive efficiency – that is, the maximization of outputs from labour effort – as distinct from allocative efficiency. Various sources for this increased productivity have been suggested. They include the coercive pressure on workers who face an increased cost of job loss where their jobs are paid above market levels; the motivational effects stemming from greater worker commitment to high-paying employers; the savings in direct supervision costs associated with increased trust between employer and employee; and the savings associated with reduced labour turnover.

The pay-off between higher pay and increased productivity implied by efficiency wage theories suggests that a competitive market might tolerate a spread of inter-firm differences in pay levels, as a result of either deliberate or random choices by employers. Empirical tests of efficiency wage theory are so far inconclusive (Groshen 1991). They will remain so until the factors underlying the decisions of employers to position themselves differently in terms of the pay–productivity pay-off can be specified more clearly. Despite this, there is considerable value in the central proposition that pay should be seen to play a part not only as a market price for labour, but also as a means by which managements can elicit productive effort from their workforce.

The Employer's Role in Pay Determination

The discussion so far has described how economists' conceptions of pay have shifted, somewhat uncertainly, to focus increasingly on the distinctive role played by the firm as the employer of labour. Starting from the undeniable fact of substantial inter-firm pay dispersion, so unsatisfactory for orthodox labour market theory, attention has moved to consider the pay-fixing behaviour of firms when they possess a degree of product market power, when they bargain with trade unions, and when they can use pay to elicit productivity.

This admission that the employer may have a distinctive role in pay determination is, however, only a starting point. Before discussing the many aspects of the role it is necessary to establish four important empirical points about the competitive constraints under which labour is managed and paid. The first is that, in a world of imperfect competition, the influences of the product market are in contest with those of the labour market in determining pay, and employers have to mediate between them. Second, the degree of discretion offered to an employer by product market conditions is permissive and not imperative. The third point is that a firm's choice of pay and employment strategy is constrained by its broader production strategy. Finally, within a firm's employment strategy, it is misleading to isolate pay from other complementary instruments of motivation and control.

The first point concerns the tensions that arise between the allocative and the productive properties of pay. So long as employers have to recruit and retain labour, they cannot wholly free themselves from the influences of the external labour market. If pay for a particular skill falls too far out of line with the external market, its turnover may rise. But, in the context of an internal labour market, raising the pay of one group may have disruptive effects on established differentials with other groups in the firm's workforce. It may be prohibitively expensive to solve the problem by conceding the pay rise for all groups. This has, for example, in the past been a common issue in petrochemical refineries where traditional notions of internal equity dictated that all time-served craftsmen should be paid on the same rate even though the earnings of their different trades in the outside labour market might be very different. Instrument artificers are likely to be paid more than painters. In practice, personnel managers struggle to maintain a compromise, with discriminating use of training, overtime and promotion, among other things, in order to preserve a balance between the acceptability of the internal wage structure and the pressures of the external labour market.

The second important point about employer discretion is that it is not automatically moulded by product market circumstances. An employer's monopoly strength is not necessarily reflected in relatively high wages. American studies have shown how companies in strong market positions have often been able to resist conceding high wages over long periods because, for example, the relatively few employers in the product market have found it relatively easy to combine to resist union demands (Levinson 1966; Ozanne 1968; Zappala 1994).

Furthermore, if an employer's monopoly strength *is* reflected in relatively high wages, one should not conclude that this is necessarily the result of a deliberate employer strategy. A study of ten British engineering firms demonstrated that some of them paid relatively high wages over periods of many years simply because their piece-work payment systems were hopelessly out of management's control. Their product markets were too undemanding, often because sales price was not the main factor in competition, to force their managements to undertake the difficult industrial relations task of regaining control (Brown 1973). The dominant influence was not a shrewd 'efficiency wage' strategy but was instead sheltered, high inertia, managerial incompetence: an illustration of the general maxim that, in industrial relations, cock-up theories are often safer than conspiracy theories.

The third point is that a firm's policy on employment and pay will be influenced by a number of broader strategic choices. The management of a firm is a complex, skilled activity. Variations in productivity and labour performance are not simply reducible to differences in factor inputs (Clark 1980; Hodgson 1982). Even firms in direct competition with each other may adopt very different approaches to production and to labour control. Firms whose production is based on high value added, where competition tends to be quality-based, are likely to emphasize high standards of work performance, an ability to work with discretion, and low labour turnover. This, in turn, is likely to be reflected in levels of pay which are high relative to those prevailing locally because of the potential costs of employee disaffection (Ramaswamy and Rowthorn 1991). This will contrast with firms whose competitive strategy is based on the production of low value added, standardized goods where competition tends to be cost- rather than quality-based. It will contrast again with firms whose production is relatively capital intensive, which will tend to provide relatively good terms of employment, including pay, in order to ensure uninterrupted production.

Finally, pay is usually used not as an isolated device, but as part of a package of complementary devices to elicit worker productivity. A central source of such differences in productivity lies in the variable nature of the output of labour. Labour cannot simply be hired and blithely set to work. In practice, managements have to devise an integrated bundle of coercive and motivational devices to elicit productive effort from the workers they have hired. Pay is usually an important component of this, but to varying extents. Its importance is likely to be greater where, for example, the work is intrinsically unrewarding, and less so where there is, for example, a strong vocational element.

In sum, a combination of factors prevents employers from being simply the passive recipients of pay rates from the labour market. Employers differ in the compromises they make in protecting internal wage structures from the external labour market. They operate in product markets which offer them different degrees of discretion, and they respond to that discretion in different ways. They adopt different competitive strategies in their product markets. They use pay to different extents and in different ways in trying to win productivity from their workforces. The key to understanding the dispersion of pay between firms thus lies in investigating management's active use of pay as a means of securing productive effort. We address this by first looking at the management of payment systems and structures, before moving on to discuss the much wider issues involved in pay bargaining with trade unions.

Managing Pay as a Motivator

Payment systems are sets of rules with which employers link pay rates not only to job descriptions, but also to any of a great variety of indicators related to issues such as employees' competence, performance, and career expectations. For as long as there has been employment, payment systems have been the object of endless experimentation. Why is the choice and management of payment systems intrinsically difficult, and why is pay so fickle a motivator?

A recurrent theme in the literature on pay is the stability of relative pay levels over prolonged periods of time (Phelps Brown and Hopkins 1981). Authors who have been actively involved in the bargaining process have long commented on the dominance of custom in shaping conceptions of 'fair' relative pay levels, and thereby contributing to this stability (Clay 1929). Relative pay is often closely linked to social status and thereby to employee self-esteem. Consequently, for both employer and employee, one enters a motivational minefield when one strays from the pattern of relative pay which, whatever its origins may have been, has become consolidated by custom. This is a major reason why relative pay levels generally respond sluggishly, if at all, to changes in the relative demand for different occupations in a labour market.

If we look inside the firm, the stability of the pay structure becomes even more important. Employees' sensitivity to relative pay is all the more acute because they are in daily contact with the people in their comparative reference groups. The closer the point of comparison, the closer it is watched. Unless they accept that some rationale of 'fairness' underlies the disturbance of established internal pay differentials, employees are liable to become distressed, demotivated and thereby less productive.

It is, consequently, important for employers to avoid discordant disruptions of internal pay structures. If there are managerial reasons to introduce alterations, it is important that it is done on some sort of basis of rational justification. This is commonly done by means of a 'job evaluation' procedure. Although these come in many types, they generally combine systematic job analysis with some degree of employee involvement in establishing acceptable relative pay levels. Job evaluation generally incorporates a procedure to review alterations to job content so as to maintain the acceptability of the structure of relative pay under changing circumstances (Quaid 1993).

The maintenance of an acceptable internal pay structure is, in large part, a political exercise. When correctly used, job evaluation provides a means of maintaining and legitimizing a negotiated order. It provides a means for establishing criteria with which to assess the 'fairness' of relative pay, with implicit conceptions of fairness which are specific to the individual firm or bargaining unit. What makes the management of an internal pay structure so demanding is that external changes, in technological, organizational and in market circumstances, alter relative power relationships within the workforce. This, in turn, affects employees' relative pay aspirations and their conceptions of fairness (Brown and Sisson 1975). In brief, it is not simply that a stable internal pay structure is a precondition for a well-motivated workforce from management's point of view, although that is a useful starting point. The particularly demanding management skill is achieving an acceptable level of stability when changing circumstances alter what is acceptable.

The danger that mismanaged pay will demotivate a workforce is all the greater when the payment system has some sort of performance related component. This is not the place to embark on a discussion of pay systems (Brown and Walsh 1994). Let it suffice to say that payment by results and performance related pay systems are notoriously fickle and short-lived. As shown in chapter 11, they are difficult to monitor, often have dysfunctional side-effects, and can generate demotivating pay anomalies. Whether at the level of the individual worker or of the enterprise, incentive pay schemes are usually, at best, a relatively minor, and highly fallible, part of a wider motivational package.

Important to this paradoxically minor role that incentive payment schemes play in eliciting productivity is the fact that the main vehicle of long-term, sustained productivity growth is technological change. Much technological innovation affects labour productivity in an almost stealthy way, changing jobs piecemeal, incrementally and irregularly. Managers tend to cope with this by manipulating grading structures pragmatically, with fresh job grades being created and old ones suppressed with the passage of time.

An important corollary is that the size of any ostensibly productivity related pay increases that workers gain from this pragmatic tinkering by management bears little relationship to any actual improvement in their productivity, however that might in practice be assessed. The pay rises that accompany technologically driven innovation owe much more to the scale of social and psychological disruption that the innovation has caused the workers involved, and to the consequent need to buy or bargain their consent (Brown and Nolan 1988).

In summary, pay plays a complex part in the productive use of labour, and if not managed astutely can be a powerful demotivator. This is true whether or not workforces are organized in trade unions. Larger non-union firms frequently use job evaluation in order to protect internal wage structures, and they experiment, often obsessively, with incentive payment systems. The presence of unions does, however, have a very distinctive impact on the management of pay. Whether or not workers are unionized may not influence their sense of grievance when a sensitive pay differential is adversely altered, but it does affect their ability to take action over it. Managements deal with them through collective bargaining, to which we now turn.

The Restructuring of Collective Bargaining

'Collective bargaining' is the term used when employers deal directly with the trade unions representing their employees in order to regulate the conduct and terms of their work. The Webbs originally conceived of collective bargaining as an essentially economic activity in which workers substitute a group negotiation over wages for individual bargains. Flanders (1975) argued that it was best seen as a political rather than an economic process, observing that the conclusion of a collective agreement does not bind anyone to buy or sell any labour. It sets out the terms and conditions that will prevail if and when labour is engaged. Collective bargaining is joint regulation. Pay rates are only a part of the resulting web of rules, which usually also covers issues such as job descriptions, working practices and hours of work. Collective bargaining is thus concerned with the joint governance not only of pay but also, to a greater or lesser degree, of important determinants of labour productivity.

Trends in bargaining levels

In Britain collective bargaining had, until the 1980s, enjoyed official support, with successive governments throughout the century upholding at least the principle of extending its coverage. Just what proportion of the workforce was covered by a collective agreement at any time has been less clear, though it has always been substantially greater than the proportion in union membership. By 1968 the first New Earnings Survey (NES) suggested that at least two-thirds of employees were covered and intermittent inquiries by its successors suggest that by 1973 this had risen to 73 per cent; but it began to fall from the mid-1970s, to 70 per cent in 1978 and to 64 per cent in 1985 and tumbled sharply to perhaps 47 per cent in 1990 and with every sign that the decline was continuing (Beaston 1993). By the mid-1990s only a minority of British employees are covered by a collective agreement.

What is the nature of the collective agreements which have undergone this change? A fundamental strategic issue for an employer committed to collective bargaining concerns the choice of bargaining unit, by which is meant the categories of workers which are to be covered by a particular collective agreement. This has far-reaching economic implications because of the standardization of wage rates and conditions of employment that is implied across all those employees covered.

The most critical question on bargaining structure for employers is whether they should bargain as a united group, with an industry-wide agreement, or whether they should bargain independently, concluding agreements that are exclusive to some or all of their own employees. The attraction of industry-wide bargaining arrangements comes from their potential to encompass whole product markets at regional or national level. From the early days of collective bargaining both unions and employers have appreciated the chance this offers to pass on some of the cost of wage rises in price rises, traditionally referred to as 'taking wages out of competition'. For unions, industry-wide bargaining has the attraction of establishing the notion of the 'rate for the job' and of encouraging the identification of their members with their wider occupational and labour market collective interests. It avoids much of the awesome loneliness that faces a workforce which bargains with its firm in isolation. For employers, besides the protection against being picked off by unions separately, there are additional benefits which have strong productivity implications. These are, first, that industry-wide agreements tend to reduce the influence of the union in the workplace and thus limit union impact upon detailed job control. Second, industry-wide agreements, with their accompanying standardization of job descriptions, make easier the industry-wide management of training which helps deal with the problem of 'free-riding' employers who do not train.

Until the 1960s there were few open challenges to this argument in the British private sector. Although there were some notable exceptions of companies which had their own 'single-employer' agreements, the overwhelming majority of employees were covered by industry-wide ('multi-employer') agreements. But post-war full employment was placing these under excessive strain. At workplace level across much of the private sector there was a growing if covert challenge reflected in the 'wage drift' of earnings away from the rates decreed by increasingly unrealistic industry-wide agreements. Informal workplace bargaining was tending to sap management control over work. In 1968 the Donovan Royal Commission, having pointed out the weakness of some of the larger industry-wide agreements, argued that for many employers the best solution would be to break away into single-employer, or what is now commonly called 'enterprise', bargaining.

This provided official blessing to an emerging trend which has come to dominate British collective bargaining. Broad estimates of the trend are given in table 5.1. In the 1960s there was still a strong majority of employees covered in the private sector who relied upon multi-employer (industry-wide) agreements. During the 1970s single-employer arrangements became dominant. Drawing on the

Table 5.1 Estimated private-sector bargaining structure in Great Britain, 1950–1990

Extent and nature of collective bargaining (c.b.)	Percentage of private-sector employees covered (manufacturing and services)					
	1950	*1960*	*1970*	*1980*	*1984*	*1990*
Pay *not* fixed by c.b.	20	25	30	30	40	50
Pay fixed by c.b.	80	75	70	70	60	50
c.b. is multi-employer (industry, regional etc.)	60	45	35	30	20	10
c.b. is single-employer (company, factory etc.)	20	30	35	40	40	40
Source on which estimate is based	various	various	various	WIRS 1	WIRS 2	WIRS 3

Workplace Industrial Relations Surveys (WIRS) it can be estimated that by 1984, of the six in ten private sector employees covered by pay bargaining agreements, four were single-employer and two were multi-employer. By 1990, of the somewhat under five out of ten employees then covered by a collective agreement, for four in ten they were still single-employer, but for only one in ten were they multi-employer agreements (Brown 1993).

At the time of Donovan it had been possible to speculate that multi-employer agreements might come to provide the base of a 'two-tier' bargaining system, such as has been successful elsewhere in Europe, with industry-wide agreements being explicitly supplemented by single-employer additions. This has not happened. Both CBI and WIRS surveys confirm that, during the 1980s, most firms that had earlier adopted two-tier arrangements decided to abandon them (CBI 1988; Millward et al. 1992).

The rise of enterprise bargaining

Why should there have been so widespread a move to enterprise bargaining when the arguments for industry-wide agreements once seemed so strong? As noted in chapters 2 and 4, employer solidarity has always had shallower roots in Britain than in most other European countries. Britain has generally had weaker wage agreements and training arrangements and none of the employer association sanctions and strike insurance schemes that are often to be found elsewhere. In any case, the advantages of an agreement constrained by national frontiers diminish when, as chapter 3 shows, international trade brings international product markets. For an ever-increasing range of goods and services, wages can no longer be 'taken out of competition'.

The positive reasons for adopting enterprise bargaining come less from any benefits on the wages front than from the potential it offers employers to improve labour's productivity in the light of their own business circumstances. It allows employers to cultivate internal labour markets. When much skill acquisition is on-the-job and when technological change is constant and incremental, there are advantages in having fluid job titles, predictable career trajectories, and stable internal salary structures. Enterprise bargaining fits in with the more individualistic treatment of employees which is associated with the decline of manual employment and it provides a ready base for enterprise related incentive schemes.

How is enterprise bargaining structured? It had been workplace bargaining which had initially undermined industry-wide agreements, and many employers regained control by concluding single-employer agreements at the level of individual establishments. Establishment-level bargaining has continued to be the dominant form in manufacturing, covering about half of employees with bargaining arrangements, but this proportion did not alter substantially between 1984 and 1990. In the service industries, however, multi-establishment firms in industries such as banking and retailing have been moving towards multi-establishment rather than single-establishment bargaining on withdrawal from industry-wide agreements. Taken as a whole, the unionized sector has not seen a further increase in establishment bargaining in recent years. 'Rather than lead to more plant-level negotiations, the move away from multi employer negotiations was accompanied by an increase in negotiating structures at enterprise or company level' (Millward et al. 1992: 355).

Not only has further fragmentation of the bargaining structure of the private sector been arrested in recent years, behind the scenes the centralization of control over bargaining by head offices is greater than is implied by this alone. It had been shown in a 1985 survey that in two-thirds of cases where the establishment was ostensibly the most important level of pay bargaining, the local manager was subject to higher level guidelines (Marginson et al. 1988). Nor was higher level control relaxing. Between 1984 and 1990 the WIRS surveys found that there was no overall change in the extent of consultation with higher level management on pay negotiations. Before the start of negotiation about three-fifths of managers in both surveys consulted with their superiors regarding manual pay negotiations. For non-manual pay negotiations the proportion was about half in both surveys (Millward et al. 1992).

This account of the recent change of the bargaining structure of the British private sector has concentrated on pay bargaining. But we would be missing the extent to which these reforms have been concerned with gaining control over productivity if we failed to mention how there has been a change in the range of other issues covered by agreements and also an increase in 'concession bargaining'. The 1992 Company Level Survey (Marginson et al. 1993) found that in 60 per cent of large companies the range of matters subject to negotiation had decreased. Confirming more fragmented case study evidence, the WIRS surveyors similarly concluded that 'when we were able to compare the scope of bargaining between one survey and another the indications were that its scope had declined within the unionized sector. Broadly speaking, fewer issues were subject to joint regulation in 1990 than in 1980, although most of the change appears to have occurred in the early part of the decade.' (Millward et al. 1992: 353).

If the range of issues has narrowed, their linkage to pay has been increased. Ingram (1991) found from CBI data that one in four manufacturing wage negotiations included changes in working arrangements, with evidence of higher wage settlements where productivity concessions were made. Marsden and Thompson (1990) found productivity concessions to be linked to decentralized bargaining. Tighter management control over bargaining has led to pay rises becoming increasingly conditional upon productivity improvements.

Withdrawal from collective bargaining

Until the 1980s it was almost unheard of for employers to withdraw from collective bargaining or, as it is usually termed, to 'derecognize' trade unions. It was common enough for unions to fail to win recruits in a workplace, or to succeed in that but to fail to gain recognition from management for bargaining purposes, but once collective bargaining had become established it was generally felt not to be worth the effort and acrimony involved in unravelling arrangements and scrapping agreements. This was despite the fact that British labour law is remarkable in international terms in its failure to provide unions with rights to organize.

In the early 1980s, despite the government's hostility to collective bargaining, acts of derecognition were rare and were generally confined to a narrow range of industries, notably newspapers, coastal shipping, and docks (Claydon 1989; Smith and Morton 1990; Turnbull 1991). But by the end of the decade it was becoming more widespread. In a broad-ranging survey of 558 companies, Gregg and Yates (1991) found that partial derecognition was becoming far more common in multi-establishment companies in the later 1980s, with 13 per cent of the sample reporting steps to derecognize unions in at least one of their establishments.

Valuable light has been cast on the question by the WIRS surveys with their use of a matched panel of workplaces from one survey to another (Millward et al. 1992; Millward, 1994). This showed that union recognition had been withdrawn at 9 per cent of the panel sample between 1984 and 1990. In many cases it appeared that negotiating rights had not been withdrawn as a deliberate management strategy but had withered through lack of support from employees. This is implied by the fact that rights were lost in 1990 from workplaces which had reported low or falling unionization in 1984, with half having lost all their members by 1990. A move from full recognition to partial recognition was rare; when managements withdrew recognition they generally did so comprehensively.

Part of the explanation of the decline in union recognition lies in the changing population of workplaces. Plants that closed between 1984 and 1990 were no more likely to have recognized unions than the rest. But there was a substantially lower likelihood of newer establishments recognizing unions; only 30 per cent did so compared with 40 per cent of all workplaces in 1990. This was partly because newer workplaces had characteristics that predisposed them to non-unionism, being smaller, in service industries, and with less skilled and more part-time workforces. But comparison with the 1980 survey suggested that, even allowing for this, probability of recognition was lower than in the 1970s, with an especially sharp decline in manufacturing.

These findings are confirmed by the 1992 Company Level Survey which suggests that the decline in recognition was most marked when companies opened new sites. Of the 140 companies opening at least one new site since 1987, 59 per cent reported that union recognition had not been granted to the largest occupational group in the workforce, while 35 per cent of companies had not recognized unions at any new site (Marginson et al. 1993). The workplace and company surveys suggest that recognition was strongly associated with bargaining arrangements that cover all the establishments in a company. It is also associated with British companies. Recognition was reported for only 18 per cent of overseas-owned companies. Further evidence comes from a matched comparison of new plants and long-established plants in the Northern Region (Peck and Stone 1992). Two-thirds of the new plants were non-union compared with little more than a third of the established plants, with non-unionism particularly strong among firms newly set up by local entrepreneurs.

The series of snapshots offered by the workplace and company level surveys thus provide some clues to the dynamics of changing employer policy towards pay bargaining and union recognition. One is that there is a distinct association between decentralized, site-level, pay bargaining arrangements and movements away from union recognition. Another arises from the fact that the withdrawal of firms from multi-employer agreements, which necessarily involve some form of union recognition, had created the initial opportunity to develop non-union arrangements for determining pay. Apparent employer hostility towards union recognition at new sites, reflected in a decline in the extent of comprehensive recognition across companies, suggests that such an opportunity is now being pursued. That this might be a conscious strategy on the part of large employers is indicated by the extent to which they report that decisions on union recognition are centralized (Marginson et al. 1993). Observing that the causes of the change to derecognition in Britain appear to be general and pervasive, Millward concludes from the workplace surveys that 'prime candidates appeared to be the removal of the statutory support for union recognition and the decline in the presumption by managements and the state in favour of collective bargaining between trade unions and employers' (Millward 1994: 102).

The picture of withdrawal from collective bargaining in Britain which emerges is historically remarkable. As is discussed elsewhere in this volume, collective bargaining is not being replaced in any systematic way by sophisticated alternative ways of representing employees' interests, channelling their conflicts, and pre-empting their grievances (see chapters 4, 11 and 12). Trade unionism is not being displaced by refined human resource management. As Millward concludes,

> the recent growth in inequality in wages and earnings which has been widely observed to be greater in Britain than in almost all other developed economies is being matched by a widening in the inequalities of influence and access to key decisions about work and employment. Many would argue that this is a welcome sign that Britain is moving towards the type of unregulated labour market that economic success requires. Others would see it as a reversion towards the type of economy that gave rise to the birth of trade unionism in the last century. (Millward 1994: 133)

Collective Bargaining and Pay Determination

The recent restructuring of collective bargaining has been on a scale that has no precedent in British industrial history. Where trade unions have not been excluded altogether, employers have tolerated them in far more constraining institutional structures than in the past. How does this affect the charge once so frequently made, that the upward pressure placed by unions on wages was the main force behind the British inflationary problem?

Wage push?

Evidence on income distribution certainly supports a view of declining union influence over pay. Atkinson (1993) concludes that official estimates of income equality

> show inequality in the UK as increasing between the mid-1970s and the mid-1980s, a reversal of the previous downward trend. Evidence from the Family Expenditure Survey shows that there can be little doubt that inequality was higher in 1985 than in 1975. The increase in measured inequality is large by historical standards, and there are grounds to believe that the rise between 1985 and later years in the 1980s was even more marked.

The New Earnings Survey makes clear that the earnings dispersion has widened steadily since the late 1970s, as did the gap between manual and non-manual earners. The ratio of top to bottom decile of gross weekly earnings for all full-time workers rose from 3.0

in 1980 to 3.4 in 1993. For men alone the ratio of the top to the bottom decile, which was 2.5 in 1970 and still 2.5 in 1980, rose to 3.1 in 1990 and 3.2 in 1993. This British picture does not, Atkinson demonstrates, reflect an international trend towards increased inequality over the period. Other countries' experience in this respect has been diverse.

Higher earners have done particularly well in recent years. The earnings of the top decile rose from 167.5 per cent of the median in 1975 to 187.4 per cent in 1993. The top 10 per cent of family incomes rose over the 1980s at the expense of other decile groups (Stark 1992). Those at the very top of the distribution, top executives and directors, have done even better (IDS 1993). In the five years to 1992, the top directors of Britain's hundred largest companies are reported to have received salary increases averaging 133 per cent, several times greater than the average employee (IPPR 1993). These and other findings have prompted McCarthy (1993) to argue that 'bottom-up' wage drift has been replaced by 'top-down' pay drift, with the interlocking membership of company directors' pay review committees fuelling a new inflationary process with self-serving and self-reinforcing awards. What used to be called 'wage push' inflation has, it is suggested, been replaced by 'top salary pull'.

There is other evidence that collective bargaining has been tending to follow rather than lead the wage setting process in recent years. In a study using the CBI's data set on wage settlements in manufacturing industry between 1979 and 1989, Ingram (1991) found that the average level of settlements was considerably higher in non-unionized than unionized firms. He also found that the range of wage increases in any given year was higher in non-union firms and suggested that wage changes here may be influenced to a greater extent than in unionized firms by firm-specific factors.

These findings were only partly supported by Gregg and Machin (1992) in a study of wage growth in 279 British firms between 1982 and 1988. They found that lower wage growth occurred in unionized firms either if there was a change in union status (derecognition or the removal of a closed shop), or if there was an increase in product market pressures, or both. Where neither occurred, there was no difference between the wage growth of union and non-union firms. They concluded that the major explanatory variable was not a reduced potential by unions to achieve wage gains *per se*, but a change in the product market circumstances of the firm.

This evidence suggests, at least, that trade unions and collective bargaining did not play a lead role in the British inflationary process during the 1980s. But there is an equally important consequential question. How far have British employers taken advantage of their apparent new-found grasp of pay determination in order to strengthen the macroeconomic circumstances of the country?

There is a growing economic literature debating the extent to which national macroeconomic success is enhanced by some form of nationally centralized or coordinated pay bargaining. As discussed in chapter 8, the most institutionally sophisticated exposition of the debate is by Soskice (1990) who argues that what matters is not formal centralized bargaining but strong *de facto* coordination of either employer organizations or unions, whichever is the stronger. This behind-the-scenes centralization permits a consideration of the inflationary and employment consequences of pay bargaining which can never be achieved by a multiplicity of individuals bargaining in isolation.

This is an aspect of employer policy in Britain which has been remarkable for its absence. We have noted the rapid decline of British industry-wide employer solidarity reflected in the collapse of industry-wide agreements. From an international point of view, it is the fact that British employers have never cultivated solidarity at the national level that deserves comment. British employers are resolutely individualistic in this respect. They may in due course be judged by their successors to have missed an historic opportunity offered by the ebb of collective bargaining.

Employer strategy beyond national boundaries

However backward British employers might be at devising national bargaining strategies, the strong multinational traditions of many of them, and increasing European integration, raise a final question concerning their international strategies. A number of commentators have suggested that European integration will lead to greater centralization and coordination of pay bargaining (Grahl and Teague 1992; Henley and Tsakalotos 1992; Marsden 1992). If so, it has been suggested that it is most likely to be of significance in firms with common European product divisions or with production integrated across more than one country (Marginson 1992).

Early signs are contrary to this prediction. The great majority of companies with businesses in Europe appear to favour nationally specific bargaining arrangements, and are disinclined either to coordinate bargaining or to standardize pay structures across their European operations (Wood and Peccei 1990). A study of British-based multinationals found that a number were using common job evaluation systems for white-collar and managerial employees across Europe, indicating that there may be advantages in harmonizing career and control structures within a company. But this is quite separate from the issue of harmonizing pay levels. The multinationals surveyed were acutely aware that differences in pension arrangements, taxation, social security, and other legal regulations seriously inhibited the scope for harmonization of salary structures in any sort of cash terms, even for highly mobile categories of senior management (Walsh et al. 1994).

Firms were generally hostile to the thought of European coordination of pay bargaining across their companies, partly because of the risk of wage comparability claims from their trade unions. Furthermore, the strategic focus of many British-based multinationals appears to be 'global' rather than distinctively European, with few companies perceiving 'subglobal' regional economic integration as a salient commercial or industrial relations issue.

The international equalization of wage structures within multinational companies, even on a regional basis, is effectively constrained by the costs involved in raising occupational wage levels to those of the highest-paying country. Even when international pay levelling is restricted to managerial or technical personnel, this can provoke resentment among local employees doing similar work at lower, non-international pay levels (Ryan 1991). Moreover, there is considerable evidence to suggest that multinational companies prefer to take advantage of, rather than suppress, national variations, choosing to locate different types of productive activity in different European Union member states, often in response to variations in wage and productivity levels (Nolan 1989; Knell 1993).

Finally, there is little evidence of effective trade union pressure to achieve international wage levelling. For all the efforts that have been made over the years, the achievements of international trade union cooperation in collective bargaining have been slight (Abbott 1994). The organizational problems confronting those efforts recall, greatly amplified, the problems that had bedevilled more modest post-war attempts to develop 'combine committees' of shop stewards, attempting to link different workplaces within a single company within Britain (see chapter 7). When collective sacrifices are required, sentiments of solidarity do not flow easily across linguistic and national boundaries. Even within the contours of multinational companies, and even within a tighter European Union, the convergence of pay and bargaining arrangements across national frontiers remains more in the realm of speculation than of reality.

In this chapter we have described the transformation which is still underway in the conduct of pay bargaining in Britain. The rise of enterprise bargaining in a country where collective bargaining as a whole is in retreat reflects a profound change in the policy of employers towards the management of labour. It would have been possible to discuss this without reference to economic theory. But to do so would have been to leave out the crucially important role that has been played in the shaping of employer strategies by the markets in which they compete. It would have been to leave unchallenged an account of pay determination which places undue, and deeply socially damaging, reliance upon the efficiency of the labour market. An understanding of pay bargaining of any value to practical policy can only come through the integration of economic and institutional analyses.

References

Abbott, K. 1994: The European Trade Union Confederation. Ph.D. Thesis, University of Cambridge.

Akerlof, G. 1984: Gift Exchange and Efficiency Wage Theory: Four Views. *American Economic Review* (Papers and Proceedings), 74, 2, 79–83.

Akerlof, G. and Yellen, J. 1986: *Efficiency Wage Models of the Labor Market.* Cambridge: Cambridge University Press.

Atkinson, A. B. 1993: What is Happening to the Income Distribution in the UK? 1991 Keynes Lecture, Faculty of Economics and Politics, Cambridge University. Mimeo.

Beaston, M. 1993: Trends in Pay Flexibility. *Employment Gazette*, September, 405–28.

Blanchflower, D., Oswald, A. and Garrett, M. 1990: Insider Power in Wage Determination. *Economica*, 57, 2, 143–70.

Brown, C. 1980: Equalising Differences in the Labor Market. *Quarterly Journal of Economics*, 94, 1, 113–34.

Brown, W. 1973: *Piecework Bargaining.* London: Heinemann.

Brown, W. 1993: The Contraction of Collective Bargaining in Britain. *British Journal of Industrial Relations*, 31, 2, 189–200.

Brown, W. and Nolan, P. 1988: Wages and Labour Productivity: The Contribution of Industrial Relations Research to the Understanding of Pay Determination. *British Journal of Industrial Relations*, 26, 3, 339–61.

Brown, W. and Sisson, K. F. 1975: The Use of Comparisons in Workplace

Wage Determination. *British Journal of Industrial Relations*, 13, 1, 23–53.

Brown, W. and Walsh, J. 1991: Pay Determination in Britain in the 1980s: The Anatomy of Decentralisation. *Oxford Review of Economic Policy*, 7, 1, 44–59.

Brown, W. and Walsh, J. 1994: Managing Pay in Britain. In K. Sisson (ed.), *Personnel Management in Britain*, 2nd edn. Oxford: Blackwell.

Brown, W., Hayles, J., Hughes, B. and Rowe, L. 1980: Occupational Pay Structures Under Different Wage Fixing Arrangements: A Comparison of Intra-occupational Pay Dispersion in Australia, Great Britain and the United States. *British Journal of Industrial Relations*, 18, 2, 217–30.

Brown, W., Hayles, J., Hughes, B. and Rowe, L. 1984: Product and Labour Markets in Wage Determination: Some Australian Evidence. *British Journal of Industrial Relations*, 22, 2, 169–76.

Carruth, A. and Oswald, A. 1989: *Pay Determination and Industrial Prosperity*. Oxford: Oxford University Press.

CBI (Confederation of British Industry) 1988: *The Structure and Processes of Pay Determination in the Private Sector*. London: CBI.

Clark, K. B. 1980: The Impact of Unionization on Productivity. *Industrial and Labor Relations Review*, 33, 4, 451–69.

Clay, H. 1929: *The Problem of Industrial Relations and Other Lectures*. London: Macmillan.

Claydon, T. 1989: Union Derecognition in Britain in the 1980s. *British Journal of Industrial Relations*, 27, 2, 214–24.

Doeringer, P. B. and Piore, M. J. 1971: *Internal Labor Markets and Manpower Analysis*. Boston: Lexington.

Employment Department 1992: *People, Jobs and Opportunity*. Cm 1810. London: HMSO.

Flanders, A. 1975: *Management and Unions: The Theory and Reform of Industrial Relations*. London: Faber.

Freeman, R. 1989: *Labour Markets in Action*. New York: Harvester Wheatsheaf.

Grahl, J. and Teague, P. 1992: Integration Theory and European Labour Markets. *British Journal of Industrial Relations*, 30, 4, 515–28.

Gregg, P. and Machin, S. 1992: Unions, the Demise of the Closed Shop and Wage Growth in the 1980s. *Oxford Bulletin of Economics and Statistics*, 54, 3, 53–71.

Gregg, P. and Yates, A. 1991: Changes in Trade Union and Wage Setting Arrangements in the 1980s. *British Journal of Industrial Relations*, 29, 3, 361–76.

Groshen, E. 1991: Five Reasons Why Wages Vary among Employers. *Industrial Relations*, 30, 3, 350–81.

Henley, A. and Tsakalotos, E. 1992: Corporatism and the European Labour Market after 1992. *British Journal of Industrial Relations*, 30, 4, 567–86.

Hicks, J. 1932: *The Theory of Wages*. London: Macmillan.

Hodgson, G. 1982: Theoretical and Policy Implications of Variable Productivity. *Cambridge Journal of Economics*, 6, 3, 213–26.

IDS (Incomes Data Services) 1993: *Reports*, 647, 648.

Ingram, P. 1991: Ten Years of Manufacturing Wage Settlements: 1979–89. *Oxford Review of Economic Policy*, 7, 1, 93–106.

IPPR (Institute of Public Policy Research) 1993: *The Justice Gap*. London: IPPR.

Knell, J. 1993: Transnational Corporations and the Dynamics of Human Capital Formation: Evidence from West Yorkshire. *Human Resource Management Journal*, 3, 4, 48–59.

Lester, R. A. 1952: A Range Theory of Wage Differentials. *Industrial and Labor Relations Review*, 5, 4, 483–500.

Levinson, H. M. 1966: *Determining Forces in Collective Wage Bargaining*. New York: Wiley.

Lindbeck, A. and Snower, D. 1986: Wage Setting, Unemployment and Insider–Outsider Relations. *American Economic Review*, 76, 2, 235–9.

McCarthy, W. E. J. 1993: From Donovan Till Now: Or Twenty-five Years of Incomes Policy. *Employee Relations*, 15, 6, 3–20.

Mackay, D., Boddy, D., Brack, J., Diack, J. and Jones, N. 1971: *Labour Markets Under Different Employment Conditions*. London: Allen & Unwin.

Marginson, P. 1984: The Distinctive Effects of Plant and Company Size on Workplace Industrial Relations. *British Journal of Industrial Relations*, 22, 1, 1–14.

Marginson, P. 1992: European Integration and Transnational Management–Union Relationships in the Enterprise. *British Journal of Industrial Relations*, 30, 4, 529–46.

Marginson, P., Edwards, P. K., Martin, R., Purcell, J. and Sisson, K. 1988: *Beyond the Workplace: Managing Industrial Relations in the Multi-Establishment Enterprise*. Oxford: Blackwell.

Marginson, P., Armstrong, P., Edwards, P., Purcell, J. and Hubbard, N. 1993: *The Control of Industrial Relations in Large Companies: An Initial Analysis of the Second Company Level Industrial Relations Survey*. Warwick Papers in Industrial Relations, 45. IRRU, University of Warwick.

Marsden, D. 1992: Incomes Policy for Europe? *British Journal of Industrial Relations*, 30, 4, 587–604.

Marsden, D. and Thompson, M. 1990: Flexibility Agreements and their Significance in the Increase in Productivity in British Manufacturing since 1980. *Work, Employment and Society*, 4, 1, 83–104.

Millward, N. 1994: *The New Industrial Relations?* London: PSI.

Millward, N., Stevens, M., Smart, D. and Hawes, W. R. 1992: *Workplace Industrial Relations in Transition*. Aldershot: Dartmouth.

Nolan, P. 1989: Walking on Water? Performance and Industrial Relations under Thatcher. *Industrial Relations Journal*, 20, 2, 81–92.

Nolan, P. and Brown, W. 1983: Competition and Workplace Wage Determination. *Oxford Bulletin of Economics and Statistics*, 45, 3, 269–87.

Ozanne, R. 1968: *Wages in Practice and Theory*. Madison: University of Wisconsin Press.

Peck, F. and Stone, I. 1992: *New Inward Investment and the Northern Region Labour Market*. Employment Department Research Series, No. 6. London: HMSO.

Phelps Brown, E. H. and Hopkins, S. V. 1981: *A Perspective of Wages and Prices*. London: Methuen.

Quaid, M. 1993: *Job Evaluation: The Myth of Equitable Assessment*. Toronto: University of Toronto Press.

Ramaswamy, R. and Rowthorn, R. 1991: Efficiency Wages and Wage Dispersion. *Economica*, 58, 4, 501–14.

Rees, A. and Schultz, G. P. 1970: *Workers and Wages in an Urban Labor Market*. Chicago: University of Chicago.

Reynolds, L. 1951: *The Structure of Labor Markets*. New York: Harper.

Robinson, D. 1968: *Wage Drift, Fringe Benefits and Manpower Distribution*. Paris: OECD.

Ryan, P. 1991: The European Labour Market: Meaning and Prospects. In L. Hantrais, M. O'Brien and S. Mangen (eds), *Education, Training and Labour Markets in Europe*. Aston University Cross National Research Group. Birmingham: Aston University.

Slichter, S. 1950: Notes on the Structure of Wages. *Review of Economics and Statistics*, 32, 1, 80–91.

Smith, P. and Morton, G. 1990: A Change of Heart: Union Exclusion in the Provincial Newspaper Sector. *Work, Employment and Society*, 4, 1, 105–24.

Soskice, D. 1990: Wage Determination: The Changing Role of Institutions in Advanced Industrialised Countries. *Oxford Review of Economic Policy*, 6, 4, 36–61.

Stark, T. 1992: *Income and Wealth in the 1980s*. Working Group Papers. London: Fabian Society.

Stewart, M. 1990: Union Wage Differentials, Product Market Influences and the Division of Rents. *Economic Journal*, 100, 4, 1122–37.

Streeck, W. 1989: Skills and the Limits of Neo-Liberalism. *Work, Employment and Society*, 3, 2, 89–104.

Thomson, A. and Sanjines, C. 1990: Earnings by Size of Company and Establishment. In M. Gregory and A. Thomson (eds), *A Portrait of Pay, 1970–82*. Oxford: Clarendon Press.

Turnbull, P. 1991: Labour Market Deregulation and Economic Performance; the Case of Britain's Docks. *Work, Employment and Society*, 5, 1, 17–35.

Walsh, J. 1993: Internalisation v. Decentralisation: An Analysis of Recent Developments in Pay Bargaining. *British Journal of Industrial Relations*, 31, 3, 409–32.

Walsh, J., Zappala, G. and Brown, W. 1994: *European Integration and Pay Determination: British Multinational Management Strategy in the European*

Labour Market. Discussion Paper in Industrial Relations and Human Resource Management, 94/01, School of Business and Economic Studies, University of Leeds.

Weiss, A. and Landau, S. J. 1984: Wages, Hiring Standards and Firm Size. *Journal of Labor Economics*, 2, 4, 477–500.

Wood, S. and Peccei, R. 1990: Preparing for 1992? Business-Led versus Strategic Human Resource Management. *Human Resource Management Journal*, 2, 1, 94–109.

Zappala, G. 1994: The Structure–Unionism–Wage Paradigm in Labor Economics: Resolving the Stalemate. *Journal of Economic Issues*, 28, 3, 819–46.

6

Trade Unions: Growth, Structure and Policy

Jeremy Waddington and Colin Whitston

Two major recessions since 1979, dramatic shifts in economic structure, and the impact of neo-liberalism on public policy have had wide-ranging effects on levels of unionization, the political legitimacy of unions, and the confidence and ability of unions to adjust. Since 1979, membership has declined every year. As discussed elsewhere in this book, legislation has restricted union activity and functions (chapter 9), and employers have introduced a range of workplace changes which have undermined bargaining power (chapters 4 and 7).

Broadly, analyses of the effects of these changes on unions fall into two categories: those that stress decline and those for which continuity is the key, with the result that some commentators see unionism being 'tamed', or in terminal decline, while others view it as undergoing a process of renewal. The purpose of this chapter is to review these arguments. It argues that the debate between decline and continuity too often obscures the contribution of unions themselves in the process of change, and tends to reduce organized labour simply to the object of external changes. It shows that political change and managerial practice have exposed tensions in unions between unifying and divisive tendencies. While unionists are attempting to establish a new agenda and practices to bolster cohesion, this chapter contends that this process has only just begun and that its outcome remains in the balance.

The development of organized labour is a complex social process based on changes in the economy and the ways in which people, in historically determined circumstances, define and pursue their interests. The possibility of collective organization is immanent in capitalist relations of production, which simultaneously divorce the worker from the means of production, and make production dependent on the social organization of labour. Yet both the extent and the form of unionism has varied widely over time and between societies. This chapter examines variations within Britain in relation to the three connected crises of unionism identified by Müller-Jentsch (1988): of workers' loyalty towards their unions; of systems to represent workers; and of means of aggregating workers' interests into a coherent programme.

Unemployment and the changing composition of the workforce can be seen as contributing to a crisis of interest aggregation as traditional areas of union strength have declined, and new occupations and employment patterns have disrupted the bases of traditional solidarity. ('Interest aggregation' refers to the process of taking workers' diverse interests and combining them into an organized programme of demands.) Winchester (1988: 494) ascribes the 'new realism' tendency which developed among some unions in the early 1980s to the 'assumption that changes in the labour market, reflecting new government policies, management strategies, and members' (and potential members') attitudes, required a substantial shift in trade union practice'. This formulation indicates the assumption that structural change in the economy was so deep as to have altered the ground on which collectivism defined itself.

However, interpretation of data on union membership can too easily become dominated by the apparent rationale of market forces, with a consequent underestimation of the social agencies involved. Kelly (1988) compared the relatively good performance of British unions in the 1980s with the much larger membership losses during the 1920–23 slump, which also followed a period of exceptional growth, and pointed to the recovery in union membership after 1934 as part of a well-established cycle of growth and decline. Similarly, shifts in the composition of the workforce are not new; Gardiner (1981: 330) has explained the stagnation of union membership in the 1950s and 1960s by the declining share of employment in older industrial sectors with historically high rates of unionization. Even in industries which became associated with the unions' manufacturing 'heartlands' in the post-war period there were examples of long-term resistance to union penetration (for example, in the case of chemicals, see Whitston 1991). What can appear historically as a straightforward cycle also includes a reorganization of working class structure and organization, and new forms of interest formation and bargaining. During the 1970s these compositional changes were partly a challenge, but also partly a source of union growth as women and white-collar workers in particular were drawn into membership.

Any crisis of membership loyalty must be assessed in the same way. Membership decline and the growth of non-union areas in employment cannot be considered as simply evidence of a decline in attachment to collective organization. Some schools of thought argue that economic restructuring has been accompanied by the growth of conditions conducive to an individualism which renders labour collectivism historically redundant. Such an espousal of individualism has been the prescriptive core of neo-liberal policy in industrial relations, but it is also discernible among analysts of the centre and left.

For example, Piore and Sabel (1984) argued that 'flexible specialization' would replace mass production, disrupting the links between monopolized production, state regulation, and management of effective demand, in ways which are beneficial to capital, labour, and society at large. The similarities between this approach and neo-liberal economic theory are obvious, not least in the inference that conflict between labour and capital arises not from the commodity status of labour, but from market imperfections which diminish the returns to labour. In fact, this optimistic reading of industrial restructuring is highly selective and misleading Although, as chapter 8 shows, there has certainly been a breakdown of the post-war consensus of full employment and the legitimation of trade union power, it does not follow that there has been a complete shift in the context of unionism. As chapter 4 shows, moves towards flexibility have been small and uncertain, and the social division of labour remains largely dependent on the power of multinationals and oligopolistic competition. Also, chapter 3 highlights the growth of low-paid and often casual jobs: the production of what Gorz (1989: 156) has described as a 'servile class', which is in the flexibility model seen, rather fantastically in view of the decline in manufacturing employment, as marginal. As that chapter also shows, models based on wider ideas of flexibilization have severe difficulties.

What is at issue is not the fact of new management practices and production methods, or the pressure of global markets; rather, it is the place occupied by human agency, and collectivism in particular, in economic change. Therefore debates on union membership loyalty are closely interwoven with the degree to which particular patterns of employment and labour management are seen as inevitable (and therefore rational), or conjunctural (and therefore amenable to alteration), and also to the degree to which they are perceived as redefining class interests. It follows that the 'crisis of representation' extends beyond employment structure and the workplace, reflecting problems of the social legitimacy of trade unions and their ability to represent a broad coalition of labour interests.

One attraction of the 'flexibility thesis' to the left in Britain lies in the exhaustion of the post-war compromise which can appear, from the perspective of the mid-1990s, as a 'golden age for unions'. However, the extension of union influence, both nationally and industrially, was far less extensive than is often supposed, and far more contradictory. In many ways the growth in the unions' sphere of influence represented a mechanism to curtail the challenge arising from the erosion of full employment, and inflation, in which unions as national institutions were to be recruited as agents of wage restraint and industrial modernization, in pursuit of a national interest which, while accommodating some working class aspirations, was in the main the property of capital. Far from altering the nature of the state, trade unions were profoundly affected by it. Nevertheless, the reflection of pluralist thinking in public policy, and in internal union organization as well, made a major contribution to the growth of union membership and the consolidation of union influence. The collapse of this supportive culture challenged the perception of both unions and union members of relations between themselves and employers, and the state.

These arguments are addressed in three sections, each of which refers to the peculiarities of the 1970s to facilitate analysis of events during the 1980s and 1990s. The first section maps the extent of membership decline, highlights the areas into which recruitment must be extended if membership decline is to be reversed, and reviews leading explanations of membership change in view of developments during the 1980s. The second section examines the attempts by the TUC to retain its position as the central coordinating agency for British unions, and the diversity in the policies adopted by affiliated unions in mergers and restructuring. The final section addresses two central issues to the future of unions in Britain: their diverse attempts to extend recruitment bases, and the new tensions between pressures towards centralization and decentralization.

The Dimensions and Explanations
of Membership Decline

This section charts the dimensions of the decline in unionization during the 1980s and reviews explanations of this decline. It establishes where unions have retained a presence, and the extent of this presence, during the 1980s. This section also identifies the areas into which unionization must be extended if the decline of the 1980s is to be reversed. Union responses to the decline in unionization are examined in subsequent sections. During the 1980s the rate of decline in unionization differed markedly between the earlier years of the decade (1980–3) and the later years (after 1983). In addition, the composition of union membership changed during the 1980s in much the same manner as during the 1970s, with increases in the proportion of white-collar and women members. These compositional changes featured in the development of union membership throughout the post-war period, irrespective of aggregate membership growth or decline.

The dimensions of decline

Unionization can be measured either absolutely or relatively. The number of trade union members is the absolute measure of unionization, whereas its relative measure is the number of trade union members expressed as a proportion of potential union members, a ratio referred to as union density. Potential union membership can also be measured in a number of different ways, hence resulting in a number of union density measures. Two measures of union density are used here: labour force density, in which union membership is expressed as a proportion of the labour force including the registered unemployed but excluding employers, the self-employed and members of the armed forces; and employment density which expresses union membership as a proportion of those in employment but also excludes the registered unemployed. The use of these two measures facilitates examination of the effects of unemployment on union membership during the 1980s. As far as is possible, all union membership data exclude retired and unemployed people who retain union membership. These data also refer to Britain only and thus exclude Northern Ireland. The principal source used here is

Table 6.1 Aggregate union membership and density in Great Britain: selected years, 1948–1987

Year	Union membership		Labour force			Employment		
	Number (000s)	Annual % change	Number (000s)	Annual % change	Labour force density level (%)	Number (000s)	Annual % change	Employment density level (%)
1948	9,102		20,270		44.9	19,994		45.5
1950	9,003		20,591		43.7	20,318		44.3
1955	9,460		21,438		44.1	21,258		44.5
1960	9,437		21,755		43.4	21,450		44.0
1965	9,715		22,895		42.4	22,619		43.0
1970	10,672		22,540		47.3	21,993		48.5
1975	11,561		23,042		50.2	22,213		52.0
1976	11,905	+3.0	23,326	+1.2	51.0	22,048	−0.7	54.0
1977	12,226	+2.7	23,516	+0.8	52.0	22,126	+0.4	55.3
1978	12,497	+2.2	23,635	+0.5	52.9	22,273	+0.7	56.1
1979	12,639	+1.1	23,687	+0.2	53.4	22,638	+1.6	55.8
1980	12,239	−3.2	23,452	−1.0	52.2	22,458	−0.8	54.5
1981	11,628	−5.0	23,021	−1.8	50.5	21,386	−4.8	54.4
1982	11,138	−4.2	23,315	+1.3	47.8	20,916	−2.2	53.3
1983	10,766	−3.3	23,615	+1.3	45.6	20,572	−1.6	52.3
1984	10,336	−4.0	23,611	0.0	43.8	20,741	+0.8	49.8
1985	10,282	−0.5	24,061	+1.9	42.7	20,990	+1.2	49.0
1986	9,995	−2.8	24,209	+0.6	41.3	21,073	+0.4	47.4
1987	9,874	−1.2	24,105	−0.4	41.0	21,325	+1.2	46.3

Waddington 1992a for data between 1948 and 1987. Data after 1987 are drawn from the *Annual Report* of the Certification Officer, the *Employment Gazette* and the *Labour Force Survey*.[1]

Aggregate unionization   Table 6.1 shows the movements in unionization between 1948 and 1987. Three distinct periods of unionization can be identified: 1948–68, 1969–79 and 1980–7. Between 1948 and 1968 union membership increased by an average of 32,000 per year, though both density measures declined. Membership thus increased at a slower rate than either the labour force or employment. During the second period, 1969–79, density increased. Membership increased by an annual average of 264,000 to peak at over 12.6 million in 1979. Labour force density increased by 10.5 percentage points and employment density by 11.9 percentage points in the same period. Between 1980 and 1987 most of the increases recorded during the 1970s were lost. By 1987 membership and employment density had declined to lower levels than recorded in 1969, while labour force density stood at its lowest level since 1948. The pattern of unionization between 1948 and 1987 was thus one of stagnation, followed by sharp increase, followed by equally sharp decline.

While actual union membership and both measures of union density fell during each of the years between 1980 and 1987, there are signs that the character of this decline varied. Between 1980 and 1983 union membership fell by an annual average of 468,000 members per year, compared to only 223,000 during 1984–7. The average annual membership loss was thus halved during the later period. Labour force density also fell more steeply during 1980–3 than during 1984–7. The reverse is the case for employment density: a higher average annual decline was recorded for 1984–7 than for 1980–3. These data indicate that when employment expanded after 1983, unions failed to recruit members in sufficient numbers in areas of employment expansion to offset membership losses from contracting sectors.

Between 1988 and 1992 (the most recent date for which data are available) the annual rate of membership loss increased, reaching 537,000 members or 5.6 per cent in 1992 (*Employment Gazette*, June 1994). Union membership in Britain fell to 7,682,000 by the autumn of 1993 and employment density to 31 per cent (*Labour Force Survey*). The fall in the period since 1979 is now the longest continuous decline on record.

Table 6.2 Union membership and density by sex in Great Britain: selected years, 1948–1987

Year	Men			Women			Employment Density for women/density for men ×100 (%)
	Union membership (000s)	Employment (000s)	Employment density	Union membership (000s)	Employment (000s)	Employment density	
1948	7,454	13,273	56.2	1,648	6,721	24.5	43.6
1950	7,353	13,447	54.7	1,650	6,871	24.0	43.9
1955	7,633	13,810	55.3	1,827	7,448	24.5	44.3
1960	7,558	14,031	53.9	1,879	7,418	25.3	46.9
1965	7,617	14,565	52.3	2,099	8,055	26.1	49.9
1970	8,089	13,706	59.0	2,583	8,287	31.2	52.9
1975	8,297	13,240	62.7	3,263	8,973	36.4	58.1
1976	8,477	13,097	64.7	3,428	8,951	38.3	59.2
1977	8,660	13,076	66.2	3,566	9,050	39.4	59.5
1978	8,907	13,100	68.0	3,590	9,173	39.1	57.5
1979	8,818	13,183	66.9	3,822	9,455	40.4	60.4
1980	8,468	13,018	65.0	3,771	9,440	39.9	61.4
1981	7,934	12,278	64.6	3,694	9,107	40.6	62.8
1982	7,552	11,930	63.3	3,586	8,985	39.9	63.0
1983	7,271	11,670	62.3	3,495	8,901	39.3	63.1
1984	6,866	11,619	59.1	3,470	9,123	38.0	64.3
1985	6,812	11,677	58.3	3,470	9,313	37.3	64.0
1986	6,567	11,610	56.6	3,428	9,463	36.2	64.0
1987	6,415	11,623	55.2	3,459	9,702	35.7	64.7

Male and female unionization As can be seen from table 6.2, the extent of female participation in the labour market was a key influence on the pattern of unionization. In 1948 women constituted 34 per cent of the employed. By 1969 this proportion had risen to 37 per cent, and by 1987 to 46 per cent. Between 1948 and 1987 the number of women in employment had risen by almost 3 million or 44 per cent. Over the same period the number of men in employment declined by over 1.6 million.

These changes in the relative participation rates in the labour market influenced the pattern of unionization. Between 1948 and 1968 the number of women union members increased by 35 per cent while the number of men rose by 7 per cent. Corresponding figures for 1969–79 were increases of 62 per cent for women and 15 per cent for men. A substantial portion of the increase in aggregate membership during the 1970s thus resulted from increased unionization of women. Between 1979 and 1987, movements in the relative rates of unionization continued to differ: the number of men in membership fell by 2.4 million (27 per cent), while the number of women members declined by 363,000 (10 per cent).

Data from the Labour Force Survey suggest the continuation of this pattern into the 1990s. Between 1989 and 1992 the number of men employees declined while the number of women employees rose. The decline in employment during this period was almost entirely due to the employment of fewer men. Over the same period the number of men trade union members fell by almost 700,000 and the number of women in membership decreased by about 200,000. In other words, between 1989 and 1991 both potential union membership and actual union membership became relatively more feminized.

Manual and white-collar unionization Table 6.3 illustrates the different trends in the unionization of manual and white-collar workers. Since 1951 the manual labour force and manual employment have tended to contract: by 20 per cent and 31 per cent respectively. In contrast, white-collar potential union membership expanded sharply over the same period: the white-collar labour force increased by 92 per cent and white-collar employment rose by 76 per cent. By 1980 the majority of the labour force was white-collar.

Until 1966, manual membership declined faster than potential membership; among white-collar workers membership grew, but more slowly than the potential figure. Density thus fell for both groups. From 1966 to 1979, membership grew among both, but

Table 6.3 Manual and white-collar union membership and density in Great Britain: selected years, 1951–1987

Year	Manual			White-collar			Employment W.-C. density/manual density ×100 (%)
	Union membership (000s)	Employment (000s)	Employment density	Union membership (000's)	Employment (000s)	Employment density	
1951	7,096.9	13,818	51.4	2,149.3	6,708	32.0	62.3
1961	6,970.6	13,504	51.6	2,526.4	8,285	30.5	59.1
1971	6,914.7	12,003	57.6	3,742.3	9,645	37.8	65.6
1975	7,085.8	11,520	61.5	4,474.8	10,693	41.8	68.0
1976	7,278.0	11,237	64.8	4,627.0	10,811	42.8	66.0
1977	7,401.6	11,079	66.8	4,824.0	11,047	43.7	65.4
1978	7,501.1	10,953	68.5	4,995.7	11,320	44.1	64.4
1979	7,517.0	10,930	68.8	5,122.2	11,708	43.7	63.5
1980	7,147.7	10,641	67.2	5,091.0	11,817	43.1	64.1
1981	6,605.5	9,942	66.4	5,022.9	11,444	43.9	66.1
1982	6,231.2	9,655	64.5	4,906.7	11,261	43.6	67.6
1983	5,947.2	9,429	63.1	4,819.3	11,143	43.2	68.5
1984	5,591.7	9,439	59.2	4,744.8	11,302	42.0	70.9
1985	5,527.8	9,484	58.3	4,753.8	11,506	41.3	70.8
1986	5,260.3	9,452	55.7	4,734.8	11,621	40.7	73.1
1987	5,119.7	9,495	53.9	4,753.8	11,830	40.2	74.6

much more rapidly among white-collar workers, who accounted for three-quarters of the rise in aggregate membership.

From 1979 to 1987 there were declines in total membership for both groups, though that for white-collar workers (7 per cent) was much smaller than that for manual workers (32 per cent). White-collar members comprised 48 per cent of total membership in 1987, compared to 41 per cent in 1979 and a mere 24 per cent in 1951. After 1987, constant employment density for white-collar workers and further declines among manual workers continued this trend.

Unionization by sector   Table 6.4 shows the development of unionization in the principal sectors of the British economy since 1948.[2] It is apparent that unionization varied markedly across sectors, though manufacturing and the public sector have been consistently the most heavily unionized. Since 1948 sectoral changes in unionization tended to follow the aggregate pattern, in that labour force density and employment density declined for all sectors except agriculture, forestry and fishing between 1949 and 1968; increased for all sectors except agriculture, forestry and fishing between 1969 and 1979; and universally declined during the period 1980–7.

Relative unionization by sector underwent some considerable changes in the post-war period. After 1948 British unionism became more firmly established in the public sector. In 1948 there were almost half a million more members in manufacturing than in the public sector. By 1987 trade union members in the public sector outnumbered those in manufacturing by more than 1.8 million. Furthermore, employment density in the public sector stood at over 80 per cent in 1987 compared to 60 per cent in manufacturing.

Only in manufacturing and the public sector did employment density increase between 1948 and 1987. In construction, and in agriculture, forestry and fishing, total membership declined rapidly, producing concomitant falls in density. In private services, membership grew but more slowly than employment so that density fell here too. For some sectors of unionism, prolonged decline was not a new feature of the 1980s.

Differences in the manner of data collection prohibit consistent comparisons between data before and after 1987. However, after 1987 employment in manufacturing, in agriculture, forestry and fishing, and in construction continued to fall at a higher rate than employment nationally (*Employment Gazette*, June 1994). The

Table 6.4   Union membership and density by sector in Great Britain, 1948–1987

	1948					1968				
Sector	Union member-ship (000s)	Labour force (000s)	Labour force density (%)	Employ-ment (000s)	Employ-ment density (%)	Union member-ship (000s)	Labour force (000s)	Labour force density (%)	Employ-ment (000s)	Employ-ment density (%)
Public sector	3,284.7	4,637.4	70.8	4,598.4	71.4	3,716.7	5,536.9	67.1	5,463.3	68.0
Utilities	218.8	324.3	67.5	322.4	67.9	305.5	419.3	72.9	413.7	73.8
Public services	1,464.3	2,472.2	59.2	2,445.5	59.9	2,248.5	3,800.2	59.2	3,764.4	59.7
Manufacturing	3,722.0	7,290.4	51.1	7,182.4	51.8	4,125.3	8,285.9	49.8	8,136.1	50.7
Manual	3,549.6	6,123.9	58.0	6,033.2	58.8	3,790.5	6,139.9	61.7	6,037.6	62.8
Whitecollar	172.4	1,166.5	14.8	1,149.2	15.0	334.8	2,146.0	15.6	2,099.2	15.9
Construction	611.2	1,325.8	46.1	1,289.7	47.4	472.0	1,570.7	30.1	1,476.2	32.0
Agriculture, forestry and fishing	224.5	988.9	22.7	980.2	22.9	131.1	516.8	25.4	505.7	25.9
Private services	665.2	4,578.4	14.5	4,524.9	14.7	771.3	6,042.0	12.8	6,006.5	12.8

level of employment density in manufacturing also fell by more than three percentage points between 1989 and 1992, while that in non-manufacturing declined by a single percentage point (*Labour Force Survey*, 1993). The manufacturing core of unionism thus further contracted after 1987 in terms of both potential and actual union membership.

Unionization by industry   Table 6.5 presents membership and density data disaggregated by industry for 1948, 1979, 1982 and 1987. The extent of unionization varies widely between industries. In 1948, 11 of the 31 industries recorded employment density levels of more than 70 per cent, whereas two industries were less than 30 per cent unionized – distribution, and entertainment and miscellaneous services. Between 1949 and 1979 a further six industries became 70 per cent unionized. Not one of the 11 industries which were 70 per cent unionized in 1948 dropped below this level before 1979. The two industries that were less than 30 per cent unionized remained so in 1979. Membership growth until 1979 was thus marked by an increase in the number of highly unionized industries.

Where unionism was entrenched prior to 1980 it remained so until 1987. In 1987, 15 industries recorded over 70 per cent employment density, for 8 of which the level of employment density was

	1979					1987		
Union membership (000s)	Employment (000s)	Labour force density (%)	Employment (000s)	Employment density (%)	Union membership (000s)	Employment (000s)	Employment density (%)
5,130.3	6,297.2	81.5	6,130.9	83.7	4,871.4	5,964.0	81.7
326.5	351.9	92.8	344.2	94.9	275.4	285.8	96.4
3,758.5	4,837.3	77.7	4,720.3	79.6	3,801.1	4,815.3	78.9
5,152.6	7,385.8	69.8	7,068.7	72.9	3,042.9	5,058.9	60.1
4,209.5	5,273.5	79.8	5,047.1	83.4	2,437.4	3,723.4	65.5
943.1	2,112.3	44.6	2,021.6	46.7	605.5	1,335.5	45.3
519.7	1,415.2	36.7	1,255.2	41.4	306.4	1,028.2	29.8
85.9	378.3	22.7	356.4	24.1	42.0	301.9	13.9
1,267.4	7,283.6	17.4	6,991.7	18.1	1,250.6	8,685.1	14.4

higher than 90 per cent. Metals and engineering and footwear were the two industries that fell below the 70 per cent threshold. This relative stability among the highly unionized industries contrasted with the position in areas of weak organization. The two industries with less than 30 per cent density in 1979 were joined by timber and furniture, and construction, by 1987, as union weaknesses became more widespread.

Of concern for the future are the relative rates of employment growth and contraction in the industries of strength and weakness. Between 1979 and 1987 employment in the ten most unionized industries declined from 8 per cent of aggregate employment to 7 per cent. In contrast, employment in the four least unionized industries expanded rapidly from 34 per cent to 42 per cent, a rise accounted for by the growth in distribution and in entertainment and miscellaneous services. Where unions were well established in 1987, employment was contracting; where they were weak, employment was expanding. Industrially disaggregated data are not directly compatible before and after 1987. However, survey data suggest that the trends identified before 1987 persisted until 1993, in that employment density declined in most industries and the number of industries where union organization was weak increased (Millward et al. 1992: 107; *Labour Force Survey* 1994).

Table 6.5 Union membership and density by industry in Great Britain, 1948, 1979, 1982 and 1987

	1948			1979		
Industry	Union membership (000s)	Employment (000s)	Employment density (%)	Union membership (000s)	Employment (000s)	Employment density (%)
Food, drink and tobacco	273.3	610.6	44.8	474.4	676.3	70.1
Chemicals	141.5	392.9	36.0	295.9	473.0	62.6
Metals and engineering	1,913.7	3,458.1	55.3	3,038.5	3,658.4	83.1
Cotton and man-made fibres	277.7	348.2	79.8	100.0	107.9	92.7
Other textiles	197.9	508.0	39.0	175.2	341.1	51.4
Leather, leather goods, fur and clothing	169.4	451.2	37.5	146.5	327.8	44.7
Footwear	92.8	118.8	78.1	65.2	77.3	84.3
Bricks and building materials and pottery	102.4	234.4	43.7	126.7	185.6	68.3
Glass	29.8	65.5	45.5	46.6	68.2	68.3
Timber and furniture	122.2	268.6	45.5	92.6	254.3	36.4
Paper and board	60.8	162.7	37.4	116.2	198.8	58.5
Printing and publishing	208.7	271.6	76.8	307.4	338.0	90.9
Other manufacturing	89.6	218.4	41.0	143.0	312.9	45.7
Coal-mining	691.4	798.4	86.6	284.3	286.2	99.3
Other mining and quarrying	42.2	73.4	57.5	24.2	49.1	49.3
Gas	101.1	136.7	74.0	95.5	103.4	92.4
Electricity	101.0	156.7	64.5	169.6	175.9	96.4
Water	16.7	29.0	57.6	61.4	64.9	94.6
Construction	611.2	1,289.7	47.4	519.7	1,255.2	41.4
Distribution	325.8	2,069.2	15.7	469.8	2,749.4	17.1
National government	375.3	696.8	53.9	588.9	612.4	96.2
Local government and education	884.7	1,229.6	72.0	2,187.3	2,811.3	77.8
Health services	204.3	519.1	39.4	982.3	1,296.6	75.8
Post and telecommunications	283.2	321.0	88.2	418.9	417.9	100.2
Railways	474.6	532.9	89.1	202.2	203.3	99.5
Road transport	481.8	513.8	93.8	409.4	427.3	95.8
Sea transport	112.2	141.9	79.1	74.0	81.4	90.9
Port and inland water transport	140.6	147.8	95.1	59.8	68.7	87.0
Air transport	11.9	30.4	39.1	80.1	90.3	88.7
Insurance, banking and finance	137.1	350.4	39.1	403.7	707.7	57.0
Entertainment and miscellaneous services	202.2	2,105.3	9.6	393.9	3,534.6	11.1

1982			1987		
Union membership (000s)	Employment (000s)	Employment density (%)	Union membership (000s)	Employment (000s)	Employment density (%)
369.6	604.9	61.1	331.1	531.4	62.3
261.0	413.3	63.2	211.8	387.7	54.6
2,202.6	2,909.2	75.7	1,641.8	2,394.5	68.6
57.8	58.8	98.3	38.4	41.1	93.4
106.1	240.6	44.1	88.9	227.8	39.0
94.3	236.3	39.9	89.0	230.6	38.6
43.9	57.2	76.7	35.9	54.6	65.8
82.0	152.3	53.8	75.8	135.6	55.9
36.3	54.2	67.0	30.5	45.9	66.4
65.8	202.2	32.5	52.8	211.9	24.9
69.2	155.7	44.4	42.5	138.4	30.7
309.1	337.4	91.6	297.2	345.4	86.0
106.0	237.3	44.7	85.3	248.3	34.4
253.6	259.6	97.7	133.0	135.9	97.9
25.3	65.2	38.8	21.8	65.7	33.2
97.0	103.5	93.7	78.3	82.9	94.5
106.2	162.8	98.4	145.4	148.0	98.2
61.3	64.6	94.9	51.7	54.9	94.2
353.0	1,024.4	34.5	306.4	1,028.2	29.8
417.4	2,655.8	15.7	399.9	3,077.0	13.0
518.6	575.9	90.1	459.4	606.3	75.8
2,346.6	2,660.3	88.2	2,333.3	2,825.9	82.6
986.9	1,395.0	70.7	1,008.4	1,383.1	72.9
415.0	421.8	98.4	401.5	438.0	91.7
187.4	191.6	97.8	150.8	156.8	96.2
347.5	383.7	90.6	306.9	400.9	76.6
56.1	56.5	99.3	21.5	23.5	91.5
47.4	51.7	91.7	35.4	42.8	82.7
70.2	71.4	98.3	74.3	89.4	83.1
467.9	784.4	59.7	487.4	906.0	53.8
358.2	3,718.7	9.6	363.3	4,702.1	7.7

Summary Declining union density after 1979 reversed previous growth. Labour force density declined more rapidly than employment density during 1980–3, whereas during 1984–7 the reverse was the case. After 1987, membership losses accelerated again, particularly as unemployment began to rise from 1990. These declines occurred in all five main sectors of the economy. Where unions were well organized in 1979, they remained so during the 1980s, but employment contracted most rapidly in these sectors. The size of the weakly unionized sectors increased, and the contrast between heavily and weakly organized industries became more marked. Changes in the structure of unionism, however, continued longer-term trends as women and white-collar workers comprised growing proportions of membership.

Explanations of the decline in unionization

There are thus two phenomena to explain: the initial steep decline and the slower rate of decline thereafter. Four broad explanations of these phenomena have been advanced: the effects of legislation; employers' policies; the business cycle; and the changing composition of employment. While there are interrelationships between these explanations they are considered separately for ease of explanation. It is argued that legislative effects and the impact of employers' policies cannot explain the sharp downturn in aggregate unionization during the early 1980s. These effects may be more influential in explaining the failure of unions to increase membership when unemployment declined between 1983 and 1990. The business cycle and the changing composition of employment are shown to be important influences on membership decline throughout the 1980s.

The effects of legislation Arguments that government policy was the cause of membership decline are expressed most forcibly in terms of the impact of legislative change. The abolition of a statutory recognition procedure in 1980; the gradual removal of immunities protecting the closed shop, culminating in 1988 with the withdrawal of any legal protection for closed shops; and restrictions on secondary industrial action are all cited as promoting membership decline (see chapter 9). Freeman and Pelletier constructed an index of the 'favourableness of labour laws to unionism' and through its application in multivariate analysis claimed that legislative change between 1980 and 1986 accounted for 'effectively the entire decline in UK density in that period' (1990: 155). While other explanations acknowledge an impact on unionization from the law, they tend to highlight its operation in conjunction with other factors (Price and Bain 1983). The unique feature of Freeman and Pelletier's argument is that they assign an independent effect to legislation.

It is this direct linkage between legislation and unionization that is the key weakness of Freeman and Pelletier's position. Disney (1990), for example, argued that density started to decline before the initial legislation was enacted and that this decline made it politically more feasible to introduce it. The effects of the legislation enacted during the early 1980s were uneven and contradictory (IDS 1987; Brown and Wadhwani 1990). If legislation was the sole influence on the initial decline in unionization, the rate of decline would be expected to rise under the cumulative weight of successive legislative measures. As table 6.1 shows, this did not occur; actual membership losses tended to slow until 1987.

The case of the closed shop further illustrates these points. Legislation on the closed shop was assigned a strong negative effect by Freeman and Pelletier. However, between 1980 and 1984 almost all of the 25 per cent decline in the closed shop was due to compositional and structural effects rather than legislative reform (Millward and Stevens 1986: 306). Furthermore, the rate of decline of closed shop arrangements increased between 1984 and 1990 (Millward et al. 1992: 96–101). Yet during this period the rate of membership decline was lower than during the early 1980s. Increases in the rate of membership decline and the termination of closed shop arrangements fail to coincide.

Legislation appears to have had more effect on unionization in enabling employers to prevent any membership growth during the mid-1980s when employment expanded. Union density at workplaces established since 1980, for example, was markedly lower than that at older establishments (Millward et al. 1992: 64). This effect was associated with other influences rather than being an independent effect of the law, not the least of which is the impact of employers' policies.

Employers' policies   Recognition of unions by employers and union membership growth were viewed as key elements of a 'virtuous circle' of cause and effect which promoted unionization during the 1970s (Bain and Price 1983: 18). Arguments that employers' policies in the 1980s adversely affected unionization come in two broad variants: first, that employers have undermined union organization at established workplaces; second, that employers have prevented unionization at greenfield sites. This section shows both of these arguments have some substance, but that neither is a plausible explanation of the sharp decline in union membership between 1980 and 1983.

Derecognition is the clearest case of the undermining of existing union organization. As discussed in chapter 7, it was not widespread for the 1980s. In particular, it was rare during the period of sharp membership decline to 1983. It was also not a general phenomenon but was concentrated in certain industries and occupations. It thus does not explain the membership decline of the early 1980s.

Where derecognition and the failure of unions to secure recognition at greenfield sites may be more influential is in explaining the absence of membership growth between 1983 and 1990 when employment expanded. Successive WIRS have shown that the proportion of establishments at which a union was recognized increased from 64 per cent to 66 per cent between 1980 and 1984, before declining to 53 per cent in 1990. The decrease in recognition thus came after 1984, and was concentrated in the private sector. Some of this decline resulted from derecognition which became more widespread during the late 1980s (Millward et al. 1992: 74–7; Smith and Morton 1993).

A further inhibitor of membership growth between 1983 and 1990 was the failure of unions to secure recognition or recruitment at recently established sites, particularly those that were small and independent. While evidence suggests that some employers in manufacturing resisted union recruitment initiatives (MacInnes and Sproull 1989; McLoughlin and Gourlay 1991) survey evidence rejects employers' antipathy towards unions as being 'the major reason' for the absence of union members in large parts of the private sector (Millward et al. 1992: 69). It would appear that weaknesses in union organization limited the spread of recognition. Inadequate resources and inefficient organization restricted union efforts to recruit at new sites (Kelly and Heery 1989). Furthermore, at some sites where unions were recognized during the late 1980s employment density declined as unions struggled to maintain existing organization (Gregg and Yates 1991; Millward et al. 1992: 70–5).

While a number of employers derecognized unions during the 1980s, this did not account for the vast decline in membership during the early 1980s. The overt anti-unionism of some American employers was not replicated on a widespread basis in Britain. Evidence from the late 1980s, however, suggests that the 'virtuous circle' of union recognition and union membership growth has been broken with little immediate prospect of its renewal. The marked decline in the proportion of establishments at which unions are recognized indicates that the failure of unions to secure recognition accounts for some of the decline in density during the late 1980s.

Business cycle explanations   Business cycle explanations of unionization have proved to be fairly robust in explaining post-war trends. Although there is considerable variation in the specification of business cycle models (see, for example, Bain and Elsheikh 1976; Booth 1983; Carruth and Disney 1988), three variables are incorporated in most models: prices, wages and unemployment. All other things remaining equal, rising prices are associated with increases in union membership as workers join unions to protect their standards of living. This effect may be dampened if money wages are rising at a rate that is sufficient to compensate for price increases. The relationship between prices and wages is thus central to most business cycle explanations. Increasing rates of unemployment also tend to be associated with membership decline. While some unions have traditionally retained limited numbers of unemployed workers in membership, the post-war development of social security eroded such membership retention, with the consequence that unemployment and unionization are inversely related. Business cycle models explain a substantial proportion of the movements in unionization. Combined with a dummy variable to represent anti-union government policy, a recent business cycle model, developed for 1896–1970, explained fluctuations in the level of employment density between 1971 and 1987 (Carruth and Disney 1988; Disney 1990).

Movements in business cycle indicators are consistent with those in unionization during the 1980s. During the 1970s both prices and earnings rose rapidly. Real earnings, however, increased only slowly. In contrast, between 1980 and 1991 the rise in earnings consistently outstripped that of prices with the consequence that real earnings increased substantially. This increase in real earnings is consistent with business cycle explanations in that it is associated with lower levels of aggregate unionization.

These effects were particularly marked among white-collar workers. The massive increase in white-collar membership during the 1970s was coincidental with the 'squeezing' of the white-collar/manual earnings differential by flat-rate increases dictated by successive income policies, an effect that was compounded by a non-indexed progressive tax system (Price and Bain 1983). The white-collar/manual earnings differential fell from 99 in 1969 to 87 in 1974 before rising to 93 in 1979. During the 1980s this differential steadily rose and reached 117 in 1991, thus reversing the 'squeezing' of the 1970s. In other words, white-collar workers joined unions to protect their living standards during the 1970s, but were not encouraged to do so during the 1980s, as their living standards improved in real terms and by comparison with those of their manual counterparts.

Business cycle explanations are also supported by the different levels of unemployment during the 1970s and 1980s. Between 1969 and 1979 the average annual level of unemployment was 3.9 per cent and changes in its annual level varied from -0.9 percentage points to $+1.5$ percentage points. Compared with the 1980s, these levels of unemployment were low and the variation within narrow bounds. Between 1979 and 1983 the level of unemployment rose from 5 per cent to 12 per cent. The level of unemployment remained higher than 11 per cent until 1986 after which it fell, reaching 6 per cent in 1990.

Furthermore, during 1980–3 unemployment was concentrated in the membership heartlands of unionism. As table 6.1 shows, labour force density fell more rapidly than employment density, as former union members became unemployed and left their unions. Crucially, unemployment reached 13 per cent in 1982 in manufacturing. Unions were often unable to retain the unemployed in membership. A substantial proportion of the decline in unionization during the early 1980s was accentuated by rising levels of unemployment.

Business cycle models remain effective explanations of the decline in unionization. The rise in real earnings, particularly among white-collar workers, inhibited recruitment during the 1980s, and the persistently high levels of unemployment restricted opportunities for workers to unionize.

The effect of changes in the composition of employment The thesis underpinning the final explanation of membership decline is that during the 1980s employment contracted where union membership was concentrated and expanded where membership was sparse. The data presented above provide some support for this explanation. In 1979, for example, manufacturing was heavily unionized, but employment in this sector contracted throughout the 1980s, whereas employment expanded in the sparsely unionized private services. In addition to these sectoral shifts, advocates of an explanation based on the changing composition of employment point to increases in the employment of women, white-collar workers and part-time workers. The rate of unionization among each of these groups has historically been lower than that of men, manual workers and full-time workers. Similarly, the spatial shift in employment from the heavily unionized north to the weaker areas of organization in the south is cited as exacerbating these trends (Stevens and Wareing 1990).

A problem with this explanation is that many of these compositional changes were in evidence before 1980. Furthermore, during the 1970s unionization increased despite adverse changes in the composition of employment. The changing composition of employment cannot thus be the sole explanation of the decline in unionization. Methodological problems mean that compositional effects are also difficult to measure. Several of the processes mentioned above are interrelated, with the result that the effects on unionization of the different compositional effects cannot simply be added together. For example, compositional shifts towards private services are associated with increases in the employment of women, white-collar and part-time workers. The evidence for compositional effects on unionization is also sensitive to the base year on which calculations are made and the definition of the compositional effect. Using a base year of 1979, for example, Booth (1989) attributed 5.25 percentage points of a total 12.5 percentage points decline in density until 1987 to compositional changes. In contrast, no significant compositional effects were shown in the period 1980–3 (Carruth and Disney 1988), a view confirmed over the longer period 1980–6 (Freeman and Pelletier 1990).

The data tabulated above allow assessment of three compositional effects: sexual, occupational and sectoral employment shifts. Had the sexual composition of employment remained the same in 1987 as it was in 1948, employment density would have been 2.2 percentage points higher in 1987; and it would have been 3.1 percentage points higher in 1987 had the occupational composition remained constant, and 4.6 percentage points higher in 1987 if the sectoral composition had remained the same (Waddington, 1992a). Long-term shifts in employment composition from a base of 1948 thus point to some adverse effects on union density. Using 1979 as the base year allows direct comparison with the studies mentioned above. Calculating compositional shifts from this base year reveals significant effects. These were particularly marked in the period 1980–3, which accounted for most of the compositional effects between 1980 and 1987. These data thus indicate significant compositional effects during the period of the steepest decline in membership. The impact of a wider range of compositional shifts was calculated for 1983–9 (Green 1992).[3] Over this period the impact of specific compositional effects was small, but their combined effect accounted for about 30 per cent of the fall in density during the period.

The changing composition of employment helps to explain both the sharp decline in unionization during the early 1980s and the persistence of membership loss thereafter. However, union membership increased during the 1970s against compositional changes, and during the 1980s these changes account for only a portion of the decline.

Overview The gains in unionization secured during the 1970s were wiped out during the 1980s. Between 1980 and 1983 the rate of this decline was particularly steep. The composition of union membership changed as it declined: union membership became more feminized and more white-collar. Union membership remained concentrated in the public sector and manufacturing. Employment in both these sectors contracted throughout the decade. In contrast, where unionization was sparse, particularly in private services, employment expanded but unions were unable to achieve commensurate increases in membership.

No single influence is sufficient to explain these trends. Furthermore, the different effects are necessarily interrelated and difficult to separate. It is clear, however, that legislative effects and the impact of employers' policies are relatively weak explanations of the sharp decline in union membership during the early 1980s. While these explanations may have accounted for some of this initial decline, movements in the business cycle and changes in the composition of employment were responsible for a substantially greater share of this decline. In particular, the sharp rise in unemployment and real earnings coupled to the contraction of employment in manufacturing had strong negative effects on unionization. During the later 1980s, business cycle models tended to over-predict unionization (Booth 1989; Disney 1990), and changes in the composition of employment accounted for about one-third of the decline. It would thus appear that the effects of legislation and employers' policies came more to the fore during the late 1980s. The failure of unions to secure recognition and membership in the expanding private services during this period is consistent with such a development.

Trade Union Structure: Crisis or Realignment?

If the main contours of the economic and political problems facing trade unions are relatively easy to define, characterization of union responses is less so. In part this is a reflection of union diversity, both in terms of structure and tradition, and in the uneven impact of employment and workplace changes. In the private manufacturing sector, unions have not only faced rapid reductions in membership and the pool of potential recruits, but changes in work organization which have undermined traditional demarcations between white-collar, skilled, and general unions. In the public sector, privatization, competitive tendering and changes in bargaining structures necessitated the reappraisal of union practices which were established around national bargaining. In addition to falling numbers, therefore, unions faced a crisis of interest aggregation which rendered traditional structures problematical. This section addresses union responses to these challenges by looking at the changed role of the TUC, and the structural reforms implemented through union mergers. Chapter 7 discusses representation at workplace level; chapter 16 looks at privatization in particular.

The TUC and the inter-union consensus

Before 1980, inter-union relations had become firmly established around the TUC. Except for powers of suspension and expulsion the TUC has never had any direct constitutional authority over affiliated unions (Martin 1980). Some authority over affiliated unions accrued to the TUC from its resolution of inter-union disputes by reference to the Bridlington Principles, originally agreed at the 1939 Congress. With the development of tripartism the TUC assumed a central role as a conduit to government from which it also derived some authority. The authority gained from these functions compensated for the TUC's lack of direct constitutional authority over affiliated unions and facilitated the TUC's involvement in public policy formation. Some later analyses drew a picture of the years before 1979 as a 'golden age' when union involvement in public policy formulation through a united TUC produced substantive gains for a labour movement with a defined social purpose (see, for example, Leadbeater 1987).

After 1980, as chapter 8 shows, the TUC lost its role as a conduit to government as successive Thatcher-led administrations withdrew from tripartite institutions. The labour movement was effectively excluded from public policy forums. Furthermore, affiliated unions expressed concern over the utility of the Bridlington Principles. In other words, after 1979 many of the functions from which the TUC derived authority over affiliated unions were lost or eroded. Those who see this loss as a crisis in the maintenance of an inter-union consensus refer to cases where the TUC failed to find a compromise between affiliated unions: for example, the failure to reach a common position towards the legislation enacted during the early 1980s, in particular regarding ballots and their funding (Sherman 1986); and the expulsion of the Electrical, Electronic, Telecommunications and Plumbing Union (EETPU) at the 1988 Congress.

In order to argue that an inter-union consensus is breaking up, it is necessary to make the case that such a consensus existed in the first place. Two arguments are developed here which show that this consensus has always been illusory. First, presentations of the 'golden age' gloss over the tensions and competing interests that marked the activities of TUC and its affiliated unions during the 1970s. Second, the influence of the TUC in public policy formation during the 1970s is much overstated.

The TUC remains the principal national trade union centre and, by comparison with its European counterparts, is among the most comprehensive in its coverage (Visser 1989). Attempts to form competing centres have been restricted to occupationally or industrially specific groups of unions. Furthermore, only the EETPU was expelled from the TUC in the 1980s. During the 1970s, expulsions from the TUC were more common; several major unions, for example, were expelled for complying, against TUC policy, with the registration procedure of the Industrial Relations Act 1971. In 1993, despite considerable opposition, and some unresolved conflicts, the EETPU was readmitted to the TUC after its merger with the Amalgamated Engineering Union (AEU). Also noteworthy are the recent affiliations of the Society of Radiographers and the Chartered Society of Physiotherapists, the first significant new affiliations since the 1970s. Currently, the only major unions that remain outside are the Royal College of Nursing (RCN) and the Association of Teachers and Lecturers (ATL). The coverage of the TUC thus remains comprehensive.

Throughout the 1970s the TUC's role in inter-union relations remained pragmatic rather than inspired by the establishment of an overarching consensus. Intervention in industrial disputes, for example, was directed towards the restriction of any political damage arising from initiatives launched by individual affiliates rather than the coordination of actions. On numerous occasions, however, even this limited objective was beyond reach. The TUC also failed during the 1970s to establish an agreed basis for union structural reform, restricting its role to advice on specific mergers. Tensions between competing viewpoints were a consistent feature of TUC policy formulation.

As chapter 8 explains, it is also open to question whether the TUC exerted any significant influence through tripartite institutions. The TUC, despite a resolution formally opposing a wage limit, did nothing to mobilize against the imposition of a limit in 1975. Living standards declined and unemployment rose until 1977, as the TUC's advocacy of mild reflation was ignored (Minkin 1992: 106–16). A substantial minority of unions also opposed tripartite involvement, while in those that accepted it internal tensions grew. These were symbolized by the defeat of Jack Jones, one of the architects of the Social Contract, at the Transport and General Workers' Union (TGWU) Biennial Delegate Conference. Eventually, the Social Contract dissolved in the 'winter of discontent' as even a semblance of union consensus disappeared.

The question remains whether the TUC can remain at the centre of British unionism and maintain some authority. Two phases may be identified in the TUC's pursuit of this objective: 1980–7, and 1987 to date. During the first of these the TUC anticipated the re-election of a Labour government which would repeal the legislation enacted during the period. While TUC policy was to reject state funding for ballots, the AEU and the EETPU sought such funding, thus raising internal tensions. An initiative to review TUC practices, policies and procedures was much curtailed by the effects of the miners' strike of 1984/1985. However, the General Council was reformed in 1983 to reflect some of the changes in the composition of affiliated membership. Some internal reform was thus achieved in the early period, but wider policy initiatives faltered.

The third consecutive electoral defeat for the Labour party in 1987 pre-empted some significant changes in TUC policy, several of which were *inter alia* intended to restore the TUC's authority.

Prominent among these were additional internal reform; assigning a higher profile to involvement in Europe; and the establishment of a Special Review Body (SRB). Some of the key proposals arising from the SRB are examined in the section on recruitment below. Internal reform in 1989 further increased the representation of women, white-collar and public-sector workers on the General Council. However, reform of the Bridlington Principles in 1988 was superseded by the provisions of the Trade Union Reform and Employment Rights Act 1993 (TURERA), particularly those measures which allow an employee greater freedom to join the union of his/her choice. It remains open to question whether subsequent proposals (TUC 1993) will be longer-lasting. Also, in response to perceived weakness the TUC developed a policy towards Europe intended to secure for Britain the platform of social and workplace protections proposed in the European Union, many of which had been removed by Conservative governments of the 1980s. Subsequent political developments have thwarted the achievement of this goal. Furthermore, the extent of the protections available through European-level institutions has been questioned (Wedderburn, 1990). However, irrespective of the substantive gains available through European participation, it is clear that the TUC is attempting to become the principal conduit to Europe and thereby establish authority over affiliated unions. It remains to be seen whether this initiative will be successful, as several unions have established, or intend to establish, their own offices in Brussels in order to maintain direct links independently of the TUC.

Other fragmentary pressures are also in evidence. The merging of unions has resulted in the formation of several organizations with the capacity to deliver bargaining services and training independently of the TUC. More importantly, the merger process has concentrated membership in a smaller number of unions with wider recruitment ambitions and the prospect of independent activity in the area of public policy both domestically and in Europe. It is to these structural reforms that we now turn.

Trade unions and the merger process

Continuous membership decline in the 1980s led to the reform of trade union structure. While membership decline had remarkably little effect on the distribution of membership among unions of different sizes, it promoted a sharp decline in the number of unions through mergers. Mergers were encouraged, but not coordinated, by the TUC with the result that a range of merger policies were pursued within competing unions. Thus the notoriously complex structure of British unionism was not simplified, but remained characterized by a multiplicity of industrially and occupationally overlapping recruitment bases. This section examines the major features of these structural reforms and highlights the diversity of merger policies.

The distribution of membership   Table 6.6 shows the distribution of trade union membership in 1979 and 1992. In 1979 there were 454 unions, 11 of which recruited more than 250,000 members and organized almost 64 per cent of total membership. By 1992 the total number of unions had fallen to 268; and the 9 unions with over 250,000 members organized about 60 per cent of total membership. The number of unions with fewer than 10,000 members fell by over 44 per cent between 1979 and 1992, but the proportion of total membership recruited by these unions remained constant. In other words, membership decline between 1979 and 1992 was spread fairly evenly across unions of different sizes.

In 1979, 109 of the total of 454 unions (24 per cent) were affiliated to the TUC. By 1991 the number of TUC-affiliated unions had fallen to 74 (27 per cent of the total). The number of non-affiliated unions thus fell at a higher rate than that of affiliated unions. Membership followed a different pattern. In 1979, 90 per cent of total membership was organized by TUC-affiliated unions, compared with 86 per cent in 1991. The expulsion of the EETPU from the TUC at the 1988 Congress explains some of the steep decline in membership. Compounding this effect were the industrial and occupational concentrations of membership losses which were particularly hard felt by TUC-affiliated unions.

A primary reason for the sharp decline in the overall number of unions was the high rate of mergers. Unlike the 1970s, when a large number of unions were newly formed, there were very few formations during the 1980s. The effect of mergers on the total number of unions was thus mitigated during the 1970s but not during the 1980s, hence the particularly sharp decline in unions in the latter period.

The high rate of merger activity during the 1980s and 1990s represents a continuation of a trend established since the mid-1960s (Waddington 1992b). During the 1970s the acquisition of small

Table 6.6 The distribution by membership size of British unions

Membership size	1979				1992			
	Number of unions	Membership (000s)	Percentage of all unions (%)	Percentage of all membership (%)	Number of unions	Membership (000s)	Percentage of all unions (%)	Percentage of all membership (%)
under 500	197	34	43.3	0.2	92	16	34.3	0.2
500–2,499	105	127	23.2	1.0	71	97	26.5	1.1
2,500–9,999	67	312	14.8	2.3	42	214	15.6	2.3
10,000–24,999	26	448	5.8	3.3	15	236	5.6	2.6
25,000–99,999	32	1,566	7.0	11.6	28	1,326	10.5	14.6
100,000–249,999	16	2,387	3.5	17.7	11	1,710	4.1	18.9
250,000 and more	11	8,624	2.4	63.9	9	5,449	3.4	60.2
Total	454	13,498	100	100	268	9,048	100	100

Sources: Employment Gazette, January 1981 and June 1994.

unions – most of which were not affiliated to the TUC – by their larger TUC-affiliated counterparts was the dominant pattern. The establishment of this pattern followed the enactment of the Trade Union (Amalgamations, etc.) Act 1964. This Act allowed a merger to be ratified when ballot among the membership of the 'transferor' union produced a simple majority in favour. The acquisition of smaller unions persisted during the 1980s. In addition, several larger unions were acquired in the merger process and the number of mergers from which a new union emerged also increased.

Diversity in merger policies Table 6.7 shows the memberships of unions with more than 100,000 members in 1992 and their memberships in 1979. Twelve of the 20 unions listed in the table lost members between 1979 and 1992. The rates of membership loss reflect the different concentrations of membership; unions sustaining the largest losses organized manual workers in manufacturing. Only four of the eight unions that increased membership did so without extensive involvement in mergers: the National and Local Government Officers' Association (NALGO), Royal College of Nursing (RCN), National Association of Schoolmasters / Union of Women Teachers (NAS/UWT), and the Association of Teachers and Lecturers (ATL). Irrespective of the direction of membership change, there was marked variation in the merger policies pursued to reform union structure. Examination of this diversity shows that traditional recruitment priorities have been abandoned by many large unions in attempts to establish ever broader recruitment bases with the objective of spreading the membership load. This ensures that membership losses concentrated in a specific industry or occupation do not undermine entire organizations.

Financial stringency arising from membership decline promoted many mergers during the 1980s. Several unions were caught between rising administrative expenditure and reduced income from membership contributions. Where competition for members was intense it was difficult to raise subscriptions without adversely affecting recruitment. However, trade union structure was not 'simplified' by these mergers, as competition between an 'industrial logic' and a 'political logic' influenced most merger policies. Resolution of this competition differed between unions with the result that a wide range of merger policies were implemented. This tension and its effect on some of these policies is examined below.

During the 1970s the TGWU was one of the most active 'acquirers' of unions (Undy et al. 1981: 203–14). This continued into

Table 6.7   UK unions with more than 100,000 members, 1979[a] and 1992

Union	1979	1992
Transport and General Workers' Union (TGWU)	2,086,281	1,036,586
Amalgamated Engineering and Electrical Union (AEEU)	1,309,553[b]	884,463
GMB	967,153[c]	799,101
National and Local Government Officers' Association (NALGO)	753,226	764,062
Manufacturing, Science, Finance (MSF)	691,054[d]	552,000
National Union of Public Employees (NUPE)	691,770	527,403
Union of Shop, Distributive and Allied Workers (USDAW)	470,017	316,491
Royal College of Nursing (RCN)	161,692	299,157
Graphical, Paper and Media Union (GPMU)	111,541[e]	269,881
National Union of Teachers (NUT)	290,740	213,656
Confederation of Health Service Employees (COHSE)	212,930	195,519
National Association of Schoolmasters / Union of Women Teachers (NASUWT)	152,222	190,637
Union of Communication Workers (UCW)	203,452	178,862
Union of Construction, Allied Trades and Technicians (UCATT)	348,875	157,201
Banking, Insurance and Finance Union (BIFU)	131,774	153,562
Association of Teachers and Lecturers (ATL)[f]	87,762	152,795
National Communications Union (NCU)	125,723[g]	126,376
Civil and Public Services Association (CPSA)	223,884	124,504
National Union of Civil and Public Servants (NUCPS)	107,957[h]	111,831
National Union of Rail, Maritime and Transport Workers (RMT)	170,294[i]	105,146

[a] In 1979, the following unions also organized more than 100,000 members: Association of Professional, Executive, Clerical and Computer Staff (APEX), Amalgamated Society of Boilermakers, Shipwrights, Blacksmiths and Structural Workers (ASBSBSW),

National Union of Tailors and Garment Workers (NUTGW), Iron and Steel Trades Confederation (ISTC), Institution of Professional Civil Servants (IPCS), National Union of Mineworkers (NUM), Society of Graphical and Allied Trades (SOGAT), National Graphical Association (NGA), and the Electrical, Electronic, Telecommunication and Plumbing Union (EETPU). Since 1979 APEX, ASBSBSW and the NUTGW were acquired in mergers by the GMB; SOGAT and the NGA merged to form the GPMU; the EETPU was absorbed by the AEU in forming the AEEU; and ISTC, NUM and IPCS remain independent but with less than 100,000 members.

b In 1979, the Amalgamated Union of Engineering Workers included Construction, Engineering and Foundry Section, but excluded the Technical, Administrative and Supervisory Section (TASS) which became part of MSF in 1988. The Amalgamated Union of Engineering Workers became the Amalgamated Engineering Union in 1984 which merged with the EETPU in 1992 to become the AEEU. In 1979 the membership of the EETPU was 443,621.

c In 1979, the National Union of General and Municipal Workers (NUGMW).

d MSF was formed in 1988 by the merger of the Association of Scientific, Technical and Managerial Staffs (ASTMS) and the Technical Administrative and Supervisory Section (TASS). In 1979 the memberships of these unions were 491,000 (ASTMS) and 200,054 (TASS).

e In 1979, the National Graphical Association (NGA). The NGA merged with the Society of Graphical and Allied Trades (SOGAT) to form the GPMU. The membership of SOGAT in 1979 was 205,784.

f The title ATL was adopted in 1993, the union having earlier been called the Assistant Masters' and Mistresses' Association (AMMA).

g In 1979, the Post Office Engineering Union (POEU).

h In 1979, the Society of Civil and Public Servants (SCPS).

i In 1979, the National Union of Railwaymen (NUR).

Source: Annual Report of the Certification Officer, 1980 and 1993.

the early 1980s with, for example, the acquisition of the National Union of Agricultural and Allied Workers which became a TGWU Trade Group. After 1982, however, the GMB became the more successful of the traditional general unions in the merger process, acquiring 12 unions in the textile and garment industry as well as the Association of Professional, Executive, Clerical and Computer Staff (APEX), the boilermakers' union and the Greater London Council Staff Association. Though many of these unions had declining memberships, their acquisition represented a considerable broadening of the GMB's representational base. The GMB also adopted a structure of sections, similar to the TGWU's Trade Groups. This offered a degree of autonomy to merger partners and helped to make the GMB attractive to them. By aligning the structures of the two main general unions, it also encouraged the idea of a merger between them; if successful, such a merger would unify the successors of the 'new unions' of 1889.

Mergers among traditional craft-orientated unions also further expanded recruitment bases. This was particularly the case among engineering unions where the abandonment of any occupational restrictions to recruitment accompanied the widespread adoption of sectional structures allowing some form of post-merger autonomy. During the 1980s, the Amalgamated Union of Engineering Workers Engineering Section (AUEW-ES), the Technical, Administrative and Supervisory Staffs section (TASS) and the EETPU all made acquisitions. The character of the merger policies pursued within these unions differed markedly in terms of the extensions to recruitment bases and the maintenance of political affiliations. Political differences between TASS and AUEW-ES representatives underpinned the withdrawal of TASS from the AUEW following action in the High Court during 1984. The remaining three sections of the AUEW (Engineering, Construction and Foundry) merged in 1984 to transform a federal structure, in which each section maintained its pre-merger constitution, into a section-based structure. This adoption of a single constitution was integral to a process involving financial centralization; it was introduced to curtail costs and bring the union into surplus (see Willman et al. 1993: 154–69).

Opposition between the right-of-centre AEU and the left-led TASS was not restricted to the latter's withdrawal from the AUEW, but extended to competition for merger partners among the small unions in engineering with traditional craft recruitment bases. As each of the small unions was also left-led, TASS competed successfully. TASS thus became a rallying point for those unions politically opposed to the AEU, a position which enabled the predominantly white-collar TASS to acquire four unions that recruited manual grades.[4] A 'political logic' thus overcame an 'industrial logic'. Each union acquired in this process became a Sector within TASS, enjoying some bargaining autonomy.

A different political position informed the merger activity undertaken by the right-of-centre EETPU. This activity focused on the acquisition of management and professional associations which tended to remain apart from the TUC. In all, 19 associations were acquired between 1980 and 1992. These acquisitions were integral to a policy directed towards the establishment of a recruitment base among more senior white-collar staff, a group with a substantial potential membership. In other words, unlike the AUEW-ES and TASS which acquired only TUC-affiliated unions, most of which recruited in engineering, the EETPU extended its recruitment both occupationally and industrially through the acquisition of non-affiliated unions. Furthermore, following the expulsion of the EETPU from the TUC in 1988 for failing to comply with Disputes Committee decisions (see Waddington 1988), the EETPU also acquired organizations that had broken away from TUC-affiliated unions. While these acquisitions distanced the EETPU from the TUC, they also allowed further extensions to the EETPU's recruitment base. A 'political logic' was thus central to the EETPU's attempts to extend its recruitment base into areas of potential membership growth.

Extensions to the recruitment bases of the AUEW-ES, TASS and EETPU only mitigated the effects of employment contraction in their core memberships, each of which declined. Further mergers were thus sought, resulting in the formations of Manufacturing, Science, Finance (MSF) in 1988 and the Amalgamated Engineering and Electrical Union (AEEU) in 1992. In both these instances a political and an industrial logic informed merger decisions. The merger of the Association of Scientific, Technical and Managerial Staffs (ASTMS) and TASS to form MSF combined two left-led unions that organized the majority of white-collar engineering grades. Similarly, the AEEU united two right-of-centre unions that recruited predominantly manual grades. In both instances technological change and the reorganization of the labour process had eroded historical distinctions between memberships.

The formations of MSF and the AEEU 'simplified' union organization in engineering. Several unions with substantial memberships, however, remain in the sector. Only in printing was industrial or-

ganization achieved through merger with the formation of the
Graphical, Paper and Media Union (GPMU) in 1992. This 'simplification' resulted from two discrete strands of merger activity. The
first of these comprised only craft unions, but overcame geographical
recruitment demarcations and combined letterpress and lithography
trades in the form of NGA82. The second strand comprised primarily non-craft organizations and produced SOGAT82. As in engineering, many workshop demarcations in print were eroded by
technological change. However, attempts by the GPMU (and its
predecessors) to incorporate other unions whose memberships were
affected by the same technology were unsuccessful. The National
Union of Journalists, for example, elected a General Secretary whose
principal campaign platform was opposition to a merger. Merger
activity among the broadcasting unions followed a similar pattern to
that in printing, culminating in 1991 with the formation of the
Broadcasting, Entertainment, Cinematograph and Theatre Union
(BECTU).

In other areas of the private sector merger activity continued
apace, but with no apparent simplification of union structure. The
Banking, Insurance and Finance Union (BIFU) and ASTMS (after
1988 part of MSF) competed to acquire staff associations in banking, insurance and the building societies. ASTMS was the more
successful of the two in the 1970s. During the late 1970s, however,
BIFU's constitution was reformed to allow acquired associations
some form of sectional representation and bargaining independence.
Latterly, as a result, BIFU has been as successful an acquirer as
ASTMS/MSF. Attempts by the TUC to restrict BIFU to the acquisition of banking associations and ASTMS/MSF to insurance associations came to nothing. Insurance unionism, in particular, is now
divided between the two unions and large numbers of independent
staff associations.

In contrast to intense merger activity throughout the private
sector, structural reform in the public sector was relatively subdued.
Stability in public sector membership did not create the same pressures towards mergers. Political divisions – regarding TUC affiliation, policies towards strikes, and whether representation should be
through a union or a professional association – led to an increase in
the number of organizations representing teachers. In the Civil Service repeated attempts to merge the Society of Civil and Public
Servants (SCPS) with the Civil and Public Services Association
(CPSA) were thwarted by the effects of the internal political shifts

within the CPSA. The SCPS, however, merged with the Civil Service Union to form the National Union of Civil and Public Servants (NUCPS).

The effects of privatization (both realized and anticipated), however, promoted both constitutional and structural reform among public-sector unions. Many unions that were exclusively public-sector organizations in 1979 amended constitutions to enable recruitment in the private sector, and hence to retain members working in privatized enterprises. Privatization has also influenced some structural reform designed to retain recognition or to position the post-merger organization to compete for recognition. The formation of UNISON in 1993 – through the merger of NALGO, the National Union of Public Employees (NUPE) and the Confederation of Health Service Employees (COHSE) – to form the largest current British union is the most substantial illustration of the point. The formation of UNISON enables it to campaign for recognition where compulsory competitive tendering (CCT) had removed members from Local Authority employment. The combination of the three unions reduces competition for such recognition. Similarly, in the Health Service if Hospital Trusts embark on the widespread reform of existing recognition procedures, UNISON will attempt to represent administrative, clerical, manual and professional grades. Competition for recognition will be sharp in both these areas. The GMB and TGWU will compete for recognition in newly established CCT enterprises, while in the Health Service the RCN is the largest nursing organization, and health professionals are largely organized by independent professional associations.

Overview   Throughout the 1980s the TUC attempted to re-establish the basis of its authority over affiliated unions after the loss of its role as a conduit to government. While internal reforms intended to reflect the changing composition of TUC-affiliated membership were agreed, the effects of policies towards Europe remain in the balance. Concurrent with these developments were reforms of trade union structure by mergers. Competition for merger partners and the considerable diversity in merger policies precluded any simplification of union structure. Increasing membership heterogeneity, centralized financial control, and a wider range of forms of sectional representation and bargaining autonomy, however, characterize many of the larger unions as a result of these mergers. Merger activity has been used to reform union structure, but has only mitigated the effects of membership loss. During the 1980s absorbed unions tended to decline after merging. In other words, while mergers may provide unions with opportunities for growth in new sectors, these opportunities have yet to be realized.

Adapting to Change:
Recruitment and Representation

Neither changes to TUC policy nor union structures have provided the key to membership revival, though they do address important shifts in employment and management and bargaining structures. To understand the pattern of union adaptation to change, two further areas must be addressed: approaches to recruitment, and forms of representation.

During the 1970s the issue of union growth was addressed mainly in terms of factors external to unions themselves: economic structure and conditions, management policy, and the political and legal framework. The explanatory power of these variables is considerable, and was reviewed in the first part of this chapter. This approach does, however, treat unions almost exclusively as objects, rather than subjects, of their own history, and as Undy et al. (1981) argued, leadership commitment and appropriate decision-making structures may also influence membership levels. Mason and Bain (1993: 333) have characterized these approaches as 'structural determinist' and 'union interventionist'. It is not necessary to accept Mason and Bain's construction of these ideal types to appreciate the central point they make: that complacency or fatalism can also affect membership levels. Indeed, as Hyman (1983) points out, academic analysis has largely failed to link the active role of unions and their members, and the material forces which shape their activity. It is precisely this integrated challenge that unions face in attempting to recruit and represent members today; and their understanding of these factors, and the policies they pursue, will have a real impact on both the coverage and the purposes of unionism.

An orientation to recruitment

Some unions, particularly those like the Union of Shop, Distributive and Allied Workers (USDAW) whose area of organization is characterized by high labour turnover, have always been very active recruiters. By the mid-1980s, however, unions were becoming increasingly aware that membership and density levels had not improved even with falling unemployment. The growth of non-unionism was identified as both a problem of changing employment patterns, and of social attitudes and union purpose. The TUC Special Review Body and the 1991 'Towards 2000' consultative conference developed an influential analysis linking labour market developments with the perceived 'new' needs of 'new' members in 'new' areas of potential union organization. The question of recruitment was thus seen as involving more than simply a matter of organizational commitment and resourcing. Three issues are considered here: the impact of labour market changes; the identification of membership needs; and implications for organization.

Analyses of labour market changes emphasized the lack of opportunities available to replicate the organizational successes of previous periods. As well as influencing the merger process, change has led unions to consider how to 'place' themselves in relation to growth employment areas. This is not a simple matter. One problem is the question of the identity and previous orientation of unions, as for example the attitude to be adopted by industrial or craft unions. Another is the polarized nature of the labour market; growth occupations are clustered in two particular occupational areas; professional and technical occupations, and low-paid and often insecure service sector manual jobs. Some smaller unions organizing in the former area have attempted to define a unionism based on horizontal status solidarity, aimed at the particular characteristics of managerial and professional employment. For example, in 1989 the Institution of Professionals, Managers and Specialists (IPMS) proposed a federation of small and medium-sized specialist unions whose strength would lie in 'the calibre of its membership and its party political neutrality'. The construction of such a horizontal occupational appeal is problematical, however. First, it reopens in new forms arguments about organizing rights. Second, it may run contrary to pressures to reduce the numbers of unions recognized by employers. Many professionally based unions already have a 'tail' of membership in other occupational groups and this would be likely to increase in the event of penetration into new areas, with the possible outcome that unions would lose their professional appeal or, alternatively, have sections of membership alienated from the principal concerns of the organization.

General and craft unions which have attempted to recruit among the low-paid faced a variation of the same problem. Both the GMB and the TGWU contain craft and white-collar workers, but represent, predominantly, less skilled, lower-paid manual workers. Unions such as the merged AEEU have a tradition and organization heavily influenced by differential bargaining and exclusivity. Sectional organization and bargaining autonomy may help to reconcile different interests, but difficulties remain, in terms of organizational culture, resource allocation, and recognition. General unions, for example, have found it hard to increase their membership levels among higher occupational groups to a level where they may be seen as natural contenders in this area. At the same time, these unions are committed to extending membership among the least advantaged workers in the lower occupational groups. There is no fundamental reason why this should prove impossible, but it poses new questions about the ability of unions to construct an identity of interest that transcends older boundaries.

It is this question of constructing interests that has contributed to the attention paid to the individual characteristics of potential members. This has happened in two main ways: first, in terms of defining new collective needs, so that gender, race, age, and contract status become increasingly central to policy; and second, in terms of offering individual, often non-work-related, services to individual members.

In the first case unions have been engaged in a number of initiatives, most typically at national level, to make space for the development of the interests of groups outside the formerly male full-time core of members. Many unions now have officers with national responsibility for ethnic and gender equality as well as committees of officers and lay members at regional level. In addition to employment equality issues, attempts are being made to find a union role in social representation: for example, USDAW has negotiated a national agreement offering workplace breast cancer screening. At a more general level, TUC support for a national minimum wage, although previously opposed by several major unions, reflects a renewed interest in the position of low-paid part-time workers, who are predominantly women. John Edmonds (1986) emphasized the political importance of this move, arguing that:

> This will put [us] on the side of the oppressed and disadvantaged, which is a side of the argument we haven't actually been on for some time. It also puts us on the side of women . . . and it puts us on the side of short service and mobile workers in the service sector.

At the same time, new attention to the needs of new members also reflects a sense of insecurity about the strength of traditional collectivism, and assumptions that areas of potential recruitment are characterized by a growing individualism. This was reflected in the findings highlighted in the Second Report of the SRB (TUC 1989). First, it was suggested that recruitment among managerial and professional groups needs to be accelerated, particularly as employment of such groups was predicted to expand in the long term and, therefore, constitute a major source of potential membership. Second, the SRB recommended that financial services packages be offered by unions to attract workers. Implicit in the adoption of these packages was the assumption that recruitment will be more individualized, rather than reliant on more traditional collective methods. The TUC thus recommended the adoption of the same individualized approach that characterized much management thinking during the 1980s.

This analysis led to the widespread adoption by unions of discount and financial services schemes to supplement more traditional benefits. The Unity Trust Bank, formed in 1984 to handle union funds and investments, was used to extend a variety of services, including personal pensions, mortgages, and personal loans to union members. Individual unions also introduced, or extended existing, personal benefits, and some have promoted the 'Unionlaw' scheme providing reduced-cost legal advice on non-work matters. These schemes were widely regarded by unions as a 'hook' for 'non-union minded people', and incorporated such services into their recruitment material, NALGO at one point adopting the slogan 'Join NALGO and save £100'.

What implications does this orientation to recruitment have for union organization? It is impossible to assess its specific impact on membership levels since this would entail distinguishing between efforts aimed at membership retention at established sites, success and failure rates in gaining recognition at new sites, and the results of more generalized recruitment drives. Some general points may be made, however.

Unions have begun to address recruitment, but face many problems in allocating resources and identifying obstacles. Polls taken in the late 1980s suggest that the main reason non-members had not joined was because they had not been asked (Mason and Bain 1993). While this undoubtedly reflects organizational shortcomings it cannot be taken to mean that unions have been careless of recruitment opportunities. Current research by the authors (Waddington and Whitston 1993) shows that, at established union sites, workplace representatives are active and effective recruiters. At the same time, large proportions of new members of unions claim to have joined on their own initiative, rather than as the result of an approach from the union. This is particularly true of senior white-collar occupational grades: in a survey of new members of unions organizing throughout the labour market, as many as 40 per cent of these grades made contact themselves, as against 14 per cent for other occupational groups. (Waddington and Whitston 1993). Differences in the role of the union and local representatives between different groups of workers seem to reflect variations in relations with management, and the degree of local union organization, which is more extensive where local, as opposed to national or company, bargaining exists; in these circumstances, potential members also tend to be aware of union activity.

Differential success at established sites points to the importance of resourcing for recruitment, and this is particularly true on non-union sites where lay activists have very little impact. Individual union campaigns, such as the 'Flare' campaign by the GMB, or TUC-coordinated drives including the 'Union Yes' campaigns in London and the North-West, have aimed to raise the profile of unions and to extend membership into previously unorganized areas and firms. They have had little success. Longer-term efforts to establish a presence and recognition at new sites rely on the use of full-time officers, and may consume considerable time and resources whether successful or not. Kelly and Heery (1989) showed that officers were motivated in recruitment, but were inhibited by resourcing difficulties and organizational obstacles. This is confirmed by current research which highlights the extent of membership-servicing demands on individual officers, and the degree to which changes in local bargaining and decentralization of management inhibit recruitment work by officers.

Kelly and Heery's findings have a point of greater general significance, however. They say that the most striking feature of their research lies in 'the difference in priorities between superiors and lay members. The evidence suggests that lay committees are much *less* concerned with recruitment than their superiors, and are much more concerned with pay and job protection' (1989: 203).

This disjuncture between the perceived needs of organizations to reorientate towards recruitment, and the composition, traditions and immediate concerns of established membership structures, is central to the uneven pace and direction of change within and between unions. To the extent that reorientation is leadership driven there remains a problem of the ownership of issues which can militate against adaptations in the crucial area of bargaining priorities and practice. Dickens and Colling (1989) have argued that the actual ground of bargaining is too limited to address effectively the concerns of women, that existing pay, grading, and promotion structures encourage equality issues being seen as minority or sectional interests, and that these problems are exacerbated by the parochialism of much local and company bargaining.

Nor is this divorce between more traditional local organizational priorities and national level reorientation addressed by the perceived growth of individualism among members and potential members. Waddington and Whitston (1993) echo earlier findings (Millward 1990) which show that support at work and better pay and conditions remain the most important incentives for membership of a union. In this survey of 2,844 new members from a range of occupational groups, two reasons were central to union joining irrespective of occupation: 'support if I had a problem at work' and 'to improve pay and conditions'. The consistency in this result across two occupational groups confirms other occupationally undifferentiated findings (Millward 1990; Kerr 1992). Interestingly, despite the fact that white-collar staff tend to be more secure in their employment and are more highly paid, they assign both these issues greater importance than other occupations. A further solidaristic issue was ranked third in the reasons for joining by white-collar staff: belief in trade unionism. This belief tends to be more firmly established among white-collar staff than among those in other occupations. This divergence between occupational groups appears to have been present since at least the 1970s, though there is no single explanation of its occurrence (Klandermans 1986).

Individualistic instrumental reasons for joining were not strongly supported by any occupational group. Training and education services barely influenced recruitment at all. Benefits and services (including financial services packages) were cited as a reason for joining by fewer than 10 per cent of white-collar staff and only 12 per cent of other occupations. In other words, benefits and services do not have a significant effect on union joining. This result, therefore, questions the use of financial services packages to increase recruitment and suggests that the SRB's initial recommendation for their introduction was without foundation (see also Sapper 1991). It may be the case that financial services packages assist in the retention rather than the recruitment of members, but this does not alter the main point: a recruitment orientation which is based on assumptions that collectivism is in decline are not only unlikely to succeed, but may undermine existing strengths.

A final point needs to be made. Whatever the impact of reorientation by unions to recruitment, however diverse the strategies adopted, and whatever the implications for broader policy, the biggest obstacle to a restoration of union membership, and in particular its extension into new employment sectors and companies, remains the ability of employers to withhold recognition, or to marginalize union influence at the workplace. It remains the case that significant progress is dependent on an improved legal framework on recognition (McCarthy 1991: 19). The broader implications of this argument are addressed in the concluding section. The next section, however, extends the discussion of the nature of union adaptation and the formation of interests by examining the associated issue of representation.

Representation: new forms of old tensions

The standard description of British unionism during the 1970s contrasts the bureaucracy of national union structures with local workplace activism. The resulting problems of interest aggregation are felt to have been exacerbated by developments during the 1980s: the weakening of shop stewards, the decentralization of collective bargaining, and government efforts to 'return unions to their members' by altering the law on unions' internal democracy (see chapter 9). It is argued here that the classic description of 1970s unionism masked internal variation and downplayed the existence of alternative forms of union organization. Also, tendencies towards centralization and decentralization are shown to remain in tension, but are expressed in different forms.

The characterization of British unionism as decentralized and 'activist-driven' only ever applied to a small number of unions. In engineering, the docks and printing, for example, local organization retained some autonomy from union head offices, became more important than the national level in the setting of pay and conditions, and often opposed national priorities. This form of organization tended to be concentrated in areas dominated by male workers in manual and full-time employment. Public sector, white-collar, and private-sector services unions, for example, operated on different models (Terry 1982; Kessler 1986; Armstrong et al. 1986). Where national pay and conditions were set only through national bargaining, union organization tended to be more centralized. Similarly, where there was a high turnover in membership, or where workplaces were small and geographically spread, there was a greater reliance on full-time officers than on active lay members. Those referring to a crisis of British unionism use as their point of reference only one of many forms of organization.

While autonomous workplace organization was not as widespread as suggested, some developments during the 1980s did lead to greater centralizing pressure, arising from legislation and the merger process. Although the rhetoric underpinning laws enacted since 1980 suggested that unions were to be returned to their members, the actual effects have promoted union centralization (see chapter 9). In many unions they reproduced existing constitutional provisions. The principal effect in these circumstances was to supplement constitutional authority, which had been challenged by workplace organization in the 1970s, with external legal sanctions and financial penalties. Centralization also resulted from two aspects of the merger process: first, by uniting two (or more) union memberships within the authority of a single union executive; and second, by ensuring that financial control within post-merger organizations rested with the central executive. While this financial centralization extends a pattern extant since the 1960s, the impact of the law accentuated its effect after 1980.

Decentralizing tendencies have also shifted in character and influenced internal union relations. The withdrawal of employers from national bargaining has been particularly influential, though privatization and compulsory competitive tendering have also contributed to the trend. Prior to 1980 national officers in many unions, particularly in the public sector, relied on national bargaining as a source of authority through which union cohesion could be promoted. The role of active lay members was restricted to the local enforcement of nationally agreed terms and conditions and the pursuit of cases of individual representation. Decentralization of bargaining redefined the role of some active lay members: increasingly, local unionists are required to participate more fully in the setting of terms and conditions, rather than only the enforcement of terms settled elsewhere.

Some commentators have suggested that these developments have allowed local union organization to adopt some of the characteristics of 'activist-driven' unionism and facilitated resistance to management-led initiatives (Fairbrother 1989; Heaton and Linn 1989). Countervailing trends are also apparent. Survey evidence suggests that full-time officers are increasingly being drawn into local negotiations because local representatives have received insufficient training (IRRR 1992, 1993). Furthermore, several unions – for example, the National Union of Teachers (NUT), NUCPS, IPMS and the Society of Telecom Executives (STE) – have established regional offices staffed by full-time negotiating officers through which local activities can be more closely coordinated and serviced. Other unions have facilitated the access of workplace representatives to research and legal support by appointing specialists outside of head offices.

These developments reflect efforts to address the links between national and local levels within unions. As shown in chapter 7, there was concern at a gap between the two in the 1970s, as local activists in well-organized workplaces challenged national bureaucracies. During the 1980s, managerial reform was widely felt to encourage a form of company unionism in which local representatives identified with the interests of the firm and were disconnected from the wider labour movement. If unions in the 1980s and 1990s have so far maintained a durable core presence in the face of difficult circumstances, that core itself now faces new problems of isolation and orientation. Where workplace organization remains, is revived or is introduced, a restructuring of relationships between it and the wider union will be essential to the character of unionism in the coming years.

Together with the challenge of non-unionism, the question of representation in its broadest form – how workers define and pursue their interests at work and in society as a whole – has dominated debates within unions as well as among commentators. It has long been the fashion to discuss unionism in terms of conflicting perspectives of the left and right. At times, this distinction was associated with particular sets of policies: on management of the economy or industrial democracy, for example. At other times, the ground was harder to discern, and far more dependent on context: appeals to 'free collective bargaining' have been made on occasion by both right and left. While important differences of emphasis remain, and can arouse passionate debate, recent years have seen the diminution of faction, and an (often muddled) emergence of a degree of orthodoxy.

There are three main planks of this redefinition: relations with employers, a legal platform of individual rights, and social dialogue with a European dimension. None of these represents a radical departure from the long-term practice of British unions. Writing in the wake of the General Strike, Citrine (1929), then TUC General Secretary, advocated a form of 'cooperative' unionism which presupposed a continuum of influence from the workplace to the national government, and the subordination of sectional interests to broader economic goals. The new orthodoxy is an attempt to recast the parameters of cooperation within a more restrictive framework which limits the social horizons of union aspirations. It remains fraught with difficulties: policy thrust, both corporate and public, remains hostile, and the establishment of a new space for unions between employers and the state itself implies a struggle to impose cooperation, rather than a simply defensive posture.

A hostile environment has led to a renewed emphasis on a bargaining practice which enhances the competitive position of employers, and facilitates change at the workplace. It is in this area of relations with employers that changing union perspectives are most complex. Cooperation is nothing new; what has changed is the power relationship underlying its pursuit, driven by the need to minimalize marginalization. Responses have ranged from widespread acceptance of single union agreements, to attempts to encourage single table bargaining (the practice, discussed in chapter 4, whereby several unions bargain as a group), to accepting dilute forms of union representation through company councils, and the reduced collective control of job regulation often implicit in changed working practices. 'We must', argued John Edmonds (Edmonds et al. 1992), 'recognise the frustration of managers who find it hard to achieve radical and continuous change through existing union structures.' In doing so, explicit appeals to traditions of worker control or industrial democracy are dissolved into a new bargained partnership based on the upgrading of labour through training and investment, opportunities for personal development, and adaptation to, rather than control of, market developments.

Part of this promotion of a new form of partnership is reflected in the importance assigned to individual over collective legal rights for workers. This does not mean an abandonment of collective rights: legal reform of recognition procedures is a core demand around which a new social settlement is proposed, and individual rights are seen as a springboard which 'unions must use to provide additional services to members in both traditional and new areas' (McCarthy 1991: 19). There has been, nevertheless, a considerable shift in emphasis, at national level at least, in the frontiers of collectivism, which has facilitated, for example, the abandonment of the closed shop as a valid form of worker autonomy. A system of individual rights policed by, and validating, union organization puts the development of an autonomous worker interest on a different and more restricted footing.

The unifying element here is the adaptation to both the political possibilities of the European Union, and a European pattern of social partnership. The vicissitudes of the Maastricht Treaty and the future of the Social Chapter notwithstanding, unions have turned to the limited social regulation of market systems advocated by European liberalism in reaction to the explicit exclusion and coercion associated with the New Right in Britain. What has proved attractive, even within a framework largely alien to British industrial relations practice, has been the entrenchment of an institutional framework for negotiation at company and societal levels.

This emerging orthodoxy is not a radical break from the past and is essentially defensive. But it does point to a central contradiction in the regulation of labour. The appeal of a new social dialogue reflects, as chapter 4 shows, the failure of British capital to develop a coherent model to replace the proceduralism of the 1970s. The aspirations of large groups of workers are thus not being addressed. The call for social dialogue is an implicit recognition of this problem. For unions, the contradiction is between the maintenance of a cooperative stance in the face of continuing erosion of membership and confidence, and the opportunity to channel and articulate collective dissent.

Conclusions and Future Prospects

Since 1979, British unions have been thrown on to the defensive. Isolation from the centre of political life, membership loss coupled to financial weakness, the intensity of management change, and the decentralization of bargaining structures rendered problematic union policies and practices developed for use during the 1970s. The 1980s were the most recent of a series of cycles of expansion and contraction of union influence. However, unions have not just been passive recipients of environmental effects; they implemented a wide range of policies intended to address the particular circumstances they face. As this chapter shows, these measures have, at best, only started to address the policy challenges that confront unions; they have certainly not reversed union decline. Furthermore, the measures implemented by unions are not without their own contradictions. Mergers, for example, have not markedly slowed the rate of membership decline, yet they have raised questions of representation as they have resulted in more heterogeneous memberships.

In terms of the three crises of unionism introduced at the start of this chapter, there is little evidence to suggest that the first – workers' fundamental loyalty to unions – has been destroyed by the Conservatives' political project. Individualism was not central to union decline, and collective issues remain at the core of workers' demands of unions. Indeed, as chapter 11 shows, individualism and collectivism in industrial relations are not opposed principles. The 1980s and 1990s have, however, been marked by an alteration of the relationship between the principles. This process has involved the economic and political environment of unions and has also shaped their internal dynamics. Systems of representation and interest aggregation have thus come under increasing pressure. In adjusting to this pressure, three tensions impinge on the nature of internal union reforms: between decentralization and centralization; between different representative structures; and between attempts by the state and employers to impose more widespread individualization and the collectivism that underpins union activity. These tensions will be worked out differently between and within unions with the result that union policies and practices will remain differentiated; but how they are resolved will influence the future development of the trade union movement in Britain.

While we cannot be specific about the manner in which these tensions will be worked out, they will be subject to environmental influence. The political complexion of the government will be particularly influential. The Conservative government elected in 1992 remains committed to the policies dominant since 1979. The Trade Union and Employment Rights Act 1993 contains two measures of widespread importance to trade union development. First, 'check-off' procedures, whereby members' subscriptions are deducted at source by employers on behalf of unions, must now be renewed every three years. Second, the Act includes provisions to wind down state funding for ballots and trade union education. These measures will heighten concern about union financial viability, and bring into question unions' capacity to maintain existing membership and extend membership to hitherto unorganized sites. The difficulties of reversing the recent decline of unionism are thus likely to continue under a Conservative government.

The election of a Labour government would be likely to provide some opportunities for unions to extend recruitment. The Labour party is currently committed to some form of statutory recognition procedure which may enable more extensive recruitment in expanding areas of employment. In addition, Labour party policy includes the introduction of a legal platform of workers' rights. While it remains to be seen how this development will affect unions, as it is uncertain whether unions have the expertise and resources to ensure that the rights are enforced, such a platform of rights also has the potential of transforming the purpose and direction of trade union activity. The introduction of a platform of workers' rights, for example, would require unions to reassess their relations with the Labour party and to examine their reliance on collective bargaining as the means whereby members are protected.

Regardless of the political climate, however, changes in the structure of employment and in employer policy pose continuing challenges. They call for imaginative responses in the organization and representation of groups of workers and in the aggregation of these interests into a wider social agenda.

Notes

1 There are some key differences between the data sources. Data from the Certification Officer and the *Employment Gazette* are based on information provided by the trade unions. These data include membership in Northern Ireland and no attempt is made to exclude retired or unemployed persons that retain union membership. The Labour Force Survey is a survey of about 65,000 private households throughout the UK. The results of the survey are grossed to estimates of the national population using data from the Office of Population, Census and Surveys for Great Britain and the Department of Economic Development in Northern Ireland. The Labour Force Survey excludes unemployed, retired and otherwise inactive union members.

2 Unemployment data disaggregated by industry were not published after 1982. It is thus not possible to calculate industrially disaggregated labour force and labour force density figures from this date.

3 Included in compositional effects examined by Green are sex, age, employment status (full-time or part-time), establishment size, industry and occupation.

4 Between 1981 and 1985 TASS acquired the National Union of Gold, Silver and Allied Trades; the National Union of Sheet Metal Workers, Coppersmiths, Heating and Domestic Engineers; the Associations of Patternmakers and Allied Craftsmen; and the National Society of Metal Mechanics.

References

Armstrong, P., Carter, B., Smith, C. and Nichols, T. 1986: *White Collar Workers: Trade Unions and Class.* London: Croom Helm.

Bain, G. S. and Elsheikh, F. 1976: *Union Growth and the Business Cycle.* Oxford: Blackwell.

Bain, G. S. and Price, R. 1983: Union Growth: Dimensions, Determinants, and Destiny. In G. S. Bain (ed.), *Industrial Relations in Britain.* Oxford: Blackwell.

Booth, A. 1983: A Reconsideration of Trade Union Growth in the United Kingdom. *British Journal of Industrial Relations*, 21, 3, 379–91.

Booth, A. 1989: What do Unions do Now? Discussion Paper in Economics, No. 8903, Brunel University.

Brown, W. and Wadhwani, S. 1990: The Economic Effects of Industrial Relations Legislation since 1979. *National Institute Economic Review*, 131, 57–70.

Carruth, A. and Disney, R. 1988: Where Have Two Million Members Gone? *Economica*, 55, 1, 1–19.

Certification Officer, various dates: *Annual Report.* London: The Certification Office.

Citrine, W. 1929: The Next Step in Industrial Relations. In W. Milne-Bailey (ed.), *Trade Union Documents.* London: G. Bell and Sons Ltd.

Dickens, L. and Colling, T. 1989: *Equality Bargaining – Why Not?* London: HMSO.

Disney, R. 1990: Explanations of the Decline in Trade Union Density in Britain: An Appraisal. *British Journal of Industrial Relations*, 28, 2, 165–78.

Edmonds, J. 1986: New Wave Unions: An Interview with Beatrix Campbell. *Marxism Today*, September 1986.

Edmonds, J., Jordan, B. and Steinkuhler, F. 1992: Industrial Relations in Europe. *Die Mitbestimmung in Europe: Conflict and Cooperation.* English Edition of the Journal of the Hans-Bockler Foundation.

Fairbrother, P. 1989: *Workplace Unionism in the 1990s: A Process of Renewal.* London: Workers' Educational Association.

Freeman, R. and Pelletier, J. 1990: The Impact of Industrial Relations Legislation on British Union Density. *British Journal of Industrial Relations*, 28, 2, 141–64.

Gardiner, J. 1981: The Development of the British Working Class. In S. Aaronovitch (ed.), *The Political Economy of British Capitalism: A Marxist Analysis*. London: McGraw-Hill.

Gorz, A. 1989: *Critique of Economic Reason*. London: Verso.

Green, F. 1992: Recent Trends in Trade Union Density. *British Journal of Industrial Relations*, 30, 3, 445–58.

Gregg, P. and Yates, A. 1991: Changes in Wage-setting Arrangements and Trade Union Presence in the 1980s. *British Journal of Industrial Relations*, 29, 3, 361–76.

Heaton, N. and Linn, I. 1989: *Fighting Back: A Report on the Shop Steward's Response to New Management Techniques in TGWU Region 10*. Barnsley: Northern College and TGWU Region 10.

Hyman, R. 1983: Trade Unions: Structure, Policies and Politics. In G. S. Bain (ed.), *Industrial Relations in Britain*. Oxford: Blackwell.

IDS (Incomes Data Services) 1987: Tales of the Unexpected. *IDS Focus*, 44, August.

IRRR (Industrial Relations Review and Report) 1992: The Changing Role of Trade Union Officers 1: The Devolution of Pay Bargaining. *Industrial Relations Review and Report*, 526, December, 5–12.

IRRR (Industrial Relations Review and Report) 1993: The Changing Role of Trade Union Officers 2: Collective Bargaining and Working Practices. *Industrial Relations Review and Report*, 527, January, 3–11.

Kelly, J. 1988: The Decline of British Trade Unionism? *The Industrial Tutor*, 4, 7, 5–17.

Kelly, J. and Heery, E. 1989: Full-time Officers and Trade Union Recruitment. *British Journal of Industrial Relations*, 27, 2, 196–213.

Kerr, A. 1992: Why Public Sector Workers Join Unions: An Attitude Survey of Workers in the Health Service and Local Government. *Employee Relations*, 14, 2, 39–54.

Kessler, I. 1986: Shop Stewards in Local Government Revisited. *British Journal of Industrial Relations*, 24, 3, 419–41.

Klandermans, B. 1986: Psychology and Trade Union Participation: Joining, Acting, Quitting. *Journal of Occupational Psychology*, 59, 3, 189–204.

Labour Force Survey, annual: London: HMSO.

Leadbeater, C. 1987: Unions Go to Market. *Marxism Today*, September, 22–7.

McCarthy, W. 1991: *Towards 2000: A Consultative Document*, Section 2, Part One. London: Trades Union Congress.

MacInnes, J. and Sproull, A. 1989: Union Recognition and Employment Change in Scottish Electronics. *Industrial Relations Journal*, 20, 1, 33–46.

McLoughlin, I. and Gourlay, S. 1991: Transformed Industrial Relations? Employee Attitudes in Non-Union Firms. *Human Resource Management Journal*, 2, 2, 8–28.

Martin, R. 1980: *TUC: The Growth of a Pressure Group 1868–1976*. Oxford: Clarendon Press.

Marxism Today 1986: New Wave Unions. TUC Special Edition, September.

Mason, B. and Bain, P. 1993: The Determinants of Trade Union Membership in Britain: A Survey of the Literature. *Industrial and Labor Relations Review*, 46, 2, 332–51.

Millward, N. 1990: The State of the Unions. In R. Jowell, S. Witherspoon and L. Brook (eds), *British Social Attitudes: the 7th Report*. Aldershot: Gower.

Millward, N. and Stevens, M. 1986: *British Workplace Industrial Relations 1980–1984*. Aldershot: Gower.

Millward, N., Stevens, M., Smart, D. and Hawes, W. R. 1992: *Workplace Industrial Relations in Transition*. Aldershot: Dartmouth.

Minkin, L. 1992: *The Contentious Alliance: Trade Unions and the Labour Party*. Edinburgh: Edinburgh University Press.

Müller-Jentsch, W. 1988: Industrial Relations Theory and Trade Union Strategy. *International Journal of Comparative Labour Law and Industrial Relations*, 4, 3, 177–90.

Piore, M. and Sabel, C. F. 1984: *The Second Industrial Divide: Possibilities of Prosperity*. New York: Basic.

Pollert, A. (ed.) 1991: *Farewell to Flexibility?* Oxford: Blackwell.

Price, R. and Bain, G. S. 1983: Union Growth in Britain: Retrospect and Prospect. *British Journal of Industrial Relations*, 21, 1, 46–68.

Sapper, S. 1991: Do Members' Services Packages Influence Trade Union Recruitment? *Industrial Relations Journal*, 22, 4, 309–16.

Sherman, B. 1986: *The State of the Unions*. Chichester: Wiley.

Smith, P. and Morton, G. 1993: Union Exclusion and Decollectivisation in Contemporary Britain. *British Journal of Industrial Relations*, 31, 1, 97–114.

Stevens, M. and Wareing, A. 1990: Union Density and Workforce Composition. *Employment Gazette*, 98, 8, 403–12.

Terry, M. 1982: Organising a Fragmented Workforce: Shop Stewards in Local Government. *British Journal of Industrial Relations*, 20, 1, 1–19.

TUC 1989: *Organising for the 1990s: The SRB's Second Report*. London: Trades Union Congress.

TUC 1993: *The Future of the TUC*. London: Trades Union Congress.

Undy, R., Ellis, V., McCarthy, W. and Halmos, A. 1981: *Change in Trade Unions: The Development of UK Unions since the 1960s*. London: Hutchinson.

Visser, J. 1989: In Search of Inclusive Unionism. *Bulletin of Comparative Industrial Relations*, 18, 1–12.

Waddington, J. 1988: Trade Union Mergers: A Study of Trade Union Structural Dynamics. *British Journal of Industrial Relations*, 26, 3, 409–30.

Waddington, J. 1992a: Trade Union Membership in Britain: Unemployment and Restructuring. *British Journal of Industrial Relations*, 30, 2, 287–324.

Waddington, J. 1992b: Trade Union Mergers. In D. Cox. (ed.), *Facing the Future*. Nottingham: University of Nottingham.

Waddington, J. and Whitston, C. 1993: Why do White-Collar Staff Join Unions? Some Evidence on the Tension Between Individual Activity and Collective Organisation. Paper presented to Conference on 'Unions on the Brink', Cardiff Business School, September.

Wedderburn, K. (Lord) 1990: *Social Charter, European Company and Employment Rights*. London: Institute of Employment Rights.

Whitston, C. 1991: Chemical Unions in the United Kingdom and Germany. In A. Martinelli (ed.), *International Markets and Global Firms: A Comparative Study of Organized Business in the Chemical Industry*. London: Sage.

Willman, P., Morris, T. and Aston, B. 1993: *Union Business: Trade Union Organisation and Financial Reform in the Thatcher Years*. Cambridge: Cambridge University Press.

Winchester, D. 1988: Sectoral Change and Trade Union Organization. In D. Gallie (ed.), *Employment in Britain*. Blackwell, Oxford.

7

Trade Unions: Shop Stewards and the Workplace

Michael Terry

Trade unions in the United Kingdom are structured, organized and resourced, to an extent unparalleled elsewhere in Europe, around and by unpaid volunteer activists, sometimes referred to as shop stewards. These activists provided British unionism and workplace industrial relations with many of their particular characteristics, not least among which is a claim that the democratic nature of shopfloor unionism – its closeness to the membership – enables it directly and accurately to reflect employees' interests and concerns; to provide them with a clear and accurate 'voice'. This line of argument was certainly accepted by the Donovan Commission whose report, anticipating the later work of Freeman and Medoff (1979), urged managers to foster and take advantage of democratic workplace unionism to improve productivity and the management of change. As shown in chapters 2 and 4, during the 1980s a significantly different managerial approach has been pursued. One direct consequence has been that the union shopfloor 'voice' has become increasingly muted. While this decline clearly operates to the detriment of unions and, equally plausibly, to those they represent, it raises two further linked and intriguing questions. First, does it also work to the disadvantage, at least over the medium term, of employers and managers denied the union 'voice' and, second, if it does, why have they pursued the policies they have done? The first of these questions is touched on in several places in this volume (especially in chapters 4 and 13), and the second is directly examined here. First, however, it is necessary to sketch in some of the background.

In the early 1980s, when the first edition of this book was being written, it was possible to begin any essay dealing with workplace trade union organization in the United Kingdom with the observation that it had grown and developed more or less continuously since the 1950s (see Terry 1983). By the late 1970s such organization and its active representative members (shop stewards, or sometimes 'staff representatives' for white-collar unions) were to be found in virtually all workplaces where trade unions had a presence. Expanding outwards from its early base in the engineering industry, the docks, and one or two other sectors, workplace unionism spread into the rest of manufacturing and, especially during the 1970s, into much of the public sector. The gaps were only really to be found in small firms and in private services, where trade unions were in any case historically weakly organized.

By the end of the 1970s British trade unionism had developed widespread decentralized, relatively autonomous structures at workplace level. Tens of thousands of shop stewards performed the detailed tasks of recruiting members, participating in workplace committees dealing with such matters as health and safety and job evaluation, representing members in disciplinary and dismissal hearings and, crucially, bargaining with managers over pay and other conditions of employment.

Fifteen years later, the picture had changed, though at first glance significant similarities remain. The 1990 Workplace Industrial Relations Survey (Millward et al. 1992, especially chapter 4) reveals a falling-off in steward organization in line with union decline more generally, being most marked in small firms and in places where union density was low. In larger workplaces, with relatively high union densities, the formal indices of shop steward organization have remained more or less unchanged.

Despite this apparent continuity, however, few analysts would argue that workplace union organization plays as significant a role in industrial relations in the early 1990s as it did fifteen years before, or that shop stewards are as powerful. Rather, much recent research speaks of the 'marginalization' or the 'roll-back' of shop stewards; of their powerlessness to prevent the managerial drive to recapture unilateral control over work and employment relations. Something clearly has been taking place beneath the surface of the statistical calm. This chapter will describe and explain some of these changes and the reasons for them. It focuses on the nature of steward representation; chapter 12 takes up the effects on the organization of work. First, however, it is necessary to describe the growth in shop steward coverage and authority that took place during the 1970s, since in doing so it will be possible to identify some of the reasons for the subsequent decline.

The 1970s: Growth and Hidden Weaknesses

Growth

By the late 1970s shop stewards were to be found in 73 per cent of manufacturing sector establishments with more than 50 employees, with metal manufacturing showing the strongest presence at 90 per cent and textiles the weakest at 49 per cent (Brown 1981: 52). The situation was much the same in the public sector, with a marked growth in public services (Terry 1983: 68–9). White-collar as well as manual workers established shop-steward-based systems of local representation.

The factors contributing to this growth have been widely discussed (Brown 1981: 51–78; Batstone 1988: 33–71). Within an environment of (relative) economic and industrial stability, employees, unions, employers and governments all played a part. As shown in chapter 6, employees, especially white-collar and public service workers, joined unions in unprecedented numbers, often looking to their unions to campaign for higher pay either to restore traditional differentials eroded by manual union successes or to fight against government incomes policies, on occasion instituted in collaboration with national union leaderships.

Within trade unions a growing consensus confirmed the centrality of steward-based systems. They were seen as an effective and democratic form of unionism, appropriate to the environment of the time. The 1960s debates and struggles for control between stewards and national union leaders (often, but not always accurately, characterized as struggles between 'left' and 'right') were largely over. The 'swing to the left' in several major unions representing primarily manufacturing sector workers had resulted in the election of national leaders who themselves endorsed the development of steward organizations. Of particular significance were the elections of Hugh Scanlon as President of the AUEW (as it then was) in 1967 and of Jack Jones as General Secretary of the TGWU in 1968 (Taylor 1980: 179, 208–9). Such leaders worked during the 1970s both to extend the spread of steward organization and to bring it more firmly within the ambit of union rule-books and constitutions. It was a period in which stewards lost much of their unofficial, almost clandestine, status and become accredited union officials, with defined rights and responsibilities. This process led to the debates concerning the 'incorporation' of stewards into official union structures (and by implication their associated loss of independent militancy) and the 'bureaucratization of the rank-and-file' (Hyman 1979). Both these tendencies reflected the greater institutionalization and professionalization of rank-and-file unionism. In the public sector a similar process occurred, a few years later, following widespread rank-and-file revolt against leadership acquiescence in incomes policy norms during the 1970s.

Unions, in conjunction with the Workers' Education Association, the TUC and many colleges, developed a wide range of union education provision; tens of thousands of stewards received training in bargaining skills; in representing union members; in building organization; and in recruitment. Shop stewards became in many ways the pivotal figures of British trade unionism. Indeed, in large workplaces in industries such as engineering they often relegated union-employed full-time officials to a secondary role of back-up and assistance (Batstone et al. 1977).

It was not only events in trade unions, however, that were contributing to this growth. Employers too were playing a major part. The widespread managerial acceptance of the Donovan recommendations for the formalization of collective bargaining at plant and company level was an important part of this. For this was still a period of large workplaces and mass production in manufacturing (in 1979 41 per cent of all employees in manufacturing worked in establishments of more than 1,000 people, compared with 28 per cent a decade later). Systems of work measurement and job evaluation that lent themselves to joint regulation and collective bargaining were increasingly common. Employers keen to introduce new technologies and payment systems saw plant-level collective bargaining as an appropriate medium. The idea of the managerial 'sponsorship' of shop steward organizations was developed to describe this process, most visible in industries such as food and drink where steward organization spread rapidly, and in the public services where the traditional 'good employer' model of widespread union recognition and union-based consultation and negotiation was being extended to the workplace (see Terry 1978; Willman 1980; Marchington and Parker 1990: 18–20).

Employer support for workplace union organization was tangibly reflected in the increasing facilities made available for stewards. Office space, telephones, photocopying, as well as time off for union duties, frequently in excess of that stipulated in Social Contract legislation, were all provided in increasing volume. A growing number of stewards, estimated to be as many as 10,000 by the late 1970s, spent all their time on trade union duties, their wages paid by the companies who had originally taken them on as workers.

More broadly still, the role of the state was crucial. This was a period in which support for collective bargaining and trade unionism was, under both Labour and Conservative governments, still the norm. The Donovan Commission's reform message had been broadly accepted by both major parties, and government agencies – in particular the Commission on Industrial Relations and its successor, ACAS – promulgated the message of recognizing unions and developing formal bargaining structures at plant and company level. The 1974–9 Labour government went significantly further in introducing legislatively based support for shop steward organization, including rights to time off for specified union activities and to training. In addition, the 1974 Health and Safety at Work Act, giving statutory backing to the election or appointment of union safety representatives at local level in firms where unions were recognized, gave an organizational fillip to the establishment of local structures (Brown 1981: 75). Finally, in the public services shop steward organization grew rapidly under the influences of local union resistance to incomes policies and a degree of bargaining devolution associated with the introduction of local bonus schemes.

Taken together with relatively low levels of unemployment, these factors combined to facilitate the development of local forms of organization. Steward-based bargaining appeared to be successful in producing pay increases for members, and generally in providing an effective form of union representation. Collective bargaining over pay and other conditions of employment was increasingly devolving away from national multi-employer bargaining towards steward-based single-employer bargaining in the private sector, and in the public sector where a degree of devolution was also occurring. In addition, stewards were taking on an ever-increasing load of individual employee representation through grievance and disciplinary procedures. Indeed, despite the greater attention paid to collective bargaining, anecdotal evidence indicated the vital importance of such individual interest representation in winning membership loyalty and commitment.

The shortcomings of 1970s steward organizations

Its obvious successes notwithstanding, there were inadequacies in the union representation afforded by steward-based systems, some of which were apparent at the time, others of which would become clearer during the 1980s. The problems were organizational, structural and ideological.

In terms of coverage, steward organization was significantly less well developed in the private service sector than elsewhere. In part this reflected the significantly lower membership of trade unions generally, but even where unions were to be found (in parts of the finance and retail sector, for example), steward systems were under-developed, reflecting both the small establishment size and the lack of opportunity for effective local bargaining. Second, there were indications that stewards generally were failing properly to represent groups such as women and black workers. There was a significantly lower proportion of women and black stewards than of unionized members. There were examples of stewards organizing overt resistance to these groups' grievances – in the breaking of black workers' strikes at Imperial Typewriters and Mansfield Hosiery (Miles and Phizacklea 1981: 254–5) – and of covert subversion – in collusion with management to forestall the effective implementation of the Equal Pay Act (Snell et al. 1981: 66).

Structurally, the key feature of stewards' organizations was their decentralization. The work group was the basis of the steward constituency and often commanded greater loyalty than the wider steward organization itself. Steward organization was invariably based around the individual factory or workplace, but even at that level it often displayed tensions, between skilled and semi-skilled or between white- and blue-collar unions. Steward efforts, even in the supportive environment of the 1970s, to establish permanent structures – 'combine committees' – at higher levels (of the multi-plant company or operating division, for example) often foundered in the face of employer and official union hostility on the one hand, and workplace-level steward indifference on the other (see Terry 1985).

The decentralization of steward organizations was also reflected in their often distant relationship with the outside union, in particular unions' full-time officials. Steward independence and autonomy were part of the engineering stewards' tradition, and were also valued in parts of the public sector (Batstone et al 1984: 254–67). For many stewards the involvement of a full-time official in a local matter constituted almost an admission of 'failure'; for many full-time officials one key organizing objective was to help bring into being 'self-sufficient' steward organizations that would no longer require their services.

In many workplace trade union organizations the writ of the external national union did not run very deep, a fact of key importance during certain periods of incomes policy when national union compliance was rejected in favour of local membership pressure for larger increases. In such situations of tension between national union policy and membership demands, stewards' loyalty was almost always to the latter. This was one reason for the often-heard comment that 'to the membership the steward *is* the union' (Marsh 1963: 20): not simply a provider of services and the immediate face of unionism but the active representative of membership interests directly expressed.

These structural features, in particular the closeness of the relationships between stewards and members and the distance between stewards and the 'official' unions, were intimately related to steward ideology (or more accurately, the lack of a clear ideology).[1] One important characteristic of the bargaining behaviour of shop stewards was a certain narrowness of vision: a limitation of purpose and ambition. As noted above, shop stewards' main democratic point of reference was their constituents (the work group or occupational group) and the second one was the factory or workplace. Giving primacy to the objectives of these groups was characterized as 'sectionalism', or as 'factory consciousness': a 'sophisticated understanding of how [workers] were exploited in the factory and how they could best combat management there' (Beynon 1973: 98–9). Furthermore, giving primacy to the representation of localized groups inevitably meant also giving priority in bargaining to their directly expressed interests and claims. Frequently, this meant prioritizing bargaining over pay; hence the claim that shop-steward-based unionism was 'economistic' in character and often short-term in its thinking. Issues of health and safety provide a simple illustration. Frequently, confronted by a safety hazard or dirty working conditions the response of stewards would be to bargain for 'danger money' or 'dirt money' rather than to alleviate the conditions.

There were exceptions to this rule of relatively limited, constrained, objectives. Famous examples, early in the 1970s, were the steward-organized 'work-ins', in particular at Upper Clyde Shipbuilders, which not only protested at job loss but constructed a broad alliance of support to argue the social and industrial costs of closure. Yet more striking was the 'Alternative Plan' developed by stewards at Lucas Aerospace in the mid-1970s, again to strengthen their campaign to resist redundancies (Wainwright and Elliott 1982). This initiative displayed great sophistication in arguing the potential for new product development and for company restructuring. Yet perhaps the very exceptionalism of these cases reinforces our perception of the limitations of routine steward-based activity.

The 1970s in retrospect

During the 1970s, shop steward organization developed to the extent that by 1979 it was to be found in effect wherever unions operated. Employers, official unions and governments accepted the argument that stewards had a legitimate role as company and workplace representatives in collective bargaining, and the policies of all three were directed at achieving and regulating this process, with the intention of exerting a degree of control over steward activity. The logic was that of regaining managerial control through sharing it via formal agreements with shop stewards and to reduce the level of unofficial strikes with which shop stewards were associated by providing better, more formal, and 'fairer' procedures for resolving grievances.

Such evidence as exists suggests that the strategy did not produce the benefits hoped for by managers, despite the fears of those who commented on, and criticized, the 'incorporation' of stewards into management and union hierarchical systems (Hyman 1979). Edwards (1983: 213–14), for example, noted that there was very little evidence of a reduction in unofficial strike levels during the 1970s that could be attributed to these reforming tendencies. Indeed, both he and Hyman (Hyman 1989: 204–5) suggest that the very process of reform itself, by changing the status quo, actually precipitated an increase in such action. More adventurous calculations made by Batstone (1984: 128–45) indicate that there were neither significant reductions in wage movements nor improvements in labour productivity during the 1970s that might testify to the impact of reform. Although there are major difficulties in separating the effects of reform from those of other changes in the economy there was at least prima facie evidence to which employers and managers could point if they wished that by the end of the 1970s their enhanced recognition of shop stewards in extended plant level bargaining had failed to 'deliver'. This had important implications for what was to follow.

In addition, however, it is clear that, even at their peak, shop steward power and influence were limited and constrained by structural and ideological factors, in particular the decentralization and relative autonomy of steward organizations and the associated focus of their attention on the short-term bargaining of pay and conditions. This 'narrowness' of activity was in turn reinforced by a continuing managerial refusal to widen the scope of formal bargaining and consultation, in particular to issues of 'managerial relations'. On matters such as work organization, staffing levels, the speed and intensity of working, despite widespread informal bargaining in some sectors, managers continued to resist formalization, being unwilling to concede *de jure* rights to unions (Sisson and Brown 1983: 148–50). This too was to be important in the following decade.

The 1980s: Shop Stewards in Decline

The 1980s started with a flurry of interest and speculation about what rapidly came to be labelled 'macho management', a term used to denote a new type of manager no longer prepared to accept the extent of shop steward influence and prepared to take tough action to get their way. Far and away the most spectacular example of this was the sacking in November 1979 by British Leyland of Derek Robinson, the convenor of their Longbridge factory, as part of the campaign to push through radical changes to working practices (Edwardes 1983: 114–31). This event, and the fact that the workforce did not, for whatever reason, take action against the decision, were taken by some as evidence of a sea-change in workplace industrial relations.

Other examples, albeit less sensational, followed. For this was the period of the first 1980s recession, when jobs in manufacturing industry were being lost at a staggering rate, and widespread factory

Table 7.1   Workplace trade union representation

	All			Private manufacturing			Private services			Public sector		
	1980	*1984*	*1990*	*1980*	*1984*	*1990*	*1980*	*1984*	*1990*	*1980*	*1984*	*1990*
Establishments with recognized trade union:												
as per cent of all estabs.	64	66	53	65	56	44	41	44	36	94	99	87
as per cent of estabs. with union members	88	91	83	84	83	77	81	82	78	95	99	89
Estabs. (per cent of those with a recognized union) where workers represented by:												
1 or more workplace reps.	82		71		98	90		67	57		84	73
Senior rep. if 2 or more present	19		22		46	40		9	12		14	23
Full-time rep.	2		2		5	2		1	2		3	2

Source: Millward et al. (1992: tables 3.7, 4.1).

closures were taking place (see chapter 3). Stewards' demands were sometimes met with a managerial threat to close a factory if strike action took place, a threat that experience showed was by no means always empty. Less dramatically, stories of full-time shop stewards being put back to work, of significant reductions in steward facilities and time off, and of alleged victimization all strengthened the 'macho management' view.

Survey evidence

In fact, when detailed survey work was carried out in the mid-1980s it revealed a picture of considerable organizational stability (Millward and Stevens 1986; Batstone 1988). In both manufacturing and the public sector, steward coverage of unionized workforces remained as extensive as before, and the arrangements for steward activities and for local collective bargaining appeared remarkably unscathed, leading some writers (Batstone 1988: 207–31; MacInnes 1987: 92–107) to argue that there had been few if any fundamental changes.

The 1990 WIRS, by contrast, suggests significant changes as well as continuities. On the latter, as table 7.1 shows, where a union was recognized representation by a steward continued to be the norm. This was particularly true of private manufacturing, where a steward was present in 90 per cent of these establishments. The presence of 'senior' representatives was a little more common overall, while that of full-time stewards was unchanged, albeit very rare. However, as noted below, the latter two figures conceal some significant changes. Moreover, even where there was recognition, the presence of stewards declined. Combined with the fall in recognition, this meant that, among all establishments in the survey, a steward was present in 54 per cent in 1984; by 1990, this had fallen to 38 per cent (Millward et al. 1992: 110).

Millward and his colleagues argue that, in private manufacturing in particular, union density helps explain the decline. In that sector most of the fall in local representation was in workplaces with low union density. In such workplaces, it is suggested, there are fewer facilities provided by management. The lack of membership interest and of management support may then combine to deter volunteers from taking on steward jobs. If such low-density establishments are left out of the equation, then again the situation looks stable, as indeed it does in the public sector where there was 'little or no change in the presence of representatives when . . . establishments with similar union density [are compared]' (Millward et al. 1992: 112). In the private service sector, density appeared to have no particular effect. More significantly, the fall would have been more dramatic still had it not been for the shift into the private service category of several large and well-organized privatized industries.

These declines, combined with falls generally in union membership and in employment levels, especially in the traditionally highly organized sectors of employment, have contributed to what Millward et al. describe as a 'substantial' fall in the number of stewards in British industry. However, union membership as a whole has been falling still faster, with the result that, on average, there are fewer members for each steward to represent. In that limited sense, at least, steward representation has 'improved'.

The survey also revealed some decline in managerial support for local unionism. This was particularly evident in the case of shop steward training, in which managerial initiative and involvement had declined considerably (Millward et al. 1992: 120). However other indices of such support – time off for union activity, office and other facilities – remained roughly stable, as did the proportion of employers who had arrangements for the automatic deduction of members' union subscriptions from their pay. Other measures of stability at the workplace, such as steward meetings at a variety of organization levels, again showed little change. An important change seems, however, to have occurred in the presence of senior representatives, often taken as an index of organizational sophistication. Despite the overall stability mentioned above, Millward et al. (1992: 118) also highlight a decline in their presence for the largest negotiating group: down from 67 per cent of all establishments to 38 per cent, with a particularly rapid fall among white-collar unions. The possible significance of this point will be developed below.

The survey evidence, therefore, suggests both that there has been a degree of change, albeit of a gradual kind, and that in many workplaces plant-level union organization has been relatively unaffected by the changes of the 1980s in those establishments and companies where it was already well established. However, it is equally clear that the 1970s expansion of trade union organization in general, and of shop stewards as part of that, has been stopped in its tracks. It has fallen away in weakly organized manufacturing companies; it has declined from an already low base in the expanding private service sector, and it has made at best limited advances on 'greenfield sites' in manufacturing industry (Smith and Morton 1993: 101).

These setbacks aside, the overall picture does not seem to bear out claims that shop steward organization has been severely weakened during the 1980s. However, the survey data only tell one part of the story. It has been argued elsewhere (Terry 1986) that, even by the mid-1980s, case study evidence was telling a more dramatic story in which considerable changes in the activities and influence of shop stewards were taking place.

Case study evidence

The case study material is, inevitably, patchy and incomplete; much less such work was done in the 1980s than in the preceding decade. But generally it appears to confirm, most noticeably in manufacturing, a decline in the influence that stewards wield over managerial decisions. Several authors (Terry 1989; Marchington and Parker 1990) refer to the 'marginalization' of shop stewards as increasingly characteristic of the 1980s. Managers, it seems clear, have been increasingly prepared to introduce change and to take decisions without prior negotiation; they have replaced negotiation with consultation; and they have increasingly deployed methods of workforce communication and participation that do not depend on the single channel of shop steward trade union organization.

In many manufacturing companies this marginalization or exclusion of steward influence has been most marked over issues of managerial relations (it was noted above that this was an area in which management had been reluctant to concede formal bargaining rights to stewards in the 1970s). The dismissal of Derek Robinson took place in the context of a managerial effort specifically directed at re-establishing unilateral control over issues of work organization. Similar efforts to re-establish managerial prerogatives took place over much of manufacturing industry (motor vehicles, steel and shipbuilding being well known examples). By the late 1980s both case study work (Terry 1989; Elger 1991) and survey work (Edwards 1987) appeared to confirm that managers had a freer hand in implementing organizational change than had been the case earlier. The 1990 WIRS showed that only a small minority of managers in private manufacturing establishments (10 per cent of all establishments) reported any union constraint on their ability to 'organize work among non-managerial employees' (Millward et al., 1992: 332). At the same time, it made clear that managers in non-union companies felt that their hands were even freer.

Further case study evidence concerning the limited role played by stewards in the 1980s and 1990s comes from 'greenfield' sites where unions have been recognized, and where managers have, in effect, been able to draw up their industrial relations strategies from scratch. The most frequently cited of these are the agreements reached between single unions and Japanese inward-investing multi-nationals. Examining here the effect on unions, with the pattern of workplace relations being considered in chapter 12, it is clear that managers exercise unilateral control over 'managerial relations' with unions agreeing in advance to full flexibility of workers. In addition, local union representatives frequently play little part in negotiation or consultation through so-called factory or company councils (Oliver and Wilkinson 1992: 298).

Such 'formalized marginalization' of stewards is not universal, even on greenfield sites. The industrial relations arrangements established by Pirelli in South Wales give stewards and other union representatives a significantly more important role, which may be one reason why 'around 80 per cent of employees covered by the agreement are [union members], compared with Nissan, where only about 30 per cent of the workforce are estimated to be members of the AEU' (Yeandle and Clark 1989: 38). Nevertheless, the Pirelli situation too makes clear the limited scope for union engagement with managerial relations; the agreement specifies the need to the union to 'cooperate actively with the introduction of change, whether in products, materials, techniques or working practices'.

Finally, in attempting to chart the changed position and influence of shop stewards in the 1990s we can refer to the mounting evidence of stewards' increasing reliance on support from union-employed full-time officers. The 1990 WIRS confirmed that

> [external] trade unions in 1990 were much more heavily involved in workplace-level matters than they were in 1984. All levels of the union were affected, it seems, from the local paid officials being more likely to represent members in the absence of lay representatives, or to be in contact with representatives that still existed, up to union national officers being much more commonly consulted directly by establishment-based representatives. (Millward et al. 1992: 130)

Further research suggests that at least one reason for this contact is the increasing vulnerability of stewards in the face of tougher management:

> In some instances, management attitudes are making union members reluctant to stand as lay representatives. As one NALGO officer . . . puts it, 'it is becoming more difficult to find stewards as they now feel more vulnerable to macho management'. Feeling less confident and much more 'vulnerable to attack', lay representatives require much more support from the FTO [full-time official], according to an MSF officer. (IRRR 1993: 4)

Further detailed research suggests that despite this increased contact, and the improvement in relationships between employed and lay union officials that takes place as a result (discussed in greater detail below), shop stewards still feel increasingly vulnerable and isolated (Waddington and Whitston 1992).

The case study evidence therefore tends to support the analysis hinted at by the survey data, namely that shop stewards and their organizations have been weakened and marginalized, and that stewards themselves are more vulnerable and less self-confident than they were in earlier periods. A preliminary conclusion might be that shop steward organizations that derived at least some of their support and stability from managerial systems during the 1970s have found it increasingly necessary to revert to their unions for support when management's has been withdrawn or reduced.

The Reasons for the Diminution of Stewards' Influence

This section will look at four broad sets of interrelated influences on shop stewards during the 1980s: those deriving from economic and industrial changes, from government action, from management behaviour, and from within the unions themselves.

Economic and industrial changes

Steward organization and bargaining power were facilitated during the 1960s and 1970s by a number of factors external and internal to the firm. They included tight labour and product markets that increased workers' bargaining power and put employers under pressure to settle disputes; workplaces employing large numbers of people, especially manual workers performing relatively routine jobs; and assembly-line production organization that enabled small groups of striking workers to bring entire factories to a standstill. Clearly, not all of these factors obtained in all workplaces during the 1970s – hence in part the suggestion that some steward organizations that developed during the decade owed at least something to managerial 'sponsorship'.

During the 1980s all of these factors changed in some degree. First, despite continuing shortages of certain skilled crafts, high levels of unemployment generally weakened workers' bargaining position. But for many it was the changes in product markets that were more important (see Edmonds 1984; Hyman 1989; Terry 1989). The recession of the early 1980s and the general vulnerability of UK manufacturing throughout the decade both increased workers' nervousness at the prospect of taking collective action and reduced the bargaining threat posed to employers by a reduction or cessation in production.

Second, as discussed in chapter 4, the average size of employing unit fell dramatically, under the twin impacts of job loss and displacement by new technologies. All previous survey work has shown a direct association between workforce size and the existence and sophistication of steward organization. Although the linkages have never been precisely clarified, the argument that larger workforces throw up enough shop stewards to enable them to form a 'critical mass' capable of self-sustaining organization has been widely accepted (see Brown et al. 1978: 142). By implication, a reduction in average establishment size, as has clearly taken place during the 1980s, may lead to organizational weakness.

Two further changes have contributed to the changed bargaining position of local trade unionism. The first is the gradual abandonment of production line technologies and their replacement by more flexible production systems; the second is a significant increase in productive flexibility within firms and competition between them from within the UK and from other countries. The first has, as indicated in chapter 12, perhaps contributed to a reduction in worker solidarity by introducing new distinctions in the organization of work, affecting concepts of both 'craft' and 'non-craft' work. In addition, new forms of flexible working have rendered more problematic employee- and union-based approaches to job control. The second factor has reduced stewards' bargaining leverage. Although just-in-time systems apparently make employers more vulnerable to local stoppages, concomitant changes weaken the value of such a tactic. Employers are increasingly able to close plants at short notice and to open new ones. At the same time, competition means that other firms can capture markets; stewards' awareness of this fact has reduced their desire to use bargaining sanctions.

Few if any of these considerations apply to steward organization in the public services, since their 'market' and bargaining contexts are, and have always been, very different. In this sector it has been government, and more especially, employer, policies that have had the greater impact, and it is to these that we now turn.

The role of the state

The United Kingdom and Ireland are the only two countries in the European Union in which there are no legal rights underpinning some form of collective employee representation at the workplace level. Arguably, this is the most important element in understanding the importance (or lack of it) of the role of the state, since it has left the field clear for the unfettered operation of managerial and union preference – very much the former during the 1980s. Such legal supports as did exist for the establishment and maintenance of shop steward organization have been weakened or abolished. The repeal of the statutory union recognition procedures in 1980 contributed to the failure of unions to extend their recognition base into new areas. A further implication was that ACAS, which had taken on the role of the Commission on Industrial Relations in, among other things, advising companies on their industrial relations strategy, ceased advocating Donovan-style systems of formal plant- and company-level collective bargaining as their preferred model of labour relations (Armstrong and Lucas 1985: 198–203). More direct legal effects included the weakening and then abolishing of the closed shop, and from the 1989 Employment Act's reductions in time-off rights for union activities. Such changes have reduced, though perhaps not greatly, the organizational stability of shopfloor unionism.

The full impact of legal innovation on the power and stability of shopfloor unionism has yet to be seen. Perhaps the three most important changes are recent: the 1990 Act's extension of balloting and other requirements for lawful industrial action to unofficial strikes; the making lawful the *selective* dismissal of employees involved in industrial action (the implications for local 'leaders' are obvious); and the requirement in the 1993 Trade Union Reform and Employment Rights Act that the check-off system has to be reapproved individually by union members every three years.

At least as important as any legal change was the Thatcher governments' open distaste for trade unions and collective bargaining. This helped legitimate private- and in particular public-sector employers' moves to weaken bargaining structures and to reduce the influence and status of trade unions, including that of shop stewards (see Ferner 1989: 7–12). The extensive decentralization and restructuring of public services that took place during the 1980s have provided opportunities for steward organizations to develop an enlarged local role (see Fairbrother 1990: 152–60). On the other hand in some sectors, and the health service provides one clear example, decentralization has often been accompanied by a managerial desire to exert effective unilateral control over pay and conditions – for example, in self-governing Health Service Trusts (Seifert 1992: 378–88). The potential for local bargaining in such decentralization has frequently been negated by managerial hostility.

Finally, the government policy of compulsory competitive tendering discussed in chapter 16 has caused real problems for many steward organizations in local government and the health service in particular, both with their members and with the outside unions. Faced with the threat of outside tenders for work, stewards have on many occasions found themselves constrained into helping organize a bid on behalf of their members in order to retain the work 'in-house'. On occasion, this has been done in defiance of national union policy, and it has almost always meant stewards agreeing to – sometimes even been perceived as proposing – deteriorations in their members' terms and conditions of employment in order to put in a competitive bid:

> in the 1980s the ancillary unions [in the health service] spent much time and effort defending jobs and resisting privatization measures. In practice most union stewards ended up involved in negotiations over in-house tenders. This was due to ambivalence among members, confusion among many stewards, and a realization that they had to live and work there whatever the TUC or national union had to say. (Seifert 1992: 381)

There is some evidence that, in other situations, unions have shown considerable resilience at local level (Fairbrother 1990;

Darlington 1994)*. Although the conditions permitting such continued activism have yet to be established with certainty, particular factors seem influential – notably, relatively slowly changing economic conditions and a well-entrenched tradition of local activism (as in one of Darlington's examples, the Post Office in Liverpool). In general, however, such resilience depends on very particular circumstances.

New approaches by employers

Employers' approaches have been the key factors in influencing shop steward organization and behaviour. As employers' bargaining power increased they, aided by a supportive legislative and political framework, and unconstrained by extensive union legal rights at the workplace, have generally acted to contain and reduce the authority of stewards and the influence of workplace unionism.

There has been no single employer approach, but two underlying guides to their action may be widely perceived. First, employers believed they had to regain significant or total control over technological innovation and the organization of production if they were to compete successfully (their earlier refusal to follow the Donovan recommendations of formalizing bargaining in this area has been noted already). Second, they increasingly argued that the single channel of union representation and information dissemination was inadequate to serve managerial purposes.

In the early 1980s in particular, in manufacturing industry and in parts of the public sector (telecommunications, steel, coal, the railways), managers took action to restore effective control over 'managerial relations'. On some occasions, as at British Leyland (BL), this meant working to break the power of the shop stewards (see Scarbrough 1986: 101–10), and more widely managers took tough action against stewards and threats of strike action to achieve this objective.[2]

In these cases managers often went to hitherto unprecedented steps to 'get their message' across to the workforce, over the heads of the stewards, the long-accepted sole or dominant channel of communication (see Edwardes 1983: 146–52, for details from BL in the late 1970s and early 1980s). Employers argued that they could not allow their 'message' to be entrusted solely to union mechanisms; to do so would be an abdication of managerial responsibility. The habit of using 'union-free' methods of communications during the 1980s spread with the development of techniques of 'human resource management' (HRM) and they grew in extent and sophistication.

At the same time as these moves towards the 'marginalization' of stewards was taking place, however, managers were retaining at least the form, and often a significant part of the content, of steward-based systems for the handling of collective bargaining over pay and conditions, though plant-level bargaining was increasingly being abandoned in favour of multi-plant corporate or divisional bargaining. As noted above, stewards have traditionally experienced serious problems in sustaining stable organization at such levels, especially in the weakened position of the 1980s.

Such new managerial strategies have been facilitated by their enhanced bargaining power and by the technological and organizational restructuring of production and service work driven by the fierce competitive pressures of the 1980s. Employers' retreat from collective bargaining has been crucial in a country where it has limited legal underpinning. The 1970s showed how in a supportive economic and political environment stewards could exert effective power despite their partial reliance on employers. The 1980s has shown how conditional that power was, and how significantly it can be undercut when employers withdraw their 'goodwill'.

The contribution of shopfloor unions

The events of the 1980s raised serious problems for stewards and their organizations of a qualitatively different kind from those encountered earlier. Rarely did they take the form of all-out attack; rather, they reflected a managerial determination to reduce or eliminate steward influence over certain issues, and to construct alternative channels of communication to and from the workforce. Shop stewards were confronted by employers arguing in detail the need not only for job loss but for the rapid introduction of new technology, the development of functional flexibility (multi-skilling), the introduction of new forms of employment (part-time, temporary employees, subcontracting), more intensive working patterns such as bell-to-bell working, and other changes associated with a drive for increased labour productivity. Frequently, the need for radical change was driven home by managerial propaganda direct to employees, emphasizing the seriousness of the problems faced by the company and the urgency of such change.

The problem for stewards was that they had neither the organizational nor the ideological resources to respond. Such initiatives and the arguments that accompanied them required a strategic response, coordinated at company level, that engaged with issues of production and work organization. But, as noted above, stewards lacked strength at company or divisional level, and rarely developed a clear trade union position on issues other than terms and conditions of employment. In other words, their 'sectionalism' and 'economism' were sources of weakness in their search for a way to respond on behalf of their members. This contributed to a broad pragmatic acceptance of the logic of managerial action (Terry 1989; Colling and Geary 1992), with a consequent weakening of their oppositional role and an increased risk of loss of membership credibility.

Stewards have also been uncertain about how and on whose behalf to respond to certain new initiatives for another reason. Issues such as increases in part-time working, and flexible working hours, for example, may have attractions for some employees, many women for example, but not others. Stewards, in common with other trade union negotiators, have rarely articulated the interests of women, of part-time and temporary workers, often reflecting instead those of full-time, permanent employees, predominantly men, who may perceive such initiatives as constituting threats to their own security. The need for unions to pay more attention to the interests of other employees (members and potential members) and to look at such issues as work organization and health and safety from a different perspective has become increasingly accepted by the TUC and affiliated unions, but has not widely percolated down to shopfloor negotiators.

Similar uncertainties can be discerned in the evolution of stewards' responses to new managerial techniques of human resource management. An initial profound distrust of a managerial strategy perceived as excluding and weakening unions has been replaced increasingly by a 'pragmatic acceptance' of the new HRM (see Martinez Lucio and Weston 1992; Bacon and Storey 1993). In some ways, this change reflected the absence of a clear-cut set of arguments to resist such managerial innovation; put crudely, stewards who had for years criticized managers for failing to listen to the shopfloor expertise of their members found it difficult to argue against initiatives (team working, quality circles) that claimed to achieve just that. Stewards' responses continue to reflect the inevitable underlying ambivalence: on the one hand suspicion and mistrust reflected in hostility to these initiatives; on the other cooperation and an effort to secure union influence within the new structures (IRRR 1992).

The response of many stewards' organizations to new managerial initiatives, both substantive and procedural, reflects in part their continuing dependence on managerial support (recognition, facilities, check-off arrangements). Lacking independent legal support for their own organization for collective bargaining, stewards have had to respond with one eye always on maintaining or obtaining employer recognition. Similar considerations have underlain union attempts to gain recognition on greenfield sites, through signing agreements that constrain union activities. In some cases, this 'organizational interest' has conflicted with, and may have taken priority over, direct response to membership interests. In so far as this too may risk undermining one traditional claim of shop steward democracy, it may on occasion jeopardize membership legitimacy.

Against these organizational and ideological problems have to be set other factors that are working to assist and maintain steward organization. The first is that for many employers, despite the adoption of 'union-free' approaches, no thoroughgoing alternative to steward-based collective bargaining has been pursued. The basic infrastructure for wage and conditions bargaining remains intact in many areas. Second, as noted above, the increased importance of the workplace may provide opportunities for stewards to develop new approaches (see Spencer 1989; Fairbrother 1990). Third, the tougher working conditions for many workers in the 1980s, discussed in chapters 12 and 16, have contributed to a continuing demand for stewards' services as representatives on individual problems and issues. Finally, there is strong evidence of a reconstruction of relationships between shop stewards and full-time union employed officers in which a more collaborative and cooperative relationship is beginning to displace the 'arm's-length' relationship of earlier periods (see Heery and Kelly 1990; IRRR 1992, 1993). Part of the reason lies in the need to create union structures for pay and conditions bargaining at corporate or divisional levels. But the move also indicates a perceived need for support in day-to-day union activities at local level.

Conclusion: The Prospects for Shop Steward Organization

British unions have no feasible alternative to the shop steward model, not least at a time when managerial and government action continues to decentralize decision-taking. British unions continue to rely on stewards for their basis – to recruit, organize and represent the membership. Unions do not have the resources, even if they had the inclination, to replace them with other structures.

Faced with this commitment, unions have no alternative but to seek to reinforce and maintain steward organization. A clear example can be found in the organizational structures established for the new public services union UNISON. This massive union deliberately sought to base itself on a steward network based on direct account-ability to members. In addition, stewards were to reflect all sectors of the membership, with direct and supportive access to the external union. Unions, and also many managers, see no alternative to a shop-steward-based unionism.

It is likely, therefore, that steward systems will continue to be found wherever unions are found. Nevertheless, it has been argued here that considerable changes may take place. First is a greater integration of stewards into official union systems, not just as powerful figures on national executive committees but as partners with full-time officials on a range of representative activities. This development goes along with the financial centralization introduced in many unions, discussed in chapter 6. In this they may become more like many of their continental European counterparts, with less organizational autonomy than they enjoyed in the 1980s, and perhaps with a less reactive, less economistic, approach.

At the same time, and irrespective of the future of steward systems in established sectors, there is little likelihood under present circum-stances of effective steward organization extending to the growing service sector. Arguably, it is unlikely ever to be able to do this without legislative support; the organizational, political, market and technological conditions that favoured growth in manufacturing and the public sector during the 1960s and 1970s will not be replicated there.

Notes

1   Many shop stewards were politically active in Labour, Communist or other left-wing groups, but their politics rarely found direct expression in their steward activities. Batstone et al. (1977) argue that the more effective shop stewards were those who operated to a set of 'trade union principles', but these principles could not really be characterized as essentially socialist or communist in nature.

2 At the same time, as chapter 5 shows, employers were also prepared to pay significant pay increases, at least in manufacturing industry, in exchange for the trouble-free introduction of change and for the abandonment of job controls. This is important in assessing the overall change in industrial relations, but it does not contradict the fact that widespread changes in workplace practice have been introduced.

References

Armstrong, E. and Lucas, R. 1985: *Improving Industrial Relations: The Advisory Role of ACAS*. London: Croom Helm.

Bacon, N. and Storey, J. 1993: Individualization of the Employment Relationship and the Implications for Trade Unions. *Employee Relations*, 15, 1, 5–17.

Batstone, E. 1984: *Working Order*. Oxford: Blackwell.

Batstone, E. 1988: *The Reform of Workplace Industrial Relations*. Oxford: Clarendon.

Batstone, E., Boraston, I. and Frenkel, S. 1977: *Shop Stewards in Action*. Oxford: Blackwell.

Batstone, E., Ferner, A. and Terry, M. 1984: *Consent and Efficiency*. Oxford: Blackwell.

Beynon, H. 1973: *Working for Ford*. Harmondsworth: Penguin.

Brown, W. (ed.) 1981: *The Changing Contours of British Industrial Relations*. Oxford: Blackwell.

Brown, W., Ebsworth, R. and Terry, M. 1978: Factors Shaping Shop Steward Organisation in Britain. *British Journal of Industrial Relations*, 16, 2, 139–59.

Colling, T. and Geary, J. 1992: New Management Initiatives and Workplace Union Responses. Paper presented to Industrial Relations in the European Community Conference on Changing Systems of Workplace Representation in Europe, Dublin, November.

Darlington, R. 1994: *The Dynamics of Workplace Unionism: Shop Steward Organization in Three Merseyside Plants*. London: Mansell.

Edmonds, J. 1984: The Decline of the Big Battalions. *Personnel Management*, March, 18–21.

Edwardes, M. 1983: *Back from the Brink*. London: Pan.

Edwards, P. K. 1983: The Pattern of Collective Industrial Action. In G. S. Bain (ed.), *Industrial Relations in Britain*. Oxford: Blackwell.

Edwards, P. K. 1987: *Managing the Factory*. Oxford: Blackwell.

Elger, T. 1991: Task Flexibility and the Intensification of Labour in UK Manufacturing in the 1980s. In A. Pollert (ed.), *Farewell to Flexibility?* Oxford: Blackwell.

Fairbrother, P. 1990: The Contours of Local Trade Unionism in a Period of Restructuring. In P. Fosh and E. Heery (eds), *Trade Unions and their*

Members. Basingstoke: Macmillan.

Ferner, A. 1989: Ten Years of Thatcherism: Changing Industrial Relations in British Public Enterprises. *Warwick Papers in Industrial Relations*, 27. Coventry: Industrial Relations Research Unit.

Freeman, R. and Medoff, J. 1979: The Two Faces of Unionism. *The Public Interest*, 57, 69–73.

Heery, E. and Kelly, J. 1990: Full-time Officers and the Shop Steward Network: Patterns of Cooperation and Interdependence. In P. Fosh and E. Heery (eds), *Trade Unions and their Members*. Basingstoke: Macmillan.

Hyman, R. 1979: The Politics of Workplace Trade Unionism. *Capital and Class*, 8, 54–67.

Hyman, R. 1989: *Strikes*, 4th edn. Basingstoke: Macmillan.

IRRR (Industrial Relations Review and Report) 1992: The Changing Role of Trade Union Officers 1: The Devolution of Pay Bargaining. *IRS Employment Trends*, 526, December, 5–12.

IRRR (Industrial Relations Review and Report) 1993: The Changing Role of Trade Union Officers 2: Collective Bargaining and Working Practices. *IRS Employment Trends*, 527, January, 3–11.

MacInnes, J. 1987: *Thatcherism at Work*. Milton Keynes: Open University Press.

Marchington, M. and Parker, P. 1990: *Changing Patterns of Employee Relations*. Hemel Hempstead: Harvester Wheatsheaf.

Marsh, A. 1963: *Managers and Shop Stewards*. London: Institute of Personnel Management.

Martinez Lucio, M. and Weston, S. 1992: The Politics and Complexity of Trade Union Responses to New Management Practices. *Human Resource Management Journal*, 2, 4, 77–92.

Miles, R. and Phizacklea, A. 1981: The TUC and Black Workers, 1974–76. In P. Braham, E. Rhodes and M. Pearn (eds), *Discrimination and Disadvantage in Employment*. London: Harper and Row.

Millward, N. and Stevens, M. 1986: *British Workplace Industrial Relations 1980–1984*. Aldershot: Gower.

Millward, N., Stevens, M., Smart, D. and Hawes, W. R. 1992: *Workplace Industrial Relations in Transition*. Aldershot: Dartmouth.

Oliver, N. and Wilkinson, B. 1992: *The Japanization of British Industry*, 2nd edn. Oxford: Blackwell.

Scarbrough, H. 1986: The Politics of Technological Change at British Leyland. In O. Jacobi, B. Jessop, H. Kastendiek and M. Regini (eds), *Technological Change, Rationalisation and Industrial Relations*. London: Croom Helm.

Seifert, R. 1992: *Industrial Relations in the NHS*. London: Chapman and Hall.

Sisson, K. and Brown, W. 1983: Industrial Relations in the Private Sector: Donovan Re-visited. In G. S. Bain (ed.), *Industrial Relations in Britain*. Oxford: Blackwell.

Smith, P. and Morton, G. 1993: Union Exclusion and the Decollectivization of IR in Contemporary Britain. *British Journal of Industrial Relations*, 31, 1, 97–114.

Snell, M., Glucklich, P. and Povall, M. 1981: *Equal Pay and Opportunities*. Department of Employment Research Paper, 20. London: Department of Employment.

Spencer, B. 1989: *Remaking the Working Class?* Nottingham: Spokesman.

Taylor, R. 1980: *The Fifth Estate: Britain's Unions in the Modern World*. London: Pan.

Terry, M. 1978: *The Emergence of a Lay Elite? Some Recent Changes in Shop Steward Organisation*. Industrial Relations Research Unit Discussion Papers, 14. Coventry: Industrial Relations Research Unit.

Terry, M. 1983: Shop Steward Development and Managerial Strategies. In G. S. Bain (ed.), *Industrial Relations in Britain*. Oxford: Blackwell.

Terry, M. 1985: Combine Committees: Developments of the 1970s. *British Journal of Industrial Relations*, 23, 3, 359–78.

Terry, M. 1986: How Do We Know If Shop Stewards Are Getting Weaker? *British Journal of Industrial Relations*, 24, 2, 169–79.

Terry, M. 1988: Introduction: Historical Analyses and Contemporary Issues. In M. Terry and P. K. Edwards (eds), *Shopfloor Politics and Job Controls*. Oxford: Blackwell.

Terry, M. 1989: Recontextualizing Shopfloor Industrial Relations: Some Case Study Evidence. In S. Tailby and C. Whitston (eds), *Manufacturing Change: Industrial Relations and Restructuring*. Oxford: Blackwell.

Waddington, J. and Whitston, C. 1992: Workplace Change and Union Organization: Preliminary Survey Results. Paper presented to Industrial Relations in the European Community Conference on Changing Systems of Workplace Representation in Europe, Dublin, November.

Wainwright, H. and Elliott, D. 1982: *The Lucas Plan: A New Unionism in the Making?* London: Allison and Busby.

Willman, P. 1980: Leadership and Trade Union Principles: Some Problems of Management Sponsorship and Independence. *Industrial Relations Journal*, 11, 4, 39–49.

Yeandle, D. and Clark, J. 1989: Growing a Compatible IR Set-up: Pirelli General's Single Union Agreement in South Wales. *Personnel Management*, July, 36–9.

8

The State: Economic Management and Incomes Policy

Colin Crouch

The central thrust of the government's role in industrial relations since the Conservative Party's victory in 1979 can be summarized briefly: disengagement from communication and interaction with the parties to industrial relations, especially on the labour side; and weakening the trade unions. To some extent this has been achieved through changes in industrial relations law, as discussed in chapter 9. There have also been important developments in the government's role as an employer (see chapter 10). But it has also operated through general economic management.

The changes can readily be interpreted in terms of the government's general neo-liberal ideology, which implies avoidance of entanglements with organizations that are, at least in part, devoted to interfering with pure market forces. It can, however, also be explained in terms of the dilemmas appearing in British industrial relations in the preceding period, which in turn help explain why the Conservative Party turned so strongly to neo-liberalism.

Elsewhere (Crouch 1994) I have proposed a classification of industrial relations systems of the kind summarized in figure 8.1. This embodies the following assumptions. First, the most important variables are (1) the strength of organized labour; and (2) the extent to which both labour and capital have organizations with central coordinating capacity. Labour strength (which can be measured by union membership and legal and bargained rights) is an important determinant of the extent to which workers are able to express their interests, and of whether employers need to come to terms with that strength. The importance of coordinating capacity will become clear in the following discussion.

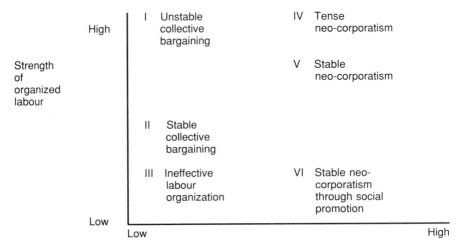

Figure 8.1 Different forms of industrial relations systems

Second, it is assumed that the organization of labour presents a problem to a market economy, as in the simplest case workers use their organizations to seek better wages and conditions than the market makes possible. In a pure market economy the consequence of this will be unemployment for the workers concerned. In a Keynesian economy, where government has the avoidance of unemployment as a policy priority, it will take fiscal and monetary measures to avoid this occurring. If the unemployment is being partly caused by labour-market pressure through organization, the consequence will be inflation.

Third, where organizations of both capital and labour have some kind of central coordinating capacity, they may become aware of these likely inflationary consequences, perceive them as problems, and have the capacity to take action to moderate their own behaviour. A centralized organization that represents a high proportion of a given workforce cannot easily ignore the consequences of its actions, as these are large enough to be perceptible and the organization knows it has the capacity to do something about them. Where there is no coordinating capacity, a mass of small-scale groups is each able to claim that its own particular actions have no measurable effect, and no-one is in a position to do anything about the cumulative effect.

Following this logic, figure 8.1 shows that where coordinating capacity is weak, the only form of regular interaction possible is collective bargaining; at low levels of labour strength this can be a stable model (II), but as labour's strength grows its bargaining power will cause macroeconomic problems which the system lacks the capacity to accommodate, rendering the system unstable (I). At the extreme of labour weakness, workers may not be able to insist on any interaction at all (III).

When labour and capital possess capacity for both strategy and *articulation* they are likely to develop neo-corporatist structures (IV and V). By 'articulation' is meant a systematic linkage between the levels of an organization (in the case of unions, for example, between national leaderships and the shopfloor). These make it possible to contain workers' strength at higher levels of labour's organizational power than under weakly coordinated systems, though there will still be tension as this rises in level IV. (The only other point that requires to be demonstrated is the possibility of coordinative ability by weak labour movements (VI). According to most theories, including that outlined so far above, labour acquires a coordinating capacity only as it develops organized power. The exception occurs in societies where, for some exogenous reason, the state (or possibly employers) needs to give organized labour a place of recognition that its industrial strength does not strictly 'deserve'. This is not a model that is relevant to the UK.)

Implicit in this model is a curvilinear relationship between stability (measured by inflation, industrial conflict, etc.) and degree of organization of the labour market, as shown in figure 8.2. Coordinating capacity and union strength have been presented as independent variables in figure 8.1, but it is possible to see them combining in a complex way to form a single indicator of organization in the sense of departure from a pure market. The more that workers are able to organize, the more there is such a departure; but, given that an essential feature of the market is an absence of coordination, then the possession of coordinating capacity by unions and employers' associations is also a departure. The polar opposite cases are therefore: a pure labour market in which workers have no organizations at all, and hence no coordinating capacity; and a highly organized system in which a central organization has authority on behalf of the mass of employed persons. Under these circumstances, there will be stability either where organization is very weak (because workers cannot disrupt effectively) or where there is central

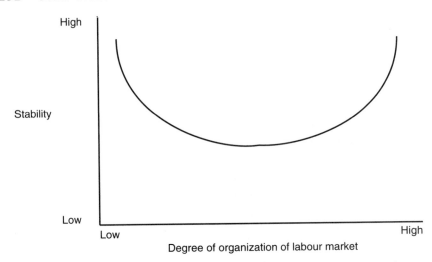

Figure 8.2 Organization and stability in the labour market

coordinating capacity. In between these poles, where there is uneven organization, or powerful organization with poor coordination, there is likely to be a higher level of disruption.

Two important theoretical contributions during the 1980s suggested this curvilinear approach. In a work that has been highly influential with the neo-liberal campaign to weaken organizations of interests, Mancur Olson (1982) argued that, when interests organized, they generally did so in order to externalize on to the general public any costs of pursuing their own ends. Societies' main hopes of avoiding this problem lay in the fact that organizing interests was a difficult task, taking several years. This led him to the paradoxical conclusion that societies with disrupted histories were likely to have higher rates of economic growth and better economic prospects: disrupted pasts meant the destruction of organizations and therefore weaker organizations. He used the theory in particular to explain why the two defeated nations in the Second World War, West Germany and Japan, enjoyed stronger economies than the victors, the UK and the United States.

Olson did, however, allow an exception: where organizations were so encompassing in their membership that they included within them a large proportion of the public, they would find it more difficult to externalize their damage. This accounted for the economic success of peaceful, heavily organized societies of the Scandinavian kind. Olson still believed that there was a danger of stagnation in such economies because of the extensive consultation required by large organizations, but his theory was distinctly curvilinear: either very weak organizations or very strong, centralized ones; not intermediately organized and decentralized ones.

A similar conclusion was reached by Calmfors and Driffill (1988), who plotted various indicators of disruption against indices of corporatism or of the coordinating power of organizations, again finding a curvilinear relationship. Several other studies have taken a similar approach (for example, Dell'Aringa and Lodovici 1992; Crouch 1993).

Soskice (1990) has queried the viability of the left-hand side of the curve (that is, that there can be high stability with completely uncoordinated, weak labour systems). He bases his objection primarily on the fact that two of Calmfors and Driffill's uncoordinated cases are France and Japan. Soskice argues that, while in the former case organizations of labour are not important to coordination, the state possesses the ability to regulate the economy enough to pursue stability. In the case of Japan he argues that the recourse to internal labour markets of the giant Japanese corporations insulates them from external labour market forces. This leaves the UK and the United States as the only candidates for inclusion as low-coordination cases, and their inflation record is not particularly good, especially in the case of the UK. It may still be argued, however, that a fully deinstitutionalized labour market would be stable, and that the UK has simply not yet been able to reach such an end point. This chapter addresses these questions by first outlining efforts before 1979 to achieve coordination. Trends in the opposite direction since 1979 are then examined in detail. Finally, the success of these efforts is evaluated.

Before 1979: Attempts at Coordination

Arguments about the role of coordination featured increasingly prominently in debates about industrial relations in the UK from about 1940 until the end of the 1970s. This was a period of strong government commitment to Keynesianism and to recognition of the organization of labour, starting during the period of intense national solidarity of the Second World War, but extending long afterwards into a very different period. Initially, trade unions and organizations of employers had characteristics necessary for seeking stability at the high-coordination pole. Although British unions had historically been highly decentralized, national organizations had acquired a stronger role during the 1930s, fighting a rearguard defence of pay and conditions during the prolonged depression, a time when little could be achieved by local action. Their involvement at government level in helping to organize the war economy strengthened this tendency enormously under very different economic and political conditions. Employers' associations, to which firms had traditionally been reluctant to grant much authority, similarly acquired a new role in wartime management. These conditions lasted into the early years of post-war recovery (Middlemas 1979; Davies and Freedland 1993: ch. 2).

However, the decentralized character of British industrial relations institutions gradually reasserted itself as early reconstruction gave way to the years of a full employment that was increasingly taken for granted. As Davies and Freedland show, the fundamental characteristic of British industrial relations institutions was that of what Otto Kahn-Freund (1954) had called 'collective laissez faire', which did not really accept coordinating or corporatist action (see McCarthy 1992: 4–11). Their own traditions and structures gave neither unions nor, as explained in chapter 4 above, employers' associations an autonomous base for central coordination. The incentives from government to behave that way declined as the Conservative governments of the 1950s, while Keynesian and not neo-liberal, had less use of national planning mechanisms that gave a role to coordinating organizations of business and labour. These were, however, the years of strong economic recovery, what Davies and Freedland call 'the easy decade'. In general, the level of economic growth kept pace with workers' aspirations, only a minority of workers had developed strong, autonomous shopfloor bargaining groups, and there was stable collective bargaining.

But by the early 1960s union strength was increasingly concentrated at a disaggregated shopfloor level, where more or less informally organized groups of workers bargained opportunistically in conditions of a tight labour market. Initially a form of organization limited to skilled workers, the shopfloor model spread to the production line in the then flourishing motor vehicle sector and other parts of engineering (see chapter 7). By the end of the decade it was beginning to be practised by employees in the public services, long considered to be incapable of doing so.

Governments became increasingly concerned at the inflationary implications of this kind of bargaining in a full-employment economy, at the strike level that sometimes seemed to be associated with it, and at the difficulties for employers in negotiating improvements in working practices with well-organized shopfloor groups. The policy conclusion of the debate was usually to try to increase the coordinating capacity of the two sides of industry so that they could play a neo-corporatist role. This continued to be the essential pattern throughout the 1960s and 1970s. Changes of government would cause changes of emphasis, changes of direction, a reshuffling of the councils, committees and boards within which the coordination was supposed to take place; statutory incomes policies alternated with voluntary ones; attempts at cooperation alternated with angry rejection. But there was a basic continuity in the pattern (Crouch 1977; Middlemas 1979).

Meanwhile, on the ground, the decentralized character of British collective bargaining and the lack of coordination capacity among unions and employers' associations continued and indeed intensified. The Donovan Commission discussed in detail the 'two systems' of industrial relations that had come to prevail in several industries in Britain: the formal system of branch-level bargaining between unions and employers' associations, and informal shopfloor system (Crouch 1977: part 3; Davies and Freedland 1993: 238–67). It urged a reconciliation of the two (Donovan 1968), but its arguments avoided confronting the issue that a major reason for such a reconciliation would be to enable central organizations to cooperate in a coordination of national bargaining. In practice, many unions' and firms' subsequent attempts at achieving the reconciliation seemed mainly to give greater prominence to the shopfloor level.

Following the major international rises in the prices of oil and other commodities in the 1970s, the threat to economic stability posed by inflation became acute. Government increasingly tried to pull the Trades Union Congress (TUC), the Confederation of British Industry (CBI) and their national affiliates towards the high-coordination pole; the rise in shopfloor bargaining increasingly resisted those attempts. Britain was thoroughly trapped in the middle of the curve of figure 8.2. By the so-called 'winter of discontent' of January 1979 attempts at moving towards the high-coordination pole had reached a crisis.

Behind this story, which can be told primarily in terms of industrial relations institutions themselves, lies something more general about the British political and economic context. The British political legacy of the mid-twentieth century has had two components. The first of these has comprised an incoherent mix of the following: (1) the country's past as the first industrial nation, with a heavy inheritance of manufacturing industry that had become inflexible; (2) the pattern of compromise and give-and-take in industrial relations between employers and unions, combined with the generally decentralized, non-strategic pattern of organization of collective laissez faire discussed above; (3) the country had also developed, after the Second World War, a strong welfare state, which in its way fitted into the country's general record of expansive, benign institutions and a genial care for a public interest, conceived in a non-strategic way.

The general character of this side of the British legacy was relaxed, even incoherent. Nothing united the different components in a way that might make possible a national strategy, since the only thing that really brought them together was their incapacity for strategy. The general mix has become known in a vague way as the post-war consensus, but it was not a real consensus in the sense of a true agreement, orientated to widely discussed, chosen goals. Rather, it was the kind of consensus that arises when various groups put the avoidance of struggle beyond the search for agreement. This was not the kind of consensus that would make for stability at the high-coordination pole; but it could not produce the attack on labour's rights and capacities that would be involved in a switch to the opposite approach described in figure 8.2 (Fox 1985: 360–72).

The second model, which was internally far more coherent, also has its heart in the unforced character of the British industrial revolution, but not in its legacy of old manufacturing industry; rather, in the idea of laissez faire capitalism. Markets should be unimpeded by institutions and should move smartly and flexibly. The acme of this side of British life was the City of London and its associated financial sector, a set of markets geared to very rapid decisions and short-term calculations. This model informed British company law, with its emphasis on shareholding and short-term bank-lending and dividend calculations, where the hostile take-over was an accepted part of business life and prevented managers from undertaking long-term investments that might push the real assets of a company above its quoted value (see Ingham 1984; Fine and

Harris 1985: ch. 2). There was a further hostility, or at least indifference, to industrial interests in the role of the pound sterling and its over-valuation, and in the City's international orientation.

The second face of Britain was clearly at loggerheads with the first. Within industrial relations it would clearly imply the achievement of stability at the 'weakened labour' pole. But for many years the two Britains coexisted. This was possible because both models shared a lack of interest in long-term strategy: the former because it had no capacity for it, the second because it had no need for it, being geared to the very short term. This coincidence of interest was expressed in the particular form of British Keynesianism. The Treasury manipulated a few central policy instruments to sustain demand and therefore employment (favouring the interests associated with the first Britain), but having done that it left the economy alone to be run by virtually free market forces (the second Britain). Keynesianism by itself was a short-termist policy.

As the manufacturing sector visibly deteriorated from at least the 1960s on, governments tried various interventions, but none that succeeded in reconciling the gap between the two Britains. An attempt at indicative planning by the Labour governments of 1964 and 1966 was undermined by a postponement of a devaluation of the pound sterling that was at least partly in deference to the City's need for an exceptionally strong and stable home currency.

After 1979: Seeking Stability through the Weakening of Organized Labour

The winter of discontent and subsequent fall of the Labour government in 1979 marked a major turning point. The signal achievement of the Conservative governments after 1979 was to break the log-jam by siding unequivocally with the second Britain of finance-driven laissez faire. An attack on the public service and on a whole set of other institutions flowed from that, to make the choice of model unequivocal: British public institutions had to be forced out of all commitments that contradicted the short-term market model. Public expenditure that both detracted from market forces and, in some of its forms, imposed expensive costs of infrastructure investments had to go. Other institutions that did not follow the rules of the short-term market either had to reform themselves in the desired direction or decline. The second model held together a far more integrated and coherent set of forces than the first; once it gained the upper hand it was able to drive home its logic and victory.

Within industrial relations this clearly meant trying to move steadily towards the opposite pole from the attempts of the preceding decades. Stability and low inflation came to be sought, not through coordination, but through the weakening, if possible the destruction, of workers' organizing capacity.

The post-1979 Conservative governments have had a strong neo-liberal ideology. This has predisposed them: to reject Keynesian demand management and the search for full employment; to oppose policy deals with trade unions that would involve taking action incompatible with neo-liberal principles; and to reject relations with organizations of interests – on both sides of business but especially on the labour side – that interfered with neo-liberal policy priorities.

Meanwhile, more general changes in the economy were rendering the central coordination model more difficult to achieve irrespective of past success or failure and current political ideology. Employment in manufacturing industry, the traditional heartland of solidaristic trade unionism, was declining. An increasing number of firms was seeking company autonomy in planning their human resource management and wanted interference from neither an external trade union nor even an employers' association (see chapter 5). The company, not the industrial branch, was increasingly becoming the important unit. Even countries where central coordination had enjoyed years of success, such as in Scandinavia, began to experience strains in central coordination (Kjellberg 1992). Strains were even more likely to lead to a collapse of the system in a situation like that in the UK, where there was no great record of past coordination to sustain confidence during lean years.

Further, as the years have passed, so Conservative governments have felt confident that they could take risks with social stability. This is an important socio-political point, often forgotten by industrial relations analysts, especially in the UK, where social order is taken for granted. In a number of advanced industrial countries there is often concern among governing elites to ensure that social stability will not be threatened by social groups feeling alienated from and therefore hostile to the socio-political order. This may be because of recent past histories of civic unrest or of dissident regional groups (as in Belgium, France, Italy and Spain), or general anxieties about a longer past (as in Austria, Germany and Japan), or the recency of establishing a stable democratic order (Spain, or the new countries of Eastern Europe).

In these situations even governments that are essentially hostile to the aspirations of organized labour nevertheless retain for it a role of national consultation and respectability. Britain, as a country with a long history of social stability, is among those in which these issues have low priority. During the 1980s they faded even further, as the traditional issue of ensuring that the working class was nationally integrated, that had dogged earlier Conservative governments, became a thing of the past. The decline in the strength of the industrial working class assisted this. So did the temporary collapse of the Labour party as a political force and the defection from it of leading figures on the right of the party who were later instrumental in establishing the Social Democratic party in 1981. For the whole of the 1980s the party of organized labour ceased to be a serious political force.

The occupational group most noted for militant resistance, the coal miners, was involved in the fiercest challenge to social order of the post-1979 period in its year-long dispute of 1984–5. This involved the usual accoutrements of civil disorder – massive police action, fighting, even deaths. But the National Union of Mineworkers was itself bitterly divided; most of the confrontation and violence was between miner and miner (Adeney and Lloyd 1986). The defeat of the strike probably ended an era of working class political challenge, and it had ended in a bitter intra-union struggle. Social alienation continued to be an issue in Britain, but it affected either the unemployed and marginally employed, who do not form part of a labour movement challenge, or ethnic minorities, who are small in number (Gallie 1988). Even then, it is significant that virtually the only occasion when Margaret Thatcher, as Prime Minister, met the General Council of the TUC for a discussion of general issues was in the wake of severe urban rioting in ethnic minority communities in 1982.

During the 1980s, therefore, the government acquired both the motives and the opportunities that might lead it to shift British industrial relations to the 'weak organization' pole of the Olson or Calmfors–Driffill curve. It was a change of major importance and with many detailed implications. These include the legal changes analysed by Dickens and Hall in chapter 9. The aims of weakening the scope for unions' action and preventing wider solidary action were consistent with the government's more general aims of weakening and localizing collective organization.

On the other hand, the imposition of needs for ballots for union officers' elections and for major strike decisions, and the need for union leaders to accept responsibility for or disown unofficial strikes, while consistent with the former aim, also sowed seeds for a potential recentralization of unions wishing one day to enjoy a new coordinating role. The need for ballots imposes a need for extensive communications between leaders and movement, a characteristic familiar to northern European solidaristic unions but foreign to the opportunism of the British – as the miners' strike showed.

Also consistent with the policy have been the measures directed at public employment, discussed by Winchester and Bach (chapter 10). This has been the only sector in which the government has maintained an incomes policy, but it has also pursued a strategy of privatization, competitive tendering and hiving off, designed partly to break up national bargaining structures and replace them by small local agreements or, when privatization has occurred, no agreements at all (chapter 16).

In the present chapter we concentrate on the contribution of general economic management to the 'weakening and localizing' strategy. This has primarily taken four forms: (1) prioritizing the conquest of inflation over the avoidance of high unemployment; (2) encouraging the dismantling of collective bargaining, especially at levels above the individual firm; (3) ceasing to encourage the pursuit of 'good' industrial relations; and (4) gradually abolishing all tripartite mechanisms for addressing economic questions.

The priority of counter-inflation

Demoting the full-employment commitment, and prioritizing instead the conquest of inflation, was a prerequisite for cutting free from dependence on central coordination. Once it was possible for the commitment to be dropped, monetary policy needed to give less attention to wage-push inflation.

Looking at it from another point of view, some years ago I raised the question of what it was that unions who behaved in a neo-corporatist manner achieved that was different from what would be achieved by their disappearance – since such unions seemed to be primarily engaged in stopping the conflict and inflation that their members would probably cause if the unions did not behave in that manner (Crouch 1985). Castles (1987) answered my question by showing, as have several others since (see Dell'Aringa and Lodovici 1992; Crouch 1993: ch. 1), that neo-corporatist unions seemed to secure lower unemployment and higher social benefits than those who concentrated on conflictual bargaining or outright contestation. British unions, not having delivered neo-corporatist cooperation, could no longer expect the reward of official commitment to full employment.

In fact, an important breach of that commitment had already occurred under the 1974–9 Labour government. The twin pressures of high inflation and what in retrospect we can now see as having been increasing difficulty in sustaining full employment in high-wage Western economies, led that government in 1976 to adopt quantitative control over the money supply as an alternative to the priorities of Keynesian demand management. Wholehearted pursuit of such a strategy was, however, made much easier by the election of the Conservatives in 1979, as that party's electorate was both occupationally and geographically less vulnerable to the unemployment that was likely to follow such an abandonment. In fact, when this occurred, in the collapse of Scottish, northern and midlands manufacturing industry in the early 1980s, there was further electoral insulation from the consequences by the split in the Labour party. Monetarism could be endorsed as a politico-economic strategy with relatively low fears of social and electoral discontent.

Monetarism as such – that is, the pursuit of target growth rates for the quantity of money in circulation – was not pursued very consistently. Critics warned that the supply of money alone did not control expenditure patterns; there was also the velocity of circulation (Kaldor 1982). Further, measurements of money became dubious exercises at a time when new forms of credit were expanding very rapidly. Various different measures of money supply have been developed, and governments in various countries seem to have adopted whichever they found most convenient. The British government seemed eventually to be happiest with the measure known as M0, which measures notes and coin. While the crudest available measure, this has the advantage of being likely to move most slowly at a time of expanding use of credit cards, bank transfer arrangements and the cashless economy.

More important than the technical device of monetarism were the dropping of both the stated aim of and the political need to seek full employment, and pursuit of a strategy of reductions in public expenditure that was also disinflationary. The political situation was again important here. High public spending, which is largely welfare spending, is in large part demanded politically by and on behalf of less wealthy parts of the electorate. The weakening of the Labour party as a political alternative made easier this break with the past.

Associated with cuts in public spending were reductions in direct taxation. One explanation of the wage militancy of the late 1960s had been that workers were seeking to restore through wage increases real income that they had lost through the rapidly rising rates of income taxation during that period (Wilkinson and Turner 1972). An important limb of economic strategy during the 1980s and 1990s was to reduce levels of taxation in general and of direct taxation in particular.

The motives for this were of course by no means limited to questions of industrial relations. The government has believed as a general matter of ideology that public expenditure should decline in relation to private; this requires reductions in both public expenditure and taxation. It has also believed that during the post-war decades inequalities had been too much reduced. Since direct taxation has been a source of income redistribution, it was logical to reduce it, especially for higher incomes.

Indirect taxation sometimes rose during the period, having a directly inflationary impact. This was particularly the case with a major increase in value added tax (VAT) in 1980. This occurred, however, at the outset of the early 1980s recession and had no major industrial relations impact. Throughout the 1980s and early 1990s direct taxation as measured by the standard rate of income tax fell gradually.

In fact, the period of Conservative government has not been one of thoroughgoing low inflation. A particular problem has been a tendency for wages to rise rapidly in skilled sectors during economic recoveries. This has largely been a result of the neglect of training and other elements of skill provision during recessions, leading to skill shortages which firms seek to resolve through wage rises (see chapter 17). Since the rises cannot lead to an increase in skilled labour supply, there has been inflation.

The government and business have no counter to this process other than an attempt to prevent pay rises in one establishment or locality from spreading to others. As chapter 5 shows, for many years a rule of comparability governed much pay-fixing in both unionized and non-union sectors. According to this norm, workers are entitled to the wages and conditions enjoyed by workers in other firms and localities who are doing what is considered to be broadly comparable work. For unions and workers a norm of 'fairness' requires this, and workers feel a grievance if their pay drops demonstrably below that of people doing similar work. Employers in non-union situations have, however, often followed the same norm, partly because even in the absence of unions, perceived unfairness may cause low morale. Also, whether unionized or not, large firms often seek to insulate themselves from fluctuations in the external labour market, by re-cruiting at only certain points and by seeking to retain employee loyalty and long service. They are then likely to use pay scales for purposes other than pure labour-market responses: for example, to indicate the structure of the organizational hierarchy and to build career paths (Brown 1989). Across an industry, companies may seek stable inter-company rates of pay in order to protect their internal labour markets from external competition.

There are also economic arguments for restraining the extent to which workers' pay rises depend on their individual, or their com-pany's, productivity rather than sectoral or national rates. It is often difficult to allocate accurately the source of a productivity improve-ment. Even if it is possible to do so, scope for improvement or even scope for measurement of improvement may vary considerably be-tween the departments of an individual firm, and there could be considerable distortion if the pay of employees were to be affected by these characteristics.

There are also reasons for resisting wide pay disparities between different regions of a country. If wages rise consistently slower in poor districts, consumption declines, local shops and other services decline, and unemployment rises. Meanwhile, inflation takes place in the prosperous areas. Labour cannot respond easily to market signals by relocating, as the movement of people across regions of the country is cumbersome and disruptive. It does take place; over the years the population of Britain's prosperous regions has grown strongly through migration, and that of poor districts has declined. (This in turn creates a need for expenditure on new social infrastruc-ture – roads, schools, hospitals, etc. – in the prosperous areas; and for expenditure in the poor areas to try to counteract decline.) But population movement does not take place quickly enough to prevent unemployment in some areas and labour shortages and inflation in others.

If this is to be avoided, it is necessary for expanding sectors and regions not to consume all the proceeds of all their increased wealth. Relatively standard national terms and conditions achieved by collective bargaining, and levels of taxation that enable public-service employees to benefit from growth, can contribute to this. In some countries, mechanisms of this kind are more-or-less built in to the bargaining system. In Britain they have never worked very effectively, because neither unions nor employers have been organized in a sufficiently coordinating way. In recent years the departure from what elements of such a structure did exist, while it has enabled some problems to be tackled (as discussed below), has intensified the vulnerability to inflation of some skill-specific, sectoral and geographical labour markets. This has in turn required an even sterner macroeconomic counter-inflationary stance.

Dismantling inter-company collective bargaining

This discussion indicates a further important characteristic of the drive to weaken organization and coordination: the decline of collective bargaining above the level of the company. This is discussed in several other chapters in this volume. We here concentrate on its place in government economic management. Within the public service, government has encouraged the disbanding of national pay settlements and the use of comparisons between public- and private-sector pay to determine the scope for rises in the latter, as Winchester and Bach describe (chapter 10). In the economy at large it has encouraged a general breakdown of institutional arrangements in general (Purcell 1993), and has specifically discouraged the use of comparability in mechanisms for conciliation and arbitration. An early casualty of the 1979 government was the Standing Commission on Pay Comparability that had been established by the previous Labour government to apply comparability criteria to public-sector disputes. This was abolished in 1980.

In 1982 the government formally denounced the UK's earlier adherence to Convention 94 of the International Labour Organization that commits signatory governments to observing parity with terms and conditions in the private sector in their role as a public employer (Davies and Freedland 1993: 540–1). Between 1986 and 1993 it gradually reduced the powers of and abolished the Wages Councils that for most of the twentieth century maintained minimum standards in designated low-paid industries (see chapter 18).

Meanwhile, its general national strategy of allowing firms and industries in difficulties to decline led to major divergences in the fortunes of different regions. The fact that several industries were in a very non-competitive position combined with the British electoral situation to intensify these developments. Conservative support is increasingly concentrated in the heavily populated south of the UK, and the British first-past-the-post voting system by geographical constituencies is one that rewards geographically concentrated parties and imposes little need to attract support nationally. In general, therefore, the economies and living standards of the poorer regions declined sharply during the early 1980s recession, while those in the south climbed.

It was in this context that inter-firm bargaining virtually collapsed. Again, several other causes apart from government policy came together to produce this outcome. First, the strains of maintaining national structures, or even company structures, of pay when local labour markets were becoming so divergent, were often unsupportable. Despite the arguments above concerning the damaging effects of wide regional pay disparities, if regional fortunes begin to diverge widely then workers in poorer regions stand a chance of employment only if their relative wages are reduced. Pressures to do this broke several industry-wide agreements.

Second, as already noted, new managerial doctrines of the promotion of company culture and the pursuit of human resource management led companies to want to depart from inter-firm arrangements and stamp their own identity on their payment systems. Third, large companies with complex internal bureaucracies were increasingly trying to resolve their problems of inflexibility by granting local plant or divisional managers limited autonomy over pay and conditions. Managers might be given a cash budget and a set of basic rules, and told to resolve their labour-market problems how they liked within that frame. This could lead to considerable divergence in practice; it certainly created a disincentive for firms to cooperate in inter-firm agreements.

Political preference, regional divergence, managerial strategies and the almost unmanageable changes happening in the economy therefore combined to weaken the role of organizations and further push moves to resolve British stability crises towards the left-hand pole of the curve in figure 8.2.

The fate of 'good' industrial relations

The central labour-market aim of the Conservative governments has been a certain kind of flexibility. This means reducing as much as possible all restrictions on the deployment of labour, whether from unions, employers' organizations or protective legislation giving workers rights either at work or against its loss. In all this, as in the law reforms, the government's central aim has been to restore the initiative to employers (as opposed to either unions or the government itself). In so doing, it is concerned to ensure that employers' freedom is strongly structured by market incentives.

The state's preferences among alternative models can be seen in the choices government has itself made when given the opportunity: it has gone primarily for an employment relationship based on numerical flexibility (especially temporary and part-time contracts), a low level of established rights, and avoidance of stipulated minimum standards. This can be traced from the denunciation of ILO resolution 94 to the refusal to sign the Social Protocol to the Treaty of Maastricht.

For many years British governments maintained a concept of 'good industrial relations', which they claimed to follow in their own conduct as employers and which they imparted to other employers through the practices of national conciliation and mediation agencies and in the general stance of the Ministry of Labour and its successor the Department of Employment (DE). This approach was prominent during the Second World War, when firms could only acquire government contracts for war equipment if they recognized unions and followed other 'progressive' employment policies. At the other end of the pre-1979 period, similar concepts were embodied in the *Industrial Relations Code of Practice* of the Conservative government of 1970–4 (Department of Employment 1972), even though this was within the context of an overall approach to industrial relations considered by the unions to be hostile to them.

There is no longer a government concept of 'good' industrial relations. There is no expressed preference for union recognition, or for the provision of stable conditions of employment.

The abandonment of tripartitism

As part of the same logic, government has gradually abandoned most elements of tripartite cooperation and has ceased to encourage any bipartite cooperation among unions and employers. This has happened partly at the political level (Middlemas 1991). Ministers rarely see union leaders; and early in the 1980s the government announced that it was ending the previous principle of twentieth-century government whereby trade union leaders were often members of government inquiries, committees, commissions and so forth. (The aim of this earlier practice had been to ensure some kind of voice for representatives of working people in a system otherwise dominated by business, the professions and professional politicians.) Henceforth, it was announced, unions would be involved in public business only where matters concerning them as organizations were concerned. Unions' contact with government, especially contact through meetings and personal visits, has declined steadily since 1979 (Mitchell 1987; Middlemas 1991; Marsh 1992).

Apart from these ad hoc developments, at the outset of the 1980s there were four main channels for tripartitism: the National Economic Development Council (NEDC), the Manpower Services Commission (MSC), the Advisory, Conciliation and Arbitration Council (ACAS) and the Health and Safety Commission (HSC). The fourth has been largely uncontroversial. The varied fates of the other three will be considered in turn.

The National Economic Development Council   Tripartite institutions in Britain do not have a good record of longevity, incoming governments tending to break up the arrangements of their predecessors. The NEDC was remarkable for having been established in 1961 but enduring until the late 1980s. It was often argued that it survived because it avoided involvement in controversial issues like incomes policy or industrial relations law reform. What it did was to provide a regular forum, including an elaborate network of sectoral and other subcommittees, that brought government, unions and employers together on a regular basis to consider problems of the British economy as a whole and of individual branches or special issues. Its associated staff, the National Economic Development Office (NEDO), produced independent evaluations of issues, drew up and analysed statistics, and kept the three partners mutually informed by the same sets of data and argument.

The Thatcher government retained the NEDC for most of the 1980s. Its meetings were often acrimonious, as the gulf between unions and government was so wide. Its business increasingly lacked point because government had neither industrial policy nor tasks for the union and employer organizations that could provide a serious agenda. CBI representatives, although they would often criticize government policy, were careful to avoid the political trap of responding to TUC overtures to make joint statements and draw up joint reports that might isolate a government which employers in general favoured.

It must also be remembered that during this period the CBI was fighting a rearguard action against the Institute of Directors (IoD), which was far closer to the circle of advisers around the Prime Minister and was far more an aggressively ideological right-wing propaganda body rather than an expert organization that looked at statistics and discussed them judiciously with trade union leaders (Grant 1993: 110–18). The IoD was not part of NEDC and did not want to be. It did not believe in talking to unions, and did not believe that government should have any involvement in business matters. It could therefore wrong-foot the CBI in the eyes of the business community if the Confederation were seen to be consorting with the TUC and lending unions an influence and a legitimacy that they were rapidly losing.

The NEDC therefore achieved even less than in the past, though the NEDO's independent reports continued to be significant. During the 1987 election campaign the Conservatives announced that NEDC would in future meet far less often. Then, in 1992, the Chancellor of the Exchequer abruptly announced that it would be abolished altogether. The NEDO staff were disbanded. Nothing was done to replace the organization. There is no longer any forum, formal or informal, at which government, unions and employers meet together to consider economic questions.

The Manpower Services Commission   The MSC had been established in 1973 by a Conservative government to give new impetus to training and manpower policy. It formed part of a general policy move of that time, overlapping a Labour and a Conservative government, to take the central functions of the DE – manpower policy (training and employment services), conciliation services and occupational health and safety – and place them under tripartite control. This resulted in the formation of the MSC, ACAS and the HSC respectively. The aim was to involve employers' and workers' organizations more deeply in the administration of labour-market and industrial relations issues. It was a highly corporatist concept, based on Swedish models. Representatives of government, the CBI and the TUC or their affiliates participated in these bodies.

The role of the MSC expanded slowly under the subsequent Labour government. After 1979, as expected, its role was downgraded. Its budget was cut and the number of Industrial Training Boards (ITBs) under its responsibility considerably reduced. However, from around 1983 the situation changed dramatically, and for four years the MSC became the most dynamic and proactive agency of government. It was being used for two purposes: first, to secure changes in the education system that the Department of Education and Science seemed reluctant to pursue; second, to secure reductions in the wages of trainees and increases in the pressures imposed on young unemployed people to seek training rather than unemployment pay.

Both purposes were controversial: the former between government departments, the MSC being within the remit of the DE; the latter between government and employers on one side, the unions on the other. The education and training activities generated a wide range of new policies and functions, and increasing parts of the education budget were transferred to the Commission. Its initiatives, initially limited to vocational education as such, began increasingly to affect the normal school curriculum. All this was happening outside the scope of education policy as such, and ministers at Employment found it useful to have the active support of CBI and TUC representatives in their critique of the lack of vocational preparation in the education system. In 1986 an education white paper, *Working Together: Education and Training* (HM Government 1986), issued jointly by the Departments of Education and Employment spelt out the major role for the MSC and its programmes in the government's education and vocational training strategies.

The tendency of government to use MSC training schemes in a series of attempts to reduce the wages of young workers obviously met with far less agreement within the Commission, as union representatives were strongly opposed (Davies and Freedland 1993: 541–5; 601–6; Marsh 1992: 125–34). There were in fact frequent moves by some unions to seek a TUC withdrawal from MSC on these grounds. However, it was through their participation that unions were able to ensure that trade union membership was discussed in MSC training programmes for new workers, and more generally to sustain a role in an important and growing area of government policy at a time when they were otherwise losing their public place.

Then, in 1987, policy changed abruptly. The Conservative general election manifesto for that year, besides promising a reduced role for the NEDC, also declared the party's intention to reduce union representation on the MSC while increasing that of employers. It would also restrict the Commission's role to training, removing from it responsibility for the employment services which earlier policy had sought to associate with training in order to establish a comprehensive manpower policy agency. Davies and Freedland (1993: 610) argue that a major motive for the change may have been the government's intention to pursue more rigorous policies than the tripartite MSC would have supported to exclude categories of unemployed persons from entitlement to benefit. The Employment Act 1988 implemented these changes, renaming the MSC the Training Commission to demonstrate the abandonment of the broader concept of manpower policy and placing it under the direct control of the DE.

But within the year policy had again changed fundamentally. The new commission adopted a programme of job experience for the long-term unemployed which some unions saw as coming close to labour conscription. The TUC Congress later in the year voted to boycott the commission while this policy was in force. The government responded with the Employment Act 1989, abolishing the commission and replacing it with a Training Agency directly controlled by government. Meanwhile the Department of Education had regained the initiative in education policy with its development of plans for a national curriculum and the Education Reform Act 1988. These would gradually squeeze out many of the MSC's schemes, and reordered government views on the need to challenge the education department's priorities.

As discussed in chapter 17, within another two years the Training Agency itself had been abolished and an uncoordinated national network of local Training and Enterprise Councils (TECs), or Local Enterprise Councils in Scotland, established in its place. These were to be run by boards of local business leaders, chosen as individuals and not as representatives, able to coopt a small number of local trade union leaders and local education authorities' chiefs or head teachers – all serving as individuals, not as representatives – if they so chose. In practice only a tiny number have done so (Marsh 1992: 133). The link between manpower policy and industrial relations organizations had now been completely severed.

The Advisory, Conciliation and Arbitration Service ACAS was established in the early 1970s as part of the same wave of corporatist thinking that informed the establishment of the MSC, though as Davies and Freedland point out (1993: 409), it was also an attempt at rescuing the old 'voluntarist' model of industrial relations from government attempts to impose ideas of incomes policy on its own mediating institutions. The ideas for ACAS developed within the CBI and TUC, seeking a means of establishing such institutions free of the DE. It was, however, formally set up by the Labour government of 1974. It brought together a wide range of dispute resolution services that government has provided either systematically or in an ad hoc view for over a century, but again under tripartite rather than purely governmental control.

ACAS continues to exist and do its work. It has, however, lost a considerable number of functions. The whole comparability exercise discussed above, which had been a major part of its burden, was dropped. Many of its informal adjudication activities were replaced by law. It also lost its ability to adjudicate in disputes over union claims for recognition, though this had long been an ineffective part of its remit. At the time of writing, ACAS was coming under pressure to adopt a more commercial approach to its services, even though research has repeatedly shown that ACAS advice was strongly valued by managements and unions and that the free and independent nature of the advice was very important in giving it status and legitimacy (Kessler 1992).

Conclusions

The combined effects of all these strategies has been to move Britain sharply towards the left-hand pole of figure 8.2. There can be debate whether the result has been a new stability as predicted there. Inflation has certainly been reduced. Trends in industrial relations indicators such as productivity and strikes have also been widely seen as indicating improvement. However, as chapters 13 and 14 below show, it is not clear whether there has been any greater change here than occurred in many other countries. More fundamentally, how far the underlying dynamics of the workplace have changed is also open to serious question.

In relation to the state's management of the economy, four issues may be highlighted. First, as we have seen, the counter-inflationary strategy has remained fragile. In particular, the laissez faire approach to regional labour markets, which is itself central to the general strategy, produces regional imbalances and skill shortages that create inflation at early stages of recoveries.

Second, heavy dependence on 'pure labour market' (that is level of employment) means for containing inflation, seem to imply continuing suboptimal employment levels and reliance on 'flexible' or insecure forms of employment that do not create a base for sustained growth.

Third, because the counter-inflation strategy embodies its own weaknesses, there has been excessive reliance on holding down pay (perhaps by reducing numbers of employees) in the public sector as a means of support for the strategy. Not only does this weaken morale among public employees, but as more and more of the public sector is privatized it leaves a rather small tail trying to wag the dog, especially as most privatized corporations remain monopolies or oligopolies.

Finally, the erosion of the institutional base of the economy, which is fundamental to the leftward shift along the figure 8.2 curve, may have wider implications. In saying this it must be recalled that the state of British institutions in 1979, in the trough of figure 8.2, was also highly suboptimal. Yet recent shifts diminish the capacity of the British economy to make more general uses of cooperative and coordinating institutions, not only between business and labour but even within business. This occurs because, for example, as supra-company bargaining declines, so employers' associations decline, and so does the capacity of business interests to engage in any collective-goods provision, apart from lobbying for their own interests. This may diminish the business cooperation that would otherwise lead to enhanced performance in occupational training, research and development, joint export promotion, and other issues in a manner common in some other economies. The loss of both a strategic and a representative voice in vocational training policy as TECs replaced the MSC network is an outstanding example of the price that has been paid in order to 'deinstitutionalize' the British industrial relations system and, by extension, the British economy.

References

Adeney, M. and Lloyd, J. 1986: *The Miners' Strike, 1984–5.* London: Routledge and Kegan Paul.

Brown, W. 1989: Managing Remuneration. In K. Sisson (ed.), *Personnel Management in Britain.* Oxford: Blackwell.

Calmfors, L. and Driffill, D. J. 1988: Bargaining Structure, Corporatism and Macro-Economic Performance. *Economic Policy*, 6, 1, 13–62.

Castles, F. 1987: Neo-Corporatism and the Happiness Index. *European Journal of Political Research*, 15, 381–93.

Crouch, C. 1977: Class Conflict and the Industrial Relations Crisis. London: Heinemann.

Crouch, C. 1985: Conditions for Trade Union Wage Restraint. In L. N. Lindberg and C. S. Maier (eds), *The Politics of Inflation and Economic Stagnation.* Washington, DC: Brookings Institution.

Crouch, C. 1993: *Industrial Relations and European State Traditions.* Oxford: Clarendon Press.

Crouch, C. 1994: Beyond Corporatism: The Impact of Company Strategy. In R. Hyman and A. Ferner (eds), *New Frontiers in European Industrial Relations.* Oxford: Blackwell.

Davies, P. and Freedland, M. 1993: *Labour Legislation and Public Policy.* Oxford: Clarendon Press.

Dell'Aringa, C. and Lodovici, M. S. 1992: Industrial Relations and Economic Performance. In T. Treu (ed.), *Participation in Public Policy-Making: The Role of Trade Unions and Employers' Associations.* Berlin: Walter de Gruyter.

Department of Employment, 1972: *Industrial Relations Code of Practice.* London: HMSO.

Donovan 1968: Royal Commission on Trade Unions and Employers' Associations. *Report.* Cmnd 3623. London: HMSO.

Fine, B. and Harris, L. 1985: *The Peculiarities of the British Economy.* London: Lawrence and Wishart.

Fox, A. 1985: *History and Heritage.* London: Allen and Unwin.

Gallie, D. 1988: Employment, Unemployment and Social Stratification. In D. Gallie (ed.), *Employment in Britain.* Oxford: Blackwell.

Grant, W. 1993: *Business and Politics in Britain*, 2nd edn. Basingstoke: Macmillan.

HM Government 1986: *Working Together: Education and Training.* Cmnd 9823. London: HMSO.

Ingham, G. K. 1984: *Capitalism Divided?* London: Macmillan.

Kahn-Freund, O. 1954: Legal Framework. In A. Flanders and H. Clegg (eds), *The System of Industrial Relations in Great Britain.* Oxford: Blackwell.

Kaldor, N. 1982: *The Scourge of Monetarism*. Oxford: Oxford University Press.

Kessler, I. 1992: An Independent Look at ACAS' Advisory Services. *Personnel Management*, March, 45–7.

Kjellberg, A. 1992: Sweden: Can the Model Survive? In R. Hyman and A. Ferner (eds), *Industrial Relations in the New Europe*. Oxford: Blackwell.

McCarthy, W. E. J. 1992: The Rise and Fall of Collective Laissez Faire. In W. E. J. McCarthy (ed.), *Legal Intervention in Industrial Relations*. Oxford: Blackwell.

Marsh, D. 1992: *The New Politics of British Trade Unionism*. Basingstoke: Macmillan.

Middlemas, K. 1979: *Politics in Industrial Society*. London: Deutsch.

Middlemas, K. 1991: *Power, Competition and the State, iii. The End of the Postwar Era: Britain since 1974*. Basingstoke: Macmillan.

Mitchell, N. 1987: Changing Pressure Group Politics: The Case of the TUC, 1976–1984. *British Journal of Political Science*, 17.

Olson, M. 1982: *The Rise and Decline of Nations: Economic Growth, Stagflation and Social Rigidities*. New Haven, CT: Yale University Press.

Purcell, J. 1993: The End of Institutional Industrial Relations. *Political Quarterly*, 64, 1, 6–23.

Soskice, D. 1990: Wage Determination: The Changing Role of Institutions in Advanced Industrialized Countries. *Oxford Review of Economic Policy*, 6, 4, 1–23.

Wilkinson, F. and Turner, H. A. 1972: The Wage–Tax Spiral and Labour Militancy. In D. Jackson, H. A. Turner and F. Wilkinson, *Do Trade Unions Cause Inflation?* Cambridge: Cambridge University Press.

9

The State: Labour Law and Industrial Relations

Linda Dickens and Mark Hall

Introduction

The first forerunner of this textbook, published in 1954, contained
the since oft-quoted view that:

> There is, perhaps, no major country in the world in which the law has
> played a less significant role in the shaping of industrial relations than
> in Great Britain and in which today the law and legal profession have
> less to do with labour relations. (Kahn-Freund 1954: 44)

In the 1970 textbook Hugh Clegg was able to repeat this dictum
with the comment 'this remains true despite substantial additions to
statute law' (Clegg 1970: 344), and disposed of labour law in just
two pages. Students coming to industrial relations in the mid-1980s
found that not only did the contemporary text in this historical line
(Bain 1983) have two lengthy chapters on the law, but that it had
been necessary to produce a companion text, *Labour Law in Britain*
(Lewis 1986).

Faced with writing about labour law and industrial relations in the
current volume we have had to abandon any hope of providing
comprehensive coverage of statute law and how it is being interpreted in the courts, or of detailing the development of the law which
has led to the swelling textbook coverage indicated above.[1] Rather,
we aim to provide an overview of the current legal framework as it
has developed since 1979 and some understanding of what went
before. We focus not only on the rationale for particular types of
legal intervention but also on the impact which that intervention has

had on industrial relations practice, thereby contributing to the debate concerning the role of law in industrial relations.

Our starting point of 1979 corresponds to the beginning of a period of unbroken Conservative government which has seen frequent, far-reaching and controversial changes to Britain's labour law framework. The period has seen the final death of voluntarism, under which law was essentially an adjunct to an autonomous, self-regulated system of industrial relations. The government's sustained 'step by step' legislative programme, comprising a major statute every two years or so, has dramatically increased the extent of legal regulation in British industrial relations. But the sheer *volume* of labour legislation is not the central issue. The traditional emphasis on voluntarism did not imply the complete absence of statutory intervention. As is made clear later in the chapter, action to legalize basic trade union activities in the face of common law liabilities was central to the voluntary system. Auxiliary legislation to support and supplement collective bargaining (including measures to regulate the terms and conditions of vulnerable groups of workers, the individual employment relationship and health and safety standards) was seen as consistent with the tradition of voluntarism. It is the *nature* and *function* of the legislation enacted since 1979 which has transformed the legal environment in which relations between employers, employees and trade unions are conducted.

The major thrust of the legislation since 1979 is clear: to weaken trade union power, to assert individualist rather than collective values and to reassert employer prerogative. As Wedderburn (1986: 84–5) comments, 'for the first time in a century . . . labour law is directed not towards amendment or reform of the collective bargaining system . . . It points in a different direction. It does not accept the legitimacy of collective labour power'. A much greater emphasis than in previous periods has been placed on law in the pursuit of government economic and social objectives, with particular fiscal and economic policies (for example, monetarism and reliance on the operation of the 'free market') helping to shape the labour law agenda and with law being seen as a key instrument facilitating labour-market restructuring. The stated aim of many of the government's labour law measures has been to improve the operation of the labour market. Unions' wage bargaining strategies were held to have an adverse impact on employment: workers were 'pricing themselves out of jobs'. As unions' bargaining strength was considered to stem from their immunities in relation to industrial action and the 'coercive power' of the closed shop, these became central targets of the government's legislative programme. 'Fair wage' mechanisms and the wages councils were seen as creating inflexibility in pay and were abolished. The government also tends to view the statutory rights of individual employees not as essential minimum standards but as 'burdens on business' (particularly in respect of small employers) which deter the employment of more people. This belief underpins the sustained emphasis on the 'deregulation' of the employment relationship.

The obvious affinity of the legislative programme (and the statements of ministers in presenting it) with the ideology of the so-called 'new right' has led some to suggest that ideological considerations have been to the fore in shaping the legislation, with the work of Hayek being seen as a key influence (Wedderburn 1986). Others place rather more emphasis on pragmatic, often short-term considerations (Auerbach 1990). It is likely that the answer is not ideology *or* pragmatism but both, with an ideological impulse finding expression opportunistically. Davies and Freedland (1993: 521) suggest that the measures against the closed shop were more ideologically driven than those aimed at industrial action, where opportunistic considerations played a greater part. Opportunism can be found both in terms of responding to particular industrial disputes and in the influence of political considerations (electoral and internal party). What is clear, as we shall see, is that the government's justification for intervention and legislative change came to rest increasingly on unsubstantiated statements of ideological belief rather than empirical research.

In seeing 1979 as the start of a new era in labour law, it is important not to neglect continuities with earlier periods. The voluntary system (as noted in chapters 2 and 8) had been under strain in the 1960s and 1970s as tensions emerged between 'collective laissez faire' and the state's increasingly active role in the area of economic management. The 1969 White Paper *In Place of Strife* had indicated that a Labour government was prepared to consider legal restrictions on industrial action; the Conservatives' Industrial Relations Act 1971 (IR Act) was an ambitious but unsuccessful attempt at the comprehensive legal regulation of industrial relations. A modified form of voluntarism – but one which embraced significant legislative innovation – had been reasserted under the Labour governments in the 1970s.

Moreover, the government has also had to act within the constraints imposed by the UK's membership of the European Community. In particular, there is a clear tension between provisions introduced into domestic labour law to comply with the requirements of EC law and those reflecting the government's 'home-grown' policy objectives. The EC's collective labour law agenda in particular predominantly reflects mainstream continental regulatory models with a heavy emphasis on the statutory regulation of employment relations (see Hall 1994). EC measures pre-dating the election of the Conservative government have continued to have a significant – and, in the government's eyes, disruptive – impact on its domestic labour law programme. As we discuss later, the need to conform to EC legislation has placed limits on the extent to which the government can pursue its deregulatory ambitions. In a succession of instances, the UK government has been forced – by threatened or actual infringement proceedings before the European Court of Justice – to take legislative steps it would rather have avoided, in order to comply with EC requirements. In each case, the government has adopted a 'routinely minimalist response' (Davies and Freedland 1993: 583) often coupled with deregulatory measures. While generally opposing further EC social policy intervention, UK ministers have also found it politic to accede to the adoption of certain new directives proposed under the social charter action programme. Thus, a significant proportion of the Trade Union Reform and Employment Rights Act 1993 reflects EC requirements.

Despite the importance of EC legislation for UK labour law developments, its impact has been confined to certain areas such as sex discrimination, pay equality and employment protection. Key aspects of the government's industrial relations agenda – especially the restriction of the freedom to take industrial action and the statutory regulation of trade union government and administration – have essentially been unrestrained by EC requirements. On occasion, international standards which *have* impinged on the government's scope to pursue its objectives in these areas, primarily ILO conventions and the Council of Europe's European Social Charter 1961, have been 'denounced' by the UK. On a range of issues, the UK has been held to be in breach of international standards to which it remains a signatory. Unlike the EC, however, neither the ILO nor the Council of Europe has effective mechanisms for enforcing rulings against offending countries.

The remainder of the chapter is in three main parts, discussing legal intervention over the 1980s and 1990s in terms of the relationships between employer and worker, employer and trade union, and trade union and member. In each case, the rationale, nature and impact of the law is addressed. Any such division risks playing down the fact that a particular measure can have multiple intentions and more than one site of impact. This should also be borne in mind in respect of table 9.1 which lists the relevant statutes and indicates their key provisions, categorizing them according to the area they sought to address. The chapter concludes by offering an overall assessment of the significance of the changing pattern of British labour law.

The Employer–Worker Relationship

Rationale for legal intervention

A 1986 White Paper asked why it is 'necessary to depart from the basic principle that terms and conditions of employment are matters to be determined by the employer and the employees concerned (where appropriate through their representatives) in the light of their own individual circumstances' (DE 1986: para. 7.2). One argument is that statutory regulation that constrains the freedom of the contracting parties is justified because it counteracts the inequality of bargaining power which is inherent in the employment relationship. The individual employee's position is one of subordination, though the asymmetry in power is clothed 'by that indispensable figment of the legal mind known as the contract of employment' (Kahn-Freund 1983: 18).

Under the voluntarist system collective bargaining was seen as the primary method of addressing this inequality and the regulatory function of law was limited. Statutory regulation was not used to provide a code of substantive rules to govern terms and conditions of employment, but played a supplementary role, filling in the gaps left in collective bargaining protection. This generally meant statutory protections for those groups (predominantly women and young people and those in certain trades) who fell outside the ambit of collective organization.

This supplementary protection historically concerned health and safety standards, the method and calculation of wage payment,

Table 9.1   Key legislative changes, 1979–1994

Statute/statutory instrument	*Employer–worker relationship*
Unfair Dismissal (Variation of Qualifying Period) Order 1979	qualifying period increased from 6 months to 1 year
Employment Protection (Handling of Redundancies) Variation Order 1979	
Employment Act 1980	protection against unfair dismissal further weakened, including qualifying period of two years for workers in small firms existing maternity rights limited new right to time off for antenatal care
Transfer of Undertakings (Protection of Employment) Regulations 1981	continuity of employment and existing terms and conditions where change of employer*
Employment Act 1982	
Equal Pay (Amendment) Regulations 1983	equal pay for work of equal value introduced*

Employer–union relationship	Union–member relationship
statutory redundancy consultation period reduced	
enforceability of closed shop restricted	public funds for union secret ballots secret ballots
statutory procedures for union recognition and extension of established terms and conditions repealed	protection against unreasonable exclusion or expulsion from union membership
picketing away from own workplace unlawful	
secondary industrial action restricted	
right to hold secret ballots on employers' premises	
consultation with recognized unions over business transfers★	
enforceability of closed shop further restricted	
unions – as opposed to union officials – liable for unlawful industrial action	
statutory definition of trade dispute narrowed, limiting the scope for lawful industrial action	
more selective dismissal of strikers permitted	
ban on contractual arrangements and industrial action designed to ensure work is done by unionized companies or workers	

Table 9.1   *(cont.)*

Statute/statutory instrument	*Employer–worker relationship*
Trade Union Act 1984	
Unfair Dismissal (Variation of Qualifying Period) Order 1985	qualifying period increased to two years
Wages Act 1986	law on payment of wages and deductions reformed scope and functions of wages councils reduced
Sex Discrimination Act 1986	restrictions on women's working hours and other conditions removed coverage of sex discrimination legislation extended★
Employment Act 1988	
Employment Act 1989	equal treatment for men and women regarding access to employment, vocational training vocational training and promotion and working conditions★

Employer–union relationship	Union–member relationship
industrial action unlawful without secret ballot	five-yearly secret ballots for union executive committee elections union political funds subject to ten-yearly secret ballots
discriminatory clauses in collective agreements void*	
dismissal for non-membership of a union prohibited in all circumstances all industrial action to enforce union membership unlawful separate strike ballots required for each workplace involved	right of union members to seek court orders to restrain unballoted industrial action disciplinary action by unions against members refusing to take part in industrial action prohibited right of members to inspect union accounts postal, independently scrutinized ballots for election of union executive members, president and general secretaries Commissioner for the Rights of Trade Union Members established to assist members in legal action against unions
right to time off for trade union duties narrowed	

Table 9.1 *(cont.)*

Statute/statutory instrument	Employer–worker relationship
	protective restrictions on employment of women and young people repealed small firms exempted from requirement to provide written statement of disciplinary procedures
Employment Act 1990	
Trade Union and Labour Relations (Consolidation) Act 1992	
Trade Union Reform and Employment Rights Act 1993	employees' right to written information on terms and conditions extended* pregnancy and maternity rights improved* protection against dismissal for exercising statutory employment rights check-off subject to three-yearly written consent right to join any union organizing appropriate class of employee, overriding TUC Bridlington rules wages councils abolished

* Denotes legislative change prompted by EC requirements.

Employer–union relationship	Union–member relationship
unlawful for employers to refuse employment on grounds of union membership or non-membership, outlawing pre-entry closed shop	tighter strike ballot procedures CROTUM enabled to assist members alleging breach of union rules
all secondary industrial action unlawful	
unions liable for unlawful industrial action called by any union official – including shop stewards – and any union committee	
selective dismissal of employees taking unofficial industrial action permitted	
consolidated existing collective labour law provisions	consolidated existing trade union law provisions
unions to provide employers with at least seven days' notice of industrial action	postal, independently scrutinized ballots on industrial action and union mergers
citizen's right to seek court orders to restrain unlawful industrial action	ballot funding scheme phased out annual financial statements to members
redundancy and business transfer consultation requirements extended*	

and the level of wages in 'sweated trades' (Kahn-Freund 1983: 37–51; Hepple 1983a: 404–13). The mass of piecemeal legislation in the health and safety area gave way to a more comprehensive system following the Health and Safety at Work Act 1974, which emphasizes self-regulation within a framework of state inspection and enforcement.

In the 1960s and 1970s, individual contractual rights were supplemented increasingly by statutory rights, generally enforceable via a tripartite industrial tribunal system, linked to the ordinary court system (Dickens and Cockburn 1986). There was still no general statutory regulation of substantive terms and conditions such as minimum wages, holidays or hours of work, but there was a marked increase in the extent to which the law sought to restrict managerial prerogative in handling the employment relationship, particularly in the areas of recruitment (through discrimination law) and dismissal.

The previous gap-filling role of law gave way to a more 'universal' approach, albeit one which some argued was still in keeping with the voluntarist tradition in that employment rights were seen as constituting a statutory floor upon which collective bargaining might build (Wedderburn 1971: 8, 16). Rights relating to notice of termination, redundancy and unfair dismissals were enacted in the 1960s and 1970s and the Labour government's Employment Protection Act (EPA) 1975 'accomplished the crucial transition from a statutory floor of rights concerned primarily with the termination of employment to a statutory floor of rights concerned (also) with the content of the employment relationship' (Davies and Freedland 1984: 347).

The legal intervention of the 1960s and 1970s reflected also the importance attached to the role of individual legal rights in wider strategies of industrial relations reform, and the use of statutory regulation as a means of promoting efficient management and reducing industrial conflict. These additional rationales for legal intervention can be seen particularly in the redundancy payments and unfair dismissal legislation (Fryer 1973; Anderman 1986: 433; Dickens et al. 1985).

As noted in the introduction, legal intervention in the employment relationship reflected not only national concerns but also increased supra-national influence through the UK's membership of the European Community. In particular, developments in equal pay and sex discrimination legislation in the 1980s reflected EC influence as domestic law failed to keep pace with European Court of Justice's progressive development of Community law (Davies 1992: 343). In the 1970s and 1980s, European legal instruments (usually legally binding Directives) were used as a means of addressing disparities between levels (and costs) of employment protection legislation in different member states, and as part of the 'social dimension' of the single European market. These inevitably impinged on the nature and content of national law affecting the employer–worker relationship.

In contrast, Conservative governments in Britain from 1979 aimed to reduce or remove workers' statutory employment rights in order, it was argued, to promote employment, enhance the flexibility seen as crucial to competitive success, and to create 'a climate in which enterprise can flourish' (DE 1985, 1986, 1988, 1989). The 1980s thus saw a shift towards an increasingly 'contractualist' approach which, in the writings of the 'new right', treated freedom of contract as if it were a social fact rather than a conceptual apparatus of the law (for example, Hanson and Mather 1988: 39).

It was declared, however, that the government had 'no intention to dismantle the whole framework of employment protection in current legislation' (DE 1986: para. 7.2). What was at issue was redressing the balance between the needs of employers and employees, which the government felt to be too heavily weighted in favour of the employee and to impose cost burdens on employers (particularly small employers) which worked to the disadvantage of job creation, and thus of those not in employment. Similarly, it was felt that downward pressure on wages would stimulate employment growth. Measures (whether in labour law or in social security provision) which acted to provide a floor to wages were therefore seen as undesirable.

While committed to deregulation, the UK had to increase employment rights in some areas to meet its European obligations. The deregulation policy manifested itself in relation to Europe as opposition to a range of draft Directives which would have led to enhanced rights for workers (for example on parental leave, and rights for atypical workers); a refusal to adopt the Community Charter of Fundamental Social Rights (the 'Social Charter') and opposition to the broader social dimension of the single European market. Where measures could not be prevented, the UK government generally played a significant part in the dilution of European proposals (apart from mainstream health and safety measures) and/or sought to give effect to them in a minimalist way. This latter approach led to the UK being charged by the Commission with lack of effective implementation, and the need for further legislation, for example in the areas of sex discrimination and equal pay.

Employment rights and deregulation

Currently, individual statutory employment rights include the right to a minimum period of notice of termination; a statement of principal terms and conditions of the contract of employment, and of discipline and grievance procedures; the right to receive an itemized pay statement; the right to a statement of reason for dismissal; the right not to be unfairly dismissed; the right not to be unfairly discriminated against on grounds of race or sex; the right to maternity pay and the right to return to work after leave for childbirth; a right to time off for various public and trade union duties and for ante-natal care; a right to equal pay and other contractual terms as between men and women; the right to a severance payment in the event of redundancy; rights relating to trade union membership and activity, and to non-membership; and rights on the transfer of undertakings. There are in addition general health and safety at work protections.

This list is not so different from that which applied in 1979. Some areas remain virtually unaffected by direct deregulation, notably protection from sex and race discrimination. What is notable here is rather a failure to adopt the extensive reform proposals suggested for strengthening the existing legislation or making it more user friendly (such as EOC 1990). Indirectly, however, various deregulatory measures have had a disproportionately adverse impact on women. Further, a levelling down approach rather than a general improvement in standards was adopted by the government, to bring about the equality urged by the EC (Deakin 1990). One clear change is the abolition of wages councils in 1994, which at the time covered some 2.5 million employees, mainly women. The EPA 1975 had increased the powers of these bodies; in the Wages Act 1986 they were reduced substantially. As discussed in chapter 18, weakening of the wages councils' powers was driven by a concern that they set unduly high wages; a major effect was the worsening of women's pay.

The specific and limited nature of deregulation in the employer–worker sphere, which fell short of the government's rhetoric, can be explained by considering the experience of the individual employment rights enacted in the 1960s and 1970s. The scope and nature of protection they afforded was limited and, although presented as conferring benefits on employees and costs on employers, in practice they operated in ways which were beneficial to management (Dickens 1994).

Employees benefited from the enactment of individual employment rights in that many sought and gained redress at industrial tribunals in circumstances where previously none would have been available. Arbitrary 'hire and fire' approaches to discipline were curbed; 'due process' and corrective procedures were instituted. Those losing their jobs through no fault of their own are compensated. Pay structures have been revised and de-sexed with the use and threat of equal pay actions providing a lever to reform. The gender pay gap has narrowed. Discrimination legislation has curbed the most overt discriminatory practices, especially in recruitment; has indicated how less overt, taken for granted, practices can be discriminatory; and has given a push to the development of equal opportunity policies. Maternity rights facilitate mothers' interaction with the labour market.

These positive achievements must be seen in perspective, however. Research into the operation of major employment protection rights (for example, Daniel 1980; Hepple 1983b; Dickens et al. 1985; Gregory 1987; Leonard 1987), and the official tribunal statistics, show that individuals make limited use of their legal rights to seek redress, with limited success and with limited redress for those who are successful. Broader examination indicates little impact (direct or indirect) of the legislation in terms, for example, of enhanced employee job security or greater equality of opportunity in employment.

The unfair dismissal law does not go very far in challenging managerial prerogative and has afforded only limited protection to employees, putting a relatively low 'price on dismissal' rather than offering job security (Dickens et al. 1985; Anderman 1986). The redundancy legislation was only ever intended to compensate for job loss, not to prevent it; any talk of enhanced job security or 'job property rights' here is misplaced. As the dismissal law was applied by the tribunals it became clear that the job security interests of workers were recognized, but only so far as they are consistent with managerial objectives (Forrest 1980: 379; Dickens et al. 1985: 106).

Achievements of the discrimination and equal pay legislation appear slight when placed in the context of evidence of continuing discrimination and the continued pay and labour market disadvantage of women and ethnic minorities discussed in chapter 15. What law may achieve here is necessarily limited, but there are considerable weaknesses in the legal provisions, procedures and enforcement mechanisms, and in the assumptions underlying the legislation, which restrict its potential impact (Dickens 1992).

The extent to which statutory rights deliver gains for workers will be affected by the degree to which workers are able to avail themselves of such rights. Looked at narrowly, this relates to the ease of enforcing rights. Applicants are often relatively disadvantaged at tribunals (Dickens et al. 1985; Justice 1987) and inspectorates generally suffered a reduction in resources in the 1980s. But, more broadly, it relates to the context within which rights operate. Fiscal, welfare and social policies in the 1980s which reinforced women's domestic role and underpinned inequalities in the home, for example, served to undermine rights to equality at work without any deregulatory change to the legislation. A right to return after maternity leave is only a formal right for women with no access to childcare (Daniel 1980).

There is evidence that individual statutory rights have provided a floor for collectively bargained improvements (though there are also indications that the 'floor' may form a 'ceiling', with employer provision restricted to that required by legislation). For those outside the union-organized sectors, however, there is no bargaining to improve on the floor, nor any union to ensure the floor is actually provided. Employee statutory rights do not appear to have prevented employers from pursuing the competitive strategies they wished to adopt. In as much as compensation for job loss facilitates the smooth handling of redundancies and restructuring, they may have even been of assistance (Fryer 1973). Certainly, despite the legal protections afforded to their workers, employers retained sufficient scope in the 1980s to pursue quantitative and qualitative flexibility in labour utilization and to introduce technological and other change (Napier 1992; Dickens 1994).[2]

The impact of the legislation on employers has not been to weaken their control over hiring and firing (indeed it has served to legitimate it) but, rather, has tended to foster improvements in managerial efficiency in the handling of job terminations, and the development of 'good employment practice' or more professional personnel policies. This was seen, for example, in greater care being taken over recruitment, and in the development and reform of disciplinary rules and procedures (which remain managerially determined), with consequent restrictions on the freedom of action of lower-level management and enhanced importance, at least initially, of the personnel function (Dickens et al. 1985: 232–42, 256–8, 263–9). Similar impacts can be attributed to the discrimination legislation (Hitner et al. 1982; chapter 15 below).

Given this experience, deregulation has been concerned less with abolition than with reducing the scope of individual protections, though in some cases the substantive content also has been weakened. In practice such rights have never been 'universal'. Access to most rights, apart from discrimination and health and safety legislation, rests on 'employee' status and the legal tests do not always afford protection to those who, as subordinated labour, have need of it (Hepple 1986: 69–83; Collins 1990: 371–4). Employees who deviate from the so-called 'typical' or 'regular' employment pattern of full-time continuous work for one employer may find themselves unable to fulfil the various qualifying conditions, relating to continuous service and minimum hours, attached to the statutory rights (Dickens 1991).

In the 1980s the required length of continuous service was increased and the size of the so-called 'unregulated' labour force grew. Labour Force Survey data for 1988 suggested that after the changes some 55 per cent of part-time workers and 29 per cent of full-time workers were excluded from unfair dismissal (and other employment protections) because of the hours and length of service qualifications (Hakim 1989; Disney and Szyszczak 1989). Deregulation removed certain legal protections from those least likely to be organized in unions and covered by collective bargaining. Unorganized employment is now often unregulated employment (Dickens 1988).

The unfair dismissal legislation, introduced by a Conservative government in 1971, had been strengthened in the mid-1970s. Deregulation measures, in addition to a reduction in coverage, included special provisions relating to small firms; removed the burden of proof from the employer; and permitted lower compensation awards, and the introduction of various 'filters' and deterrents to proceeding with a case. These measures were designed to shift the balance of advantage towards the employer, unfair dismissal protection having been identified by the government as the statutory protection imposing the greatest burden on business (Evans et al. 1985: 2–3).

Impact

As noted above, the scope of employment protection rights was narrowed, access to rights was made more difficult and some protections were abolished. Clearly, the legal position of some workers deteriorated. The compensatory impact was to be found, the government contended, in job creation. The deregulation argument is that reduction in the legal protection afforded to workers will stimulate employment growth. A problem in seeking this kind of impact is that the deregulation measures were based more on ideological belief or neo-classical economic theory in terms of their impact on jobs, rather than on clear evidence as to any employment-inhibiting effects of the existing legal provisions. In fact, all the available empirical evidence indicated that employment protection legislation was not having a general employment-inhibiting effect.

Research showed no proven link between minimum wages levels and reduced employment prospects for young people (Keevash 1985: 229; Dolding 1988: 93; IPM 1991: 43). Numerous studies, covering firms of all sizes, including the smallest, failed to find that the employment protection legislation, as it stood prior to the deregulation measures, acted to prevent job creation or to inhibit recruitment (Daniel and Stilgoe 1978; Clifton and Tatton-Brown 1979; Evans et al. 1985; Curran 1989), or that changes made in the 1980s led to more jobs (Evans et al. 1985). Comparative surveys too found that British employers did not feel particularly constrained by employment protection legislation. In one 1985 survey, conducted prior to some of the main deregulation measures, Britain was the only country whose employers viewed obstacles to the termination of employment contracts as 'insignificant' (Emerson 1988: 791).

Even the government study most often pointed to as 'proof' that employment protection rights harm employment (DTI 1985) found that only a very small proportion of employers (15 out of 200) mentioned employment protection as something hindering their business without being prompted. Those few who did think it a problem did not see it as a very serious one (ibid.: 35; McCarthy 1992: 60).

Although legal change relating to the employer–worker relationship fits into the general picture of deregulation (or return to regulation by common law), it was a limited, pragmatic deregulation and the rhetoric often outstripped action. We have argued that this is perhaps to be expected given the limited nature of the protection afforded in practice by statutory rights and the fact that, while affording some protection to workers, employment protection rights also serve employer (and state) interests. Further, in a comparative European context, even after the increased statutory intervention of the 1970s, the employment relationship in the UK was still relatively unregulated by law; thus there was little to deregulate. The main target was the social regulation provided via collective organization and bargaining, to which we now turn.

The Relationship between Trade Union and Employer

At the heart of the union–employer relationship is collective bargaining. This section examines the way in which the law in Britain has been used to affect the extent and conduct of collective bargaining and the relative bargaining power of the parties. In particular, a key aim of government policy since 1979 has been to reduce trade union bargaining power *vis-à-vis* employers. The dismantling of statutory support for collective bargaining and the restriction of industrial action have been recurrent themes as the government's 'step by step' legislative programme evolved over the 1980s and early 1990s. First we examine the law relating to organizing in trade unions, gaining recognition from employers, and union security. We then turn to the freedom to take industrial action.

Union organization, recognition and security

Rationale for, and nature of, legal intervention   Throughout the twentieth century, until the late 1970s, public policy in Britain had been to encourage and support collective bargaining; joint regulation of the employment relationship was seen as the best method of conducting industrial relations (for example, Donovan 1968: para. 224).

Davies and Freedland (1984: 127) identify three fundamental provisions as the core of a legal policy designed to encourage the growth of collective bargaining. The first is the freedom to organize in trade unions, without interference by state or employer. This freedom of association includes protection of actual and potential trade unionists from discriminatory acts by employers because of trade union membership or activities. The social function of this positive right of association is distinct from that of the 'negative' right (the right *not* to be a union member). The former right supports collective bargaining, which the latter is 'designed to frustrate' (Donovan 1968: para. 599).[3] Second, the law can require or encourage employers to recognize unions and enter into joint regulation and can support and affect the 'quality' of the bargaining process. Third, legal provisions may ensure that collective bargaining agreements are observed.

The voluntarist tradition in Britain meant that there was very limited legal development in any of these three areas. The growth of collective bargaining in Britain owed little to legal supports, and the unions themselves generally did not seek legal intervention in this area. Law was used in an auxiliary fashion to lend support to collective bargaining (for example, state-funded voluntary dispute settlement machinery), but provisions were limited and often linked to attempts to tackle other problems (such as fair wages measures). In the public sector, certain corporations were under legal duties encouraging them to establish machinery for collective bargaining and for joint consultation. In practice, such provisions were more significant as expressions of policy than as a basis for enforceable legal obligations and stood alongside other state measures which fostered a climate supportive of collective bargaining (Dickens and Bain 1986: 80).

It was only following the Donovan Commission in the 1960s that direct legal support was enacted, linked to the reform of collective bargaining. The reform emphasis was evident in the Conservative government's IR Act 1971 which first enacted legal measures relating to the three fundamental provisions above. The Act provided rights of association, *and* dissociation; established a statutory procedure to determine recognition issues (including those referred by employers); and made collective agreements legally binding for the first time, a provision nullified in practice by the parties opting out (Weekes et al. 1975).

The Labour government's legislation of the mid-1970s was less reform orientated and more concerned with extending (albeit orderly) collective bargaining. The EPA 1975 enacted a new statutory recognition procedure and provisions (Schedule 11) whereby unions could require employers who were not parties to the agreements to observe collectively agreed or 'going rate' terms and conditions of employment. Legal enforceability of collective agreements was removed. Unions were given new statutory rights to have information needed for collective bargaining provided by the employer and to consultation over intended redundancies. Consultation rights in other areas (health and safety, transfer of undertakings, and occupational pensions) were enacted subsequently, with EC Directives providing some stimulus.

The EPA was also significant in seeking to protect and support trade union membership and activity at the workplace. The right to dissociate was removed; protection against dismissal or victimization (though not in recruitment) on the grounds of trade union membership or activity was strengthened, and, for the first time, lay officials of independent recognized trade unions had a right to paid time off for industrial relations and related training duties, and union members were given a right to unpaid time off to engage in union activities. One distinguished commentator described these measures as constructing a collective right to associate 'out of the bricks of certain "individual" employment rights' (Wedderburn 1976: 169).

Since 1979, legislative intervention in this area has had a different rationale. As noted, public policy support for collective bargaining has been reversed with a move away from collectivism in industrial relations towards individualism. Legislative intervention after 1979 was presented as enhancing individual freedom, freeing employers from abuses of union power and improving efficiency and competitiveness. The Conservative legislation emphasizes the individual rather than functional (collective) approach to freedom of association (von Prondynski 1984: 10). This clearly fits in with the government's wider objective of weakening unions in the workplace, moving the balance of power towards the employer by marginalizing collective bargaining and individualizing the employment relationship.[4]

The move to individualism Since 1979 legislative supports to collective bargaining have been removed. The recognition procedure was repealed almost immediately (except in Northern Ireland) as was Schedule 11, and the fair wages provisions were rescinded. The repeal of the recognition procedure did not simply return unions to the position prior to the 1970s, however, since their task of achieving recognition for collective bargaining was made harder by legislative curbs on certain tactics: the use of their collective strength in one employing organization to put pressure on another employer to recognize a union was made unlawful, as was action to secure clauses in commercial contracts which required contractors to recognize unions or employ union labour. Together with the reintroduction of the right not to be a union member (and enhanced remedies for those denied this right), the measures constituted 'rights to disorganize' (Lewis and Simpson 1982).

The Conservative governments of the 1980s also sought to promote non-unionism, enacting 'the most comprehensive and most effective statutory protection for non-union employees that we have ever had' (Tebbit, then Secretary of State, quoted in Wedderburn 1989: 23). Part of this involved the removal of legal support for compulsory union membership (the closed shop). The position inherited from the previous Labour government was that employers and unions were free to conclude union membership agreements under which workers could be required, as a condition of employment, to be a member of a specified trade union. Closed shops often developed with management support, following high levels of voluntary membership.

The legal undermining of the closed shop in the 1980s is a good example of the 'step by step' approach, with each statute building on its predecessor and pushing restriction a little further until the Employment Act (EA) 1988 made protection from dismissal, or lesser detriment, for the non-unionist absolute – whether or not a closed shop agreement was in existence, and whether or not it had been approved by the vast majority of employees in a recent ballot (Dickens 1989: 41). In 1990 it was made illegal for employers to refuse job applicants on the grounds that they were not union members (outlawing the less common pre-entry closed shop). A similar protection is enacted for union members, but, intentionally, not for union activists, thus conferring a formal equality only (Simpson 1991: 419).

A further assault on union security came in the Trade Union Reform and Employment Rights Act 1993 (TURERA) which threatens the continued viability of check-off arrangements, whereby currently around 6 million union members have their union subscriptions deducted from their pay by the employer and handed to the union. Many unions fear adverse impacts on membership levels and subscription income. The threat to check-off is one of a number of areas (including ballot financing, discussed later) where the financial base of unions is being undermined.

Union consultation rights have been narrowed (where the increasing requirements of European law allow) and union officials' rights to time off were restricted. Inasmuch as rights depend on prior union recognition, deregulation of the statutory rights was not always necessary; they could be reduced by the refusal or withdrawal of recognition, which was facilitated by other legal changes.

The declining coverage of collective agreements and increased negotiation of pay on an individual basis, with new forms of individual performance based pay being introduced, are all seen by the government as 'valuable and healthy developments' (DE 1992: 37). Some employers have offered financial inducements to encourage employees to give up union membership and move away from collective bargaining in the determination of their terms and conditions of employment (Evans and Hudson 1993). When the statutory right not to be discriminated against on the grounds of union membership appeared to be about to prevent employers offering enhanced pay to those willing to move to 'individual' contracts, the government quickly stepped in with legal amendment.[5]

Impact Assessing the impact of the legislative switch to individualist rather than collectivist relations is extremely difficult. Survey evidence shows a declining proportion of workers covered by collective agreements and declining union membership (Millward et al. 1992) and, as chapter 11 shows, there is evidence too of growth in more individualized techniques in managing labour. But legislative changes can only be a part of the explanation, along with structural shifts in industry and labour markets, and the inhospitable macroeconomic context (see chapter 6).

There is no legal hurdle for employers wishing to derecognize unions and some have done so, either completely or, more commonly, on particular sites or in respect of particular categories of staff (Claydon 1989; Smith and Morton 1990; Gregg and Yates 1991). Unions have experienced difficulty in extending collective bargaining into new or traditionally under-organized areas. The legal framework is such that new entrant or 'greenfield site' employers, particularly foreign multinationals, who wish to pursue a non-union strategy may do so.

Alternatively, the law allows recognition to be offered on the employer's terms – sometimes 'no strike' deals with the employer's choice of single union. Where collective bargaining remained in place, there has been greater decentralization and 'domestication' (Brown and Wadhwani 1990: 64). The quality or scope of bargaining may well have deteriorated within continuing bargaining structures (Batstone 1984; Terry 1988). A number of companies 'rolled back' shopfloor organization, with fewer rights and facilities being afforded to fewer shop stewards at a time when the relevant legal rights were being narrowed (Terry 1983: 55; chapter 7, above).

These trends to more individualist managerial approaches cannot be explained by legislative change but they have been assisted by the removal of positive legal support for collective organization. In some cases, the symbolic function of the legislative change may have been as important as the change itself, helping foster an anti-collectivist culture. This is the case in those areas where the rights or achievements in practice were limited. The interpretation by the courts of the EPA provisions concerning trade union membership and activities, for example, revealed large holes in the protection they provided for nascent collective bargaining (Fenley 1984; Dickens et al. 1985: 244–7) and the recognition procedure had almost run aground at the time of its repeal, hampered by restrictive judicial interpretation and other problems (Dickens and Bain 1986: 93).

Union organization and recognition cannot be imposed by legal sanctions (Dickens and Bain 1986: 103–4). Indeed, there are arguments that statutory recognition procedures may be counterproductive (Townley 1987). Law can play a part, however, in facilitating union organizing and recruitment activity, upon which union recognition depends, and can help tip the balance of employer decision towards entering into collective bargaining, including ways not tried in the UK.[6] Alternatively, it can help promote nonunionism and the marginalization of joint regulation. Since the 1970s, legal policy in Britain has been designed with the latter objective in mind.

The abolition of legal supports for compulsory union membership came at a time when the closed shop was declining in importance, due to the structural shifts outlined earlier (Brown and Wadhwani 1990: 63). Assessment of the extent to which the abolition of the closed shop has aided the removal of restrictive practices and so enhanced efficiency and competitiveness, as it was argued it would, is hampered by the fact that there was no firm evidence to support the contention that the closed shop was linked to such practices. Indeed, high levels of union membership were correlated positively with the introduction of change (Daniel 1987; Brown and Wadhwani 1990: 66). Employers have not always welcomed the new emphasis on individual freedom to be a non-member of any or a particular union, fearing the instability this might cause to established arrangements.

Overall, we can see that at a time when sectoral and labour-market change increased the unions' need for positive legal support to aid organization, such support was removed. At a time when unions are weakened by recession and declining membership, their economic and organizational security is reduced by legislative change. In a context where some employers are questioning the appropriateness or functional value of collective bargaining, some of the tactics which in the past have been part of the unions' legitimate armoury of persuasion have been made unlawful, and non-unionism is increasingly supported by law.

A further impact of legal change in this area, as in others, has been to widen the gap between UK legislation and international standards. Some of the developments discussed above required the UK to denounce ILO Conventions and it has been found to be in breach of others, including those relating to freedom of association (Ewing 1989; Brown and McColgan 1992: 271).[7] The unitarist, individualist approach of current UK legislation, and broader public policy, contrasts also with the emphasis on social dialogue between the social partners characteristic of most other EU member states, and provides an inhospitable context for the operationalization of European measures which are predicated on the existence of worker representatives at the workplace (Hall 1992).

Restricting industrial action

A key and recurring element of the post-1979 government policy of reducing trade union bargaining power has been the restriction of the scope for unlawful industrial action. The freedom to take industrial action traditionally has been seen as offering the prospect of some kind of countervailing social power for employees via effective trade unionism, recognizing the disparity between the bargaining position of the individual employees and that of their employer (Kahn-Freund and Hepple 1972: 6).

In Britain, there is no right to strike as such. Instead, the freedom to take industrial action is conferred by granting trade unions, their officials and representatives 'immunities' or statutory protections from the common law which otherwise would make their action unlawful. Without these protections, the organizers of industrial action would be liable for civil wrongs including that of inducing breach of employment contracts, and would thus be exposed to court orders and claims for damages. As a mechanism for keeping industrial disputes out of the courts the immunities, dating from the Trade Disputes Act 1906, were central to the voluntarist character of British industrial relations. Functionally, the immunities can be seen as 'negative' law: 'to remove legal obstacles to the smooth functioning of the social institutions of industrial self-governance' (Davies and Freedland 1993: 11–12). Without 'negative' statutory intervention, 'the freedom of employees . . . to apply collective sanctions against employers would, in fact, have been subject to detailed regulation by the common law, to the point where self-regulation would have appeared to be a wholly one-sided system in the employer's favour' (1993: 15).

One problem with relying on immunities is that their effectiveness has frequently been undermined by the development by the courts of new common law liabilities outflanking the scope of the existing statutory protections. Judgements of this kind led to the Trade Disputes Act 1965, introduced to restore the intended effect of the 1906 legislation. The provisions of the Trade Union and Labour Relations Acts 1974 and 1976 also took account of judicial decisions in seeking to re-establish the system of immunities which had been displaced by the IR Act 1971. A further bout of judicial creativity in the late 1970s fuelled the political controversy over the scope for lawful industrial action.

The legal form of the immunities, and the fact that, having sought to exclude the common law from industrial disputes, the 1906 Act did not impose any statutory restrictions on the use of industrial action, meant that Conservative politicians and commentators increasingly came to characterize the statutory immunities as 'unique privileges' which put trade unions 'above the law' – terminology designed to 'create an impression of unwarranted legal status' (Fredman 1992: 26). Some on the right urged the complete abolition of the immunities, arguing that the political, social and economic conditions underlying the 1906 settlement no longer applied in the 1980s (Tur 1985), and that an efficiently functioning labour market, freed from the distortion of 'organised collective action by unions using the strike-threat', offers the best prospects for individual employees (Hanson and Mather 1988: 82). Short of this, Conservative governments have aimed to redraw radically the boundaries of lawful industrial action. As we explore in this section, major changes have been made in the legal rules governing who is allowed to strike, when and in what circumstances, where and how. New sanctions have been introduced against unions who overstep the new, tighter boundaries, and they may be triggered by a wider range of parties. Rejecting the replacement of the traditional immunities by a new legal framework, as was tried in the 1971 legislation, the Conservative governments since 1979 have instead narrowed the scope and application of the immunities through successive pieces of legislation, thus increasingly restricting the lawfulness of industrial action. In 1989 the British legislation on strikes was adjudged to fall below the minimum standards set by the ILO conventions (Ewing 1989).

Since the beginning of the 1980s, industrial action has been restricted by a number of different techniques. One approach has been to remove immunity from particular types of industrial action. Thus, picketing away from the pickets' own workplace was made unlawful by the EA 1980. So too was industrial action by workers whose employer is not party to the dispute, except in those instances where such 'secondary' action was targeted at supplies going to or from the employer in dispute, or at business transferred from the employer in dispute to associated employers. This exception was later removed and all secondary industrial action was made unlawful by the EA 1990.

A second approach has been to limit the issues about which industrial action can lawfully be organized. Industrial action can only be lawful if taken 'in contemplation or furtherance of a trade dispute', and the EA 1982 introduced a narrower, enterprise-specific definition of what constitutes a trade dispute, requiring a trade dispute to be between workers and their own employer and wholly or mainly related to industrial relations issues as opposed to 'political' motives. In addition, immunity has been withdrawn from industrial action over the employment of non-unionists (EA 1988), over the dismissal of employees taking part in unofficial industrial action (EA 1990), and to promote the use of union recognition requirements in commercial contracts (EA 1982).

The third approach was to make unions liable for unlawful industrial action. Previously, liability had extended only to the individuals organizing the action. Under the 1982 Act unions became liable for damages of up to £250,000 for each unlawful industrial action authorized or endorsed by the president, general secretary, executive committee or others empowered to do so by union rules, and by other employed officials or committees to which they reported unless they were prevented from doing so by union rules or 'repudiated' by the union's national leadership. The 1990 Act extended the scope of union liability to include industrial action organized by any official or committee of the union, including shop stewards, and laid down a more onerous repudiation procedure if unions are to avoid liability for the acts of officials and committees acting outside union rules. Making trade unions rather than individuals liable for the consequences of action deemed to be unlawful removes the risk of making martyrs of jailed shop stewards (as happened under the IR Act) and poses a threat to union finances of the kind the Trade Disputes Act of 1906 was designed to avoid, following the famous Taff Vale decision.

The fourth approach was one which linked the lawfulness of industrial action to demonstrable support from workers concerned. The Trade Union Act 1984 made immunity for industrial action authorized or endorsed by unions conditional on majority support of the members concerned in a secret ballot. The EA 1988 and 1990 added considerably to the complexity of the procedural requirements relating to pre-strike ballots, including the contents of the voting paper which, among other things, had to inform those voting that industrial action constituted a breach of their contract of employment. The TURERA 1993 required union industrial action ballots to be by full postal voting only, and to be independently scrutinized. Workplace or 'semi-postal' voting is not allowed if the immunity is to be retained. In addition, unions were required to provide employers with at least seven days' notice of official industrial action, sufficiently identifying those employees who would be taking the action and stating the dates on which action will take place.

Fifth, the government has widened the range of potential litigants in cases of unlawful industrial action. In addition to the possibility of common law proceedings by an employer or anyone else party to a contract which would be broken or interfered with by unlawful industrial action, the 1988 Act enabled union members to apply for court orders where unions call on them to take industrial action without a properly conducted ballot. Moreover, TURERA 1993 established a 'citizen's right' for individuals deprived of any goods or services because of unlawful industrial action to seek a court order restraining the organization of the action – dubbed the 'Disgusted of Tunbridge Wells provision' (Hendy 1993: 64). It also provides for a new Commissioner for Protection against Unlawful

Industrial Action to assist financially individuals wishing to exercise this right.

In addition, the government has used a variety of other means of deterring industrial action. Changes in social security provision in 1980 led to deductions from the entitlements of strikers' families corresponding to a fixed amount of strike pay whether the union actually provided it or not. The 1982 Act allowed employers to be more selective than hitherto in dismissing groups of workers involved in industrial action, and the 1990 Act enabled employers selectively to dismiss employees taking unofficial industrial action. The 1988 Act also introduced a right for union members not to be disciplined unjustifiably by their union for, among other things, refusing to take part in industrial action. Codes of Practice concerning picketing and ballots on industrial action introduced by the government under new powers give 'practical guidance' which can be – and on occasion has been (Davies and Freedland 1993: 461) – taken into account in relevant court proceedings. The provisions of the Codes are in places more restrictive than the legislation they purport to amplify, as in the case of the 'six picket maximum', widely considered a legal provision but, in fact, guidance in the Code of Practice on Picketing.

Impact: (1) Legal action by employers In several key disputes during the 1980s, extensive use of the law by employers had a major and possibly decisive impact. Examples included the 1983 dispute between Messenger Newspapers and the NGA, the 1986 dispute between News International and the print unions, and the 1988 dispute between P. & O. Ferries and the NUS, each of which resulted in heavy fines followed by the sequestration (legal confiscation) of the unions' assets arising from contempt proceedings because of union non-compliance with court orders. In the 1984–5 mining dispute, during which the NUM also had its funds sequestrated, the most significant legal actions against the union stemmed not from the post-1979 legislation but from disaffected union members exercising common law rights to enforce the observance of union rules. This dispute was notable also for the extensive use of criminal and public order law rather than labour law (Benedictus 1985; Wallington 1985; Ewing 1985).

More generally, even though legal action by employers during disputes remains the exception rather than the rule (Elgar and Simpson 1993), the law has been used with considerably higher frequency than during the 1970s. This is despite the widespread belief initially that, as during the IR Act period, employers would refrain from invoking the law because to do so might inflame the dispute as well as causing longer-term damage to their industrial relations. One study (Evans 1985, 1987) identified over 100 injunctions issued over the period from September 1980 to April 1987. Of these, 28 cases related to picketing, 27 to secondary industrial action and 47 (post-1984 Act) to the absence of pre-strike ballots.

It appears that the relative simplicity of the 'strike ballot' provisions compared to the earlier, complex restrictions on the lawfulness of industrial action accounts for the fact that unballoted industrial action became the most common grounds for employers seeking injunctions. Employer action in such cases could be presented also as acting in the interests of their employees, ensuring democratic procedures were followed. The available information on subsequent injunction cases is less systematic (LRD 1990, 1991) but suggests, if anything, a slight decline in their frequency. This may be accounted for by unions' increasing use of pre-strike ballots (see below).

But employers' increased readiness to resort to legal action compared to the IR Act period is not simply a result of the different legal provisions. It is also likely to reflect differences in the economic and industrial context. As Weekes et al. (1975: 210) pointed out, in their study of that Act, the early 1970s was a period of general economic growth and employers were generally content to avoid 'legal entanglement' which might have risked prolonging the dispute. By contrast, in the recession of the first half of the 1980s, use of the law appears to have been more attractive to employers, particularly those pursuing radical restructuring and cost-cutting in the face of union opposition. This is borne out by the fact that the bulk of the injunction cases occurred in three sectors – printing, shipping/transport and public services – particularly affected by restructuring (Evans 1987).

In most cases, the objective of employers in resorting to legal action is to stop the industrial action in question by means of securing an injunction. Employers generally have shown little interest in going beyond the injunction stage to pursue claims for damages against unions (Evans 1987), and very few have set out to use the law strategically to undermine effective industrial action during disputes. What does appear to be the case, though, is that employers are willing, in the current climate, to consider legal action

– and certainly the threat of legal action – as a potentially worthwhile tactic in disputes (LRD 1990; Elgar and Simpson 1993).

Impact: (2) The union response Union responses to legislative changes inevitably reflected the experience of those high profile disputes in which the law played a significant part, in particular the demonstration of the damaging consequences of sequestration orders as a means of enforcing injunctions. Trade union leaders' initial stance on the 1980 and 1982 Acts had been strongly influenced by unions' successful opposition to the Industrial Relations Act 1971. A programme based on non-cooperation with the new legislation was adopted by a special TUC conference at Wembley in 1982. However, the policy masked underlying differences between unions. In particular, while some unions were prepared to countenance non-compliance with the law, others were not. The ambiguity in this respect of the central element of the Wembley conference policy – that the TUC General Council could coordinate assistance by other unions in support of a union facing legal action under the new laws – was put to the test during the bitter Messenger Newspapers dispute. By a narrow majority the General Council declined to organize the support requested by the union concerned because to do so would risk the TUC itself being held in contempt of court. Thus, despite strong criticism from a number of major unions, it was established that TUC policy stopped short of non-compliance with the law. Indeed, it is clear that unions have become more cautious in the tactics they adopt during disputes, and that because of the greater risks of court action union leaders have tended to strengthen central union control over how and when industrial action should be called and who should be empowered to authorize it (Evans 1987; Martin et al. 1991).

But the most direct and extensive impact of the post-1979 legislation concerns unions' use of pre-strike ballots. Even allowing for undercounting, the 951 pre-strike ballots noted by ACAS during the three years from 1987 to 1989 (Brown and Wadhwani 1990: 61) amounted to only a fraction of the overall number of industrial disputes. But by 1990 ACAS reported that 'in our experience, the practice is now universal' (ACAS 1990: 13). Moreover, a recent survey of the 18 largest TUC unions (LRD 1993) suggests that in the year to August 1992 more than twice as many ballots were held than recorded instances of industrial action, even though in the vast majority of cases the vote went in favour of industrial action.

Impact: *(3) Implications for collective bargaining* While recent research has cast doubt on suggestions that unions have often used
strike ballots 'tactically' (to get members to vote for action they are
not actually prepared to take), it suggests that ballots can none the
less be valuable during negotiations, acting as a 'low cost' way of
demonstrating the strength of membership feeling to management
(Martin et al. 1991). In 92 per cent of the strike ballots recorded by
ACAS during 1987–9 the outcome was a vote in favour of industrial
action; in the great majority of cases the employer then settled
without a strike occurring (Brown and Wadhwani 1990: 61). ACAS
has commented that 'in many instances, ballots have helped to
strengthen the negotiating position of trade unions' (ACAS 1990:
13). This perception is supported by union negotiators themselves
(Martin et al. 1991; Elgar and Simpson 1993). It may also be that
ballots mean that members are more willing to participate in any
subsequent industrial action (Martin et al. 1991). These outcomes
can hardly have been consistent with the government's expectations.
More generally, the research by Martin and colleagues suggests that
the legislation requiring pre-strike ballots, though formally 'de-col-
lectivizing' decisions about strikes, has not in itself affected traditional sources of union cohesion. The point needs to be made,
however, that this verdict relates primarily to workplace ballots; the
1993 Act now requires strike ballots to be fully postal. Whether this
has a greater impact in terms of 'de-collectivization' remains to be
seen.

Impact: *(4) The incidence of industrial action* More difficult to assess
is the impact of the legal changes on the actual incidence of industrial action. As noted above, any impact is likely to vary according to
sector and other factors; and other legal developments, for example
in social security, may also play a part. While some elements of the
law affect only particular tactics during industrial action (such as
secondary action and 'off-site' picketing), the potential lawfulness of
primary strikes is affected by the restricted definition of 'trade dispute' and by the balloting requirements. Surveys of union negotiators and workplace representatives appear to suggest that legal
constraints have affected union members' willingness to resort to
industrial action (LRD 1990; Elgar and Simpson 1993). Some
econometric studies have suggested that the number of strikes has
been reduced by the legislation (Metcalf 1990), but the impact on
the size and length of strikes has been less clear. Brown and
Wadhwani's (1990: 60) comparison of international strike statistics

covering 20 leading industrialized countries for the period 1978–87 show that most countries saw a greater proportional decline in days lost through strikes than the UK. McCarthy (1992) is also sceptical about the claimed impact of legal restrictions on the overall volume of strike activity, arguing that this continued to be governed by factors other than the law (see chapter 14).

The Union–Member Relationship

A key element of the traditional 'voluntarist' framework of British industrial relations was the limited statutory regulation of trade unions' internal affairs. In Kahn-Freund's words, 'it [had], on the whole, been common ground that in [the] dilemma between imposing standards of democracy and protecting union autonomy the law must come down on the side of autonomy' (Davies and Freedland 1983: 274). With the exception of the statutory requirements governing the administration of unions' political funds (contained in the Trade Union Act 1913) and union amalgamations (Trade Union (Amalgamations etc.) Act 1964), unions were generally free to devise their own rules and procedures without interference from statute.

The position, however, has been altered radically by the enactment over the 1980s and early 1990s of a series of measures regulating unions' internal affairs, each more detailed and interventionist than the last. Moreover, this legislation reflects a highly individualistic conception of the rights and obligations associated with trade union membership (McKendrick 1988: 141). The underlying aim – like that of the legislative provisions regulating industrial action discussed above – appears to have been to discourage collectivist or solidaristic behaviour by union members, promoting a view of trade unions not as collective organizations but as mere aggregates of individuals (Dickens 1989: 44). The extension of the rights and protections of union members *vis-à-vis* their unions contrasts sharply with the reduction of the rights and protections of employees in relation to their employer (see above). Moreover, the internal affairs of employers, the other party to collective bargaining, have not been subject to greatly increased regulation.

The legislation

The primary focus of measures in this area has been to promote the use of secret ballots by unions in elections and before taking industrial action. The stated rationales for this policy concern both its internal and external impacts (Auerbach 1990: 118). The basic internal justification for intervention was to make unions more democratic and responsive to the wishes of their members. This in turn was expected to have important external effects: more representative (and, implicit in the government's own analysis, more moderate) union leaderships, and the use of strike ballots, were expected to help restrain industrial action.

Both before and after the Conservatives assumed office in 1979 there were intra-party tensions over whether the more extensive use of secret ballots was to be achieved by voluntary or compulsory means. Under the incoming government's first employment secretary, James Prior, the emphasis was on encouraging secret ballots in non-mandatory ways. The EA 1980 confined itself to making public funds available towards the cost of postal ballots, and requiring employers to allow their premises to be used for the holding of workplace ballots. Prior's subsequent Green Paper *Trade Union Immunities* (DE 1981) canvassed opinion on the possibility of legislating for membership-triggered strike ballots; other forms of compulsory strike ballots were, by implication, rejected (DE 1981: 62–3). However, following Prior's replacement as employment secretary by Norman Tebbit, this cautious approach gave way to a more radical agenda. A pre-election Green Paper *Democracy in Trade Unions* (DE 1983) discussed various proposals for legislation on secret ballots for union elections, ballots before industrial action, and unions' political activities. The government's justification for this initiative was that trade unions had refused to reform their internal procedures voluntarily; in particular, TUC-affiliated unions had maintained a boycott of the ballot funds scheme established under the 1980 Act. But it is also apparent that there was a strong political motivation behind the essentially populist secret ballots project. As Norman Tebbit later confirmed, the Green Paper was perceived as 'part of a struggle for trade unionists' votes in the forthcoming general election' (Tebbit 1988: 198). In its manifesto for the June 1983 general election the Conservative Party committed itself to legislation in each of the three areas discussed in the Green Paper.

The Trade Union Act 1984 required five-yearly secret ballots for the election of union executive committees, and presidents and general secretaries if they had voting rights in decision-making by executive committees. As noted above, the Act also made industrial action called without a secret ballot unlawful. The third strand of the 1984 Act was to make the continuation of unions' political funds subject to ten-yearly 'review' ballots, with a wider definition of 'political objects', expenditure on which must come from a properly constituted political fund.

Following a further pre-election Green Paper, *Trade Unions and their Members* (DE 1987), the EA 1988 extended the statutory election requirements to all union general secretaries and presidents (prompted at least in part by Arthur Scargill's evasion of the 1984 Act's provisions by relinquishing his casting vote as president of the NUM), and stipulated that union election and political fund ballots should be fully postal and independently scrutinized. Citing workplace balloting irregularities in the 1984 TGWU and 1986 CPSA elections for general secretary (both of which were re-run after independent inquiries commissioned by each union), the government's case for fully postal balloting was that it is the method least susceptible to malpractice. This outweighed any concern about lower levels of membership participation in postal ballots; the government's view was that the evidence on this was inconclusive (DE 1987: 24).

Moreover, the 1984 Act's requirement that unions had to compile and maintain a register of their members' names and postal addresses meant that all unions should now be in a position to hold fully postal ballots. The 1988 Act also provided a range of statutory rights for individual union members enforceable against their union with the financial or other assistance of a new 'Commissioner for the Rights of Trade Union Members' (CROTUM). Reflecting experience during the 1984–5 mining dispute, these included the right to apply for court orders against being called on to take unballoted industrial action, new rights in relation to union finances, and – highly controversially – the right not to be 'unjustifiably disciplined' by a union for refusing to take part in industrial action, even where there has been a majority in favour of industrial action in a ballot. As Fredman (1992: 35) comments, here 'individualism takes precedence over democracy'.

Further refinements to the law affecting trade union government and administration have been made by subsequent statutes. For example, the EA 1990 enabled the CROTUM to assist union members in court proceedings over a union's alleged failure to observe the requirements of its rule-book. The TURERA 1993 requires ballots before industrial action to be fully postal and independently scrutinized. It also includes highly detailed provisions on the storage and distribution of ballot papers, the counting of votes, and the appointment and functions of independent scrutineers for election, industrial action and political fund ballots. Unions' financial affairs are also subject to further regulation.

Impact

Although trade unions have been strongly opposed to the extension of statutory controls on internal union affairs, they have adapted to successive legal requirements with varying degrees of reluctance but little resistance. After an initial flurry in 1986 – the first full year of the 1984 Act's operation – the number of union members' complaints to the Certification Officer (CO) that their union had failed to comply with the Act's requirements slowed to a trickle. For the most part, the complaints upheld by the CO have concerned minor lapses in balloting procedure, and the unions concerned have readily taken the necessary remedial steps. There were only isolated instances of unions deliberately adopting a policy of non-compliance with the legislation (including COHSE, NALGO and TASS). While this resulted in decisions against them by the CO, these were not followed up, as is provided for in the Act, by legal action for an enforcement order. However, they were seized upon by the government, which strengthened the 1984 Act's complaints/enforcement procedure (by establishing the CROTUM) despite the cooperation of the great majority of unions with the legislation (Hall 1988: 204).

The possibility of enforcement orders from the courts has remained a virtually redundant procedure. No enforcement order has ever been made, and in the only recorded instance of an application to the High Court being pursued, in 1990, the union (UCATT) decided to re-run the ballot in question following an interim court hearing (CO 1991: 28). Similarly, the modest number of cases in which the CROTUM grants assistance to potential litigants (Morris 1993: 105) lends credence to union – and employer – arguments that the range of statutory rights for union members included in the 1988 Act and subsequent legislation, and the particular role of the CROTUM, are in practice unnecessary.

The central balloting provisions of the legislation have none the less had a significant impact on union practice, though the more individualistic conception of union democracy promoted by the legislation has not significantly altered the political character of trade union leaderships. The electoral systems of many unions were transformed by the 1984 Act, which prevented the use of indirect elections for union executive committees, but in few unions has this resulted in radical change in the political composition of the executive. Similarly, the requirement for the election and periodic re-election of union general secretaries ruled out the practice, common particularly among white-collar unions, of appointing the union's senior full-time official. But this has resulted in only two cases to date in which an incumbent general secretary has been defeated in an election (NATFHE and NUJ). If, as was implicit in its analysis (DE 1983), the government expected that one consequence of its prescribed balloting procedures would be to encourage a general shift to the right in the result of union leadership elections, then it will have been disappointed. Smith et al. (1993) show that the political complexion of most unions has been largely unaffected by the legislation. Moreover, where change has occurred, the outcome has been inconsistent across unions and contingent on internal union dynamics. Thus, in a number of unions (for example, the TGWU and the NCU) left wing factions have consolidated their position on the executive. Moreover, in UCATT, the use of postal ballots and a new membership register for the 1991 executive elections led to the creation and victory of a Labour-left/communist faction. This contrasts with the growing hold of the 'moderate' faction within the CPSA on the executive committee (Smith et al. 1993).

This picture is consistent with earlier research (Undy and Martin 1984) which suggested that a move from indirect to direct electoral systems places a premium on the organization of factions to campaign for slates of candidates, and that direct elections tend to favour the better-organized faction rather than political 'moderation'. The more recent research into the impact of the 1984 and 1988 Acts also found that, whereas the workplace ballots allowed by the 1984 Act and favoured by most unions tended to strengthen workplace union organization and the relationship between union representatives/activists and members, the imposition of postal ballots for union elections by the 1988 Act led to a decline in levels of participation (Smith et al. 1993). As members having little identification with the union may be less likely to vote in a postal ballot, this may in turn reinforce the importance of factional organization in elections irrespective of politics.

Similarly, against initial expectations, unions were successful in every case in winning the necessary ballots to maintain existing political funds. A number of unions which had not previously had political funds also held ballots to establish them, prompted by the 1984 Act's extension of the definition of political activity. The success of the political fund ballots campaign represented a considerable achievement for the unions concerned. It required the use of sophisticated membership communication strategies on a potentially problematic issue, and the establishment of effective administrative systems and campaign organization (for details see Steele et al. 1986; Blackwell and Terry 1987). The political fund campaign served to overcome some of the unions' fears about the new emphasis on ballots. It remains to be seen whether the first-round success will be repeated on each ten-year anniversary.

The introduction of the 1984 Act's compulsory balloting requirements also led the TUC to drop its previous policy of boycotting the postal ballot funds scheme, though not before a damaging internal row over decisions by the then AUEW and EETPU to apply for such funds had overshadowed the 1985 annual Congress. Extensive use was made subsequently by TUC-affiliated unions of the ballot funds scheme (postal ballots for executive elections and political fund review ballots having been made mandatory by the 1988 Act). Following the 1993 Act's provision making the postal method compulsory for strike ballots too, the government is to phase out the ballot cost reimbursement scheme by the end of March 1996, a move likely to weaken further trade union finances.

It may be too early to come to a definitive assessment of the way in which legislation in this area will affect the nature of British trade unions. However, it does not appear premature to note that the terrain of debate concerning democracy in trade unions has shifted. Discussions of alternative representative and participative forms of democracy now appear academic; the vocabulary has been captured and union democracy is in practice now firmly equated with a requirement for individual balloting.

Conclusion

The employment relationship in Britain has traditionally been regulated by a mix of legal and social regulation. The latter, resulting from collective bargaining, was seen as the primary method in the voluntarist system, and the state as legislator stood back. Such social regulation rests on trade union organization, autonomy and recognition and on workers' freedom to exercise collective strength. Since 1979, labour law has moved away from this position; the legitimacy of collective labour power is no longer accepted. As Davies and Freedland note (1993: 657) 'government saw no legitimate place for collective bargaining in the regulation of labour relations, except perhaps at enterprise level to help management achieve its goals'. As noted earlier, the main thrust of the post-1979 legislation has been to weaken trade union power, assert individualist rather than collective values and to reassert employer prerogative.

The move, therefore, has not been away from joint regulation through collective bargaining to legal regulation of the terms and conditions of employment, but, rather, from joint regulation to increased *unilateral regulation* by the employer, under the banners of freedom of contract and deregulation to aid restructuring and economic regeneration. Certain measures in the post-1979 legislation were aimed at removing supports for extending social regulation and restricting any extension of workers' collective strength beyond that of their own enterprise (through limitations on secondary and sympathetic action etc.). At the same time, legal protections for those beyond the reach of social regulation diminished. Other measures attacked the established territory of social regulation with severe curbs on the freedom to take industrial action, and increasingly onerous requirements were imposed on unions in respect of their decision-taking procedures. The ability of both social and legal regulation to protect workers *vis-à-vis* their employers and to determine the terms and conduct of the employment relationship diminished, except where European law demanded otherwise.

Such developments were not an inevitable consequence of dissatisfaction, which was not limited to the Conservative government, with the traditional voluntarist approach. But different solutions appeared less viable or desirable. One alternative approach, for example, might have been the adoption of a legally regulated, social partnership model of the continental type. However, in the context of the apparent failure of corporatist arrangements of the Labour governments of the 1970s and the Conservatives' ideological commitment to deregulate product and money markets, which inevitably was reflected in labour-market policy, this was not politically acceptable to the government.

In this chapter we have explored the impact of the legal changes in the particular areas of relationships between employers and workers, employers and trade unions, and trade unions and their members, noting that non-legal considerations (such as union membership loss through economic restructuring and recession) played as great, and often a greater, role than legal change. Rather than rehearse the particular impacts again here, we consider instead the overall change in the perceptions of the role which law might play in industrial relations.

No return to the voluntarist autonomous system is likely. The nature of the legislative agenda may change, whether because of the election of a different government, the need to comply with European Union standards, or pressure from particular groups. But there can be little doubt that the debate has switched from *whether* the law should play a role in industrial relations to *what* role it should play.

The legislative provisions enacted since 1979 have not always accorded with employers' own perceptions of industrial relations problems and their desired solutions. But if employers did not necessarily advocate the measures enacted, and have not always sought recourse to the legal procedures and remedies provided, nor are they calling for their removal. As noted, the law has been used to curb union strength and thus reduce social regulation not replace it, and employer freedom of action has been enhanced. Any call for a 'return to voluntarism' from employers is likely to occur only if there is a move to a highly legally regulated employment relationship. In such a context, 'voluntarism' is likely to be equated with 'leaving it to employers' rather than a demand for a return to a system allowing the free play of collective forces and the extension and strengthening of social regulation. This is the meaning currently given to voluntarism by the British government in opposing European measures – the voluntarist system being narrowly (mis)defined as simply the absence of legal regulation.

Union demands for a statutory national minimum wage, enhanced legal protections for workers, statutory union representation rights, and the advocacy of an extensive EU social policy agenda, stand in stark contrast to the characteristic union response given to the Donovan Commission in the mid-1960s by the then general secretary of the NUR. When asked about the possible extension of legal regulation, he replied:

I would be happier, with great respect to you, my Lord, if we didn't have anything to do with the law at all.

The Labour movement's commitment to voluntarism has always been based as much on pragmatism as theory. But this change is more than simply a shift in the boundaries of voluntarism. There has been a pronounced shift in the industrial relations policy stance of the TUC and of the Labour party over the 1980s (see, for example, Labour Party 1990). The unions have learnt to live with the law not only in terms of a pragmatic adjustment to the restrictive legal regime of the 1980s, but through a more fundamental reassessment of union attitudes to the role of law in industrial relations which embodies an acceptance that there is a need for the state to do more than just provide procedural safeguards for a voluntary system and to plug a few gaps (Dickens 1989: 49).

Until the heavy defeat of Labour in the 1983 general election, TUC and Labour party policy had been essentially to return to the legal position of the mid-1970s. After that defeat, and with the crumbling of the unions' strategy of opposition to the new labour laws, the TUC and the Labour party began redrawing the labour movement's industrial relations policy. By the 1990s, Labour's industrial relations programme had undergone substantial change. A future Labour government would revise rather than totally repeal the labour laws enacted by the Conservatives since 1979 but would introduce some important innovations in British labour law, notably a statutory minimum wage, which would extend the legal regulation of the employment relationship rather than leave it to unilateral employer regulation.

In identifying the death of voluntarism, and the changed roles of the state, and law, in industrial relations in Britain since the 1960s, the differential effects of legal regulation as between organizations and with respect to different aspects of industrial relations should be emphasized. As the discussion in this chapter has indicated, the line between state intervention and the autonomy of employers and unions has shifted towards state intervention. However, labour law has impinged upon the autonomy of trade unions as organizations to a far greater extent than it has upon employers. In a number of areas, legal requirements or norms now dictate behaviour (most obviously perhaps in the sphere of internal union government and administration). Further, while legal rules and procedures inform what occurs within enterprises, replacing or reshaping voluntary norms (for example, in the handling of discipline and dismissal and in the planning and conduct of lawful industrial action), it is important to note that an increased role for law has not led to legal regulation rather than collective bargaining shaping the employment relation. The legislative assault on collective organization and collective bargaining created a space filled less by statutory determination of terms and conditions of employment than by unilateral employer decision. The legal principles promulgated since 1979 have been compatible with, and encouraging of, increased scope for the exercise of managerial prerogative.

Notes

The authors thank Graham Moffat for his comments on an earlier draft.

1 For detailed expert treatment of the law and its interpretation, see Wedderburn 1986; for exposition of post-war labour legislation and public policy, see Davies and Freedland 1993.

2 More recently, the Transfer of Undertakings regulations (arising from an EC Directive on acquired rights) have affected contracting out. The regulations affect the terms on which it is undertaken, preventing immediate deterioration in the terms and conditions of transferred employees. It remains to be seen how this will impact on the extent of this practice.

3 The ILO Conventions do not include protection of non-membership, though it is not necessarily excluded from other international (European) standards (Lewis 1986: 47–51; Ewing 1991: 11).

4 For discussion of the affinity of this approach to Hayekian philosophy, see Wedderburn 1989.

5 Amendment made at third reading to TURERA following reversal by the Court of Appeal of *Associated Newspapers* v. *Wilson* 1992 [IRLR] 440 EAT; *Associated British Ports* v. *Palmer* 1993 [IRLR] 63 EAT.

6 For example, imposing high norms by law and allowing derogation from them only by collective agreement. For discussion of issues in this area, see Ewing 1990.

7 The ILO Committee of Experts has criticized Britain for, among other things, the sacking of public employees who refused to give up union membership after the removal of collective bargaining rights at Government Communication Headquarters (GCHQ) in 1983; the abolition of collective bargaining rights for schoolteachers in 1987); and the lack of protection from dismissal for workers taking industrial action (Brown and McColgan 1992). The provision in TURERA relating to personal

contracts reduces yet further the modest protection offered by law to freedom of association in Britain.

References

ACAS (Advisory, Conciliation and Arbitration Service) 1990: *Annual Report 1989*. London: ACAS.

Anderman, S. 1986: Unfair Dismissals and Redundancy. In R. Lewis (ed.), *Labour Law in Britain*. Oxford: Blackwell.

Auerbach, S. 1990: *Legislating for Conflict*. Oxford: Clarendon Press.

Bain, G. (ed.) 1983: *Industrial Relations in Britain*. Oxford: Blackwell.

Batstone, E. 1984: *Working Order: Workplace Industrial Relations over Two Decades*. Oxford: Blackwell.

Benedictus, R. 1985: The Use of the Law of Tort in the Miners' Strike. *Industrial Law Journal*, 14, 3, 176–90.

Blackwell, R. and Terry, M. 1987: Analysing the Political Fund Ballots: A Remarkable Victory or the Triumph of the Status Quo? *Political Studies*, 35, 4, 623–42.

Brown, D. and McColgan, A. 1992: UK Employment Law and the International Labour Organization: The Spirit of Cooperation? *Industrial Law Journal*, 21, 4, 265–79.

Brown, W. and Wadhwani, S. 1990: The Economic Effects of Industrial Relations Legislation since 1979. *National Institute Economic Review*, 131, 57–70.

Claydon, T. 1989: Union Derecognition in Britain in the 1980s. *British Journal of Industrial Relations*, 27, 2, 215–24.

Clegg, H. 1970: *The System of Industrial Relations in Great Britain*. Oxford: Blackwell.

Clifton, R. and Tatton-Brown, C. 1979: *Impact of Employment Legislation on Small Firms*. DE Research Paper 7. London: HMSO.

CO (Certification Officer) 1991: *Annual Report 1990*. London: Certification Office for Trade Unions and Employers' Associations.

Collins, H. 1990: Independent Contractors and the Challenge of Vertical Disintegration to Employment Protection Laws. *Oxford Journal of Legal Studies*, 10, Autumn.

Curran, J. 1989: *Employment and Employment Relations in the Small Firm*. Occasional Paper 6. Kingston: Kingston Polytechnic.

Daniel, W. 1980: *Maternity Rights: The Experience of Women*. London: Policy Studies Institute.

Daniel, W. 1987: *Workplace Industrial Relations and Technical Change*. London: Policy Studies Institute and Frances Pinter.

Daniel, W. and Stilgoe, E. 1978: *The Impact of Employment Protection Laws*. London: Policy Studies Institute.

Davies, P. 1992: The Emergence of European Labour Law. In W. McCarthy (ed.), *Legal Intervention in Industrial Relations*. Oxford: Blackwell.

Davies, P. and Freedland, M. 1983: *Kahn-Freund's Labour and the Law*, 3rd edn. London: Stevens.

Davies, P. and Freedland, M. 1984: *Labour Law: Text and Materials*, 2nd edn. London: Weidenfeld & Nicolson.

Davies, P. and Freedland, M. 1993: *Labour Legislation and Public Policy*. Oxford: Clarendon Press.

DE (Department of Employment) 1981: *Trade Union Immunities*. Cmnd 8128. London: HMSO.

DE (Department of Employment) 1983: *Democracy in Trade Unions*. Cmnd 8778. London: HMSO.

DE (Department of Employment) 1985: Consultative Paper on Wages Councils.

DE (Department of Employment) 1986: *Building Businesses . . . Not Barriers*. London: HMSO.

DE (Department of Employment) 1987: *Trade Unions and their Members*. Cm 95. London: HMSO.

DE (Department of Employment) 1988: *Employment for the 1990s*. Cm 540. London: HMSO.

DE (Department of Employment) 1989: *Removing Barriers to Employment*. London: HMSO.

DE (Department of Employment) 1992: *People, Jobs and Opportunity*. London: HMSO.

Deakin, S. 1990: Equality under a Market Order: The Employment Act 1989. *Industrial Law Journal*, 19, 1, 1–19.

Deakin, S. and Wilkinson, F. 1989: *Labour Law, Social Security and Economic Inequality*. London: Institute of Employment Rights.

Dickens, L. 1983: The Advisory, Conciliation and Arbitration Service: Regulation and Voluntarism in Industrial Relations. In R. Baldwin and C. McCrudden (eds), *Regulation and Public Law*. London: Weidenfeld & Nicolson.

Dickens, L. 1988: Falling through the Net: Employment Change and Worker Protection. *Industrial Relations Journal*, 19, 2, 139–53.

Dickens, L. 1989: Learning to Live with the Law? The Legislative Attack on British Trade Unions since 1979. *New Zealand Journal of Industrial Relations*, 14, 1, 37–52.

Dickens, L. 1991: *Whose Flexibility? Discrimination and Equality Issues in Atypical Work*. London: Institute of Employment Rights.

Dickens, L. 1992: Anti-discrimination Legislation: Exploring and Explaining the Impact on Women's Employment. In W. McCarthy (ed.), *Legal Intervention in Industrial Relations*. Oxford: Blackwell.

Dickens, L. 1994: Deregulation and Employment Rights in Great Britain. In R. Rogowski and T. Wilthagen (eds), *Reflexive Labour Law*.

Deventer: Kluwer.

Dickens, L. and Bain, G. 1986: A Duty to Bargain? Union Recognition and Information Disclosure. In R. Lewis (ed.), *Labour Law in Britain*. Oxford: Blackwell.

Dickens, L. and Cockburn, D. 1986: Dispute Settlement Institutions and the Courts. In R. Lewis (ed.), *Labour Law in Britain*. Oxford: Blackwell.

Dickens, L., Hart, M., Jones, M. and Weekes, B. 1981: Re-employment of Unfairly Dismissed Workers: The Lost Remedy. *Industrial Law Journal*, 10, 160–75.

Dickens, L., Weekes, B., Jones, M. and Hart, M. 1985: *Dismissed: A Study of Unfair Dismissal and the Industrial Tribunal System*. Oxford: Blackwell.

Disney, R. 1990: Explanations of the Decline in Trade Union Density in Britain: An Appraisal. *British Journal of Industrial Relations*, 28, 2, 165–77.

Disney, R. and Szyszczak, E. 1989: Part-time Work: A Reply to Catherine Hakim. *Industrial Law Journal*, 18, 4, 223–9.

Dolding, L. 1988: The Wages Act 1986: An Exercise in Employment Abuse. *Modern Law Review*, 51, 1, 84–97.

Donovan, 1968: Royal Commission on Trade Unions and Employers' Associations. *Report*. Cmnd 3623. London: HMSO.

DTI (Department of Trade and Industry) 1985: *Burdens on Business*. London: HMSO.

Elgar, J. and Simpson, B. 1993: *Union Negotiators, Industrial Action and the Law*. Mimeo. London School of Economics.

Emerson, M. 1988: Regulation or Deregulation of the Labour Market. *European Economic Review*, 32, 2, 775–817.

Employment Gazette 1981: Proposals for Industrial Relations Legislation. *Employment Gazette*, December, 510–14.

EOC (Equal Opportunities Commission) 1990: *Equal Pay for Men and Women: Strengthening the Acts*. Manchester: EOC.

Evans, S. 1985: The Use of Injunctions in Industrial Disputes. *British Journal of Industrial Relations*, 23, 1, 133–7.

Evans, S. 1987: The Use of Injunctions in Industrial Disputes: May 1984–April 1987. *British Journal of Industrial Relations*, 25, 3, 419–35.

Evans, S., Goodman, J. and Hargreaves, L. 1985: *Unfair Dismissal Law and Employment Practice in the 1980s*. Research Paper 53. London: Department of Employment.

Evans, S. and Hudson, M. 1993: *Standardized Packages Individually Wrapped?* Warwick Papers in Industrial Relations, 44. Coventry: Industrial Relations Research Unit.

Ewing, K. 1985: The Strike, the Courts and the Rule Books. *Industrial Law Journal*, 14, 3, 160–75.

Ewing, K. 1989: *Britain and the ILO*. London: Institute of Employment Rights.

Ewing, K. 1990: Trade Union Recognition – A Framework for Discussion.

Industrial Law Journal, 19, 4, 209–27.

Ewing, K. 1991: *The Employment Act 1990: A European Perspective*. London: Institute of Employment Rights.

Fenley, A. 1984: Trade Union Activists – an Endangered Species? *Employee Relations*, 6, 3, 26–32.

Forrest, H. 1980: Political Values in Individual Employment Law. *Modern Law Review*, 43, 4, 361–80.

Fredman, S. 1992: The New Right: Labour Law and Ideology in the Thatcher Years. *Oxford Journal of Legal Studies*, 12, 1, 24–44.

Freeman, R. and Pelletier, J. 1990: The Impact of Industrial Relations Legislation on British Union Density. *British Journal of Industrial Relations*, 28, 2, 141–64.

Fryer, R. 1973: Redundancy, Values and Public Policy. *Industrial Relations Journal*, 4, 2, 2–19.

Gregg, P. and Yates, A. 1991: Changes in Wage-setting Arrangements and Trade Union Presence in the 1980s. *British Journal of Industrial Relations*, 29, 3, 361–76.

Gregory, J. 1987: *Sex, Race and the Law*. London: Sage.

Hakim, C. 1989: Employment Rights: A Comparison of Full-time and Part-time Employees. *Industrial Law Journal*, 18, 2, 69–83.

Hall, M. 1988: Annual Report of the Certification Officer 1987. *Industrial Law Journal*, 17, 3, 203–5.

Hall, M. 1992: Behind the European Works Councils Directive: The European Commission's Legislative Strategy. *British Journal of Industrial Relations*, 30, 4, 547–66.

Hall, M. 1994: Industrial Relations and the Social Dimension of European Integration: Before and after Maastricht. In R. Hyman and A. Ferner (eds), *New Frontiers in European Industrial Relations*. Oxford: Blackwell.

Hanson, C. and Mather, G. 1988: *Striking Out Strikes: Changing Employment Relations in the British Labour Market*. London: Institute of Economic Affairs.

Hayek, F. A. 1960: *The Constitution of Liberty*.

Hendy, J. 1993: *A Law unto Themselves*. London: Institute of Employment Rights.

Hepple, B. 1983a: Individual Labour Law. In G. S. Bain (ed.) *Industrial Relations in Britain*. Oxford: Blackwell.

Hepple, B. 1983b: Judging Equal Rights. *Current Legal Problems*, 36, 71–90.

Hepple, B. 1986: Restructuring Employment Rights. *Industrial Law Journal*, 15, June.

Hepple, B. 1990: Social Rights in the European Economic Community: A British Perspective. *Comparative Labour Law Journal*, 11, 4, 425–40.

Hepple, B. 1992: The Fall and Rise of Unfair Dismissal. In W. McCarthy (ed.), *Legal Intervention in Industrial Relations*. Oxford: Blackwell.

Hitner, T. et al. 1982: *Racial Minority Employment: Equal Opportunity Employment Policy and Practices*. Department of Employment Research

Paper 35. London: HMSO.

IPM (Institute of Personnel Management) 1991: *Minimum Wage: An Analysis of the Issues*. London: IPM.

Justice, 1987: *Industrial Tribunals: A Report by Justice* (Chair of Committee, Bob Hepple). London: Justice.

Kahn-Freund, O. 1954: Legal Framework. In A. Flanders and H. A. Clegg (eds), *The System of Industrial Relations in Great Britain*. Oxford: Blackwell.

Kahn-Freund, O. 1983: *Labour and the Law*, 3rd edn (P. L. Davies and M. Freedland). London: Stevens.

Kahn-Freund, O. and Hepple, B. 1972: *Laws against Strikes*. Fabian Research Series 305. London: Fabian Society.

Keevash, S. 1985: Wages Councils: An Examination of Trade Union and Conservative Government Misconceptions about the Effect of Statutory Wage Fixing. *Industrial Law Journal*, 14, 4, 217–42.

Labour Party 1989: *Meet the Challenge, Make the Change*. London: Labour Party.

Labour Party 1990: *Looking to the Future*. London: Labour Party.

Leonard, A. 1987: *Judging Inequality: The Effectiveness of the Industrial Tribunal System in Sex Discrimination and Equal Pay Cases*. Cobden Trust.

Lewis, R. 1983: Collective Labour Law. In G. S. Bain (ed.), *Industrial Relations in Britain*. Oxford: Blackwell.

Lewis, R. 1986: The Role of Law in Employment Relations. In R. Lewis (ed.), *Labour Law in Britain*. Oxford: Blackwell.

Lewis, R. and Simpson, B. 1982: Disorganising Industrial Relations: An Analysis of Sections 2–8 and 10–14 of the Employment Act 1982. *Industrial Law Journal*, 11, 4, 227–44.

LRD (Labour Research Department) 1990: Are the Anti-strike Laws Working? *Labour Research*, September, 11–12.

LRD (Labour Research Department) 1991: Unions in a Legal Minefield. *Labour Research*, October, 19–21.

LRD (Labour Research Department) 1993: The Tories' Union-ballot Mania. *Labour Research*, February, 14–16.

McCarthy, W. 1992: The Rise and Fall of Collective Laissez Faire. In W. McCarthy (ed.), *Legal Intervention in Industrial Relations*. Oxford: Blackwell.

McKendrick, E. 1988: The Rights of Trade Union Members – Part I of the Employment Act 1988. *Industrial Law Journal*, 17, 3, 141–61.

Martin, R., Fosh, P., Morris, H., Smith, P. and Undy, R. 1991: The Decollectivisation of Trade Unions? Ballots and Collective Bargaining in the 1980s. *Industrial Relations Journal*, 22, 3, 197–208.

Metcalf, D. 1990: *Industrial Dispute Incidence, Laws, Resolution and Consequence*. Working Paper 65. Centre for Economic Performance, London School of Economics.

Millward, N., Stevens, M., Smart, D. and Hawes, W. 1992: *Workplace*

Industrial Relations in Transition. Aldershot: Dartmouth.

Morris, D. 1993: The Commissioner for the Rights of Trade Union Members – A Framework for the Future? *Industrial Law Journal*, 22, 2, 104–18.

Napier, B. 1992: Computerisation and Employment Rights. *Industrial Law Journal*, 21, 1, 1–14.

Simpson, B. 1979: Judicial Control of ACAS. *Industrial Law Journal*, 8, 2, 69–84.

Simpson, B. 1991: The Employment Act 1990 in Context. *Modern Law Review*, 54, 3, 418–38.

Smith, P. and Morton, G. 1990: A Change of Heart: Union Exclusion in the Provincial Newspaper Sector. *Work, Employment and Society*, 4, 1, 105–24.

Smith, P., Fosh, P., Martin, R., Morris, H. and Undy, R. 1993: Ballots and Union Government in the 1980s. *British Journal of Industrial Relations*, 31, 3, 365–82.

Steele, M., Miller, K. and Gennard, J. 1986: The Trade Union Act 1984: Political Fund Ballots. *British Journal of Industrial Relations*, 24, 3, 443–67.

Tebbit, N. 1988: *Upwardly Mobile*. London: Weidenfeld & Nicolson.

Terry, M. 1983: Shop Stewards through Expansion and Recession. *Industrial Relations Journal*, 14, 3, 49–58.

Terry, M. 1988: Recontexualising Shopfloor Industrial Relations: Some Case Study Evidence. In S. Tailby and C. Whitston (eds), *Manufacturing Change*. Oxford: Blackwell.

Townley, B. 1987: Union Recognition: A Comparative Analysis of the Pros and Cons of a Legal Procedure. *British Journal of Industrial Relations*, 25, 2, 177–99.

TUC–Labour Party Liaison Committee 1986: People at Work: New Rights, New Responsibilities. London: TUC / Labour Party.

Tur, R. 1985: The Legitimacy of Industrial Action: Trade Unionism at the Crossroads. In W. McCarthy (ed.), *Trade Unions*, 2nd edn. Harmondsworth: Penguin.

Undy, R. and Martin, R. 1984: *Ballots and Trade Union Democracy*. Oxford: Blackwell.

von Prondynski, F. 1984: Freedom of Association in Modern Industrial Relations. *Industrial Relations Journal*, 15, 1, 9–16.

Waddington, J. 1992: Trade Union Membership in Britain, 1980–1987. Unemployment and Restructuring. *British Journal of Industrial Relations*, 30, 2, 287–324.

Wallington, P. 1985: Policing the Miners' Strike. *Industrial Law Journal*, 14, 145–59.

Wedderburn, K. W. (Lord) 1971: *The Worker and the Law*. Harmondsworth: Penguin.

Wedderburn, K. W. (Lord) 1976: The Employment Protection Act 1975:

Collective Dimensions. *Modern Law Review*, 39, 2, 169–83.

Wedderburn, K. W. (Lord) 1986: *The Worker and the Law*, 3rd edn. Harmondsworth: Penguin.

Wedderburn, K. W. (Lord) 1989: Freedom of Association and Philosophies of Labour Law. *Industrial Law Journal*, 18, 1, 1–38.

Weekes, B., Mellish, M., Dickens, L. and Lloyd, J. 1975: *Industrial Relations and the Limits of Law*. Oxford: Blackwell.

10

The State: The Public Sector

David Winchester and Stephen Bach

Since 1979, Conservative governments have attempted to uproot traditional patterns of public-sector industrial relations. The origins of these changes lay in the unprecedented levels of conflict in the public sector during the 1970s, culminating in the notorious 'winter of discontent', which brought into sharp relief the importance of public-sector industrial relations. During the 1980s and early 1990s industrial relations remained centre stage, most visibly through a series of bitter disputes involving civil servants, health workers, teachers and, most dramatically, coal miners. These disputes reflected largely unsuccessful union attempts to safeguard jobs and pay in a harsher economic and political climate. The landscape of the public sector has also been transformed: privatization of former nationalized industries and public utilities decreased its size; contracting out of services blurred the boundaries between public and private provision; and the establishment of NHS trusts, grant maintained schools and civil service executive agencies fragmented the traditional monolithic pattern of public-sector organization.

At the heart of these changes lay a deep distrust of the contribution that the public sector could make towards the British economy. The Conservative belief in the superiority of market provision and the necessity of competition to sharpen performance sat uneasily with the post-war trend of a growing proportion of government expenditure and employment being absorbed by the public sector. Government ministers reserved their greatest hostility for the public-sector trade unions, arguing that their members worked in services protected from the rigours of competition and used their privileged position to extort excessive pay rises out of hapless governments. Conservative criticism was not confined to trade unions; public service managers were also implicated for failing to rectify this situation. They were viewed as too passive and acquiescent in responding to the demands of professional staff and trade unions. Consequently, a central theme of Conservative policy has been the need to strengthen the management function in the public sector and to ensure greater efficiency, value for money and responsiveness to public needs. This philosophy underpinned the managerial and organizational restructuring which has radically altered the context in which industrial relations are conducted.

These changes have altered the management of industrial relations in the public services and the former public enterprises. This chapter focuses on the core services that have remained in the public sector: namely, the civil service, the National Health Service (NHS) and local government. It begins with a consideration of the significance and character of the state as employer. It then examines the changes in management and organization of the public services, before analysing the consequences for the structure of pay determination, patterns of conflict and changes in working practices. Chapter 16 examines parallel themes for the privatized sectors.

The State as Employer

The significance of the state in its role as employer stems from the large numbers of employees in the public sector and the distinctive set of employment practices, which has set an example for the private sector (Fredman and Morris 1989: 25). The state remains directly or indirectly responsible for nearly 5.5 million employees, representing 22 per cent of the workforce (Pearson 1994). As table 10.1 indicates, local government is the largest sector with more than 2.6 million employees providing social services, education, police, fire and other services. The NHS has more than 1 million employees of which nearly half are nursing staff. The civil service employs close to 600,000 employees; and most of the other public-sector employees work in the surviving nationalized industries such as the Post Office, British Coal, British Rail and in other public corporations.

Conservative policies have changed the size and composition of the workforce. Across the public sector the government has been

Table 10.1   UK public-sector employment, mid-1993 (thousands)

	Total	Male	Female Full-time	Part-time
Total public sector	5,828	2,638	1,677	1,513
Public corporations	532	432	77	23
Central government, of which:	2,245	917	792	536
National Health Service	1,185	260	473	452
HM forces	271	252	19	0
Other (e.g. civil servants)	789	405	300	84
Local authorities, of which:	2,680	1,089	716	875
Education	1,201	264	381	556
Social services	398	56	134	208
Police	207	172	26	9
Construction	90	85	4	1
Other	784	512	171	101
Grant funded education	371	200	92	79

The figures for public corporations refer mainly to nationalized industries. National Health Service figures include NHS trusts. Grant funded education includes universities, and further/higher education establishments and grant maintained schools previously within the control of local authorities.

Source: adapted from Pearson 1994.

committed to reducing staff numbers, with the greatest reductions occurring in the civil service. Local government and the NHS were less directly controlled by the government and in both sectors employment remained relatively stable throughout the 1980s. More recently, redundancies have become a more common feature of employment practice in these sectors as a consequence of the market-style reforms.

The generally stable pattern of employment disguises important changes in the composition of the workforce. Two aspects stand out. First, there has been a sharp decline in the numbers of ancillary staff employed in the public sector, reflecting the policy of competitive tendering where employees have to compete for their jobs against outside competition. Regardless of whether the service is contracted out or not, the competitive tendering process invariably leads to reductions in the number of staff employed. For example, in the

NHS where cleaning, catering and laundry services have been subject to mandatory competitive tendering since 1983, ancillary staff numbers have fallen from 172,000 in 1981 to 86,000 by 1991 (Department of Health 1993). The extension of competitive tendering to the civil service and to white-collar services in local government can only lead to an acceleration of this trend.

Second, there has been an increase in the number of management staff in the public sector and in their remuneration. The NHS has been particularly beset by controversy, with the commercialization of the health service used to increase sharply the pay of trust chief executives in contrast to the pay restraint faced by other health workers. Chief executives at the first 57 trusts established in April 1991 enjoyed an average rise of 8.7 per cent in the year to March 1993 (IDS 1993). These pay increases, coupled with figures showing that the number of NHS managers has risen from 6,091 in 1989–90 to 20,478 in 1992–3, have fuelled controversy about the government's reforms (*Guardian*, 9 March 1994). For critics of government policy these figures indicate the bureaucracy associated with the 'market style' reforms, the misguided importance attached to management at the expense of direct service providers, and the lack of accountability of trusts in setting managers' pay with little direct public scrutiny.

A distinctive characteristic of public-sector employment is the relatively high proportion of women in the workforce, accounting for 3 million of the 5.5 million employees. As in other sectors, women are often employed on a part-time basis and concentrated at the bottom of the employment hierarchy; as a result there is an acute low-pay problem (see chapter 18). None the less, the public sector also employs substantial numbers of women in professional and managerial grades. There are important implications for public-sector trade unions whose membership is drawn heavily from women. More generally for the trade unions in a period of retrenchment, membership in the public services remained far higher than in the private sector and has not been subject to the same degree of decline. Trade union density in national and local government and within hospitals has hovered around 60 per cent (Bird et al. 1993) and 78 per cent of employees are covered by collective agreements (Millward et al. 1992: 93–4). This pattern of high trade union membership has been attributed to the concentration of public-sector employment in large, bureaucratic undertakings and government encouragement for employees to join trade unions (Bain and Price 1983).

The decline of the model employer

Since the end of the First World War British governments have recognized the need to act as a good employer to promote stable industrial relations. This concern was not confined to state employees, for successive governments believed that the employment practices adopted for their own employees should act as a model for the private sector. The government did not simply rely on exhortation; as a major purchaser of private-sector services it used its position to require private-sector contractors to pay fair wages when carrying out government work (Fredman and Morris 1989).

For the government's own employees the philosophy of the good employer meant tangible benefits, such as high levels of job security, good pensions and sick leave benefits and procedures to resolve grievance and disciplinary issues. It also signified a willingness to recognize trade unions. The institutional position of trade unions was reinforced through the establishment of national joint industrial councils (Whitley Councils) where trade unions negotiated over terms and conditions of employment. This collective bargaining model spread from the civil service to local government and the NHS. Collective bargaining rights were backed up by encouraging individuals to join trade unions, helping to ensure support for the outcomes of the bargaining process. The good employer model also influenced the pay determination process where emphasis was placed on ensuring that fair comparisons were made with the private sector so as not to disadvantage public-sector workers. Finally, when disputes between management and trade unions emerged there was a commitment to use extensive arbitration procedures to resolve these differences without reverting to overt conflict (Winchester 1983).

This approach was not universally or evenly applied and the long-standing concerns of public-sector trade unions with problems of low pay indicate that some groups fared better than others. None the less, the idea of the good employer remained an aspiration of government policy even when not translated fully into practice. The good employer model also implied a limited role for management in the conduct of industrial relations. The centrality of national collective bargaining meant that managers were detached from the pay determination process and their role was largely confined to administering the detailed regulations that emerged from national agreements (Beaumont 1992). Managers also had only a limited role in the crucial area of recruitment and selection; in the civil service a separate commission carried out this function, while in the NHS the appointment of professional staff was rarely viewed as a concern of line management. One legacy of this philosophy was an underdeveloped management function, which impeded later government attempts to decentralize collective bargaining.

It was not simply the political consensus in the post-war period that sustained the good employer model; it was buttressed also by a favourable economic situation. In the 1950s and 1960s continuous economic growth and low inflation enabled growing government revenues to be channelled into the expanding welfare state. This economic prosperity allowed the public sector to pay wages that were comparable to the private sector, safeguard job security and provide opportunities for promotion. From the late 1960s, however, this position was undermined as economic growth faltered, unemployment rose and inflation increased substantially. As the economic situation worsened, exacerbated by the oil crisis of the early 1970s, the consequences for the philosophy of the good employer became apparent.

First, the rise in inflation, which peaked at 26 per cent in 1975, had serious consequences for the public-sector pay bill. As public-sector pay increases were indirectly linked to movements in the retail price index, soaring inflation undermined the government's ability to control its expenditure. Second, governments tried to contain expenditure through a series of incomes policies and public expenditure reductions. Trade unions and their increasingly restive members responded through industrial action, and in the process banished their traditionally moderate image. Finally, in the wake of the 1979 winter of discontent, a Conservative government was elected on a wave of anti-union sentiment, committed to breaking the power of public-sector trade unions, reducing public expenditure and reversing the employment practices associated with the model employer.

For the government, the scale of public expenditure hindered economic prosperity as the financing of the public sector required high taxation and pushed up interest rates and inflation. The priority was therefore to curb public expenditure and to reduce employment levels. Shortly after taking office the Conservatives targeted staffing levels in the civil service and subsequently the NHS. The government was initially frustrated by its inability to curb expenditure in local authorities, which enjoyed greater autonomy from central government intervention. Consequently, a series of legislative and administrative measures were introduced to control local authority spending, leading to a significant centralization of government power (Cochrane 1993).

The primary instrument of public expenditure control was the system of cash limits. This broke with the previous system of volume planning, which had allowed policymakers to plan services in volume terms and receive additional resources to meet unanticipated increases in wage costs and prices. In contrast, cash limits were less flexible; they allocated a fixed amount of money for service provision, and required services managers to accept the responsibility for staying within predetermined budgets. Cash limits had a significant impact in shaping the conduct of industrial relations (Winchester 1987).

First, the government abandoned its position of good employer and encouraged a more abrasive style of public-sector management. In lengthy disputes in the early 1980s government ministers used direct and indirect intervention to defeat union claims. Second, cash limits forced union and employer negotiators to confront the trade-off between income and employment. The cash limit included a pay assumption which, if breached, required the additional costs to be funded by job losses, higher productivity or service reductions. Finally, cash limits required a more active management participation in the negotiating process; local services managers needed to communicate their priorities to employers negotiating at national level to ensure that pay awards could be implemented within the financial constraints they faced at local level.

Management practice and organizational restructuring

Since 1979 there has been a radical change in the way in which public services have been managed and organized (Stewart and Walsh 1992; Farnham and Horton 1993). During the 1970s, governments largely confined their interest to problems of public-sector pay determination and the industrial strife that stemmed from the precarious state of the British economy. The distinctiveness of the 1980s was not that these concerns diminished, but rather that the Conservatives intervened more actively to reshape the management and organization of the public services. Underlying these changes was the belief that more forceful management, organized on a decentralized basis and held accountable for performance, would ensure greater control of expenditure and lead to better public services. For all parts of the public sector this involved major structural changes.

The Civil Service   As civil servants are employees of the Crown, the government has greater direct control over their management than over other public services. The Conservatives entered office convinced that the civil service's monopoly position had produced a large, inefficient organization whose employees enjoyed privileged terms and conditions of employment. The government moved rapidly to enhance managerial efficiency and curb civil service expenditure. Manpower targets were established which aimed to decrease the number of civil servants from 742,000 in 1979 to 642,000 by 1982. By 1990 civil service numbers had been reduced by 20 per cent (Horton 1993). A related initiative was Mrs Thatcher's establishment of an Efficiency Unit under Sir Derek Rayner of Marks and Spencer, which organized value for money audits (Rayner Scrutinies) and identified financial savings. In addition to raising efficiency, these scrutinies signalled the importance that the government attached to senior civil servants' management responsibilities to ensure value for money. This message was reinforced by the Financial Management Initiative which devolved budgetary responsibility to individual cost centres and made departments more accountable for expenditure and performance.

The most radical change stemmed from a critical report by the head of the Efficiency Unit, Sir Robin Ibbs, which reviewed the impact of the government's management reforms in the civil service. The report, entitled *Improving Management in Government: The Next Steps* (Ibbs 1988), stated bluntly that 'the civil service is too big and too diverse to manage as a single entity'. It criticized the neglect of management and service delivery, compared to the attention given to policymaking. This neglect discouraged the effective use of resources and was compounded by the inflexible and centralized systems of financial and personnel management which prevented effective management. The solution advocated was to reorganize executive activities of government, as distinct from policy advice, into separate agencies with specific responsibilities and targets. These agencies, headed by chief executives often recruited from outside the civil service, were granted greater flexibility over financial and personnel matters to enable them to meet their performance targets. The growth of executive agencies has been very rapid and by the end of 1993 there were 92 agencies, together with 64 executive units and offices within Customs and Excise and the Inland Revenue which operate along the principles of agencies. Together, these organizations employ around 350,000 civil servants, about 60 per cent of the total (Next Steps Review 1993).

There are important variations between the agencies in terms of size, the range of activities they undertake, the financial regimes they operate under and the type of links they retain with their sponsoring department (Corby 1993). These factors have influenced the degree to which individual agencies have been able to exercise their new personnel and financial freedoms. Some agencies, such as HMSO, have a financial regime akin to a commercial organization, enabling them to develop new pay and grading structures incorporating a performance management system and measures to harmonize terms and conditions of employment (IRS 1993a).

The longer-term significance of the *Next Steps* initiative is becoming apparent with the government's confirmation that executive agencies mark a transition phase towards privatization or contracting out of services (Next Steps Review 1993). As the civil service becomes dominated by agencies, which are developing their own distinctive personnel practices linked to their business needs, the survival of a unified civil service with career progression through different departments has been jeopardized (Corby 1993). These organizational and management changes have resulted in a smaller and more fragmented civil service and have prepared the ground for more radical industrial relations changes during the 1990s.

The National Health Service   In the Conservatives' second decade of office the most contentious changes have been the market-based reforms introduced into the NHS. The NHS continues to be funded by central government which thus retains responsibility for overall policy and management. As in other areas of the public sector the government has used this influence to enhance managerial control in the name of increased efficiency. A variety of initiatives were implemented to produce financial savings. Health authorities were encouraged to be more commercial and raise additional revenue, for example by expanding private-patient provision in hospitals. Manpower targets were used as a crude means to reduce health authorities' wages bills, an approach that has continued with regional health authorities instructed in 1993 to limit their HQ staff to 200. However, this policy made less headway than in the civil service, and in response to constantly rising demand for health care the NHS still has over 1 million employees.

Mandatory competitive tendering for cleaning, catering and laundry services introduced from 1983 had a greater impact. Although the majority of contracts remained in-house, competitive tendering enabled general managers to alter employment practices and to undermine terms and conditions of employment (Bach 1989). With hindsight, it is apparent that by encouraging health service managers to concentrate on the specification and purchase of health services rather than their provision, these developments foreshadowed the later development of the internal market.

One of the most important initiatives during the 1980s was the introduction of a general management role into the NHS. This followed a government inquiry into NHS management chaired by Roy Griffiths, a senior manager from J. Sainsbury plc (Griffiths Report 1983). The report criticized the consensus style of management and the absence of clear responsibility for decision-making in the NHS. General managers, employed on fixed term contracts with a performance related pay element, were subsequently appointed at each level of the NHS. The introduction of general management has established a tighter managerial regime, dominated by the requirement to stay within financial targets, and with managers increasingly willing to challenge the working practices of professional staff. General management was an essential prerequisite for the establishment of an internal market as the NHS became more amenable to political influence through the creation of a management regime of decree and compliance (Butler 1994).

Since April 1991, an internal market has operated in the NHS with the separation of the purchasing of health care, carried out by district health authorities and some general practitioners, from the provision of health services, undertaken by hospitals and community units. The majority of hospitals have opted out of district health authority control to become NHS trusts. Trusts have greater potential autonomy to manage their own affairs: employing staff directly; establishing their own terms and conditions of employment; and devising new industrial relations procedures.

These changes have had a major impact on the climate of NHS industrial relations. NHS trusts' revenue is dependent on competing effectively to gain sufficient contract income from a range of purchasers who renew their contracts on an annual basis. Salaries and wages accounted for 76 per cent of health authorities' net revenue expenditure in 1990 (Office of Health Economics 1992) and therefore managers have identified labour savings as a means to enhance competitiveness: reducing staffing levels; challenging traditional working practices; and tightening procedures in areas such as discipline and sickness (Seccombe and Buchan 1994). In the 1990s the NHS has evolved from an integrated, professionally dominated bureaucracy into a plethora of separate organizations, where managers hold the purse-strings and make decisions using increasingly financial criteria. These reforms have undermined employees' job security and challenged traditional employment practices.

Local government More than 2.5 million employees are employed directly by individual local authorities, covering a wide range of activities in education, social services, environmental health, housing and transport. This complex and diverse workforce includes low-paid ancillary and clerical workers alongside professional occupations; most notably, over 400,000 teachers. Two features distinguish local government from the civil service and the NHS. First, local authorities are not totally dependent on central government funding, as they raise a proportion of their expenditure by levying local taxes. Second, local government is run by elected members who may not share the political affiliation of the party in government. These characteristics of local government frustrated the Conservatives who believed that their policies to reduce inflation and curb public expenditure were being undermined by profligate local authorities. The Thatcher administration introduced a series of reforms: rate capping; the abolition of the predominantly Labour-controlled metropolitan authorities; and the establishment of a uniform business rate. These measures curbed the power of local authorities, ensuring that they spent only as much as central government considered appropriate.

The most important changes have arisen from the government's policy of compulsory competitive tendering (CCT). The initiative started slowly, but the Local Government Act 1988 extended CCT into cleaning services, refuse collection and maintenance functions and in 1991 the government unveiled plans to establish tendering for white-collar services (Treasury 1991). The tendering exercise has required authorities to separate the client role, which draws up the specification, manages the CCT process and monitors the contract, from the contractor role, which directly provides the service. As the discussion in chapter 16 indicates, the impact of the policy has been profound. There have been job losses, extensive alterations to terms and conditions of employment, and radical restructuring of internal management and organization which has fragmented the traditional unified structure of local government (Colling 1993).

Services less directly affected by CCT have not been immune from management changes. In housing and transport the role of local authorities has diminished with the establishment of non-elected quangos to oversee the provision of these services. For social workers, reforms of community care have introduced the purchaser/ provider split, radically changing the roles they perform. The 1988 Education Reform Act introduced the Local Management of Schools (LMS) which delegated some of the responsibility for financial and staff management to governing bodies. Schools have been encouraged to opt out of local authority control and the government is fostering competition between schools for pupils (Department for Education 1992). These changes, and the pressures generated by central government intervention to restructure the national curriculum and introduce 'league tables' and other performance indicators for schools, have exposed 'the crucial importance of school management and the need to improve it' (STRB 1993: ix).

The new managerialism

Changes in all parts of the public services have radically altered the management process and organizational context. New financial and performance targets have been introduced to increase managerial accountability upwards to central government, through a proliferation of performance indicators and league tables which compare the relative efficiency of organizations. At the same time, the government has emphasized the importance of responsiveness and accountability to the customers of public services with targets established under the Citizen's Charter initiative (Cabinet Office 1991). This emphasis on performance has been reinforced by establishing internal markets to stimulate greater competition between the providers of public services. The specific character of these internal markets and the degree of competition generated has varied substantially depending on the political sensitivity of the service, the level and type of funding policies, and the degree of flexibility in the contracting arrangements.

Effective implementation of these complex organizational reforms has required the transformation of the management process. Traditionally, public services have been characterized by bureaucratic, hierarchical management structures designed to deliver a standardized service in a uniform manner to clients. Centralized industrial relations procedures mirrored the management process and personnel managers ensured local managers adhered to national rules. Service managers concentrated on channelling inputs to professional staff who used their discretion to determine the service provided.

To establish a more performance-orientated and efficient public service required a new breed of managers to fulfil a number of functions. The first aim was to curb the power of interest groups, not only trade unions, but also professions, such as doctors and school-teachers. Professional staff were believed to be indifferent to the need to use resources more cost-effectively and were insufficiently accountable for their performance. Second, in a more restrictive financial climate, managers were to adjudicate between competing claims on resources and ensure value for money. Finally, the devolution of decision-making to managers was designed to allow the government to distance itself from the operational problems of the public sector. Awkward decisions, for example about closures of hospitals or schools, could be presented as rational managerial decisions or the outcome of market forces rather than the consequences of political judgements.

These managerial changes have been associated with the decentralization of management authority and the internal restructuring of public service organizations into separate business units. Managers are accorded greater authority over finance and personnel policy and are expected to shape their organization and employment practices to be responsive to the market conditions and business targets they confront. The strengthening and delegation of management authority within a strict framework of financial accountability has encouraged diverse responses from managers between and within the public services, fragmenting the traditional patterns of industrial relations in the public services. Managers have broadened their industrial relations preoccupations beyond traditional concerns with bargaining structures and processes to an emphasis on ensuring improved individual performance and work effort at local level. This has encouraged widespread experimentation in personnel practice with the spread of appraisal, an emphasis on direct communication with employees and the adoption of total quality programmes.

Nevertheless, the degree of change has been variable. Managers have had to confront the historical legacy of the model employer and have frequently faced opposition from powerful groups of professional staff. Doctors, nurses, schoolteachers and the police in their differing ways have all proved effective in slowing the pace of change. Moreover, the complexity of government reforms and the pace at which they have been introduced have placed new demands on managers that cannot always be met. A common theme permeating official reports has been the limited competence and resources available to public services managers to implement this radical agenda of change (Audit Commission 1994; STRB 1994).

The changes have been justified in terms of a comparison of traditional public service management with private-sector 'best practice'. They have thus challenged a widespread belief about the distinctiveness of 'management in the public domain' (Stewart and Ransom 1988). While recognizing the diversity of private-sector management practice, it can be argued that public service management practice differs fundamentally from that in the private sector, in terms of objectives, the context in which it operates and the constraints upon performance. Stewart and Ransom are not alone in thinking that there are dangers in an uncritical adoption of private-sector management practice and rhetoric, not only in respect of competition and market mechanisms, but also in terms of the emulation of decentralized pay determination.

Pay Determination and Conflict

As managers have been forced to achieve greater control of their labour costs, inevitably they have questioned the relevance of the national pay and conditions arrangements that have provided the framework for public-sector industrial relations since the 1950s. Many public service managers no doubt shared government ministers' hostility to the system of centralized collective bargaining involving strong trade unions committed to the principle of pay comparability and standardized conditions of employment. As the rest of this chapter shows, however, the creation of a decentralized system of pay determination, responsive to the needs of managerial efficiency, labour-market conditions and employee performance, has proved to be a difficult enterprise.

The decentralization of pay determination has developed in a piecemeal and uneven manner. This can be explained partly by disagreements within each of the three main parties to the process, as well as between them. First, government policy has been inconsistent; the overwhelming priority of the Treasury for tight budgetary control has undermined ministerial exhortation on the advantages of local pay flexibility. Second, public service managers have also been divided on the pace and direction of reform. All managers wanted greater freedom from centralized and prescriptive agreements, but many recognized that flexibility and management discretion were possible within reformed national pay structures. A substantial investment in organizational resources and management skills, especially in the area of personnel management, would have been necessary for a more decisive shift to local pay determination. Finally, trade union leaders invariably resisted proposals to dismantle national pay agreements, though some local officials and activists anticipated that they would benefit from the exploitation of new bargaining opportunities.

The slow and erratic pace of bargaining reform can be explained also by important variations in the institutional forms and substantive content of national agreements. These arrangements have been shaped by past conflicts between central government, public employers and trade unions, and they also reflect the diverse labour market characteristics of different occupations in public service employment. It is useful, therefore, to explore the changing patterns of public-sector pay determination by comparing the experience of the civil service, the NHS and local government. In each case, differences in pay principles and bargaining structures can be linked with variations in pay outcomes and conflict.

The civil service

From the mid-1950s until the early 1980s, the terms and conditions of employment of more than half a million civil servants were determined within a highly centralized institutional framework. National negotiations between the Treasury or Cabinet Office and the trade unions produced a detailed pay and conditions code which had to be applied uniformly throughout the service. There was also a unique pay determination system. The recommendation of the Priestley

Commission (1955) that 'the primary principle for determining the pay of civil servants should be fair comparison with the current remuneration of outside staffs employed in broadly comparable work' was accepted. The comparability principle often caused problems for governments' incomes policies in the 1960s and 1970s, but it survived as the centrepiece of the system of pay determination.

The Conservative government sought a fundamental change in the priority accorded to different principles of pay determination when it withdrew from the civil service pay agreement in 1981. This precipitated a 20-week dispute in which coordinated strike action by civil service unions imposed significant costs on government, especially by delaying the collection of tax revenue. As part of the eventual settlement, the government established an inquiry into civil service pay and successfully influenced its findings. The Megaw report recommended a system of 'informed collective bargaining' in which pay comparisons 'should have a much less decisive influence than in the past' (Megaw Report 1982: para. 113). In a reformed system, affordability, defined by cash limits, should constrain overall pay increases. Thereafter, the requirements of managerial efficiency should prevail; pay structures should be designed 'to recruit, retain and motivate [staff] to perform efficiently the duties required of them at an appropriate level of competence' (para. 91).

In the middle of the decade, the government experimented with piecemeal 'flexibility' initiatives to deal with recruitment and retention problems, and the introduction of a performance related pay scheme for senior management grades. It was not until 1987, however, that individual civil service unions and the government began to reach agreements involving a more systematic reform. As Kessler (1993: 306) has argued, these agreements 'incorporated the two competing traditions of pay determination – one rooted in a concern for comparability, the other in the pursuit of flexibility as a management tool'.

On the first issue, the trade unions were able to secure a safety net for annual pay increases, namely, that they should fall within the inter-quartile range of pay *movements* for non-manual employees in the private sector, and also that they should be influenced by data from surveys of pay *levels* and benefits of comparable jobs conducted at least every four years. In practice, the unions were disappointed that across-the-board pay increases were usually close to the lower quartile level of settlements elsewhere. Second, the government was able to introduce more flexible pay structures in the separate agreements negotiated with individual unions for the main occupational groups. The existing grades were assimilated into a new pay spine, or grouped into broader pay spans, allowing management to respond to local recruitment difficulties under the terms of a general flexibility clause.

The agreements also introduced performance related pay schemes. In most parts of the civil service, the operation of these schemes has produced less union opposition than the original proposals. As Kessler noted, 'the timescales involved and the relatively small amounts allocated have produced a benign system viewed simply as providing long service awards' (1993: 307). For this reason, departmental managers became more disillusioned with the schemes; the substantial investment of management time in conducting staff appraisal and administering the schemes produced only a limited impact on employee motivation and performance.

By the beginning of the 1990s, collective bargaining procedures had become less centralized and more sensitive to the occupational and organizational characteristics of different departments. Also, the priority accorded to the principle of comparability had been eroded. The degree and pace of change, however, had been relatively limited and slow. All of the parties had been forced to compromise, not least in the face of internal divisions, and the initiatives had not eliminated the conflicts between them.

The structure and principles of pay determination will change much more significantly from the mid-1990s as a result of the reorganization of the civil service into semi-autonomous agencies and the extension of market-testing noted earlier. The Civil Service (Management Functions) Act 1992 enables the Treasury to delegate its responsibility for setting pay and conditions to individual departments and agencies. More than twenty agencies employing more than half of the civil service staff had been given delegated responsibility by April 1994. As part of the government's wider commitment to 'performance management', managers in delegated departments and agencies will be expected to develop their own grading, appraisal, training, promotion and performance related pay schemes.

While civil service unions have been unable to prevent pay delegation, they have begun to reorganize their representational structures and support services to coordinate their input into more dispersed bargaining activities and to maintain existing terms and conditions of employment. Their desire to minimize the fragmentation of bargaining may be helped by the Treasury; it will continue to set expenditure limits and paybill targets and it may also impose conditions on the delegation of management functions, such as the approval of new job evaluation schemes (IRS 1993a).

It is inevitable that the pace and direction of change will vary according to the size, activities and financial regimes of delegated agencies and departments. Resistance to change may be greater in the larger agencies involved in mainstream policy and operations of their departments, such as the Employment Service, Benefits Agency and Inland Revenue, each of which employs around 50,000 staff, than in the smaller more peripheral agencies and those providing specialist services to departments. The latter group, which includes the main candidates for privatization, has been more innovative in developing new pay and employment policies and more successful in eroding the effectiveness of union representation. Despite these differences, and others based on the strength of trade unions and the career background of chief executives, Corby (1993) found examples of managers 'seeking to reject traditional employee relations processes' in all of her case studies.

The National Health Service

From the establishment of the NHS in 1948 until the early 1980s, the system of pay determination for health service employees had many of the same characteristics as that of the civil service. First, it was rooted in the common tradition of 'Whitleyism': the principle that joint agreement between employers and employees should be reached whenever possible, and that the two sides should seek to resolve their differences within an agreed procedure that included arrangements for arbitration. In the NHS the most important decisions on terms and conditions of employment were negotiated in ten functional Whitley Councils. Second, the structure of collective bargaining was highly centralized and detailed changes in the terms and conditions of employment, after approval from the Secretary of State, were applied in a prescriptive and uniform way. Third, the pay of health service employees was linked formally or informally with a number of external comparators, mainly in the civil service or local authorities.

The structures and processes of collective bargaining, however, had to confront distinctive problems arising from the size and complexity of the workforce and the multi-tiered organizational structure of the NHS. The enormous diversity of occupational groups was reflected in the multiplicity of staff organizations, about forty of which had national recognition. Staff-side representation was divided between TUC-affiliated unions, often competing for health service membership as well as members outside the service, and non-affiliated professional associations which recruited mainly health care staff. Intense organizational rivalry and conflict over bargaining objectives and tactics in defence of narrow occupational or professional interests complicated both national negotiations and local consultation (Corby 1992: 34). These difficulties were exacerbated by the representational problems on the 'management side'. While membership has changed over time, it has been dominated by Health Department civil servants and regional NHS managers: 'employers who do not pay and paymasters who do not employ', in the words of McCarthy (1976: 11).

The Conservative government's determination to elevate the criterion of affordability above that of comparability precipitated a lengthy dispute in the NHS in 1982. The unions coordinated a nine-month campaign of demonstrations and 'days of action', avoiding the public hostility that had accompanied the disruption of health services in the winter of discontent three years earlier. Research by Morris and Rydzkowski (1984) found evidence of widespread cooperation between local management and unions in minimizing the impact of the dispute on patient care. The eventual pay settlements, however, were lower than expected and nurses were awarded a higher settlement than other staff. More importantly, by establishing two new pay review bodies for nurses and midwives and other health service professionals, the government seemed to offer 'special treatment' to half the NHS workforce 'on the understanding that such generosity would be reciprocated by peace in the health service' (Bailey and Trinder 1989: 28).

The pay review body for nurses, like its three predecessors covering the armed forces, doctors and dentists, and the 'top salaries' of a small group of senior military officers, civil servants and judges, is a standing body able to develop an independent judgement on medium-term pay developments. Each year it takes evidence from government departments, health service managers, trade unions and other interested parties, reviews the information and arguments, and makes recommendations to the government. The presumption that the government will accept the recommendations, unless there are 'clear and compelling reasons for not doing so', has been broadly realized in practice. The full implementation of recommended pay increases, however, was delayed or staged following four of the first nine reports, thus reducing the annual paybill costs substantially. As Buchan (1992: 14) noted, the 'tension between accommodating public opinion and assuaging the Treasury continues to be a political factor'; in three of the five years in which full implementation occurred a general election was held.

The methodology and impact of the nurses' pay review body during the 1980s has influenced wider debates on pay determination in the public services. First, in comparison with the experience of national pay bargaining, the review process has encouraged a more systematic analysis of the parties' arguments and the employment and pay data on which they are based. It has assessed the conflicting arguments on affordability and comparability, developed a detailed review of recruitment and retention data, and considered arguments about motivation, morale and workload. The publicity accompanying the parties' evidence, and the publication of annual reports, has turned the nurses' pay review process into a form of 'arm's length bargaining' in which the review body has been sometimes unwilling to accept the expenditure control priorities of central government.

The generally positive evaluation of the pay review process for nurses made by health service unions has been based not only on its independence and methodology, but also on its impact on relative pay. The pay review system has been associated with a significant improvement in nurses' real income, invariably matching average annual increases in earnings for non-manual staff, and improving their pay relative to other health service employees.

Several caveats should, however, be attached to this positive assessment of the review process (Buchan 1992; Thornley 1993). First, the most significant uplift in relative pay arose from the clinical grading review in 1988 conducted by the nurses' and midwives' Whitley Council; the review body role was limited to recommending its implementation. Second, the recommendations of the review body have been much more favourable to qualified nursing staff and nurse managers than to the large number of nursing auxiliaries. Third, the improvement in pay relativities *vis-à-vis* other health service staff and external comparators should not disguise gendered occupational segregation; that is, the pay of mainly female nurses has improved only in comparison with the relatively low pay of women employed in the NHS and elsewhere.

The nurses' pay review system created a dilemma for government ministers and the senior health service managers who believed that pay determination should be decentralized to become more responsive to local labour market conditions. The review body was relatively unsympathetic to the demand for 'flexible pay supplements' and cautious in its assessment of the impact of the pilot schemes that were introduced at the end of the 1980s, arguing that local pay supplements could not compensate for more general supply side problems. As Buchan (1992: 28) has argued, the relationship between pay levels and nurses' labour-market behaviour is complex.

> There is no single national labour market for nurses, but rather a series of interlinked and overlapping geographical and skill based labour markets of varying sizes and dimensions. The age, gender, marital status, career history, basic and post basic qualifications and employment status (full or part time) of each individual nurse all play a part in determining in which labour market she or he is located.

It is not clear, therefore, how simple 'market forces' arguments can be applied to nurses' pay determination, either at national or local levels. Moreover, it can be argued that expenditure decisions, influencing both the demand for health care services and the supply of trained nurses, have allowed government to exploit its monopsony power in setting pay levels.

Elsewhere in the NHS, the national structures of pay determination survived the 1980s relatively intact. The level of national pay awards for most groups, however, was depressed by the strict application of cash limits. The most dramatic dispute arose from the sustained but unsuccessful attempt of ambulance staff in 1989–90 to establish a pay indexation formula similar to that enjoyed by the other 'emergency services', fire and police (Kerr and Sachdev 1992; Nichol 1992). By the early 1990s most of the national agreements had reformed wage and salary structures to produce less rigid job definitions and to facilitate local pay supplements. These were designed mainly to deal with recruitment and retention problems relating to particular occupations rather than to reward individual performance.

The national pay agreements thus became less important in two respects: local managers had the 'flexibility' to pay more to relatively few staff for market-related reasons, but they had to find ways of reducing the total paybill to stay within tight budgets. A more confident cadre of general managers used competitive tendering to impose more efficient working practices. They also sought cost savings through 'reprofiling' or skill-mix reviews, encouraged by the creation of a new grade of 'health care assistant' and the symbolically important insistence of the NHS Management Executive that the pay and conditions of the new grade should be excluded from any of the national agreements and should be determined locally.

The creation of an 'internal market' for health care threatened a further diminution in the regulatory effect of the national pay arrangements and the emergence of a more diverse pattern of enterprise-level industrial relations. Seifert (1992: 339) argues that power will devolve to workplace trade union representatives as well as local managers, and that this may lead to pay leap-frogging, labour poaching and hoarding, inefficient management and increased unofficial industrial action. The rhetorical commitment of many NHS managers to radical change supported such a prediction, but the limited moves towards pay determination implemented by the trusts established in 1991 and 1992 suggested a different pattern of change (IRS 1993b).

In the first few years of trust status, managers often achieved labour cost savings through changes in work organization, staffing levels and skill-mix, and patterns of working time. While many negotiated the procedural reforms necessary for the introduction of decentralized pay determination, they were discouraged from implementing local pay agreements by government caution prior to the 1992 general election, and the pay restraint policies imposed in the two years following the election. The evidence suggests that a more fragmented pattern of enterprise-level industrial relations is none the less beginning to emerge.

Organizational variables, especially the size, range of medical services provided, success in winning contracts under the new funding arrangements, and the way in which senior management exercises a degree of 'strategic choice', will influence the pace and direction of reform. Moreover, the impact of more developed pay determination on different occupational groups will be influenced by variations in the policies of unions and professional associations and the different labour-market conditions faced by their members. The political sensitivity of health care funding and outcomes will inevitably lead to continuous and unpredictable forms of government intervention that will constrain local initiatives.

Local authorities

The large and occupationally diverse workforce employed in local government services has been covered by a fairly centralized system of pay determination for nearly fifty years. There are significant differences, however, between the most important of the twenty or so national pay determination arrangements. In the late 1970s, fire service staff, after a prolonged dispute, and the police, after an inquiry that was set up to avert threatened (and unlawful) industrial action, were awarded large pay increases and the introduction of an indexation formula related favourably to earnings movements in the economy. Two factors help to explain the origins and survival of these exceptional methods of pay determination. First, police and fire service staff have a high degree of occupational homogeneity and a distinctive service commitment sustained by the nature of work in 'emergency services'. Second, in both cases the division of the employers' role between central and local government produced tension and conflict within the employers' side of the negotiating bodies. This latter issue also contributed to the abolition of schoolteachers' bargaining machinery in 1986, as will be discussed later.

More generally, the national agreements covering the largest groups, such as manual workers and administrative, professional, clerical and technical staffs (APT & C), became less prescriptive during the 1980s. This increasing flexibility arose partly from the structure of local government; higher- and lower-tier authorities vary in their functions and the size and composition of their labour forces. Each authority belongs to one of three local authority associations which attempts to represent its interests in national negotiations. As Kessler (1991) has shown, inter-organizational conflict on the employers' side increased in the 1980s, with disagreements arising from differences in policies, local labour-market conditions and the conflicting political orientations of individual councils and the associations. The latter dimension of conflict surfaced directly in the 1989 APT & C dispute, allowing the main union NALGO to undermine the employers' attempts to introduce changes in the national agreement that would have provided even greater local flexibility on grading.

Although the main trade unions have generally supported the continuation of national agreements, strongly organized, larger branches in urban areas have periodically sought a more decentralized bargaining system. Where local labour market conditions and the authorities' financial position allowed, they have also negotiated increases in earnings through 'soft' bonus schemes and 'grading drift' since the 1960s. These opportunities diminished significantly in the 1980s; the centralization of financial control and the implementation of compulsory competitive tendering combined to produce much tighter control of labour costs by local managers. The pressure for local pay supplements and a looser framework of national agreements in the late 1980s came not from local union activists, but from the employers' side, especially from Conservative-controlled councils in the south-east of England, struggling to recruit and retain qualified technical and professional staff in tight labour markets.

The future of national collective bargaining for the majority of local authority employees is uncertain. The research conducted by Kessler (1991) suggested that particular groups within the main bargaining units may be moving away from nationally agreed terms, whereas for the majority of staff, national agreements retain an important regulatory effect, subject to some local modification. He argued that this had led to 'the emergence of more dynamic and sophisticated forms of workplace industrial relations', rooted in broader managerial and organizational changes, and in which 'the scope of the unions had either been incorporation into the management process or restriction to a consultative role' (1991: 29). This marginalization of unions has taken an extreme form in some of the 40 councils which have opted out of national bargaining and developed local pay determination systems in which unions play only a consultative role.

In comparison with other local authority services, the education sector has been the focus of the most significant changes in the process of pay determination since 1985. The removal of polytechnics and further education colleges from local authority control in the early 1990s was accompanied by conflict over changes in lecturers' contracts. These were designed to undermine some of the existing nationally agreed terms and conditions of employment and to offer local managers greater flexibility in allocating teaching hours. Government policy towards education in schools, however, generated more disruption and led to more fundamental changes in pay determination and the management of schoolteachers.

Until its abolition in 1987, the Burnham Committee brought together representatives of six teachers' unions, more than a hundred local education authorities, and central government. The direct involvement of government departments in negotiations, and the legal provision that recommendations on pay increases would be implemented through statutory instruments only if they were approved by government, were unique and destabilizing characteristics of the system. For more than twenty years, the Burnham Committee rarely achieved agreement between the parties. Increases in pay and periodic changes in the salary structure were determined at national level, but often by means of arbitration, special inquiries or the imposition of government pay norms.

Two sources of inter-organizational conflict were endemic to the system: conflict between the teachers' unions reflected unresolved status distinctions within the schools sector and intense competition for membership; and the local authority associations were divided by party political conflict over educational reforms and bargaining tactics, only occasionally joining together to defend the interests of local authorities against the encroachment of central government. These problems were exacerbated by the exclusion of terms and conditions of service other than pay from the remit of the Burnham Committee. By the mid-1980s, separate negotiations on working hours, class size, cover for absent teachers and other conditions of service that affected teachers' workloads and job security broke down and a lengthy dispute took place (Saran 1992).

The dispute led to the abolition of national collective bargaining. The Teachers' Pay and Conditions Act 1987 empowered the Secretary of State for Education to impose new terms and conditions of employment for teachers, subject only to recommendations from an interim advisory committee and consultation with interested parties. The revision of teachers' contracts was designed to make unlawful 'cut price' forms of industrial conflict (such as the refusal to cover for absent colleagues) and to pursue broader policies of pay flexibility. For example, the 1990 award revised the salary structure and extended the incentive allowance system, giving local managers the discretion to reward outstanding classroom teachers and pay more to fill vacancies in particular subject areas. These initiatives coincided with the wider education reforms discussed earlier; governing bodies and headteachers were encouraged to develop a school-level management system with greater freedom from local authority control.

The process of pay determination was revised again by the School Teachers' Pay and Conditions Act in 1991. This established a statutory School Teachers' Review Body which was 'charged with making recommendations not only on pay, but on conditions of service which relate to school-teachers' professional duties and working time' (STRB 1993: 1). While the pay recommendations of the second and third reports of the review body were affected by government pay restraint policies, the annual remit received from the Secretary of State has directed attention towards the development of performance related pay within a more devolved and flexible structure of pay determination.

There is little evidence to suggest that headteachers and school governors agree with this agenda for reform. While they have been forced by budgetary constraints to employ younger staff, encourage early retirement and increase the number of short-term contracts, headteachers have been reluctant to use flexible payments in recent years and their representatives have argued that performance related pay would be divisive (Sinclair et al. 1993). Similarly, while headteachers have presided over an increase in the size of classes, they implicitly supported the 1993 teachers' unions' boycott of the new national curriculum tests, recognizing that the workload of teachers had increased significantly as a result of recent educational reforms.

More generally, the momentum towards local pay determination generated by market-led reforms in some parts of the public services has less force in schools. In comparison with hospital trusts and local authority direct service organizations, most schools are very small organizations engaged in limited competition for pupils, not for multi-million pound contracts. School managers none the less face a plethora of government education policy initiatives and severe budgetary constraints. They cannot easily avoid confronting a strongly unionized workforce with proposals for changes in work organization and teaching practice that challenge established conceptions of professional autonomy and erode conditions of employment.

Conclusions

Many of the distinctive features of public service industrial relations remained intact throughout the 1980s and early 1990s. National systems of pay determination became more flexible, but the principle of comparability was not completely undermined and the extension of the pay review body system to nurses and schoolteachers strengthened rather than weakened the system. Trade unions lost members, especially among manual and senior management grades, but membership density remained much higher than in the private sector. Public service industrial conflict declined from the historically high levels of the 1970s, but trade unions retained a capacity to coordinate national pay disputes and local resistance to planned changes in employment conditions and working practices. Finally, while government ministers ridiculed the failure of past incomes policies and celebrated their disengagement from direct involvement in pay determination throughout the 1980s, they were unable to resist the reimposition of an overt public-sector pay policy in the early 1990s.

Beneath the surface of institutional stability and the continuation of many past practices there have been significant changes since 1979, and more radical changes in public service industrial relations will occur from the mid-1990s. There can be no doubt about the pressures for change. As the first half of this chapter argued, the government has initiated a programme of reforms that have significantly reshaped the context, organization and policies of most public services. The political and economic rationale of the reforms has been clear for some time, but the organizational and managerial capacity to implement change did not exist in the early 1990s. The time-consuming process of creating new structures, funding mechanisms and managerial regimes, and the political sensitivity of many of the reforms, persuaded government ministers to postpone some planned changes and to limit competition by extensively regulating the new internal markets for public services.

Furthermore, government policy on pay determination has been inconsistent. The rhetorical support for market-sensitive and performance related pay clashed with the Treasury's preference to retain central control. The advocates of decentralized pay determination were disappointed by the very few attempts to abandon national systems during the 1980s (Beadle 1993) and the imposition of the 1.5 per cent ceiling on public-sector pay increases in 1993 reinforced the view of many managers that little could be gained from a move towards local pay determination. As was noted earlier, managers confronted by tight budgets sought to achieve paybill reductions through staff reductions, skill-mix changes, improved working practices and reformed bonus systems. These initiatives were encouraged further by the 1994 incomes policy in which the government insisted that public-sector paybills should be frozen and that pay increases should be funded by productivity or efficiency improvements.

The apparently greater flexibility of this policy still produced several problems associated with past incomes policies. First, the attempt to mimic the private sector in linking affordability and performance in pay settlements has to overcome formidable difficulties in defining and measuring productivity and efficiency in public services (Bailey 1994). Second, the policy effectively penalized those organizations that had made most progress in increasing efficiency previously. Third, the hypothetical freedom to pay increases significantly above the 'going rate' (in practice, 2–3 per cent) was constrained by the awareness that any such agreement would be subject to close government scrutiny. At the time of writing (mid-1994), disputes involving Railtrack signal staff, further education lecturers and other public service staff suggest that the government's commitment to reduce its very high Public Sector Borrowing Requirement through a public-sector incomes policy will produce widespread discontent. It is difficult to predict whether this will be expressed in a resurgence of overt industrial conflict or in staff demoralization and an accompanying reduction in service standards.

More generally, there is clear evidence of increasing fragmentation and diversity between and within different parts of the public services (Bach and Winchester 1994). Even though the government may continue to cushion the impact of increased competition on staff and service users, the logic of its overall strategy seems inescapable; there will be 'winners' and 'losers' in the new public service internal markets. While all providers will face continuous downward pressure on labour costs, the pay, career prospects and working conditions of staff are likely to diverge more significantly than in the past, and the most vulnerable 'losers' will be swept aside in a continuing process of restructuring.

The problems facing public service managers are formidable. They have been encouraged to develop and integrate new business and human resource management strategies whilst struggling to meet tight and unpredictable short-term budget constraints. The future prospects for many public service employees are also uncertain; surveys of employee attitudes and exit interviews have revealed widespread stress and demoralization arising from work intensification, job insecurity and deteriorating career prospects.

It seems unlikely that a new and coherent system of industrial relations will emerge to reconcile the interests of government, managers, employees and service users across the public services. The prospect is of a more fragmented pattern of industrial relations shaped by variations in organizational resources, management strategies and the individual and collective responses of employees.

References

Audit Commission 1994: *Trusting in the Future: Towards an Audit Agenda for NHS Providers*. London: HMSO.

Bach, S. 1989: *Too High a Price To Pay?* Warwick Papers in Industrial Relations, 25. Coventry: Industrial Relations Research Unit.

Bach, S. and Winchester, D. 1994: Opting Out of Pay Devolution? Prospects for Local Pay Bargaining in UK Public Services. *British Journal of Industrial Relations*, 32, 2, 263–82.

Bailey, R. 1994: Annual Review Article 1993: British Public Sector Industrial Relations. *British Journal of Industrial Relations*, 32, 1, 113–36.

Bailey, R. and Trinder C. 1989: *Under Attack? Public Service Pay over Two Decades*. London: Public Finance Foundation.

Bain, G. and Price R. 1983: Union Growth: Dimensions, Determinants and Destiny. In G. Bain (ed.), *Industrial Relations in Britain*. Oxford: Basil Blackwell.

Beadle, R. 1993: *Public Sector Pay in Search of Sanity*. Paper no. 16. London: Social Market Foundation.

Beaumont, P. 1992: *Public Sector Industrial Relations*. London: Routledge.

Bird, D., Beatson, M. and Butcher S. 1993: Membership of Trade Unions. *Employment Gazette*, May, 189–96.

Buchan, J. 1992: *Flexibility or Fragmentation? Trends and Prospects in Nurses' Pay*. Briefing Paper 13. London: King's Fund Institute, 7–40.

Butler, J. 1994: Origins and Early Developments. In R. Robinson and J. Le Grand (eds), *Evaluating the NHS Reforms*. London: King's Fund Institute.

Cabinet Office 1991: *The Citizen's Charter: Raising the Standard*. Cm 1599. London: HMSO.

Cochrane, A. 1993: *Whatever Happened to Local Government?* Buckingham: Open University Press.

Colling, T. 1993: Contracting Public Services: The Management of CCT in Two County Councils. *Human Resource Management Journal*, 3, 4, 1–15.

Corby, S. 1992: Industrial Relations Developments in NHS Trusts. *Employee Relations*, 14, 6, 33–44.

Corby, S. 1993: How Big a Step is 'Next Steps'? Industrial Relations

Developments in Executive Agencies. *Human Resource Management Journal*, 4, 2, 52–69.

Department for Education 1992: *Choice and Diversity: A New Framework for Schools*. Cm 2021. London: HMSO.

Department of Health 1993: *Health and Social Services Statistics for England*, 1993 edn. London: HMSO.

Farnham, D. and Horton, S. (eds), 1993: *Managing the New Public Services*. Basingstoke: Macmillan.

Fredman, S. and Morris, G. 1989: The State as Employer: Setting a New Example. *Personnel Management*, August, 25–9.

Griffiths Report 1983: NHS Management Inquiry. *Report*. London: DHSS.

Horton, S. 1993: The Civil Service. In D. Farnham and S. Horton (eds), *Managing the New Public Services*. Basingstoke: Macmillan.

Ibbs, R. 1988: *Improving Management in Government: The Next Steps*. London: HMSO.

IDS (Incomes Data Services) 1993: Management Pay Review 154: NHS Trust Chief Executives' Remuneration. December, 2–5.

IRS (Industrial Relations Services) 1993a: Agenda for Delegation in the Civil Service. *Employment Trends*, 549 (December), 4–11.

IRS (Industrial Relations Services) 1993b: Local Bargaining in the NHS: A Survey of First- and Second-wave Trusts. *Employment Trends*, 537 (June), 7–16.

Kerr, A. and Sachdev S. 1992: Third Among Equals: An Analysis of the 1989 Ambulance Dispute. *British Journal of Industrial Relations*, 30, 1, 127–43.

Kessler, I. 1991: Workplace Industrial Relations in Local Government. *Employee Relations*, 13, 2, 1–31.

Kessler, I. 1993: Pay Determination in the British Civil Service since 1979. *Public Administration*, 71, 3, 301–18.

McCarthy, W. 1976: *Making Whitley Work*. London: HMSO.

Megaw Report 1982: Inquiry into Civil Service Pay. *Report*. Cmnd 8590. London: HMSO.

Millward, N., Stevens, M., Smart, D. and Hawes, W. 1992: *Workplace Industrial Relations in Transition*. Aldershot: Dartmouth.

Morris, G. and Rydzkwoski, S. 1984: Approaches to Industrial Action in the National Health Service. *Industrial Law Journal*, 13, 3, 153–64.

Next Steps Agencies in Government Review 1993: Cm. 2430. London: HMSO.

Nichol, D. 1992: Unnecessary Conflict: NHS Management's View of the 1989–90 Ambulance Dispute. *British Journal of Industrial Relations*, 30, 1, 145–54.

Nurses' Pay Review Body 1993: *Tenth Report*. Cm. 2148. London: HMSO.

Office of Health Economics 1992: *Compendium of Health Statistics*, 8th edn. London: HMSO.

Pearson, N. 1994: Employment in the Public and Private Sectors. *Economic*

Trends. 483, 92–8.

Priestley Report 1955: Royal Commission on the Civil Service (Chairman: Sir Raymond Priestley). *Report.* Cmnd 9613. London: HMSO.

Saran, R. 1992: The History of Teachers' Pay Negotiations. In H. Tomlinson (ed.), *Performance Related Pay in Education.* London: Routledge.

Seccombe, I. and Buchan, J. 1994: The Changing Role of the NHS Personnel Function. In R. Robinson and J. Le Grand (eds), *Evaluating the NHS Reforms.* London: King's Fund Institute.

Seifert, R. 1992: *Industrial Relations in the NHS.* London: Chapman and Hall.

Sinclair, J., Ironside, M. and Seifert, R. 1993: The Road to Market: Management and Trade Union Initiatives in the Transition to School Level Bargaining under Local Management of Schools. Paper to BUIRA annual conference, University of York, July.

Stewart, J. and Ransom, S. 1988: Management in the Public Domain. *Public Money and Management,* 8, 1, 13–19.

Stewart, J. and Walsh, K. 1992: Change in the Management of Public Services. *Public Administration,* 70, 4, 499–518.

STRB (School Teachers' Review Body) 1993: *Second Report.* Cm 2151. London: HMSO.

STRB (School Teachers' Review Body) 1994: *Third Report.* Cm 2466. London: HMSO.

Thornley, C. 1993: Pay Determination for Nurses: Pay Review, Grading and Training in the 1980s. Unpublished Ph.D. thesis, University of Warwick.

Treasury 1991: *Competing for Quality: Buying Better Public Services.* Cm 1730. London: HMSO.

Winchester, D. 1983: Industrial Relations in the Public Sector. In G. S. Bain (ed.), *Industrial Relations in Britain.* Oxford: Blackwell.

Winchester, D. 1987: Labour Relations in the Public Service in the United Kingdom. In T. Treu (ed.), *Public Service Labour Relations: Recent Trends and Future Prospects.* Geneva: ILO.

PART III

Issues and Processes

11

Individualism and Collectivism in Theory and Practice: Management Style and the Design of Pay Systems

Ian Kessler and John Purcell

When Mrs Thatcher proclaimed in *Woman's Own* that 'there is no such thing as Society. There are individual men and women, and there are families' (31 October 1987), she was reflecting the views of the New Right on the value of individualism in modern post-industrial society. The political debate was couched in terms of stereotyped opposites. For the New Right or libertarian individualists, collectivism is a pejorative term. Here, it is claimed, individuals are inhibited from pursuing their own self-interests either because of a Durkheimian sense of 'collective consciousness' (as in the term 'Society'), or because institutions like the welfare state, trade unions or collective bargaining bodies restrict the freedom of the subject by making regulations on their behalf. The contrast is individualism where, following Samuel Smiles, 'the spirit of self-help is the root of all genuine growth in the individual'. Enlightened self-interest for individualists becomes the driving force for progress; the role of the state is to attack collectivist regulation imposed in an earlier age and so to 'empower' individuals to take informed action to maximize their self-interest. All intermediary or secondary institutions which claim a representative role whether between the individual and the state, or between the individual employer and the worker, are viewed with suspicion.

Industrial relations has been caught in this debate because of its traditional focus on collective labour organizations (trade unions *and* employers' associations) and the importance attached to collective bargaining as the most desirable and normal way of regulating the employment contract. As chapter 8 shows, during the 1980s there was a conscious move away from the collectivism of corporatism. Attention also turned to human resource management, which is seen to embody the new individualism (Guest 1987, 1990). Here management techniques of direct communication, appraisal and assessment, target setting and performance related pay are assumed to encourage individual responsibility for quality and performance. Authority is shifted downwards and vested in teams and individuals. Employees are thus expected simultaneously to be committed and empowered to pursue their enlightened self-interest. There is no role in this model for the collective labour organization, or for the institutions of collective bargaining or collective consultation. Collectivism is here the enemy of individualism. By implication, the one is the antonym of the other.

To collectivists, however, 'the core function of collective bargaining [is] to generate pressure for the enhancement of the dignity, worth and freedom of individuals in their capacity as workers' (Harbison 1951). Their starting point is the unequal nature of the employment relationship and the need for workers to develop collective labour organizations in order to gain sufficient power to advance their interests. From this perspective, 'individualism' is seen to isolate individuals; the 'freedom' from collective representation, far from empowering them, reduces their ability to tilt the employment relationship more in their favour. Here individualism is again portrayed as the opposite of collectivism but for quite different reasons.

The purpose of this chapter is first to argue, and then to illustrate, that this dichotomous imagery of individualism and collectivism is misplaced and highly damaging to the study of industrial relations. In the first section the case for individualism and collectivism as opposites is explored in greater depth. The second section argues that aspects of individualism and collectivism can be found simultaneously within the workplace, since they relate to different aspects of the employment relationship: the employee as individual worker, and as part of a collective represented by a trade union or works council. This leads on to an examination of the types of choices that employers make in the way labour is to be managed. Here the management style models proposed by Storey and Bacon (1993) and Purcell and Ahlstrand (1994) are used to explore a number of interconnections between collectivism and individualism. The next section uses the example of current thinking and practice in the design of payment systems, especially performance related pay (PRP), to show how in practice individualistic and collectivist modes of regulation are applied. In the conclusion we consider where firms are moving on the dimensions of individualism and collectivism.

Individualism versus Collectivism

Under the adversarial imagery of the frontier of control between management and labour (Goodrich 1975), the battle between individualism and collectivism is conducted on two fronts. At the ideological level the question is which is the better way to organize the employment relationship. At the practical level the issue focuses on the extent to which employers support or oppose aspects of collectivism as part of their policies for the management of labour and the ability of labour to make inroads into management control. Collective bargaining can only exist if there is a collective labour organization able to represent employees. Any action taken by employers or the government to weaken sources of solidarity is thus an attack on collectivism. The most recent obvious example here is the last-minute amendment to the Trade Union Reform and Employment Rights Act 1993 to allow employers to offer a financial inducement to an employee covered by a collective agreement to accept a personal contract.

Personal contracts have become lauded as exemplars of individual freedom. Here, according to the right-wing Institute of Economic Affairs, 'workers become in various ways more like capitalists: they hire their capital assets of natural or acquired talents, skill, experience, information and advice to competing buyers or "employers"' (Hanson and Mather 1988: 36). The evidence of the use of personal contracts collected by Evans and Hudson (1993) paints a very different picture. The privatized firms they examined generally refused to negotiate with individuals or their representatives but provided 'standardized packages, individually wrapped'. Far from being negotiated between equal parties, personal contracts represent a reassertion of the managerial prerogative and unilateral control.

It is often assumed that individualism is closely associated with certain personnel techniques like individual performance pay and direct communication with employees. It is through these mechanisms that the trade union comes to be marginalized and collectivism weakened. As shown in more detail below, such a straightforward assumption is too simplistic, however. For example, in certain circumstances the trade union might be actively involved in determining the regulations surrounding the performance related pay scheme which the membership positively support. Direct communication with employees might be associated with increased flows of more strategic information to the union and members of a joint consultative committee so that the total volume of information is greater. Indeed recent research has demonstrated that there is a much greater likelihood that forms of direct communication to individual employees will be used in companies where unions are recognized (Marginson et al. 1993). It is not possible to associate a particular technique such as direct communication with the growth of individualism or the decline of collectivism.

There is a simple model of motivation behind the use of personal contracts and other individualist policies. This has, in a different context, been described by Fox as 'atomistic individualism'. Here it is assumed that it should be possible for:

> individuals not only to pursue their own enlightened self-interest (which they define themselves) but do so with no concerted action between them, each acting as an atomistic, independent self-responsible unit and being treated as such. (Fox 1985: 192)

Fox was describing a form of Tory philosophy which emerged in the two decades before the First World War. It only became the dominant Tory logic in the 1980s under Mrs Thatcher. Before then, in the period of the inter-war years and the post-war settlement,

> Conservative thought and action, seeing collectivism as irreversible, sought ways of rendering it harmless by incorporating it into a society unified from above by imperial glory, economic protectionism and statutory social welfare. (Fox 1985: 193)

If the role of government since 1979 has been to sweep away institutions and regulations which stood in the way of individualism, it was for the employers to provide the conditions where individuals could determine their own self-interest. The government White Paper *People, Jobs and Opportunity* (1992) expressed this succinctly, and in a partisan way not until then found in such official documents.

> There is new recognition of the role and importance of the individual employee. Traditional patterns of industrial relations, based on collective bargaining and collective agreements, seem increasingly inappropriate and are in decline. Many employers are replacing outdated personnel practices with new policies for human resource management which put the emphasis on developing the talents and capacities of each individual employee. Many are also looking to communicate directly with their employees rather than through the medium of a trade union or formal works council. There is a growing trend to individually negotiated reward packages which reflect the individual's personal skills, experience, efforts and performance.

Storey (1993) describes the emerging pattern, when new approaches under the guise of human resource management (HRM) mix with traditional collectivist industrial relations, as 'dualism'. Here, innovative employer action and policy is focused on the individual manager and employee while 'old' style institutional regulation is slowly eroded. He lists 27 points of difference between the dominant collective style of personnel and industrial relations and the new essentially individualist HRM. Purcell has argued elsewhere that the danger with lists of human resource practices is that, like the debate on collectivism, they 'idealize the future and stereotype the past' (Purcell 1993: 513). This assumption that all regulation and procedure is outmoded and restrictive has been questioned also by Clark (1993).

The force of the rhetoric of 'new individualism' is not easily challenged. An emphasis on common goals, flexibility and personal performance which allows individuals to achieve commitment to their job and the firm is intuitively attractive. Here, management control is achieved via employee commitment – the ultimate dream of the self-managed workforce. The assumption is that what was previously covered by collective regulation is now both unilaterally determined by the employer and focused on or targeted to each employee. The worker is assumed to have neither the interest nor the ability to combine with others, but will strive to maximize his or her own interests which coincide with, or are complementary to, those of the employer. This is the atomized individual given the freedom to pursue 'enlightened self-interest'.

Individualism with Collectivism

There are two main objections to this portrayal of individualism as the antithesis of collectivism: it depends on a distorted image of collectivism; and it reduces the employment relationship to one of rule making, or contract. Fox argues that individualism is rooted deeply in the attitudes and beliefs that both employers and employees bring to the employment relationship. By this he meant that worker solidarity (and indeed employer solidarity) was conditional, and collectivism in Britain always was instrumental not ideological. In 'instrumental collectivism', as he called it,

> individuals, who still perceive self-interest as their criterion of judgement and action, find it expedient to concert with others on those issues where collective action yields better results. (Fox 1985: 192)

Here, collectivism is not the romanticized socialist ideal of working class solidarity but a hard-headed, conditional response to the economic circumstances that the worker experiences in employment. It is quite possible in these circumstances to respond to some employer initiatives as an individual and to others as a member of a collective protecting the interests of all employees. This historical or cultural depth to instrumental collectivism accords with the test of individualism conducted by Hofstede (1980) as part of his study of cultural differences. The countries with the highest individualism scores were the Anglo-Saxon nations: the United States, Canada and Great Britain. We will note later that employee attitudes toward performance related pay strongly endorse individualist principles as the basis for pay system design.

It is misleading in these circumstances to assume that collectivist action on behalf of workers must always be preferable to individualism. The limited or instrumental nature of collectivist beliefs would be less important if the whole of the employment relationship were regulated by collective bargaining, since there would be no choice. But it never was nor ever could be, since employment relations has a much broader meaning than the contract of employment. Gospel (1983) has defined human resource management in terms of three sub-processes: work relations, employment relations and industrial relations. Taken together, these cover the plans and policies used by management to direct work tasks, to evaluate, discipline and reward workers, and to deal with trade unions. (Gospel's terminology differs from that in this book, which sees industrial relations as including 'employment relations'. Gospel's more limited definition of industrial relations is signalled by placing it in quotation marks.) Work relations covers the organization of technology and social processes at work. Employment relations includes job structures, and tenure, remuneration and reward systems. 'Industrial relations' is focused on union–management relations and the processes of negotiation, consultation, communication and participation.

It is clearly possible to develop the collective aspects of labour regulation in the 'industrial relations' sub-process while simultaneously pursuing individualist policies as part of employment relations, for example in job descriptions and performance appraisal, and different types of work arrangements, perhaps based on team working, under work relations. This threefold classification of human resource sub-processes becomes reflected in the traditional distinction between personnel management and industrial relations that still applies in some universities and in practice in some companies. Personnel management was concerned with the recruitment, retention and reward of individual employees, while industrial relations focused on conflict, collective bargaining and consultation. Meanwhile, the design of jobs and work processes was the responsibility of operational and production management. Modern initiatives in management such as process re-engineering and total quality management are designed to break down the barriers between functions. It is absurd to try to manage, let alone understand, the employment relationship by demarcating between work, employment and industrial relations, or by treating individualism and collectivism as opposites.

Models of Individualism and Collectivism

Various attempts to integrate individualism and collectivism have been made in recent years. These attempts often draw on the idea of a distinct 'style' of management. The value of this idea depends on the use to which it is put. As chapter 4 argues, it is difficult to identify coherent and self-contained *practices* of British management that could be called styles. The present aim, as figure 11.1 highlights, is to indicate *preferred* managerial approaches. The issue of the wider value of the concept of styles is taken up in chapter 20.

Storey and Bacon (1993) have utilized Gospel's classification to suggest that three different forms of collectivism and individualism can be experienced in employing organizations. They see collectivism in 'industrial relations' in terms of the employer's policy toward trade unions and, where unions are recognized, the nature and scope of collective bargaining. They suggest further that collectivism can be defined in a second way as a form of group or social cohesion, as in the Japanese sense of collective consciousness. They apply this to design of work and work relations. They suggest that collectivism in work organization is found where the division of labour is low, job methods are group-based and jointly determined by the group, and where there is extensive movement between jobs. Thus 'a collective social organization of work involves working in teams, a low division of labour and low job segmentation' (ibid.: 675). The type of team working found in Total Quality Management (Hill 1991) and sometimes associated with cell manufacturing or process re-engineering typically requires extensive team work and mutual support. In contrast, individualism in work relations, Storey and Bacon assert, is associated with hierarchical control and the extensive division of labour. Individualism and collectivism can be seen in a third sense, they suggest, in aspects of personnel management systems. Collectivist personnel management, for example, is associated with job tenures, standardized terms and conditions, high job security and internally segmented yet permanent labour markets. Performance pay, they suggest, however, is symptomatic of individualism in personnel policies.

There is a confusion, however, between the three types of collectivism proposed. The third type, a classification of HR/personnel policies, is a measure of outcomes rather than processes or the beliefs that inform them. The second, the social cohesion mode of collectivism in work organization (as in team work) is clearly important in differentiating between American and Japanese cultural stereotypes, but in application the ideas seem to cut across forms of individualism. For example, a performance appraisal system and related merit pay is often used to emphasize the need for each employee to take part in group activity: to be good team players. The group or team is seen as a key element in work organization collectivism, but the performance review and appraisal is clearly individualistic.

This use of collectivism to mean team spirit is reflected in the debates on company cultures that emerged in the early 1980s in the

United States (Ouchi 1981; Kanter 1983). Here, the pursuit of strong company cultures required commitment of an extraordinary nature.

> Although shared beliefs and values might blur the boundaries between staff and organization, such commitment was said to imply no loss of individualism or autonomy. In fact, strong cultures were said to actually enhance autonomy, since well socialized employees would be trusted to act in the organization's best interests. (Barley and Kunda 1992: 383)

There is an obvious close fit here with Fox's atomistic individualism. Barley and Kunda suggest that 'ultimately, advocates promised, strong cultures would transform organizations into full-fledged collectives'. They quote Kanter that employees in strong culture companies 'gain an experience of . . . communitas' (Kanter 1983: 119). This type of 'communitas' is something different from the everyday experience of working life inside the factory or office. What Kanter meant is a culture *directed* by management: a strongly unitarist, even monist, frame of reference. 'Enlightened managers were said to be capable not only of formulating value systems but of instilling those values in their employees' (Barley and Kunda 1992: 383). In this formulation of collectivism the employee identifies completely with the firm which itself becomes the all-embracing collective organization. There is no room for dual commitment to the firm and the trade union. These claims to a new type of 'collectivist' firm need to be taken seriously and subjected to rigorous research, but for our purposes they confuse the debate. We need to return to the basics in the definition of collectivism in industrial relations.

The standard use of the term 'collectivism' in the field of employment relates to the existence of independent, or quasi-independent, organizations founded to represent and articulate the interests of groups of employees within the employment unit, the firm, the industry, sector, country or community. In the classic industrial relations sense, then, our concern is with trade unions and other types of independent representative organizations such as works councils, where they exist with established rights and powers as in most of the European Union. Purcell and Ahlstrand (1994) prefer this formulation since it allows them to differentiate between firms, or industries, and even countries, on the type of relationship that might exist between management and union. In some cases the relationship is adversarial, where 'distributive bargaining' (Walton and McKersie 1965) is used to determine contractual rules. In another firm, or country, the history of collective labour relations might encourage forms of cooperation. This cooperativeness might include the use of joint working parties to seek to solve common problems: what Walton and McKersie call 'integrative bargaining'. At the level of the state, a form of corporatism might develop based around the exploration of areas of common interest (Crouch 1993). Some firms (and a few countries), however, may positively seek to avoid trade unions and any form of collective labour representational body.

In short, types of collectivism can be classified by looking at the underlying approach of management to the union or works council: avoidance, adversarialism or cooperativeness. This is used by Purcell and Ahlstrand (1994) to form one of the axes in their Management Style Matrix (figure 11.1).

The other dimension of their style matrix is 'individualism', since firms can vary in their approach to the individual employee. Some might provide benefits to employees superior to those normally found in industry, and spend time and effort seeking to maximize employee potential through training and development. Their aim is to focus on the worth and value of each employee along the lines

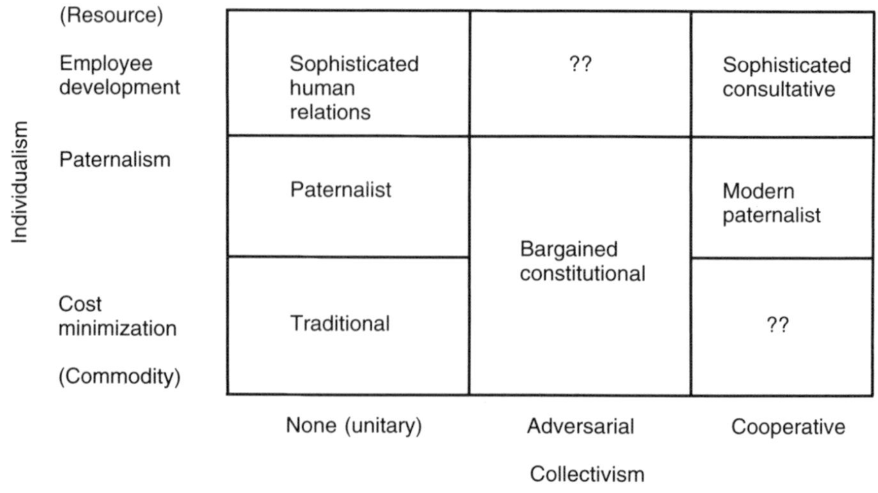

		None (unitary)	Adversarial	Cooperative
(Resource)				
	Employee development	Sophisticated human relations	??	Sophisticated consultative
Individualism	Paternalism	Paternalist	Bargained constitutional	Modern paternalist
	Cost minimization	Traditional		??
(Commodity)				
			Collectivism	

Figure 11.1 Typology of management styles (after Purcell and Ahlstrand 1994)

suggested by Fox's atomistic individualism where 'soft' HRM policies come to be introduced. Others adopt an approach to employees based around the minimization of cost and the exploitation of labour. These employers have little interest in providing the conditions for employees to follow enlightened self-interest, apart from the requirement of keeping a job. In other words, we can classify firms according to the extent to which the management are prepared to invest in their employees, as Marchington and Parker (1990) put it. This means that employers can and do operate on the dimensions of individualism and collectivism simultaneously, as shown in figure 11.1 and explained with illustrations in table 11.1.

Three explanatory remarks are significant. First, as noted above, style is a preferred way of managing employees which may be amended in practice. Second, firms may have no real style, being essentially opportunistic in reaction to events. The matrix represents how those firms which do have a clear style of labour management can be classified. Third, styles may differ in relation to different groups of employees, notably managers, highly skilled employees and peripheral workers. Inconsistency can be a problem here.

The type of individualistic policies developed by the firm will influence the nature of the collective relationship with a union or works council. Similarly, the type of collectivism in action may well influence the nature of the firm's policies toward, and expectations of, individual employees. It is unlikely, for example, that a sophisticated form of employee development based around investment in employees would emerge in a firm locked into a highly adversarial relationship with the trade union, if only because of the tension for dual commitment imposed on the employees as union members and valued employees. In the matrix in figure 11.1, this problematic interconnection between high individualism and adversarial collectivism is shown as ?? in the top central box.

The other problem style is more straightforward (bottom right on the matrix). Here, a cooperative relationship is envisaged with the trade union or works council, while simultaneously the policy of the firm towards individual employees is based on cost minimization, numerical flexibility and the exploitation of labour. The relationship would be much more likely to turn into adversarialism, or workers would leave the union in disgust.

The interconnection between individualism and collectivism has a profound effect on the design and implementation of the type of

Table 11.1 Characteristics of management styles in employee relations

Sophisticated Human Relations (employee development / no collectivism)

Employees (excluding short-term contract or subcontract labour) viewed as the company's most valuable resource. Great care taken with selection. Above-average pay. Internal labour-market structures with promotion ladders common, with periodic attitude surveys used to harness employees' views. Emphasis on flexible reward structures; employee appraisal systems and development and training; teamwork; competences; and extensive networks and methods of communication. The aim is to inculcate employee loyalty, commitment and dependency. As a by-product these companies seek to make it unnecessary or unattractive for staff to unionize.

Most often found in American electronic/information firms and high technology / professional service firms. Typical of the aims of greenfield sites opting for no trade unions or works councils. Many firms seek to develop managers through this style.

Sophisticated Consultative (employee development / cooperative)

Similar to the sophisticated human relations companies except that unions or company councils are recognized. Attempt to build 'constructive' relationships with the trade unions. Broad-ranging discussions are held with extensive information provided to the unions on a whole range of decisions and plans including aspects of strategic management, but the 'right of last say' rests with management. Emphasis also on enhancing individual employee commitment to the firm and the need to manage change (profit sharing, briefing or cascade information systems, joint working parties, quality or productivity circles/councils, training and development).

Most often found in greenfield site companies recognizing single unions with 'no strike' deals or where traditional manufacturing firms have sought a radical change in work organization and industrial relations. Similar to Japanese corporations.

Paternalist (paternalism / no collectivism)

Welfare caring image projected which focuses on the employee's place in the firm. Emphasis on loyalty and downward communication. Fixed grade structures through job evaluation. Often a high proportion of lower grade women employees. Little internal mobility or promotion across grades. Job training provided. Stability, order and hierarchy with everyone knowing his/her place. Conflict seen as a failure of communication. Unions avoided.

Most often found in service/financial/distribution firms.

Modern Paternalist (paternalist / cooperative)

Emphasis on 'constructive' relationships with trade unions with extensive information provided and a network of collective consultative committees within the context of a caring welfare image. Fixed grade structures based on job evaluation with union–management review teams and appeal bodies. Average pay. Little internal mobility. Overall emphasis on stability, order and hierarchy with employees knowing their place.
Most often found in large, relatively stable process industries, such as foods, oil.

Traditional (cost minimization / no collectivism)

Labour is viewed as a cost or factor of production and employee subordination is assumed to be part of the 'natural order' of the employment relationship. Fear of outside union interference. Unionization opposed or unions kept at arm's length. Often low pay and low job security. The prime driving force in employment policies is cost minimization. Little or no training provided.
Most often found in labour-intensive contract/franchise firms, hotel and catering.

Bargained Constitutional
(paternalist or cost minimization / adversarial)

Somewhat similar to the traditionalists (or paternalists) in basic value structures (an emphasis on cost minimization or welfare provision) but unions have been recognized for some time and accepted as inevitable. Employee relations policies centre on the need for stability, control and the institutionalization of conflict. Management prerogatives are defended through highly specific collective agreements and careful attention is paid to the administration of agreements at the point of production. The importance of management control is emphasized with the aim of minimizing or neutralizing union constraints on both operational (line) and strategic (corporate) management. Relations with trade unions range from conflictual (collective bargaining restricted to terms and conditions of employment) to stable, more formalized relationships where the rules of employment are determined.
Most often found in public service sector, mass production or large batch manufacturing firms or firms with large workforces with a high proportion of manual workers, such as the postal service.

Note (1) Firms may have no preferred style, being essentially opportunistic and reactive to internal and external events and pressures. Attempts to change styles are shallow and based on the beliefs of the Chief Executive or the Board in the light of the current trends. Styles may vary between departments and in different periods according to the personal leadership style of each manager (authoritarian, democratic etc.).
(2) More than one style can be used for different groups of employees, such as managers, highly skilled employees, process/routine employees, clerical staff, peripheral workers. Inconsistencies and boundary problems are likely with mixed styles. This is especially true of core–periphery firms.
(3) The style boxes marked ?? are unlikely to exist and if they do are liable to be highly unstable, unless relations are focused outside the firm as in multi-employer bargaining.

employment policies pursued by the firm. Here we use the example of pay system design, especially modern forms of performance related pay, to illustrate the way in which models of individualism and collectivism provide a framework to interpret shifts in pay systems. It will be evident from our arguments so far that it is naive to try to associate a particular policy (performance pay) with a particular approach to individual employees. The same pay system might be used for very different purposes, and provide different means for union involvement or exclusion.

Individualism and Collectivism in Practice: Pay Systems

Much attention has been drawn in recent years to the fact that substantial changes are taking place in how employees are paid (ACAS 1988; Murliss and Wright 1993). The evidence suggests that the changes have primarily involved a shift towards relating pay more directly to individual characteristics and away from a reliance on pay for grade or job. The emergence of individual performance related pay schemes has been striking. According to WIRS, 45 per cent of establishments have either individual payment-by-results or merit-based schemes, while Casey et al. (1991: 57) conclude their review of pay systems in two regional labour markets, Leicester and Reading, by noting that 'an individualization of pay systems has indeed occurred'. Meanwhile, the proportion of establishments in the industrial and commercial sector with profit-sharing schemes rose from 18 to 43 per cent between 1984 and 1990 (Millward et al. 1992: 264).

There are strong grounds for suggesting that in general terms performance pay schemes constitute a challenge to collectivism. These schemes rely upon mechanisms for uprating pay which lie beyond the scope of collective bargaining and are often dependent upon the exercise of managerial discretion. Many examples from the past highlight the ways in which managements have explicitly used such systems to weaken collective institutions and rules. Writing at the end of the nineteenth century, for instance, Schloss (1898: 282) cites examples of employers in the coal and iron industries using profit-sharing in this manner. As he notes:

> In the well-known case of the Briggs Collieries, in which a scheme on profit sharing lines was introduced in 1865, the business being, at the

same time, turned into a limited company, in which a large number of workmen held shares, and on whose Board of Management the employees were presented by one out of five directors, it had been hoped by Messrs. Briggs that Profit Sharing would be accepted by their workmen as a substitute for trade union organization, they, on their part, abstaining from joining any combination of employers for the regulation of wages.

Formal trade union hostility to performance pay across the decades is a further indication of the perceived threat posed to collective bargaining and collective organization. There was considerable union opposition to the initial introduction of piecework schemes both in Britain and the United States (Lewchuk 1987). More recently, concerns about the implications of profit sharing for the future of collective bargaining have been raised by a number of unions. As one union notes:

> The real danger of profit related pay . . . is that it is often an attempt to take part of the paybill out of the collective bargaining arena, where employees through their unions have a voice in negotiations, into the domain of management discretion and unilateral decision making. (IPCS 1988: 3)

In addition, there has been considerable union concern about merit pay, reflected in a number of unions, including NALGO, the Transport Salaried Staff Association and the Association of University Teachers, instituting national policies of outright opposition to the principle.

Performance pay schemes are not, however, peculiar to non-union organizations. WIRS, for example, found that some form of incentive pay was almost as common in unionized establishments (49 per cent) as in non-union ones (54 per cent).

Union leaders have also had to confront the fact that the *principle* of pay for performance sometimes finds strong support among the workforce. A survey of employees at Scottish Amicable found that 96 per cent of staff felt rewards should recognize job performance, while 90 per cent indicated support for the view that unsatisfactory performers should not expect to receive pay awards as high as other members of staff (PBB 1992). This finding is reinforced by our own research on pay systems in a number of private- and public-sector organizations. It shows that employees strongly favour the use of individual performance as a means of determining pay increases even relative to more traditional criteria such as cost of living, and internal and external comparisons. Indeed, this same research suggests that, while views on PRP vary according to age, length of service and, to a lesser extent, gender, they are not affected by trade union membership (see also Thompson 1993).

In discussing the impact of these developments upon the balance between individualism and collectivism at the workplace, attention needs to be given not only to the formal, structural characteristics of performance pay systems but also to contextual circumstances, managerial needs and operational practices. More specifically, any assessment of the way in which performance pay is used as an expression of a particular managerial style must initially assess the intentions lying behind the use of such a pay system. It then becomes possible to assess whether and in what ways the collective and individual dimensions of industrial relations are challenged or supported.

We may identify three sets of managerial goals underpinning the use of performance pay schemes: pay flexibility goals; soft, development goals; and hard, exclusion goals. These goals not only help characterize management style but also influence the way in which schemes are designed, implemented and operated.

Pay flexibility

There has been debate about how much considered thought has been given by management in the move towards performance pay (Smith 1992). It has been suggested, for instance, that in some companies the move was simply dictated by fashion. One commentator, referring to merit pay, notes that 'many organizations were vague and uncertain about what they were doing; some were swept away by the mood of the time' (IDS 1991: 6).

More typically, the introduction of performance pay has been seen either as part of a more strategic approach to pay determination or as an opportunistic, ad hoc response to immediate organizational pressures. Central to the concerns of the 'opportunists' has been the issue of pay flexibility, the need to make pay more sensitive to prevailing labour-market pressures and organizational financial difficulties. Indeed, the issue of reduced costs has figured prominently, suggesting perhaps that in this guise performance pay has reflected a style of management dominated by cost minimization concerns.

Cost minimization has been a central management concern in some of the more traditional performance pay schemes. Piecework, for example, involves the establishment of a direct link between pay and output. The employer pays for the achievement of a specific task or standard and therefore avoids the need to reward for less tangible expressions of employee performance like commitment or cooperation. In the non-union situation and as a reflection of the traditional managerial style, this approach is still prevalent in certain older industries, such as footwear and textiles, that use a high proportion of female workers often working at home or on a 'sweated' workshop basis (Rainnie 1989: 120–1; Cannell and Wood 1992).

Merit pay has also provided organizations with flexibility by clearly giving scope to reward staff on a selective basis. In part, this flexibility has been used to respond to labour-market pressures, as a means of attracting and keeping those in short supply. The initial enthusiasm for merit pay coincided with a tight labour market in particular regions and for specific occupations in the mid- to late 1980s. Surveys of employers at the time found that recruitment and retention were the major concerns prompting the introduction of merit pay (LACSAB 1990a). In addition, however, the ability to reward on a selective basis has been seen as a more efficient use of the paybill, providing better 'value for money' than across-the-board increases, especially when organizations are facing difficult financial times.

It is at the point where performance pay is used to introduce greater pay flexibility at the expense of negotiated across-the-board increases that the tension between individualism and collectivism is at its height. Moves towards greater pay flexibility in these terms have been seen to fuel managerial attempts to break up national bargaining (Walsh 1993) and there are examples of employers seeking to move from general, bargained increases, embodied in the collective agreement, to all-merit increases typical of the personal contract.

Yet the use of performance pay in a relatively ad hoc and reactive manner suggests that it has not been employed as part of a concerted attempt to undermine collectivism. The break-up of national bargaining, for example, has led to devolved company or establishment bargaining, not an absence of bargaining. Moreover, where performance pay has been introduced in a unionized context, companies have often allowed negotiation on the size of the pay pot, as at Scottish Equitable and Robert Bosch (IDS 1993c, 1993d). Others have sought flexibility at the margins, retaining negotiated, general increases, but using performance pay in the form of a 'top-up' or non-consolidated bonus. The latter approach has generally run alongside collective bargaining and therefore has gained qualified acceptance from the unions. Indeed, some unions have used this sort of pay flexibility to try to strengthen the bargaining process, arguing that if members' pay depends on company performance, for example, they should have a say in strategic business decision-making (see, for instance, IPCS 1988).

In addition, the use of performance pay as a means of enhancing pay flexibility should not be seen solely in terms of cost mini-mization. As a reflection of a much more considered managerial approach to pay determination which is more in line with an em-ployee development orientation, some organizations have sought to link pay flexibility to task flexibility. This has taken the form of skills acquisition or competence-based pay. It has been used mainly for craft workers, in some cases on brownfield sites such as at Amersham International, or more commonly on greenfield sites such as those set up by Pilkington Glass, Venture Pressing and Pirelli Cable (IDS 1992). Although it is an approach which clearly differ-entiates pay rewards between individual employees, as a system relating pay to an identifiable aspect of performance and providing career opportunities for blue-collar workers, it has tended to be regarded more favourably by the unions than the other forms of performance pay.

A concern with employee development has, however, been much more to the fore in the use of performance pay to pursue the second set of managerial goals.

Soft, development goals

This set of goals is founded upon management's use of performance pay as a key lever in dealing with the individual employee at the workplace. The potency of performance pay in this respect is seen to lie in the connection between it and the development of certain employee skills, attitudes and values.

First, and particularly in the case of merit pay, the direct link between pay and assessed performance is based upon a managerial assumption that employee motivation will be enhanced. This con-cern has figured prominently in the reasons given by management for introducing merit pay. A survey of 48 private- and public-sector organizations indicated that this was the most important stated reason (Thompson 1993). Second, other developmental benefits have derived from the procedures and systems which help define performance pay schemes. The need for the manager to establish performance criteria and to evaluate performance often forces a dialogue with employees which may have been absent in the past. It also encourages management to develop certain skills, in particular the ability to communicate with employees, to make judgements on employee performance, to support those judgements with pay decisions and if necessary to defend those decisions in the face of staff complaints (Kessler and Purcell 1992). Finally, the processes related to performance pay schemes have been seen as a way of developing greater employee commitment to the organization. Surveys have consistently highlighted the importance of creating greater employee loyalty as a reason for introducing profit sharing (Smith 1986; Poole 1989). As the 1986 government Green Paper on profit sharing noted, 'PRP schemes should lead to a closer identification of the employees with the companies in which they work' (para. 9).

These development aims have significant implications for collective institutions and rules. Placing important pay-related decisions in the hands of line management, opening up a direct dialogue between workers and managers, and basing pay awards on how the company or the individual performs, can be seen to challenge collective bargaining as the main means of pay determination. It consequently casts a shadow over the traditional role of trade unions. None the less, this set of managerial goals is 'soft' in the sense that it is not designed to challenge directly the collective dimension of industrial relations, unless collectivism is defined exclusively in terms of the union controlling every aspect of the employment relationship.

Much of the evidence suggests that the introduction of performance pay has been characterized by this 'soft' approach. Drawing upon information from 18 local authorities, LACSAB (1990b: 16) found that 'The authorities with one exception were adamant that it [performance pay] was not part of a deliberate attempt to marginalize trade unions.' Thompson's (1992: 42) more broadly based case study work led to similar conclusions:

> Overall there was limited evidence that PRP had been used as part of a process of de-recognizing trade unions and de-collectivizing the values of the work environment by replacing them with more individualized arrangements for pay determination and communication.

Performance pay cannot typically be seen, therefore, as a broad frontal assault upon the collective dimensions of industrial relations. Its introduction is often founded upon the assumption of an ongoing managerial engagement with collective institutions and rules. It is apparent, however, that the role played by the unions (and other collective institutions) in the development and operation of such schemes is often more difficult than in straightforward adversarial annual pay bargaining. The union role is sometimes contingent, qualified and limited. In other words, there remains considerable scope for variation as to whether an adversarial or cooperative collectivism predominates. Much depends on management's interpretation of an appropriate role for the union to play in the development of performance related pay, and on the union's reaction to the principle of PRP and the details of their involvement in each case.

The *principle* of pay for performance seldom appears to be open for discussion (LACSAB 1990b: 18; Thompson 1992: 42). There are only rare cases where the principle has been jointly agreed (Mumford and Bailey 1988: 74). It is much more common for management to have unilaterally decided to adopt performance pay with union involvement contingent upon an acceptance of it. This is in line with the observation that management are willing to 'invite the unions to the party' but are quite prepared to start it without them if they fail to turn up (Storey 1992: 25).

Confrontation with the principle of pay for performance presents the unions at the workplace level with a dilemma. They can either swallow a principle which may be contrary to union policy but in so doing become involved in shaping the operation of the scheme; or they can reject it, thereby retaining their ideological integrity but at the expense of any influence over future developments and possible loss of support from the membership. Both options have been taken. There are examples of concerted union campaigns against the introduction of performance pay. At GPT, the GEC- and Siemens-owned telecommunications company, for example, opposition was so strong that it stimulated the first company-wide joint union organization (IDS 1993b).

In many instances, however, unions appear to have been prepared to become involved in the design and implementation of schemes. This involvement has taken various forms. There are cases where the *design* of performance pay schemes has been subject to detailed negotiation. This is particularly the case where management is seeking longer-term organizational change through consensus. In an earlier paper (Kessler and Purcell 1992), we cited the case of a pharmaceutical company which, keen to develop a performance driven culture but aware of union strength and genuinely welcoming union involvement in the change process, set up a joint working party to discuss the implementation of performance pay. A comparable joint approach was also taken at the Wellcome Foundation on the introduction of performance pay for laboratory staff (PBB 1992: 4–6). Findings from local government similarly confirm that the unions are more likely to negotiate over performance pay where such a scheme is related to broader organizational change strategies (LACSAB 1990a: 77):

> The unions had acquired influence, therefore, in the context of a generally participative approach to the management of change. The frequently encountered claim that communication with individual employees is an alternative to the use of the union channel was not supported by the evidence.

Elsewhere, the degree of union and employee involvement allowed for by management can be much more superficial, sometimes taking the form of consultation, in other cases simply information-giving or, as we shall see, in some instances no role at all.

Despite long-standing evidence that employee participation in the design and implementation of a payment scheme contributes to the scheme's longer-term effectiveness (Bowey and Thorpe 1986), many organizations still choose to take a route which limits employee and union involvement. The IMS survey revealed that in only around half of the public- and private-sector organizations covered had the introduction of PRP been agreed with the unions. The LACSAB survey found that while in 10 per cent of local authorities the introduction of PRP had been negotiated with the unions, in 44 per cent there had been consultation and in a quarter simply the provision of information. This variety is indicative of the degree of choice management had in the late 1980s and early 1990s, and the inability of unions to mount effective national opposition.

Once a trade union has some involvement in the design and implementation of performance pay, it is usual, but not inevitable, for them to have a degree of participation in the *operation* of the schemes. In the case of the pharmaceutical company identified earlier, for instance, the unions secured an ongoing role in the process of pay determination by ensuring that merit pay supplemented rather than replaced the bargained general pay increase. Some organizations see benefits from union participation in the operation of performance pay in terms of employee legitimation and procedural effectiveness. In some cases, unions have retained a role in negotiation or consultation over the size of pay pot or the uprating of scale minima and maxima. In others they have represented members with pay grievances. In some instances they have monitored the operation of schemes through the receipt of related information, a task which has become increasingly important as evidence points to the potential for sexual or racial discrimination (Bevan and Thompson 1992).

Yet there are instances where management feel that once negotiated the operation of a scheme should be subject solely to the exercise of managerial prerogative. Following negotiations on the introduction of merit pay schemes at Boots, for example, the unions relinquished direct pay bargaining rights (IDS 1993a).

The pursuit of soft development goals to improve employee performance has therefore been based upon management's appreciation of the potency of performance pay as a means of developing the employee at the workplace. At the same time, however, there has been little attempt to confront collectivism directly, allowing different local solutions to be reached on union involvement in the design, implementation and operation of schemes. In terms of the style matrix, the prime management objective has been to use performance pay as one means of seeking to develop employees: in other words, moving up the vertical axis. In some cases, but not all, this has involved shifting the relationship with trade unions to a more cooperative, consultative basis. There are very few examples of modern performance pay systems being developed via adversarial distributive bargaining. The ability of unions to mount effective opposition is very limited. Management thus tends to emphasize consultation and communication with unions much more than negotiation. This is a good illustration of how the cooperative segment of the style matrix gives emphasis to management power to determine final outcomes. This consultative and information-giving approach, which might be described as 'European-style human resource management', does provide unions and representative committees with a collective representational role but rarely with the power of veto. This is not the case always, as our last category shows.

Hard, exclusion goals

The hard, exclusion goals are distinguished from the previous set of objectives by an unambiguous attempt by management to use performance pay to undermine the collective dimension of industrial relations. Central to this approach is a desire to exclude the trade unions from the process of pay determination with expectations that membership will wither away. The use of performance pay in this way can be related to the management style matrix in two ways: as an identifiable position within the matrix, and as a reflection of management's clear intention to move from a collective approach to a unitary one.

One of the major distinctions drawn between unitary managerial styles is between those managers who accept a commonality of interest between the constituent groups within the organization as an unproblematic given, and those who recognize that there may well be distinctive employee–management interests, which have to be addressed and broken down (Purcell and Sisson 1983). The latter approach conforms with a sophisticated human relations style of management. Here there is a well-considered attempt to shelter employees from external labour-market pressures and from any need for employees to seek outside representation.

Some non-union companies adopt considered approaches to industrial relations with these union exclusion ends in mind. McGoughlin and Gourlay (1992), for example, found that the predominant managerial style amongst non-union high-tech companies was what they termed high strategic integration / high individualism. Management were using a range of employment relations techniques centred upon the individual employee, including profit sharing and merit pay, in a concerted way.

There are a number of well-publicized cases where the use of PRP to exclude trade unions has taken place (Smith and Morton 1993). Some of these 'attacks' have been broadly based. At British Rail, for example, individual performance related pay was introduced and the unions derecognized, for 10,000 middle and junior managers (Involvement and Participation 1990). In this and similar cases, performance pay is seen as an important mechanism for forcing a change in organizational culture in a dramatic and proactive way (Kessler and Purcell 1994b).

This hard, exclusion approach is usually restricted to senior managerial grades in the first instance. In these cases, merit pay is part of a package of measures including individual contracts and the derecognition of the unions. This has occurred at a number of organizations including British Telecom, Thames Water and Amersham International. All these companies have moved from the public to the private sector and the changes may consequently reflect attempts to undermine a collective dimension to industrial relations which simply never existed to the same degree for senior managers in private-sector companies.

Unions with a strong membership presence in the rest of the workforce within these privatized companies have sometimes been prepared to relinquish their pay bargaining role for senior managers with little resistance; by so doing they hope to preserve bargaining rights for the bulk of their members. For unions with a more restricted membership, however, derecognition represents a more profound threat. The Society of Telecom Executives (STE), for example, is a union with membership clearly restricted primarily to management grades at British Telecom. Any threat to bargaining rights has major implications for its future role. Yet even in these circumstances the unions have adapted and tried to retain a peripheral collective dimension to industrial relations. Thus, the STE and other unions have undertaken regular surveys of members, partly to highlight the perceived problems with schemes and to generate information on the level and range of pay increases.

The effects of PRP

Performance pay can therefore be seen as an expression of different managerial styles with intentions or goals having a significant impact upon the way individual and collective dimensions of industrial relations are combined. A concern with pay flexibility, particularly as an ad hoc response to immediate labour-market or financial pressures, may reflect a cost minimization approach. Individuals are given little choice and the purpose of PRP is to reduce the paybill and identify low performers. It is sometimes closely allied to the traditional style of non-union labour exploitation. Elsewhere, however, it forms yet another twist to standard patterns of industrial relations. Like piecework schemes popular after the Second World War, the 'new' pay arrangements become part of the bargaining agenda in a typical adversarial way. In contrast, the use of performance pay to pursue softer goals is explicitly informed by attempts to develop the individual employee. The use of performance pay as part of a high individualism policy in these ways has important implications for collective rules and institutions, but the crucial point is that neither approach involves a direct assault upon collective rules or institutions. There is no deliberate intention to undermine collectivism, and many unions have therefore been willing and able to involve themselves in different aspects of schemes, albeit often on a limited or contingent basis.

Performance pay has also been seen as a powerful mechanism for changing management style and there are examples where it has been used to exclude unions from pay determination. However, what has not been considered in the case of exclusion and more generally in relation to other approaches is how effectively management has been able to use performance pay to change or support management styles.

Many of the classic, early industrial relations studies (Lupton 1963; Brown 1973) highlighted the ways in which the managerial intentions underlying the use of a certain payment system were often undermined in practice. These studies warned against the treatment of payment systems as a set of uncontentious, static and formal rules or procedures, and drew attention to the fact that in operational terms they were driven by the interplay of competing shopfloor pressures. It is important not to overlook the insights provided by these early studies in any consideration of more recent developments in pay systems, particularly as a reflection of managerial style.

A number of more recent works (Cannell and Wood 1992; Thompson 1992; Kessler and Purcell 1994b) have drawn attention to the operational difficulties that have arisen in the use of performance pay schemes, weakening the intended impact on individual performance and support for the collective dimensions of industrial relations. In the case of a national newspaper, for example, the tension caused by a new and highly contentious pay scheme, introduced with the explicit managerial aim of weakening union influence and perhaps moving towards a sophisticated human relations style of management, actually resulted in an increase in NUJ membership and a further deepening of adversarial relations (Kessler and Purcell 1992). More generally, Bevan and Thompson (1991) have stressed that the use of 'judgemental' appraisal in the pay context can actually serve to undermine the use of appraisal for 'developmental' purposes. Employees may mask weaknesses which ought to be addressed through training if they know that their pay increases may also be at stake.

These operational problems raise more general issues related to measuring the effect of performance pay schemes. The difficulties of isolating the impact of a single industrial relations variable, in this case a payment system, upon the behaviour or attitudes of individual workers or upon the performance of organizations are notorious.

They may well account for the fact that a comprehensive trawl of American literature on performance pay found 'virtually no research on merit pay that directly examines its effects' (National Research Council 1991: 77). In Britain, evidence from attitude surveys suggests that merit pay has very little positive influence upon employee motivation or commitment (Richardson and Marsden 1991; Thompson 1993), though it is interesting to note that it does not necessarily appear to sour staff–management relations or undermine teamwork (Kessler and Purcell 1994b). It is important to recall, however, that performance pay, particularly as a means of furthering management's soft, development or hard, exclusion goals, is often part and parcel of a much broader assault on employee attitudes, values and attitudes. As such, management is much less likely to take a short-term, calculative view of its impact. Management may be more inclined to evaluate its effects from an extended temporal perspective and in terms of its symbolic contribution to the longer-term process of organizational change. This issue of the use of a specific device to symbolize a wider cultural change is taken up in chapter 20.

Conclusion

The need to consider operational details clearly extends beyond performance pay systems. Any assessment of shifts in the relationship between individualism and collectivism must examine the impact of changing policies on the individual and the organization. Management intentions, however grandiosely described as strategies, often prove difficult to realize. In the case of payment systems especially, the type of inconsistencies and inequities which accumulate over a period eventually lead to the collapse of the system and the search for a 'new' approach. Bowey and Thorpe (1986: 148) concluded, after exhaustive research into payment system effectiveness, that the most important factor was 'the degree of effort put in by management to consultation, and the consequent modification of the schemes prior to introduction and during implementation'.

The debate about collectivism and individualism in the 1980s and 1990s shows that policy decisions to include or exclude trade unions and other representative bodies are not likely to be influenced by technical research providing evidence in favour of consultation or joint problem solving (Kessler and Purcell 1994a). The agenda of the libertarian New Right is principled not pragmatic. Robert Taylor, the labour correspondent of the *Financial Times*, judged that:

> What Mrs Thatcher and her like-minded Cabinet colleagues were intent on doing was to destroy once and for all the post-war industrial relations settlement. In every aspect of domestic policy the objective was to individualize the collective, to deregulate and stimulate competition, to diminish the public sector through privatizing industries and services, and to encourage personal ownership of shares, property and capital. . . . The world that Mrs Thatcher and John Major have sought to create has no obvious role for trade unions at all. (Taylor 1993: 319)

The action of government since 1979 has polarized the debate between individualism and collectivism. We have tried to show in theory and through the practice of payment system design that it is more fruitful to see individualism and collectivism as separate components of the employment relationship. Employers may seek to develop policies in favour of greater individualism and simultaneously to redefine the collectivist relationship with the workforce through a trade union or works council. Alternatively, they may wish to seek to abolish all traces of collectivism. We have shown how some, but not many, employers have used performance related pay for this purpose, while others have sought to build in a role for the union in any or all of the stages of design and operation of the scheme.

In terms of the management style matrix (figure 11.1), the impression of movement in the years since 1979 is of a decline in the adversarial 'bargained constitutional' type of industrial relations and a reduction in paternalism, as economic forces have come to bear on most employers in the public as well as the private sectors. The rhetoric of 'soft' human resource management is associated with the rise of individualism in terms of the development of each employee to the maximum of their potential. This has a particular appeal, since it comes close to the utopian world of the high commitment, high performance, team-based, self-regulated workforce. An employer pursuing policies which are designed to achieve these ends, as in total quality management and process re-engineering, is likely to be impatient with traditional adversarial approaches to collective representation. Some have sought new relationships with trade unions more akin to consultation on a wide range of issues and negotiation on a few, while others have preferred to seek to develop a non-union workforce, if need be by offering inducements to employees to give up union recognition.

This image of the high performing, satisfied worker may apply, probably as it always has, to the professions, but it has proved to be a difficult species to track down among manual, clerical and technical employees. The conclusion of the 1990 Workplace Industrial Relations Survey has been widely reported to the effect that what is measurably new in industrial relations is to be found in the low-pay, low job security, non-union firms. In terms of the style matrix the growth has been in the bottom left-hand, 'traditional', box. It is here, for example, that competitive tendering has placed large numbers of cleaners, school cooks and canteen workers. For them, as chapters 16 and 18 show, individualism is the freedom to scramble for a (part-time) job, and performance pay a means for the employer to get 'value for money'.

The intriguing question for the late 1990s and the millennium is the prospect of a reassertion of government intervention in the labour market, if only to assert minimum rights. The battle over the European Works Council has only just begun, while other parts of the Social Chapter of the European Union aspire to establish minimum conditions of work. The New Right seek to portray these regulations as a return to the worst form of socialist, collectivist regulation of the 1960s and 1970s and a retreat from the high point of individualism under Mrs Thatcher. It could be argued, however, that the underlying purpose of this interventionism is to develop a new form of collectivism that allows for greater flexibility and individualism while providing minimum rights. The precise outcome, like that of performance related pay, will be likely to vary from workplace to workplace, since neither legislation nor management strategies can determine what actually happens in the world of work.

References

ACAS (Advisory, Conciliation and Arbitration Service) 1988: *Developments in Payment Systems*. Occasional Paper 45. London: ACAS.

Barley, S. R. and Kunda, G. 1992: Design and Devotion: Surges of Rational and Normative Ideologies of Control in Managerial Discourse. *Administrative Science Quarterly*, 37, 3, 363–99.

Bevan, S. and Thompson, M. 1991: Performance Management at the Crossroads. *Personnel Management*, November, 36–9.

Bevan, S. and Thompson, M. 1992: *Merit Pay, Performance Appraisal and Attitudes to Women's Work*. University of Sussex: IMS.

Bowey, A. and Thorpe, R., with Hillier, P. 1986: *Payment Systems and Productivity*. Basingstoke: Macmillan.

Brown, W. 1973: *Piecework Bargaining*. London: Heinemann.

Cannell, M. and Wood, S. 1992: *Incentive Pay*. London: Institute of Personnel Management.

Casey, B., Lakeu, J., Cooper, H. and Elliot, J. 1991: Payment Systems: A Look at Current Practices. *Employment Gazette*, August, 53–8.

Clark, J. 1993: Procedures and Consistency versus Flexibility and Commitment: A Comment on Storey. *Human Resource Management Journal*, 4, 1, 79–81.

Crouch, C. 1993: *Industrial Relations and European State Traditions*. Oxford: Clarendon.

Evans, S. and Hudson, M. 1993: *Standardised Packages Individually Wrapped? A Study of the Introduction and Operation of Personal Contracts in the Post, Transport and Electricity Supply Industries*. Warwick Papers in Industrial Relations, 44. Coventry: Industrial Relations Research Unit.

Fox, A. 1985: *History and Heritage – The Social Origins of the British Industrial Relations System*. London: George Allen and Unwin.

Goodrich, C. L. 1975: *The Frontier of Control*. London: Pluto.

Gospel, H. 1983: Management Structures and Strategies: An Introduction. In H. Gospel and C. R. Littler (eds), *Managerial Strategies and Industrial Relations*. London: Heinemann.

Guest, D. E. 1987: Human Resource Management and Industrial Relations. *Journal of Management Studies*, 24, 5, 503–22.

Guest, D. E. 1990: Human Resource Management and the American Dream. *Journal of Management Studies*, 27, 4, 377–98.

Hanson, C. and Mather, G. 1988: *Striking Out Strikes: Changing Employment Relations in the British Labour Market*. London: Institute of Economic Affairs.

Harbison, F. H. 1951: *Goals and Strategy in Collective Bargaining*. New York: Harper.

Hill, S. 1991: How Do You Manage a Flexible Firm? The Total Quality Model. *Work, Employment and Society*, 5, 3, 397–416.

Hofstede, G. 1980: *Culture's Consequences*. London: Sage.

IDS (Incomes Data Services) 1991: *Focus*, 16, December.

IDS (Incomes Data Services) 1992: Skill Based Pay. *Study*, 55.

IDS (Incomes Data Services) 1993a: *Report*, 636, March.

IDS (Incomes Data Services) 1993b: *Report*, 641, May.

IDS (Incomes Data Services) 1993c: *Report*, 646, August.

IDS (Incomes Data Services) 1993d: *Report*, 650, October.

Involvement and Participation 1990: BR Take the PRP Line. *Involvement and Participation*, Autumn, 12–13.

IPCS (Institution of Professional Civil Servants) 1988: *Fair Share? Negotiator's Guide to Profit Sharing.* London: IPCS.

Kanter, R. M. 1983: *The Change Masters: Innovation and Entrepreneurship in the American Corporation.* New York: Simon and Schuster.

Kessler, I. and Purcell, J. 1992: Performance Related Pay – Objectives and Application. *Human Resource Management Journal*, 2, 3, 34–59.

Kessler, I. and Purcell, J. 1994a: Joint Problem Solving and the Role of Third Parties: An Evaluation of ACAS Advisory Work. *Human Resource Management Journal*, 4, 2, 1–21.

Kessler, I. and Purcell, J. 1994b: *The Templeton Performance Related Pay Project: Summary of Key Findings.* Management Research Paper 94/3. Templeton College.

Kinnie, N. and Lowe, D. 1990: Performance Related Pay on the Shopfloor. *Personnel Management*, November, 45–9.

LACSAB (Local Authorities Conditions of Service Advisory Board) 1990a: *Performance Related Pay in Practice.* London: LACSAB.

LACSAB (Local Authorities Conditions of Service Advisory Board) 1990b: *Performance Related Pay Case Studies.* London: LACSAB.

Lewchuk, W. 1987: *American Technology and the British Vehicle Industry.* Cambridge: Cambridge University Press.

Lupton, T. 1963: *On the Shopfloor.* Oxford: Pergamon.

McLoughlin, I. and Gourlay, S. 1992: Enterprise without Unions: The Management of Employee Relations in Non-Union Firms. *Journal of Management Studies*, 29, 5, 669–91.

Marchington, M. and Parker, P. 1990: *Changing Patterns of Employee Relations.* Hemel Hempstead: Harvester/Wheatsheaf.

Marginson, P., Armstrong, P., Edwards, P. K. and Purcell, J., with Hubbard, N. 1993: *The Control of Industrial Relations in Large Company: Initial Analysis of the 2nd Company Level Industrial Relations Survey.* Warwick Papers in Industrial Relations, 45. Coventry: Industrial Relations Research Unit.

Millward, N., Stevens, M., Smart, D. and Hawes, W. 1992: *Workplace Industrial Relations in Transition.* Aldershot: Dartmouth.

Mumford, J. and Bailey, T. 1988: Rewarding Behavioural Skills as Part of Performance. *Personnel Management*, December, 33–7.

Murliss, H. and Wright, V. 1993: Decentralizing Pay Decision: Empowerment or Abdication? *Personnel Management*, March, 28–33.

National Research Council 1991: *Pay for Performance.* Washington: National Academic Press.

Ouchi, W. G. 1981: *Theory Z: How American Business Can Meet the Japanese Challenge.* Reading MA: Addison-Wesley.

PBB 1992: Industrial Relations Services, *Pay and Benefits Bulletin*, 306 (June).

Poole, M. 1989: *The Origins of Economic Democracy.* London: Routledge.

Poole, M. and Jenkins, G. 1990: *The Impact of Economic Democracy.* London: Routledge.

Purcell, J. 1993: The Challenge of Human Resource Management for Industrial Relations Research and Practice. *International Journal of Human Resource Management*, 4, 3, 511–28.

Purcell, J. and Ahlstrand, B. 1994: *Human Resource Management in the Multi-Divisional Firm.* Oxford: Oxford University Press.

Purcell, J. and Sisson, K. 1983: Strategies and Practice in the Management of Industrial Relations. In G. S. Bain (ed.), *Industrial Relations in Britain.* Oxford: Blackwell.

Rainnie, A. 1989: *Industrial Relations in Small Firms: Small Isn't Beautiful.* London: Routledge.

Richardson, R. and Marsden, D. 1991: *Does Performance Pay Motivate?* London: LSE.

Schloss, D. 1898: *Methods of Industrial Remuneration.* London: Williams and Norgate.

Smith, G. 1986: Profit Sharing and Employee Share Ownership in Britain. *Employment Gazette*, September, 380–5.

Smith, I. 1989: *People and Profits.* London: Croner.

Smith, I. 1992: Reward Management and HRM. In P. Blyton and P. Turnbull (eds), *Reassessing Human Resource Management.* London: Sage.

Smith, P. and Morton, G. 1993: Union Exclusion and the Decollectivization of Industrial Relations in Contemporary Britain. *British Journal of Industrial Relations*, 31, 1, 97–114.

Storey, J. 1992: *Developments in the Management of Human Resources.* Oxford: Blackwell.

Storey, J. 1993: The Take-up of Human Resource Management by Mainstream Companies: Key Lessons from Research. *International Journal of Human Resource Management*, 4, 3, 529–49.

Storey, J. and Bacon, N. 1993: Individualism and Collectivism: Into the 1990s. *International Journal of Human Resource Management*, 4, 3, 665–84.

Taylor, R. 1993: *The Trade Union Question in British Politics: Government and Unions since 1945.* Oxford: Blackwell.

Thompson, M. 1992: *Performance Related Pay: The Employer Experience.* Brighton: Institute for Manpower Studies, University of Sussex.

Thompson, M. 1993: *Performance Related Pay: The Employee Experience.* Brighton: Institute for Manpower Studies, University of Sussex.

Walsh, J. 1993: Internalization v. Decentralization: An Analysis of Recent Developments. *British Journal of Industrial Relations*, 31, 3, 409–22.

Walton, R. E. and McKersie, R. B. 1965: *A Behavioral Theory of Labor Negotiations.* New York: McGraw-Hill.

Willman, P. and Winch, G. 1985: *Innovation and Management Control: Labour Relations at BL Cars.* Cambridge: Cambridge University Press.

12

Work Practices: The Structure of Work

John F. Geary

In recent years, employers have made earnest efforts to reform work practices, and have in doing so challenged many established assumptions and traditions of labour regulation. The environment of intensified competition and a government hostile to trade unions has provided employers with a unique opportunity to institute a new, more formalized system of work organization. That significant changes have taken place is unquestionable. New technology has been introduced and employers speak eagerly of the benefits to be derived from team work, just-in-time (JIT), human resource management (HRM), total quality management (TQM) and lean production. And, as chapter 7 shows, the once-common practice of exhaustive negotiations with trade unions and bargaining for change has been subjected to increasing attack.

The question remains, however: how complete has this change process been? Has there been a transformation in the manner in which work is organized or are there significant continuities with past practice? This chapter examines the evidence of change in work structures in Britain. More specifically, the discussion will cover a number of issues: the position and influence of shop steward organization; changes to authority relations; levels of effort, autonomy and participation; the extent to which such changes have led to a transformation in employees' attitudes towards their employers; the persistence or otherwise of custom and practice; and, finally, the implications for conflict. The significance of these initiatives will be examined by firstly providing some account of the *quantitative* extent of new participative forms of work organization. Much of this evidence has been discussed at length elsewhere (Millward et al. 1992:

175–80; Geary 1994) and will only be presented in brief here. The next section will explore whether these supposed changes to work practices have actually had a *qualitative* impact on the nature of work in Britain. Here the analysis will rely primarily on evidence from case study research. An attempt will be made to review a variety of employment sectors, but considerably more space will be given over to manufacturing as most research has been conducted here.

The chapter argues that although changes in work organization have been widespread, their effect has been modest, so that they do not amount to a transformation of employment. The need to empower employees and enhance their skills by granting them increased autonomy and providing them with more training has been less significant than the pressures to adapt to new production technologies, to accommodate reductions in numbers employed and to reduce the cost of supervision. The extent to which these new work structures have successfully won over employees' commitment is also questioned. Moreover, management have not relied solely on the 'softer' participatory techniques to attain order on the shopfloor; traditional mechanisms of labour regulation have remained important. That there has been a shift in the balance of power cannot be denied, but the extent to which management have successfully used this to institute a new model of employment must remain open to doubt.

Reclaiming Control of the Effort Bargain: Managerial Strategies and Objectives

Conflict and the control of effort

In an attempt to understand how new forms of work organization have impinged on existing forms of labour regulation, commentators have tended to conceptualize developments in one of two ways. On the one hand, there are those who speak of a shift in managerial strategy from imposing control to eliciting commitment (Walton 1985). Management, it is thought, are no longer content to rely on merely securing employees' compliance through a narrow conception of the labour contract, but seek instead to win over employees' hearts and minds by developing broad job descriptions, encouraging greater flexibility and engendering employees' involvement in the affairs of the enterprise. On the other hand, there are scholars who are less enthusiastic about the level and significance of change and urge caution in the manner in which apparent change is to be interpreted (Elger 1990; Kelly and Kelly 1991; Geary 1993a). It is argued that management are more concerned to root out shopfloor challenges to their right to manage than to transform the manner in which work is organized. There is, these authors contend, little evidence of change to a degree which would suggest that workplace industrial relations has assumed 'a model of transformation'.

The 'optimistic' recipe is utopian; an analysis which concentrates on consensus and cooperation to the exclusion of conflict and control is a simplistic interpretation. Such dichotomies are false: conflict is an inherent feature of the employment relationship. Acceptance of this does not discount the possibility that employees and management may share similar concerns, as chapter 1 explains; rather, it is that cooperation and conflict coexist and are normal features of workplace relations. A central task, therefore, of this chapter is to attempt a dual analysis of conflict and cooperation, to investigate how conflict is organized and to examine by what means it is given or denied expression. Space will also be given to explore the use of custom and practice: the existence or otherwise of effort bargaining and the degree to which employees are able to exercise some control over the labour process.

The benchmark for change is the traditional pattern of workplace relations. In some sectors, this involved a developed form of bargaining between first-line managers and shop stewards (see chapter 7). This was, however, rare, but more generally firms preferred to settle issues at the point of production: as chapters 2 and 4 show, there was a reluctance to develop systematic structures to control the effort bargain. Recent change has involved, not the replacement of one model by another, but a rebalancing of forces within the negotiation of effort.

Contemporary analyses of change in the workplace reveal, perhaps not unexpectedly, an increase in management's prerogative and a concomitant decline in the exercise of union and worker controls which had hitherto restrained managerial action (Elger 1990; Purcell 1991; Millward et al. 1992). One important aspect of management's attempts to reassert control is their rationalization of work organization to ensure minimum waste and maximum efficiency. The new production methodologies of JIT, TQM and lean production would seem to have had some profound effects on the manner in which employers seek to extract effort from their employees, particularly as they rely less on informal rules and understandings and more on strictly defined procedures and norms.

There are likely, however, to be limits to the extent to which this rationalization process has purged the workplace of custom and practice and informal bargaining. First, the wage–effort bargain will always – in part at least – remain indeterminate. Any effort on management's part to tap employees' discretionary effort and creative talents may in turn require them to enter some informal bargaining relationship. Second, and independently, new sources of leverage are likely to emerge which employees may choose to use. Third, and more fundamentally, new forms of work organization evolve within a given arena of opportunities and constraints. Existing institutions, formal and informal rules of behaviour, modes of understanding and ways of managing will all have a bearing on the shape assumed by new work practices. One would, therefore, expect the introduction of change to involve ongoing negotiation, entailing continual definition and redefinition of relationships between the parties. And as long as employees and their representatives possess sufficient power and bargaining awareness, it is probable that the use of custom and practice will persist, in some form at least.

Employer strategies

Since the end of the 1960s, employers have used a variety of initiatives to alter the shape of industrial relations on the shopfloor. As noted in chapter 3, the early 1970s were characterized by formalization of the shopfloor, with productivity agreements becoming a key instrument for introducing change, often containing clauses on the nature of work involving the dilution of job boundaries between crafts and between skilled and non-skilled employees (Ahlstrand 1990). Studies indicate that the 'old industrial relations' was not as inflexible as it is sometimes portrayed, and that cooperation with management in the introduction of change has long been a feature of many trade unions (see, for example, Batstone et al. 1987). Thus, the introduction of new forms of work organization should not be considered a novel phenomenon.

With the huge job losses experienced during the late 1970s and early 1980s, there were further changes to work practices (Edwards 1987; Batstone 1988). The depth and degree of change in work structures, however, would seem to have been quite modest. Edwards, for instance, noted that changes which were aimed at dismantling job demarcations and challenging trade union restrictive practices were notably less common in comparison to those changes in work practices which were associated with new technology and increasing the efficiency of existing equipment. Other studies, too, found that the attainment of flexibility, particularly between skilled groupings, had proved somewhat elusive (Daniel 1987; ACAS 1988; Cross 1988). Where cross-trade working did occur it was normally across tasks requiring comparable skill levels or downward job enlargement within the ambit of a narrow range of enterprise specific skills, rather than any general enhancement of knowledge. More radical change was rarely sought by management. Thus, as Lane (1988) has noted, British management's interest in functional flexibility has not been accompanied by a commitment to increase employees' skill levels. The increased training costs and a preference for maintaining a particular specialization in skills were often thought to outweigh any perceived benefits which may have accrued from pursuing flexibility further. Thus, while many workplaces would have seen some change in work practices, the proportion of any given establishment's workforce experiencing significant change of a qualitative form is likely to have been small.

It is clear also that the lack of stable markets and the continuous erosion of organizations' competitive position has compelled employers to look again at the manner in which their productive processes function and the efficiency of their work organization strategies. These new pressures have forced employers, in the public and private sectors, to seek reductions in labour costs, raise production output and quality, introduce new technology, and achieve greater flexibility in the deployment of labour. The need for such changes is given added urgency by the belief that Japanese competitive advantage is crucially dependent not only on the organization of production processes but also on the greater involvement of employees in their work. Thus, we witness the implementation of a number of task participation initiatives (Geary 1994). The most notable of these were quality circles (QCs) and semi-autonomous work groups (SAWGs), both of which were adopted by a significant number of organizations (Batstone 1988; Collard and Dale 1989). In the mid-to late 1970s, for example, QCs were a rare phenomenon, but by the mid-1980s their number had increased to about 400 (IDS 1985). Batstone found that, while only three of his 130 large manufacturing firms had operated QCs before 1978, by 1983 the proportion had increased to 19 per cent. The same study found that 20 per cent of firms had SAWGs, though in a later publication the author was to admit that this figure exaggerated their popularity (Batstone 1989). Another study found that, of a range of employee involvement initiatives, SAWGs were the least widely used and showed the smallest increase over a five-year period (Batstone and Gourlay 1986). WIRS3 found that only 2 per cent of establishments had SAWGs in 1990. The significant growth of quality circles in the early 1980s has been matched only by their equally impressive decline (Hill 1991) – though WIRS3 did find, surprisingly perhaps, that QCs had increased from a low of less than 0.5 per cent in 1984 to 5 per cent of manufacturing firms in 1990 (Millward et al. 1992). None the less, they remain confined to only 2 per cent of all enterprises. Furthermore, the available evidence would suggest that QC programmes rarely spread throughout the organization and are more likely to dwindle away, usually from a lack of managerial commitment to their development (Collard and Dale 1989).

In more recent years, there has been much talk about innovations in production methodologies and work practices like cellular manufacturing, TQM and team working. Evidence of their diffusion, however, is limited and of varied quality, but we can be reasonably assured that they remain rare (IDS 1990; Geary 1994). Furthermore, many of the organizations which claim to have adopted these techniques have only done so recently. Team working, for instance, especially in its more sophisticated forms, is largely confined to a small number of well-publicized organizations, many of which were originally established on greenfield sites (IDS 1985). In such instances, management's efforts are aided by negotiating single-union agreements, recruiting a young, green workforce and by adopting exhaustive recruitment procedures. The adoption of team working principles in older, brownfield sites has, of necessity, been more gradual. Recent examples where management and unions have agreed to introduce team working include Ford, IBC, BP Chemicals (IDS 1988a), Cadbury Schweppes, Wandsworth Health Authority (IDS 1988b), Rover, Vauxhall and Rolls Royce (IDS 1992). In most cases, it is still too early to assess whether these agreements have seen the development of team working on the shopfloor. We know little, too, of the extent to which organizations in Britain have adopted cellular manufacturing and TQM.

Another broader issue here, as revealed in WIRS3, is employers' seeming preference for seeking employees' involvement through communicative media. The use of briefing groups and two-way communication, for instance, is noticeably more common than SAWGs or QCs. The proportion of establishments reporting use of the former initiatives had also increased since 1984. But, despite this increase, there was only a very small rise in the number reporting an increase in the amount of information being communicated to employees. Thus, management may have been more concerned to use these initiatives to tap the knowledge which employees possess of the production process than to extend their decision-making powers.

In summary, the evidence suggests that employers' interest in employee involvement and flexibility has been confined to the margins of existing work practices, and attempts to embrace new forms of work organization have been notably modest and piecemeal. Management's efforts would seem to have had more to do with the removal of traditional skill boundaries than with making an investment in new skills structures.

New Forms of Work Organization on the Shopfloor

The role and influence of trade unions

Chapter 7 charts the general decline of trade unions in the workplace. The following section considers the role of trade unions in relation to changes in work structures. There are two important issues to be addressed. First, when management introduce new work structures, are employees' representatives invited to participate or do management actively seek to marginalize their influence? Second, where change does include a role for trade unions, what conditions encourage such an outcome?

Survey evidence shows a significant decline in the range of issues over which management negotiated with unions in the early 1980s (Millward and Stevens 1986). Subsequent years, however, have witnessed a stabilization of union influence in these matters. A recent study of 3,500 employees found that, over a range of issues, trade union influence was weakest with respect to work organization, even though a majority of respondents felt that union influence had remained unchanged in this area over the previous five years (Gallie and White 1993). Case study research also indicates that management have become tougher in their dealings with trade unions. In Lucas, for instance, the introduction of team working and cellular manufacturing was aggressive and vigorous, with unions only being dealt with in a selective manner (Elger and Fairbrother 1992). On the other hand, there is evidence to show that trade unions can have a significant role in the introduction of new forms of work organization (Colling and Geary 1992; Hendry 1993).

The conditions which influence one outcome above another are clear. Unions are more likely to be marginalized where they are weak or divided and where they encounter an assertive management. Where unions adopt an uncooperative stance, a similar outcome is likely. On the other hand, where a union offers to work with management, and especially where it is an inclusive, strong but flexible body, and where there is a history of cooperation, then it is more likely to gain managerial support (Geary 1993c).

Thus, Hendry's investigation has shown that the major factors favouring trade union involvement in the introduction of changes in work organization were the history of cooperative relations between management and trade unions, the unified approach of the various unions, and the pragmatic approach adopted by the union leadership. Colling and Geary found that management both in manufacturing and local authorities relied almost exclusively on shop stewards to convince the rank-and-file of the necessity of implementing changes in work organization. It was claimed that the success of the programme was dependent on extensive trade union involvement. Here, too, management was aided by a strong inclusive trade union organization. The case of Cadbury's is also revealing here (Smith et al. 1990); although management set about forcefully to reassert its authority and rid itself of an obdurate industrial relations infrastructure, this new assertiveness was accompanied by continual efforts to win shop stewards' consent for management's goals. In short, management had not sought, or wished, to dismantle representative structures completely.

In instances, then, where management and trade unions cooperate in the introduction of new work structures, what influence do unions exercise? The available evidence would indicate that there is a clear division in the role and influence management permit to unions. First, management have typically reserved the right to decide whether the changes are worthy or desirable. Rarely have such issues entered a negotiating forum where employees are provided with a say in the decision to adopt these new initiatives (Daniel 1987; Marsden and Thompson 1990). Second, however, employers often willingly communicated the reasons for such action to the trade unions and their members. It is here that 'involvement' and 'participation' become the key concern, with employers seeing trade unions playing a crucial role in convincing employees of the need for, and the desirability of, change. Once unions accept the need for change, it is easier for management to justify the changes to the shopfloor. In this way, trade unions are incorporated further into the communication process.

Union leaders have, in the main, been realistic enough to know the folly of over-using their diminishing power resources and generally have resigned themselves to accept changes in work organization. It is not that employee representatives had become more docile, but rather that they came to identify their interests more with the success of the enterprise and the preservation of jobs than the maintenance of restrictive practices (Geary 1993c). For both parties, then, the development of a cooperative relationship is based on a pragmatic appreciation of the benefits which accrue from mutual support. It is a relationship informed by rational self-interest and one which may appropriately be termed *neo-voluntaristic*, in the sense that, while it takes place under management hegemony, employers see cooperation with trade unions as the most beneficial way of responding to pressures emanating from the marketplace.

A challenge to the traditional role of trade unions?

Despite this level of trade union involvement, it is clear that changes to the organization of work have challenged traditional assumptions of industrial relations practice. First, there is the shift from collective bargaining to consultation. While one may cite a variety of managerial concessions to trade union demands as evidence that work organization changes assume a *bargained* character, the paradox of such *initial* agreements is that they often contain clauses which prohibit further negotiations over subsequent changes in work practices. One of the most distinctive features of British industrial relations – where the deployment and organization of the labour force was subject to continuous collective bargaining – has been superseded by the need to accept managerial views on what forms of work practices are required. Moreover, many of the new task participation initiatives – but particularly team working, with its attendant values of consensus and shared interests – requires employees and their representatives to submit to a reasoned and harmonious discussion of the needs of the enterprise and accept the need for constant revision and change in work practices. In this sense, 'team working' is an assertive polemic which argues with, and challenges the legitimacy of, separate divisional interests and collectivities. In short, it is clear that management have tried in recent years not only to implement changes in work practices, but also to remould the ideological domain of collective bargaining (Terry 1989), to narrow its agenda and to reorientate trade union priorities therein.

Second, there is the difficulty for trade unions that, having advocated increased employee involvement for decades, they are now faced with a managerial strategy which purports to grant employees greater discretion and participation at work. Suspicion of what these initiatives conceal is a frequent response. This is particularly the case with TQM, where management have deliberately sought to couch their objectives in a language which trade unionists find difficult to discredit (Martinez Lucio and Weston 1992; Geary 1993b).

Third, changes to work structures are normally accompanied by attempts to rationalize and consolidate payment systems. So, with the removal of payment by results, for example, which traditionally lent shop stewards considerable power, the scope for workplace bargaining is substantially reduced.

Fourth, there is the manner in which employees are encouraged to work as a team, to identify with the production of a product and thereby relinquish their identity with a particular profession or trade. In manufacturing, craft identification is to be replaced by a team and/or product identification. Such tensions are likely to be exacerbated where union membership is spread across a number of unions. Within such teams, team members are typically encouraged to approach their supervisor if they have a grievance, and not their shop steward as they may have done in the past. Here, we can see that management are not engaged in a direct attack on the existing institutions of employee participation; these are allowed to remain intact. Rather, it is a case of management going around them, of bypassing the shop steward's organization and communicating directly with the shopfloor: a 'form of temporary derecognition' in Smith and Morton's (1993) words.

Finally, the identity and existence of trade unions is often threatened by the formation of new skill structures which accompany changes in work practices. Traditionally in British industrial relations, unions have defined their membership around particular occupations, 'job territories' and specific technologies. In certain situations, particularly with a number of the craft unions, control over training extended across the national labour market (see chapter 17). The establishment of new work structures, however, is often associated with the creation of enterprise specific skills. Instead of looking for people who possess a single craft skill, employers are often more concerned that people develop a portfolio of skills which are congruent with the production needs of the business. No longer, therefore, are modes of job regulation and training mutually reinforcing as they have been in the past.

But such outcomes are not predetermined. Four aspects deserve special mention here. First, while it is undoubtedly significant that management should attempt to by-pass established forms of employee representation, it is by no means inevitable that employees will desist from seeing their shop steward as the appropriate medium of communication. As discussed below, employees often remain distrustful of management. In such instances, one might reasonably expect employees to continue going to their trade union representative to acquire some understanding of (the possibly hidden agenda in) management's actions.

Second, shop stewards have shown themselves to be resilient and imaginative in their responses. In Heaton and Linn's (1989) study, for example, stewards were capable of enforcing a role for themselves where the content and means of management's communication could be monitored and its impact controlled. Indeed, in some cases, the outcome of management's initiatives was the opposite of that intended and actually resulted in a strengthening of the unions' position. In British Telecom, for example, although management's TQM initiative initially 'wrong-footed' the trade unions, in the end it provided them with some new opportunities for workplace bargaining, whereby the resourcing of the provision of a quality service allowed them to manipulate the slogan 'where are the resources I need to do a quality job?' to their advantage in negotiations with management (Ferner and Colling 1991). In local government, the devolution of decision-making and the accompanying changes in work practices has also had something of an equivocal effect on trade union influence (Fairbrother 1991).

Third, the introduction of these new techniques may not succeed in constraining negotiation at the point of production. There are two important factors here. First, although management may be successful in removing work organization issues from a collective bargaining forum and in impressing upon senior shop stewards the need to accept new working practices, it represents a different challenge to convince local shop stewards. The latter may well insist that what constitutes appropriate work behaviour is open to debate and negotiation. This is the case in a number of research sites currently under investigation by the author. Second, this type of informal negotiation may re-emerge because of line management's inability, or perhaps unwillingness, to utilize the initiative that their senior colleagues have presented to them. A number of studies offer support for this possibility. In British Rail, for example, it was found that, in spite of senior management's efforts to reduce trade union influence over working practices, local management, who lacked the necessary expertise to reconstruct work organization, needed to call upon trade union representatives to design and implement the changes (Pendleton 1991). Esso's management at Fawley encountered similar problems with the negotiation of two open-ended productivity agreements in the 1970s and 1980s (Ahlstrand 1990). As a consequence, changes in work practices remained marginal and temporary. In these cases, then, the scope for workplace bargaining was considerably enhanced and the influence of shop stewards was retained.

Finally, while particular unions may suffer as job boundaries are dismantled, trade union influence as a whole may increase as membership becomes concentrated in a smaller number of unions and inter-union hostilities are suspended or substantially reduced. Thus, an unwished-for result of such work organization changes may be an increase in the homogeneity of workers' interests, making it easier for shop stewards to mobilize support. Lucas is an interesting case here. While the introduction of cellular manufacturing was found to have weakened the occupational identity of craft employees and reduced the influence of their shop stewards, the grouping of employees into production teams increased the importance of operators within the manual unions, and in effect, it would seem, led to a more solidaristic union organization (Elger and Fairbrother 1992).

In summary, there can be little doubt that new forms of work organization do pose a potential challenge to the traditional role of trade unions. It is not inevitable, however, that they should eventually lead to the erosion of trade union influence or render existing forms of employee participation impotent. It seems possible – though more research is needed to state with more certainty – that the factors listed above may maintain or restore, to some degree at least, shop stewards' influence at the point of production.

New Work Structures: The Effect on Employees' Working Lives

What effect have these changes in work practices had on employees' working lives? Have authority relations changed? Are employees working harder? Is there participation within work teams, what form does it take and what issues are significantly influenced by worker participation? Have management increased their control over the labour process? And, finally, has there been a transformation in employees' attitudes towards their employers?

Participation in new forms of work organization

Both case study and survey evidence suggest that the development of new working arrangements has not improved the lot of semi-skilled and unskilled workers a great deal (Lane 1988; Elger 1990; Bratton 1991; Elger and Fairbrother 1992; Gallie and White 1993). Skilled workers have been far more likely to experience skill enhancement and increased responsibility. And as women continue to occupy the majority of unskilled and semi-skilled jobs, the gender divide, too, would seem to have been left relatively untouched. Thus, established forms of work organization and hierarchical relations continue to be reproduced. Despite this, however, it would be unwise to think that management have not directed their efforts towards defining the parameters of acceptable work behaviour for skilled employees too. In Cadbury's, for example, Smith et al. (1990) note that intermediate specialist groups, like engineers, accountants and skilled manual employees, who formerly enjoyed considerable autonomy, had many of their privileges withdrawn. In an attempt to bring these groups under tighter managerial control, they were transferred to line positions and exposed to the regulation of production. In becoming subject to line management disciplines their occupational controls were steadily undermined. Thus, the paradox of 'team working' for these employees at least was that it not only restricted their autonomy, but it also fragmented their collective identity and isolated them from their colleagues.

Employee discretion: a free rein?

New forms of work organization ostensibly extend workers' control over decisions that relate to the organization of work. It may also be, of course, that such managerial strategies serve to shape employee participation in a particular way such that they enable, or perhaps more accurately prescribe, one form of participation by delimiting another. So, what happens when employees participate in these new working practices? The available survey evidence suggests that an increase in employees' skills and responsibilities does not have any clear implications for autonomy (Gallie and White 1993): in comparison with those employees whose skills had remained unchanged, there was both a higher proportion that had seen supervisory controls slacken and a higher proportion that had seen supervision tighten. It was also the case that, although close control over employees' work was not being exercised in a majority of cases, supervisors continued to communicate to their subordinates the organization's performance standards. Furthermore, the authors concede that the most revealing feature of their study was the rarity with which employees participating in a QC or similar group were involved in decisions affecting changes in work organization. Only a third had such a say and nearly half remained dissatisfied with their level of influence.

Although we have relatively few detailed qualitative analyses, they show that management place discrete and definite limits on the autonomy given to employees, and expectations are clearly defined and monitored closely. As shown elsewhere (Geary 1994), studies of new work structures show that they often accompany other changes in the organization of production, like a move to JIT production, modular and cellular manufacturing, or TQM. In a study of cellular manufacturing, Bratton (1991) found that, although operators were given increased discretion over a number of work organization issues, the parameters for such freedom were set by the company's computer. The computer, in turn, provided management with the necessary information on the flow of production and employees' performance. There was, therefore, little need for close supervision; in its place was an unobtrusive form of surveillance. It has also been found, in a research project undertaken by the present author, that as one moves from a single cell module to a module containing two or more cells (that is, where each cell is responsible for a discrete part of the products' manufacture), the level of overall coordination and task interdependence increases and employees' discretion over the pace and methods of work is constrained.

The introduction of JIT, too, has been found to have ambiguous effects on employees' autonomy. Unlike traditional methods of production which permit the insertion of buffer inventories between successive stages of the production process and allow for variations in the timing and pacing of production, JIT seeks to reduce slack and variability by establishing a high degree of standardization throughout the production process. Thus, as a mechanism of process control, JIT impinges on group and individual autonomy by withdrawing the discretion employees had hitherto enjoyed over the pace and method of working (Tailby and Whitston 1989; Klein 1991).

Similar outcomes have been reported with the introduction of new technologies, like CNC (computer numerical control), CADCAM (computer-aided design and manufacture) and other flexible automation systems. The literature in this area is extensive and will be commented upon in brief here. The first point to note is that British industry has not made a systematic shift to flexible automation (Jones 1988). Those organizations which have adopted these new technologies, particularly in their most advanced form, remain rare and confined to particular sectors, and are more common in greenfield sites than in brownfield establishments. Yet within these enterprises, peoples' experience of these new technologies has varied tremendously. Some continue to perform repetitive tasks and have seen little change in their work roles. Others, however, have seen their responsibilities and skills enlarged. But despite this variation, there remains, it would seem from Jones's review, one constant: traditional lines of authority remain intact and 'the widely predicted autonomous workgroups have yet to appear' (1988: 469). In those infrequent instances where responsibility had been devolved to the work group it had been as a pragmatic response to particular operational contingencies. Other studies confirm that, despite the potential of new technology to create new forms of work organization, management seem unable or, perhaps more accurately, have been unwilling to consider seriously the alternative of relinquishing operational control to shopfloor employees (McLoughlin and Clark 1988).

It has also been found that, where management have introduced new participative forms of work organization, they do not rely on them alone to persuade workers to work hard. Geary (1993a) studied SAWGs in a US electronics plant in Ireland and found that the self-control permitted to employees was located within a larger structure of control which clearly delineated what type of work behaviour was expected. Close, over-the-shoulder type of supervision may have been absent, but management's expectations of employees were clearly defined in job descriptions and enforced at appraisal time.

There is also a considerable amount of evidence to indicate that disciplinary regimes have been tightened both in manufacturing and in the services sector (Edwards and Whitston 1993). Trevor's (1988) study of Toshiba found that although employees were granted substantial discretion and flexibility in their work, their time-keeping and attendance were closely policed. So too at Nissan, where it is claimed that the introduction of team working has transformed the social relations of production (Wickens 1987), management continue to maintain close forms of supervision – a ratio of 20:1 (IDS 1988b). It would seem, then, that conventional forms of authority relations persist even where one might most have expected team working to have ordained the reverse. The significance of these findings is that work behaviour rules continue to be enforced by non-team members. The disciplinary system does not reside within the work groups but is enforced from without. Thus, while some employers emphasize team working and employee participation, alongside them exists a regime that is overtly based on an assertion of managerial control.

Stress and effort intensification

There is considerable evidence from both case study and survey research that the implementation of new forms of work organization has given rise to increased stress and effort levels. With JIT, for instance, customary notions of 'hard work' are replaced by other activities involving more intense levels of effort to improve the production process (Dawson and Webb 1989), often resulting in increased anxiety and stress (Turnbull 1988). With TQM, too, as established workplace standards are dispensed with, employees are not only expected to work with more commitment, but are also required to supervise their colleagues' work performance (Delbridge and Turnbull 1992; Webb 1993). Traditional workplace disciplines are, therefore, remoulded to suit new production arrangements. In Japanese firms, the ambiguous effects of team working have been recognized. Berggren (1993) has argued that, as against Womack et al. (1990), 'lean' production is more appropriately understood to be 'mean', compelling workers to work hard at boring, repetitive tasks for long hours and to work overtime, often at short notice. This has led to significant health problems. In my own research, female employees working in a cellular manufacturing system were found to suffer similar illnesses, but refused to disclose their suffering, fearing that management would terminate their employment. This added fear led to more stress. Evidence reviewed in chapter 16 also points to an intensification of work associated with the privatization of public-sector organizations.

These undesirable consequences would not seem to be confined to a small number of case study sites. Gallie and White's (1993) survey found that while an increase in skill requirements did have some benefits for employees – increased variety of work, increased responsibility and better opportunities for self-development – it had also led to a marked intensification of work effort. The majority of respondents were working harder than they had been ten years previously. Stress levels had also increased, and were intimately connected with upskilling and the devolution of responsibility.

Some commentators have argued that job intensification has not simply been an unintended consequence of new work structures, that management's primary objective in enlarging jobs and in increasing labour's flexibility has been to increase work loads and reduce the amount of spare or free time available to employees (Elger 1990). A word of caution needs to be entered here: to deduce an inevitable intensification of effort levels may be mistaken. In addition, one cannot presume *a priori* that employees will necessarily perceive this to be undesirable or unacceptable (Geary 1994). First, as the introduction of new work practices is often accompanied by the removal of piece rates, the pressure on unskilled and semi-skilled employees in particular will have been reduced. Second, if the reorganization of production leads to a more systematic and better planned manufacturing process and to a reduction in overtime working, it is conceivable that employees would also look upon this as a decrease in effort levels. In the past, where work had been poorly organized, effort may have been expended in an uneven, and at times frantic, manner. New arrangements may require workers to spend more of the day working, but in a more even and organized way. Third, while effort may have increased, workers may accept this and may gain in terms of job security and better working conditions. Another possibility is that with the introduction of new work structures employees are infused with a new willingness to work harder and are happier to work more diligently.

Two other points need to be stressed. First, as Guest (1990) suggests and is apparent in the case of Toshiba (Trevor 1988), increases in employees' effort levels are often bound up with the introduction of new technologies and improvements in the technical organization of work, such that it is sometimes difficult to isolate the effort component. Moreover, increased effort levels may not have been sought after by management, but may have arisen as a consequence of other changes. As intimated earlier, such improvements may lead workers to have a higher regard for management and they may willingly work harder. The second conclusion follows from this. It would be wrong to adopt a simple zero-sum view: effort may have increased, but employees may have welcomed this.

Whither Japanization?

Throughout this chapter, reference has been made to a variety of industrial relations and manufacturing practices which, it is often claimed, were developed and mastered by Japanese employers. It has become popular to speak of the Japanization of British industrial relations. Discussion as to the relevance of this concept and the appropriateness of attributing changes in work structures to a *Japanese effect* has raged for some years (Ackroyd et al. 1988; Oliver and Wilkinson 1992; Elger and Smith 1994). In evaluating the significance of Japanization for new work structures, the present discussion will examine these issues by focusing on three principal questions: (1) Are British firms adopting 'Japanese-style' practices? (2) Are the work structures adopted by Japanese companies in Britain different from those of other firms? (3) Finally, and very briefly, are Japanese firms in Britain different from Japanese firms in Japan? The analysis will also examine whether this Japanese effect is exercised in a direct or an indirect manner.

At present there are two surveys of Japanese-style industrial relations practices in Britain. Oliver and Wilkinson (1992) examined the practices of 118 manufacturing companies. Of these, 52 were Japanese-owned and were predominantly established on greenfield sites. Many of the remaining 66 firms were in the *Times 1,000* index and would, therefore, constitute large, relatively prosperous firms. Together, then, these companies operated under conditions, one might assume, most appropriate for the development of new forms of work organization. Over a range of practices like cellular manufacturing, QCs, continuous improvement, JIT production and total quality control the authors found little difference between British- and Japanese-owned companies. Where British firms did differ from their Japanese counterparts was in the degree of fit between personnel policies and manufacturing practices. It was found that, while many of the changes to manufacturing practices were informed by a 'Japanese' model, personnel practices were adapted in an uneven manner and driven by a variety of models and forces.

Wood and Mundy's (1993) study of personnel policies and work practices in a representative sample of non-Japanese manufacturing plants and a comparable sample of Japanese-owned transplants found that the latter were using far more of the practices associated with a so-called high commitment management (HCM) model. Apart from this 'quantitative' difference, the authors found 'no appreciable qualitative difference' in the two samples' employment policies. Of more interest, however, was the finding that there was no independent Japanese effect at work, as foreign-owned non-Japanese plants were found to practise HCM to a greater extent than the Japanese companies. Thus, there was nothing particularly distinctive about Japanese plants' practices when compared with other foreign-owned transplants. Wood and Mundy's study also involved case study analysis, and here there was some evidence to suggest that there were differences in the approach of Japanese and non-Japanese management. Of specific interest was the finding that, whereas team working constituted a fundamental organization principle in Japanese plants, elsewhere it was used merely as an exhortation for more team cooperation. On a number of other factors, however, like QCs, functional flexibility and job design there was little difference between Japanese and non-Japanese companies. In sum, then, the evidence would suggest that certain Japanese practices have become quite common, with a trend towards common patterns, with few – albeit some significant – UK–Japanese differences. Caution is required here, however: the industrial relations practices of Japanese firms in the UK are a variant of a home-country approach, and while UK firms have copied certain techniques, any deeper Japanization is highly questionable.

Other evidence, too, questions the uniqueness of the 'Japanization' employment model. First, there is considerable evidence that many Japanese firms rely on traditional mechanisms of labour regulation. For example, shopfloor discipline is reported to be very strict (Trevor 1988); effort levels are demanding; employees are not given the freedom to change things for themselves (Berggren 1993); plants locate in economically depressed areas and recruit a young, inexperienced workforce (Garrahan and Stewart 1992) and are adept both at manipulating divisions between unions to establish contests for recognition and in marginalizing their influence by use of management-controlled forms of participation. Many Japanese enterprises in Britain continue to seek flexibility through more traditional routes (Peck and Stone 1992). Oliver and Wilkinson (1992), for instance, found that 57 per cent of Japanese companies made substantial use of temporary workers. Second, Japanese transplants are largely assembly operations, recruiting a predominantly unskilled workforce, and therefore lack the range of skills and occupations to support a sophisticated form of work organization and opportunities for advancement within the firm. Finally, studies of employees' attitudes reveal that the basis of their cooperation resides less in a qualitative transformation in the manner in which the employment relationship is managed and more in a pragmatic and instrumental response (Garrahan and Stewart 1992). It is evident then that the so-called three pillars – permanent employment, enterprise unions and extensive training programmes – ascribed to the Japanese model are more notable by their absence in Japanese transplants in Britain.

The foregoing criticisms of the Japanization model, though valid, are revealing only in part. An analysis which compares the practice of Japanese firms in Britain with some ideal model, or with practices in Japan, itself runs the risk, as Smith and Elger (1993) point out, of seeing the former as exemplifying a deviant case. It is more likely that the logic of corporate strategy requires a particular spatial division of labour and form of personnel practice. In this sense, it may be that the 'deviation' in personnel practices in Britain is the outcome of a deliberate management strategy, and is designed to 'fit' within a specific local environment. The consequent variations in Japanese practice outside Japan suggest, therefore, that 'Japanization' is too unwieldy a concept to permit sufficient consideration for the influence of different regimes of labour regulation, management strategy and trade union response. It may be more appropriate, then, to ask whether Japanese firms operating in Britain are becoming 'Anglicized'.

One further point needs to be raised here, however. While the direct effect of Japanese employment practices would appear to be limited, it seems clear that it has had a noticeable indirect effect by arming British employers with a powerful vocabulary with which to justify their actions. As has been emphasized in this chapter, there is little that is new in management's employment strategies; attacks on union demarcations and the quest for greater flexibility are old concerns, but when cloaked in the language of HRM and with the need to compete with the Japanese, they are given added legitimacy and impetus.

The Re-Regulation of Work

The analysis thus far would suggest that management's strategy in introducing new forms of work organization has been an attempt to redraw the parameters of acceptable work behaviour, to redefine work standards and to police them closely. With this reformulation of workplace rules, management have grown more concerned to bring these understandings into view, to challenge them and to restrict employees' ability to exercise control over the effort bargain. It must be said, however, that this reorganization and re-regulation of management control is a larger-firm phenomenon. As chapter 19 shows, small companies' managements are more likely to use tried and tested methods. The evidence presented here would suggest that management has achieved considerable success with little overt conflict. But it would be a mistake to think that this has been the whole picture. There are three issues which have yet to be explored. First, how far have management gone towards redefining work behaviour and at what stage has following such a route ceased to be to their advantage? Second, have workers been able to resist, have they wished to, and if so, what influence have they been able to exercise over the terms of the effort bargain? Third, what does all this say about the place of conflict and cooperation?

Although informal bargaining has been reduced, management may not seek to abolish it. First, managers, as much as workers, can gain from vagueness and fluidity. Second, the more that authority is devolved to line managers, the more likely are new local precedents. Third, firms rely on workers' cooperation. As Edwards and Whitston (1993) found in British Rail, managers need a willingness to work overtime at short notice and thus have to 'give' something if workers are to grant this cooperation.

Employees have been able to exercise control over their efforts by other means. An interesting case is that of an engineering company currently being studied by the present author. Management believed that they could obtain greater control over the effort bargain by disposing of piecework. Their success was only partial, however, for employees continued to work to the old piece rate times, fearing that management intended to return to this method of remuneration as soon as productivity increased. Moreover, the new emphasis on total quality provided shop stewards with the opportunity to bargain for more training (and hence more pay) so that a quality product could be produced. Thus, quantity was replaced by quality as the main constituent of employees' effort bargain. Robertson et al. (1992) have also found that team working has not only given employees a sense of solidarity, but it has also provided them with a conduit for advancing interests which are sometimes incongruent with those of management. They have, to a degree at least, successfully appropriated team working to further their own interests.

It is evident, then, that there are a number of conditions which allow workers and their representatives to contest the purpose and functioning of new work structures, thereby enabling them to retain some influence over the labour process: the type of work organization; the structure of management control (centralized or decentralized); the extent to which management choose to formalize work procedures; and the degree to which management depend on employees' expertise and discretion. Their influence is likely to be mediated by the level of bargaining awareness which exists among employees. Thus, while management's strategy of introducing team work, for instance, may lead to a new shopfloor identity, its mobilization in pursuit of sectional demands is dependent on employees' willingness to contest management and to create some space for themselves. Such a process may be assisted or constrained by a number of those facilitative factors listed above, but in the absence of a bargaining awareness, a different workplace regime is likely to emerge.

Furthermore, there is little evidence that employees' commitment has been won over. Geary (1993a), for instance, examined the implementation of new work structures in two electronics plants, in a sector in which trade union organization was weak, effort bargaining poorly established and organized worker action rare, but found evidence of overt discontent. Conflict was present in both organizations: in one site, the success of SAWGs was undermined by operators' refusal to be flexible between work tasks, and in the other, employees refused outright to participate in QCs.

Similar findings have been reported in a variety of other studies. Kelly and Kelly's (1991) review of a variety of employee involvement initiatives indicates that employees' trust in management has not increased significantly: the 'them and us' syndrome remains stubbornly persistent. Also, a number of detailed case study examinations of a variety of participative techniques have found that the differences in attitudes between those employees who do participate and those who do not is not significant (Bradley and Hill 1983; Hill 1991). Similarly, longitudinal studies of SAWGs and QCs found that, although employees enjoyed the new work practices and the attendant responsibilities, there was no lasting change in employees' attitudes or commitment to the organization (Wall et al. 1986; Griffin 1988). Geary (1993a) also found that one unanticipated consequence of SAWGs was that employees' commitment and loyalty was directed inwards towards the immediate work team and cooperation between work groups was prevented as a result. Thus, in these studies employees' favourable response to team working was not generalized to affect their wider relationship with management. In other studies, employees' initial enthusiasm for team working was found to be frustrated by a lack of resources given to training, which prevented them from acquiring a wider repertoire of skills to rotate between work tasks (Elger and Fairbrother 1992). The flattening of job hierarchies, too, has been found to induce discontent amongst employees by removing promotion opportunities. Thus, there is an inherent tension between the need to reduce the number of job descriptions in order to promote flexibility, and the need to retain these job hierarchies so as to enlist employees' ideological and normative commitment (Ahlstrand 1990). Even at so-called leading-edge companies, like Nissan in the UK and CAMI in Canada, there is evidence of growing disenchantment among employees, and participation in team working would not seem to have transformed their attitudes towards management (Garrahan and Stewart 1992; Robertson et al. 1992).

In brief, then, there is little evidence that employees have grown more committed to their employers' objectives. Management, for their part, have grown more assertive, challenging former assumptions of industrial practice, and have undoubtedly been successful in attaining greater control over the labour process. But this period of increased managerial power has not witnessed a fundamental transformation in the organization of shopfloor order. Elements of the past remain. We have seen how management still rely, albeit on a much reduced basis, on custom and practice. This would point to definite limits to the extent to which management have been able to define unilaterally acceptable work behaviour. Employees continue to challenge managerial logic, and while the space for custom and practice and employee resistance has been substantially reduced, it has not been eliminated.

Conclusion

It is clear that the changing nature of competition has forced British employers to look closely at their work organization strategies. To suggest, however, that these pressures have led to a qualitative transformation in the way in which labour is managed would be to err. Management are certainly determined to eradicate any obstacles that may prohibit them from improving the manner in which effort is extracted from labour. But they are *against* restrictive practices and inflexibilities, rather than positively *for* creating new skill structures. New forms of work organization have not led to groups of polyvalent workers charged with responsibility for managing the production process. Nor has their introduction affected employees' lives a great deal. There has been little significant upskilling and, for the main part, task specialization and gendered divisions of labour have remained as they were. Under team working, TQM and lean production, as under more traditional forms of work organization, management remain opposed to extending employees' autonomy (as opposed to increasing their discretion, which is amenable to managerial control), or to any other moves that might impair management's ability to define the content and boundaries of acceptable work behaviour.

Traditional modes of control have remained important, too. Close forms of supervision, job intensification, and strict policing of attendance and of hours coming to and from work would all suggest that the manner in which the shopfloor order is constructed bears a close resemblance with past practice. To this extent, the new marks a return to the old, albeit within a sophisticated guise: a collage of practices, one moment endorsing a move towards increased skills and greater employee participation, another reinventing and rewriting older practices. This conflation of strategies exemplifies the essentially conflictual nature of the labour process, where management are divided between two opposing imperatives: attempts to control employees continually endanger the possibility of fostering their commitment to managerial goals, while empowering workers conversely runs the risk of reducing management control.

What has changed, then, is less management's approach to work organization than the wider industrial relations scene. The present inhospitable economic and political climate has weakened unions and induced a compatibility of interests between them, their membership and employers. Distinct common interests do bind them together, but this cooperative relationship, informed by a pragmatic acceptance of the other party's objectives, has not prevented confusion, disenchantment and conflict. Employees remain, for the main part, mistrustful of management, and continue to question the logic of the demands placed upon them. As for management, there has been great pressure to remove inflexibilities and restrictive practices, but this has not been flanked by a willingness or an ability to invest in new skill structures. It must be concluded, therefore, that the current managerial means of labour regulation do not constitute a fundamental departure from past practice.

References

ACAS (Advisory, Conciliation and Arbitration Service) 1988: *Labour Flexibility in Britain: The 1987 ACAS Survey.* Occasional Paper, 41. London: ACAS.

Ackroyd, S., Burrell, G., Hughes, M. and Whitaker, A. 1988: The Japanization of British Industry? *Industrial Relations Journal,* 19, 1, 11–23.

Ahlstrand, B. W. 1990: *The Quest for Productivity: A Case Study of Fawley after Flanders.* Cambridge: Cambridge University Press.

Batstone, E. 1988: *The Reform of Workplace Industrial Relations: Theory, Myth and Evidence.* Oxford: Clarendon.

Batstone, E. 1989: New Forms of Work Organization in Britain. In P. Grootings, B. Gustavsen and L. Hethy (eds), *New Forms of Work Organization in Europe.* New Brunswick: Transaction.

Batstone, E. and Gourlay, S. 1986: *Unions, Unemployment and Innovation.* Oxford: Blackwell.

Batstone, E., Gourlay, S., Levie, H. and Moore, R. 1987: *New Technology and the Process of Labour Regulation.* Oxford: Clarendon.

Berggren, C. 1993: Lean Production – the End of History? *Work, Employment and Society,* 7, 2, 163–88.

Bradley, K. and Hill, S. 1983: 'After Japan': The Quality Circle Transplant and Productive Efficiency. *British Journal of Industrial Relations,* 21, 3,

291–311.

Bratton, J. 1991: Japanization at Work: The Case of Engineering Plants in Leeds. *Work, Employment and Society*, 5, 3, 377–95.

Collard, R. and Dale, B. 1989: Quality Circles. In K. Sisson (ed.), *Personnel Management in Britain*. Oxford: Blackwell.

Colling, T. and Geary, J. F. 1992: Trade Unions and the Management of Change in the Workplace. Paper presented at the IREC Network Conference, Changing Systems of Workplace Representation in Europe, Dublin, 5–6 November.

Cross, M. 1988: Changes in Working Practices in UK Manufacturing, 1981–88. *Industrial Relations Review and Report*, 415, 2–10.

Daniel, W. W. 1987: *Workplace Industrial Relations and Technical Change*. London: Pinter.

Dawson, P. and Webb, J. 1989: New Production Arrangements: The Total Flexible Cage? *Work, Employment and Society*, 3, 2, 221–38.

Delbridge, R. and Turnbull, P. 1992: Human Resource Maximization: The Management of Labour under Just-in-Time Manufacturing Systems. In P. Blyton and P. Turnbull (eds), *Reassessing Human Resource Management*. London: Sage.

Edwards, P. K. 1987: *Managing the Factory: A Survey of General Managers*. Oxford: Blackwell.

Edwards, P. K. and Whitston, C. 1993: *Attending to Work: The Management of Attendance and Shopfloor Order*. Oxford: Blackwell.

Elger, T. 1990: Technical Innovation and Work Reorganization in British Manufacturing in the 1980s: Continuity, Intensification or Transformation? *Work, Employment and Society*, Special Issue (May), 67–101.

Elger, T. and Fairbrother, P. 1992: Inflexible Flexibility: A Case Study of Modularization. In N. Gilbert, R. Burrows and A. Pollert (eds), *Fordism and Flexibility: Divisions and Change*. London: Macmillan.

Elger, T. and Smith, C. 1994: Global Japanization? In T. Elger and C. Smith (eds), *Global Japanization?* London: Routledge.

Fairbrother, P. 1991: In a State of Change: Flexibility in the Civil Service. In A. Pollert (ed.), *Farewell to Flexibility?* Oxford: Blackwell.

Ferner, A. and Colling, T. 1991: Privatization, Regulation and Industrial Relations. *British Journal of Industrial Relations*, 29, 3, 391–409.

Gallie, D. and White, M. 1993: *Employee Commitment and the Skills Revolution: First Findings from the Employment in Britain Survey*. London: Policy Studies Institute.

Garrahan, P. and Stewart, P. 1992: Management Control and a New Regime of Subordination. In N. Gilbert, R. Burrows and A. Pollert (eds), *Fordism and Flexibility: Divisions and Change*. London: Macmillan.

Geary, J. F. 1993a: New Forms of Work Organization and Employee Involvement in Two Case Study Sites: Plural, Mixed and Protean. *Economic and Industrial Democracy*, 14, 4, 511–34.

Geary, J. F. 1993b: Total Quality Management: A New Form of Labour

Management in Great Britain? In M. Ambrosini and L. Saba (eds), *Participation and Involvement in Great Britain*. Milan: FrancoAngeli.

Geary, J. F. 1993c: A New Voluntarism or Trade Union Marginalisation?: The Role of Trade Unions in the Introduction of New Work Structures. Paper prepared for the Cardiff conference: Unions on the Brink? The Future of the Trade Union Movement, September.

Geary, J. F. 1994: Task Participation: Employees' Participation Enabled or Constrained? In K. Sisson (ed.), *Personnel Management: A Comprehensive Guide to Theory and Practice in Britain*. Oxford: Blackwell.

Griffin, R. 1988: Consequences of Quality Circles in an Industrial Setting. *Academy of Management Journal*, 31, 3, 338–58.

Guest, D. E. 1990: Have British Workers been Working Harder in Thatcher's Britain? A Re-consideration of the Concept of Effort. *British Journal of Industrial Relations*, 28, 3, 293–312.

Heaton, N. and Linn, I. 1989: *Fighting Back: A Report on the Shop Steward Response to New Management Techniques in TGWU Region 10*. Barnsley: Northern College.

Hendry, C. 1993: Personnel Leadership in Technical and Human Resource Change. In J. Clark (ed.), *Human Resource Management and Technical Change*. London: Sage.

Hill, S. 1991: Why Quality Circles Failed but Total Quality Management Might Succeed. *British Journal of Industrial Relations*, 29, 4, 541–68.

IDS (Incomes Data Services) 1985: *Ever Increasing Circles*. Study, 352.

IDS (Incomes Data Services) 1988a: *Flexible Working*. Study, 419.

IDS (Incomes Data Services) 1988b: *Teamworking*. Study, 419.

IDS (Incomes Data Services) 1990: *Total Quality Management*. Study, 457.

IDS (Incomes Data Services) 1992: *Teamworking*. Study, 516.

Jones, B. 1988: Work and Flexible Automation in Britain: A Review of Developments and Possibilities. *Work, Employment and Society*, 2, 4, 451–86.

Kelly, J. and Kelly, C. 1991: 'Them and Us': Social Psychology and the New Industrial Relations. *British Journal of Industrial Relations*, 29, 1, 25–48.

Klein, J. A. 1991: A Reexamination of Autonomy in Light of New Manufacturing Practices. *Human Relations*, 44, 1, 21–38.

Lane, C. 1988: Industrial Change in Europe: The Pursuit of Flexible Specialization in Britain and West Germany. *Work, Employment and Society*, 2, 1, 141–68.

McLoughlin, I. and Clark, J. 1988: *Technological Change at Work*. Milton Keynes: Open University Press.

Marsden, D. and Thompson, M. 1990: Flexibility Agreements and their Significance in the Increase in Productivity in British Manufacturing since 1980. *Work, Employment and Society*, 4, 1, 83–104.

Martinez Lucio, M. and Weston, S. 1992: The Politics and Complexity of Trade Union Responses to New Management Practices. *Human Resource*

Management Journal, 2, 4, 77–91.

Millward, N. and Stevens, M. 1986: *British Workplace Industrial Relations 1980–84*. Aldershot: Gower.

Millward, N., Stevens, M., Smart, D. and Hawes, W. 1992: *Workplace Industrial Relations in Transition*. Aldershot: Dartmouth.

Oliver, N. and Wilkinson, B. 1992: *The Japanization of British Industry: New Developments in the 1990s*, 2nd edn. Oxford: Blackwell.

Peck, F. and Stone, I. 1992: *New Inward Investment and the Northern Region Labour Market*. Employment Department, Research Series, 6. London: HMSO.

Pendleton, A. 1991: The Barriers to Flexibility: Flexible Rostering on the Railways. *Work, Employment and Society*, 5, 2, 241–57.

Purcell, J. 1991: The Rediscovery of the Management Prerogative: The Management of Labour Relations in the 1980s. *Oxford Review of Economic Policy*, 7, 1, 33–43.

Robertson, D., Rinehart, J. and Huxley, C. 1992: Team Concept and Kaizen: Japanese Production Management in a Unionized Canadian Auto Plant. *Studies in Political Economy*, 39, 77–107.

Smith, C., Child, J. and Rowlinson, M. 1990: *Reshaping Work: The Cadbury Experience*. Cambridge: Cambridge University Press.

Smith, P. and Morton, G. 1993: Union Exclusion and the Decollectivization of Industrial Relations in Contemporary Britain. *British Journal of Industrial Relations*, 31, 1, 97–114.

Tailby, S. and Whitston, C. 1989: Industrial Relations and Restructuring. In S. Tailby and C. Whitston (eds), *Manufacturing Change: Industrial Relations and Restructuring*. Oxford: Blackwell.

Terry, M. 1989: Recontextualizing Shopfloor Industrial Relations: Some Case Study Evidence. In S. Tailby and C. Whitston (eds), *Manufacturing Change: Industrial Relations and Restructuring*. Oxford: Blackwell.

Trevor, M. 1988: *Toshiba's New British Company*. London: Policy Studies Institute.

Turnbull, P. J. 1988: The Limits to Japanization: Just-in-Time, Labour Relations and the UK Automotive Industry. *New Technology, Work and Employment*, 3, 1, 7–20.

Wall, T. D., Kemp, N. J., Jackson, P. R. and Clegg, C. W. 1986: Outcomes of Autonomous Work Groups: A Long-Term Field Experiment. *Academy of Management Journal*, 29, 2, 280–304.

Walton, R. E. 1985: From Control to Commitment in the Workplace. *Harvard Business Review*, 53, 2, 77–84.

Webb, J. 1993: Quality Management and the Management of Quality. Paper presented at the eleventh Labour Process Conference, Blackpool.

Wickens, P. 1987: *The Road to Nissan: Flexibility, Quality and Teamwork*. London: Macmillan.

Wilkinson, A. 1992: Total Quality Management and Employee Involvement. *Human Resource Management Journal*, 2, 4, 1–20.

Womack, J., Jones, D., Daniel, T. and Roos, D. 1990: *The Machine that Changed the World*. New York: Rawson Associates.

Wood, S. and Mundy, J. 1993: *Are Human Resource Practices in Japanese Transplants Truly Different?* Paper presented at the BUIRA Conference, York.

13

Industrial Relations and Productivity

Peter Nolan and Kathy O'Donnell

Britain's productivity profile has been the subject of long-standing controversy. Linked to a wider set of concerns about the competitiveness of British-based industry, the productivity record has commonly served to direct attention to the possible sources of domestic under-performance. The historical evidence shows that the United States opened up a significant productivity gap with Britain early in the twentieth century, and since 1945 most major Western European economies have eclipsed Britain's record. Successive post-war governments strove to check the problem but with limited success, and by the late 1970s talk of a deep-seated crisis in production was commonplace. By the mid-1980s, however, the climate of opinion had begun to change. The government of the day, with notable academic support, claimed there had been a productivity breakthrough. With official statistics showing a domestic growth rate of over 4 per cent, Britain was said to be top of the league table in Europe, ahead of the United States, and on a par with Japan.

Coinciding with a radical shift in the character of state policy, these performance gains were linked by many commentators (for example, Crafts 1988; Maynard 1988; Metcalf 1989a) to the changes in industrial relations triggered by Mrs Thatcher's policies after 1979. The traditional pattern of 'adversarial' industrial relations, it was said, had for far too long been a scourge on business. Some accounts (Nichols 1986) highlighted the shortcomings of management, but overwhelmingly the burden of responsibility for Britain's inferior productivity record was attributed to the behaviour of workers and their trade unions.

In the period since 1979 union membership has shrunk, employees have been disciplined by mass unemployment and restrictive legislation, and employers have striven to reassert their authority (see chapters 6, 9 and 12). This chapter investigates the significance of these changes in production relations. The first part highlights conceptual and measurement problems in comparative studies and places the productivity record in context. Subsequent sections examine the arguments and evidence adduced in support of the view that performance was impeded by industrial relations before 1979, and enhanced by Conservative policies thereafter. The analysis looks at the record in manufacturing and takes the coal industry as a specific case study of the effects of power shifts in production. In contrast to many accounts, which compare the 1980s only with the 1970s, particular attention is given to the long-run linkages between industrial relations and productivity; this is essential if the character of developments since 1979 is to be understood. Our interpretation of the links between industrial relations and productivity in Britain is presented in the concluding section.

The Productivity Record

Measurement issues

The analysis of productivity across time, establishments, industries and national frontiers is fraught with problems. How should productivity be measured; what are the relevant procedures for aggregating heterogeneous inputs and outputs; and how, in time series studies, should trend and cyclical movements be disentangled? Given that productivity is the outcome of a collective social process, what significance should be assigned to the politics of production relations? This issue has scarcely been addressed, still less resolved, in the empirical research literature which has been directed at the measurement of outcomes.

The most commonly used statistics are labour productivity and total factor productivity. Labour productivity measures output per employee or employee hour, usually in price rather than physical units, and is often presented as a rough and ready index of labour efficiency. Do British employees work, on average, as efficiently as their counterparts overseas? Comparative data on labour productivity are often cited to support the view that they do not, yet such a conclusion may not be warranted. Is the quality of management in Britain comparable to that elsewhere, are domestic factories equipped to the same standards, do British workers receive the same levels of training? Without a consideration of such issues, few meaningful conclusions can be drawn from the figures on labour productivity.

Total factor productivity (TFP) is thought to be a more robust performance indicator, especially if the focus is on the causes of increasing labour productivity (Oulton and O'Mahoney 1994). It is defined as the rate of output growth minus the weighted sum of the growth of the inputs, the weights being determined by each input's share of total income. Interpreted as a broad indicator of technical progress, TFP is said to capture the output gains accruing from changes in the methods of capital and labour utilization rather than changes in the quantities themselves. Critics of TFP note that it is estimated as a *residual* and hence tends to serve as a crude 'catch all' term, not least because it is usually the largest element in the estimated equation. Among other things, it is said to embrace 'advances in knowledge, personal characteristics such as effort and experience, union power, government regulation' (Alford 1988: 18); and one might add the improvements in industrial relations allegedly induced by the Conservatives' policies (cf. Muellbauer 1986).

The analysis of TFP is predicated on a number of key assumptions: that the economy is characterized by homogeneous factor inputs, perfect competition, and hence marginal productivity factor pricing and constant returns to scale. While some advocates of TFP analysis (or growth accounting as it is sometimes known) accept that these assumptions are rather limiting, and may put at risk the reliability of the interpretations of the estimated residual (Feinstein 1988), more usually such problems are ignored. Yet the issues are of no small significance. One crucial problem concerns the measurement of capital. Marginal productivity theory assumes that profit rates are determined by the marginal contribution of capital to net output. But how is the total amount of capital to be measured? In growth accounting, capital is aggregated across firms in price terms. The only way of estimating the value of capital is to include an estimate for the rate of profit. Profit must already be included in advance of its having been determined at the margin by the contribution of 'capital'. The approach is plainly circular, as demonstrated many years ago by the Cambridge critique (see Harcourt 1972).

Similar problems arise in respect of the aggregation of the labour input, once the assumption of homogeneity is dropped. There is a further problem, however: labour productivity is usually calculated on the basis of an *extensive* measure of labour – the number of people or hours worked – but the *intensity* of work is also relevant. If the human effort expended per worker hour is raised, for whatever reason, then the total input of labour would have increased. In failing to capture this increase, a focus on the extensive use of labour would result in biased estimates of the true relationship between output and labour input. Two implications follow from this. First, improvements in measured labour productivity may not imply a corresponding improvement in labour efficiency: what matters for efficiency is the ratio of output to input including changes in labour intensity. Second, comparative productivity measures over time and place which fail to factor in relative intensities must be judged deficient.

Turning to the measurement of output, the problem is how to aggregate all the different products and services that are produced. The usual procedure is to value them in nominal prices, which are then adjusted by an appropriate price deflator to yield a measure of the real value of output. Two possible difficulties may arise with the procedure. First, value added may be distorted if the price of inputs rises at a rate different from that of the price of output (fuel would be an obvious example). To avoid such difficulties, Bruno (1984) and Stoneman and Francis (1992) have argued that separate (or 'double') deflators for inputs and outputs should be applied. Second, the existence of different price regimes in different countries introduces a further complexity when the value of output is converted into a common currency. Recent studies (van Ark 1990) have tried to address this problem by calculating purchasing power parity (PPP) exchange rates. The latter are formed on the basis of ratios of ex-factory prices for matched samples of products in each pair of countries under comparison. The effect is to remove distortions in the valuation of output, country-by-country, that would otherwise surface as a result of exchange rate fluctuations. Table 13.1, which places Britain's labour productivity record in a wider international context, is based on this method.

Productivity trends

Table 13.1 reveals a substantial and enduring shortfall in productivity levels in the United Kingdom as compared to the United States and the other European countries. The gap with the United States opened up early in the twentieth century, and remains in excess of 100 per cent. By contrast, Britain emerged from the Second World War as a relatively high productivity economy within Europe, yet within the space of two decades that position of comparative advantage had been converted into a significant productivity deficit, currently of the order of 25 and 40 per cent. Table 13.2 presents the comparative data on total factor productivity. Taken at face value the figures suggest that Britain under-performed during the 1960s and the 1970s but improved in the 1980s, achieving something close to the average European performance, but remain-

Table 13.1   Gross value added per person hour in manufacturing in The Netherlands, France, West Germany and the USA as a percentage of the UK, selected years 1960–1988 (UK = 100)

	UK	*Netherlands*	*France*	*West Germany*	*USA*
1960	100	98.5	80.7	105.3	242.5
1970	100	124.8	111.7	133.1	223.7
1975	100	142.4	119.8	141.9	216.7
1980	100	173.5	144.2	164.3	227.2
1984	100	165.5	130.8	146.8	209.6
1988	100	144.1	125.5	136.8	207.0

Source: van Ark 1990.

Table 13.2   Total factor productivity growth in the business sector, average annual percentage change

	1960–1973	*1973–1979*	*1979–1990*
United States	1.6	−0.4	0.1
Japan	5.9	1.4	2.0
France	4.0	1.7	1.5
Germany	2.6	1.8	0.9
United Kingdom	2.3	0.6	1.3

Source: OECD, *Economic Outlook*, December 1992.

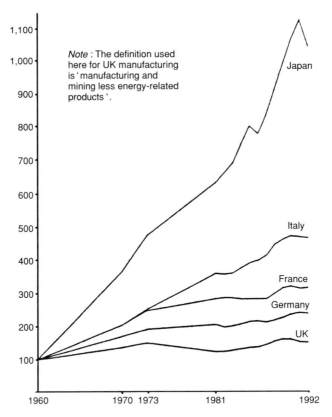

(*Source*: Bureau of Labor 1994)

Figure 13.1 Manufacturing output, 1960–1992 (1960 = 100)

ing some way short of Japan's record. How should the better performance record of the 1980s be interpreted?

Labour productivity changes are the product of differential movements in output and employment. Productivity may be rising because output is growing faster than employment. It may have
increased because the technology of production has changed: more
advanced machinery, improvements in organization, or better
trained workers may have supplanted less efficient combinations of
inputs. A third possibility is that workers and/or machinery are being
used more intensively. Figure 13.1 helps to put Britain's productivity record in perspective. In comparative terms, Britain's output growth rate is inferior to all the other countries shown. It makes
clear that the productivity gains that have been secured since the
early 1970s do not derive from increases in manufacturing output,
which has risen by only 1 percentage point since 1973.

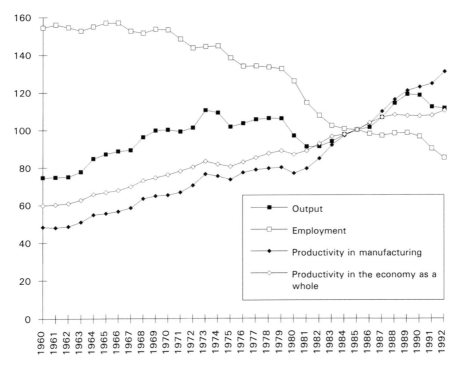

(*Source*: CSO 1993)

Figure 13.2 Output, employment and labour productivity,
1960–1992 (1985 = 100)

Figure 13.2 charts the movements in labour productivity, output
and employment in manufacturing since 1960. It also gives the
growth of productivity for the economy as a whole. What it shows is
a transformation in the output–employment ratio since 1979. The
collapse in output in 1979–80 was followed in 1981 by an even larger
collapse in employment. Output began to recover in 1982, but
employment continued to fall. Manufacturing output returned to its
1979 level in 1987 (and its previous peak of 1973 in late 1988); but
with many fewer workers engaged in manufacturing, productivity
was bound to rise.

Did the productivity advances of the 1980s represent a fundamental shift in supply side performance? Darby and Wren-Lewis (1988)
tackled this question by correcting the time series data for the effects
of firms' 'incorrect' output expectations which they claim led to a
rise in hoarded labour services in the 1970s. They concluded that the
'recent underlying productivity growth . . . is not out of line with
earlier behaviour' in the 1960s: it was the performance of the 1970s

that was aberrant. Stoneman and Francis's reworking of the official productivity series for 1979–89 points in the same direction. Using the method of double deflation accounting, they found that the official series (based on single deflators) significantly overstated the growth of productivity at 51 per cent compared to their estimate of 34 per cent. While an average annual rise of 3 per cent represents a substantial advance on the 1970s, it is very much in line with the performance of the 1960s. The next section puts these data in historical context.

The Politics of Productivity

The historical context

The United States, as noted, established a commanding productivity lead over Britain early in the twentieth century. Many commentators (Chandler 1966; Lazonick 1991) have linked the success of American business to four connected developments: the early and rapid diffusion of the techniques of 'scientific' management and the associated subjugation of craft unions; the decisive shift in key industries to capital-intensive methods of production; the growth of the vertically integrated firm; and the monopolization of markets which permitted the fuller exploitation of economies of scale. By contrast, in Britain's staple industries (cotton, coal, steel, shipbuilding) techniques of production were not radically transformed, craft practices partially survived, markets remained fragmented, and firms retained their traditional structures rendering them on average small in scale and scope.

Some writers account for the delayed modernization of British industry almost exclusively in terms of the character of industrial relations. Pencavel (1977), for example, estimated that the growth of unionism in the coal industry – from 66 per cent in 1900 to 88 per cent in 1913 – reduced output significantly: other things being equal, 'a totally unionized coal field produces some 22 per cent less output than a completely ununionized coal field' (1977: 145). But Pencavel did not stop there. On the basis of his estimates for the coal industry – remember, for the period 1900–1913 – he was willing to 'conjecture' that this figure of 22 per cent was probably 'a lower bound' estimate of the economy-wide output losses stemming from unionism in the 1970s. Assuming that he might be correct, how, one might ask rhetorically, would he account for the failure of output to grow in manufacturing in the 1980s given that union membership virtually halved?

Other research in any case suggests that Pencavel's analysis over-states the unity, coherence and power of the miners' union in the coal industry. Fine et al. (1985), for example, highlight the diversity of mining conditions, wages and working hours, and the obstacles which this diversity posed to the formation of common and coherent campaigns at local, regional and national level. The struggle nation-ally to impose limits on the working day was eventually successful, culminating in 1908 with the passage of an eight hour Bill. But struggles within collieries and coalfields to lift wages and improve safety and underground conditions continued to be inhibited by the division of labour, which so often placed haulier and hewer, for example, in conflict. Resistance to management was uneven, spor-adic and often ineffective. Although the growth of output was evi-dently constrained by the primitive techniques used underground, it is difficult to sustain the view that the union had the power to inhibit change.

This is especially true of the inter-war period. Despite the heavy defeat sustained by the miners' union in 1926, investment in mech-anized coal cutting machinery after 1926 fell by as much as 60 per cent (Supple 1987). With the union in disarray, and in the face of increased overseas competition (particularly from France and Belgium), the colliery owners had both the power and incentive to modernize methods of production. Instead, they opted to take ad-vantage of the weakened position of the union by further degrading wages and working conditions. Productivity and profitability were thus lifted through pay cuts and enforced extensions in the working day, while investment in new methods and machinery stagnated. By 1938 mechanized coal cutting accounted for only 55 per cent of output in Britain, as compared with 97 per cent in Germany, 98 per cent in Belgium and 88 per cent in France.

These conflicting interpretations of the impact of unionism in the early twentieth century coal industry reflect two very distinct cur-rents in the literature on industrial relations and productivity. The more common position, as exemplified by Pencavel, treats unions as a potent source of production inefficiency. Fine and his colleagues, by contrast, argue that union weakness and defeat do not necessarily correlate with higher rates of investment and sustainable increases in productivity and output growth. On the contrary, they may lead to the postponement of investment in modern techniques as employers pursue other (for example, low wage, effort-intensive) routes to profitability. While such strategies may help lift productivity in the short run, their effects on efficiency and competitiveness in the longer term may be pernicious. And so it proved in coal and other key industries.

The post-war period

The accumulated weaknesses of domestic industry, especially the legacy of under-investment in new techniques and methods during the inter-war years, were rudely exposed during the Second World War. The incoming post-war Labour government attempted to deal with the most glaring deficiencies – in gas, electricity, coal and the railways – through nationalization. But, as discussed in chapter 2, for the bulk of industries, particularly manufacturing, which remained under private ownership, exhortation rather than direct intervention was the chosen lever for change.

In a context of severe labour shortages, the Labour government assigned a high priority to lifting industrial productivity (Tomlinson 1991). But its initiatives met with limited successes. Labour's Production Campaign, which involved media advertising, conferences and factory newsletters, was launched in 1946. It was followed with plans to establish tripartite development councils to promote rationalization and renewal in key industries, but in the face of strong opposition from employers only four such councils were eventually created (Tomlinson 1991: 46–7). With American encouragement, notably from the Economic Cooperation Administration which was established to administer Marshall Aid, Labour set up in 1947 the Anglo-American Council on Productivity (AACP). The Council sought to promote awareness of American production methods, particularly Scientific Management and mass production, by organizing visits (66 in total between 1949 and 1952) for British employers and trade unionists to American factories.

The Reports that flowed from these missions identified major obstacles to the 'Americanization' of British industry: not the restrictive practices of labour as Crafts (1988) alleged, but rather the shortcomings of management (see Coates 1994). Tomlinson points out that the AACP Reports attracted hostility from the industrial community, particularly the Federation of British Industry, which had come to regard Labour's productivity drive cynically as the 'thin end of the wedge' and an attempt by the government to lay the blame for Britain's ills solely on management. With the return to power of the Conservatives in 1951, the findings of the AACP were shelved. Indeed, during the 1950s there were no further major state-sponsored initiatives in respect of productivity, though it was apparent to many commentators that productivity growth rates elsewhere were such that Britain's relative position was seriously at risk. What, if any, forces for modernization were at play?

Many analysts of this period stress the buoyant market conditions, at home and abroad (Kilpatrick and Lawson 1980; Grant 1991; Tomlinson 1991), which they claim served to weaken the pressures on firms to upgrade products and processes. This argument, which meshes in important ways with Reid's account of the factors behind management's sloppy approach to industrial relations (discussed in chapter 3), has become almost an orthodoxy. Yet it does not help to explain why the techniques and business structures pioneered in the United States were so enthusiastically embraced elsewhere, in France for example. Nor does it explain why the forces of competition, both domestic and international, were subverted. Even in buoyant market conditions, it must surely be to the advantage of at least some firms to exploit modern techniques to gain competitive advantage?

With the benefit of hindsight, it is possible to see that the sources of domestic industry's developing weaknesses in the post-war period were complex, yet the character of contemporary analysis and debate was such that many crucial considerations were crowded out by the search for immediate panaceas. In and of itself, the argument about market conditions is insufficient as an explanation of the increasingly sclerotic character of domestic industry. The other favoured explanation was (and remains) labour, or more particularly union obstructionism.

Typical of the genre was the 1958 pamphlet, *A Giant's Strength*, produced by the Inns of Court Conservative and Unionist Society, which recommended the erosion of the legal immunities which had protected trade unions since 1906 from criminal prosecution for most torts (civil wrongs). This argument, which drew upon and helped promote a developing consensus, was premised upon the belief that union power and obstructionism were the root cause of Britain's industrial malaise. Within a decade, despite the absence of systematic evidence – indeed almost any evidence at all – this perspective had become entrenched as a conventional wisdom.

As discussed in chapters 2 and 8, the Donovan Commission, set up by Labour in 1965, focused primarily on the sources of workplace 'disorder'. Shortly before the Commission began its work, Hugh Clegg, the principal architect of the final report, had this to say on the issue of 'restrictive' practices:

> Under-employment of labour is one of the major scandals of the British economy. There may be few workers – outside of the newspaper industry – who are paid to do nothing at all, but throughout British industry there must be hundreds of thousands of workers who are paid to do nothing for a considerable part of their working time . . . Then there are the new machines and changes in technology – many of them in use in other countries – which would be introduced here but for the limits placed by workers on their output. (Clegg 1964)

In the event, the Commission's report did not lay the blame for disorder solely at the feet of the unions. The analysis was more subtle. Senior management were held culpable for neglecting industrial relations issues and allowing foremen and supervisors to enter into covert and cosy deals with the rapidly expanding ranks of shopfloor trade union representatives. Stressing that management alone could put the situation to right, the Donovan Report argued for comprehensive factory agreements, the formalization of industrial relations procedures, and the integration of shop stewards into the machinery of collective bargaining.

As shown in chapter 7, formalization was indeed an important consequence of the changes sought by management in the 1960s and 1970s. Strategies of internalization were more pervasive and pronounced, as indicated in chapter 3, and greater efforts were made to cut costs by introducing work study techniques, job evaluation, and pay policies more closely tailored to the needs of the enterprise. Yet the weaknesses in industrial performance became more, not less, striking. The substantive improvements in labour productivity that were expected to accompany the workplace reforms prescribed by the Donovan Report did not materialize, perhaps, as Metcalf (1989b) has suggested, because the benefits of formalization were subject to significant lags and only became apparent in the changed conditions of the 1980s. Others, for example Edwards (1983), have argued that the reform process itself may well have been self-defeating; attacks on the status quo may have provoked resentment and increased conflict in the workplace. In addition, it must be recognized that the performance of enterprises in Britain, as indeed elsewhere, would have been affected by wider developments in the international economy: monetary instability, oil price rises, and the generalized profit and productivity slowdown which some (Boyer 1988) associate with the exhaustion of Fordism.

Whatever the true explanation – and part of it must be that the anticipated performance gains from formalization were massively overstated in the first place – the fact is that the apparent failure of the post-Donovan industrial relations reforms served only to build support for the case that more radical policies were required to attenuate the allegedly deleterious effects of union 'bosses' and their lay representatives in the workplace. Many thought that the solution lay in the enactment of new laws designed to restrict unionism, and the 1971 Industrial Relations Act was the first major shift in that direction. Although its subsequent repeal in 1974 was erroneously thought to constitute clear evidence that the voluntarist tradition in British industrial relations was firmly embedded, support for tougher measures against unions continued to grow. The clearest manifestation was the election of Mrs Thatcher in 1979.

Production politics and productivity

What theories and evidence were mobilized to support the case against workers and their unions? An examination of the literature for this period reveals a dearth of systematic and dispassionate findings. In relation to theory, the investigation of the connections between workplace struggles and accommodations, their wider effects on the economy, and the role of mediating forces such as economic competition, was (and still is) remarkably primitive. What are the relevant bridging concepts in moving from isolated incidents in the workplace (strikes, job controls and so on) to developments at company, industry and economy-wide level? The debate focusing on the productivity consequences of industrial relations institutions has tended to draw from neo-classical economics – albeit selectively and often inconsistently – yet this analytical framework, as its most accomplished exponents would readily concede, has virtually nothing to say about conflicts in production, the relative performance consequences of different institutional bargaining arrangements or trade union structures.

One of the most immediate consequences of the lack of relevant theory is that the analysis of the impact of industrial relations on productivity has usually lacked specificity. What is the nature of the charge against British workers and unions? When exactly did unions develop the capacities to block change, and what is the nature of these capacities which supposedly enabled unions – however localized and partial in presence – to impede the forces of competition? These questions, some might say, are in fact being addressed in the contemporary quantitative research literature on unions. That claim is investigated below, but first it is necessary to sift the findings of an earlier period. What exactly prompted Hayek (1980), among others, to allege that 'unions were the main reason for the decline of the British economy' prior to Mrs Thatcher's election?

One obvious place to look is in the voluminous research reports provided for the Donovan Report. Unfortunately, as discussed elsewhere (Nolan 1993), the Commission did not explicitly investigate the nature of the connections between particular workplace practices, systems of job regulation and their performance consequences. It took for granted that there was a connection, which is entirely understandable in the circumstances of the time and given the pressures that led to the Commission's establishment in the first place. But it did not attempt to unravel the relevant causal linkages.

The research papers do contain important pointers: for example, McCarthy's authoritative work on the nature of shop steward organizations, which suggested that they were more a 'lubricant' in the change process than an 'irritant'. And there were other contemporary studies (Mackay et al. 1971) which, like Donovan, focused on developments in engineering in the first half of the 1960s. Allegedly, these were the years of spiralling work group power on the shopfloor, yet Mackay and his research team found that in the workshops of Glasgow, Birmingham and North Lanarkshire – three areas with firmly established industrial traditions – management prerogative remained firmly intact (see also chapter 5). While noting the complacency of the managements which they studied, in line with Reid's thesis (see chapter 3), there is little support in their work for the conventional wisdom about the misuse of union power.

Other research on the car industry, which for many commentators had by the mid-1960s come to symbolize the British malaise, pointed to a complex set of connections between management strategy, the organization of work, and company performance (Turner et al. 1967). On the specific issue of the impact of strikes on output and productivity, Turner and his colleagues found a strong 'clear but inverse connection between striker days and production'. Their interpretation of this finding was that management used strikes as a way of regulating output in an industry that experienced acute seasonal shifts in demand.

Re-examining the evidence some twenty years later, Tolliday (n.d.) noted that the 'the interruptions of production due to disputes do not seem to have had very serious effects on car-makers' performance'. By the 1960s, the manufacturers' 'main problem was not inadequate volumes of production but being able to sell the cars they made at a profit and "beneficial strikes" could avoid the pile-up of unsaleable cars'. On the question of the impact of workers' job controls on productivity, he concluded that 'under piecework the pace and intensity of work were generally high', but the low levels of pay in the industry 'made it less attractive' for the manufacturers 'to invest in capital intensive methods'. The low cost of labour was in effect functioning as a barrier to the exit of inefficient firms.

These contemporary studies none the less failed to dislodge popular perceptions about the damage inflicted on industry by inefficient industrial relations practices, and before long there was new evidence – generated by economists with rather different concerns – which helped breathe new life into the conventional wisdom. There were three major studies, which have become stock reference points in the leading textbooks and are often treated as authoritative sources, yet the conclusions which they reached have been judged seriously flawed.

For the early 1970s, Pratten (1976) investigated the determinants of labour productivity differentials in 100 international firms with factories in Britain, France, Germany and the United States. He found that, as compared to Britain, labour productivity was higher by 50 per cent in the United States, 27 per cent in Germany, and 15 per cent in France, and labour 'problems' emerged as a significant factor. Strikes, restrictive practices and staffing levels, according to Pratten, accounted for 11 per cent of the differential with the United States, 12 per cent of the differential with Germany and 6 per cent of the differential with France. Caves (1980), through regression analysis, examined the causes of productivity differentials in 71 matched industries in Britain and the United States for the period 1967–72. He found that the factors which best explained the productivity shortfall in Britain were the number of strikes and days lost through strikes, the proportion of employment in Britain in 'older industrial regions', and the extent of the coverage of male manual employees by collective agreements. With Davies, seven years later, he carried out a similar investigation but found that the productivity effects of industrial relations were 'rather unclear' (Davies and Caves 1987).

Prais (1981) studied 10 matched industries in Britain, Germany and the United States, and concluded that two factors had impaired Britain's performance: the inefficient size of plants, and under-investment in training. Union practices were held to be the root cause of both problems. First, a history of damaging conflicts in large plants had led to a skewing of production towards small units, which in turn inhibited the exploitation of economies of scale. Second, the compression of pay differentials between skilled and unskilled work-ers, fought for by 'open' unions such as the Transport and General Workers, had served to blunt the incentive for workers to acquire new skills. The supporting evidence for these claims is thin, however.

Nichols (1986) has concluded that the studies by Pratten and Caves contained so many weaknesses that their conclusions could not be judged safe. Among other things, Pratten relied almost exclusively on information provided by management, he did not observe directly the performance of labour in any of the plants included in his study, and the numbers that he presented which derived from subjective impressions were not, on his own admission, 'hard' data in the usual sense. Nor, one might add, was he able to control for interactions between the various 'labour' and non-labour variables embraced by his study. Caves's study was flawed by serious data limitations: no information on strikes for the United States or on the quality of management in Britain; and his dependent variable, output per worker, was not adjusted for the effects of price and exchange rate variations as discussed above.

The study by Prais has been considered authoritative (see Crafts 1991) but it is at odds with the more detailed accounts of the history of domestic industry by business historians such as Hannah (1976) and Channon (1973). These point to various factors, including the enduring character of family-owned and managed firms, which stalled the rise of the modern integrated company, hierarchical M-form management systems, and monopolized markets – surely necessary preconditions for the successful exploitation of economies of scale? Unions may have been a factor, perhaps, but why ignore these other well-documented dynamics? 'Too often', Prais con-cluded, 'management seems not to be free to decide on how many [workers] to employ per machine, nor is it free to decide on what work to employ them' (1981: 269), yet he made no effort to check these perceptions with the relevant workers nor specify clearly in what ways workers had blocked change.

Kilpatrick and Lawson (1980), writing from a position far removed from orthodoxy, traced the causes of Britain's long-run industrial decline to two self-reinforcing processes: successful worker resistance to cost cutting changes in production, and Britain's insertion into the world economy as a major imperialist power. On the one hand, workers in Britain are reckoned to have been better placed than their overseas counterparts to mount defensive struggles against employers' cost cutting initiatives. On the other hand, British firms' privileged access to the protected markets of the Empire are said to have weakened the incentives for management to launch a determined offensive against workplace practices.

Kilpatrick and Lawson highlighted three distinctive features of the British system of industrial relations which served to consolidate workers' relative strength. First, the acceptance of the principles of collective organization before the turn of the twentieth century facilitated the 'growth of real power by workers to resist changes and to defend standards . . . [particularly craft] customs and norms which existed before the introduction of mass production techniques' (1980: 87). Second, British unions had not suffered major political defeats at the hands of authoritarian states in the same way that autonomous trade unionism had in, for example, Spain, Italy and Germany. Third, Britain's decentralized structure of collective bargaining had militated against long-term corporate planning and coordinated management decision-making. Workers' self-activity at shopfloor level had, in consequence, succeeded in delaying 'the adoption and diffusion of new techniques and [lifting] staffing levels above what they would otherwise have been' (1980: 86).

Unquestionably, the strengths of Kilpatrick and Lawson's thesis, which presumably account for its enduring appeal, lie in the fact that it does not analyse the role of unions in conventional terms. Unions are not blamed for blocking technological advances; they are commended for their efforts in resisting the pressures for degradation in the class struggle. Management are not held to account for their sins of omission, they are judged passive victims of their circumstances. But there are still major problems with their argument.

First, Kilpatrick and Lawson, as Hyman and Elger (1981) noted, are inclined to over-romanticize the strength of work group power and resistance. Hyman and Elger mobilized evidence from four industries (steel, railways, cars and print) which shows that at decisive moments unions capitulated to offers of enhanced job security or pay in return for concessions over staffing levels, work organization or technology. Second, as Coates (1994) has pointed out, there is a lack of attention in the analysis – which, after all, covers no less than a century of British industrial relations history – to the details of the ebb and flow of trade union power. Is it really plausible, Coates asks, to suggest that unions always offered such effective resistance, for example after the employers' offensive launched in the 1890s against trade union rights? Would the organizational capacities of unions at workplace level have survived the force of mass unemployment in the inter-war years? And if not, was their character such in the aftermath of the Second World War that they could be held to account for the sluggish performance of the 1950s?

Linked to these points are the criticisms of Fine and Harris (1985), who note that there is a major inconsistency in Kilpatrick and Lawson's argument in respect of the role of competition. We are told that the Empire helped forestall the pressure on industrialists to modernize. But why, in the declining years of Britain's role as an imperial power, were the harsh winds of international competition so ineffectual? Why, to return to a question posed at the outset of this section, was it the case that firms in Britain were not cajoled into modernization by firms less exposed to the pressures of unionization? British manufacturing, as Fine and Harris note, was never completely unionized, so does the evidence reveal superior performance in areas of non-unionism? Why, if unions posed such a powerful obstacle to change, were they not progressively eroded by the expansion of more productive and profitable non-union companies?

The Impact of Conservative Reforms

Mrs Thatcher's governments sought to remove, weaken or radically reform those institutions which in their view had created and fostered an adversarial industrial relations system. But did they succeed in providing the appropriate 'signal' to employers to reassert the principle of managerial prerogative and to refashion the character of the employment relationship to their lasting advantage? Some commentators, for example Purcell (1993) and Gregg et al. (1993), have answered this question in the affirmative but the evidence, as reviewed below, is less clear-cut. Early commentaries on the Thatcher

years tended to highlight the stability of established industrial relations structures and procedures, but, as discussed in chapters 7, 12
and 14, as new evidence has accumulated these earlier conclusions
seem premature: union membership and influence have been
severely cut, the closed shop has been abolished, and strikes are at
an all time low. The productivity record is cited by some (for
example, Metcalf 1989a) as further evidence of the progressive
effects of Thatcher's policies. Does this assessment stand up to close
scrutiny?

Theoretical controversies

Theoretically, the most recent research on the connections between
industrial relations and productivity has been informed by two distinct currents. These are the conventional neo-classical view of
unionism, and a predominantly American based economics literature which has sought to challenge the one-dimensional perspective
of unionism in neo-classical theory.

Neo-classical economics treats unions unambiguously as a source
of inefficiency. They are regarded in the first instance as monopoly
sellers of labour which distort otherwise efficient markets. They are
then accused of producing technical inefficiencies in production,
and they also stand charged of pursuing narrow, sectional gains in
the political arena at the expense of the common good. In each
instance these charges can be shown to derive from a particularly
narrow conception of the economy.

Consider first the labour market, which is thought of as an arena
free from information costs and other frictions, including the exercise of power. Individuals are said to contract with one another
voluntarily in pursuit of selfish interests, and the myriad transactions
that emerge are judged to be optimal (or 'first-best') in terms of the
allocation of resources. Unions are believed to frustrate the efficient
workings of the market in order to gain a limited benefit for their
members. While they may prove successful in this venture, the
consequences will be reduced job opportunities, as employers
substitute alternative inputs for relatively expensive unionized
labour, and output reductions, as firms take steps to bring their
inflated costs in line with given revenues. Initially confined to unionized establishments, these effects will be amplified as the displaced
unionized workers are gradually re-employed at lower wages in
relatively labour-intensive, low productivity jobs in non-union firms.

The effects of unions in production are less clearly specified, yet they are none the less thought to lead to major output losses (Rees 1963). Seeing the work process as a predetermined technical relationship between inputs and outputs, neo-classical theory regards the attempt by work groups to influence the character of the labour process as an unacceptable abrogation of management prerogative. Strictly speaking, in its most refined forms, economic theory has little or nothing to say about the functions, processes and 'prerogatives' of management. As any student of the subject would explain, it is the market mechanism which governs the selection and deployment of factor services in production: managers are mere ciphers, prisoners of underlying market and technological forces (see chapter 4). But in practice, most economists tend to deviate from this highly abstract view, which after all amounts to a denial of one of the most salient institutions of modern capitalism. Relying more on pragmatic judgement than the underlying theory, they would typically argue that the management hierarchies and authority structures which characterize modern organizations developed as an *efficient* response to prevailing deficiencies in the utilization of information, technology and productive resources. Hence they should not be subject to challenges from unions.

These propositions should be treated with considerable caution. For they are derived from a model of the economy which is highly abstract, ahistorical, and preoccupied with static, allocative questions. The method of neo-classical theory construction involves, in the first instance, the elaboration of the allocative and distributive properties of a perfectly competitive economy. Prominent institutional features of actual economies, including firms and unions, are ruthlessly excised. Then, by taking the individual as the basic unit of analysis, and assuming away all transactions costs, the theory is able to demonstrate the existence of an equilibrium price vector which allows all mutually beneficial trading opportunities to be fully exploited.

The best exponents of this approach, of course, readily concede that the model is merely an 'ideal type', a device to better understand the workings of the real economy. Yet in practice, the real economy is judged against the properties of the model rather than the other way round. Unions and other key institutions are inserted into the analysis as 'imperfections', in other words as unwelcome sources of variance from the 'first-best' world of perfect competition. Not only is this conclusion predetermined at the outset by the assumptions of the model, it is also generated without any consideration of the dynamic properties of the system. What are the sources of economic change, and what role do historically forged collective institutions play in the developmental process? These questions are all but ignored in modern economic analysis. Finally, no attempt is made by modern economic analysis to investigate the root causes of conflicts of interest in production and exchange (see chapters 1 and 12 above). Evidence that such tensions pre-dated the formation of unions, indeed that they helped spur the growth of worker combinations, is swept aside in a relentless effort to ascribe to unions the blame for strikes, wages struggle and associated industrial relations difficulties. To concede that conflicts may be deeply rooted in our industrial system would expose the folly of directing exclusive attention to its institutional manifestations through unions and other interest groups.

The main challenge to the orthodox position has come from a group of economists at Harvard, which sought to demonstrate that American trade unions have been good for productivity and economic efficiency (Freeman and Medoff 1984). Their work revives many of the key insights of the American institutional labour economists writing in the 1940s and 1950s (Slichter et al. 1960): in particular, the twin propositions that unions may reduce lateral tensions within the workforce and hence function as a force for improved morale; and that they may shock management into adopting 'best practice' techniques and production organization. On the first point, unions act to provide 'voice' by aggregating individual workers' preferences. The usual empirical outcome associated with this is the level of absence or quits. These actions are seen as costly forms of 'exit', for which the union voice mechanism acts as an alternative. Freeman and Medoff cite empirical work which finds that in unionized plants absence and quitting are lower than in non-union plants.

On the second feature, the idea that well-organized unions may 'shock' management into adopting 'best practices', unions are said to induce managements to introduce new technology and to organize the production process more efficiently. Again, there is empirical evidence in support of this contention (Clark 1980). This has also attracted interest in the context of the British economy. Some analysts (Nolan and Marginson 1990; Evans et al. 1992) have suggested that the absence of a sufficiently powerful shock effect in Britain, whether from unions or other industrial relations institutions, may help to account for the preservation of high exit barriers to inefficient production in so many industries, before and after 1945.

Until relatively recently, the Harvard empirical studies had limited impact on the British debate, but this work is now beginning to gain wider attention. One of its attractions is that, in emphasizing the potential efficiency gains resulting from the presence in the workplace of an effective collective voice mechanism, the studies force to the forefront many of the traditional concerns of pluralist industrial relations. A central conclusion of the Harvard studies is thus that 'unionism per se is neither a plus nor a minus to productivity. What matters is how unions and management interact at the workplace' (Freeman and Medoff 1984: 179). In principle, the way is open for an assessment of the dynamic interplay between firms and employees. However, much of the empirical evidence comes from a more restricted methodology.

The evidence

The idea that Conservative policies in the early 1980s may have engendered a productivity breakthrough was first mooted by Muellbauer (1986). Although he was unable to specify the precise nature of the connections, his investigation pointed to a trend shift in TFP after the third quarter of 1980. According to Muellbauer, TFP averaged 2.76 per cent annually between 1980 and 1985 as compared to 0.62 per cent between 1973 and 1979. Because, as noted above, TFP is estimated as a *residual* it is open to a number of possible interpretations. The one that was seized upon, by Maynard (1988) among others, was that the Thatcher government's tougher approach to the unions had allowed previously unexploited gains in efficiency to be realized.

Metcalf echoed this perspective in his wide-ranging review of the changing character of post-war British industrial relations (Metcalf 1989a). Government policies – anti-union legislation, the freeing of market forces, and the permissive stance towards high unemployment – had effected a profound change in workplace behaviour and practices. Workers had been disciplined by the 'fear' of unemployment and plant closures, and were no longer in a position to resist change. In the exceptionally brutal conditions of the early 1980s, management had seized the initiative and subordinated their employees to harsher work routines which demanded higher levels of work effort and productivity.

While these arguments were in line with the available evidence – for example the reported rise in the Percentage Utilization of Labour (PUL) index (Bennett and Smith-Gavine 1988) – far more controversial was Metcalf's claim that Thatcher's policies were succeeding. Comparing their effects with the pluralist reform strategy of the 1960s and 1970s, Metcalf concluded that, whereas the latter had failed to yield any significant productivity improvements, Thatcher's policies 'seem to have done the trick' (1989a: 27). Some writers agreed. Crafts (1991), for example, claimed that the 'get tough' approach to the unions had yielded significant benefits for the economy, which might endure 'if the bargaining power of workers over manning levels remains weak'. Others, for example Nolan and Marginson (1990), took issue with Metcalf's interpretation of the evidence and suggested that Thatcher's reforms might be promoting short-term gains at the expense of the more fundamental structural reforms, including investment in plant, people and technology, urgently required to reinvigorate the economy.

In a separate review of the evidence, Metcalf reported that there was little support for the 'Harvard' proposition that unions are good for productivity (Metcalf 1989b). On the contrary: 'the weight of the evidence suggested that union presence is associated with lower labour productivity'. Is this conclusion borne out by the most recent evidence?

Nickell et al. (1989) and Wadhwani (1990) looked at the impact of unions on rates of productivity growth. Using data culled from the accounts of 124 manufacturing companies between 1972 and 1986, they were able to track changes in productivity during the second half of the 1970s (a period of relative union 'strength') and the first half of the 1980s (a period of union 'weakness'). Wadhwani found that unions in the 1970s, and the 'pro union' legislation of that period, did not discourage investment or inhibit productivity growth; while both studies noted that unionized firms in the first half of the 1980s experienced faster productivity growth than their non-union counterparts.

These results are consistent with different interpretations. It is possible that unionization was positively correlated with faster productivity growth in the first half of the 1980s, not because of unionization *per se* but because of other forces acting within and without the companies in question. It is also possible, as the authors note, that the faster rates of growth were the product of the removal of obstacles to work reorganization. Yet the interpretation which

Wadhwani and Nickell et al. stress is that 'there is no simple association between unionism and productivity growth . . . Contrary to what is alleged, unions do not consistently reduce productivity growth' (Nickell et al. 1989). Wadhwani is even more emphatic: 'there is no evidence . . . for the view that unions reduce productivity growth' (1990: 382).

Machin and Wadhwani (1991) reported a 'positive association between unionism and organizational change' for the period 1981–4. Organizational change is defined as 'substantial changes in work organization or work practices not involving new plant, machinery or equipment'. Their study focused on 721 private-sector establishments of which 27 per cent had experienced some form of organizational change. Machin and Wadhwani interpreted their results in two ways. On the one hand, the higher incidence of change in unionized establishments may have reflected the removal of restrictions on managerial discretion. On the other hand, it is possible that union voice effects, by improving communications in the workplace, may have encouraged organizational change. Noting that there is evidence for both explanations the authors 'incline towards the view that *both* the above channels combine to give us a positive association between unionism and organizational change' (1991: 852).

Unfortunately, Machin and Wadhwani are unable to tell us why unions are associated with positive voice effects in some establishments and damaging restrictive practices in others. Presumably, as the Harvard economists have argued, the effect of unionism in any given situation will reflect the character of management–labour relations. Attempts to rip unions from that wider context and attribute to them sole responsibility for particular organizational change outcomes may thus be ill-advised.

Two further points are relevant in this context. First, the WIRS data used by the authors are solely based on the qualitative responses of management; hence what is being reported is management's perceptions of the change process. Second, it would have been helpful to know something about the incidence of change in non-union firms. Evidence of widespread changes in such firms would, of course, challenge the motivating assumption of this study that output restrictions are more pervasive in unionized organizations.

The final study of note, by Gregg et al. (1993), develops the theme that the harsher environment of the 1980s led managers to reassert their authority, among other things by repudiating union membership agreements. This change of approach, we are told, represented a clear 'signal' to employees to work harder. Recalling a theme of Metcalf's earlier work, the authors claim that the higher productivity levels observed in the 1980s stemmed from the removal of restrictive practices in unionized firms. Their evidence, which is derived from a regression analysis of company accounts and the data on changing union status generated by Gregg and Yates's earlier postal survey (Gregg and Yates 1991), relates to 328 companies, the majority of which were in manufacturing.

In common with much of the recent work on this issue, this study unfortunately tells us nothing about productivity dynamics and the effects of Thatcher's policies in the expanding non-union sector. Unionized firms are said to have outperformed non-unionized firms between 1985 and 1989, and there is further evidence that the process of union derecognition gave a further fillip to productivity. But why was the performance of non-union firms inferior? Presumably, the authors would argue that the growth of productivity will be higher in unionized firms because there is more scope for improvement. But that was also the implication of the results of the earlier studies for the first half of the decade. In short, we are asked to accept that throughout the entire duration of Thatcherism non-union firms performed less well on average than their unionized counterparts. It is also of note that some 70 per cent of firms reported no organizational change in the early 1980s (Machin and Wadhwani 1991), and that the WIRS data show that 47 per cent of establishments reported neither organizational nor technical change in respect of manual workers (Millward et al. 1992: 15). Might this not suggest that the harsh winds of competition failed to promote upgrading, except in unionized firms where perhaps the Harvard positive voice effects were at work?

Evidently, the focus of recent research has been on developments in manufacturing, largely because there are available published data for this sector. Yet, for the most spectacular changes in productivity during the Thatcher years, it is necessary to look beyond manufacturing to the British coal industry, which has of course experienced a major upheaval in its established patterns of industrial relations.

Industrial Relations and Performance in the British Coal Industry

Since 1985, in the aftermath of the year-long strike, the coal industry has achieved rapid productivity growth – indeed, far in excess of the record for manufacturing industry, as is revealed by figure 13.3.

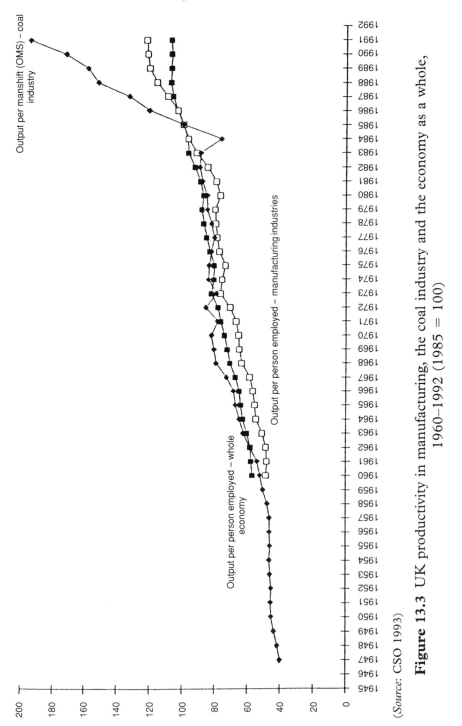

(*Source*: CSO 1993)

Figure 13.3 UK productivity in manufacturing, the coal industry and the economy as a whole, 1960–1992 (1985 = 100)

Between 1960 and 1983 the performance of manufacturing industry and coal mining were closely matched, but more recently the trajectory of productivity changes in coal has diverged radically from the rest of the British economy.

This 'renaissance' of coal coincided with a radical shift in the power balance between the mineworkers and British Coal (BC) management. Many writers observed this coincidence of events and have sought to account for BC's productivity achievements with reference to the changes in industrial relations following the defeat of the miners in the 1984–5 strike. It is difficult to deny that the industry's record of productivity growth is remarkable: labour productivity increased by 10 per cent per annum between 1985 and 1994 and in 1993–4 it rose by 38 per cent (British Coal 1994). What accounts for this record? Our analysis suggests that changes in industrial relations have indeed been important, but not for the reasons that have been put forward in the literature to date. In addition, our research points to the critical role of investment in capital equipment and new mining methods, and of shifts in the regulatory framework governing the industry. It also suggests that the productivity figures are overstated, and it is to this issue that we turn first.

In 1983, BC forecast a growth rate for labour productivity of 29 per cent for the decade 1981–90, equivalent to an average of 3 per cent per annum. They argued that over 50 per cent of the increase would stem from the introduction of heavy-duty capital equipment, a third would be due to new mines such as Selby, and the rest would occur because of closures. Of course, these figures were reckoned without the strike, but none the less there is a major discrepancy between BC's forecast and the actual outcome.

How is coal productivity measured? The published data measure output per manshift (OMS) – that is, a physical measure of tonnes of coal per measure of labour input. The fact that coal is not a homogeneous product has prompted the use of a standard measure of energy value – the calorific value per gigajoule. With respect to the labour input, the denominator for labour productivity is the manshift, where one shift has a fixed length of 8.5 hours, as prescribed by the 1906 Coal Act. All production workers are included in the overall OMS figures including surface workers, transport underground and face workers, but not supervisory and white-collar workers.

The official series on OMS overestimates performance on two counts: it excludes overtime working and the use of contract labour.

In the case of contractors, although their output is included in the OMS figure, they are not included by BC in the total head count for productivity. The use of contractors grew rapidly after 1985, and in 1994 the number stood at around 4,500 as compared to 10,000 BC employees. Our estimates (O'Donnell 1994) suggest that the exclusion of contractors has the effect of lifting the OMS figures by approximately 3 per cent per annum.

Turning to overtime working, between 1985 and 1990 there has been a 350 per cent increase in overtime working, with average overtime worked per week in the region of 12–14 hours per miner. This translates into the equivalent of a seven-day week and in many ways is reminiscent of the industry in the early post-war years when the Essential Works Order was in operation (Fine et al. 1985). With respect to the OMS figures, overtime shifts are not included. Traditionally, this was justified on the grounds that most overtime was scheduled for maintenance work and not coal production. In recent years, however, there has been a shift towards weekend and extended shifts in order to cut coal. It is difficult to calculate precisely the impact of overtime working on the OMS figures, but on the basis of survey data (O'Donnell 1994) a lower bound estimate would be 2 per cent per annum.

Even allowing for these measurement errors, a considerable record of productivity growth remains to be explained. Immediately following the 1984–5 dispute, attention focused on the impact of the closure of the so-called tail of 'uneconomic' pits. Echoing the 'batting average' hypothesis, studied in relation to manufacturing, it was argued that the closure of the least productive collieries would result in productivity gains without involving an improvement in the efficiency of remaining pits. Glyn (1988: 173) carried out a shift-share analysis of BC's collieries before and after the 1984–5 dispute and concluded that 'less than one sixth of the productivity increase after the strike reflected the direct effect of closing low productivity pits'. The closures between 1987 and 1992 are thought to have boosted productivity by a further 8 per cent (British Coal 1993). Since 1992, a further 35 collieries have been closed but given the industry's almost horizontal supply curve, as depicted in figure 13.4, their impact on average productivity will have been almost negligible. In short, what is clear is that the vast proportion of the productivity changes arises from improvements in remaining pits.

Richardson and Wood (1989) studied productivity change in the South Yorkshire coalfield between 1982 and 1986 and found that

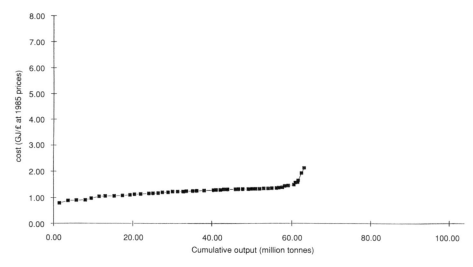

(*Source*: O'Donnell 1994)

Figure 13.4 Cumulative output and unit costs of British Coal at constant (1985) prices, 1991/92

the average productivity increased by 49 per cent. In explaining this performance they give little weight to closure effects, in line with Glyn and British Coal. But they also argue that technical change and capital investment were of little significance. For them the critical issue was that managers 'have much more power now to manage production' (1989: 50). On this basis, they conclude that:

> we are indeed in a new era of industrial relations and it is most unlikely that performance levels will slip back to those of the 1970s, although the rate of improvement will certainly slow down. Our judgement is that the change has resulted largely from management taking advantage of a unique opportunity (1989: 52).

Richardson and Wood singled out in particular the Doncaster option (essentially a pit-based incentive scheme) as the major factor in the improved performance of the South Yorkshire pits where it had been introduced. The gains were attributed to the emergence of more individualistic attitudes among the workforce and were judged symptomatic of a wider shift to 'new' industrial relations. But two points are relevant in this context. First, the rate of change of OMS was as high during the operation of the National Power Loading Agreement, which was a national day-wage scheme introduced during a previous phase of major technological investment. Second, other coalfields, for example South Wales, which adhered to the district agreement in 1985–6 (the year of Richardson and Wood's study), achieved faster growth than in South Yorkshire.

It is likely that other changes in patterns of working have been more crucial. Of particular relevance is the 'incentive' effect stemming from BC's increased deployment of contractors. In most pits, contractors are used primarily on 'drivages' to develop new coal faces and typically they work in competition with BC's direct employees. This arrangement has created a two-way disciplinary dynamic. BC employees are under the constant threat of further contractors being employed, and outside contractors have to meet the new targets set by BC for their own workforce.

While these changes have been important there are clear limits to the gains in productivity from labour intensification. We return to the issue of 'new' industrial relations below. Capital expenditure is a vital, yet hitherto neglected part of the explanation of BC's post-strike record. Wage costs as a proportion of total operating costs have fallen from 68 per cent in 1947 to 36 per cent in 1992. At the same time, the relative proportion of capital expenditure per colliery has risen substantially, leading for example to an increase in the proportion of 'retreat' mining faces from 20 per cent in 1982 to 66 per cent in 1992 and a wider diffusion of heavy-duty equipment (shearers and shield supports), with over 70 per cent of faces utilizing these techniques. Retreat mining and heavy-duty equipment have had the effect of doubling productivity, but there appears to be a three-year lag between the capital expenditure and its positive effects on productivity (O'Donnell 1994).

Were such capital investment changes impeded before the defeat of the miners in 1984–5? The position of the National Union of Mineworkers (NUM) has been one of support for technological investment, often on the grounds of the improvements in health and safety which such investments bring, but also in terms of sustaining miners' wages. There is no persuasive evidence of resistance at colliery or official levels to productivity-enhancing innovations.

To understand the timing and pattern of investment in coal it is necessary to take account of the changing character of the regulatory framework which has governed the industry since nationalization. Of particular significance here is the financing of investment. BC has had limited autonomy to raise external finance and has had to rely on Treasury-controlled sources. As discussed elsewhere (O'Donnell 1988), the restriction of government expenditure has had substantial knock-on effects and constrained the options open to management. It has led to the scrapping of major capital expenditure schemes such as the 1974 Plan for Coal and to massive closure programmes, notably in the 1960s. In the 1980s, however, BC received increased financial support from government which financed its capital up-grading strategy as well as funding the costs of rationalization (for example, redundancy payments, capital write-offs). Doubtless, the government's desire to privatize coal has been critical in this shift of policy.

Indeed, it is in the context of impending privatization that the changes in industrial relations should be placed. Is there a 'new industrial relations' system emerging in the industry, as some have claimed? There have been major changes, to be sure, including the unilateral scrapping in 1986 of the 1946 conciliation scheme agreement which gave the NUM sole bargaining rights. More use has been made of direct communication with the workforce through group meetings, quality circles and newsletters, but survey evidence (O'Donnell et al. 1994) failed to reveal any improvement in the character of production relations. This is consistent with the analysis of developments in manufacturing provided in chapter 12.

Far more striking was the perception by miners that they were experiencing a return to the inferior conditions of the pre-nationaliz-ation era: new contracts extending the length of a shift; widening pay differentials; increased overtime; and the erosion of health and safety conditions. Equally evident is the fact that the growth of multi-unionism – scarcely an indicator of new industrial relations – has prevented the mineworkers from staging effective resistance. It re-mains to be seen whether these adverse developments serve to re-create the economic incentives which gave rise to the disastrous pre-1945 productivity record.

An Interpretation

We have attempted to highlight the main critical fault lines in the long-running debate about the impact of industrial relations on productivity. Too often, unions have been ripped from their social context and treated as an exogenous determinant of productivity. Far better to acknowledge that their practices will reflect the charac-ter of the social structures in which they are embedded. Too often, the evidence adduced in support of the argument that unions have been a prime cause of productivity under-performance depended on the subjective perceptions of management – scarcely a disinterested party. And too often, the evidence was found to be insensitive, theoretically and empirically, to the forces of competition. How is it that isolated, decentralized plant-based work groups can impede the advance of plants, companies, industries, indeed the whole economy – not merely over five or ten years, but according to some writers over the course of a century? Why was the position of unionism not eroded by the forces of competition? Reference to the disincentive effects of the Empire – a theme surfacing in much of the literature and which is mimicked in inverted form in the latest work emphasizing Thatcher's free market reforms – is too imprecise, and in any case has little purchase in the 1950s and beyond when Britain's postwar relative decline began in earnest.

We would not deny, however, that industrial relations – the interplay of relations between state, workers, unions and employers – have affected the performance trajectory of the British economy. But we do strongly reject the conventional wisdom. For the post-war period, it is difficult to find any persuasive evidence that supports the argument that management was severely hamstrung in its attempts to modernize. The evidence suggests, on the contrary, that all too often management did not seek to innovate. Even in the strike-torn car industry of the 1960s, which had a profound influence on the Donovan Commission, the evidence points to the output-restricting strategies of management. Difficult to quantify and model within a regression equation, may be, but this sort of rich qualitative evidence should not be disregarded.

In the 1970s, the years in which union power and influence allegedly reached its zenith, the wages of British workers continued to fall in relative terms. Britain became a centre for cheap and divided labour available to be exploited by both indigenous and international companies. Perhaps not surprisingly, the tendency for companies in Britain to produce with relatively labour-intensive methods was consolidated during this time, again probably not because powerful work groups resisted modernization – though in a context of growing job insecurity that resistance may have been real – but because of the incentives for firms to specialize in low wage, low value added and hence low productivity areas. That specialization, which was already in evidence immediately after the Second World War, has proved remarkably difficult to dislodge (see chapter 3). Commentaries on the 1970s, which make much of the growth of union power, rarely mention the fact that most of that growth occurred in the public sector. Yet the main focus of the argument about industrial relations and productivity is manufacturing.

Coming to the 1980s, a large element in the controversy turns on the issue of whether or not the changes in industrial relations – particularly the erosion of union membership and influence – have resulted in a more dynamic, productive and efficient economy. Even if it is accepted that productivity has increased more rapidly – the work of Darby and Wren-Lewis (1988) and Stoneman and Francis (1992) suggests that there are good reasons for looking at the record with some caution – it need not follow that the economy is more efficient. Metcalf and others have stressed that workers are working harder. An unambiguous case for an efficiency improvement would exist if more output had been produced from the same quantity and quality of inputs, perhaps as a result of the modernization of production. Evidence has not been produced to show that this was the case; indeed, it points in the opposite direction for manufacturing (Glyn 1992).

By contrast, in coal, the evidence presented above emphasized the significance of capital investment and the transformative effects of this investment on colliery performance. By the time that the latest closure programme was announced in 1992 most of the former high-cost collieries had become average performers. The events in the coal industry demonstrate graphically the complex nature of the relations between state, labour and business. Although there has been a marked improvement in productivity, most of the industry's capacity has been buried. There is no evidence of new industrial relations, if that is taken to imply a move to a more cooperative structure of employee relations. As indicated, the fear must be that in private hands, without state sponsored investment, and in the presence of a greatly weakened workforce, private operators will make profits at the expense of long-term development. Could there be a clearer case of the past striking back?

Elsewhere – in private services and manufacturing – despite the enthusiasm with which recent productivity advances have been greeted, there must surely be legitimate grounds for concern that the gains have not been underwritten by investment; that management practices in the absence of effective union voice will deteriorate; and that the gains of the recent past will be converted into a widening long-term productivity deficit. At present, it is too early to tell, but the evidence reviewed at the beginning of this chapter highlights a still substantial productivity differential with the more regulated economies of Western Europe.

References

Alford, B. W. E. 1988: *British Economic Performance 1945–1975*. London: Macmillan.

Bennett, A. and Smith-Gavine, S. 1988: The Percentage Utilization of Labour Index. In D. Bosworth (ed.), *Working Below Capacity*. London: Macmillan.

Boyer, R. 1988 (ed.): *The Search for Labour Market Flexibilities*. Oxford: Clarendon.

British Coal 1980–1994: *Annual Reports and Accounts*.

Bruno, M. 1984: Raw Materials, Profits and the Productivity Slowdown. *Quarterly Journal of Economics*, 99, 1, 1–30.

Bureau of Labor 1994: *Monthly Labor Review*. US Bureau of Labor, January, table 49.

Caves, R. E. 1980: Productivity Differences among Industries. In R. E. Caves and L. B. Krause (eds), *Britain's Economic Performance*. Washington, DC: Brookings Institution.

Chandler, A. D. 1966: *Strategy and Structure*. New York: Anchor Books.

Channon, D. 1973: *The Strategy and Structure of British Enterprise*. London: Macmillan.

Clark, K. B. 1980: The Impact of Unionization on Productivity: A Case Study. *Industrial and Labor Relations Review*, 33, 4, 451–69.

Clegg, H. A. 1964: Restrictive Practices. *Socialist Commentary*. Cited in *Productivity Bargaining and Restrictive Labour Practices*, Research Paper 4, Royal Commission on Trade Unions and Employers' Associations. London: HMSO, 1968.

Coates, D. 1994: *The Question of UK Decline: The Economy, State and Society*. Brighton: Harvester Wheatsheaf.

Crafts, N. 1988: The Assessment: British Economic Growth over the Long Run. *Oxford Review of Economic Policy*, 4, 1, i–xxi.

Crafts, N. 1991: Reversing Relative Economic Decline? The 1980s in Historical Perspective. *Oxford Review of Economic Policy*, 7, 3, 81–98.

CSO 1993: *Economic Trends Annual Supplement*. London: HMSO.

Darby, J. and Wren-Lewis, S. 1988: *Trends in Manufacturing Labour Productivity*. National Institute of Economic and Social Research Discussion Paper, No. 145.

Davies, S. and Caves, R. 1987: *Britain's Productivity Gap*. Cambridge: Cambridge University Press.

Donovan 1968: Royal Commission on Trade Unions and Employers' Associations. *Report*. Cmnd 3623. London: HMSO.

Edwards, P. K. 1983: The Pattern of Collective Industrial Action. In G. S. Bain (ed.), *Industrial Relations in Britain*. Oxford: Blackwell.

Evans, S., Ewing, K. and Nolan, P. 1992: Industrial Relations and the British Economy in the 1990s: Mrs Thatcher's Legacy. *Journal of Management Studies*, 29, 5, 571–89.

Feinstein, C. 1988: Economic Growth since 1870: Britain's Performance in International Perspective. *Oxford Review of Economic Policy*, 4, 1, 1–13.

Fine, B. and Harris, L. 1985: *The Peculiarities of the British Economy*. London: Lawrence & Wishart.

Fine, B., O'Donnell, K. and Prevezer, M. 1985: Coal before Nationalisation. In B. Fine and L. Harris, *The Peculiarities of the British Economy*. London: Lawrence & Wishart.

Freeman, R. B. and Medoff, J. L. 1984: *What Do Unions Do?* New York: Basic.

Glyn, A. 1988: Colliery Results and Closures after the 1984–85 Coal Dispute. *Oxford Bulletin of Economics and Statistics*, 50, 2, 161–74.

Glyn, A. 1992: The Productivity Miracle: Profits and Investment. In J. Michie (ed.), *The Economic Legacy 1979–1992*. Academic Press, pp. 77–90.

Grant, W. 1991: Government and Manufacturing Industry. In G. Jones and M. Kirby (eds), *Competitiveness and the State*. Manchester: Manchester University Press.

Gregg, P. and Yates, A. 1991: Changes in Wage Setting Arrangements and Trade Union Presence in the 1980s. *British Journal of Industrial Relations*, 29, 3, 361–76.

Gregg, P., Machin, S. and Metcalf, D. 1993: Signals and Cycles? Productivity Growth and Changes in Union Status in British Companies 1984–89. *Economic Journal*, 103, 4, 894–907.

Hannah, L. 1976: *The Rise of the Corporate Economy: The British Experience*. Baltimore: Johns Hopkins University Press.

Harcourt, G. 1972: *Some Cambridge Controversies in the Theory of Capital*. Cambridge: Cambridge University Press.

Hayek, F. 1980: *Unemployment and the Unions*. London: Institute of Economic Affairs.

Hyman, R. and Elger, T. 1981: Job Controls, the Employers' Offensive and Alternative Strategies. *Capital and Class*, 15, 115–49.

Kilpatrick, A. and Lawson, T. 1980: On the Nature of Industrial Decline in the UK. *Cambridge Journal of Economics*, 4, 1, 85–102.

Lazonick, W. 1991: *Business Organization and the Myth of the Market Economy*. Cambridge: Cambridge University Press.

Machin, S. and Wadhwani, S. 1991: The Effects of Unions on Organisational Change and Employment. *Economic Journal*, 101, 3, 835–54.

Mackay, D., Boddy, D., Brack, J., Diack, J. and Jones, N. 1971: *Labour Markets under Different Employment Conditions*. London: Allen and Unwin.

Maynard, G. 1988: *The Economy under Mrs Thatcher*. Oxford: Blackwell.

Metcalf, D. 1989a: Water Notes Dry Up: The Impact of the Donovan Reform Proposals and Thatcherism at Work on Labour Productivity in British Manufacturing Industry. *British Journal of Industrial Relations*, 27, 1, 1–31.

Metcalf, D. 1989b: Trade Unions and Economic Performance: The British Evidence. *LSE Quarterly*, 3, 21–42.

Millward, N., Stevens, M., Smart, D. and Hawes, W. R. 1992: *Workplace Industrial Relations in Transition*. Aldershot: Dartmouth.

Muellbauer, J. 1986: Productivity and Competitiveness in British Manufacturing. *Oxford Review of Economic Policy*, 2, 3, 1–25.

Nichols, T. 1986: *The British Worker Question: A New Look at Workers and Productivity in Manufacturing*. London: Routledge & Kegan Paul.

Nickell, S., Wadhwani, S. and Wall, M. 1989: *Unions and Productivity Growth in Britain 1974–86: Evidence from Company Accounts Data*. Centre for Labour Economics Discussion Paper, 353, August. London School of Economics.

Nolan, P. 1989: The Productivity Miracle?. In F. Green (ed.), *The Restructuring of the UK Economy*. Brighton: Harvester.

Nolan, P. 1993: The Past Strikes Back: Industrial Relations and UK Competitiveness. *University of Leeds Review* (ed. G. Pitt), 36, 195–210.

Nolan, P. and Marginson, P. 1990: Skating on Thin Ice? David Metcalf on Trade Unions and Productivity. *British Journal of Industrial Relations*, 28, 2, 227–47.

Nolan, P. and O'Donnell, K. 1991: Flexible Specialisation and UK Manufacturing Weakness. *Political Quarterly*, 62, 1, 106–24.

O'Donnell, K. 1988: Pit Closures in the British Coal Industry: A Comparison of the 1960s and the 1980s. *International Review of Applied Economics*, 2, 1, 62–77.

O'Donnell, K. 1994: Pitfalls in Measuring Productivity Performance in the British Coal Industry. Mimeo, School of Business and Economic Studies, University of Leeds.

O'Donnell, K., Nolan, P. and Harvie, D. 1994: Industrial Relations and Performance in British Coal. Mimeo, School of Business and Economic Studies, University of Leeds.

OECD 1991: *Historical Statistics 1960–1990*. Paris: OECD.

Oulton, N. and O'Mahoney, M. 1994: *Productivity and Growth: A Study of British Industry, 1954–86*. Cambridge: Cambridge University Press.

Pencavel, J. 1977: Distributional and Efficiency Effects of Trade Unions in Britain. *British Journal of Industrial Relations*, 15, 2, 137–56.

Porter, M. 1990: *The Competitive Advantage of Nations*. London: Macmillan.

Prais, S. J. 1981: *Productivity and Industrial Structure*. Cambridge: Cambridge University Press.

Pratten, C. F. 1976: *Labour Productivity Differentials within International*

Companies. Cambridge: Cambridge University Press.

Purcell, J. 1993: The End of Institutional Industrial Relations. *Political Quarterly*, 64, 1, 6–23.

Rees, A. 1963: The Effects of Unions on Resource Allocation. *Journal of Law and Economics*, 6, 2, 69–78.

Reid, G. 1968: Economic Comment on the Donovan Report. *British Journal of Industrial Relations*, 6, 3, 303–15.

Richardson, R. and Wood, S. 1989: The Coal Industry and the New Industrial Relations. *British Journal of Industrial Relations*, 27, 1, 33–54.

Slichter, S. H., Healy, J. J. and Livernash, E. R. 1960: *The Impact of Collective Bargaining on Management*. Washington, DC: Brookings Institution.

Stoneman, P. and Francis, N. 1992: *Double Deflation and the Measurement of Output and Productivity in UK Manufacturing 1979–1989*. Warwick Business School Discussion Paper.

Supple, B. 1987: *The History of the British Coal Industry, Volume 4, 1913–1946*. Oxford: Oxford University Press.

Tolliday, S. n.d.: High Tide and after: Coventry Engineering Workers and Shopfloor Bargaining, 1945–80. In B. Lancaster and T. Mason, *Life and Labour in a 20th Century City: The Experience of Coventry*. Cryfield Press.

Tomlinson, J. 1991: A Missed Opportunity? Labour and the Productivity Problem, 1945–51. In G. Jones and M. Kirby (eds), *Competitiveness and the State*. Manchester: Manchester University Press.

Turner, H. A., Clack, G. and Roberts, G. 1967: *Labour Relations in the Motor Industry*. London: George Allen and Unwin.

van Ark, B. 1990: Comparative Levels of Manufacturing Productivity in Postwar Europe: Measurement and Comparisons. *Oxford Bulletin of Economics and Statistics*, 52, 4, 343–73.

Wadhwani, S. 1988: *Union Presence and Company Performance*. Centre for Labour Economics Discussion Paper. London School of Economics.

Wadhwani, S. 1990: The Effects of Unions on Productivity Growth, Investment and Employment: A Report on some Recent Work. *British Journal of Industrial Relations*, 28, 3, 371–85.

14

Strikes and Industrial Conflict

Paul Edwards

> The one clear unassailable fact about labour relations over the past
> twenty years is that there has been a dramatic change for the better . . .
> every reasonable indicator of labour unrest, everything that we can
> count, shows that the operating environment of Ford factories is
> vastly better than it was twenty years ago. (Hougham 1992: 233)

As discussed in chapter 1, conflict is one of the major underlying
principles of relations between managers and workers. The links
between the wider processes of conflict and overt disputes are rarely
discussed in IR texts, which tend to state the inevitability of conflict
in an introduction but then focus in the empirical analysis not just on
strikes but on strike statistics. Yet strikes are not the only form of
conflict, which can be expressed in quitting, absenteeism and many
other ways. Moreover, the links between such concrete behaviour
and conflict are complex. Quitting reflects job opportunities elsewhere as well as discontent with one's present employer. Even the
strike reflects conflict in varying ways. In sectors where strikes were
an accepted means of pursuing bargaining objectives they had a
quite different meaning from situations where disputes were rare and
where a stoppage could reflect a major breakdown of means of
handling industrial relations. A celebrated example of the latter is a
strike at the Pilkington glass company in 1970 (see Lane and Roberts
1971).

Conflict thus means an element of workplace relations, which may
be termed conflict at work, as well as overt industrial conflict, which

may take an individual or a collective form. A detailed discussion of conflict at work is beyond the goals of this book (for introductions see Batstone 1988; P. Edwards 1988). However, this deeper sense of conflict has run through several chapters, notably chapter 7 on the role of the shop steward and chapter 12 on the reorganization of work tasks. As for specific actions, there is limited evidence on some of them, such as quitting. Some comments on their significance, in terms of the balance of emerging workplace regimes, are, however, made in the concluding chapter. Strikes merit particular attention because statistics can chart developments over a long period (in Britain, since 1893) and because they have been widely seen as a leading indicator of change, for example as the 'litmus test' of government efforts to curb union power (Kessler and Bayliss 1992: 207). It is thus important to assess the statistical record, though in doing so the chapter tries to relate the figures to the changing meaning and significance of strikes.

A reduction in strike activity can come about for many reasons. Going backwards in the stages leading to a strike, the previous stage is the existence of a dispute between a group of workers and their employers. A dispute need not lead to a strike if there are alternative means of resolving differences. Going back a stage, whether or not an organized dispute occurs depends on two things. First, there are facilitating conditions. Thus workers need some degree of collective organization to sustain a strike, which generally means that they are unionized. Lower unionization would thus tend to reduce the number of strikes. Second, other factors shape the willingness to strike. They include depressed economic conditions which are generally held to make workers cautious. They also include the series of laws introduced since 1979 which have restricted the freedom to strike. Finally, the structure of the economy has shifted, with formerly strike-prone sectors such as coal and the docks experiencing massive job losses. Union organization and economic, legal and structural forces could all reduce strike levels without affecting any underlying 'disputatiousness' of workers and managers.

Many commentators wish to go further. The statement quoted above, from Ford's then executive director of personnel, suggests that the quality of working relationships has improved. There is the significant risk of circularity here. Some popular discussions argue, in effect, that better industrial relations mean fewer strikes and that the decline in strikes shows that relations are indeed better. What is needed is independent evidence that relations are 'better' and that there has been an effect on strikes over and above those mentioned in the previous paragraph. The argument can also be taken further by differentiating between industries. It is possible that reduced strike rates at Ford reflected improved working relationships; elsewhere, strikes may have fallen for other reasons, or not fallen much at all.

The reasons why workers went on strike in the past also help to show the significance of the fact that they do so much less. Many strikes can be traced to an environment which promoted disputes and the assumption that a strike was a normal means to try to press a case. The reduction of strikes may mean that some of the motivations to pursue a dispute have been removed. It does not necessarily mean that a more positive atmosphere has been created. Obvious sources of difficulty have, it will be argued, been removed, but eliminating these things is not the same as creating a sense of commitment.

This chapter starts with the pattern of strikes, showing that strike rates have been declining and also that strikes have become shorter. It then examines the causes of the pattern, in aggregate and in relation to three strike-prone sectors. The final section considers the implications for conflict: does the decline in strikes mean merely that the balance of power has shifted, or that there are fewer concerted grievances, or even that the base of conflict in day-to-day working relationships has been eroded?

Trends in Industrial Action

To understand the pattern of industrial action calls for a knowledge of the key statistics and a sense of what they mean. This section thus begins by describing the main strike measures and then outlines the main trends of strikes and non-strike collective action. The final subsection looks more qualitatively at the forms of behaviour underlying the numbers.

Measures of strikes

Strikes are counted by the Employment Department, which uses reports from Unemployment Benefit offices, returns from some public sector organizations, and newspapers and other sources, to identify stoppages. Three main measures are identified: the number of separate stoppages; the number of workers involved; and the number of days 'lost' (a potentially emotive and inaccurate term, since days on strike may be recouped later, a fact leading some observers to prefer the term striker days). Each measure has its technical difficulties which have been extensively debated (Shalev 1978; Franzosi 1989). The key point is that the official agencies have used standard definitions and means of gathering information, the result being that the strike measures are reliable; that is, they measure the same sort of thing from one year to the next. Increases and decreases can thus be taken as genuine.

Each measure reflects a different aspect of the strike picture. The number of strikes can be taken as an index of how often negotiations involve stoppages. Strikes may be large or small; this is taken into account in the measure of how many workers have become involved in strikes. Striker days measures both the extent of worker involvement and how long strikes have lasted. It is an index of the overall 'volume' of strike action. It is a convenient summary measure, but because it merges number, involvement and duration it can be hard to interpret.

The measures are not necessarily valid in the sense of measuring what they claim to measure. There are two aspects of this: whether they include all strikes falling within the official definition (in Britain, only those lasting at least a day and involving at least ten workers, unless a total of 100 or more striker days is involved); and whether this measures all strikes. A survey of manufacturing in 1977–8 estimated that only 62 per cent of strikes meeting the official definition were in fact counted (Brown 1981: 99). When strikes outside this threshold are included, the official number would have to be multiplied by 4 in order to estimate the true number of all strikes. Since, however, manufacturing was particularly prone to small and short strikes that are hard to detect, the factor for the whole economy may be considerably smaller. Data for days lost were also found to be much more complete, since most days lost occur in the largest and most visible strikes.

To assess change, it would be necessary to have a more recent survey. The extent of official recording has not been addressed, but some indication of the balance between short and long strikes can be derived from the Workplace Industrial Relations Surveys (WIRS). The data are reproduced in table 14.1. The proportion of establishments reporting a strike of less than a day, in relation to the proportion reporting a longer strike, did not change between 1980

Table 14.1 Establishments reporting strikes or industrial action, 1980–1990

	1980	1984	1990
Any strike action	13	19	10
Strike less than 1 day	6	14	4
Strike 1 day or more	9	12	7
Any non-strike action	16	18	5
Overtime ban/restriction	10	11	3
Work to rule	7	8	2
Any industrial action	22	25	12

	Manufacturing		Services	
	1980	1990	1980	1990
Any strike action	26	4	12	11
Any non-strike action	24	7	16	4

The percentages represent establishments where either a manager or a worker representative reported industrial action in the 12 months prior to the interview.

Source: Millward et al. 1992: 279, 314; 1980 sectoral distribution calculated from Daniel and Millward 1983: 229.

and 1990. This suggests that there was no dramatic change in the distribution of strikes by length, and therefore that the earlier estimates of the validity of the official data still stand.

Overall strike trends

Figures on the three strike indices are shown in table 14.2, while figure 14.1 presents some of the information graphically. The table separates the coal industry from all others, because coal accounted for a very high proportion of strikes during some periods (up to three-quarters of all disputes in the late 1950s) so that the overall figures obscure trends in the majority of industry. Following the analysis of Durcan et al. (1983), years can be grouped together into distinct phases of strike activity.

The late 1940s were characterized by relative peace on all three dimensions of strikes. During the 1950s, there were the first national stoppages since the General Strike of 1926 in industries such as engineering. The 1960s were marked by a rapid rise in the number

Table 14.2   Strike trends in the United Kingdom, 1946–1993
(annual averages)

	All industries			Non-coal industries		
	Strikes	Workers involved (000)	Days lost (000)	Strikes	Workers involved (000)	Days lost (000)
1946–52	1,698	444	1,888	625	228	1,318
1953–59	2,340	790	3,950	608	551	3,407
1960–68	2,372	1,323	3,189	1,451	1,189	2,872
1969–73	2,974	1,581	12,497	2,723	1,447	9,881
1974–79	2,412	1,653	12,178	2,141	1,555	11,147
1980–85	1,276	1,213	9,806	1,022	1,046	5,830
1986–89	893	781	3,324	656	705	3,166
1990	630	298	1,903	543	283	1,844
1991	369	177	761	340	170	729
1992	253	148	528	243	145	520
1993	211	385	649	206	371	622

Source: 1946–73: Durcan et al. (1983). Subsequent years: annual articles on
stoppages of work in *Employment Gazette.*

of small disputes, particularly in the vehicles and related sectors.
Combined with the continuing occurrence of large-scale disputes,
this produced a peak of strike numbers in 1970 when 3,906 strikes
were recorded. During the 1970s, strike numbers fell, but the pres-

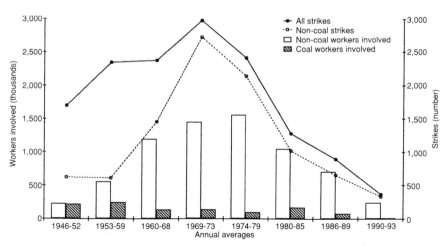

Figure 14.1 Strikes and workers involved, 1946–1993

ence of large disputes kept the levels of worker involvement and days lost very high. The pattern became notorious with the labelling of a series of large disputes in 1978–9, including a national stoppage in engineering and several public service strikes, as the 'winter of discontent'. During the 1980s all the main indicators fell, so that by the end of the decade the number of strikes was similar to that in the 1940s, though worker involvement and days lost were still higher. The 1990s saw a further substantial shift to levels of activity that were the lowest of the post-war period on all three dimensions. At 211, the number of strikes in 1993 was a mere one-twentieth of the 1970 peak number.

These figures may be put in perspective by looking at the longer-term trend. It is necessary here to control for changes in the level of employment. In the 1990s there were about 20 strikes per million workers, a historically low level attained in the 1920s but not at any other time since 1893. The number of days lost per thousand employees was about 50 in the 1990s; this was about half the rate of the previous low recorded during the 1930s. Worker involvement figures are less consistent, but the 1990s level is again lower than most on record.

Britain is not unique in this experience. Strike rates have fallen rapidly in countries such as the United States and France, though others, notably Sweden, have recorded increases compared with the 1950s and 1960s (Shalev 1992; P. Edwards and Hyman 1994). At least some of the forces reducing strike rates have not been peculiar to Britain.

An important element of the picture concerns the duration of strikes. As figure 14.2 shows, strikes lasting no more than a day continued at a relatively steady level. The most dramatic decline was in stoppages of three days or more. There were only 51 such stoppages in 1993, compared with around 1,400 in the early 1970s. The lengthy setpiece battle had become a rarity.

In addition to the decline in duration, the issues in strikes have changed. Some care has to be taken in analysing the data, which rest on a classification by Employment Department officials of the 'principal reason' for a dispute. Strikes have many causes, and the ostensible reason given may hide a more fundamental and less clearly articulated sense of grievance (Hyman 1989: 119–32). Moreover, official figures probably underestimate the extent of disputes on immediate workplace issues, since these are often small and short.

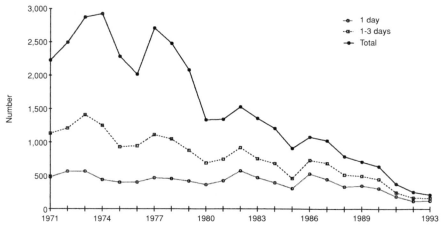

Figure 14.2 Strikes by duration, 1971–1993

None the less, since means of classification have remained unchanged, trends in the figures indicate the broad ways in which issues provoking disputes have changed. In the 1970s, about 60 per cent of all recorded strikes related to pay. Since the major battles of the period were pay-related, the proportion of striker-days in pay disputes was even higher (up to 90 per cent in some years). During the 1980s, pay strikes formed a declining proportion of the total. A growing percentage was accounted for by stoppages over immediate workplace issues. These are counted under the three heads of 'working conditions and supervision', 'manning and work allocation' and 'dismissal and disciplinary measures'. Since 1986, disputes on these issues have outnumbered pay strikes; they accounted for about half of all stoppages in the period 1987–90 and 42 per cent in 1990–3, compared with about a third during the 1970s. When workers now go on strike, it is likely to reflect discontent over the organization of work and to be a brief protest rather than a lengthy battle.

Distribution by industry

As shown elsewhere (P. Edwards and Hyman 1994), the distribution of strikes between the three broad sectors of mining, manufacturing and services (both public and private) changed considerably between 1960 and 1989. The most dramatic trend was a rise in the role of services, which were virtually strike-free during the early 1960s. By the late 1980s they accounted for a fifth of all strikes, and the number of striker days per employee reached 70 per cent of the national average. There was a corresponding though less clear-cut decline in the role of manufacturing. The decline here was clearest from the 1970s, with days lost per employee falling from twice the national average to just over the average by the late 1980s. The reason for the complexity is the uneven trend in mining. As noted above, the number of strikes here fell sharply during the 1960s but then rose again. During much of the 1980s, miners maintained their strike propensity while strike activity was declining elsewhere.

The rise in activity in services is illustrated by the official category of 'public administration, sanitary services and education'. From the mid-1980s, while the overall number of strikes fell, the number in this sector remained more or less steady, so that by 1991 it was greater than the number in the whole of manufacturing. There were two broad types of action. First, large national disputes affected a whole sector; for example, in 1985 there was a long-running dispute involving teachers over pay and conditions of service. Second, there appear to have been several more localized disputes over new working practices and the like. Although little research on the reasons for such disputes has been conducted, certain general themes can be identified. As shown in chapter 10, in the public services there has been a long history of work reorganization and commercial pressures. These have eroded a public service ethos and made issues of discipline and work performance more prominent.

In the private services, too, traditions of job security have been eroded, and major changes in work organization have been initiated (Rees and Fielder 1992). Such developments do not determine the occurrence of strikes. They are conditioning forces which may be offset by other factors, such as levels of job security which continue to be higher than those of manufacturing, and a need for organization before a specific grievance reaches the level of a strike. A debate on the banks illustrates the point. Cressey and Scott (1992) underline structural changes including job losses and reduced promotion opportunities. Gall (1993) contends that such developments have produced workforce militancy, but Cressey and Scott (1993) counter that strike rates remain very low and that job losses erode the possibility of collective action. A reasonable conclusion is that the possibility of action is greater than it was in such sectors, because labour is subject to the controls that used to characterize manufacturing, with a division between manager and worker being more marked. But many other factors prevent this possibility from leading to a high level of strikes.

Action short of strikes

The all-out stoppage is not the only form of industrial action. Discussing the situation in the 1960s, Flanders (1970: 112) identified a growing 'use of "cut price" industrial action such as overtime bans, working to rule or going slow'. Since the 1970s, a series of workplace surveys have asked managers and union representatives about such action. The most recent data are summarized in table 14.1. As Milner (1993a) shows, any non-strike action seems to have been about twice as common as strikes. The overtime ban is a particularly favoured weapon. Workplace studies show, however, that it calls for a substantial level of workplace union organization, for an overtime ban requires coordinated and disciplined action in the face of a potentially hostile employer; more weakly organized groups are more likely either to be quiescent or to use spontaneous walk-outs (P. Edwards and Scullion 1982).

As for trends in action, Milner draws on CBI Pay Databank figures on disputes over pay issues in manufacturing to argue that the relative popularity of non-strike action has increased. The implication is thus that the official strike figures exaggerate the decline in industrial action. His results are apparently contradicted by the 1990 WIRS figures, which show a steep decline in non-strike action: setting the proportion of plants reporting a strike at 100, the proportion with non-strike action fell from 123 in 1980 to 50 in 1990. The obvious reason for the difference is that the CBI data cover only manufacturing and refer only to pay disputes. As table 14.1 shows, the relative popularity of non-strike action rose in manufacturing. In services, strike action stayed almost constant while non-strike action fell rapidly. The less obvious reason is that the CBI figures cover action associated with annual pay rounds, and they thus relate to relatively large-scale and formal bargaining. It thus seems that, in such bargaining, unions find the overtime ban a useful tactic, not least because it is less constrained by the law than is the strike (as chapter 9 explains). More generally, however, overtime bans have been hard to sustain, which may reflect the point made above, that non-strike sanctions require extensive organization; as chapter 7 shows, workplace union organization has been weakened.

Conclusion: behind the numbers

Up to the end of the 1970s, three types of strike typified the British pattern. The first was the short and small dispute over an immediate workplace grievance; it was most common in the unionized manufacturing sector, notably the vehicle industry, and in sectors like the docks. A study of a strike-prone plant (Batstone et al. 1978: 48) revealed that the leading reasons for striking were beliefs that management was breaking agreements or acting in bad faith, and concerns about such issues as work allocation. It was also important not to show weakness: a concession now might mean that the other side strengthened its demands the next time an issue arose. This kind of strike was as much about the whole effort bargain as about its ostensible issues. Strikes thus reflected a continuing power relationship in a situation of low trust, and they were intimately bound up with the conduct of this relationship.

The second type was a larger dispute, often over wages. This involved not a particular work group but the whole of the group recognized by management for purposes of formal collective bargaining. Negotiations could drag on for some time. Such a strike was less directly connected with the politics of bargaining and was a more straightforward result of a failure to reach agreement on basic wages and conditions.

Third, there was the public sector. Although parts of the nationalized industries, notably coal, displayed, as discussed below, strikes of the first two types, much of the public sector remained generally strike-free. As shown in chapter 10, bargaining was conducted at national level and there were few issues that were settled through workplace negotiation; moreover, workers lacked the tradition and organization to sustain action at this level. There were also bureaucratic systems through which to appeal against disciplinary action, so that many issues that provoked disputes in the private sector, such as changes in workloads or the sacking of a shop steward, arose rarely. Workplace-based action was thus rare. As chapter 10 again explains, however, the major national dispute became increasingly common.

The first two types merged during the 1980s. The former became less common for reasons discussed in the following section, but workplace issues of working conditions and discipline became proportionately more important causes of strikes. At the same time, the will and ability to sustain long wage disputes also fell. Workers might have a deep sense of grievance but found that they were unlikely to win and were willing to settle quickly.

As for the public sector, the scale of national stoppages was reduced during the 1980s, though some significant disputes continued to occur, notably in 1989 on the railways and in the ambulance service as well as the largest dispute of the period, the 1984–5 coal strike. As discussed below, there is some evidence of a shift in the pattern of disputes, with relatively more small-scale disputes.

With the decline in activity in private manufacturing, the emerging pattern throughout the economy may involve two types. First, there is a small number of short disputes, often about an immediate issue of work conditions. They may reflect a build-up of grievances, which eventually result in a short protest. Second, there are a few larger stoppages arising out of major pay negotiations. Their occurrence is by nature unpredictable, though in the short term they seem likely to remain rare.

The Causes of Strikes

As noted above, there are five possible explanations for falling strike rates: economic conditions; the shift of employment away from strike-prone sectors; legal restrictions; improved means of dispute resolution; and 'better industrial relations'. These are first considered at the aggregate level before they are examined in more detail in three leading former strike-prone sectors.

Explanations of strike trends

There is a long tradition of analysis relating strikes to measures of the labour market, a widely held view being that low levels of unemployment strengthen workers and unions and thus encourage strikes. The theoretical basis for the view has been the subject of considerable dispute. The causal chain running from unemployment through bargaining power to the level of strikes is lengthy; low unemployment can raise bargaining power and mean that workers can gain their demands without the need for a stoppage (see Mayhew 1979; Shalev 1980). The argument also works only for the number of stoppages, with other indices of strike activity being very difficult to predict. Any empirical linkage is far from universal, with high unemployment being associated with low strike rates in countries like

Britain and the United States but high rates in some other European countries (Davies 1981).

Up to the 1970s, two aspects of the economy were found to affect strikes in Britain. Examining the period 1966–75, Davies (1979) found that unemployment reduced the number, but that it was not a high level of unemployment but increases in the level which reduced strikes. It was also found that high levels of inflation encourage strikes, the explanation being that inflation leads to concerns about maintaining real income. Some unpublished work by the present writer extended the model to 1984. It found that the effects of increasing unemployment and of inflation continued to be significant. The view that declining inflation helped to reduce discontent while rising unemployment weakened workers' bargaining power thus receives some support.

The changing structure of employment is also likely to have had an effect. Since the strike-prone sectors have lost jobs, there are simply fewer workers subject to whatever special forces operate within them. A particularly clear indication of the size of the effect is given by the coal industry, which was among the most strike-prone sectors and experienced one of the sharpest reductions in size. We may take its actual number of strikes per employee and calculate the number of strikes that it would have experienced had it stayed at the same size that it had in 1971 and in 1981. During the period 1986–90, there would have been over 300 more strikes per annum on the 1971 employment level, and around 200 more on the 1981 level. This would have increased the number of strikes in Britain as a whole by about two-fifths and a quarter respectively. Sectoral shifts are not the sole factor, however. As noted above, there were also developments within them, with manufacturing moving close to the national average in its strike propensity.

On the role of the law, it is important, as chapter 9 shows, to distinguish between effects on the character and the extent of strike action. In summary, the character of industrial action has been shaped by the law: the use of injunctions by employers, though still far from frequent, is a recognized tactic which was virtually absent in the past; and the conduct of industrial disputes turns on the deployment of ballots of workers. The taking of action is a much more considered choice than it used to be. On extent, as chapter 9 again noted, some studies (reviewed by P. Edwards 1992) have tried to measure the impact of the law once the effects of labour-market forces and the structure of the economy have been taken into account. No consistent results for worker involvement or days lost have emerged, though the number of stoppages seems to have been reduced. It is not clear, however, that indices of the law are measuring only the specific effects of legislation. An index of legal restrictiveness will be correlated with wider political and social developments such as the government's privatization programme. To show that it is associated with a decline in strike numbers is not to show that specific statutory provisions have directly affected workers' willingness to strike, but to indicate that the law, as part of a complex of other changes, has indirectly shaped assumptions about the desirability and efficacy of action. As the studies cited in chapter 9 also suggest, the effects are likely to vary considerably between industries.

The fourth factor, improved procedures, has two elements: voluntary procedures for the resolution of disputes, and the strike ballots that have been legally required since September 1984. The former are unlikely to have had much effect. The greatest growth in formal dispute resolution procedures occurred during the 1970s, not the 1980s. The notable development during the latter decade was the 'no-strike deal' but this remained too rare for there to be much effect on the aggregate strike figures. A study of these deals could find only 101 of them (Milner 1993b).

Strike ballots, by contrast, are generally recognized to have been one of the major influences of the 1980s legislation. As chapter 9 explained, ballots have become an accepted part of negotiations. The fact that most cases of ballots have not in the end involved a strike (Brown and Wadhwani 1990) suggests that disputes which might have led to a strike are now settled without one. However, the majority of strikes, namely, the small and short ones, do not involve ballots: ACAS sources, summarized by Kessler and Bayliss (1992: 222), recorded 1,274 ballots in the four years from 1987 to 1990, a figure which is 40 per cent of the number of recorded strikes. Thus the incidence of at least 60 per cent of strikes will have been unaffected. And ballots did of course exist before 1984: the question is not whether some disputes are now settled without strikes but whether more ballots are now held, and whether the percentage of cases settled without a strike has increased. There may have been some tendency in this direction, though there is little hard evidence on the point. Finally, ballots can be used to signal to the employer the seriousness of a union's resolve, which may in turn promote an improved offer. In terms of substantive outcomes, therefore, the avoidance of a stoppage may have little effect.

The final influence is the most general, and the most difficult to assess. 'Better industrial relations' can mean at least three things: some general increase in trust, commitment and cooperation within the workplace; a reassertion of managerial prerogative so that, in addition to the effects of the external environment, workers do not strike because of the fear of the costs; and a pragmatic reordering of the workplace such that some of the past encouragements to strikes have been removed without this necessarily implying any more fundamental shift in attitudes. There is some evidence for a mixture of the second and third, but not the first.

Many other chapters point to the weakness of the first. Chapter 4 shows that a 'high commitment' route has rarely been followed by management in the private sector, and chapter 10 that the public sector has been marked by managerial domination and the demands of commercialism. Chapter 11 argues that any individualization of the employment relationship is often underpinned by managerial demands and not by any deeper commitment. Chapters 12 and 16 underline the power of managements in pressing through change, which was often accompanied by an intensification of work. One relevant indicator from the WIRS series is an increase in the use of dismissal for disciplinary reasons (Millward et al. 1992: 201). These chapters also indicate the degree to which change has depended on managerial assertiveness, a point also underlined in chapter 7's analysis of the weakening of the role of the shop steward. But this does not mean that change has simply been imposed, a point developed in the final chapter.

It can be argued that assumptions about when it is reasonable to use a stoppage of work as a bargaining counter have changed. The normality of strikes used to be widely accepted. A useful way of examining this is Batstone's (1986: 41) argument that the usual explanation of poor economic performance in Britain in terms of 'bad industrial relations' may reverse the order of causation. In fact, events such as strikes may reflect a poor technical organization of work. For example, stoppages of production caused by technical difficulties may set off industrial relations problems of allocating workers to new tasks or payment for the time lost. Poor organization may mean that management depends on workers' cooperation in bending the rules; this can provide scope for this cooperation to be removed while also promoting a general sense of low trust in managerial competence.

The subsequent changes in the technical organization of work and in payment systems discussed in chapter 12 are likely to have removed some of these sources of friction. Payment systems that are less based on piecework and the negotiation of the effort bargain at the shopfloor level (see chapter 5) will have had a similar effect. In short, a connected set of changes within the workplace combined with a changing external environment to erode some of the conditions promoting strikes. This point may be pursued by looking at three sectors in more detail.

Three strike-prone sectors

To understand why strike activity has fallen it is sensible to consider the sectors where it was concentrated. Three industries are examined: coal and the docks, because of their prominent place in the league table of strikes, and the motor vehicle industry, because it also had a high rate of strikes and because it indicates particularly sharply the situation in manufacturing. The analysis draws on a series of studies without further attribution.[1]

Each sector was potentially affected by the five factors mentioned above. In addition, there is the question of why their level of activity was so much greater than average. There are two main explanations: institutional and structural. The leading institutional explanation is Clegg's (1979): the strike-prone industries experienced rapid fluctuations in employment levels and also a highly fragmented payments system. Fluctuating employment encouraged disputes over job losses and also promoted a sense of distrust. Fragmented pay systems meant that there were many separate bargains, with resultant possibilities of dispute, and also that each work group was concerned to maintain its position in relation to others so that there could be a cycle of disputes. Structural explanations consider the basic conditions of work. In the cases of coal and the docks, these are the danger and physical effort of the job, together with the fact that workers work in groups and often live in communities of fellow workers which help to sustain solidarity: the celebrated 'isolated mass' thesis (Kerr and Siegel 1954). In the case of cars, the monotony of assembly line work was felt to generate alienation and frustration.

Some of these explanations are questionable. The isolated mass hypothesis identifies some timeless conditions of certain industries. It thus fails to explain variations over time and also within industries. Studies of the coal industry up to the 1940s (Church et al. 1990,

1991) show that strike rates varied considerably, and also that a mine could have a high strike rate one year and a low one the next. These studies support a heavily qualified version of the thesis, namely, that community solidarity can be important in sustaining strikes once they occur but that it does not directly explain why strikes occur in the first place. Similar points apply to other factors. For example, rising demand for coal was associated with rising strike rates in the 1950s but not the 1940s. Economic conditions operate along with other factors rather than as an independent variable exerting a uniform effect.

Similar points apply to the alienation argument. Otherwise similar car plants in Britain have had very different strike rates, and in many other countries the car industry is not particularly strike-prone. Moreover, there is little independent evidence that car plants were uniquely alienating. Invoking an ungrounded alienation is not satisfactory. None the less, the technology may have been a conditioning factor, in that issues of the speed of the assembly line and the allocation of work may have provoked a more conflictual atmosphere than the more predictable environment of, say, a chemicals or food factory.

Structural influences thus have to be considered in combination with other factors. A final influence needs to be added to the list. The use of the strike can become an established habit: once it has become accepted as the means to resolve disputes, its use becomes taken for granted. As well as the conditioning factors of economic conditions and so on, the dynamics of people's views of the situation also have to be taken into account. We may now illustrate this perspective.

Coal The number of coal strikes increased during the 1950s and fell sharply during the 1960s. It stabilized during the 1970s and 1980s, before declining sharply in the 1990s: from an average of around 300 a year to only five in 1993. Even during the 1980s, miners remained massively more strike-prone than the national average, as discussed above. Large national disputes were absent until the 1970s; there were then two massive disputes, in 1972 and 1974, followed by the 1984–5 strike.

The prevalence of local disputes reflected the fragmentation of the industry's bargaining structure. Up to the 1960s, miners were paid piece rates which were negotiated at each face within each colliery. This frequent bargaining produced many disputes, which the miners' work group solidarity readily sustained in strikes. Buoyant demand for coal made stoppages an effective way for workers to draw attention to their demands. The decline in the number of strikes reflected two factors: the reform of the bargaining structure, with day rates replacing piece rates, and the worsening economic condition of the industry, which made management less willing to respond positively to the threat of strikes.

The move away from local bargaining also promoted a national orientation to miners' demands. During the late 1960s, earnings were felt to be falling behind those of other groups. The big strikes of the 1970s were over national wage claims. Their length can be explained in part by the solidarity of mining communities, for miners had the communal solidarity to sustain a long strike which other groups lacked.

Local disputes continued at a fairly high level, in part because local bonus schemes were reintroduced in the late 1970s. But they were constrained by the continuing decline of the industry. Employment fell from 360,000 in 1971 to 274,000 in 1981. Further declines in employment during the early 1980s constrained local militancy but contributed to growing fears about pit closures and mass redundancies. These fears underlay the strike of 1984–5, much the most massive and significant dispute of the post-war period. Although the causes of the strike did not lie in community solidarity, the fact that it was sustained in the face of massive counter-pressures by the employer and the government does reflect such solidarity. For example, the support for the strike by women's community groups was substantial (People of Thurcroft 1986).

The defeat of this strike was a major turning point. New work practices were introduced; though these provoked resentment, workers lacked the willingness and ability to strike over them. Bonus schemes grew, but, in contrast to the past, miners were unable to exert much bargaining pressure within them. As the industry shrank rapidly during the 1990s, the level of strikes fell rapidly (though the number of days lost per thousand employees was still five times the all-industry average).

The docks The docks stand out as the most strike-prone sector in Britain; up to the 1970s an average of one docker in two was involved in a strike each year, as against an average for all non-coal industries of one in twenty. The number of dock strikes rose unevenly during the 1960s to reach a peak in 1969; it then fell steadily throughout the 1970s and 1980s. The continuity of this decline suggests that forces peculiar to the latter decade cannot explain the industry's record.

The high rate of strikes reflected facilitating and immediate causes. A key facilitating force was a strong sense of work group solidarity, itself the product of working together in gangs. Traditional means of loading and unloading ships called for heavy and well-coordinated physical labour. Gangs organized much of the detail of the allocation of work, and managers were distant figures. Dockers were not employed permanently by one firm but were hired for each cargo. This casual system further heightened a sense of autonomy and distance from management. The economics of the industry also permitted strikes, for shipowners wanted their ships turned round quickly, and granting strikers' demands was cheaper than taking a long dispute. Immediate causes turned on the uncertainty of earnings associated with piecework payment and the casual system of employment.

From the 1960s, technical change, in the form of roll-on, roll-off ferries and standard containers, revolutionized work on the docks. It eroded traditional dockers' skills based on the manual stowing of cargoes and it was also associated with the rise of a small number of large employers in place of a multitude of small firms. A related development was the removal of much work from the docks themselves: containers were packed and unpacked where they were used, not on the quayside. This last trend provoked a series of large-scale and bitter disputes during the 1970s, as dockers strove to retain control of traditional dock work. In general, they lost.

These trends continued into the 1980s as employment fell steadily: from around 21,000 in 1980 to half that figure in 1989, compared to about 80,000 during the 1950s. The number of strikes fell from 90 in 1980 to 15 in 1988. These disputes were increasingly desperate efforts to defend a traditional way of working in the face of employer efforts to develop new working practices. In 1989 came a final effort to preserve traditional notions of dock work, a national strike called against the abolition by the government of the National Dock Labour Scheme. The strike soon collapsed as dockers accepted either redundancy payments or new employment contracts. Technical change would probably have eventually eroded the basis of dock strikes, but the process was accelerated by the government's antipathy to the NDLS.

The car industry In contrast to coal and the docks, before the Second World War the car industry was not particularly strike-prone; but between 1946 and 1973 the number of stoppages rose tenfold, while worker involvement increased almost as rapidly. Strike rates fluctuated around a generally high level during the 1970s and then fell during the 1980s: from about 200 per year at the end of the 1970s, the number of strikes fell to an average of 65 in 1985–90, and to only 13 in 1993.

The rise of strikes to 1970 reflected intense bargaining at shopfloor level over two kinds of issue. The first was the level of earnings and in particular a concern to maintain a bargaining group's earnings relative to those of others. Piecework bargaining permitted frequent disputes. Second, there were issues of the pace of work, the allocation of work between different trades and the exercise of discipline. In line with Clegg's analysis, this bargaining was much more common in the plants using piecework, notably those of the main British-owned firms in the Midlands, than it was in the American-owned firms of Ford and Vauxhall which retained tight control of pay. During the 1970s, the former group of firms tried to reform their payments systems. This in itself led to disputes and encouraged the emergence of larger strikes involving the whole of a factory or a grade of labour. For example, most of British Leyland's toolmakers were involved in a long and damaging strike in 1977 over differentials between them and semi-skilled workers.

The decline of strikes during the 1980s reflected several forces. First, there was the continuing contraction of the industry. This had the direct effect of closing many plants. It also affected workers in those which remained open. Unlike miners or dockers, car workers had never had a tradition of solidarity to a whole industrial or occupational community, however, so that the result was not major strikes against closure but resigned acceptance. Second, management at British Leyland (BL), and to a lesser extent at some other firms, instituted an aggressive style in which new working practices were imposed and opposition repressed, as symbolized by the dismissal of the convener at Longbridge in 1979 (see chapter 7). During the early 1980s, this process helped to reduce strike levels; those disputes which remained were increasingly about immediate workplace issues. Third, later in the decade technical change was widely implemented. The studies of this (Willman and Winch 1985; Whipp and Clark 1986) do not fully explore the links with strikes but some inferences can be made. The bargaining positions of some traditional crafts, such as toolmakers and sheet metal workers, were eroded as new technology reduced their numbers and also the extent to which management was dependent on their specialized skills. Other demarcation lines crumbled. New technology also helped in the technical organization of work, so that the breakdowns and shortages of components highlighted by Batstone were less common.

Alongside these developments were schemes to promote worker involvement, such as the 'Working with Pride' programme at Austin Rover (as BL had become). As chapter 12 demonstrates, there is little general evidence that such schemes promote deep commitment. But, together with new technology and new managerialism within the plant, and a tough external environment, they may have contributed to changing assumptions about the relevance of strikes.

Conclusion

Consideration of these three industries highlights the importance of technical and organizational change in reducing strike levels. Such changes have removed some of the conditions which allowed strikes to flourish in the past. In coal and the docks, there is no evidence to suggest that there was any fundamental change in general cooperativeness. The weakening of workers' bargaining power is a sufficient explanation. In other strike-prone sectors managerial reorganization may well have increased the arena of cooperation. As managers demonstrated more technical competence in running the work process, a sense of organized opposition among workers may have been eroded even though this did not necessarily imply a wider sense of commitment. Much of the decline in strikes reflects trends in the strike-prone sectors. In the traditionally strike-free sectors, there has been relatively little change in the determinants of industrial action. Indeed, as noted above, in some parts of the service sector action has become more common, reflecting the grievances discussed in chapter 10. Although improved working relationships may be part of the story in some sectors, in others they have had no effect on the strike record.

The various causes of the reduction of strike levels have acted in combination. Economic pressures, the changing distribution of employment and organizational change within the firm exerted the most clear-cut effects. Changes in the law may have had a less direct influence, though it is hard to disentangle their effects from wider political forces. Changed procedures and institutions were less important.

Conclusion: do strikes matter?

In conclusion, some of the wider aspects of strikes may be considered. What are their outcomes and effects, how have these things been changing over time, and what is the likely future?

First, do strikes pay? There is some statistical evidence that they do. Analysis of the CBI Databank shows that about one bargaining group in forty in manufacturing went on strike during the 1980s (Ingram et al. 1993). Negotiations involving strikes had higher pay settlements than those without strikes. Whether or not such benefits outweigh the wages lost during the strike depends on assumptions about how workers discount future as against current earnings, but it does appear that there may be modest benefits from the sorts of strikes analysed by the Databank (Metcalf et al. 1993). Such outcomes should, however, be seen as an *ex post* result which it would be hard to predict in advance. In some cases, wage gains might have been available without a strike. For example, the 1989 ambulance strike, which was seen by the unions as an important victory, was claimed by the employer to be unnecessary (Kerr and Sachdev 1992; Nichol 1992). This case illustrates the wider point, that strikes are used for many reasons other than immediate economic gain, and that they emerge from a bargaining process in which politics are a key feature. Union leaders may feel that they need to strike in order to demonstrate their determination on an issue or because negotiations have developed in such a way that a strike is seen as unavoidable. The key question in analysing decisions to strike is not whether a strike is expected to pay in some measurable way but why the strike is felt to be necessary. Outcomes are often unpredictable, the ambulance dispute being a good example of a case where defeat was widely predicted at the outset but where the dispute was pursued vigorously and with results that satisfied the unions.

Up to the 1970s, strikes often 'paid' in the sense that they were felt to be required either to support a pay claim or to resist a managerial demand. Calculation in terms of costs and benefits was foreign to the thinking of many workers, who responded in relation to standards of fairness and beliefs about the employer's good faith. As for employers, there is little evidence that they had deliberate policies of fomenting strikes. The coal strike was not engineered by the Coal Board or the government. It was, rather, a matter of pursuing a policy of industrial relations change, together with awareness of, and preparedness for, a strike should one emerge. During the 1980s the nature of the terrain shifted. As noted above, the main effect of legal changes was to alter ways of thinking about industrial action, not to impact directly on workplace behaviour. Thus unions had to think more carefully about calling strikes. The new-found willingness of employers, particularly in the public sector, to take a strike rather than settle further underlined the seriousness of the issue.

Strikes were part of the bargaining landscape, the continuation of collective bargaining by other means. During the 1980s they lost at least some of this organic relationship with the bargaining process. Shopfloor action became rarer, and the remaining strikes tended to be short protests about immediate workplace issues. This, together with the closer discipline in strikes resulting from the use of ballots, may make conscious cost-benefit decisions more central than they were when strikes were more intimately connected to the politics of bargaining.

In terms of wider impacts, there was much debate during the 1970s about the costs of strikes (see Hyman 1989: 36–9). Some points became well established, for example that the direct costs of strikes cannot have been high in view of the fact that even in years of high activity an average of half a working day per worker was 'lost', a figure much smaller than losses due to absence or unemployment. What was more in debate was whether strikes constrained managers from rationalizing production and led to inefficiencies, for example the need to keep excessive levels of stocks. As discussed in chapter 13, attempts to measure such things involved asking managers in different countries about restraints on efficiency; even this very leading questioning suggested that strikes were seen as a relatively minor issue. Pratten (1976: 61), for example, found that of an average 27 per cent efficiency differential between Britain and West Germany only 3.5 percentage points were due to strikes and restrictive practices. Knight (1989) studied the strike-prone year of 1968, when any effect should have been particularly strong. He concluded that the effect of strikes was probably neutral. Dickerson et al. (1992), studying 98 industries in the period 1970–9, similarly found that strikes had no effect on productivity. Trends in the 1980s suggest that any effects will have diminished further.

There is one final aspect of strikes' impact. Historically, strikes have been important in symbolizing the aspirations of certain groups of workers. For example, the famous strike in 1888 of women making matches brought to public attention the wages and conditions of a whole group of workers. In other countries, waves of strikes have changed the basic terrain of industrial relations, as in the United States in the 1930s or Italy in the 1960s. Because strikes in Britain have been more localized, they have not had such clear effects. But they none the less gave voice to important grievances. As shown in chapter 13, shopfloor voice can be a significant stimulus to efficiency. As Knight (1989) comments, strikes can give vent to grievances, thereby leading to a resolution of the issue. To the extent that the strike ceases to be a voice mechanism, there is a danger that discontents will not be articulated and that they will go underground. It is possible to have too few strikes as well as too many.

This leads to the issue of the future. There are two possibilities, a continuation of the very low rates of strike activity of the early 1990s or some, modest, increase. The latter could be stimulated by cyclical improvements in the economy, which in the past have been associated with increases in strikes, and also by longer-term developments. These long-term forces relate to the fact that strike rates tend to move in waves (P. Edwards 1992). There were major peaks around 1920 and 1970 with subsequent steep reductions. If the wave pattern continues, 1990 may turn out to mark the bottom of a trough. But the changing structure of employment suggests that strike levels are unlikely to approach those of 1970.

Organized conflict may also take new forms. There have been suggestions that work reorganization can be met with generalized discontent, which is less overt than a strike but more collective and organized than mere grumbling. A group of workers may, for example, try to negotiate how a new shift arrangement is actually implemented. Evidence here is very slight at present, but it is possible that collective industrial action becomes increasingly fragmented and localized. Strike data would then have to be complemented with analyses of the local politics of bargaining.

Note

1 They are, for all three cases, Durcan et al. (1983); for coal, Scott et al. (1963), Adeney and Lloyd (1986), C. Edwards and Heery (1989),

Leman and Winterton (1991); for docks, Allen (1984), Phillips and Whiteside (1985), Turnbull (1992), Turnbull et al. (1992); for cars, Turner et al. (1967), Batstone et al. (1978), Willman (1984), Marsden et al. (1985).

References

Adeney, M. and Lloyd, J. 1986: *The Miners' Strike, 1984–5*. London: Routledge and Kegan Paul.

Allen, P. T. 1984: The Class Imagery of 'Traditional Proletarians'. *British Journal of Sociology*, 35, 1, 93–111.

Batstone, E. 1986: Labour and Productivity. *Oxford Review of Economic Policy*, 2, 3, 32–42.

Batstone, E. 1988: The Frontier of Control. In D. Gallie (ed.), *Employment in Britain*. Oxford: Blackwell.

Batstone, E., Boraston, I. and Frenkel, S. 1978: *The Social Organization of Strikes*. Oxford: Blackwell.

Brown, W. (ed.) 1981: *The Changing Contours of British Industrial Relations*. Oxford: Blackwell.

Brown, W. and Wadhwani, S. 1990: The Economic Effects of Industrial Relations Legislation Since 1979. *National Institute Economic Review*, 131, 57–70.

Church, R., Outram, Q. and Smith, D. N. 1990: British Coal Mining Strikes, 1893–1940. *British Journal of Industrial Relations*, 28, 3, 329–50.

Church, R., Outram, Q. and Smith, D. N. 1991: The 'Isolated Mass' Revisited. *Sociological Review*, 39, 1, 55–87.

Clegg, H. A. 1979: *The Changing System of Industrial Relations in Great Britain*. Oxford: Blackwell.

Cressey, P. and Scott, P. 1992: Employment, Technology and Industrial Relations in the UK Clearing Banks. *New Technology, Work and Employment*, 7, 2, 83–96.

Cressey, P. and Scott, P. 1993: Careers and Individual Action in Banking. *New Technology, Work and Employment*, 8, 1, 72–3.

Daniel, W. W. and Millward, N. 1983: *Workplace Industrial Relations in Britain*. London: Heinemann.

Davies, R. J. 1979: Economic Activity, Incomes Policy and Strikes. *British Journal of Industrial Relations*, 17, 2, 205–23.

Davies, R. J. 1981: The Political Economy of Distributive Conflict. Ph.D. thesis, University of Warwick.

Dickerson, A. P., Geroski, P. A. and Knight, K. G. 1992: *Productivity, Efficiency and Industrial Conflict Activity*. University of Kent Studies in Economics, 14.

Durcan, J. W., McCarthy, W. E. J. and Redman, G. P. 1983: *Strikes in Post-War Britain*. London: George Allen and Unwin.

Edwards, C. and Heery, E. 1989: *Management Control and Union Power.* Oxford: Clarendon.

Edwards, P. K. 1988: Patterns of Conflict and Accommodation. In D. Gallie (ed.), *Employment in Britain.* Oxford: Blackwell.

Edwards, P. K. 1992: Industrial Conflict. *British Journal of Industrial Relations,* 30, 3, 361–404.

Edwards, P. K. and Hyman, R. 1994: Industrial Conflict: Peace in Europe? In R. Hyman and A. Ferner (eds), *New Frontiers of European Industrial Relations.* Oxford: Blackwell.

Edwards, P. K. and Scullion, H. 1982: *The Social Organization of Industrial Conflict.* Oxford: Blackwell.

Flanders, A. 1970: *Management and Unions.* London: Faber and Faber.

Franzosi, R. 1989: One Hundred Years of Strike Statistics. *Industrial and Labor Relations Review,* 42, 3, 348–62.

Gall, G. 1993: Industrial Relations in UK Clearing Banks. *New Technology, Work and Employment,* 8, 1, 67–71.

Gallie, D. (ed.) 1988: *Employment in Britain.* Oxford: Blackwell.

Hougham, J. 1992: Law and the Working Environment. In W. E. J. McCarthy (ed.), *Legal Intervention in Industrial Relations.* Oxford: Blackwell.

Hyman, R. 1989: *Strikes.* London: Fontana.

Ingram, P., Metcalf, D. and Wadsworth, J. 1993: Strike Incidence in British Manufacturing in the 1980s. *Industrial and Labor Relations Review,* 46, 4, 704–17.

Kerr, A. and Sachdev, S. 1992: Third among Equals. *British Journal of Industrial Relations,* 30, 1, 127–43.

Kerr, C. and Siegel, A. 1954: The Interindustry Propensity to Strike. In A. Kornhauser, A. Dubin and A. M. Ross (eds), *Industrial Conflict.* New York: McGraw-Hill.

Kessler, S. and Bayliss, F. 1992: *Contemporary British Industrial Relations.* Basingstoke: Macmillan.

Knight, K. G. 1989: Labour Productivity and Strike Activity in British Manufacturing Industries. *British Journal of Industrial Relations,* 27, 3, 365–74.

Lane, T. and Roberts, K. 1971: *Strike at Pilkingtons.* London: Fontana.

Leman, S. and Winterton, J. 1991: New Technology and the Re-structuring of Pit-level Industrial Relations in the British Coal Industry. *New Technology, Work and Employment,* 6, 1, 54–65.

Marsden, D., Morris, T., Willman, P. and Wood, S. 1985: *The Car Industry.* London: Tavistock.

Mayhew, K. 1979: Economists and Strikes. *Oxford Bulletin of Economics and Statistics,* 41, 1, 1–19.

Metcalf, D., Wadsworth, J. and Ingram, P. 1993: Do Strikes Pay? In D. Metcalf and S. Milner (eds), *New Perspectives on Industrial Disputes.* London: Routledge.

Millward, N., Stevens, M., Smart, D. and Hawes, W. 1992: *Workplace Industrial Relations in Transition*. Aldershot: Dartmouth.

Milner, S. 1993a: Overtime Bans and Strikes. *Industrial Relations Journal*, 24, 3, 201–10.

Milner, S. 1993b: *Final Offer Arbitration in the UK*. Employment Department, Research Series 7. London: HMSO.

Nichol, D. 1992: Unnecessary Conflict. *British Journal of Industrial Relations*, 30, 1, 145–54.

People of Thurcroft 1986: *Thurcroft*. Nottingham: Spokesman.

Phillips, G. and Whiteside, N. 1985: *Casual Labour*. Oxford: Clarendon.

Pratten, C. F. 1976: *Labour Productivity Differentials within International Companies*. Cambridge: Cambridge University Press.

Rees, G. and Fielder, S. 1992: The Services Economy, Subcontracting and the New Employment Relations. *Work, Employment and Society*, 6, 3, 347–68.

Scott, W. H., Mumford, E., McGivering, I. C. and Kirkby, J. M. 1963: *Coal and Conflict*. Liverpool: Liverpool University Press.

Shalev, M. 1978: Lies, Damned Lies and Strike Statistics. In C. Crouch and A. Pizzorno (ed.), *The Resurgence of Class Conflict in Western Europe since 1968*, Vol. 1. London: Macmillan.

Shalev, M. 1980: Trade Unionism and Economic Analysis. *Journal of Labor Research*, 1, 1, 133–74.

Shalev, M. 1992: The Resurgence of Labour Quiescence. In M. Regini (ed.), *The Future of Labour Movements*. London: Sage.

Turnbull, P. 1992: Dock Strikes and the Demise of the Dockers' 'Occupational Culture'. *Sociological Review*, 40, 2, 294–318.

Turnbull, P., Woolfson, C. and Kelly, J. 1992: *Dock Strike*. Aldershot: Avebury.

Turner, H. A., Clack, G. and Roberts, G. 1967: *Labour Relations in the Motor Industry*. London: George Allen and Unwin.

Whipp, R. and Clark, P. 1986: *Innovation and the Auto Industry*. London: Frances Pinter.

Willman, P. 1984: The Reform of Collective Bargaining and Strike Activity in BL Cars, 1976–82. *Industrial Relations Journal*, 15, 2, 6–17.

Willman, P. and Winch, G. 1985: *Innovation and Management Control*. Cambridge: Cambridge University Press.

15

Equal Opportunities: Continuing Discrimination in a Context of Formal Equality

Sonia Liff

One aspect of the study of 'old' industrial relations in Britain was its overwhelming concern with those aspects of the employment relation which affected white male skilled workers. Changes in the composition of the workforce and the types of jobs available in the 1970s and 1980s have made it impossible to sustain this perspective as the dominant concern of the 1990s. Yet many aspects of what have been classed as 'new' industrial relations seem also to be in danger of constructing an agenda which continues to ignore the experiences of those groups who have traditionally faced discrimination in employment. This chapter describes the ways in which workplace experiences vary depending on the gender, ethnicity and other characteristics of workers and, as a result, identifies a different industrial relations agenda. This focuses on the ways in which different experiences of the employment relation persist within a context of legal equality and apparently widespread organizational commitment to equal opportunities. Chapters 18 and 19 pursue parallel themes, focusing respectively on two other areas of traditional neglect: low pay and small firms.

Three issues underpin this chapter: first, a more detailed exploration of the ways in which the legal and socio-economic context for equality has changed since the 1970s; second, the ways in which discrimination against members of certain social groups continue to be embedded in the formal and informal rules governing employment; third, the strengths and weaknesses of equal opportunity policies as a way of changing such rules. The chapter concludes with a brief discussion of likely future developments in the field.

The Changing Context for Equal Opportunity, 1975–1995

Discrimination as an issue has always been an important, if often neglected, aspect of the study of employment relations. Equal opportunities as currently understood has a much more recent history. This is not to deny the important struggles in particular workplaces over access to work, or more frequently rates of pay. However, equal opportunity policies which involve attempts to change the whole range of employment practices including the allocation of work, the assessment of performance, and the remuneration given, have largely emerged since the mid-1970s. The developments during this period are discussed below as a basis for considering their significance for changing approaches to equality in the next section.

Legal and political changes

As mentioned in chapter 9, legal changes have had an important influence on the development of employment practices. Most obvious in this field is the introduction of anti-discrimination and equal pay legislation in the 1970s. The Equal Pay Act was introduced in 1970 and came fully into force in 1975. This provided for equal pay for men and women doing 'like work' for the same employer, or doing jobs which had been rated equal by a job evaluation scheme. 1975 also saw the introduction of the Sex Discrimination Act which included provision for the equal treatment of men and women in most spheres. Discrimination was defined in two ways. Direct discrimination involved treating a person differently from the way a person of the other sex has been, or would have been, treated in the same circumstances. Indirect discrimination involves applying a term or condition equally to all, but with the effect that a substantially larger proportion of those of one sex can fulfil it than the other, and that this is to their detriment and cannot otherwise be justified. One example involved a company which made part-timers redundant before full-timers. This affected far more women than men because they were less likely to be able to work full-time and the organization was unable to provide a justification for this method of selection in terms of the work they were doing (EOC 1985a). In 1976 the Race Relations Act was passed, giving ethnic minorities identical provisions to those given to women. The 1970s also saw legislation giving at least some women protection against being dismissed while pregnant and the right to their job back after maternity leave.

The period during which anti-discrimination legislation was passed was politically favourable to the establishment of formal rights for workers. In contrast, during the 1980s Conservative governments argued that unnecessary burdens should be removed from industry. Despite this, the 1980s saw an important amendment to the Equal Pay Act providing for equal pay for work of equal value. The ability of the 1970 legislation to tackle pay differentials had been undermined by the rarity of men and women doing 'like work' or being covered by the same job evaluation scheme. The new amendment, introduced following an EC ruling on the inadequacy of British equal pay legislation, allowed a person to ask for their job to be independently evaluated against a specified job undertaken, for the same employer, by a person of the opposite sex. EC rulings have also led to other changes and the Community has been a source of pressure (frequently resisted by the British government) for improved provisions for parental leave and for enhanced rights for part-time workers.

However, the Conservatives' lack of enthusiasm for this type of legislation has not resulted in a radical reform of the 1970s provisions. Instead, it has been expressed in a reluctance to take legislation any further (not just towards EC proposals but also in a refusal to consider strengthening the Acts in ways suggested by the equality commissions). The Conservatives have also resisted pressure to extend the scope of provisions: for example, resisting pressure in the 1980s for age and disability anti-discrimination legislation.

Existing anti-discrimination legislation is frequently criticized for a range of limitations relating to its formulation, its operation in practice, and its ability to influence employer practice (for example, Leonard 1987; O'Donovan and Szyszczak 1988; Chambers and Horton 1990; Dickens 1992; Gregory 1992). Relatively few cases are brought and there is a low rate of success in proving claims (Employment Gazette 1993a). Nevertheless, its significance in terms of bringing discrimination onto the agenda of management should not be underestimated. The Sex Discrimination and Race Relations Acts also set up the Equal Opportunity Commission (EOC) and the Commission for Racial Equality (CRE). As well as pursuing cases themselves they have established Codes of Practice which, as will be discussed below, have provided the framework for most organizations' own Equal Opportunity policies.

Political changes are also evident in both the rationale for equal opportunities and the means by which they are seen as best pursued. In the 1970s the Commission for Racial Equality and the Equal Opportunities Commission were established as tripartite bodies with representatives from government, industry and trade unions. Equal opportunities was seen as an issue of social justice, and legislation provided a way of extending and supporting rights which trade unions were campaigning for on behalf of their members. Legal prosecutions and investigations by the Commissions were seen as the way to deliver equality.

These measures are still available but at the beginning of the 1990s a new body, Opportunity 2000, emerged to promote equal opportunities. Despite the fact that Conservative governments had shown little support for, or interest in, the EOC or CRE this was launched by the Prime Minister, John Major. Opportunity 2000 is employer-led and counted among its founder members 25 per cent of the *Times* Top 100 companies. While not negating the moral arguments, they stressed that they were in favour of equal opportunities because it made sound business sense. Managers were told that a key to competitive advantage was to get the best person for the job – and that best person might well be a woman. Ironically, the EOC had been making a similar argument for several years and the initiatives proposed differed little from their Code, being if anything rather stronger. However, in the changed political climate the message lacked conviction until made by employers.

Labour-market and socio-economic changes

Changing industrial structures and patterns of work have also dramatically altered the context for equal opportunities. The trend for married women to work in the formal economy both before their children were born and again once the children were established at school has increased throughout the post-war period. What has been distinctive about the more recent period has been the larger number of women working while their children are under the age of 5. This has been in part facilitated by maternity leave provisions.

However, broader changes in the availability of jobs are also important, in particular the long-term decline of employment opportunities in manufacturing relative to services. In 1993 there were 3.6 jobs in services for every 1 in manufacturing (Employment Gazette 1994a). Such jobs frequently have poorer terms and conditions than full-time manufacturing jobs, a tendency which has been exacerbated by the practice, in both public and private sectors, of contracting out services. Women are much more likely to take up these jobs than men. In 1993, women made up 57 per cent of service-sector workers (Employment Gazette 1994a). The reasons for this are complex but one factor that sustains this association is the number of such jobs which are part-time. This again is an employment pattern associated with a much higher proportion of women than men.

Social attitudes as well as practices have changed. Sixty-three per cent of the British population now feel that women should work part-time while their children are at school (Kiernan 1992). There is also some evidence that people feel more positively about women in more senior positions. In 1992 the Institute of Management surveyed their male and female managers. One of their findings was that 99 per cent of women and 94 per cent of men agreed or strongly agreed with the statement that women bring positive skills to the workplace (Coe 1992). This compares interestingly with Hunt's 1973 survey of managers formulating or implementing personnel policy. She found that only 11 per cent responded positively to the statement 'Do you think it would be a good or bad thing if more women occupied senior positions?' (Hunt 1975).

The recessions and booms of the 1980s and 1990s have also changed the context within which we need to understand equal opportunities. Calls to provide more, and better, jobs for members of previously disadvantaged groups are seen as more socially legitimate and economically rational in a boom than in a recession. In the second half of the 1980s, amid warnings of an impending labour shortage caused by the 'demographic timebomb', employers were concerned to draw on all sections of the workforce to fill vacancies and fully utilize available skills. At the end of the decade and at the beginning of the 1990s many organizations were shedding labour, and few were recruiting. Concern refocused on the existing workforce and some felt that women should not be helped to take up jobs while so many men were unemployed.

This may be one factor behind what has become known as the 'backlash' (Faludi 1992). This encompasses views such as that equal opportunity has gone 'too far', and that women are being appointed in preference to better men. Hard evidence for such claims is rarely presented, leading some women to suggest that men are simply unhappy that their previously advantageous position is being undermined.

Overview of the changes

Thus the context within which such policies have emerged and developed is complex and contradictory. Labour-market changes, which have resulted in a greater number of women workers and 'women's jobs', have raised the profile of equality issues. Changing patterns of birth rates leading to the 'baby boom' of the 1960s and the subsequent 'trough' have led women's increasing workforce participation to be seen alternatively as a 'problem' and then a 'salvation'. Recession confounded this latter perception and undermined the economic and, to some extent, the moral arguments for equality. The introduction of legislation outlawing discrimination on the basis of sex or race was clearly supportive of equality initiatives, but the subsequent political view that employment legislation is a burden on employers and counterproductive for increasing employment opportunities counteracts this tendency.

Equal Opportunity Policies

The codes of practice

The existence and prevalence of equal opportunity policies in the 1980s and 1990s need to be understood in terms of the context outlined above. Yet the precise form taken by the policies, based as they are on the application of formal rules and procedures in a uniform way for all employees, often reflects the 'old' approach to managing employment relations. The dominant approach derives from Codes of Practice issued by the Commission for Racial Equality and the Equal Opportunities Commission (CRE 1983; EOC 1985b). These outline procedural approaches to (1) avoiding discrimination and (2) promoting equality. The first part is based on the steps considered necessary to comply with the anti-discrimination legislation. The second part outlines those initiatives compatible with, but not required by, the legislation which are thought likely to enhance the opportunities of previously disadvantaged groups.

To avoid discrimination, organizations are encouraged to issue a policy statement which describes their intentions in relation to equal opportunities. Such statements range from the minimalist 'We are an equal opportunities employer' to a more elaborate statement saying which areas of employment policy are to be addressed, which social groups covered, and some of the measures that will be taken to put it into practice. The importance of such a statement is said to lie in its indication of senior management support and commitment. Organizations are also advised to instruct their staff not to discriminate and to provide them with some guidance as to how this is to be achieved. This is usually an elaboration of personnel best practice in areas such as selection. Many organizations stop at this point. However, Codes of Practice recommend that the policy should be monitored, as should the make-up of the workforce, so that any remaining problems can be identified.

In order to promote equality positively, organizations are encouraged to undertake policies which address the particular disadvantages or specific employment patterns of women and ethnic minorities. The law requires equal treatment in most circumstances, so such approaches cannot be about providing specific benefits for only certain groups (except for the provision of training in some limited circumstances) or about reserving jobs for them. Instead, it is about adapting employment practices so that they are more open to these groups.

Examples include allowing a wider range of jobs to be worked on a part-time basis; providing career breaks whereby jobs are held open during unpaid leave; advertising jobs more widely, for example in the ethnic minority press; ensuring that advertisements and publicity material show diverse images of employees; allowing flexible holidays so that workers can observe their own religious festivals; recognizing the need for leave when arrangements for child care or dependants' care break down; making buildings accessible to those with disabilities; and providing specific training for those groups who have been traditionally under-represented in a particular occupation and who lack the necessary pre-qualifications. It is also possible to establish targets for increasing the proportion of particular groups within certain occupational areas (and this is part of the Opportunity 2000 approach). This is different from setting quotas or establishing reserved places, which are illegal. Instead, the intention is to indicate what one is aiming for and to have some measure of progress.

The role of trade unions

Around three-quarters of large organizations now have EO policies in place, but there appears to be no association between those who have a formal policy and those which recognize a trade union (Marginson et al. 1993). Colling and Dickens (1989) concluded that bargaining over equality issues was rare. Their research suggested that management-initiated EO measures were often excluded from the bargaining arena. It also found that, while there was plenty of scope for collective bargaining to consider equality issues during negotiations over pay, benefits, and organizational change, in practice this did not occur. Instead, negotiations tended to stay within the confines of the existing structures rather than questioning their form.

In some cases, unions clearly have played a prominent role in getting EO policies in place or in extending their scope (Cameron 1987). Many unions have also recognized the importance of equal opportunity issues in their own membership drives and in their provision of services for members. However, as will be discussed further below, EO is not a simple 'us and them' issue where the interests of management are in straightforward opposition to those of the workforce. For management, EO may bring benefits as well as costs; for the union it may bring benefit to some of its membership at the same time as eroding advantages previously enjoyed by other members.

Analytical perspectives

What type of equality are such policies aiming for? Jewson and Mason (1986a) characterize the approach outlined in the Codes of Practice as 'liberal'. By this they mean that equality is understood as treating everyone the same. The Codes suggest meeting this objective by improving personnel practices in ways that have been elaborated above. Cockburn (1989) also discusses this approach under the title of the 'short agenda'.

Jewson and Mason (1986a) contrast the approach taken by the Codes with one they call 'radical'. In this, equality is conceived as equal outcomes. They argue that this involves a commitment to achieving fair distributions (as established by quotas) of under-represented groups within the workforce. This is likely to constitute positive discrimination and as such is usually illegal under British legislation. As such, one cannot find examples of organizations explicitly building an equal opportunity policy around such an approach, though Jewson and Mason argue that it is expressed by workers.

This dichotomy is problematic for a number of reasons. Are 'liberals' indifferent to the outcomes that flow from their fair procedures? Is it not more likely that they support equal treatment *because* they believe it is the best way of securing fair outcomes? Do radicals just want equal outcomes regardless of merit or is it not more likely that they are unconvinced of the ability of 'fair procedures' to demonstrate the abilities of under-represented groups?

There is an alternative to the radical approach which may capture better the limitations of the liberal approach. This sees equality as allowing people to compete on equal terms. Such an approach has been explored by Webb and Liff (1988) in their critique of Jewson and Mason (1986a) and is characterized by Cockburn (1989) as the 'long agenda'. It embodies the idea that although people may be treated equally this may not necessarily result in 'fair' outcomes. For example, if an able-bodied person is competing against a wheelchair user for a job located in a building with steps up to it, then although they are being treated equally, few would find the outcome fair. Fairness is not ensured by giving the person in the wheelchair the job regardless of the applicants' relative merit (which is what the radical approach seems to imply should happen), but rather, this approach suggests, by providing access to the building. The employer can then judge the applicants equally on job-related terms. Treating people 'equally' is insufficient if the terms of competition for jobs are stacked against members of one group. This can happen in many different ways; one very common example is the insistence that certain jobs be worked on a full-time basis. Dickens (1992: 127) argues that anti-discrimination legislation fails to tackle this dimension since 'it is not unfavourable treatment of women which is outlawed . . . but less favourable treatment when compared with the treatment of a man similarly situated'.

Differing experiences of the employment relation

Have anti-discrimination legislation and equal opportunity policies been effective in changing people's experience of the employment relation? This question raises difficult issues about what we would expect such policies to achieve, over what time scale as well as what we mean by discrimination.

Historically, there is little difficulty in showing that women were deliberately excluded from some areas of work and targeted for others (for example, Bradley 1989). Such exclusion was not simply the result of management preferences but was actively pursued by male trade unionists (Walby 1983). Wartime experience showed that women were able to do many jobs from which they had been previously excluded, particularly where adequate training was provided and minor adjustments made. Nevertheless, they were excluded after the war, not simply as a result of trade union agreements but also through management choice (Summerfield 1989). Trade unions long defended differential wages for women on the grounds that men needed to be able to provide for their families whereas women were 'secondary' wage earners (despite the TUC's long-standing formal commitment to equal pay). In the 1950s and 1960s Afro-Caribbean people were encouraged to come to Britain and were specifically channelled into jobs which the indigenous population considered unattractive (Deakin 1970; Fryer 1984).

The current situation in Britain may seem rather different. Legislation exists and there appears to be widespread support by both management and trade unions for treating all people equally on the basis of their abilities. Yet other types of evidence suggest that this does not happen in practice. The following sections investigate two key aspects of the employment relationship: the allocation of work, and the assessment and reward of ability and performance. They explore whether the experience of these aspects of employment differs depending on characteristics such as gender and ethnicity rather than just by individual differences in qualifications and ability. Where this does appear to be the case the processes through which this occurs will be explored.

The Allocation of Work

There is certainly extensive evidence that not only the likelihood of having a job, but also the type of jobs obtained, varies with different social group membership. The nature of this evidence varies and this is reflected in the discussion below. Differences between the employment position of men and women are regularly and fairly extensively documented in statistical sources. Statistical information is also collected about ethnic minorities, though it is far less prevalent than that on women. In both cases, such data need to be supplemented with those from occasional surveys and case studies in order to clarify the processes involved. In the case of some social groups this is the only type of data available. Often even this is limited. For example, there is considerable anecdotal evidence that gays and lesbians face discrimination in the allocation of work, and some organizations include them in their equal opportunity policies for this reason. However, there is very little systematic research which explores this issue.

Unemployment

As shown in chapter 3, since 1980 the number of women in employment in Britain has grown much faster than the number of men, suggesting that they are in an advantageous situation. Unemployment figures seem to bear this out, with December 1993 figures giving a male unemployment rate of 13.2 per cent and a female one of 5.2 per cent (Employment Gazette 1994b) among those of working age. However, such figures are different from those in all other EC countries (Bulletin 1993) and need careful interpretation. In Britain many women are unable to register as unemployed because of child care responsibilities or ineligibility for benefits. Many of these may prefer to be working. One study estimates that 900,000 women are keen to return to work but are unable to do so because of their family and caring responsibilities (Berry-Lound 1990).

Unemployment figures are higher for both men and women from ethnic minorities than for the equivalent white group. Taking an average of figures for 1989–91, white men and women over age 16 had an unemployment rate of 7 per cent whereas people from ethnic minorities had a rate of 13 per cent. There was also considerable variation between different ethnic minority groups. For example, those of Pakistani or Bangladeshi origin had an unemployment rate of 21 per cent for this period (Employment Gazette 1993b). These differences cannot be explained by differences in qualification levels. People from ethnic minorities have a higher unemployment rate than white people at each qualification level. Rather than differences disappearing when people have qualifications the discrepancy between unemployment rates is actually greater for those with higher qualifications (those above A level). A US study of black women in clerical occupations showed that the same levels of education and training led to less occupational mobility than they did for white women (Power and Rosenberg 1993).

An OPCS survey in 1988 found that there were 6.2 million adults in Britain who were disabled (though comparatively few are officially registered). Of the 2.4 million of working age, only 31 per cent are in employment despite the fact that many disabilities are comparatively mild. Seventy per cent of disabled people who are in work or seeking work became disabled during their working lives (Employers' Forum on Disability 1992).

Occupational segregation

Women in Britain now make up nearly 45 per cent of the workforce but there are many occupational groups where the distribution of men and women is very different. For example, 83 per cent of working women have jobs in the service sector compared with 57 per cent of men. Women significantly outnumber men in health and associated professions, personal services, clerical and teaching occupations. Men significantly outnumber women in science and engineering professions, in skilled trades, and as drivers and mobile machine operators (Employment Gazette 1993c). Differences are not just between occupational areas (described as horizontal segregation) but are also related to levels in the organizational hierarchy (vertical segregation). So, for example, while 27 per cent of all managers in the UK are women they make up only 1–2 per cent of senior executives, and 4 per cent of middle and senior managers (NEDO 1990).

The details of which jobs are done by men and which by women vary between countries but the existence of segregation and its general characteristics are pervasive. For example, within the EC women's share of employment in manufacturing ranges from a low of 10.9 per cent in Luxembourg to a high of 31.8 per cent in Portugal (Bulletin 1993). What is shared is an under-representation of women in this sector.

Men and women often tend to have different patterns of working. Women are much more likely to work part-time than are men in all EC countries (Bulletin 1993). Great Britain has one of the highest proportions of women working part-time, accounting in 1992 for 43 per cent of the female labour force (Employment Gazette 1993c). There is no necessary association between these different working hours and occupational segregation but in practice part-time working is much more prevalent in sectors which have an over-representation of women workers (Beechey and Perkins 1987). Thus those seeking part-time work may find themselves restricted to a limited range of occupations.

Women's participation rates vary depending on their domestic circumstances. Engagement in waged work, particularly on a full-time basis, is negatively correlated with having young children (Employment Gazette 1993c). With an ageing workforce many women are increasingly faced with responsibility for elderly or sick relatives which may also affect their ability to go out to work. These patterns vary between EC countries but in all cases are distinctive from men's engagement with waged work over their lives (Rubery and Fagan 1993). Again, there is no necessary link between these patterns and occupational segregation, but longitudinal research suggests that breaks in paid employment are associated with downward occupational mobility for women (Dex 1987).

Ethnic minorities make up less than 5 per cent of the British workforce, so it is easiest to judge whether occupational segregation exists by looking at the proportion of the ethnic minority workforce within a particular occupation compared with the proportion of the workforce overall. This shows some areas of similarities but also significant areas of difference. Thirteen per cent of white males work in the construction industry compared with 5 per cent of ethnic minority men. Twenty-nine per cent of ethnic minority men work in distribution, hotels, catering and repairs compared with 16 per cent of white males. In some ways, the occupational patterns of ethnic minority women follow those of white women: for example, there are a similar percentage in the service sector. However, there are also differences. Eleven per cent of white women work in the education sector compared with 6 per cent of ethnic minority women. Fifteen per cent of ethnic minority women work in health and related services compared with 9 per cent of white women (Employment Gazette 1993b).

Women and ethnic minorities are the groups which are most commonly considered in relation to distinctive employment patterns. However, there are other groups to which a similar analysis can be applied. Young workers are occupationally concentrated, not simply in relation to the levels they have achieved in organizational hierarchies, but also in terms of the sectors within which they work. In particular, they are concentrated in low level service sector jobs. In 1987 34 per cent of men and 40 per cent of women aged 16–19 were employed in distribution, retail, hotel and catering compared with 16 per cent of men and 26 per cent of women of all ages (Wells 1989).

Processes of recruitment and selection

Evidence of different experience is not necessarily evidence of discrimination against these social groups. Alternative explanations of differential patterns could be that they reflect the qualifications and abilities of different groups. Or that they reflect choices on the part of members of groups to engage in some areas of work in preference to others, or their degree of attachment to work and a career compared with other aspects of their lives, or to their willingness to acquire training. Studies of the recruitment and selection process provide a way of exploring the causes of the differential allocation of work.

The first part of the process relates to the methods and forms of recruitment. The Commission for Racial Equality has drawn attention to the possible consequences of recruitment methods based on internal, or extended internal, labour markets. If the current workforce is not ethnically mixed then recruiting internally will simply perpetuate this situation. Asking current workers to recommend friends or family members for vacancies is similarly likely to lead to a reproduction of the current social mix of the workforce. The suggestion is not that white people are deliberately discriminating by refusing to tell black people about vacancies. Rather, it is that people are most likely to have friends from the same ethnic group as themselves. As such, these forms of recruitment could constitute indirect discrimination. An example of the significance of where information is placed is given by one company which simply included a job centre in an area where a high proportion of people from ethnic minorities lived. This on its own led to a significantly different mix of applicants (Wild 1986). Word-of-mouth recruitment remains common: in 1984, according to WIRS2, 42 per cent of establishments recruiting semi-skilled manual workers used 'personal contacts of existing staff' (Millward and Stevens 1986: 198), and much other research underlines the continuing role of informal methods (Collinson et al. 1990: 55–9).

Sex and race discrimination legislation make it illegal, in most circumstances, to advertise explicitly for someone of a particular gender or ethnic group. In the case of disabled people it may be socially unacceptable, even if not strictly illegal, to exclude them from access to jobs. However, one large scale survey of organizations, mainly in the service sector, found that 40 per cent of employers saw disabled people as 'unsuitable employees' (PMP 1992).

In the case of age no legislation exists and it is common to see advertisements which exclude applications from, say, people over the age of 40 (Naylor 1987; Tillsley 1990).

Even where the law prevents explicit exclusion there is evidence that employers are screening incoming applications on this basis. In Britain there have been experiments whereby employers advertising vacancies have been sent a series of matched applications purporting to come from members of different ethnic groups. The jobs were non-manual or skilled manual and involved both men and women. The researchers treated as a positive response any invitation to take the application further, even if this only involved being sent an application form to complete. Forty-six per cent of employers made a positive response to all three applicants. If all applicants were treated equally one would expect all other options to get the same response. In fact, 25 per cent of employers rejected the two black candidates and only 2–3 per cent rejected the other combination of pairs of applicants. Overall, the researchers concluded that 35–45 per cent of employers discriminated against one or more of the black candidates (Brown and Gay 1985). This proportion is little changed from similar studies conducted in the past.

Interviewing has received much attention as a possible site for discrimination in the selection process. Interviews are generally criticized for being a poor method of selection. One reason is that research has shown that people tend to appoint in their own image. Other research has drawn a distinction between decisions based on specific job-related qualifications or experience – known as suitability criteria – and assessments about whether the person will fit in with the organization, other workers, or customers – known as acceptability criteria (Jenkins 1986). This has shown that acceptability criteria are particularly likely to be disadvantageous to ethnic minorities, leading to the recommendation that selection should focus on suitability criteria. More recent research by Jewson et al. (1990) again showed that acceptability criteria continue to be used to the disadvantage of ethnic minorities. However, they also found that assessment of suitability criteria was based on stereotyped assumptions about the characteristics of particular ethnic groups.

In the case of women, some research has shown that even where applicants fulfil predefined suitability criteria some managers seem to find it difficult to believe that a woman could possibly be the best candidate. Collinson et al. (1990), during detailed observation of interviews, found that managers used different (gender-based) criteria to assess whether applicants were able to meet the job requirements. For example, the same type of behaviour was described in a male applicant as 'showing initiative' and assessed as desirable, and in a woman applicant as 'pushy' and undesirable. Similarly, Curran's (1988: 344) research showed that managers often found it hard to separate the assessment of a characteristic such as leadership from the concept of masculinity, or a 'requirement for a pleasant personality and one for a pretty girl with a smile'. What is so important about these findings is that they show that for some managers at least, gender becomes part of their assessment of suitability criteria.

In other cases, suitability may be assessed by behaviour patterns that are gender-related. In Britain managers often work extremely long hours and the length of time one is at one's desk has become, for some organizations, a measure of commitment. Despite the increase in the number of women in paid work, research shows that housework, child care and care of the sick and elderly are very unevenly divided between men and women (Liff 1991; Kiernan 1992). In these circumstances fewer women than men are likely to be able to work long hours for an employer (though women's total hours of work, paid and unpaid, have been shown in a number of studies to be greater than men's). Employers may judge a woman as less suitable for promotion than a man on this basis without assessing what they have both achieved in the same hours.

One might assume that more 'scientific' approaches to selection, such as psychometric tests, would not be subject to these problems. However, research suggests that the use of many of these tests can lead to indirect discrimination. There are a number of ways in which this can occur. The simplest may just be about how familiar different groups of applicants are with taking tests and with the best approach for getting a high score. Research suggests that people do better if they have been told in advance that tests will be administered and given samples of the types of test involved so that they can prepare themselves. This is true for all applicants but seems to have a particular significance for reducing the adverse impact on ethnic minorities. Other problems can occur when a test embodies a higher language requirement than is needed for the job. For example, reasoning skill may be measured through a written test and for those for whom English is their first language it may be a perfectly acceptable method. However, some people may score badly not because they lack reasoning skills but because they have limited written language skills (Wood and Baron 1992).

Assessment and Reward of Ability and Performance

Remuneration

The most obvious way to look at whether members of different social groups gain different benefits for their performance is to look at the pay they receive. The usual way to compare pay is via a comparison of rates for similar time periods. On this basis, women's hourly pay in Britain is 72 per cent of men's in manual occupations and 67 per cent in non-manual occupations (Sefton 1993). Again, this general difference is repeated in most countries, though the percentage difference varies. Other aspects of remuneration such as membership of an occupational pension scheme are also less favourable to women (EOC 1988). There is little systematic information collected on earnings for ethnic minorities, but Bruegel (1989) draws on a range of sources which indicate that wage levels are lower than those received by white men and women at most qualification levels.

Again, there are a number of explanations of these differences in pay. One is that they are a reflection of market rates and that women and ethnic minorities are disadvantaged by being 'crowded' within certain low level occupational areas. However, even in areas of skill shortage, pay is not always equal. A statistical study of men from certain Asian ethnic groups in the United States with very high levels of qualification and high levels of pay showed they were still earning less than white men when matched for occupation and industry (Duleep and Sanders 1992).

Another explanation of such differences would be to say that pay differences are simply consequent on the occupational segregation described above. Or, in cases where individuals are doing the same job, that pay differences reflect different degrees of merit in performing those jobs rather than the consequences of discrimination. These 'explanations' raise two important questions. First, is the relative pay between different occupations based on an objective assessment of the skills and abilities needed to perform the jobs successfully? Second, are methods of assessing job holders' performance objective? Alternatively, do the methods used to assess jobs and individuals embody hierarchies based on gender and ethnicity?

Job evaluation

Equal pay legislation determined that a man and a woman whose jobs had been rated as equal under a job evaluation scheme should be entitled to equal pay. This clause proved to have limited applicability because men's areas of work were often subject to separate evaluation schemes from women's. Even where a scheme covered both areas of work the result was frequently that women's jobs were all rated in the lowest categories. Job evaluation is based on assessing the relative value of different jobs either by direct comparison or by assessing the need for different characteristics, such as mental ability, physical ability, responsibility and so on.

Research suggests that the way such comparisons were made often embodied a view that the types of skills and abilities men more commonly had, or displayed at work, were more valuable than those displayed by women. For example, the need for physical skill was rated more highly than the need for caring skills, and responsibility for money or equipment was rated more highly than responsibility for people. In this way, job evaluation schemes frequently just endorsed conventional pay hierarchies (Morris 1983; EOC 1985c). There is no 'scientific' way of determining relative value; job evaluation schemes only help to apply judgements in a systematic way. The suggestion is that such schemes tend to embody a system which values some things more highly than others, or regards some abilities as more important skills than others, because in our society male activities and behaviour are valued more highly than female ones. By rethinking these categories and their relative value, job evaluation systems can produce completely different results. For example, a local authority scheme significantly changed the differential between home helps and dustmen as a result of such a reassessment (Lodge 1987).

The 1984 Equal Value amendment has allowed existing job evaluation schemes to be questioned and allows the appointment of an external expert to assess a person's job against another nominated one with the same employer. This has led to a greater awareness of the ways in which definitions of skill are gender-biased. One study of experts' reports showed that there was very little consistency in the criteria employed and that the comparison of jobs was far from objective (Plumer 1992). Research in North America and Australia (where 'comparable worth' has a longer history) continues to demonstrate the difficulty of producing a gender neutral system and the limitations of this approach to equal pay (Burton 1991; Kahn and Meehan 1992).

Appraisal and performance related pay

Attempts to assess individuals' abilities or performance have also been subject to claims that their methods reflect wider social values. Appraisal systems raise many similar issues to those discussed under selection techniques above. The more informal the appraisal system, the greater the opportunity for bias to enter. Even when a person is being assessed against specific criteria it is possible for views of the characteristics and abilities of different social groups to affect a manager's perceptions of an individual's abilities (Townley 1990).

Unlike most selection situations, an appraiser will generally have knowledge of the appraisee over a considerable period of time. This should be valuable in overcoming the 'instant' judgements made in selection decisions. However, greater familiarity does not seem to necessarily lead to any greater objectivity. A recent study of assessment linked to performance related pay found that managers of both sexes valued different attributes in men and women (Bevan and Thompson 1992). Those attributes tended to be ones that reinforced gender stereotypes. This led to different merit awards for men and women – though not always to women's disadvantage. They also found some cases where jobs which were sex-typed as male were associated with higher than average merit increases and vice versa. Ethnic minority workers on London Underground won a case where they argued that the assessment process in their performance related pay scheme was discriminatory (Sage 1993).

Problems with Equal Opportunity Policy in Practice

The coexistence of anti-discrimination legislation, equal opportunities policies, and continuing evidence of differential experiences of the employment relation on the basis of social group membership suggests that there are some problems with the approaches commonly used to counter inequality. A number of explanations have been suggested. A fundamental question is whether the dominant 'liberal' approach is the right way to proceed or whether there is a need to try the 'radical' approach, or something entirely different.

For those who accept the validity of the 'liberal' approach, attention is usually focused on the need for a more effective approach to policy implementation as the best way forward.

At the most fundamental level this could just be a matter of doing the same things in a more committed manner: underlining the importance of senior management support for the EO policy, the need for more thorough monitoring of managers' behaviour, the need for comprehensive training, and the availability of resources to support the policy. Such approaches are common within the pre-scriptive management literature (for example, Coussey and Jackson 1991).

Other accounts show a greater understanding of the factors which make implementation difficult. One of these, the deep-seated nature of gender stereotyping and bias, has already been touched on in the discussion of selection and appraisal. Three other areas are particularly important: the relationship between line managers and personnel; the conflicts between EO and other priorities facing managers; and resistance from employees.

The primary responsibility for the implementation of EO tends to rest within the personnel department. However, many studies have shown that personnel managers are a relatively powerless group. The study by Collinson et al. (1990) demonstrates the significance of this for implementing equality measures in the recruitment and selection process. Personnel managers failed to intervene when line managers pursued lines of questioning, or proposed to make selection decisions, which contravened either the law or their policy guidelines. Personnel tended to defer to line managers on the grounds that line managers had a better understanding of their job needs, that personnel did not want to be blamed for imposing a decision which later turned out to be wrong, or because they needed to establish their legitimacy within the management structure by concurring with line managers' perceptions and priorities. Legge (1978) has discussed in a broader sense the problems personnel managers have in establishing power within organizations either through, or in distinction to, existing organizational goals. Elsewhere, she has pointed to another dimension of the problem: that personnel management is a predominantly female profession (Legge 1987).

Conflicts between management priorities raise other important problems for the implementation of equal opportunities. The choice between formal and informal methods of recruitment demonstrates these issues clearly. Informal methods have been shown to risk discrimination and all EO guides recommend a formalized approach whereby job descriptions are clearly drawn up, the post is externally advertised, and candidates are assessed systematically against predefined criteria. However, such an approach can be extremely time-consuming and costly. For a manager losing production because of staff shortages, or working on a fixed budget, such considerations are unlikely to be important. It may be particularly galling if the manager has to advertise externally when he or she believes they have a perfectly competent internal person who could be appointed. Or if they risk upsetting the goodwill of their current workforce by changing the practice whereby current employees' relatives are given preferential consideration for posts.

Similar conflicts could occur over a choice between a payment system based on equal value considerations and one based on market rates. Clearly, the degree of conflict experienced and the likely outcome will be affected by both internal and external factors and is likely to change over time. For example, in times of labour shortage managers may be less hostile to EO approaches to recruitment (Mahon 1989). This argument suggests that line managers may not be simply for or against equal opportunities. In some situations they may find it acceptable or may even be favourably disposed towards it. In other cases they may find it objectionable. Such ambiguity has also been shown to extend to workforce reactions to EO.

It is perhaps obvious that groups who currently have a dominant position within the workforce are likely to feel threatened by EO initiatives. Those who have been successful in gaining jobs and progressing up organizational hierarchies are likely to feel that they have achieved their positions as a result of their own merits. They may be quite happy for other individuals to do the same regardless of their gender or ethnicity but may be concerned about EO policies which they see as giving these groups 'special help'. A study of the London Fire Brigade demonstrated this way of reasoning. Firemen argued that if women and black people were able to make as good firefighters as white men they would already have been appointed; a change of procedures that increased the representation of these groups must therefore be about lowering the standards for some people (Salaman 1986). Such a view fails to understand that the pre-existing procedures were not operating in a neutral way.

Resistance can also be met from employees whom one would expect to welcome EO initiatives. Jewson and Mason (1986b) describe a situation where Asian employees objected to the discontinuation of an extended internal labour market which had been previously operating in their favour. Cockburn (1991) draws attention to the presence within many workforces of groups with different priorities for EO policies. In one case, ethnic minorities who were under-represented in an organization favoured a move towards external recruitment at all levels. Some white women in the same organization argued that since women were concentrated at the bottom of the hierarchy the development of internal promotion routes would be of particular benefit to them.

Whether one regards such factors as evidence of the need for more thoroughgoing implementation of existing EO approaches or as evidence of the need for a different approach perhaps depends on how intractable the problems are seen to be. In all cases, however, it is possible to think of organizational responses that might reduce the scale of the problem. Restructuring, including the allocation of responsibilities, the seniority at which appointments are made, and so on can affect the power balance between personnel and line managers. Building equality targets into the assessment of managers' performance might increase managers' commitment, and other approaches might reduce the significance of other priorities. North American experience with contract compliance certainly provides some evidence for this (IPM 1987). Forms of employee involvement and the development of an organizationally specific approach to EO might reduce employees' concerns.

Other difficulties which have been highlighted in relation to current EO approaches seem less amenable to change. At the heart of EO approaches is an attempt to control managers' behaviour by tightly specifying how they *should* carry out certain tasks and monitoring, whether they do or not. A whole range of studies have shown that managers are very adept at finding ways round such controls (Jewson and Mason 1986b; Collinson et al. 1990; Burton 1991). The wider literature on bureaucracy as a form of control suggests that such problems are not overcome by simply imposing more rules and checks (see chapter 1). Nor does it seem to be the result of a culture where there is a general disregard for EO issues. Liff and Dale's (1994) research in an organization with a high degree of commitment to EO still found cases where managers simply ignored the rules and justified their behaviour on the grounds of operational difficulties. In other, more subtle, cases managers appeared to distort selection criteria or to apply discretionary aspects of the policy selectively to achieve a preferred appointment. It is possible that in some cases managers were actively hostile to EO, but it seems more likely that they objected to procedures that made it difficult for them to make a decision they believed to be right. It is hard to see how the 'radical' approach which implies even stronger constraints on management action would overcome these problems.

Such findings are perhaps consistent with another criticism that is made of EO approaches: that they attempt to change behaviour without tackling underlying prejudicial attitudes or addressing underlying reasons for inequality. Some approaches to EO have attempted to change attitudes and beliefs through the medium of awareness training. However, racism awareness training, in particular, is often delivered in a confrontational way. While some organizations continue to include it as a significant aspect of their policy, most do not give it much prominence. Yet there are a number of reasons for thinking that it is important. Instructions, included in many codes of practice, not to discriminate suggest that such behaviour is a conscious act. Research, described above, has shown that discriminatory judgements are embedded in, for example, the selection assessment process in a far more subtle way. Unless people understand the nature of their prejudices and the ways in which these affect their judgement, then it is arguable that equality initiatives will have only a limited effect. An understanding of these processes might also reduce people's resistance to EO approaches which might otherwise be seen simply as bureaucratic encumbrances.

Critics of both the liberal and radical approaches, discussed earlier (Webb and Liff 1988; Cockburn 1989), suggest a different way forward. They point out that conventional EO approaches concentrate on trying to ensure that all candidates are assessed equally without acknowledging that social advantages and disadvantages mean that candidates are not equally able to demonstrate their ability to do a job. For example, requiring that candidates have a degree is likely to disadvantage older people and members of some ethnic minority groups, both of whom have had less opportunities for higher education. This way of assessing merit may be appropriate when specific knowledge is a job requirement. However, it will often be just an indication that a job requires particular abilities of decision-making which could be demonstrated in some other way. Although organizations which are actively promoting positive action have addressed such issues there is little encouragement to most to do so.

Neither do dominant EO approaches acknowledge that job requirements often structure the competition in favour of some groups rather than others. For example, if a woman is refused a job for which she is qualified because she wants to work part-time so that she can look after a child or elderly relative, should we classify this as discrimination? Many people would regard the fact that women are more likely to take time off to look after children than men, or need to leave work to pick up children from school rather than staying to do overtime, as reflecting a personal choice between the woman and her partner about how to organize their households. As such, it could be argued that any consequences that follow in terms of fewer opportunities in the workplace could hardly be attributed to discrimination on the part of managers. However, an alternative perspective would say that full-time work has only become the norm because it developed around male patterns of work and behaviour that have just been assumed to be a necessary part of the job or an objective way of assessing ability. Such approaches can be described as institutional discrimination, indicating that disadvantage is built into organizational structures and practices. Again, current EO approaches allow organizations to respond to these issues but they are not part of mainstream practice.

Future Opportunities?

Is there any evidence that changed circumstances will lead to a change in the experiences of disadvantaged groups or that new approaches to equality will provide improved opportunities? The significance of the broader economic context has already been noted. Current approaches to EO are structured around improving access to vacancies. As such, they are particularly ineffective in a recession. There is no theoretical reason why radical restructuring associated with cutbacks and mergers should not provide an opportunity to rethink occupational boundaries in a way which breaks down gender and ethnic divisions. However, there is no evidence of this happening in practice. In the absence of such evidence it would appear that improved economic circumstances combined with demographic trends which suggest an underlying labour shortage offer the best context for improved opportunities.

There has been much debate, and little agreement, about new approaches to the management of labour. Little of this has touched on the issue of equal opportunities and many of its themes seem to have contradictory implications. The groups considered in this chapter have, for the most part, been excluded from, or relatively poorly served by, collective bargaining. In that sense, a decline in collective bargaining is, as chapter 18 shows, probably of less relevance than the decline in state controls over management practice in the form of wages councils. Moreover, few members of disadvantaged groups are likely to be in a position to benefit from the individual contracts discussed in chapter 11. A decline in collectivism has other contradictory implications. On the one hand it could signal a recognition of different needs and interests within the workforce – a positive development for equal opportunities. But carried further it could lead to a denial of collective bases for disadvantage.

The devolution of responsibility for human resource issues from personnel specialists to line managers seems a more straightforwardly negative development for EO. Personnel managers have developed considerable expertise in this area and have had a clear interest in it having a high profile (Young 1989). In contrast, the majority of line managers are likely to have neither the expertise nor the commitment to pursue EO. But even here it is possible to envisage circumstances in which the increasing role for line managers could be advantageous for equal opportunities. If line managers take responsibility for human resource issues then EO may be treated more seriously by the organization than when promoted by marginalized personnel managers. Thus, in circumstances where line managers have something to gain from EO it may be pursued more effectively than in the past. Line managers' central role might also reduce some of the implementation problems discussed above, such as conflicting priorities and rule avoidance.

If human resource issues achieve a more strategic role within organizations then this could also be positive for equal opportunities. As we have seen, current approaches suffer from being fragmented and marginalized. Equal opportunities pervades all aspects of employment and if the EO implications of policies were systematically assessed as they were developed this could well be more effective than an attempt to maintain a separate EO policy. However, this is to assume that EO would be considered a strategic issue. Currently, for many organizations, it is not clear where the motivation would come from to give it this priority, particularly in the absence of legislative pressures.

There is some evidence of a new approach developing towards EO which draws on some dimensions of the 'new industrial relations'. This is variously described as valuing or managing diversity (for example, Greenslade 1991; Jackson 1992). Whereas conventional EO approaches try to ignore or minimize differences between members of different social groups, the diversity approach suggests that there are positive aspects to difference. Employees from different social groups can bring different perspectives and skills to the workforce. Recruiting and retaining them will involve recognizing and responding to their differing needs. This is most commonly argued with respect to ethnic minority workers in the United States, where it is suggested that they might bring knowledge of new markets, customer groups and so on. However, it has also been suggested that women managers might manage in a different style that might be particularly appropriate to some organizations (for example, Rosener 1990).

Some organizations in Britain are beginning to use the term 'diversity' instead of 'equal opportunities' when describing their programmes. However, it is not yet clear whether this signals a significant change of approach. As we have seen in this chapter equal opportunities policies have had only limited success in bringing equality to organizations, whether this is defined in the 'liberal' equal treatment sense, or the 'radical' equal outcomes sense. Where 'diversity' could prove a positive way forward would be if it led to an increased questioning of the skilled white man as the archetypical worker against whom all other workers are judged. Equal opportunities could then be less about adjusting the rest of us to rules based on his abilities and behaviour and more about restructuring the rules to reflect the reality of the current British workforce.

References

Beechey, V. and Perkins, T. 1987: *A Matter of Hours*. Cambridge: Polity Press.

Berry-Lound, D. 1990: *Work and the Family: Carer-friendly Employment Practices*. London: Institute of Personnel Management.

Bevan, S. and Thompson, M. 1992: *Merit Pay, Performance Appraisal and Attitudes to Women's Work*. IMS Report 234. Brighton: Institute of Manpower Studies.

Bradley, H. 1989: *Men's Work, Women's Work*. Cambridge: Polity Press.

Brown, C. and Gay, P. 1985: *Racial Discrimination: 17 Years after the Act*. London: Policy Studies Institute.

Bruegel, I. 1989: Sex and Race in the Labour Market. *Feminist Review*, 32, Summer, 49–68.

Bulletin 1993: *Bulletin on Women and Employment in the EC*, 2, April.

Burton, C. 1991: *The Promise and the Price.* Sydney: Allen & Unwin Australia.

Cameron, I. 1987: Realising the Dividends from Positive Action. *Personnel Management*, October, 62–7.

Chambers, G. and Horton, C. 1990: *Promoting Sex Equality.* London: Policy Studies Institute.

Cockburn, C. 1989: Equal Opportunities: The Short and the Long Agenda. *Industrial Relations Journal*, 20, 3, 213–25.

Cockburn, C. 1991: *In the Way of Women.* Basingstoke: Macmillan.

Coe, T. 1992: *The Key to the Men's Club.* Corby: Institute of Management.

Colling, T. and Dickens, L. 1989: *Equality Bargaining – Why Not?* London: HMSO.

Collinson, D. L., Knights, D. and Collinson, M. 1990: *Managing to Discriminate.* London: Routledge.

Coussey, M. and Jackson, H. 1991: *Making Equal Opportunities Work.* London: Pitman.

CRE (Commission for Racial Equality) 1983: *Code of Practice.* London: HMSO.

Curran, M. 1988: Gender and Recruitment, People and Places in the Labour Market. *Work, Employment and Society*, 2, 3, 335–51.

Dex, S. 1987: *Women's Occupational Mobility.* Basingstoke: Macmillan.

Deakin, N. 1970: *Colour, Citizenship and British Society.* London: Panther Books.

Dickens, L. 1992: Anti-Discrimination Legislation: Exploring and Explaining the Impact on Women's Employment. In W. McCarthy (ed.), *Legal Intervention in Industrial Relations: Gains and Losses.* Oxford: Blackwell.

Duleep, H. O. and Sanders, S. 1992: Discrimination at the Top: American Born Asian and White Men. *Industrial Relations*, 31, 3, 416–32.

Employers' Forum on Disability 1992: *Monitoring People with Disabilities in the Workforce.* London: Employers' Forum on Disability.

Employment Gazette 1993a: Industrial and Employment Appeal Tribunal Statistics 1991–2 and 1992–3. *Employment Gazette*, November, 527–31.

Employment Gazette 1993b: Ethnic Origins and the Labour Market. *Employment Gazette*, February, 25–37.

Employment Gazette 1993c: Women in the Labour Market. *Employment Gazette*, November, 483–502.

Employment Gazette 1994a: Table 1.4 Employees in Employment GB. *Employment Gazette*, January, S12–S13.

Employment Gazette 1994b: Table 2.2 Claimant Unemployment GB. *Employment Gazette*, March, S15.

EOC (Equal Opportunities Commission) 1985a: Sex Discrimination Decisions. No. 4: Selection for Redundancy (part-time workers). The Case of Clarke and Powell v. Eley (IMI) Kynock Ltd. Manchester: Equal Opportunities Commission.

EOC (Equal Opportunities Commission) 1985b: *Code of Practice*. London: HMSO.

EOC (Equal Opportunities Commission) 1985c: *Job Evaluation Schemes Free of Sex Bias*. Manchester: Equal Opportunities Commission.

EOC (Equal Opportunities Commission) 1988: *Behind the Fringe*. Manchester: Equal Opportunities Commission.

Faludi, S. 1992: *Backlash: The Undeclared War against Women*. London: Chatto and Windus.

Fryer, P. 1984: *Staying Power: Black People in Britain Since 1504*. Atlantic Highlands, USA: Humanities Press Inc.

Greenslade, M. 1991: Managing Diversity: Lessons from the United States. *Personnel Management*, December, 28–33.

Gregory, J. 1992: Equal Pay for Work of Equal Value: The Strengths and Weaknesses of Legislation. *Work, Employment and Society*, September, 461–73.

Hunt, A. 1975: *Management Attitudes and Practices towards Women at Work*. London: HMSO.

IPM (Institute of Personnel Management) 1987: *Contract Compliance*. London: Institute of Personnel Management.

Jackson, B. 1992: Diversity. *Human Resource Management*, 31, 1/2, 21–34.

Jenkins, R. 1986: *Racism and Recruitment: Managers, Organisations and Equal Opportunity in the Labour Market*. Cambridge: Cambridge University Press.

Jewson, N. and Mason, D. 1986a: The Theory and Practice of Equal Opportunities Policies: Liberal and Radical Approaches. *Sociological Review*, 34, 2, 307–34.

Jewson, N. and Mason, D. 1986b: Modes of Discrimination in the Recruitment Process: Formalisation, Fairness and Efficiency. *Sociology*, 20, 1, 43–63.

Jewson, N., Mason, D., Waters, S. and Harvey, J. 1990: *Ethnic Minorities and Employment Practice*. Department of Employment Research Paper, No. 76. London: Department of Employment.

Kahn, P. and Meehan, E. (eds) 1992: *Equal Value / Comparable Worth in the UK and the USA*. London: Macmillan.

Kiernan, K. 1992: Men and Women at Work and at Home. In R. Jowell et al. (eds), *British Social Attitudes: the 9th Report*. Aldershot: Dartmouth.

Legge, K. 1978: *Power Innovation and Problem-solving in Personnel Management*. Maidenhead: McGraw-Hill.

Legge, K. 1987: Women in Personnel Management: Uphill Climb Or Downhill Slide? In A. Spencer and D. Podmore (eds), *In a Man's World*. London: Tavistock.

Leonard, A. 1987: *Judging Inequality*. London: The Cobden Trust.

Liff, S. 1991: Part-time Workers: Current Contradictions and Future Opportunities. In M. Davidson and J. Earnshaw (eds), *Vulnerable Workers: Psychosocial and Legal Issues*. Chichester: Wiley.

Liff, S. and Dale, K. 1994: Formal Opportunity, Informal Barriers: Black Women Managers within a Local Authority. *Work Employment and Society*, 8, 2, 177–98.

Lodge, D. 1987: Working Equality into Manual Job Evaluation. *Personnel Management*, September, 27–31.

Mahon, T. 1989: When Line Managers Welcome Equal Opportunities. *Personnel Management*, October, 76–9.

Marginson, P., Armstrong, P., Edwards, P. K. and Purcell, J. with Hubbard, N. 1993: *The Control of Industrial Relations in Large Companies: An Initial Analysis of the Second Company Level Industrial Relations Survey.* Warwick Papers in Industrial Relations, 45. Coventry: Industrial Relations Research Unit.

Millward, N. and Stevens, M. 1986: *British Workplace Industrial Relations, 1980–84.* Aldershot: Gower.

Morris, J. 1983: *No More Peanuts.* London: National Council for Civil Liberties.

Naylor, P. 1987: In Praise of Older Workers. *Personnel Management*, November, 44–8.

NEDO (National Economic Development Office) 1990: *Women Managers: The Untapped Resource.* London: NEDO.

O'Donovan, K. and Szyszczak, E. 1988: *Equality and Sex Discrimination Law.* Oxford: Blackwell.

OPCS (Office of Population Censuses and Surveys) 1988: *The Prevalence of Disability Among Adults.* Surveys of Disability in Great Britain, No. 1. London: HMSO.

Plumer, A. 1992: *Equal-value Judgements: Objective Assessment or Lottery?* Warwick Papers in Industrial Relations, 40. Coventry: Industrial Relations Research Unit.

PMP 1992: Discrimination against Disability Continues. *Personnel Management Plus*, June.

Power, M. and Rosenberg, S. 1993: Black Female Clerical Workers: Movement towards Equality with White Women? *Industrial Relations*, 32, 2, 223–37.

Rosener, J. 1990: Ways Women Lead. *Harvard Business Review*, November/December, 119–25.

Rubery, J. and Fagan, C. 1993: Women as a Flexible Reserve?: Gender and Country Specificities in the Organisation of Employment. Paper presented to the Labour Process Conference, March.

Sage, A. 1993: Tube Staff Win Discrimination Award. *Independent*, 6 April.

Salaman, G. 1986: *Working.* London: Tavistock.

Sefton, R. 1993: Patterns of Pay: Results from the 1993 New Earnings Survey. *Employment Gazette*, November, 515–22.

Summerfield, P. 1989: *Women Workers in the Second World War.* London: Routledge.

Tillsley, C. 1990: *The Impact of Age upon Employment*. Warwick Papers in Industrial Relations, 33. Coventry: Industrial Relations Research Unit.

Townley, B. 1990: A Discriminating Approach to Appraisal. *Personnel Management*, December, 34–7.

Walby, S. 1983: *Patriarchy at Work*. Cambridge: Polity Press.

Webb, J. and Liff, S. 1988: Play the White Man: The Social Construction of Fairness and Competition in Equal Opportunity Policies. *Sociological Review*, 36, 3, 543–51.

Wells, B. 1989: The Labour Market for Young and Older Workers. *Employment Gazette*, June, 319–33.

Wild, A. 1986: Realistic Expectations of Equal Opportunities. *Personnel Management*, October, 45–50.

Wood, R. and Baron, H. 1992: Psychological Testing Free from Prejudice. *Personnel Management*, December, 34–7.

Young, K. 1989: The Space between Words: Local Authorities and the Concept of Equal Opportunities. In R. Jenkins and J. Solomos (eds), *Racism and Equal Opportunity Policies in the 1980s*, 2nd edn. Cambridge: Cambridge University Press.

16

Privatization and Marketization

Trevor Colling and Anthony Ferner

The reduction in the role of the public sector has been one of the most notable features of the political programme of Thatcherism. It has taken two basic forms: 'privatization' and 'marketization'. Under the first, most of the major public corporations have been sold off, usually through flotation on the stock exchange. As described in chapter 10, the second involves attempts to introduce competitive pressures and managerial disciplines, in the form of 'internal markets', 'executive agencies' and 'compulsory competitive tendering', into the non-traded public services.

The reform of the public sector can be seen partially as a mechanism for 'forcing management to manage'. Conservative critics have maintained that public managers were caught in a cleft stick: on the one hand, there was a pattern of pervasive government interference in managerial issues, including areas of industrial relations such as pay, conflict and working practices (Thompson and Beaumont 1978; Ferner 1988; Beaumont 1991); on the other, managers were constrained by the dead weight of supposedly monopolistic and over-powerful public-sector unions whose influence impinged on areas of managerial prerogative (for example, Veljanovski 1987: 62–4). Thus privatization and marketization would force public managers to refocus their attention, away from other public-sector actors and towards the more impersonal forces of 'the market'.

This chapter examines the consequences of privatization and marketization for industrial relations. It will be argued that the cold wind of 'market forces' has altered the traditional values and priorities of public employers, with profound, though ambiguous, consequences for industrial relations. The Whitley-based traditions of the public sector have given way to more individualized industrial relations; unions are weaker and the agenda of change is increasingly dictated by the managers of marketized public service units and of privatized companies.

Privatization: The Background

This section considers the programme of reform in the public sector generally referred to as privatization. Distinctions are drawn between the flotation of public enterprises and the commercialization of public services. Although the intention in each case has been similar, to expose organizations to competition, the form and nature of the processes have been different.

Public enterprises

Curiously, the privatization programme which now forms such a key part of the legacy of 'Thatcherism' evolved in a piecemeal, incremental way. Sell-offs of government shares, largely in companies such as British Petroleum or Cable and Wireless that already operated as private enterprises, took place in the early years of the Conservative government. But it was not until 1984 that the first major sale of a 'core' public utility took place with the flotation of British Telecom (BT). Thereafter, as table 16.1 shows, large-scale privatizations followed thick and fast.

Table 16.1 Major privatizations of public
enterprises, 1979–1993

1984	British Telecom
1986	British Gas
1987	British Airports Authority
	British Airways
1988	British Steel
1989	Regional water authorities
	(England and Wales only)
1990	Regional electricity companies
	(England and Wales Only)
1991	Electricity generating companies
	(England and Wales only)
1992	Scottish electricity companies

In addition, the nationalized ports and the shipbuilding industry (what remained of it following its catastrophic decline) were sold off piecemeal during the 1980s. So too were dozens of minor companies, many of them former subsidiaries of large public corporations like British Rail, whose catering, ferry, hovercraft and engineering subsidiaries were all 'hived off'. By 1991, the total nationalized industry workforce had fallen to 501,000, well under a third of the 1979 figure of 1,849,000.

Of the major trading enterprises in state hands at the beginning of the 1980s, only the railways, the coal mines and the postal services remained in 1993. In all of these, there were plans for total or partial privatization in the short to medium term.

Managers in the old public corporations were subject to formal ministerial powers to set objectives, approve investment and borrowing, and appoint board members. In addition, they faced a complex array of direct and indirect informal political influences, with ministers often engaging in behind-the-scenes 'arm-twisting' and 'bargaining' with public-sector managers. The privatized enterprises face an environment of decision-making very different from this highly politicized public-sector model, with far-reaching implications for the culture of industrial relations.

First, with the ending of ministerial supervision, privatized companies now have a whole new constituency to satisfy: their shareholders. This has produced a novel set of influences on managerial behaviour. The impact of decisions on share prices and 'investor expectations' has now been integrated into managerial calculations, creating pressure for changes in the culture of management and in industrial relations. It has led, for example, to the widespread abandonment of one of the characteristic features of the public enterprise sector, collective bargaining for managerial staff (see below). Shareholder pressures have also frequently provided a convenient rationale for managers seeking changes in relations with employees and unions.

Second, direct political control has been replaced by a framework of regulation for the major privatized utilities (gas, water, electricity, telecommunications). The industries' regulators have powers to oversee prices, competition and quality of service. Other state competition agencies have a role in supervising the operations of the new companies. One of the major functions of the regulator is to set the formula determining permissible price increases in the 'controlled' portion of a utility's market. The control is seen as a spur to cost reduction, since profitability cannot be increased by further price increases (Ferner and Colling 1991). In theory, at least, political control has been minimized, though governments continue to exert indirect influence through the remit of the regulator. Moreover, the political ramifications of major service defects can still be a potent factor swaying management decision-making in the core utilities. For the unregulated privatized companies – British Steel, for example – privatization has curtailed the influence of politicians over key investment decisions. As a nationalized industry, BSC had been forced by ministers to reverse a decision to scrap the major steelworks at Ravenscraig in Scotland; after privatization, the company was able to ignore the pressures of ministers and closed the works.

Third, privatization has gone hand-in-hand with changes in the competitive structure of previously monopolistic industries. The most striking example is electricity generation. The old nationalized Central Electricity Generating Board was split into competing generating companies and new entrants into the industry were encouraged under the regulatory framework. Even in state monopolies, such as telecommunications and gas, which were privatized as single organizations, a dominant market position has been eroded by new competitive forces, with the regulator playing a key role in promoting change; there has been speculation about the break-up of British Gas. This too has given added urgency to management attempts to refashion their personnel and industrial relations strategies.

Fourth, privatization has meant an end to statutory limits on the activities of privatized companies. They are now free to diversify into new sectors and to expand internationally. With the 'core' activities of the utilities restricted by regulation and competition, diversification makes increasing sense. BT and British Gas, for example, see themselves as actors on the global telecommunications and energy markets. In many cases, expansion has been through acquisition of companies with different personnel and industrial relations traditions, or through greenfield ventures, allowing management to make radical departures from the inheritance of public-sector industrial relations.

A logical consequence of diversification has been the reshaping of organizational structures towards more devolved forms of management such as subsidiaries or 'divisions' organized along business lines. For example, the retail services business of some regional electricity suppliers has been formed into separate companies, as have the ancillary services of water companies. Business units appear to have increasing autonomy over operational matters, including industrial relations.

Decentralization of authority has also been a common feature of the core activities of the privatized companies as corporate strategists have sought ways of changing from old-style bureaucratic structures of service delivery to more entrepreneurial and flexible forms. Thus line managers in power stations, gas supply and telecommunications districts, or steel product divisions have been encouraged to think of themselves as running 'mini-businesses' with responsibility for 'bottom line' performance. They have generally been handed greater powers to run their own operations, with greater control over budgets, staffing and industrial relations.

Public services

As described in chapter 10, the government has, since the late 1980s, introduced a battery of reforms which have 'marketized' public service management: 'compulsory competitive tendering' (CCT); 'market-testing', through which public employers are obliged to allow private contractors to bid for the right to carry out specified services; internal markets in education and health, to encourage competition among 'opted out' schools and among hospitals constituted as 'self-governing trusts'; and the creation of executive central government agencies which function as semi-autonomous management units. This new and still emerging environment has dramatically altered the framework for managerial decision-making with particular consequences for industrial relations. First, as in privatized enterprises, the potential for political pressure has been significantly reduced. A common feature has been the concept of arm's-length operation, removing the day-to-day management of organizations from policymakers. At national level, agencies are empowered to develop their own operations and procedures independently of ministers and government departments. At local level too, contractors are under no obligation to observe the employment policy of the local authority from which they win work. Policies relating to low pay, equal opportunities and the creation of employment have all been substantially weakened as a consequence.

Second, there has been an associated decentralization of managerial authority, particularly over areas of finance and personnel policy. The creation of agencies, self-governing trusts and grant maintained schools all resulted in devolution from departments within central and local government to chief executives and from there down the line to more junior levels. Such trends are increasingly accompanied by the decentralization of bargaining and consultation arrangements.

Third, there has been a shift in the focus of public service managers from a preoccupation with the concerns of the workforce to the those of the customer (Ridley 1988; Harden 1992; Heery 1992). Competition is partly responsible: managers newly dependent on work secured through contracts have discovered the importance of customer relations. This has given rise to a focus on treating the public (previously 'clients', 'residents', 'patients', etc.) as 'customers', an approach codified in the government's Citizen's Charter (Cabinet Office 1991) which requires the setting and monitoring of performance standards. The Charter has since been supplemented by other charters for particular services and the establishment of a central unit to oversee their development. This drive for quality often has direct implications for labour which range from the apparently trivial (the wearing of name badges, for example) to the fundamental, such as the need to meet deadlines for responses to inquiries and complaints which impinge directly upon the organization of work.

The Consequences for Industrial Relations

The combined pressures of regulation, increasing competition, and greater commercial freedom described above have been powerful forces for change in the arena of industrial relations. This section discusses the changes that have taken place in privatized companies and public services, beginning with the general impact on employment.

Trends in employment

It is often difficult to establish a direct link between changes in industrial relations and privatization or 'marketization'. In the area of employment change, for example, many water companies reduced their workforces *prior* to privatization in response to financial pressures. Job reduction in BT has also been prompted by technological change which may have been intensified by privatization but which would have proceeded regardless. In the public services, it is almost impossible to disentangle the effects of marketization from those of other administrative and policy initiatives, whose continuing budgetary pressure would undoubtedly have prompted reductions.

That said, there have been very significant falls in employment in privatized companies and in marketized public services, as table 16.2 details. BT, for example, after increasing its workforce slightly in the late 1980s to a peak of 246,000, cut it very sharply in the early 1990s. In a few cases, however, workforces have risen, as a result of merger or diversification: Thames Water, for example, increased from 7,900 at privatization in 1989 to 10,400 in 1993. A marked phenomenon was the increase in the non-UK workforce of companies like British Airways, British Gas and British Steel. British Steel, for example, had around 4,500 foreign employees as a result of post-privatization acquisitions.

In the public services, compulsory competitive tendering has led to significant reductions in workforces. It is estimated that 111,000 health service jobs, amounting to 40 per cent of the manual workforce, have been cut since tendering was introduced in 1983 (LRD 1991; PSPRU, 1992). Yet the greatest reductions in public service employment have been registered in the civil service and have not been dependent upon competitive pressures. Ministers, intent on reducing the size of the entire public sector, found it relatively easy to drive through reductions in civil service costs and employment (see chapter 10).

Table 16.2 Employment in selected privatized companies (thousands)

Company	1980	At privatization	1993
British Airways	56.9	40.7 (1987)	49.0
British Gas	104.4	89.8 (1986)	74.5
British Steel	166.0	53.7 (1988)	46.0
British Telecom	240.1	241.1 (1984)	170.7
National Power	[a]	14.5 (1991)	7.4
PowerGen	[a]	8.8 (1991)	4.9
Regional electricity companies	95.7	82.4 (1990)	82.3 (1992)

[a] Part of former unified Central Electricity Generating Board, with a total of 48,000 staff in 1980.

Changes in collective bargaining and consultation

The public sector generally, including the nationalized industries, typically had very elaborate machineries of negotiation and consultation, through which the unions exercised pervasive influence over a wide range of operational matters such as staffing levels, working practices, career structures, job mobility and pay systems, in addition to basic pay and conditions. These formal structures went hand-in-hand with a public-sector culture of change by consent, a presumption that matters would be progressed through the machinery until they had been comprehensively dealt with.

Public-sector management came to see this culture as increasingly burdensome and as a source of procrastination. In the privatized sector, commercial considerations were a powerful force for change. In most privatized companies, there have been pressures for reform of bargaining, allied to a more aggressive, confrontational managerial style.

A similar pattern of reassessment has been evident in the public services. As expenditure constraints began to bite it became increasingly difficult to coordinate bargaining and consultation at national level with the budgeting processes within employer units. Government funding decisions included assumptions about annual increases in pay. Where these were outstripped in actual negotiations employers were obliged to balance their budgets by adjusting service levels or through increased efficiency. The pressures generated by these processes led employers to seek greater flexibility in negotiating structures and collective agreements.

But the pace of change in formal structures has been relatively slow and uneven in the public services. Privatizing companies have often sought 'once and for all' change, sometimes because structural change required it, or in order to send strong signals to unions and workforces about relationships in newly commercial contexts (as in the water industry). While, informally, bargaining perspectives and behaviour have been similar, public service bargaining structures have been subject to much more gradual and incremental reform.

Decentralization and rationalization of bargaining structures There has been a general trend to break up integrated national bargaining structures and to move towards arrangements focusing upon the company and/or the business unit, but such moves have been driven by different motives and pursued with varying enthusiasm.

First, in the multi-firm industries – water and electricity – there has been a reluctance to sit at the same bargaining (or consultation) table as commercial rivals (and in some cases customers), and a desire to develop structures appropriate to their individual corporate strategies and managerial style. The outcome has been a considerable divergence in bargaining arrangements from company to company.

In water, some decentralization of the national machinery predated privatization, giving individual water authorities control over matters such as bonus and productivity schemes. The announcement of the industry's sale accelerated the break-up of national bargaining by providing 'an opportunity to further a more imaginative approach toward pay and conditions of employment', according to a representative of Welsh Water (*IRRR* (*Industrial Relations Review and Report*) 516, July 1992: 7).[1]

The national structure of union representation in electricity broke up following privatization. The privatized companies reached individual agreements with their unions on new structures, typically giving local management far greater flexibility to organize work to suit local circumstances (James 1992, 1993).

As suggested in chapter 10, the primary engine for change in health, education and central government has been increasing fragmentation and competition as a result of the introduction of internal markets and executive agencies. Indeed, it was the advantages of devolved participation and management that reformers most sought in introducing executive agencies into the civil service. While national structures remain in place, examples of devolved bargaining are increasing. In 1990, Her Majesty's Stationery Office (HMSO), one of the largest printers and publishers in Britain, became the first civil service agency to break away from national pay bargaining and establish its own pay structures (*IRRR* 484, March 1991: 6–10).

The second aspect of decentralization is that, within organizations, management has been pushing matters down to lower organizational levels (see Colling and Ferner 1992). This reflects the move to more devolved responsibilities, and the restructuring of companies and services along 'product division' lines. This devolution of representation has taken two forms. First, matters have been devolved from corporate level to individual business 'divisions', most notably in British Steel (Avis 1990) and British Telecom, where bargaining over pay and conditions now takes place *within* product divisions. Analogous arrangements are becoming common in local government. The CCT legislation requires that direct services establish trading accounts which demonstrate a rate of return. Given that, in addition, these services now compete for contracts in very diverse markets (the building cleaning market is very different from the catering market, for example) there are pressures for terms and conditions of employment to reflect the specific circumstances of the service.

These developments have had particular consequences for the role of corporate personnel specialists and their relationship with line managers. In local government, for example, personnel managers are increasingly operating as 'enablers' working from departmental level rather than as overseers of corporate policy (Kessler 1991). This emphasis on the personnel role of the line manager is underpinned by various systems of performance management incorporating individual employee appraisal, sometimes linked to pay. Agreements reached in the civil service, for example, abolish the past practice of automatic individual progression through pay scales. Instead, employees' performance is to be assessed by line managers who will then determine the level of performance bonus (*IRRR* 314, October 1992).

In many cases, organizations have taken advantage of the reform of structures to rationalize negotiating and consultation activity. One of the commonest changes has been the adoption, as in the private sector (see chapter 4), of 'single-table bargaining'; notable examples were in electricity, health, some local authorities, water and steel. Previously, it was normal for negotiations to take place in several separate machineries for manual, craft, white-collar and technical employees. The establishment of single representative bodies (often with both negotiating and consultative functions), has been prompted by a number of factors common to industry as a whole, notably the increasing flexibility of work organization and the blurring of occupational boundaries, the harmonization of manual and white-collar terms and conditions, reform of pay and grading structures, and the trend towards union mergers.

Union recognition and derecognition   In most cases, employee relations strategies have been built on the premise that the unions would continue to be the main representative body of the workforce. Even managers whose ideal world would be union-free have accepted that it is a goal unlikely to be achieved in practice. Privatized companies have found that union membership levels among the bulk of their staff have been sustained. Consequently, blanket derecognition of unions has been rare. Indeed, managers have chosen more often to negotiate change through trade union channels and to continue support for union organization.

None the less, the position of the unions has been weakened in a number of respects. First, the unions have been forced to react to aggressive managerial initiatives for change. The initiative for the break-up of the electricity and water industries' national negotiating machineries came primarily from management. Negotiations stemming from competitive tendering and the preparations for agency status have been driven by managers within very tight deadlines, with the consequence that union influence has often been minimized or absent altogether (Kessler 1991; Colling 1993a).

Second, there has been derecognition 'at the edges'. In the water industry, individual unions have lost their recognition for bargaining in certain companies: NALGO, the white-collar union, was derecognized in Northumbrian Water's holding company; NUPE, representing public-sector manual workers, was derecognized at Welsh Water. A number of BT's subsidiaries have refused to recognize unions for bargaining purposes. Elsewhere, the unions suspect that companies will use diversification out of their core activities as an opportunity for signing single-union deals in new companies, perhaps setting a precedent that may then be 'imported' into the core company. In the public services, compulsory competitive tendering has produced a growing trend towards *de facto* derecognition. Private contractors now have between 25 and 40 per cent of the market depending on the service yet very few formally recognize trade unions (PSPRU 1992). This trend can only spread as the private sector makes further inroads and as tendering is extended to more and more services.

Third, union influence on bargaining procedures has often been diluted. Northumbrian Water established a 'Company Council' in 1991 which provides only an 'advisory' role for unions. The main workforce representation on the Council is through employee councillors, one from each of the seven directly elected 'employee councils' based in the company's operating areas (*IRRR* 484, March 1991: 2). Similarly, many of the framework agreements for executive agencies within the civil service refer to consultation with 'trade unions and staff' or 'committees including trade unions'. Trusts moving to functional bargaining units are also allowing employees who are not union members to be elected onto committees.

Fourth, there has been 'creeping derecognition' of unionized managerial and professional staff. These groups were traditionally highly unionized in the public sector, and had their own collective bargaining arrangements. Now, it is increasingly considered inappropriate for managers to be trade union members. Again, explicit derecognition has been rare; the key mechanism has been the offer of personal or individual contracts often with terms more favourable than the existing collective agreements (see below). The practice is well established in health and local government but is probably most widespread in the electricity industry. The new company agreements in electricity formally exclude managers from collective bargaining. In BT, while the managerial unions retain a role, it has been severely reduced by the introduction of 'all-merit' pay rises for most managerial and professional staff (IRRR *Pay and Benefits Bulletin* 330, June 1993: 8–9).

Finally, new participative machineries have put a greater emphasis on direct forms of participation, reducing the centrality of union channels (for example, IPMS 1990). This has reflected management's wish to get across its own message about the need for a new corporate 'culture' to meet the demands of a more competitive commercial environment. Direct communication has also been linked with initiatives for team briefings, quality circles, and so on, and with new developments such as employee share schemes. The last of these has necessitated an increase in direct transmission of information to staff, not least since the successful achievement of mass employee shareholding has been an important symbol of the wider political objectives of privatization.

Such developments have led unions to complain of being bypassed and of receiving less information. Facilities agreements have been weakened and time off for union duties cut back. Full-time trade union representatives, previously common in the public services, are now being phased out. In some civil service agencies, limits of 50 per cent of the working week are being imposed. Some hospital trusts have said they will only negotiate with trade union representatives who are trust employees. This excludes full-time paid officials who would previously have expected to be fully involved in any major change. It also possibly excludes experienced lay representatives, as branch structures are often not based exclusively on one workplace or employer (*IRRR* 491, July 1991).

While there have been few radical moves to eradicate union-based forms of consultation, either in privatized companies or in the public services, survey and other evidence suggests that discussions are increasingly characterized by the assertion of managerial prerogative.

Kessler (1991) found that union involvement in ancillary services affected by tendering had either no impact or actually assisted change in over 80 per cent of cases. Case study evidence confirms this; indeed in some instances consultation with unions is only tolerated so long as it does not impede managerial action (Colling 1993a).

Reactions of the unions   Unions are facing significant challenges from these developments. It would be premature to suggest that the decline in union influence is terminal. Nevertheless, as highly centralized and bureaucratic organizations they have found it difficult to respond to restructuring and decentralization.

Unions have been slow to decentralize their own organizations. The large public-sector unions retain a substantial concentration of human and financial resources in their head offices in London. Organizational inertia provides one explanation; democratic organizations inevitably move more slowly than those based on hierarchical authority. But there have also been serious reservations about simply mimicking apparent trends. Most important among these is the potential loss of coherence and the growth of parochial, inward-looking workplace organization. Unions have consequently continued to emphasize the importance of central campaigns, information gathering and dissemination, which require the retention of resources at the centre.

This has left local negotiators exposed in the context of devolved bargaining and managerial authority. Full-time officers in the regions have experienced a rapid increase in workloads, and lay representatives in the workplace have been required to participate in much more significant negotiations than previously. Both have found negotiation increasingly difficult in the light of the increasing use of managerial prerogative described above. Most unions have responded by strengthening local organization. Branch restructuring has been a common development and there has been an increase in training and education for lay representatives. It is doubtful, however, whether these initiatives alone will ensure the long-term survival of unionism.

Some restructuring seems almost inevitable and may be delivered through union mergers, another common trend referred to earlier. Financial difficulties and the emergence of single-table bargaining have prompted the search for merger partners. The merger of NALGO, NUPE and COHSE in 1993 created Britain's largest trade union, Unison.

Unions have sought to assert new bargaining agendas. Unison, for example, is instructing negotiators to emphasize gender equality issues, a move designed to reinforce attempts to recruit within increasingly feminized workforces. The prospects for success, in a context of continuing retrenchment and cost cutting, are at best patchy.

Much more significant has been the rediscovery of legal action by unions in the light of the developing framework of European law. Thus the regime of competitive tendering and market testing has been profoundly undermined by union legal action based on the Acquired Rights Directive, which protects the terms and conditions of employees when there is a transfer of undertakings. The British government has always maintained that such regulations should not apply to the public sector and has made that explicit when drafting its own legislation (Transfer of Undertakings [Protection of Employment] Regulations 1981). Cases in the European Court have tested this narrow interpretation and provided the basis for legal challenges by unions in the domestic courts. If the Acquired Rights Directive does apply, then employers will be unable to realize savings from cutting labour costs. They will also have to alter radically current negotiating and consultation practice with recognized trade unions. Union emphasis on these points has dramatically affected employer strategies. In 1993 the Welsh Office was effectively forced to suspend tendering in the Welsh Health Authorities pending legal action. Many local authorities were assuming that TUPE regulations do apply and were including such stipulations in their contracts. Most significantly, agencies showed extreme caution in proceeding with the extension of market testing. The Inland Revenue announced its intention to protect employment conditions in its market testing programmes.

Though far from resolved, such developments may shore up union influence over important developments in the public sector and privatized companies. But it is the resilience and resourcefulness of lay structures at the workplace, and the capacity of unions to support them effectively, which will be the decisive factor in determining union influence in the future.

Work organization and flexibility

In most privatized companies and 'marketized' public service organizations, there has been extensive reorganization of the way work is done. As with employment losses, it is not always easy to attribute such changes to the consequences of privatization. For example, changes in working practice were a prominent feature of remaining public enterprises such as British Rail or British Coal throughout the 1980s (Pendleton and Winterton 1993). Similarly, changes in BT, for example, are significantly driven by a technological imperative regardless of ownership. In water, changes in work organization pre-dated the unveiling of a privatization plan for the industry (O'Connell Davidson 1990).

Yet the managerial and environmental changes described earlier do contribute specific pressures for change in how work is organized. First, the creation of a 'customer' culture in response to market pressures has driven management to seek ways of responding more flexibly to market demand. In the privatized utilities, such responsiveness is seen as necessary for avoiding the regulator's unwelcome attention, with its inherent threat of a stiffer competitive framework. Thus one of the commonest developments in recent years has been the reform of attendance patterns, in order to respond to operational demands, as in the case of the water industry (for example, *IRRR* 520, September 1992: 5), or to provide extended cover for customers, as in gas, electricity distribution, and most recently telecommunications. In 1993, BT's plans included the introduction of a scheduled weekday work span of 6 a.m. until 10 p.m. and routine weekend working.

Second, the decentralization of managerial authority has increased pressures for local adaptations in working practice to suit local circumstances. This has been aided by the reform of bargaining structures, which often allows greater scope for local initiative within overall framework agreements (as in the 'repatterning' of the work of telecommunications engineers in BT in the late 1980s). At the same time, moves to single-table bargaining have, by reducing the scope for inter-union rivalry, facilitated the introduction of functional flexibility through the elimination of skill demarcations.

Third, even where changes are technologically driven, as in telecommunications, privatization has often shifted the balance of power away from unions towards management, providing management with a more propitious climate in which to introduce changes such as the reform of exchange staffing. At the same time, the post-privatization introduction of new systems aimed at pursuing 'quality' objectives, such as BT's TQM programme, has tended to erode existing practices in the workplace by shifting the focus of action from local unions to work groups with problem-solving responsibilities.

Fourth, the growth of market mechanisms has substantially altered managerial work. It is now likely that managers' key responsibilities and the terms of their employment will be explicitly codified in a personal contract. This will often provide the basis for setting personal targets through performance appraisal systems. The extent to which such contracts are genuinely tailored to individual managers is open to doubt (Evans and Hudson 1993). Their utility for employers lies in their potential to generate commitment from individual managers unmediated by allegiances to third parties, particularly managerial trade unions, and to tighten accountability for performance. Managerial tasks are increasingly geared to contractual rather than bureaucratic systems and driven by the negotiation, delivery and monitoring of contracts. For example, a laboratory manager in a large water company would once simply have run the laboratory as a department within the overall organization. The relationship between the manager and the company is now likely to be contractual rather than bureaucratic, with the laboratory run as a devolved cost or profit centre. In addition, the manager is likely to act as the customer of the company's finance, legal, personnel and information technology departments. Such arrangements are increasingly typical of the management of organizational sub-units in local government and the privatized sector.

Finally, the development of contracting has had a very specific impact on manual employees in the remaining public services (Colling 1993a). Competitive pressure on costs has resulted in large-scale job losses, as described earlier, at a time when the quality of the service is subject to increasing scrutiny (Colling 1993b). Consequently, the quest for increased productivity and flexibility has been widespread and intense. Some improvement has been delivered through the use of new machinery and materials, such as the shift to 'wheelie bins' in refuse collection. The scope for technological improvements in highly labour-intensive services is limited, however, and most productivity improvements have come from the intensification and expansion of workloads. Crudely, there is little doubt that employees are now simply required to work harder. Cleaners have become responsible for larger areas, often working to newly specified standards in fewer hours (Bach 1989). More sophisticated initiatives have required staff to be more mobile and flexible. Employees who may previously have worked in a particular school or hospital will now often be part of peripatetic teams travelling between a number of sites. Opportunities for task flexibility have also been exploited, particularly within the growing number of multi-functional contracting organizations. Unskilled and semi-skilled employees will often be required to move between contracts without extra payment; this might involve drivers carrying out cleaning duties, for example. Skilled staff will also increasingly carry out low-grade tasks from other skilled trades. Finally, these workloads are being carried out within new working hours arrangements which are more sensitive to changes in workload. A common example is annualized hours for grounds maintenance staff which permits a longer working week over the summer months without the need for overtime payments.

Traditions of good employer practice are no longer viable in this context and the need to improve organizational and individual performance has been paramount. Yet evidence of sophisticated attempts to improve productivity and workforce commitment is scant. Rather, it seems that increased effort levels have so far been delivered through the discipline of contracts and intensified supervision. Expanded performance monitoring mechanisms are now integral to management systems and these are often augmented by strengthened disciplinary powers. Contract managers not only take great interest in the use of equipment, the timing of breaks, and the general whereabouts of staff; the appearance and attitude of employees to customers and clients is rapidly becoming a supervisory issue too (Colling 1993b).

Conclusions: Problems and Contradictions of Privatization and Marketization

The core argument of this chapter has been that the Conservative programme of public-sector reform, based on the two pillars of privatization and marketization, has had profound and probably permanent consequences, cutting large parts of the sector free of a weighty heritage of 'Whitley'-style industrial relations. Collective relations still play an important role, but increasingly they operate alongside more individual management–employee relationships, most notably in the area of managerial and professional workers. Large groups of workers who previously had the protection of union representation and collective bargaining have now been exposed to the coldest winds of private-sector market competition, and pay, conditions and employment levels have suffered as a result. Unions retain a significant presence, but their role and influence has undoubtedly diminished. The traditional highly centralized system is giving way to a much more diversified, decentralized pattern. The initiative has passed very much to the managers of privatized companies, health service trusts, local authorities and government agencies. With the unions on the defensive, managements have been able to achieve greater flexibility in employment and working practices, and to redesign bargaining and consultation machineries to suit their business needs.

In the public services the pace and relentlessness of change in itself generates difficulties for managers not usually faced by those in privatized companies apart from the frenetic pre-flotation phase. Public service managers have often had to adapt to constant financial and legislative change. There have been over 100 pieces of legislation relating to local government since 1980, many of which have had fundamental implications for its funding and operation. Aspirations to strategic management, always difficult, become practically impossible when managers are unable to count on any degree of stability.

This has had obvious consequences for employment policy. The approach to the management of labour in the public services has become much more short-term and ad hoc. For most groups of staff, issues such as training, recruitment and retention are now considered in largely pragmatic terms and are often subject to severe cost pressures exerted through competitive contracting. The pressures upon participation also become acute; there is a tendency for managers to see it as an obstacle to the rapid implementation of change, rather than as a means of increasing employee commitment.

With this important difference in mind it is possible, nevertheless, to identify a number of common dilemmas or tensions facing managers in privatized companies and public services. There are common pressures for greater quality, flexibility and responsiveness in the provision of goods and services, encouraged by increasing competition, by the scrutiny of regulators, and by the demands of the Citizen's Charter. This implies a well-trained, highly motivated workforce. Aspects of employer policy, such as more direct communications, employee shareholding or performance related pay can be seen as motivational mechanisms for winning employee commitment. In some cases – BT is an example – management has introduced wide-ranging 'total quality management' programmes designed to change the way in which employees think and work, from the top to the bottom of the organization. The emphasis is on providing a high quality of service to the 'customers', whether they are external purchasers of services or internal to the organization. Public service organizations have adopted similar programmes in response to the Citizen's Charter and the advent of the Chartermark (awarded to organizations providing a stipulated level of service). An allied development is the rush for contracting organizations to submit their management and supervisory structures to the scrutiny of the British Standards Institute (Harden 1992).

But, on the other hand, the same environment of competition and shareholder/customer expectations has, as we have described above, generated cost cutting and labour-shedding sometimes, especially in public services, having a direct and deleterious effect on pay and working conditions. These developments are likely to reduce workforce commitment and morale. There are expectations of further very heavy job cuts among the privatized companies in the coming years. The same is true in the public services. The extension of contracting to professional functions is certain to result in further job losses, as is the continuing squeeze on public expenditure.

It is unclear, therefore, that the new employment policies introduced by management will be able to achieve their objectives in a climate of fear, insecurity and a degree of demoralization. If employers have been able to square the circle of cost cutting and the introduction of massive change, it is largely because weakened unions have been unable to resist. Against a background of deep recession, unions have been forced to go along with managerial initiatives with little in the way of compensation for their members.

However, employers, particularly among privatized companies, are aware that in the future the balance of power may tilt more in favour of the unions. It is not yet clear that they will have the capacity to develop new flexible forms of participation capable of achieving consensual change. But one essential component is likely to be the ability to guarantee a measure of job security – coupled with the workforce's acceptance of job mobility and retraining – for at least a proportion of their employees.

A second set of tensions derives from the changes in organizational structure and managerial responsibility. As noted above, there has been a general devolution of managerial authority to local unit managers. Local managers are now expected to take the initiative in pushing through changes in working practices, and to play a key role in diffusing new cultures using direct communication and staff motivation. However, there are serious doubts as to how quickly such decentralization will result in genuine divergence in employment practice. The reasons are partly structural and partly cultural.

Some employers have held back from full decentralization, despite the pressures, for a number of deep structural reasons. First, employment patterns in many public service organizations can be extremely complex, with very diverse occupations represented by a wide variety of unions and professional associations. Decentralizing the discussion of employment practice in the NHS, for example, is a very complex and potentially destabilizing process (Seifert 1992). Second, even where reform has created separate and competing entities, these have often remained interdependent in practice. For example, a local authority may choose to allow its revenue collection function to operate autonomously and to make its own agreements with staff. Any dispute within the function, however, would very quickly affect the operation of other parts of the authority. Similarly, a breakdown in service in one BT business area would probably have implications for the reputation and the operation of BT as a whole. Indeed, most of the privatized companies can be described as 'network industries' to some extent, and this may temper the vogue for radical devolution of industrial relations (Colling and Ferner 1992).

As described in chapter 10, decentralizing pressures in the public services are countered to some degree by political pressures towards centralization, particularly as the government attempts to control public-sector expenditure in general and pay movements in particular. This makes it more difficult for local authorities who have withdrawn from national arrangements to deliver the improved, market-led remuneration packages to which they have committed themselves. It may also constitute a major disincentive to those employers considering decentralization who would rather not be exposed to trade union determination to claw back the shortfall when the ceilings are lifted (IDS 1992).

In the medium term, as organizations learn to adjust to their commercial circumstances, there may also be difficulties attached to the enduring culture of public service management. Those schooled in highly centralized and bureaucratized procedures may not possess the necessary skills to adopt the proactive role required of them. Their confidence is also likely to have been dented by managerial 'delayering' – the stripping out of whole organizational tiers – that has been a common feature in recent years, most notably in BT and local government.

Two contrary dangers exist from management's point of view. On the one hand, timid, unconfident managers may find themselves outmanoeuvred in negotiations by strong local workforce representatives. There may thus be, ironically, a reversion to a patchwork of inefficient local agreements and accommodations of the kind that led to a centralization of industrial relations, for example in electricity, in earlier years (Ferner and Colling 1993). On the other hand, a newly empowered, overconfident local management may misjudge the possibilities for change and push industrial relations to breaking point, provoking local conflicts which in the old days would have been defused by being 'referred up' the machinery. There is, in other words, increased scope for 'microconflict' in devolved management structures. Two scenarios are then possible: the erosion of strategic corporate personnel policies (most likely in the public services), or a renewed centralization of control over local industrial relations in the form of some kind of headquarters monitoring or coordination of local deals.

Continued centralization has been a feature of management–union relations. In some cases, a tacit alliance of the central personnel function and top union leaders, both concerned to prevent uncontrolled local developments, limits real decentralization. Within the context of wider doubts about devolved management in integrated network industries, there has been a certain amount of recentralization. BT, for example, has moved the focus of management accountability from the local tier of the management 'district' to the business sector. The autonomy of local managers over industrial relations is therefore likely to diminish, with consequent effects for local industrial relations.

A third problematic issue that arises is the extent of variation between employers. The aggressive, cost cutting, change-oriented culture of some key companies (for example, BT, British Steel and the power generators) and some public service organizations contrasts with a much more cautious approach with an emphasis on continuity in others. British Gas, for example, has seen considerable bargained change, particularly over more flexible working practices and pay structures. But there has – as yet – been little transformation of industrial relations structures or style, radical reductions in the workforce, or the sort of major industrial conflict as witnessed in BT in 1987. Indeed, an agreement with the gas company's 45,000 white-collar staff includes provisions for security of employment through 'providing alternative employment and appropriate retraining when faced with surplus staffing levels' (*IRRR* 503, January 1992: 10).

Such differences seem to be explained by the extent of restructuring required by privatization or marketization, the pace of technological change, and the political context of privatization. Thus BT's privatization was the first of the major flotations, with a symbolic importance for the whole programme. It took place against fierce union opposition including a campaign of industrial action. Union hostility marked subsequent industrial relations in BT. In later privatizations, unions bowed to the inevitable and devoted their energies to securing the best deal available rather than fighting the concept.

In short, therefore, the changes that have taken place are beset by ambiguities. It is not clear that the fragmentation and decentralization of management and consequently of industrial relations will allow a well-coordinated strategic approach either to service provision or to personnel management in the civil service or other parts of the public sector; nor that industrial relations reforms will generate the level of staff morale and commitment required to deliver high-quality services.

Note

1 Details of the consequent changes may be found in a series of articles in the IRS *Industrial Relations Review and Report* (now known as *Employment Trends*): see issues 469, August 1990, 15–18; 484, March 1991, 2; 516, July 1992, 6–15; 520, September 1992, 4–6.

References

Avis, B. 1990: British Steel: A Case of the Decentralization of Collective Bargaining. *Human Resource Management Journal*, 1, 1, 90–9.

Bach, S. 1989: *Too High a Price to Pay? A Study of Competitive Tendering for Domestic Services in the NHS.* Warwick Papers in Industrial Relations, 25. Coventry: Industrial Relations Research Unit.

Beaumont, P. 1991: *Public Sector Industrial Relations.* London: Routledge.

Cabinet Office 1991: *The Citizens Charter: Raising the Standard.* Cm 1599. London: HMSO.

Colling, T. 1991: Privatisation and the Management of IR in Electricity Distribution. *Industrial Relations Journal*, 22, 2, 117–30.

Colling, T. 1993a: Contracting Public Services: The Management of Compulsory Competitive Tendering in Two County Councils. *Human Resource Management Journal*, 3, 4, 1–15.

Colling, T. 1993b: Competing for Quality? Employee Relations in the Enabling Authority. Paper given at British Universities Industrial Relations Association Annual Conference, July.

Colling, T. and Ferner, A. 1992: The Limits of Autonomy: Devolution, Line Managers and Industrial Relations in Privatized Companies. *Journal of Management Studies*, 29, 2, 209–28.

Evans, S. and Hudson, M. 1993: *Standardised Packages Individually Wrapped? A Study of the Introduction and Operation of Personal Contracts in the Port, Transport and Electricity Supply Industries.* Warwick Papers in Industrial Relations, 44. Coventry: Industrial Relations Research Unit.

Ferner, A. 1988: *Governments, Managers and Industrial Relations. Public Enterprises in their Political Environment.* Oxford: Blackwell.

Ferner, A. and Colling, T. 1991: Privatisation, Regulation and Industrial Relations. *British Journal of Industrial Relations*, 29, 3, 391–409.

Ferner, A. and Colling, T. 1993: Industrial Relations in the Electricity Supply Industry. In A. Pendleton and J. Winterton (eds), *Public Enterprise in Transition. Industrial Relations in State and Privatised Industries.* London: Routledge, pp. 100–31.

Harden, I. 1992: *The Contracting State.* Buckingham: Open University Press.

Heery, E. 1992: Industrial Relations and the Customer. Paper Presented to British Universities Industrial Relations Association Annual Conference, July.

IDS (Incomes Data Services) 1992: Public Sector Labour Market Analysis. IDS *Report*, 630, December.

IPMS (Institute of Professionals, Managers and Specialists) 1990: *Executive Agencies: A Negotiator's Guide and Checklist for Action.* London: IPMS.

James, P. 1992: Reforming Industrial Relations in Electricity Supply. Industrial Relations Review and Report, *Employment Trends*, 521, October, 6–12.

James, P. 1993: Industrial Relations Reform in the Electricity Supply Industry. Industrial Relations Review and Report, *Employment Trends*, 533, April, 7–11.

Kessler, I. 1991: Workplace Industrial Relations in Local Government. *Employee Relations*, 13, 2, 1–31.

LRD (Labour Research Department) 1991: CCT – the Effects on Jobs,

514 *Trevor Colling and Anthony Ferner*

Wages and Conditions. *Bargaining Report*, May.

O'Connell Davidson, J. 1990: The Commercialization of Employment Relations: The Case of the Water Industry. *Work, Employment and Society*, 4, 4, 531–50.

Pendleton, A. and Winterton, J. (eds) 1993: *Public Enterprise in Transition. Industrial Relations in State and Privatised Industries*. London: Routledge.

PSPRU (Public Services Privatisation Research Unit) 1992: *Privatisation – Disaster for Quality*. London: PSPRU.

Ridley, N. 1988: *The Local State: Enabling not Providing*. London: Centre for Policy Studies.

Seifert, R. 1992: *Industrial Relations in the NHS*. London: Chapman & Hall.

Thompson, A. and Beaumont, P. 1978: *Public Sector Bargaining: A Study of Relative Gain*. Farnborough: Saxon House.

Treasury 1991: *Competing for Quality*. Cm 1730. London: HMSO.

Veljanovski, C. 1987: *Selling the State: Privatisation in Britain*. London: Weidenfeld & Nicolson.

17

Training

Ewart Keep and Helen Rainbird

Introduction: Training and the Role of Regulation

Nowhere has the pace of change within the British industrial relations system since 1979 been more rapid or sweeping than in the
field of training. In 1981 Britain possessed a training system based
on a national tripartite focus for policymaking, and statutory industrial training boards (ITBs). Today every single major element of
that system has either vanished or been radically altered. Change has
not only encompassed the institutional landscape, but has also included new methods of delivering training (such as open learning),
changing attitudes towards the role of unions in training, a massive
decline in the craft apprenticeship system, and moves towards multi-
skilling and the erosion of traditional job, skill and training demarcations in the workplace.

Given the scale and pace of change, and the often transitory
nature of many institutional mechanisms within the new British
training system, this chapter cannot cover all aspects of these developments in detail. The aim is to focus on the major underlying
trends in the structure of training policymaking and supply, some of
the most important features of new systems of training delivery in the
workplace, and the implication of these developments for relations
between employers and unions. The chapter opens by addressing
the regulation and deregulation of training and the role of the 'social
partners'. We then offer a brief account of the creation of the new
British training system. The chapter then turns to the decline of
traditional apprenticeships and new developments, such as multi-
skilling, open learning and personal development programmes,

which have consequences for the structure of occupations and the distribution of skills in the workforce. Finally, we review trade unions' changing attitudes and policies towards training.

Training policy has been viewed as a classic area for the development of corporatist arrangements, whereby the state devolves the responsibility for policy development and implementation to the representative organizations of labour and capital. The reason for this is that individual employers, acting on a rational basis, will not invest in training since they find it cheaper to recruit skilled labour from other employers. State intervention is therefore necessary in order to secure sufficient training of adequate quality to meet the needs of the economy. However, since state intervention alone is often bureaucratic and lacks adequate information, the devolution of responsibility to employers, on the one hand, and trade unions, on the other, ensures that the parties which are most directly involved in the production process have a stake in the decision-making process and thus an interest in the successful implementation of policy. Although the form of regulation varies considerably from one European country to another, most exhibit some form of state intervention and incorporation of the 'social partners' into training policy and institutions.

The ideological context framing the British debate has been bound up with the role of the state. As the first country to industrialize, Britain initially entrusted the provision of education to religious charities and training to employers. While an involvement of the state in education gradually evolved, training remained on a voluntarist basis and outside the ambit of government funding and control. By contrast, in Germany, France and Japan, the state eschewed a laissez faire approach and took the lead in stimulating industrial development and, as part of these efforts, invested in vocational education and training (VET) (Gospel and Okayama 1991; McCormick 1991). More latterly, many European states have chosen to provide some form of statutory backing to training. This often involves trade unions, for two reasons: first, to secure cooperation in changes to training programmes. Second, since union members' interests are best served through the development of skills which have wide recognition in the labour market, as opposed to the task- and firm-specific requirements of employers, the incorporation of unions is conducive to driving the training system towards meeting long-term skill requirements rather than employers' immediate needs (Streeck 1989).

In Britain the market model of training has been dominant (Campinos-Dubernet and Grando 1988). The exception was the interlude between 1964 and 1988 during which the tripartite Industrial Training Boards operated a system of training levies, and public training programmes were administered through the Manpower Services Commission (see below). Although union interests were incorporated into the policymaking process during this period, since the Conservative government came to power in 1979 there has been a systematic process of exclusion of unions from authoritative decision-making with respect to training policy (Rainbird 1990). As a consequence, individual employers are now seen as having primary responsibility for training decisions; in the residual areas of public training policy (schemes for the unemployed), employer-dominated bodies in the form of the Training and Enterprise Councils also hold sway.

A growing awareness of the relative weakness of British VET provision and its apparent effects upon economic competitiveness has led to periodic discussion about the need for reform, which has spanned the last one hundred and fifty years (Perry 1976; Reeder 1981). More recently, the difficulties posed by high levels of unemployment have added urgency to this debate. Since the late 1970s a broad consensus has emerged that improvement of the UK's skills base is a prerequisite for economic success. The means by which improvements might best be secured have not been subject to the same level of consensus, and the role of the state and degree to which training can be left to market forces has been the focus of controversy.

Changes in Policymaking and Delivery Structures

The development of the national training system prior to 1979[1]

As outlined above, until the 1960s the role of the state in training in peacetime was minimal, with responsibility for training provision resting with individual employers. However, a growing awareness of the need for improvement in Britain's training performance, and the slow pace of change being generated by voluntary training arrangements, led in 1962 to the Conservative government's White Paper on training, which in turn led to indirect state intervention in the form of the Labour government's 1964 Industrial Training Act (see

Perry 1976 for details). The Act gave ministers the power to create Industrial Training Boards (ITBs) – sectoral bodies made up of employers and trade union representatives, which were empowered to establish a levy on firms within their industry. This levy funded the Boards' operating costs and sectoral training activity via training grants to companies whose training plans and provision met standards laid down by the ITB. By 1969 there were 27 ITBs covering 15 million employees (mainly in manufacturing) out of a national workforce of 25 million (Lindley 1983).

In 1972, following criticisms about excessive bureaucracy and the inability of the ITB system to accommodate the problems and requirements of small firms, the operation of the ITBs was reviewed. As a result, the Employment and Training Act of 1973 replaced the levy/grant system with a new system based on exemptions from the levy for all small firms and for those companies whose training met criteria specified by the ITB. The state would in future meet the ITBs' operating costs (see Perry 1976; Senker 1992).

The Act also created a new national, tripartite body – the Manpower Services Commission (MSC) – to oversee manpower planning, the operation of government training schemes and employment services, and the activities of the ITBs. The MSC rapidly became involved in measures aimed at reducing persistent cyclical skill shortages in the economy, and in devising various special temporary employment measures and training schemes aimed at the unemployed (for details, see Ainley and Corney 1991; Evans 1992).

The creation of the MSC reflected a belief that there was a role for more direct state intervention in training, and that planning at national level was a necessity. Both the ITBs and the MSC also embodied the concept that training policy and delivery were best tackled via institutions that embraced both sides of industry, as well as, in some cases, the interests of educationalists and local government.

Changing policies and institutions since 1979

The election in 1979 of a Conservative government committed to ending the post-war consensus signalled a dramatic shift in training policies. The government's approach to training has been shaped by a number of beliefs. These include the assumption that market forces, rather than statutory rights and duties, are the best means of determining the type and amounts of training undertaken; that it is the responsibility of employers, and to a lesser extent individuals, to decide their levels of investment in training; that the role of the state in training should be limited to supporting provision for disadvantaged groups (such as the long-term unemployed), helping with pump-priming funding to aid innovation, and exhortation; and finally, that VET should be employer-led and employer-controlled, with the influence of educationalists and trade unions being sharply reduced (for a concise statement of government beliefs on training, see ED 1988).

This approach to training can be seen as part of a wider continuum of policies aimed at increasing the efficiency of the British labour market through increasing deregulation and greater labour-market competition. Thus the diminution of trade union influence upon training policy cannot be viewed in isolation from wider attempts by the government to weaken the power of trade unions within the British labour market.

The move from ITBs to ITOs

The initial indicator of a new approach to training came in 1981, with the decision to abolish the majority of the ITBs. Following a complex process of review and consultation (see Keep and Mayhew 1995, for details), the government announced the winding-up of 17 ITBs, and their replacement by voluntary sectoral bodies. Boards were retained in seven sectors – most importantly clothing, engineering and construction – where it was judged that the ITBs were essential to securing wider national training objectives. Ministers made clear, however, that this reprieve was only temporary, and that the ultimate aim was the abolition all the Boards. In 1988, following a further review of ITB operations, all but the Construction Industry Training Board were replaced by voluntary arrangements, while the Engineering Construction section of the Engineering Industry Training Board set up its own training board.

The voluntary sectoral bodies that have replaced the statutory ITBs were originally styled Non-Statutory Training Organizations (NSTOs), but have since retitled themselves Industry Training Organizations (ITOs). They are designed, run and financed by employers, and, in contrast to the ITBs, involvement in them by trade unions and educationalists is not guaranteed but is available only at the invitation of the employers. Employer membership of these

bodies is entirely voluntary, as is the decision to support or participate in their activities. The ITOs have no powers to raise a levy, or
to compel companies to train or to cooperate with their plans. Their
main roles have proved to be the dissemination of information on
training, helping to define future sectoral skill needs, organizing
group training schemes, and encouraging and exhorting firms to do
more training. About 90 NSTOs were established in the wake of the
1981 round of ITB abolitions, and in the early 1990s there were
about 120 ITOs operating. These cover five-sixths of the national
workforce (Berry-Lound et al. 1991: 535).

Have the new arrangements worked? Evidence to support the
government's view, that 'the Training Boards . . . have not succeeded in raising the standard and quantity of training in the sectors
they covered to the level of our major competitors overseas' (ED
1988: 34), is limited. The official reviews of ITB operation conducted in 1972, 1980 and 1981 (ED 1972; MSC 1980, 1981) all
reached the general conclusion that the ITBs had, on the whole,
made a major contribution to improving the quantity and quality of
training, but that in some important areas, such as cross-sectoral
skills, adult training and apprenticeship reform, progress had been
limited. The blame for this situation may not have rested with the
Boards. As Senker (1992) points out, their inability to take effective
initiatives in these areas often stemmed from employers' conserva-
tism and unwillingness to countenance and pay for change (see also
MSC 1981; Lindley 1983). Senker also argues that government
policies, in particular the replacement of the levy/grant system with
levy exemptions, and the tensions between the MSC's national
policies and the needs of individual sectors, made the ITBs' task
more difficult (see also Perry 1976; MSC 1980).

What is known about the performance of the ITOs does not
suggest that they represent an improvement in the effectiveness
of sectoral training arrangements in Britain. Government-
commissioned research in the mid-1980s suggested that the majority
of the voluntary sectoral bodies were ineffective when judged against
the MSC's targets for their activities (Rainbird and Grant 1985;
Anderson 1987; Varlaam 1987). There is some evidence that their
effectiveness has improved since then, but significant problems remain. One is the limited level of resources available to the ITOs. For
example, in the year 1990/1, of 78 ITOs, 54 per cent had annual
incomes of less than £200,000 (Berry-Lound et al. 1991: 539).

Moreover, when the work of the ITOs is measured against the 12-point list of 'ideal outcomes' which the ITOs have set themselves, it is apparent that progress has been halting. By 1991, only two of these 'outcomes' had been achieved by more than 50 per cent of the ITOs covered in a HOST Consultancy survey (Berry-Lound and Anderson 1991).

The development of NVQs

The second decisive development in the creation of a new training system came with moves towards a unified system of national vocational qualifications (NVQs). An MSC-sponsored review of existing vocational qualifications concluded that provision was complex, confusing to employer and trainee, offered patchy coverage, gave limited access to training for adults, made little provision for the accreditation of prior learning, and laid too much stress on the testing of knowledge rather than skills and competences (MSC/DES 1986).

A new, employer-led National Council for Vocational Qualifications (NCVQ) was set up to tackle these problems through the creation of a system of NVQs in England, Wales, and Northern Ireland. In Scotland an existing body – the Scottish Vocational Education Council (SCOTVEC) – was charged with creating parallel Scottish Vocational Qualifications (SVQs). The NCVQ adopted a radical approach, based on the formulation of an NVQ framework of employer-designed, competence-based qualifications at five (initially four) levels.

NVQs and SVQs are based on standards of competence, as defined by employers, that are needed to undertake specific jobs. NVQs must be modular, and be broken down into component 'units of competence'. The trainee acquires an NVQ by achieving the standards for each of these units, for which a credit is received. Credits can be accumulated through undertaking training, through the accreditation of prior learning (APL), or both. The competences required for an NVQ are normally assessed in the workplace, rather than the classroom or through written examinations, and assessment is generally expected to be undertaken by the candidate's supervisor or other managerial staff. As a result of this competence-based approach NVQs and SVQs are grounded on and specified in terms of the outcomes of learning, rather than the processes through which the learning takes place. They are hence specified independently of any particular location, mode and duration of training delivery (Jessup 1991).

The NCVQ does not itself design the qualifications: it simply recognizes and approves existing and new qualifications that fit within its framework. The design of the qualifications for each industry rests with employer-led Industry Lead Bodies (ILBs). To deal with areas of employment such as clerical and administrative work which cover many industries, cross-sectoral bodies have been created.

The system of competence-based NVQs is a radical innovation and a great deal of effort and political capital has been invested in its creation. The official view is that NVQs will raise the status of vocational qualifications *vis-à-vis* traditional academic qualifications, and encourage investment in training by promoting flexible provision (Debling 1991; Jessup 1991). Moreover, NVQs provide the glue that binds together the new devolved training system. As the focus of policy shifted to local delivery mechanisms, the role of national standards as a means of ensuring coherence increased. NVQs form the key element in monitoring the success of national training policies, of individual Training and Enterprise Councils (for details of which see below), and of companies' training efforts.

NVQs have not been without their critics. Some academics have accused employers of defining competences in a very narrow, task-specific way, in contrast to their European counterparts who appear to desire a broader mix of training and general education (Prais 1989; Steedman and Wagner 1989; Raggatt 1991; Callender, 1992). Some employers have echoed these criticisms (CBI 1989). It is alleged that NVQs often require the minimum level of skill needed to perform a particular job, rather than encourage broader-based learning in transferable skills (McCool 1991); and Callender (1992) suggests that there may be an inherent conflict between the short-term needs of individual employers and the longer-term needs of trainees and the national economy. There has also been concern that the levels of skill being specified are sometimes low, particularly when contrasted with those required by overseas employers. Jarvis and Prais suggest that NVQs may be creating 'a certified semi-literate under-class' (1989: 70). Doubts have also been expressed about the status and credibility of workplace assessment (Prais 1989, 1991), and about the ability of the personnel and training systems within many workplaces to deliver the support that NVQ training and assessment will require (Callender 1992). Finally, the capacity of the NCVQ to achieve a genuine rationalization of vocational qualifications is open to question (Keep and Mayhew 1995).

One of the main indicators of the likely success of NVQs is the speed with which they are adopted by employers. Current indications are not particularly encouraging. Knowledge and understanding of the new qualifications among employers and employees appears to remain limited (NTTF 1992). A survey of 171 organizations employing almost 600,000 people undertaken by the *Employee Development Bulletin* (No. 40, April 1993: 2–15) indicated that while 61 per cent of respondents had employees who were working towards or who had achieved NVQs, only 3 per cent of the people employed by the organizations were involved. The survey also revealed significant concerns among employers about over-reliance on workplace assessment; NVQs' failure to require more general educational attainment, such as proof of literacy and numeracy; low standards; bureaucracy within the NVQ system; and the apparent inability of NVQs to simplify the range of vocational qualifications on offer.

The end of the MSC, and moves to a locally-based system

In spite of the government's desire to disengage itself from responsibility for training, events during the early and mid-1980s conspired to render achievement of this goal problematic. In particular, the rise in youth and adult unemployment created a political requirement for the government to be seen to be tackling the problem via large-scale, government-funded training and work experience programmes, such as the Youth Training Scheme (YTS) (see Chapman and Tooze 1987; Jones 1988; Keep 1994). The MSC as a consequence found itself acting as the main agency for managing the problems of unemployment.

However, following the 1987 general election, and with youth unemployment no longer rising, the government fulfilled a manifesto commitment by restructuring the MSC and removing its responsibility for employment service functions – renaming the organization as the Training Commission to denote its new focus of activity. In September 1988, following a refusal by TUC representatives on the Commission to endorse the proposed Employment Training (ET) scheme for the long-term unemployed, the government announced the outright abolition of the Commission and its intention to shift decision-making away from national and sectoral levels towards a new focus on local labour markets. The chief component of the new system was to be a network of Training and Enterprise Councils (TECs) in England and Wales, and in Scotland a broadly similar set of bodies to be styled Local Enterprise Companies (LECs).

TECs and LECs are employer-led bodies, with the legal status of limited companies. Two-thirds of the members of each TEC's board must be the chairs or chief executives of private-sector companies. Trade union participation is by invitation. Members of a TEC board serve in a personal capacity and are not deemed to represent their company or organization. The functions of TECs and LECs are to administer government training and work experience schemes for the unemployed, to monitor and address skill requirements in the local labour market, to encourage companies to invest in training, and to act as a catalyst for local economic growth and regeneration. TECs and LECs have a contractual relationship with the Employment Department, from whom they receive funding for training schemes for the unemployed, plus a small basic grant to cover operating costs and promotional activities. In 1993 there were 82 TECs covering England and Wales, and 20 Scottish LECs.

TECs and LECs are the pivotal elements within the new training system. When their creation was announced, ministers suggested that:

> The creation of TECs is a truly radical step. It will give leadership of the training system to employers, where it belongs. Through their participation and involvement it will change the focus of training and bring home the importance of training for business success to every employer in the country. (ED 1988: 43)

It is important to emphasize that a distinctive feature of the TECs is that they were not constituted as representative bodies. Many TEC boards are probably not representative of local employers. Initial analysis of the composition of TEC boards (Emmerick and Peck 1991) indicated that manufacturing industry was often over-represented in relation to the proportion of employment it provided in the locality.

At a broader level, TECs have been designed by the government to be explicitly unrepresentative of other stakeholders in VET – educationalists, trade unions, community groups, local authorities and the unemployed. In November 1991 local authority representatives made up 8.5 per cent of all TEC board seats, local education authorities accounted for a further 4.2 per cent, trade unions 5.1 per cent and voluntary organizations 3.7 per cent. The government's preconditions on TEC board membership have also created problems with gender and ethnicity. Details of the make-up of TEC boards provided in November 1991 indicated that only 10.7 per cent of board members were female, and only 3.5 per cent were from ethnic minority backgrounds (Emmerick and Peck 1992: 13–14).

While some TECs have made efforts to overcome these problems and have evolved advisory structures in order to allow representation for non-employer stakeholders (IDS *Study* 485, July 1991; NTTF 1992), other TECs have done little (Emmerick and Peck 1992). Moreover, the legal status of TECs as limited companies, and the lack of any compulsory requirement for formal linkages with representative bodies in the localities within which they operate, means that their accountability to their local communities remains at best uncertain.

Information about the activities of TECs and LECs is patchy (for studies of them, see IDS *Study* 485; Barnes 1991; Emmerick and Peck 1991, 1992), and it is too early to offer any definitive conclusions about their effectiveness. Nevertheless, achievements and potential difficulties are already clearly identifiable.

To date, perhaps the greatest success of the TEC movement has been to harness the interest and energy of large numbers of senior private-sector executives (NTTF 1992; Wood 1992). As a form of 'action learning' the TECs may provide a significant opportunity to improve knowledge about, and to alter attitudes towards, training in Britain among an influential segment of the business community.

On the debit side, problems have included cuts in government funding; conflicts with the Employment Department over departmental supervision of their activities; and difficult relations with other parts of the training system, such as the ITOs. However, the greatest single problem which TECs face is that nine-tenths of the government funding they receive is committed to schemes that are, in the main, aimed at the unemployed, and which only cover entrants or re-entrants to the labour market rather than existing members of the workforce – a difficulty which has been sharply compounded by the recession and rising unemployment. It is thus open to question whether TECs will ultimately be concerned with achieving a step change in training activity in Britain, or whether their main purpose will prove to be the management of measures for the unemployed. The chief executive of one TEC has commented that: 'we seem to be caught between, on the one hand, the need to increase the skill level of the labour force, and on the other, the requirement to remove individuals from the unemployment register at any cost' (*Guardian*, 4 November 1991). The crucial issue for the future is therefore the degree to which TECs can improve training for those in employment.

New schemes and targets

The two remaining major elements of the new training system – Investors in People (IIP), and the National Education and Training Targets (NETTs) – although employer-led in their development, have included a role for participation and endorsement by the TUC.

Investors in People The Investors in People initiative (IIP) is a national standard for effective investment in employees. It was developed by the National Training Task Force, the strategic body set up to oversee the establishment and operations of the TECs, in collaboration with CBI members, the Association of British Chambers of Commerce (ABCC), the TUC, ITOs, and other training organizations. IIP was launched in November 1990. The aim is to encourage organizations to invest in training, to help them to do so more effectively, and to reward this commitment with a nationally recognized 'kitemark' of training quality.

In order to achieve IIP status an organization's owner or chief executive must make a public commitment to develop all employees in order to achieve business objectives; and the organization must regularly review the training and development needs of all its employees, demonstrate action to train and develop individuals, and provide evidence that the organization regularly evaluates and reviews its investment in training. Assessment of most organizations in England and Wales applying for IIP status is made by their local TEC, though large companies can deal with a national Employment Department unit. In Scotland, IIP assessment is undertaken by a national body – Investors in People (Scotland). The award of IIP status is made for three years, after which it is necessary for the organization to provide evidence of continued achievement and development.

IIP is important because it provides the TECs with their chief lever for attempting to improve the training of the employed workforce. Unfortunately, the pace to date at which organizations

Table 17.1 National Education and Training Targets (NETTs)

Foundation Learning

1 By 1997 at least 80 per cent of young people to attain National Vocational Qualification / Scottish Vocational Qualification (NVQ/SVQ) Level 2 or its academic equivalent in their foundation education and training.

2 All young people who can benefit should be given an entitlement to structured training, work experience or education leading to NVQ/SVQ Level 3 or its academic equivalent.

3 By the year 2000, at least half of the age group should attain NVQ/SVQ Level 3 or its academic equivalent as a basis for further progression.

4 All education and training provision should be structured and designed to develop self-reliance, flexibility and broad competence as well as specific skills.

Lifetime Learning

1 By 1996, all employees should take part in training or development activities as the norm.

2 By 1996, at least half of the employed workforce should be aiming for qualifications or units towards them within the NVQ/SVQ framework.

3 By the year 2000, half of the employed workforce should be qualified to NVQ/SVQ Level 3 or its academic equivalent as a minimum.

4 By 1996, at least half of the medium-sized and larger organizations should qualify as 'Investors in People', assessed by the relevant TEC or LEC.

have achieved IIP status has been extremely slow. By September 1992 just 76 companies had become IIPs, with a further 1,100 organizations committed to achieving the standard (*Employee Development Bulletin*, 33, September 1992: 16).

The National Education and Training Targets   NETTs form a series of performance objectives for British vocational education and training to the year 2000. These were formulated by the CBI following bilateral talks with other employers' groups, trade unions and educational bodies. The NETTs were launched in the summer of 1991 with endorsement from the TUC. The government subsequently decided to offer its support for the targets. The main targets are given in table 17.1.

The NETTs are important in the running of the training system. They establish easily identifiable strategic goals for the system, and rates of progress towards their achievement provide a set of measurable performance indicators for TECs and LECs. They also 'offer a framework that binds together a wide range of other initiatives in the education and training field and gives them coherence' (*Skills and Enterprise Briefing*, Issue 16/92, June 1992). Finally, the process of achieving the targets is hoped to foster a 'learning culture' among British employers and employees (*Labour Market Quarterly Report*, February 1992: 16).

It should be noted that the targets are ambitious, particularly those relating to the adult workforce. They are predicated on the use of the NVQ system by all employers, and their achievement would require major increases in employer expenditure on training, and a radical improvement in the planning and evaluation of in-company training activities. How achievable they are remains to be seen. It is notable that the hotel and catering industry has already concluded that the targets of half the workforce aiming for NVQs by 1996, and half the workforce qualified to NVQ level 3 by the year 2000, are unattainable in their sector, and has set itself targets at half the national level (*Employee Development Bulletin*, 40, April 1993: 3). It is rumoured that the construction industry may be forced to do the same. If sufficient significant sectors of the economy follow suit, the achievement of the targets will prove impossible.

Having examined the structural changes through which the mechanisms of training policy and delivery have been going, we now turn to see whether there are any indications that the reforms are producing concrete results in terms of changes taking place in the volume and quality of training being delivered.

The scale and scope of training activity

How much is being spent by employers on training has been an important issue in the debate about training in Britain. Unfortunately, information on this is scanty, conflicting and often open to challenge. The largest survey of training costs was undertaken, as part of a wider *Training in Britain* study, by Deloitte, Haskins and Sells for the MSC, and covered the year 1986/7 (TA 1989). This showed that in 1986/7 employers offered 64.7 million days off-the-job training and 60.7 million days on-the-job training (a total of 125.4 million days). The average duration of training per trainee was

14.5 days. The survey produced a global figure for employer spending of £18.14 billion. However, once items such as training by the agricultural sector and the armed forces, and estimates of spending by very small firms were deducted, the overall cost of training provided by employers fell to £14.43 billion, of which £9.2 billion was expended by private-sector employers.

How much credence to place upon these figures is problematic. They have been the subject of criticism, with claims that the survey may have inflated employer expenditure (see Finegold 1991; Ryan 1991b). There are problems with the survey's methodology and its analysis, particularly the calculation of the costs of off-the-job training. Other, broader, concerns focus on the difficulties of self-reporting of training activity by employers. Nevertheless, Ryan concludes that, even with corrections, total employer expenditure still exceeds £8 billion.

This estimate stands in marked contrast to two other sources of information on employers' training costs. First, the 20 company case studies of training activity undertaken as another element of the *Training in Britain* investigation produced figures indicating that about 0.76 per cent of companies' payroll costs was devoted to training (CCSC/CLA 1989: 16). This contrasts with the employers' activity survey which indicated spending equivalent to more than 8.5 per cent of payroll costs on training.

The second source that contradicts the *Training in Britain* survey is unpublished data from the Department of Employment's 1988 Labour Costs Survey (McLeish 1990). The LCS data suggest that training accounted for only a very limited proportion of total wages costs, and that in some sectors it was overshadowed by redundancy pay and the provision of benefits in kind and subsidized services (such as housing, company cars, canteens, removal expenses) to employees.

What can be deduced from these conflicting data? The answer may be: not that much. Even if we possessed firm figures for employers' spending on training, on their own they would tell us little about Britain's training performance relative to overseas competitors. Debate about Britain's relative performance needs not only to look at employers' training costs, but also to examine what that money buys in terms of both volume and quality of training.

There is, however, evidence that there has been a quite significant increase in the overall volume of training in recent years. Thus Labour Costs Survey data indicated an increase in the proportion of employers' total labour costs (excluding wages and salaries) accounted for by training, from 0.3 per cent in 1981 to 0.5 per cent in 1988 (Janes and Roberts 1990). Labour Force Survey data reinforce the view that training has increased. In spring 1984 the LFS showed that just under 2.6 million people had received some form of job-related training in the four weeks preceding the survey. By spring 1991 this had risen to 4.3 million – an increase of 73 per cent (Turner et al. 1992: 379). Gallie and White (1993: 29) also report 'a dramatic increase' in the proportion of the workforce being trained since 1987. While there are signs that the recession of the early 1990s caused some falling back in the amounts of training (Keep and Mayhew 1995), the figures suggest that employers have placed an increased emphasis on improving the skills of their employees.

How far these increases can be related to changes in the structure of the training system and delivery mechanisms is unclear. Other factors that may have contributed to the rise in training volume include the removal of the most inefficient firms in the economy during the recession of the early 1980s; the pressures generated by increases in international competition; structural shifts in employment, with the service sector demanding new levels of social and customer care skills; the spread of new technology (Gallie and White 1993); and the gradual education of employers to the value of training via government and CBI exhortation, and the popularization, via the media and management textbooks, of academic studies pointing to training's role in boosting productivity.

While the total volume of training is important in assessing Britain's overall training performance, the quality of what is being provided also influences the state of progress. The evidence on the quality of training is less encouraging than that on the volume. One indicator of quality is the qualifications towards which trainees are working. Labour Force Survey data from the summer of 1992 indicated that only a minority of trainees (37 per cent) were aiming towards a qualification, and that of those, 43 per cent of men and 44 per cent of women were working towards qualifications equivalent to or below GCSE level (*Labour Market Quarterly Report*, February 1993: 7). Figures from the autumn 1992 Labour Force Survey indicated that 36 per cent of training for male workers, and 38 per cent of training for women, lasted for three days or less (*Employee Development Bulletin*, June 1993: 16). Finally, the quality of training on the two main government-funded training schemes – Youth Training (YT) and Employment Training (ET) – as measured by qualifications gained, has not been impressive. To take the example of YT, which in various forms has been running since the mid-1980s, and which is supposed to form foundation level vocational training for all entrants to the workforce, the national average of trainees achieving qualifications fell from a peak of 41 per cent in December 1990 to just 31 per cent in March 1993 (*Labour Market Quarterly Report*, May 1993: 8).

Another note of caution concerns the distribution of training opportunities. While the overall amount of training may be increasing, access to training varies greatly. Put briefly, those employed in small firms, part-time workers, the less well-educated and qualified, the self-employed, older workers, and manual workers are all less likely to receive training. Because certain groups of people are more frequently concentrated in certain types of employment – for example, women in part-time employment – disadvantage in access to training disproportionately affects some sections of the working population. Furthermore, state training schemes have done little to break down patterns of gender segregation in occupational training (Cockburn 1987). Some commentators argue that a market-driven training system reinforces existing patterns of discrimination in access to training (EOC 1988; Payne 1990). There are also significant sectoral differences. Those employed in the public sector are more likely to be trained than those in the private sector, and, in the private sector, those employed in services are more likely to be trained than those in manufacturing, and to be trained for longer periods (TA 1989).

The weakness of training provision for some groups of workers is an important problem. In the 1987 *Training in Britain* survey, 52 per cent of employees received no training, and 20 per cent of firms offered no training whatsoever to their employees. Gallie and White underline the 'great differences in virtually every aspect of training and development, as between qualified and unqualified people, or as between those in higher-level jobs and those in jobs at the lower skill levels' (1993: 35). They point out that this 'excluded group' of 'the educationally unqualified, or those in the lowest job segment' amounts to about a third of the total workforce.

Training, skill and trade unions

Within these overall trends, one development that does need to be underlined is the decline of the craft apprenticeship system which has traditionally constituted the main form of training for skilled manual workers. Outside this, training for manual workers has primarily been provided on-the-job, with little access to structured learning. In Great Britain, the concept of 'skill' derives from the production system rather than from vocational qualifications. It is associated, in particular, with the regulation of apprenticeship by craft unions. Skilled work has therefore been associated with membership of a craft union and, since apprenticeship has normally been restricted to white male workers, access to training and to skilled work has not been open to other groups of workers. The Conservative government's policy towards the reform of the apprenticeship system in 1983 aimed to remove craft union restrictions over training. In particular, it aimed to replace traditional time-serving, the system whereby the trainee was recognized as a skilled worker on completing a number of years as an apprentice, by tested standards, and to remove restrictions limiting the age of entry to 16-year-olds. These changes, alongside the development of the Youth Training Scheme, did not have the effect of boosting the number of apprentices, but consolidated their long-term decline. Between 1970 and 1983, when the reforms were introduced, the numbers of apprentices halved from 218,000 to 102,100 and by 1990 numbers were reduced to 53,600, less than a quarter of the 1970 level (Keep and Mayhew 1995: Table 5.14). In the early 1980s these reductions partly reflected the fall in manufacturing employment and redundancies amongst trainees in particular. Nevertheless, it is clear that the decline in apprenticeships has been disproportionate to the reduction in manufacturing employment. Whereas in 1980 apprentices accounted for 2.3 per cent of the workforce, this had dropped to 1 per cent by 1990 (Keep and Mayhew 1995: ch. 5). As chapter 6 above shows, between 1979 and 1991 membership of the three main craft unions (the AEU, the EEPTU and UCATT) declined sharply.

In the same way, developments in new technology and multi-skilling have consequences for trade union organization (Rainbird 1988). British trade unions are organized along occupational lines, while multi-unionism and the existence of separate bargaining units for white-collar, manual and craft workers are common at establishment level. These structures impose constraints on occupational mobility and, in particular, limit the possibilities for unskilled and semi-skilled workers to upgrade their jobs. Where companies are restructuring or introducing multi-skilling, access to training will determine which unions benefit most from these changes and, as a corollary, the groups of employees who are most at risk from redundancy. Moves towards increased flexibility and multi-skilling may be perceived as a threat to the spheres of influence of different trade unions and bring them into conflict with each other. In practice, over and above declining membership numbers, many of the mergers between unions in recent years have been driven by an occupational logic and have had the effect of taking unions out of competition with each other for particular categories of workers (see chapter 6).

Although, as indicated earlier, access to continuing training has been limited, there have nevertheless been a number of well-publicized examples of training and education schemes which have been designed to increase workers' adaptability to change, and willingness to learn. The Ford Motor Company's Employee Development Assistance Programme (EDAP), agreed in 1987, is an example which has attracted widespread interest within the trade union movement, partly for its joint approach (it is managed through a series of joint union/management committees) and partly for its enthusiastic take-up among Ford's manual workers. Although it concerns education and personal development rather than vocational training, it has had the effect of encouraging manual workers to return to learn through the allocation of funds for courses. Other major companies such as Rover have similar personal development programmes for their employees, though they are not all jointly managed (IRRR 1992). The development of open learning methods also has the potential to open up opportunities for learning in the workplace, though this is often in the workers' own time and takes an individual rather than collective form.

Alongside this, the development of NVQs has created the possibility for unskilled manual workers to have their skills recognized. This competence-based system of accreditation, in focusing on learning outcomes rather than the learning process, has created the possibility for workers to obtain recognition of their skills acquired through experience either in employment or in the domestic sphere. It has both positive advantages and drawbacks for manual workers. In sectors where previously no qualifications existed, it has the potential to establish them. It may also mean that some groups of workers, such as women, whose skills are normally undervalued, may be able to obtain recognition for them. In so far as it assesses ability to perform tasks, it is closely allied to job evaluation methods and may therefore allow both unions and employers to make a link between the qualification system and bargaining strategies.

Union policies towards training[2]

The low levels of occupational training in Britain mean that not all unions have coherent and clearly articulated policies towards training, because their members are not accustomed to dealing with it as a workplace issue. Historically, the major form of training has been apprenticeship and, as a consequence, unions organizing skilled workers such as the Amalgamated Engineering and Electrical Union (AEEU) and the Union of Construction and Allied Trades and Technicians (UCATT) have more highly developed policies towards training than unions representing semi-skilled and unskilled manual workers, and they have been able to represent their members' interests effectively in the structures that were available to them. The general unions have had less highly developed policies on training as well as a more heterogeneous membership than the craft unions. Therefore they did not use their rights to representation on ITBs and the MSC structures as effectively as they could have done.

During the 1980s, union policies often focused on the relationship between initial training programmes such as apprenticeship and the government-funded Youth Training Scheme. Concerns have been raised by the threat to youth pay rates posed by trainee allowances and the possibility of job substitution. Craft unions have also been concerned to guarantee that apprentices complete their full period of training so that training and skill standards are maintained. In these circumstances, bargaining has focused on the wages and conditions of trainees, rather than the content of training itself (Rainbird 1990).

In contrast to initial training, which because of the history of the ITBs has been discussed to some extent at sectoral level, there has never really been any national or sectoral forum for discussing continuing training. It is in this context that unions are developing an interest in the workplace as a locus of decision-making for training and have been raising demands for workplace training committees and rights to training.

Despite the limitations to union activity in a deregulated and employer-dominated training system, unions have nevertheless sought to influence training in three main ways: through representation of members' interests where institutional structures have permitted it; through collective bargaining; and through the provision of training as a service. Paradoxically, the formal exclusion of trade union interests from training bodies has coincided with unions' increased interest in, and awareness of, training as a bargaining issue.

Representation of members' interests Although the arenas in which unions can represent their interests on training have been reduced, unions retain some representational rights. They do not have equal representation rights with employers, but in some cases they have seats by invitation on the TEC and LEC boards and their committee structures. Many unions have been involved in the development of NVQs for their sectors through their involvement in the Industry Lead Bodies. Again, this representation is by invitation rather than by right. At sectoral level, some of the voluntary ITOs (which were set up by employers' associations as a precondition for the abolition of the ITBs) offer seats to union representatives. Unions retain a minority of seats on the two remaining ITBs in construction and engineering construction. In the workplace, there are no statutory provisions for union involvement or consultation on training matters. A survey of shop stewards conducted by the Labour Research Department in 1989 found that training was agreed between the employer and the union in only 17 per cent of the workplaces responding, though 30 per cent had consultative arrangements and management provided some information in a further 31 per cent of cases (LRD 1990).

Training and collective bargaining Given the formal exclusion of union interests from training institutions, unions have increasingly turned to alternative methods of influencing training. The union Manufacturing, Science and Finance (MSF) has argued that 'as long as access to training is not a statutory entitlement, employees depend to a large degree on trade unions to secure this right for them as part of their contract of employment' (MSF 1988: 20). The TUC's preferred form of involvement is that of workplace training committees and a number of unions such as MSF and the Transport and General Workers' Union (TGWU) have incorporated this demand into collective bargaining strategies. In the run-up to the general election in 1992 the TGWU and the GMB issued a joint demand for a worker's right to five days training per year, which is now being included in bargaining strategies. In a different context, the development of NVQs provides opportunities to unions to bargain over access to training and reward for skills. However, unions organizing unskilled workers recognize that the linkage of pay to assessments of competence, especially where these are made by a workplace supervisor, may create the conditions for the development of differential pay rates and discrimination against those who do not meet the standards of competence (Rainbird 1993).

Training as a service A number of unions provide training themselves as a service to members, or see bargaining for training as a means of increasing members' job satisfaction. NALGO (part of Unison since July 1993) has long provided vocational training for its white-collar members. NUPE, which organized public sector manual workers, founded the Workbase project following negotiations with the University of London in 1978. This is now an independent organization running jointly managed courses in numeracy and literacy skills for first- and second-language speakers of English. More recently, NUPE initiated the 'Return to Learn' programme as a service to members in recognition of the barriers faced by manual workers returning to education and training. Other unions run comparable courses: for example, the Amalgamated Engineering and Electrical Union runs courses for updating electrical and electronic skills.

Origins of the growth in union interest in training A number of factors have come together to contribute to an increased interest in training. The first of these is a Labour Party and TUC analysis which identifies low levels of investment in training and education as contributing to the structural weakness of the British economy. Second, the demand for rights to initial and continuing training in the European Union's Social Charter provides a point of reference. Even though the British government 'opted out' of the Social Chapter of the Maastricht Treaty, the 'Social Dialogue' between employers' associations and unions at European level has concerned training, and this has been echoed to some extent by the TUC's endorsement of the CBI's national training targets. Third, unions have had to respond to developments such as YTS and NVQs. Although much of this has been defensive, there is some evidence of the development of more offensive strategies, particularly with respect to the development of NVQs. Fourth, the generally weakened bargaining position of unions means that bargaining strength is no longer sufficient to increase members' pay and status. Strategies towards training therefore complement wage bargaining. Finally, the development of policies towards training is part of a new relationship towards both members and employers. On the one hand, training increases the range of services offered to members. On the other hand, it is part of an approach to employers which allows unions to demonstrate their ability to cooperate in a productivist strategy.

Although these strategies are unlikely to make significant progress in the absence of statutory intervention on training, they may allow union representatives to develop effective policies and skills on workplace training committees and rights to training which could make any future attempts at state intervention more effective. There are, none the less, severe limitations to a training strategy which is dependent on collective bargaining. This is because it is most likely to be successful in unionized workplaces where the employer is already predisposed towards training. It may be unable to overcome employers' resistance to a joint approach and their lack of demand for higher levels of skill. More importantly, it excludes those workers who are most disadvantaged in the labour market – the unemployed and those in the more precarious forms of employment in non-union workplaces – who are particularly in need of modernizing and upgrading their skills.

Conclusion

What conclusions can be drawn about the changes that have taken place in the British training? The first is that training policies since 1979 have undoubtedly represented a decisive rejection of legislative backing for training, and for any notions of social partnership and tripartite control of training design and delivery. By so doing, they are in marked contrast to those common in the rest of the European Union, where legislative underpinning for training and the active involvement of the social partners are more often the norm. It can be argued that if the active participation of all stakeholders in the VET system is an essential precondition for making sustained progress in improving the supply and usage of skills in the UK, then the British training system appears to be an inadequate vehicle for securing that participation and support.

A second conclusion is that while there undoubtedly has been progress in increasing the amount of training that takes place within the British economy, doubts remain concerning the quality of what is being provided. In particular, progress at the level of intermediate skills, where many have argued Britain's skills gap compared to its overseas competitors is most acute (Ryan 1991a), has not been very marked. Indeed, the very sharp decline in the craft apprenticeship system suggests that, in the long term, the outlook for the supply of intermediate skills in manufacturing industry may actually be set to worsen.

Finally, the main thrust of policy has been to pursue sweeping institutional reform in the belief that the creation of a market-based, employer-led training system can, of itself, deliver a fundamental change in the quantity and quality of training in Britain. The pace and scale of this wave of institutional reforms and the activity which it has generated have perhaps served to focus the attention of both policymakers and commentators on the supply of training, to the detriment of the consideration of more fundamental questions concerning the often relatively weak demand for skills in the British economy. It can be argued (Keep and Mayhew 1995) that numerous structural factors within the British economy limit the demand for skills, and that unless these factors are addressed there is a danger that any increased investment in the supply of skills will produce an inadequate rate of return, whether for individuals, firms or society as a whole. Many of these structural inhibitors are identified in this book. They include developments within the labour market, such as the growth of small firms and part-time work, and the erosion of skilled manual employment (see chapters 3, 18 and 19); the structure of consumer demand within the British economy, where the large numbers subsisting on relatively low incomes force many firms to concentrate on cost-centred competitive strategies; the difficulties in calculating returns on investment in training; and, within firms, the limited adoption of HRM policies, the frequent lack of internal labour markets and opportunities for progression, the dominance of internal cost control structures, and the increasing marginality of their UK operations to many British-based multinational companies (chapters 4 and 11).

In the light of these structural brakes on demand for higher levels of skill within the economy, the need is for policies that go beyond attempts to boost the supply of skills, and which aim to address the current limits to demand. This would mean encompassing issues such as product market strategies, job design, work organization, and wider systems of personnel management and labour utilization. Thus, rather than defining the problem as being simply about the supply of education and training, a more productive approach might be a broader focus on ways in which the design and organization of production and employment can be improved, thereby enhancing demand for, and usage of, skills.

Notes

1 Parts of this section draw on material prepared for Keep and Mayhew 1995.
2 The material in this section draws on the report by Helen Rainbird and Jill Smith, 'The Role of the Social Partners in Vocational Training in Great Britain', which was prepared for the Italian Ministry of Labour, September, 1992.

References

Ainley, P. and Corney, M. 1991: *Training for the Future: The Rise and Fall of the Manpower Services Commission.* London: Cassell.
Anderson, A. 1987: *NSTOS: Their Activities and Effectiveness.* London: Manpower Research.
Barnes, G. 1991: *An Examination of the Formulation of Policies by Training and Enterprise Councils.* Small and Medium Enterprise Working Paper, 7. Coventry: Warwick Business School.
Berry-Lound, D. and Anderson, A. 1991: *Review of the Industrial Training Organisation Network.* Sheffield: Host Consultancy / ED.
Berry-Lound, D., Chaplin, M. and O'Connell, B. 1991: Review of Industrial Training Organisations. *Employment Gazette*, October, 535–42.
Callender, C. 1992: Will NVQs Work? Evidence from the Construction Industry. IMS *Report*, 228, Sussex: Institute of Manpower Studies.
Campinos-Dubernet, M. and Grando, J.-M. 1988: Formation Professionelle Ouvrière: Trois Modeles Européennes. *Formation/Emploi*, 22, 5–29.
CBI (Confederation of British Industry) 1989: *Towards a Skills Revolution.* London: CBI.
CCSC/CLA (Centre for Corporate Strategy and Change / Coopers and Lybrand Associates) 1989: *Training in Britain: A Study of Funding Activity and Attitudes. Employers' Perspective of Human Resources.* London: HMSO.
Chapman, P. G. and Tooze, M. J. 1987: *The Youth Training Scheme in the United Kingdom.* Aldershot: Avebury.

Cockburn, C. 1987: *Two-track Training: Sex Inequalities and the YTS.* Basingstoke: Macmillan Education.

Debling, G. 1991: Developing Standards. In P. Raggatt and L. Unwin (eds), *Change and Intervention – Vocational Education and Training.* London: Falmer Press.

ED (Employment Department) 1972: *Training for the Future. A Plan for Discussion.* London: HMSO.

ED (Employment Department) 1988: *Employment for the 1990s.* Cm 540. London: HMSO.

Emmerick, M. and Peck, J. 1991: *First Report of the TEC Monitoring Project.* Manchester: Centre for Local Economic Strategies.

Emmerick, M. and Peck, J. 1992: *Reforming the TECs – Towards a New Training Strategy.* Manchester: Centre for Local Economic Strategies.

EOC (Equal Opportunities Commission) 1988: Submission, House of Lords Select Committee on the European Communities, *Vocational Training and Retraining.* London: HMSO.

Evans, B. 1992: *The Politics of the Training Market – From Manpower Services Commission to Training and Enterprise Councils.* London: Routledge.

Finegold, D. 1991: The Implications of 'Training in Britain' for the Analysis of Britain's Skills Problem. *Human Resource Management Journal*, 2, 1, 110–15.

Gallie, D. and White, M. 1993: *Employee Commitment and the Skills Revolution.* London: PSI Publishing.

Gospel, H. and Okayama, R. 1991: Industrial Training in Britain and Japan: An Overview. In H. Gospel (ed.), *Industrial Training and Technological Innovation: A Comparative and Historical Study.* London: Routledge, pp. 13–37.

IRRR (Industrial Relations Review and Report) 1992: Lean Production and Rover's 'New Deal'. *IRS Employment Trends*, 514, 12–15.

Janes, M. and Roberts, B. 1990: Labour Costs in 1988. *Employment Gazette*, September, 431–7.

Jarvis, V. and Prais, S. 1989: Two Nations of Shopkeepers: Training for Retailing in Britain and France. *National Institute Economic Review*, 128, 58–74.

Jessup, G. 1991: *Outcomes: NVQs and the Emerging Model of Education and Training.* Brighton: Falmer.

Jones, I. 1988: An Evaluation of YTS. *Oxford Review of Economic Policy*, 4, 3, 54–71.

Keep, E. 1994: The Transition from School to Work. In K. Sisson (ed.), *Personnel Management in Britain*, 2nd edn. Oxford: Blackwell.

Keep, E. and Mayhew, K. 1995: *The British System of Vocational Education and Training: A Critical Analysis.* Oxford: Oxford University Press.

Lindley, R. 1983: Active Manpower Policy. In G. S. Bain (ed.), *Industrial Relations in Britain.* Oxford, Blackwell, 339–60.

LRD (Labour Research Department) 1990: *Bargaining Report*. January, 5–11.

McCool, T. 1991: Making Standards Work Together. Presentation to CBI conference 'Leading Standards Forward', London, 3 December.

McCormick, K. 1991: The Development of Engineering Education in Britain and Japan. In H. Gospel (ed.), *Industrial Training and Technological Innovation – a Comparative and Historical Study*. London: Routledge, 38–68.

McLeish, H. 1990: Who Pays for Skills? *Labour Market Briefing*, 3. London: Labour Party.

MSC (Manpower Services Commission) 1980: *Outlook on Training. A Review of the 1973 Employment and Training Act*. London: MSC.

MSC (Manpower Services Commission) 1981: *A Framework for the Future*. London: MSC.

MSC/DES (Manpower Services Commission / Department of Education and Science) 1986: *Review of Vocational Qualifications in England and Wales*. London: HMSO.

MSF (Manufacturing, Science and Finance) 1988: *Campaigning for Training*. London: MSF.

NTTF (National Training Task Force) 1992: Draft copy of the Cleaver report (mimeo). London: NTTF.

Payne, J. 1990: *Women, Training and the Skills Shortage. The Case for Public Investment*. London: Policy Studies Institute.

Perry, P. J. C. 1976: *The Evolution of British Manpower Policy*. London: Eyre and Spottiswoode.

Prais, S. J. 1989: How Europe Would See the New British Initiative for Standardising Vocational Qualifications. *National Institute Economic Review*, 129, 52–3.

Prais, S. J., 1991: Vocational Qualifications in Britain and Europe: Theory and Practice. *National Institute Economic Review*, 135, 86–92.

Raggatt, P. 1991: Quality Assurance and NVQs. In P. Raggatt and L. Unwin (eds), *Change and Intervention: Vocational Education and Training*. London, Falmer Press, pp. 61–80.

Rainbird, H. 1988: New Technology, Training and Union Strategies. In R. Hyman and W. Streeck (eds), *New Technology and Industrial Relations*, Oxford: Blackwell, pp. 174–85.

Rainbird, H. 1990: *Training Matters: Union Perspectives on Industrial Restructuring and Training*. Oxford: Blackwell.

Rainbird, H. 1993: Union Policies towards the Training of Workers with a Low Level of Qualification. Paper prepared for the workshop 'Politiques Sindicales vers la Formation des BNQ', 18–19 March, Institut de Recherches Economiques et Sociales, Paris.

Rainbird H. and Grant, W. 1985: *Employers' Associations and Training Policy*. Coventry: Institute for Employment Research.

Reeder, D. 1981: A Recurring Debate: Education and Industry. In R. Dale, G. Esland and M. MacDonald (eds), *Education and the State: Vol. 1. Schooling and the National Interest.* Lewes: Falmer.

Ryan, P. (ed.) 1991a: *International Comparisons of Vocational Education and Training for Intermediate Skills.* London: Falmer.

Ryan, P. 1991b: How Much Do Employers Spend on Training? *Human Resource Management Journal*, 1, 4, 55–76.

Senker, P. J. 1992: *Industrial Training in a Cold Climate.* Aldershot: Avebury.

Steedman, H. and Wagner, K. 1989: Productivity, Machinery and Skills in Britain and Germany. *National Institute Economic Review*, 128, 40–57.

Streeck, W. 1989: Skills and the Limits of Neoliberalism: The Enterprise of the Future as a Place of Learning. *Work, Employment and Society*, 3, 1, 89–104.

TA (Training Agency) 1989: *Training in Britain: Employers' Activities*, Sheffield: TA.

Turner, P., Dale, I. and Hurst, C. 1992: Training – A key to the Future. *Employment Gazette*, August, 379–86.

Varlaam, C. 1987: *The Full Fact-finding Study of the NSTO System.* Brighton: Institute of Manpower Studies.

Wood, L. 1992: Urgent Need Found for Government to Examine TECs' Funding. *Financial Times*, 25 March.

18

The Low-paid and the Unorganized

Jill Rubery

In common with many countries, the distribution of earnings in Britain widened during the 1980s and 1990s (OECD 1993), resulting in a significant increase in the share of the workforce receiving relatively low earnings. These developments have been associated with various labour-market developments including: a much higher level of unemployment than that which prevailed in the 1970s; a change in the composition of labour demand away from manual and unskilled work; a continued growth in part-time jobs; and finally a major increase in the share of the labour force whose pay is determined by management without the protection of minimum wage standards established by voluntary agreement or by legal regulation. More employees are now outside than within the voluntary collective bargaining system and it is among these workers that much of the low pay is concentrated.

The British industrial relations system has always been based on voluntarist regulation. Consequently, many workers have been outside the protection of collective bargaining and have not been protected by a set of minimum employment rights established by law to apply to all workers, in contrast to the position in other member states of the European Union. What changed in Britain in the 1980s was first that the scale of the unorganized sector of the labour market expanded such that the unorganized outnumbered the organized (Millward et al. 1992), and secondly that previous trends towards extending rights and protection from the organized sectors to the weaker groups were pushed into reverse. Government policy was directed towards isolating the unionized sector, thus minimizing its influence on organizations which did not wish to participate in collective regulation, and at re-establishing managerial discretion over pay levels. This policy is seen as a means towards increasing employment, albeit at low wage levels. In 1984 the then Chancellor of the Exchequer, Nigel Lawson, expounded his view that the future for Britain lay in the creation of low-paid, low-tech jobs (Lawson 1984). Low pay is thus not regarded as an unfortunate consequence of unemployment, or of policies to free up the labour market, but as an important part of the government's overall economic strategy.

The chapter begins by assessing the extent and distribution of low pay. Its central section analyses efforts before 1979 to improve the position of the low-paid and then considers deregulation during the 1980s and 1990s. The overall argument, brought together in the concluding section, is that many developments have been worsening the position of the low-paid and that only a fundamental redesign of labour-market institutions could tackle the problem.

The Low-paid

Definitions of low pay

Low pay is necessarily a relative concept. There is no absolute standard of fair pay or indeed reasonable minimum living standards; all definitions depend on the conditions specific to a particular society and time period (Wedderburn 1974). There is also the issue that discussions of low pay tend to revolve around two quite separate definitions of low pay: one relative to the earnings of other workers, and one relative to the standards of living enjoyed by other workers. Standards of living do not just depend on an individual's earnings; also important are the individual's family situation and access to other sources of income and resources. Some argue that low pay is not a problem if it does not result in the individuals who are low-paid living in poverty: low wages are only issues of social concern if the end result is the inability of families to achieve minimum acceptable consumption standards (Layard et al. 1978; Johnson and Stark 1991). The emphasis on family income draws attention away from the issue of how much effort or how much time should have to be expended to achieve reasonable living standards; should there be a maximum number of hours of labour as well as a minimum con-sumption standard? Many low-paid workers and families may get by simply by working very long hours, sometimes in a range of different jobs; and women workers may add to long hours of domestic labour by taking on paid work at low wage rates. Often these wage rates are justified by employers on the grounds that the women are working 'only for extras' or for 'pin money'.[1] Yet without these extras many more families may fall into poverty.

The principle 'a fair day's work for a fair day's pay' may be said to apply irrespective of an individual's family circumstances. The notion that pay should be proportional to the work done and not influenced by the presumed income needs of the person employed is also the basis for the principle of equal pay for equal work between men and women (a principle now included in the 1970 Equal Pay Act as well as the European Community's Treaty of Rome). Low pay is thus best defined in terms that are independent of living standards, while at the same time the impact of low pay on poverty should still be investigated (see below).

What is the extent of low pay?

Several definitions and approaches to the measurement of low pay can be used. The most common approach is to define low pay as a certain percentage of the average earnings level; the level most frequently chosen, and the one adopted as the Council of Europe's standard of decency, is around two-thirds of the mean wage level. In practice, many studies adopt the more modest definition of two-thirds of *median* earnings. Another approach is to look at what has been happening over time to the lowest 10 per cent of the labour force; has their pay been increasing or decreasing over time relative to median or average pay?

A major problem with data on earnings is that even the most comprehensive data fail to provide a fully integrated distribution of earnings in the labour market. The New Earnings Survey provides integrated data for men and women but for full-time adults only, with part-timers and those on below adult rates excluded from the integrated analysis owing to problems with the survey sample for these groups. Thus estimates of the total number of low-paid workers are often confined to full-time adult workers, a very inadequate definition, or otherwise involve ad hoc assumptions and definitions to bring about an estimate to include all employees in the labour market. Both approaches will be adopted in the tables that follow.

Despite the data problems in defining and measuring low-paid workers there are several conclusions that follow from most studies

Table 18.1   Changes in the distribution of earnings, 1979–1993

	Gross hourly earnings as a percentage of the median for each group of full-time employees on adult rates							*Part-time women's hourly earnings as a percentage of full-time women's hourly earnings*
	All employees		*All males*		*All females*			
	Lowest decile	*Highest decile*	*Lowest decile*	*Highest decile*	*Lowest decile*	*Highest decile*		
1979	n.a.	n.a.	69	167	71	165		81.3
1983	63	185	66	182	67	177		79.1
1993	58	201	58	201	61	193		74.3

Source: New Earnings Survey 1979, 1983, 1993 (London: HMSO).

of the analysis of the extent of low pay. The first is that low pay is a major problem in Britain compared to other European countries, where there are usually either national minimum wage systems or methods of extending industry-level collective agreements to non-participating firms. The results from a recent study of low pay among full-time employees, in which low pay within each country was defined as earnings below 66 per cent of the median wage for that country, show that Britain, Ireland and Spain have the highest shares of low-paid workers (CERC 1991; Bazen and Benhayoun 1992). It is notable that Britain and Ireland are the only two EU states not to have widespread protection of minimum wage levels. Spain does have a national minimum wage but the level of the minimum is lower than that set in other European states; this may account for the high share of low-paid Spanish workers. According to these estimates, some 20 per cent of full-time employees in the British labour market are low-paid. It should also be remembered that these estimates exclude part-timers who constitute a very high share of total employment in Britain and an even higher share of the low-paid workforce. If part-timers were included Britain's position would be relatively worse, though this does not take account of the fact that in some European countries low pay is dominant more among the self-employed or the informal economy.

The second conclusion is that the incidence of relatively low pay has increased during the 1980s. As table 18.1 shows, the pay of the lowest decile of full-time workers in Britain has fallen relative to the median (and even further relative to the upper quartile or highest decile). Moreover, part-time work has both increased in significance and fallen in pay relative to female full-timers' pay (while maintaining a fairly constant relationship relative to male full-timers' pay). Young workers' pay has also fallen relative to adults through the decade.

Who are the low-paid workers?

When investigating the characteristics of low-paid workers, two features stand out above all others: the majority are women and most of these are part-timers. Table 18.2 analyses the composition of the low-paid workforce in Britain in 1991 using two definitions of low pay: less than 300 pence per hour, a pay rate close to the level of legal minimum wages set by the wages councils in 1991; and less than 360 pence per hour, a rate which is approximately 60 per cent of median earnings. It also approximates to the lowest decile of full-time hourly earnings for men and women combined. Around 4 per cent of full-timers earned under 300 pence per hour, and fewer than 10 per cent under 360 pence. When part-timers are included, the share of the low-paid in employment more than doubles to over 9 per cent and over 20 per cent respectively. On both definitions of low pay there is a fairly similar composition of low-paid workers: female part-timers accounted for close to half of all low-paid workers, and male and female part-timers combined accounted for close to 60 per cent. Women, both full- and part-time, accounted for around 70 per cent of all low-paid workers. These estimates are dependent on the earnings figures for part-timers given in the New Earnings Survey being representative of all part-timers, but evidence would suggest that these figures are likely to over- and not under-estimate part-time hourly earnings. The overall incidence of low pay and the share of part-timers among the low-paid are thus if anything likely to be even higher.

It is often argued that low-paid workers are not usually living in poverty, as part-time workers are often the second income earner in a family. In particular, the government has claimed that 80 per cent of workers who until 1993 were protected by legal minimum wages set by wages councils (see below) were not vulnerable to being in poverty as they were in families with more than one income earner. However, research commissioned by the TUC (Dickens et al. 1993:

Table 18.2 Low pay by gender and working time, 1991

Percentage of low-paid[a] workers who are:	Low pay defined as	
	(i) <300 p/hr	*(ii)* <360 p/hr
Male full-timers	17.4	19.5
Male part-timers	13.5	10.9
Female full-timers	22.3	23.2
Female part-timers	46.8	46.4
Total in employment who are low-paid (%)	9.2	20.7

[a] *New Earnings Survey* sample weights used to combine estimates of low pay for those on and not on adult rates. Otherwise weighted by Census of Employment.

Sources: New Earnings Survey, Census of Employment. Own calculations.

520) found that 'single-parent families, a group with no other source of earnings, were 50 per cent more likely [than the general population] to be working in Wages Council industries'. They also estimated that abolishing the councils would reduce the wages of a significant number of workers. Using these estimates in a model of family income indicated an increase in poverty.[2] For most low income families the main route out of poverty is through work. This argument is often used to justify deregulating the labour market and allowing the creation of more jobs which the unemployed and poor may be able to move into. Yet if deregulation leads to lower wages it is on the incomes of the working poor that the main effect is felt. The impact of such policies in America has been to increase greatly the size of the population that is both in work and in poverty (Mishel and Bernstein 1993).

Where are the low-paid?

The low-paid are found in all industries and in a very wide range of occupations. Nevertheless, low pay is also concentrated by industry and occupation, with the highest concentration occurring in distribution and catering. These industries also have the highest densities of low-paid workers. The occupations in which the majority of low-paid workers are employed are not always the same as those occupations with the highest density or share of low-paid workers among the occupational labour force (table 18.3). For example, there is a relatively low incidence of low pay among female full-time clerical workers, at 12 per cent of the total female full-time clerical labour force, but this occupational category is so important for this labour force group that in fact nearly 30 per cent of all low-paid female full-timers are clerical workers. For men it is low-skilled manual jobs (categories 8 and 9) that account for 45 per cent of all low-paid male workers, while for female full-timers it is sales and clerical work that are the most important, and for female part-timers, it is other low-skill or elementary occupations (category 9) and sales that account for the highest shares of low-paid workers.

Unfortunately, there is little systematic evidence on the relationship between low pay and the characteristics of organizations in which people are employed. Such data as are available suggest that low pay is more likely to be found in small firms and in firms where pay is not regulated by collective bargaining. Various surveys have found higher rates of low pay among organizations outside the scope

Table 18.3 Occupational distribution of workers paid less than £3.60 per hour in 1991

	Share of low-paid workers in occupations			Distribution of low-paid workers by occupation		
	Male full-time	*Female full-time*	*Female part-time*	*Male full-time*	*Female full-time*	*Female part-time*
Managerial	2.0	5.1	—	4.7	2.8	—
Professional	0.5	0.7	3.4	0.7	0.3	0.2
Associate professional	1.6	3.7	4.8	2.1	2.6	0.9
Clerical	8.5	12.1	23.9	12.7	28.9	13.4
Craft	5.3	44.0	59.6	15.3	8.8	1.6
Personal and protective service	12.6	13.4	53.4	10.5	14.1	21.3
Sales	14.6	45.4	68.0	8.6	16.5	24.7
Plant and machine operatives	9.3	36.8	49.0	23.1	15.3	3.7
Other	17.3	49.6	67.3	22.1	10.7	34.1
Non-manual	3.8	11.3	34.2	28.8	53.3	48.0
Manual	10.0	43.2	63.7	71.2	46.7	52.0
All	6.8	17.2	45.1	100.0	100.0	100.0

Source: *New Earnings Survey* 1991. Own calculations.

of effective regulation (Craig et al. 1982; Craig et al. 1985; Rubery 1987; Dickens et al. 1993), with small firms being perhaps the most likely to take the opportunity to pay low wages.

The recent WIRS study, which unfortunately only looks at establishments with more than 25 employees, provides some evidence that small size and absence of unions is likely to increase the incidence of low pay (Millward et al. 1992). Thus, as table 18.4 shows, in Britain at least one low-paid worker was found in 32 per cent of establishments which did not recognize unions, as against 19 per cent where unions were recognized. Firms with under 100 employees were also the most likely to have at least one low-paid worker. The association between low pay and the share of females and the share of part-timers in the labour force was also strong, with the probability of employing at least one low-paid worker rising with the share of women or part-timers in the labour force. This relation-

Table 18.4   Proportion of establishments with any lower-paid
employees in the private sector, 1990

	Any lower-paid employees (%)
Union representation	
No recognized union	32
One or more recognized unions	19
Number of employees at establishment	
25–99	28
100–499	25
500–999	10
1000 or more	15
Percentage of workforce female	
71 or more	46
31–70	29
0–30	17
All private sector	27

Source: Millward et al. 1992: 244.

ship is stronger in the private than in the public sector, suggesting
that perhaps regulation in the public sector does something to
reduce the link between women's work and low pay.

Most non-union firms in Britain are small and adopt ad hoc and
highly personalized payment systems, conditions which can be expected to increase the risk of low pay (Rainnie 1985; Beaumont
1987; Rubery 1987). Moreover, the rapid growth of small firms in
the 1980s and the subsequent instability among small businesses as
the recession bit in the 1990s appears to have generated large areas
of employment where there is little chance of wage regulatory systems being established. While we have no direct information on
wages in establishments with fewer than 25 employees, we do have
some information on union density among employees of these establishments from the Labour Force Survey. Here we find that union
membership is much lower than in establishments with more than
25 employees (table 18.5). It is notable that men as well as women
are unlikely to be in unions if they work in small establishments or
are employed part-time.

Table 18.5   Trade union density by hours of
work, size of establishment and gender, 1991

	Men	*Women*
Hours of work		
Part-time	13	23
Full-time	43	39
Size of establishment		
<25 employees	21	18
25 or more employees	50	42

Source: *Labour Force Survey* 1991, special tabulations.

Labour-market Regulation and Low Pay

The extension of regulation and protection, 1909–1979

In Britain all parties involved in industrial relations have traditionally
been reluctant to develop compulsory systems of regulation requiring enforcement by the state (Sisson 1987). Without universal and
compulsory labour standards the labour market will almost inevitably generate areas of employment where pay levels are low and
where unions are unable or even unwilling to organize the workforce.
The 'cost' of the preference by the union movement for voluntarist
over other systems of industrial relations has thus been the tolerance
of low pay among the less well-organized groups. For many trade
unionists this may even have had the advantage of demonstrating to
union members the benefits of membership.

Although trade unions have retained an understandable ambivalence over extending efforts on behalf of non-members, the general
thrust of both trade union and government policy up until 1979 was
to extend or generalize the minimum conditions established within
the organized section of the labour market to the low-paid. This
policy was supported and promoted by the union movement, in part
because they needed to protect their own position within organized
firms against unfettered competition from unorganized firms. Such
policies were also consistent with the union movement's commitment to fair pay, social justice and income redistribution. The principles of fair pay and employment rights also fitted with the political
agenda of the welfare state and the social market espoused by both

Labour and Conservative governments up to 1979, even if these issues were given less priority than provision of benefits for those outside of the labour market.

The wages councils Instead of establishing general legal minimum wages, a policy which would have contravened the state's commitment to voluntarist labour market regulation, legal minimum wage protection was established only in those sectors where low pay or 'sweating' was regarded as a general problem and where there was no evidence of effective voluntary regulation. In 1909 four trade boards were set up; new boards, renamed wages councils in 1945, were established in other sectors. In keeping with the voluntarist principle these bodies were established as quasi-collective bargaining institutions, consisting of two 'sides', employers and workers, in practice consisting of employers' association representatives and trade union representatives even though these were largely unorganized industries. (Indeed, the only wages council that was proposed and not eventually established was that for unlicensed residential establishments, where the employers' side was so weakly organized that no representatives could be found: Bayliss 1962.) In addition to the employer and worker sides, there were independent members on the wages councils; but the independents' role was first to try to bring about a collectively negotiated rate of pay and only to intervene in the decision-making if no agreement could be reached. Even then, they were restricted to voting with one side or the other and could not put their own proposals. The wages councils only differed from collective bargaining institutions in two main respects: the independents were present to ensure that a wage rate was eventually set even if bargaining broke down, and once set the wage rates became legally enforceable through the operation of a Wages Inspectorate who had the power to inspect the wages records of any company whose business fell mainly within the scope of a wages council.

The conversion from trade boards to wages councils came in 1945 and a major expansion of the system was introduced to cover service industries as well as manufacturing. The result was that wages councils were established in most of the industries where low pay was both concentrated and dominant, in particular in retail, catering, clothing, hairdressing and laundry as well as other miscellaneous manufacturing and service trades. Similar organizations called wages boards set minimum rates of pay in agriculture. At their peak in 1953, the wages councils and agricultural wages boards together covered 4.25 million workers, compared with a workforce of about 21.5 million (Bowen and Mayhew 1990). Some smaller industries also noted for low pay were never brought within the wages council net (for example, parts of retail, dry cleaning) but also excluded were low-paid workers and unorganized firms in industries where collective bargaining was well established for the majority of firms. Thus the wages council system was set up to supplement and not to supplant the voluntary system of regulation.

Up until 1979 the main threat to the continuation of the wages councils came from the trade union movement. Pressure had begun to mount in the late 1960s to abolish certain wages councils. They were felt to set too low rates of pay, and many unions came to the view that instead of fostering collective bargaining, they discouraged firms from engaging directly in collective bargaining and workers from joining trade unions. Full employment and the general spread of collective regulation had turned wages councils into an anachronism. This view was propagated in Bayliss's classic study of the wages councils (1962: 74): 'under full employment it is no longer the prime function of wages councils to provide a legally enforced level of wages and conditions markedly above that which would otherwise prevail'. From the viewpoint of the mid-1990s many trade unionists have come to regret the time when they had such misplaced confidence in their ability to regulate the labour market without assistance from institutions such as wages councils.

Under pressure from the unions the government did agree to the abolition of a range of wages councils, mainly in manufacturing but also including one large service sector wages council, industrial and staff canteens. A study was set up to investigate to what extent the claims of the trade union movement were justified: did the abolition of wages councils lead to the development of more effective and extensive collective bargaining, and did the abolition of councils reduce, increase or have little effect on the incidence of low pay? The results showed that even before the major change in union fortunes in the 1980s, the claim that abolition would help the low-paid by bringing them properly within the voluntary collective bargaining net was unfounded (Craig et al. 1982). Not only had effective collective bargaining failed to develop in all but one of the sectors studied following abolition, but there was also evidence that a minority of workers in five industries, and possibly a majority in the case of the abolished industrial and staff canteens wages council, would have been better off if the wages councils had been maintained.

Extending collectively agreed labour standards   Wages councils constituted the main way in which workers outside the protection of voluntary collective regulation were provided with some form of wage protection. The main alternative to separate legal minimum wage systems is to make collectively agreed minima legally binding even on organizations not party to the collective agreements. This system is used in many EU member states including the large countries of Germany, Italy, France and Spain. In Britain this type of mechanism has generally not been used, in part because collective agreements are not even legally binding instruments on voluntary participants. However, there have been three exceptions to this general pattern.

The first was the series of Fair Wages Resolutions by the House of Commons. The initial resolution was passed in 1891, but its modern version was passed in 1946. This required government contractors to pay fair wages and to respect the rights of their employees to be members of trade unions. Fair wages were usually interpreted as at least equal to the minimum rates set by the relevant industry-level agreement. This provision thereby both protected public sector employees from competition based on 'unfair wages' and at the same time encouraged the extension of industry-level collective agreements to firms that otherwise might have chosen to set pay independently.

The second way in which voluntary agreements have been extended to non-participating employers was through the provisions of the 1975 Employment Protection Act, in particular Schedule 11. This act established a mechanism by which workers employed by firms which did not engage in collective bargaining could seek union recognition and the right to bargain collectively. If that failed, under Schedule 11 they could also seek the imposition on the employer of a requirement to at least match the 'general level' of pay for comparable workers in the district, a ruling in practice interpreted, when applied, as the relevant industry-level minimum rates. These provisions were not extensively used during the short period that they were available in English and Scottish law (1975 to 1980). The groups using them tended to be small, and relatively few claims came from sectors where low pay was concentrated. Moreover, the mechanisms for implementing these rights were complex and unwieldy; in contrast to other countries a separate case had to be taken for each individual firm and there was no system for imposing the minimum rates on all firms in the industry (Jones 1980).

Third, trade unions in some industries and sectors were active in extending collective regulation to non-participating firms. This action took various forms. For example, in the printing industry the unions were sufficiently well organized to sustain boycotts of non-union firms. In the public sector, unions were sometimes able, at times through the political support of councillors, to ensure that public-sector work was subcontracted to unionized firms or to those observing collective agreements. However, few unions were active in ensuring that all firms in the labour market observed the collective agreements to reduce the threat of 'unfair competition'. Particularly in the 1970s, the unions could be accused of having become complacent about collective bargaining at the industry level. Instead, they put most of their energies into the organization of bargaining at the establishment or company level. Unions were prepared in many cases to allow the industry agreement to become only a safety net, to provide a protection for workers in the least organized firms, but the unions did not consider that relegating the agreements to this function might jeopardize their continuation in the longer term. Yet if industry-level agreements disappear, a large number of employers, and their workforces, are necessarily in danger of being left outside the collective bargaining net with no guidance on minimum wage rates or the 'going rate' of wage increases in the industry. As we will see below, measures were taken in the early 1980s by the incoming Thatcher government to ensure that individual employers had the 'right' to set wages without interference from unions or collective agreements. However, it is perhaps somewhat ironic that in the majority of industries in the UK this right was already firmly established. Even employers who were members of employers' associations were often left free to interpret and implement the agreement without scrutiny from the union movement.

Individual employment rights and labour market regulation While the union movement remained attached to voluntarism in the area of collective regulation, there was from the 1960s onwards a greater interest in and pressure for the establishment of individual employment rights, many of which might be expected to be of assistance to workers outside firms covered by collective bargaining. These rights were primarily concerned with employment security, covering redundancy, notice, unfair dismissal, maternity leave etc., and did not extend to substantive rights such as minimum pay or paid holidays.

Of more direct interest to the issue of low pay, rights not to be discriminated against by gender or by race were introduced. As chapter 15 shows, the 1970 Equal Pay Act required firms to pay equal pay for the same work and to establish pay grading structures, where they already existed, which were free from sex bias. The result of this legislation was a marked narrowing of the earnings gap between men and women between 1970 and 1975, the date of implementation. As women constitute the majority of low-paid workers this development clearly had a major impact on low pay, reducing the earnings spread by raising the minimum wages previously set for women's work closer to those established for men's work. Although the principle applied to all firms, in practice it was the more regulated firms where there was a stronger effect because it was where there was a formal pay grading structure that action had to be taken to eliminate a male and a female minimum wage rate (Craig et al. 1985). Where unions were present, strong pressure was put on employers to establish the new pay structure based on the previous male minimum rate; where employers were free to establish the rate without union regulation, the new minimum rate was more likely to have been established around the previous female minimum rate. Moreover, evidence suggests that much of the impact on women's wages arose through the generalizing of the new wage structures through industry-level agreements and through wages councils (Zabalza and Tzannatsos 1985). Thus there was some reduction in low pay in the 1970s as a consequence of an effective interaction between new individual rights and the system of voluntary regulation. The widespread impact of these changes relied on mechanisms that allowed the unions to generalize the benefits to workers found in relatively unorganized as well as organized firms.

Protection against low pay may require not only direct regulation of wages for adult workers but also regulations to protect against competition from workers who may be willing to take jobs at low wage levels. Two major sources of potential competition come from the unemployed, both adult workers and young workers. In the 1970s, the unemployment benefit system could be considered to have reduced pressures on workers to take jobs at low wage levels. The unemployed were entitled not only to a basic benefit, but also to an earnings-related supplement for the first six months. Moreover, the unemployed were allowed more freedom than nowadays to turn down jobs that did not suit their income or skill requirements. Trade unions also sought to protect adult workers from competition from young people who may be willing to work at very low wages rather than remain unemployed. Trade unions in Britain have historically aimed to link youth wages to adult wages and certainly by the 1970s had succeeded in setting youth rates at relatively high percentages of adult rates (Ryan 1987; Marsden and Ryan 1991). In the 1980s, both of these methods of reducing 'competition' at the bottom of the labour market were to be challenged by the incoming Thatcher government.

Deregulation after 1979

The voluntarist system of regulation as it existed up until 1979 was by no means an ideal or effective system of protection against low pay. Much of the labour market remained outside any system of legal compulsion to pay fair wages, and even within the wages council sector pay was often low and underpayment was widespread, in part at least because of the sheer complexity of the wages council orders (Pond 1983). Trade unions failed to understand the depth of the problem of regulating pay in small firms and competitive industries and seemed content to rely on the mystical powers of full employment to keep up a reasonable floor to wages. Nevertheless, there was a general commitment to the existence and extension of labour standards. Above all there was a commitment to collective bargaining and a belief that those workers outside the collective bargaining net should be as far as possible integrated into the system and paid comparable or fair wages.

The changes that occurred in the 1980s and are still taking place in the 1990s involved a rejection of all these principles and objectives. The shortcomings of the system, that workers were only protected against low pay at their employers' discretion, became to the government the advantages of the voluntarist system. The new principle was that employers should be free to decide whether or not to recognize unions and to determine their own rates of pay according to their own individual circumstances. Any mechanisms that encouraged coordination of pay rate between firms, or that enshrined the principles of comparability or fair pay, were to be regarded as suspect. The problems with wages councils were no longer that they set too low pay and discouraged collective bargaining; instead they were deemed to set too high wage rates and to discourage employment growth. Out of this turnaround in attitudes and approach to the issue of low pay and regulation came a series of measures which reversed the tendencies described above. These policy reversals can be discussed using the same categories as above.

The dismantling of the wages councils   As wages councils represent the most blatant deviation from the notion of a free market and a voluntarist system of regulation, it is perhaps surprising that the most immediate attacks on labour-market regulation by the incoming Thatcher government were not aimed at the wages councils. Indeed, it was not until 1986 that there was a serious attempt to abolish the councils, and even then this resulted only in legislation to reduce their powers.[3] In 1988 a plan to abolish was again withdrawn and it was only in 1993 that the complete abolition of the system was effected. One reason for the survival of the wages councils must be the support that the system received from the employers' associations in the industries concerned, certainly at the time that abolition was mooted in 1986. This employer support reflected a belief that councils prevented undercutting of wages and could promote 'good industrial relations'; at the 1988 exercise, 80 per cent of replies to the government's consultation document opposed total abolition (Bryson 1989). Later that support reduced, in part because of the restrictions that the wages councils placed on Sunday trading in retailing (that is, the employers came to favour abolition for reasons other than that the councils set too high wages). With no particular constituency supporting abolition, the government perhaps felt it was too much trouble to take the steps to abolish the councils in the 1980s, especially in the run-up to the 1987 election, but in 1993, with much of their other legislation on labour markets already on the statute books, there was no good reason for further maintaining a system to which they were ideologically opposed. An additional suggestion is that abolition helped to secure political support from the Right of the Conservative party (Pond 1993).

The arguments that the government put forward in favour of abolition were threefold: first, that it would stimulate jobs; second, that the wages councils were an anachronism which no longer affected pay except for a small minority; and third, that most people who worked in wages council industries were not living in poverty, and thus there was no social justice argument for maintaining the system. We have already argued that social justice may require a fair reward for work as well as fair living standards, and that in any case there is evidence that falls in wages council rates will hurt poor-income households. The government has, however, been less than explicit about what it expects to happen to wage rates. On the one hand, it has argued that wages councils are an irrelevancy and their abolition will have little impact on pay. On the other hand, the beneficial effects of abolition on job creation are expected to come through wage cuts.

One problem in predicting the likely effects of abolition is that the 1986 reform which took young people out of wages council protection did not produce consistent evidence of a major relative decline in youth pay (Lucas 1991; Employment Market Research Unit 1993). However, the maintenance of minimum wages for adults may have served to keep up young people's pay especially when they were working alongside adults. Now there are no minimum rates; where there is also no collective bargaining, rates may begin to fall throughout the industry. One of the reasons why it has been argued that the effect of abolition may be relatively small is that most workers in wages council industries do receive rates somewhat in excess of wages council orders. However, many firms may have set their wages with regard to wages council rates and aimed to pay slightly above this floor. Once the floor to wages is removed, wages for the majority of the workforce may begin to fall. Whether such falls in wage rates for low-paid workers can be expected to lead to job creation is discussed further below. Wages council industries are in fact much less well placed to develop voluntary collective bargaining systems than they were in the 1970s or early 1980s; fewer firms recognize unions or are party to voluntary collective agreements, and thus the impact of abolition is likely to be to leave the majority even of large firms in these industries without guidelines as to basic minimum wage rates.

Narrowing the application of collectively agreed labour standards   The new Conservative regime after 1979 quickly announced its decisions to rescind the fair wages clause and to abolish the provisions for extensions of collective agreements under Schedule 11 of the Employment Protection Act. The repeal of the fair wages clause was important in paving the way for another major part of the government's economic policy – the introduction of compulsory competitive tendering into many areas of public-sector services. The explicit aim of this policy was to reduce costs, particularly in ancillary services where public-sector employers were considered likely to be paying wages in excess of the rates at which private firms could recruit workers. The repeal of the resolution removed any scrutiny of the rates set by the tendering firms. As shown in chapter 16, compulsory tendering has reduced wages both where private-sector firms have taken over services and where contracts have been retained in-house. One of the main ways that these workers have seen their remuneration package cut is in reduced holiday pay (Crompton and Sandersen 1990) and also bonuses.

In addition to limiting the influence of industry-level agreements to public sector contractors, the government took steps to prevent unions taking action against firms that refused to recognize unions, operate closed shops or respect industry-level agreements. Regulations against secondary picketing and 'blacking' reduced the ability of unions to prevent the entry of non-union firms into the labour market, for example in printing.

However, government opposition was not only to the extension of collectively agreed minima to non-participating firms but to the whole concept of industry- or occupation-based minimum wage standards. As the 1980s progressed, many industry-level collective agreements disappeared. The outcome is that the majority of employees do not now have their pay determined by collective bargaining, and many small firms in particular are left with no guidance as to what wage rates or wage increases to pay.

These regulatory changes have considerably narrowed the scope and influence of wage protection mechanisms in Britain. The pay determination system is now much more fragmented and there is no longer a web of industry-level minimum rates and wages council rates setting a floor to wages in the labour market. The impact of these regulatory changes has been enhanced by changes in the structure and composition of employment that has reduced the scope and scale of collective regulation. The move away from manufacturing employment and towards private service sector employment has tended to reduce the share of the workforce covered by collective bargaining. Other changes that have decreased the influence of collective bargaining on pay included the rapid expansion of small firms in the 1980s. Part-time work has also increased, again increasing problems of organization. Growth of female employment is also often cited as a reason for reductions in union coverage, but as we see in chapter 6 and table 18.5 the lower rates of unionization among women are more associated with the type of industry in which they are employed, and their involvement in part-time work, and not because of gender differences *per se*. However, women constitute the bulk of low-paid workers, many of them being low-paid even when covered by forms of collective bargaining. Thus the increase in female employment may itself be considered to expand the potential pool of low-paid workers.

Limiting individual employment rights, and labour-market deregulation
As discussed in chapter 9, the thrust of policy since 1979 has been to
reduce the level of individual employment rights, albeit from an
already low base, and to introduce a range of measures to increase
labour-market competition based on low wages. The link between
young people's pay and adult workers' pay was targeted in a series of
policies, including the removal of young people from the scope of
wages councils; the payment of a low allowance to young people on
the Youth Training Scheme (well below the rates previously set for
trainees in collective agreements); and the Young Workers Scheme
(in operation from 1983 to 1985), which subsidized employers who
took on young people provided they paid a wage below a fixed
amount. These measures, coupled with the impact of high unemployment among young people in the early 1980s, resulted in a
significant widening in the rates of pay between adult and youth
labour. For example, as table 18.6 shows, among female full-time
manual workers in Great Britain, those aged under 18 earned 69 per
cent of the average of the group; by 1992 the proportion was 64 per
cent.

More pressures have also been placed on the unemployed to take
low wage jobs, and the cushion of the earnings related supplement
has been removed. The large increase in the numbers of unemployed
in the early 1980s, and again in the 1990s, has in itself added
considerably to competitive pressure on wages at the bottom of the
labour market.

Table 18.6 Youth earnings in relation to adult earnings

| | Male | | | | Female | | | |
| | Manual | | Non-manual | | Manual | | Non-manual | |
	<18	18–20	<18	18–20	<18	18–20	<18	18–20
1980	45	73	35	51	69	90	55	74
1986	42	68	31	45	68	85	51	66
1992	42	65	31	42	64	81	48	74

Figures give average gross weekly earnings as a percentage of the average for all
employees in a given group.

Source: *New Earnings Survey*, various years.

Low pay: A trade-off between equity and efficiency? The deregulation of the labour market and the restrictions placed on the influence of unions and collective bargaining has been associated with an expansion of low-paid work in the economy. This association does not necessarily mean that more jobs have been created. Many of the currently low-paid jobs would be likely still to have been available if a higher floor to the labour market had been established. For example, many part-time jobs are created to reduce the total number of labour hours that the firm employs, and many firms regard the opportunity to pay part-time workers a lower hourly rate than full-timers as simply an added bonus.

Most research has examined the reverse process of raising minimum wage levels. Much of it has adopted a conventional economists' model of the labour market, neglecting wider issues of inequality. None the less, the results do not support the view that increasing minimum wages reduces jobs. In the United States, Card (1992) could find no such association. His explanation was that, at low wage levels, employers make 'monopsony profits' which are simply eroded by a rise in the minimum wage. The European evidence indicates that minimum wage protection increases the earnings of young workers and slightly reduces employment among such workers; there is no effect on the employment of other groups (Bazen and Benhayoun 1992: 632).

Nevertheless, the government sees the expansion of low wage work as evidence in support of deregulated labour markets. These arguments run counter to those of many European governments and the European Commission. This view that the future of Europe should lie in high productivity sectors was part of the reason for the inclusion of the Social Chapter in the Maastricht treaty (Sengenberger 1992). The Social Chapter is designed to provide a guarantee of basic social rights to workers and is based on a view that there are both equity and efficiency reasons for social regulation of the labour market. The equity argument stems from the notion of citizenship: if the integration of the European Union is designed to enhance the well-being of its citizens then every citizen should be at least guaranteed some basic social protection. Labour markets cannot be treated like commodity markets; employees depend on their jobs for their livelihood and as such can be subject to great pressure to accept unreasonable terms and conditions.

The efficiency argument is that without some form of regulation of the labour market there is a danger of the good employers facing unfair competition. Employers or indeed whole member states who fail to provide reasonable conditions to their workers may compete against the technologically more advanced firms and countries, undermine their competitive strength and weaken the ability of Europe to compete on the basis of advanced production methods and innovative products.

Regulatory mechanisms which provide a floor to the level of wages in the labour market provide both protection to workers and protection to those employers who provide fair terms and conditions against unfair competition. These arguments that reducing low wages can improve both efficiency and equity were deployed by the Labour party when it included a national minimum wage as part of its 1992 election manifesto. The Conservative party argued strongly against such a minimum wage and claimed that estimates showed that such a wage would lead to a major reduction in employment (DE 1990). However, many of these estimates were based on economic models which were built on assumptions that any increase in wages would significantly reduce the number of jobs; thus the estimates derive from a particular view of how economies function. Those adopting a less deterministic view of the relationship between wage levels and employment have found that a national minimum wage may reduce the viability of some jobs (Bazen 1990; Gregg 1990; Bayliss 1991; IPM 1991; Wilkinson 1992), but estimate the short-term employment loss to be around 100,000 at the wage level proposed by the Labour party in 1992. Moreover, some argue that the establishment of minimum labour standards may at the same time provide a basis for establishing higher levels of productivity and also greater stability at the bottom end of the labour market. While the price of labour may be one factor in determining Britain's ability to compete in world markets and achieve full employment, it is not necessarily the case that pay flexibility policies should be concentrated on those whose pay is already well below the average.

Conclusions and Prospects

Shortly after re-entering office in 1992, the Conservatives reaffirmed their belief in the free market and in the need for wage levels to fall even among the low-paid by abolishing the wages councils. These moves seem certain to cause yet further increases in low pay, and may lead to reversals of the gains that female workers made in the

1970s in relative pay because of the concentration of women in wages council sectors. Thus Britain seems set to move yet further away from the European model of regulation of low wages (Bazen and Benhayoun 1992; Rubery 1992).

The prospects for the 1990s are thus for yet further increases in the low-paid labour force, with perhaps the only constraint on these trends coming from the EU. One challenge to the government's policy of low wage competition has already had some success in Europe. Recent rulings suggest that workers who are transferred from the public to the private sector under the system of compulsory competitive tendering, a core part of the government's economic strategy, may be covered by the European Directive on the Transfer of Undertakings which requires employees who are transferred from one business to another not to suffer changes in terms and conditions (Napier 1993). Not only may these rulings restrict future plans for competitive tendering, as firms will not be able to compete on the basis of lower wages, it may also be the case that workers transferred before these rulings could claim compensation.

Here there is a clash of philosophies: between the view that job loss or pay reductions are part of the risks that workers have to bear in a freely operating market economy, and the view that workers have a right to protection against the impact of changes which are outside their control and which otherwise may destabilize their working and social lives. There are few grounds for believing that this clash will lead to any fundamental change in British government policy. Moreover, even if we were to have a government that put less emphasis on the free market, the effect on pay determination might be only slight, at least in the short term. Many of the institutions of labour-market regulation, where effects took many years to build up, from industry-level collective agreements to wages councils, have disappeared. It would take a major ideological shift back in favour of wage regulation at the labour-market level for the developments in the 1980s to be reversed. Policies to reduce low pay now require not the reactivation but the rebuilding and redesign of labour market institutions and regulatory mechanisms.

Notes

1 The consultative document published by the government on the abolition of wages councils indicated the fact that many of the workers

covered by wages councils were part-timers, contributing a second income to the household. This was a factor in the decision to abolish the councils.

2 The population of families includes only those where there is at least one person in work. If wages rates fell by around 10 per cent, 13 per cent of the poorest families would be affected compared to less than 5 per cent overall, and their income would fall by nearly 7 per cent compared to an average income fall of less than 4 per cent.

3 The reform of the wages councils introduced in 1986 reduced the powers of the wages councils to set anything other than a minimum rate of pay and an overtime rate. Thus, rates for skilled workers, regional differentials and holiday pay arrangements were no longer set by the councils. The other part of the reform was to take those under 21 out of the scope of the councils (previously, minimum wages were generally applied at 18, and younger workers received a lower but regulated minimum wage).

References

Bayliss, F. 1962: *British Wages Councils*. Oxford: Blackwell.

Bayliss, F. 1991: *Making a Minimum Wage Work*. Fabian Pamphlet, 545. London: Fabian Society.

Bazen, S. 1990: On the Employment Effects of Introducing a National Minimum Wage in the UK. *British Journal of Industrial Relations*, 28, 2, 215–26.

Bazen, S. and Benhayoun, G. 1992: Low Pay and Wage Regulation in the European Community. *British Journal of Industrial Relations*, 30, 3, 623–38.

Beaumont, P. 1987: *The Decline of Trade Union Organisation*. London: Croom Helm.

Bowen, A. and Mayhew, K. (eds) 1990: *Improving Incentives for the Low-Paid*. London: Macmillan.

Bryson, A. 1989: *Undervalued, Underpaid and Undercut: The Future of the Wages Councils*. Pamphlet 53. London: Low Pay Unit.

Card, D. 1992: Do Minimum Wages Reduce Employment? A Case Study of California, 1987–89. *Industrial and Labor Relations Review*, 46, 1, 22–37.

CERC (Centre d'Etudes des Revenus et Coûts) 1991: *Les Bas Salaires dans les Pays de la Communauté Européenne*, n. 101. Paris: CERC.

Craig, C., Garnsey, E. and Rubery, J. 1985: *Payment Structures and Smaller Firms: Women's Employment in Segmented Labour Markets*. Department of Employment Research Paper, no. 48. London: HMSO.

Craig, C., Rubery, J., Tarling, R. and Wilkinson, F. 1982: *Labour Market Structure, Worker Organisation and Low Pay*. Cambridge: CUP.

Crompton, R. and Sandersen, K. 1990: *Gendered Jobs and Social Change*. Unwin Hyman: London.

DE (Department of Employment) 1990: Estimating the Effect of a National Minimum Wage. A note by Officials in the Employment Department, January. London: DE. (Referenced in S. Bazen and G. Benhayoun, Low Pay and Wage Regulation in the European Community. *British Journal of Industrial Relations*, 30, 3, 623–38.)

Dickens, R., Gregg, P., Machin, S., Manning, A. and Wadsworth, J. 1993: Wages Councils: Was There a Case for Abolition? *British Journal of Industrial Relations*, 31, 4, 515–29.

Employment Market Research Unit 1993: The Pay of Young People in Wages Council Trades since the 1986 Wages Act. *Employment Gazette*, January, 690–2.

Gregg, P. 1990: A National Minimum Wage. *National Institute Economic Review*, 134, 60–3.

IPM (Institute of Personnel Management) 1991: *Minimum Wage: An Analysis of the Issues*. London: IPM.

Johnson, P. and Stark, G. 1991: The Effects of a Minimum Wage on Family Incomes. *Fiscal Studies*, 12, 3, 88–93.

Jones, M. 1980: CAC and Schedule 11: The Experience of Two Years. *Industrial Law Journal*, 9, 1, 28–44.

Lawson, N. 1984: Mais lecture, reprinted as 'The British Experiment'. *Public Money*, 4, 2, 45–8.

Layard, R., Piachaud, D. and Stewart, M. 1978: *The Causes of Poverty*. Royal Commission on the Distribution of Income and Wealth, Background Paper no. 5. HMSO: London.

Lucas, R. 1991: Remuneration Practice in a Wages Council Sector: Some Empirical Observations in Hotels. *Industrial Relations Journal*, 22, 4, 273–85.

Marsden, D. and Ryan, P. 1991: Youth Pay and Training in Industrial Countries. In P. Ryan, R. Edwards and P. Garonna (eds), *The Problem of Youth*. Basingstoke: Macmillan.

Millward, N., Stevens, M., Smart, D. and Hawes, W. R. 1992: *Workplace Industrial Relations in Transition*. Aldershot: Dartmouth.

Mishel, L. and Bernstein, J. 1993: *The State of Working America*. Economic Policy Institute, New York: M. E. Sharpe.

Napier, B. 1993: *CCT, Market Testing and Employment Rights: The Effects of TUPE and the Acquired Rights Directive*. London: Institute for Employment Rights.

OECD (Organization for Economic Cooperation and Development) 1993: *Employment Outlook*. Paris: OECD.

Pond, C. 1983: Wages Councils, the Unorganised and the Low Paid. In G. Bain (ed.), *Industrial Relations in Britain*. Oxford: Blackwell.

Pond, C. 1993: Address to the Industrial Law Society, May.

Rainnie, A. 1985: Is Small Beautiful? Industrial Relations in Small Clothing Firms. *Sociology*, 19, 2, 213–24.

Rubery, J. 1987: Flexibility of Labour Costs in Non-union Firms. In R. Tarling (ed.), *Flexibility of Labour Markets*. London: Academic.

Rubery, J. 1992: Pay, Gender and the Social Dimension to Europe. *British Journal of Industrial Relations*, 30, 4, 605–21.

Ryan, P. 1987: Trade Unionism and the Pay of Young Workers. In P. Junankar (ed.), *From School to Unemployment: The Labour Market for Young People*. London: Macmillan.

Sengenberger, W. 1992: Future Prospects for the European Labour Market: Vision and Nightmares. In A. Castro, P. Mehaut and J. Rubery (eds), *International Integration and Labour Market Organisation*. London: Academic.

Sisson, K. 1987: *The Management of Collective Bargaining: An International Comparison*. Oxford: Blackwell.

Wedderburn, D. (ed.) 1974: *Poverty, Inequality and Class Structure*. Cambridge: Cambridge University Press.

Wilkinson, F. 1992: *Why Britain Needs a Minimum Wage*. London: Institute for Public Policy Research.

Zabalza, A. and Tzannatsos, Z. 1985: *Women and Equal Pay*. Cambridge: Cambridge University Press.

19

Employment Relations in Small Firms

Richard Scase

Our knowledge of industrial relations in small firms is highly limited for two major reasons. First, small businesses have received little attention in academic social research. Second, issues of employer–employee relations have been considered to be non-problematic on the grounds that 'harmony' prevails. This chapter queries this assumption and suggests that there is a diversity of attitudes and practices within the small firms sector which, in turn, affect the character of social relations that exist between employers and employees. It argues that there is a need for further detailed comparative research that will enable us to understand more adequately the diversity of employers' strategies and how these, within different contexts, are negotiated with employees to determine varying patterns of accommodation ranging from positive commitment to sullen acquiescence. The chapter concludes with some suggestions for further research, emphasizing the need for the study of employment relations in non-traditional small businesses where contrasting interpersonal relations prevail.

Small Firms in the Economy

The study of small firms

In the EC in 1988, businesses with fewer than 10 employees accounted for no less than 92 per cent of all enterprises and for 30 per cent of total employment. The respective figures for firms with between 10 and 500 employees were 8 per cent and 41 per cent. By contrast, large-scale enterprises employing more than 500 workers accounted for only 0.1 per cent of all firms and 29 per cent of employment (Eurostat 1992). Thus, small firms constitute a dominant feature of the modern economy, with no fewer than one-third of all employees in Europe employed within very small-scale enterprises with less than 10 workers. Despite this, our knowledge of the social dynamics of small businesses remains highly limited. Why should this be? Why have social scientists been reluctant to study the work experiences of one-third of the labour force, instead concentrating their attention upon the 'other' one-third who are employed by very large organizations? There are a number of reasons.

A major factor is that, until recently, small businesses were perceived to be a declining feature of the modern economy (Goss 1991a). It was argued that forces of modern capitalism, with their inherent tendencies to the concentration and centralization of production, would lead to the growth of monopoly and quasi-monopoly enterprises, contributing to the long-term decline of small-scale forms of production. This is a predominant assumption among many Marxist writers who, in their belief in inevitable historical tendencies, considered small firms to be of little intellectual interest. Indeed, they viewed them as a 'relic' of an earlier stage within the development of the capitalist mode of production (Wright 1978). Alongside increasing concentration of economic production, it was held that there is a growing polarization of labour markets as craft forms of work become superseded by tasks that require little in the form of skills. Accordingly, the de-skilling of work went alongside the growth of large corporations, leading to the emergence of class structures wherein the petite bourgeoisie – the self-employed and the owners of small-scale enterprises – were becoming irrelevant (Scase 1982). Such theoretical assumptions among social scientists led them to focus almost exclusively upon the labour processes and the social relations of large-scale corporations, since it was these that were considered to be the 'motors' of economic development and the context within which major class struggles are acted out (Braverman 1974). The outcome has been an industrial sociology and an industrial relations which have as their underpinnings theories of labour process based on the social relations of large-scale corporations. Accordingly, with a few notable exceptions, the employment relations of small firms have been overlooked.

But there is a further reason for our lack of knowledge and understanding of small-scale enterprises. Until the closing years of the 1980s, their study was considered to be of dubious intellectual value. This was not only for the reasons stated above but because of the political rhetoric which, after the late 1970s, surrounded discussions of small business. Within the political agenda, Thatcherism was able to associate small business start-up and growth with traditional Conservative ideals of individualism, enterprise, self-reliance and anti-collectivism (Scase and Goffee 1987). To undertake research into small businesses in the 1980s, therefore, ran the risk of appearing to endorse these ideals rather than to be seen as investigating a legitimate area of academic social science research. It was not until the mid-1980s that such assumptions became less prevalent and that detailed and theoretically informed inquiries began to investigate the social dynamics of small firms. At that time, it was recognized that the economies of Western Europe and the United States were undergoing a number of fundamental structural changes such that small-scale forms of economic organization were becoming more, rather than less, prevalent. Further, it was more readily admitted by social scientists that processes associated with the internal dynamics of large-scale organizations – which had been to the forefront of their preoccupations – could only be fully understood by reference to those same structural processes associated with the growth of small firms (Piore and Sabel 1984). Hence, it became accepted that small businesses constituted a legitimate area of academic inquiry because of a range of ideological and material functions that these fulfil in modern capitalist society.

Functions of small firms

Ideologically, small firms fulfil a key function in the modern economy because they sustain notions of competition and of the free market. As such, they conceal the dominance that quasi-monopoly corporations are able to exercise within many economic sectors. Equally, the possibilities for business start-up, absent as they were in the now demised East European state socialist countries, underwrite claims that market economies are 'open' and offer opportunities for personal success for those who are prepared to extend the necessary 'effort and self-sacrifice'. Accordingly, the persistence of strata of self-employed and small-scale employers offers the 'promise' of personal achievement for those who for a variety of reasons are disadvantaged in the pursuit of more conventional careers within the more hierarchical structures of large-scale organizations (Burrows 1991).

Women and members of ethnic minorities are often attracted to entrepreneurship and small-scale business proprietorship as a result of perceiving that for reasons of prejudice, discrimination and social disadvantage, they are unlikely to obtain occupational success according to more traditional career routes (Goffee and Scase 1985). As such, business start-up – as an ideological appeal – functions as a safety valve within the capitalist order. Indeed, Thatcherism fully exploited this in the 1980s when in a period of dramatic economic restructuring, extended recession and long-term unemployment, successive Conservative governments offered business start-up as the solution not only to these macrostructural issues but also as a panacea for those individuals whose livelihoods had been destroyed by these broader economic changes.

But if entrepreneurship and small business ownership have a significant function in legitimizing the predominant capitalist order, their material contribution is even more pronounced. As noted above, small businesses employ approximately one-third of all workers in the European Union. Consequently, they fulfil a key function in determining the pay, working and living conditions of millions of workers and are thus highly significant in the structuring of labour markets. They are equally significant in the impact which they have upon the policies formulated by organizations representing the interests of large employers, unions and governments. Because of roughly one-third of workers employed in small businesses, the outcome of government policies for the economic viability of small firms cannot be neglected. Witness the role of the French farming community in the determination of EU agricultural policies, and similarly the lobbying of small business organizations in Britain in shaping the legislation affecting employment and social legislation.

But perhaps most importantly of all, small businesses often have close economic relationships with larger enterprises. Indeed, the profits and growth of the latter can be highly contingent upon their relationships with the former. Often this will take the form of subcontracting or 'out-putting', as in manufacturing, or of licensing and franchising, as in retailing. In the case of the former, various components are manufactured out-house before being assembled into completed products within large-scale work processes. Indeed, since the very beginnings of the industrial revolution, the growth of manufacturing has been characterized by the parallel processes of *centralization* and *decentralization* in productive activities. Marx was one of the first to identify such tendencies and, as he stated,

Accumulation and the concentration accompanying it are, therefore, not only scattered over many points but the increase of each functioning capital is thwarted by the formation of new and sub-divisions of old capitals. Accumulation, therefore, presents itself on the one hand as increasing concentration of the means of production and of command over labour, on the other, as the repulsion of many individual capitals from one another. (Marx 1974: 586)

In view of this observation, it is perhaps surprising that Marxists have devoted almost excessive attention to the processes of concentration but with so little concomitant interest in those of fragmentation. Within manufacturing, Fordist production methods, based upon the principles of scientific management and the standardization of products, have been heavily dependent upon subcontractors who, in competition with each other, provide the various components for later assembly. If an inherent contradiction of Fordist work methods is an increase in labour costs because of favourable conditions for the growth of organized labour and collective bargaining, the associated processes of out-putting and subcontracting can mitigate this effect. Such processes encourage the fragmentation of labour markets, the differentiation of working conditions and employment relations, and the growth of enterprise-based payment systems. They create, in other words, the very material and ideological conditions that militate against the development of collective organization, action and consciousness among employees (Sabel 1982). Centre–periphery labour markets, with the latter consisting of those engaged in lower-paid, insecure and usually unskilled jobs in small-scale enterprises, are a feature of almost all of the capitalist economies and tend to be a direct outcome of the relations of dependency and symbiosis that exist between large- and small-scale enterprises (Friedman 1977). Such features of national labour markets continue to persist, though they tend to be concealed beneath managerial rhetoric which extols the virtues of 'network' organizations, strategic alliances, joint ventures, 'externalizing' production and just-in-time methods of management. Within these managerial strategies, small businesses become increasingly locked within webs of dependency, with their economic viability determined by the purchasing capacity of their major customers.

Although not all small firms are located within such market conditions, in one way or another, the economic circumstances of the greater majority are either directly or indirectly affected. Even those geared to trading within the areas of retailing and distribution – rather than in manufacturing – are constrained by the dictates of the market as shaped by the policies and strategies of large-scale companies. Indeed, the market context of small firms and the variable relationships between them and large corporations, constitute distinct categories which have been used for the purposes of analysing small businesses. According to Rainnie, it is possible to identify four types of such firms – *dependent, dominated, isolated* and *innovative* (Rainnie 1989).

Varieties of small firm

For Rainnie, *dependent* firms are of the kind discussed above. Their economic viability is determined by their larger customers with whom they trade. However, because they act as subcontractors – as, for example, in the engineering and electronics industries – the nature of their internal work processes is also externally regulated through their purchasers' specifications about quality and quantity of output. Negotiated prices within usually highly competitive market circumstances clearly have knock-on effects for costs including level of wages, fringe benefits and, hence, employer–employee relations. Even so, such constraints merely constitute parameters within which a variety of negotiated arrangements between workers and employers can be determined. Often the owners, as subcontractors, can be little more than sub-agents for their larger customers.

Dominated enterprises, as in many sectors of retailing, compete against larger organizations on the basis of their lower operating costs. Through their intense exploitation of human labour, they are able to maintain their position in the marketplace, but according to 'rules' dictated by larger employers. Accordingly, the proprietors of these smaller businesses are compelled by their market position to offer lower rates of pay and relatively poorer working conditions. For these reasons, they tend to attract employees whose bargaining position is weak and who have limited job opportunities. Such enterprises often require relatively unskilled labour and, as a result, they tend to hire staff on a short-term, part-time and often temporary basis. Employees in such enterprises are potentially vulnerable to the exploitative demands of their employers but, again, the outcome can be a variety of employer–employee relationships, some of which are characterized by 'harmonious' modes of accommodation.

Rainnie describes *isolated* businesses as those trading in markets which larger enterprises have chosen to avoid for reasons to do with lack of profit margin or of potential for longer-term business growth. Small businesses trading in specialist and localized market niches will be constrained by costs which must be kept low since otherwise their competitive advantage will be destroyed. Many sectors of the leisure, hotel and catering industries can be described in these terms, consisting as they do of large numbers of isolated small businesses which are only able to survive because of their low prices and hence the lower wages which they offer. In these businesses there is an overwhelming tendency to employ staff on a short-term or part-time basis, offering jobs to those who are unable to obtain alternative employment.

Finally, Rainnie identifies *innovative* small businesses which operate in high risk areas because of their commitment to developing new products and services. These are the enterprises that are given the greatest prominence in political debate and it is these which are seen to offer 'solutions' to macroeconomic problems ranging from unemployment to lack of industrial innovation and modernization. They are viewed as capable of overcoming the so-called problems of large-scale enterprises because of their allegedly greater potential to respond to changing customer needs. In the 1980s, such small businesses were portrayed as the 'key' to Britain's economic rejuvenation when large sectors of manufacturing had been destroyed by a variety of global and national economic and political processes. Undoubtedly, there are some small businesses that are established by those who as engineers, scientists and other experts have identified niches in the market for new products and services. But such corporate ventures are far fewer than those which have close relations with larger corporate partners with whom they share various licensing and funding arrangements. More often than not, the innovative products and services developed by small firms are those which would be too costly or irrelevant for larger organizations to pursue. It is, for them, more cost effective to cultivate 'arm's length' relations with smaller enterprises so that when the development of an innovative product suggest profitable potential, they take equity stakes, offer distribution facilities, and even take over the production of patented commodities.

In the analysis of small firms and the understanding of their role in a modern economy it is, then, necessary to understand the economic context within which they operate and the extent to which their viability is highly contingent upon the activities of larger enterprises that are dominant within different economic sectors. However, the study of small businesses tends to be undertaken in isolation from these broader processes, and political debate is inclined to regard them as highly autonomous enterprises which, in various ways, function to *compensate* for the economic fluctuations of larger corporations. It is through such reasoning that the government's small business policies tend to be orientated towards job creation and economic renewal. But it is only by understanding wider economic processes that it is possible to identify the factors contributing to the growing popularity of small business start-ups in the 1980s and 1990s and the reasons why an increasing proportion of the labour force are now self-employed or working in small firms. It is for this reason that the study of their employment relations is now considered to be an important area of academic research.

Growth and survival

As already discussed, the inherent processes of *concentration* and *disaggregation* characterize the capitalist mode of production. But in addition to these, the growth of small firms is reinforced by forces of corporate restructuring which are leading to the break-up of forms of production that were previously assembled or manufactured 'in-house'. As noted in chapter 4, the emergence of so-called 'flexible' firms, according to which 'core' work processes are retained while all other tasks are subcontracted or outsourced, is a feature of economic change in all of the market economies in the 1990s. Through processes of organizational fragmentation, large companies are reducing their operating costs through making their former fixed-cost in-house activities into variable costs. They are able to adopt practices of competitive tendering, to exercise tight constraints over quality control and to implement methods of just-in-time management, so that they retain all the advantages of in-house assembly and production but without the associated overheads.

The processes of business start-up associated with corporate fragmentation are variable. Sometimes it takes the form of management 'buy-outs'; often it is in terms of 'sponsorship' with larger companies actively participating in the setting-up of subcontractors through equity participation or by so-called strategic alliances; while on other occasions it can be in the form of developing trading links with already existing small firms, which are then encouraged – through the offer of contracts – to expand the nature of their activities.

There are also other equally significant factors accounting for the growth of small businesses. Hand-in-hand with the relative decline of Fordism as a production process for the manufacture of standardized products for mass markets, there is a tendency for such product markets to be eroded by the growth of differentiated niches. The development of consumer markets since the 1970s has brought about changes in personal purchasing preferences. Whereas in the past, consumer concern for conformity offered ideal conditions for large-scale assembly production, a more 'postmodernist' concern with 'inner directed' individuality now prevails, particularly among those in middle class, managerial and professional occupations (Harvey 1989). Such a change offers opportunities for business start-up through the production and delivery of goods and services for these more specialized market niches. Commodities can be produced more cost effectively according to the economies of small- rather than large-scale activity and, accordingly, small firms prevail within these economic sectors.

Both the processes of corporate fragmentation and product market differentiation have encouraged the growth of small firms, and this has been reinforced by developments in, and the implementation of, new technologies. It is possible to achieve economies in subcontracting processes because management information systems and information technology enable contractors and subcontractors to be closely interrelated in their production scheduling. With these, it is unnecessary to have integrated on-site production facilities because just-in-time methods of management are equally effective. The internal operations of small businesses can be rationalized through the use of even rudimentary forms of information technology, since this enables overheads to be kept low as a result of a reduced need for administrative tasks to be undertaken by human labour. Financial management in terms of credit control, cash flow and the preparation of budgets, as well as payments to suppliers, customers and employees, can be undertaken more cost effectively with present-day information systems.

It is for these reasons that the growth of small firms is expected to continue during the 1990s. This is both in terms of their relative share in the manufacture of goods as well as in the distribution and sale of commodities and services (Johnson 1991). Indeed, the forces of organizational fragmentation are apparent not only in manufacturing but also in other key areas of economic activity. Within the financial services sector, for example, consisting of retail banking, insurance and personal savings, the deregulation policies pursued by Conservative governments in the 1980s have led to a huge increase in the numbers of those who are either self-employed as 'consultants' or engaged in partnerships and smaller business practices. Deregulation has generated greater competition between the larger financial institutions and, in a similar manner as manufacturing enterprises, costs have been reduced through 'outsourcing' tasks that were previously undertaken in-house. Equally, in different sectors of the media industries, organizational fragmentation has led to the rapid growth of freelance workers, of the self-employed, of partnerships and of other small-scale owner-managed enterprises. This trend has been particularly pronounced within the television and film industries, where the production and distribution of finished products consists of a series of interconnected cycles of work which have to be coordinated and integrated within project teams and which consist of various 'independent' small business units, many of which operate for only limited periods of time. At the end of particular programme projects or contracts, they disband with their members regrouping for new short-term ventures.

The implications of these structural changes for the nature of work, employment and labour markets are far-reaching. For some commentators, it constitutes the emergence of a postmodern industrial order within which individuals are no longer constrained by the day-to-day drudgery associated with traditional employment relations (Handy 1984). Thus, freelances and the self-employed are able to vary their work patterns according to personal preferences, work needs and life styles. According to this view, they are released from the tight supervisory control and exploitative relations associated with traditional forms of large-scale manufacturing. As a result, the emergence of such work patterns is claimed to render redundant the need for trade unions and institutional labour relations. Employment relations are becoming superseded by market relations according to which negotiations between parties determine the provision of technical, professional and expert services of one kind or another. There is, then, little need for collective bargaining as the forces of economic change are destroying the preconditions for organized and collective labour. The break-up of traditional Fordist methods of production and the increasing abolition of 'standardized' shopfloor work tasks brings with it the decline of unionism and with it, the articulation of occupational and traditional working class interests. Indeed, according to this view, in the 'knowledge-based', postmodern, 'post-industrial' society the working class ceases to exist.

For other observers, however, the shift to self-employment, the fragmentation of large-scale enterprises through the development of forms of subcontracting and the subsequent emergence of small 'independent' (in fact, in the terms introduced above, often dependent) small firms is having quite the reverse ramifications (Goss 1991a). At best, it is reinforcing the nature of dependency and exploitation in labour markets and at worst, creating an 'under-class' of the low-paid and unemployed. Although traditional Fordist methods of production were organized on the basis of rational capitalist criteria, the relative protection offered by trade unions and negotiated bargaining systems provided workers some security of employment. By contrast, the overwhelming majority of small firms, encapsulated as they are within dependent relations with larger corporations who are able to dictate the terms of trading are compelled to offer low wages, insecure employment and poor working conditions. Alongside these there are the self-employed who are forced to sell their services in a buyers' market and within the context of high unemployment. The outcome is the emergence of a labour market consisting of growing numbers who are engaged on a part-time and/or short-term basis and who, generally, receive low pay (Fevre 1991). Accordingly, it is argued that such trends – reinforced by the deregulation of labour markets and the decline of trade unionism – are leading to the polarization of earnings, the fragmentation of labour markets and the emergence of an 'under-class' of those who are more-or-less tangential to the labour market (Hartley 1991). What, then, is known of the nature of employment relations within small-scale enterprises as these become of increasing significance in modern economies?

Employment Relations in Small Firms

Problems of evidence

Despite a renewed interest in the social processes of small-scale enterprises, our knowledge remains limited. There are a number of reasons for this. In the first instance, there are problems associated with definition. How is the 'small firm' to be delineated? Is it to be defined according to market share, volume of turnover, value of turnover or numbers of employees? There are flaws in applying any of these criteria if only because 'type' of product or service will impact upon such factors in quite significant ways. Most definitions of the 'small firm', however, use criteria associated with size, particularly number of employees. But there are difficulties. In the hotels sector, for example, 50 workers could be regarded as a reasonably large number, whereas in manufacturing this would be seen as a small plant. Most definitions utilize a combination of employee numbers and economic sector. In manufacturing, firms with fewer than 200 are considered as 'small', while for establishments in retailing, distribution, hotel, catering and other so-called 'service' sectors, the respective figure is less than 20.

But this is not the end of the problem. There remain other issues of classification and conceptualization. These turn on the heterogeneous nature of the small firms sector, especially when criteria of size are regarded as of primary importance. As stated earlier, enterprises employing fewer than 10 account for roughly 30 per cent of total employment in Europe. But how is it possible to study the nature of labour relations within a size classification that incorporates such diverse activities as highly complex manufactured goods through retailing and distribution, to the provision of various financial services? Obviously, the nature of employment relations will differ between types of enterprise because of the ways in which skills, as associated with various products and services, will shape the nature of interpersonal relations; in other words, a diversity of enterprise characteristics is likely to lead to great differences in employment practices (Goss 1991a). By contrast, in the study of large-scale enterprises, it is easier to generalize to other such organizations, particularly within the same economic sector. Indeed, the evidence is so fragmentary and the theories so empirically specific that there are severe limitations to the development of cumulative small business theory.

There are also methodological difficulties in studying small firms because of problems of access and the collection of data. Since the majority of small businesses are managed by their owners, they can decide whether or not to allow access to investigators and, as a result, research has to be conducted on the proprietor's own terms. He or she is unlikely to allow the study of wage rates, working conditions and employee attitudes if these will reveal 'unfavourable', or even illegal, practices. It is for this reason that the alleged 'industrial harmony' of the small firm could be a function of access whereby only those proprietors who perceive employee relations as good will allow research inquiries to be conducted. But even if access is obtained, there are the problems of validity and reliability associated with the case study method. The understanding of small firms is largely dependent upon detailed case studies. But how *reliable* are these, in the sense that other researchers would come to similar conclusions? It is difficult to judge unless *repeat* studies are undertaken and again, problems of access can make this difficult. Equally, how *valid* are the results of case studies to the extent that the conclusions are applicable to other similar work environments? Do social surveys compensate for these problems? The indices likely to be used can produce 'superficial' findings. Precoded questions about wages rates, levels of absenteeism and quality of working conditions are likely to produce 'skewed' findings, suggesting that 'small is beautiful'. Notwithstanding such methodological issues, what are some of the findings about labour relations in small firms?

In order to review some of these, it is useful to make a distinction between 'high' and 'low' skill small firms, since associated with each of these are rather distinctive employer–employee relations (Keeble and Kelly 1986). Research has tended to focus upon low-skill manufacturing enterprises to the neglect of the other types of enterprise. This is a pity for two reasons. First, it has led to excessive overgeneralization, beyond reasonable reliability and validity, suggesting that all small firms have such characteristics. Second, it has meant that there is little data on the internal dynamics of small firms trading in high technology and those dependent upon professional, expert and creative skills of one kind or another. These firms are discussed briefly in the conclusion.

Types of low-skill firms

Small businesses trading in the more traditional, low-skill manufacturing sectors of the economy have attracted the more attention, probably because of reasons we have already discussed: namely, the nature of their dependency relationships – either directly or indirectly – with larger companies (Rainnie 1989). Their investigation, therefore, can be more readily incorporated within the traditional concerns of industrial relations and industrial sociology than other types of small firm. Hence, research has tended to be directed to the study of small-scale manufacturing or 'craft' enterprises. Even so, such a category of small firms incorporates a wide diversity of enterprises which, again, makes it difficult to generalize about the nature of industrial relations. Scase and Goffee (1982, 1987) suggested a typology of small firms based upon the nature of proprietorial roles, since it is possible to identify particular types of labour relations associated with each of these. The categories they specify are the *self-employed, small employers, owner-controllers* and *owner-directors*. Each of these, they claim, represents differences in the relative mix of capital utilized and labour employed. As such, they consider their typology to be grounded in the Marxist theory of petty capital accumulation.

The *self-employed* constitute the largest proportion of small firm owners. By definition, they formally employ no labour. They are, however, usually dependent upon the unpaid services of partners, family members and the utilization of domestic resources for trading purposes. In a sense, there are no formal employment relations, but at the same time, the unpaid input of others demands the stipulation of a rudimentary division of labour according to which duties and tasks are undertaken. Often, gender-based authority relations as found within small business families incorporate both work and domestic roles. In other words, the 'deferential dialectic' (Newby, 1977) defines not only what gets done within the home but also within the business.

Formal employment relations are obviously more explicit among *small employers*. These work alongside their employees and in addition, undertake routine administrative and managerial tasks. They both labour and own their means of production and also employ wage labour. In such enterprises, the nature of employment relations is complex and, indeed, riddled with contradictions. On the one hand, proprietors act as employers while at the same time they work alongside their staff, performing productive work as though they, themselves, are employees. They perform the functions of both capital and labour whereas in the large enterprise, by contrast, these are separately constituted. At the same time, such contradictions are reinforced by the fact that relations are personal and face-to-face. Embedded as they are within complex interpersonal networks – often incorporating 'friends' and 'family members' – there are often severe constraints to rational decision-making and, potentially, there are tensions and interpersonal frictions associated with the exercise of proprietorial authority.

Owner-controllers, in many ways, typify the old-style 'classical' capitalists. They do not work alongside their employees but are responsible for the administration and management of their businesses. Unlike the self-employed and small employers, owner-controllers are more likely to depend upon personal managerial and financial expertise rather than trade or craft-based skills. Because they do not work alongside their employees, they must devote more attention to the explicit development of employer–employee relations and, with this, mechanisms of supervisory control. Obtaining worker commitment and establishing appropriate rewards systems associated with acceptable quality and quantity of employee performance is more problematic than it is for small employers. The latter, by working alongside their staff, are able not only to nurture close personal commitment but also to exercise tight supervisory control for determining work norms.

Finally, *owner-directors* manage and control their businesses through the implementation of formalized management structures. Administrative tasks are subdivided and delegated to managers, and these proprietors no longer personally undertake all of the functions of supervision and control. These, of course, tend to be larger enterprises which, since start-up, will have experienced considerable growth. Within such enterprises, the development of employment relations will be highly variable, ranging from an emphasis upon formal and more bureaucratic forms to more personal-based strategies dependent upon the 'charisma' and personal interventions of owner-directors. Often in such businesses, mechanisms of delegation can be underdeveloped – even with the employment of managerial staff – to the extent that within such formalized structures, management styles may be similar to those found among owner-controllers.[1]

Even though it is possible to identify such types of proprietorial role, which, of course, tend to vary according to the size of small business, it is evident that they share a number of common characteristics as far as the study of labour relations is concerned. Although every business will incorporate the fundamental feature of 'mixing' capital and labour, the articulation of these forces within the small firm is negotiated within patterns of interpersonal relations. Even within owner-director enterprises, with their greater dependency upon formal mechanisms and with a more evident split between capital (managers) and labour (workers), the limited size of such enterprises is still conducive to the generation of labour relations that are particularistic, informal and rarely institutionalized. Hence, in the study of employment relations in small firms there is the need to emphasize the importance of negotiated orders and how these function within the context of personal, face-to-face relations.

The study of small business growth, as it is usually linked with small employers becoming owner-controllers, requires an emphasis upon the changes which occur within the dynamics of these negotiated orders (Scase and Goffee, 1982). Indeed, the success or failure of small business growth is often more associated with proprietors' ability to manage such transformations than it is to do with market opportunities or with various aspects of financial management. Such negotiated orders may be described in terms of *paternalistic, fraternalistic* and *autocratic* strategies, each of which describes a particular mechanism whereby, within the context of interpersonal relations, small business owners are able to obtain, or command, the allegiance of their staff. In turn, each of these is characterized by particular employer–employee relations according to which 'appropriate' work practices are established and rewards determined. However, as small businesses grow, such personal-based strategies become less relevant and while small employers and owner-controllers may be able to continue to adhere to them, this is less likely for owner-directors. Indeed, many of the key conflicts within these 'larger' small firms hinge around ambiguous expectations associated with the parallel or partial use of both *interpersonal* as well as more *impersonal* forms of managerial control.

Paternalism, fraternalism and autocracy

All of this adds caution to assuming that there is but one particular type of employment relationship. As shown in chapter 11, large firms differ widely between themselves. The following discussion elaborates on the models of style introduced there. The style of small firms is normally assumed to be characterized by employer *paternalism* and employee deference, a view which has been largely shaped by the earlier work of Lockwood (1975: 20) who, in discussing small family firms, argued that:

> The essence of this work situation is that the relationship between employer and worker is personal and paternalistic. The worker has a unique position in a functional job hierarchy and is tied to the employer by a 'special relationship' between them and not only by considerations of economic gain.

This assumption was further strengthened by Newby who, in the 1970s, studied farmers and agricultural workers in East Anglia (1977: 189). According to Newby, paternalism consists of two inter-related and reciprocated components; *differentialism* and *identification*. On the one hand, employers emphasize the fundamental differences that exist between themselves and their employees within an interdependent and cooperative division of labour. On the other hand,

> most farmers are quite prepared to construct an intricate web of paternalistic labour relations in order to obtain the identification of their workers; on the smaller farms this will occur spontaneously out of the much closer involvement of employers and employees in the work situation, whereas on the larger farms, it is often a matter of conscious or unconscious policy.

Paternalistic strategies may be appropriate in particular product and labour markets. They are most likely to be used by employers when there is relatively stable demand for their goods and when employees, for reasons ranging from the quality of their skills to geographical location, are unable to shift from one employer to another. A constant and relatively predictable demand for products enables employers to hire staff on a fairly long-term basis. There can be the delineation of work tasks and the allocation of duties and responsibilities which take on the character of 'custom and practice'. Accordingly, employees can be extended a reasonable degree of personal autonomy which is bounded by employer–employee notions of 'fairness', 'trust' and legitimate mutual obligations. For these reasons, workers will acquire a range of particularistic skills which, being primarily relevant for the duties required of them within specific enterprises, reinforce their dependency upon their employers. At the same time, however, the employers become dependent on these employees, who can only be replaced by recruiting and training others who not only have to obtain the same relevant and particularistic skills but also are capable of being 'trusted' since only then can they be given discretion and responsibility.

For these reasons, paternalism is a rational employer strategy in some work and market situations. As a result, and because of the relative indispensability of employees, such relations will often extend beyond the workplace. The cultivation of high trust within employer–employee relations of personal reciprocity will lead to the negotiation of discretionary practices that will blur the boundaries of work. They can be expressed in flexible working hours, employee use of employer resources (vehicles and equipment), and employer involvement in employees' personal welfare (Newby 1977). In return, employees are expected to reciprocate through constantly giving priority to the interests of their employers, being 'on call' to respond to emergencies and unexpected customer demands. Paternalism, as an employer strategy, therefore, is found in many traditional craft-based industries in small-scale manufacturing and in many sectors of hotel and catering as well as in other small enterprises where market niches can be carved out so that the provision of goods and services can be undertaken on a relatively long-term basis, requiring reasonably stable inputs of labour which can be hired more-or-less permanently.

There are other businesses, however, which operate in far more fluctuating markets, in which the demand for products and services is much less predictable but where proprietors are again dependent upon relatively 'indispensable' employees for the generation of profits. At the same time, these employees, because of their skills, may be potentially highly mobile and for reasons of market demand and/or geographical location are able to shift from one employer to another. Unlike the particularistic skills of those encapsulated within paternalism, such workers possess competences which are more universalistic and, therefore, transferable to other enterprises. Paternalism becomes an inappropriate owner-manager strategy, since the relationship with employees will not be long term. Accordingly, there is less emphasis upon the need to establish more permanent relations of reciprocity and high trust. And yet employee commitment has to be obtained in order to accomplish the tasks at hand if the business is to survive. In such circumstances, employers can adopt one of two strategies. The first is to pursue an almost entirely calculative and instrumental approach through the wage nexus, to offer high financial rewards – relative, that is, to competing employers – and to obtain short-term employee commitment in this way. But unless such employers are trading in markets in which there is little competition, the costs of such a strategy are likely to challenge the economic viability of the business. At the same time, such a strategy is conducive to operating inefficiencies, since employees and employers are constantly compelled to negotiate the 'rate' for the job within a context in which work tasks are generally ambiguously and broadly defined. More usually, therefore, owners will choose to adopt a second approach, that of fraternalism (Goffee and Scase 1982).

With *fraternalism*, owner-managers tend to work alongside their employees – as is the case with small employers. As a result of this working relationship, job duties and responsibilities become defined according to processes of mutual adjustment according to which hierarchical relations of the kind found under paternalism are largely absent. If, according to Newby, paternalism incorporates features of both employer–employee identification and differentiation, this also applies to fraternalism except that the emphasis between the two is somewhat different. With paternalism, employee identification is fostered within interpersonal relations of differentiation. With fraternalism, by contrast, employer strategies emphasize the overriding importance of identification and nurture interpersonal relations accordingly, with differentiation between employer and employee being defined as an inevitable but nevertheless subsidiary or secondary element in the relationship.

Employers will emphasize the importance of 'team work' and, as members themselves of such 'teams' they will demonstrate their own productive contribution to the economic welfare of their businesses. They will deliberately relegate the undertaking of administrative tasks to the evenings and weekends in order to set examples of work norms and to demonstrate that in working at the same level of output as their employees, they are not exploiting their staff for profit. Indeed, as small employers, they can often pay themselves a similar level of wages, reaping the rewards of proprietorship and compensating for the risk they endure as business owners through end-of-year profits. Even then, a strategy of fraternalism is often maintained by giving employees a share in these year-end profits so that identification is reinforced and sources of differentiation are minimized (Goffee and Scase 1982). This is also the major reason compelling employers to continue to work alongside their staff. For them to cease productive work would lead not only to an increase in costs – which could threaten the viability of the businesses – but by introducing a source of vertical differentiation into the employment relationship, it could generate resentment and feelings of low trust which can seriously reduce productivity and performance. They cannot, therefore, be seen to be 'living' off the profits created by others and as such, they feel obliged to work as competently and productively as their employees.

The fact that such small employers do work alongside their staff means that they themselves possess productive skills of one kind or another. This is often a result of the fact that they have previously been employees. Indeed, high possibilities for job mobility, whereby employees are able to become employers, further reinforce the appropriateness of fraternal strategies. In such circumstances, there will be a high degree of mutual understanding of work processes and of the difficulties and constraints which workers often face in the accomplishment of their tasks.

Of course, it is easier in some economic sectors for employees to embark upon their own business ventures than it is in many others. Such sectors will be characterized by low costs of business start-up and little capital investment. Accordingly, more business formations are likely to be found in the labour-intensive spheres where personal skills of various kinds provide the bases for trading relations. Traditional craft sectors offer such opportunities – painting, decorating, carpentry, hairdressing, pottery and interior design, as well as some sectors of retail trading. It is probably in the building industry that there are the most self-evident possibilities which are reinforced by highly fluctuating and unstable conditions of employment (Scase and Goffee 1982). Here, workers are constantly shifting from one employer to another and such experiences of personal mobility, interspersed by periods of unemployment, are likely, often by chance, to lead to many workers setting up businesses on a self-employed basis and then, because of customer demands for their work, to find themselves employing staff.

It is these former self-employed workers who, if they become small employers, respond to the bargaining capacity of their employees by adopting fraternal strategies. This may be the only means whereby they can manage their staff and as such, this can inhibit further business growth since this would require them to withdraw from controlling their workers through their own day-to-day productive activities, that is by working alongside them. With business growth, it would be necessary for them to become almost exclusively engaged in managerial and administrative activities and as owner-controllers to cultivate alternative strategies for harmonious employer–employee relations. More hierarchical control mechanisms become necessary, if only because of the employers' lack of day-to-day engagement with workers on a productive basis.

If strategies of fraternalism are driven by a variety of factors, including the market situation of employees and hence their bargaining capacity, a similar set of factors account for the *autocratic* styles found in many other small businesses. When there is fluctuating demand for the small firm's products or services and if these occur in markets which are highly competitive, proprietors will adopt either fraternal strategies (as in the building industry) or more autocratic styles. Why will they choose the latter in preference to the former? Primarily, this would seem to be conditioned by the market position of their employees. When employees possess few universalistic or particularistic skills as found under fraternalism and paternalism, they are highly vulnerable to the stipulations and commands of their employers (Goss 1988). Their market capacity is weak and, in the absence of effective unionism, they are unable to bargain with their employers. As a result, employers are able to offer extremely low rates of pay and to offer very poor work and employment conditions. This, of course, would seem to be the situation in many low-skill sectors of the economy such as in clothing and textiles, many areas of hotel and catering, and retailing (Hoel 1982). Employees have low substitute value and, being readily expendable by their small business owners, they are compelled to accept the employment relation as this is determined by their employers.

How, then, is this relationship legitimized? According to Rainnie (1989), on the basis of his case studies of small firms in the clothing and printing industries, employers legitimate their actions by reference to the competitive forces of a market economy. In other words, they will openly acknowledge to their staff that the wages which they offer are unacceptably low but claim that these reflect circumstances beyond their own personal control. Such appeals have considerable legitimacy in periods of high unemployment, especially when staff have little in the form of skills which make them either indispensable to their employers (as with paternalism and fraternalism) or capable of making job shifts between employers (as with fraternalism). For employees, it is a choice between low levels of remuneration and no jobs at all. This is particularly pertinent in circumstances when there are unfavourable preconditions for collective organization through unionism and when there is no statutory national minimum wage. As explained in chapter 18, the abolition of wages councils merely reinforces the extent to which employers can adopt autocratic strategies in their relations with staff.

The relevance of skill and market conditions shaping the nature of employer–employee relations and, hence, the adoption of particular employer strategies, can be further illustrated by the research of Goss (1991b: 161). Like Rainnie, he studied small firms in the printing industry. Unlike Rainnie, however, he identifies two quite contrasting sectors within this industry:

On the one hand, there are those firms which are concerned with high-quality, technologically sophisticated work. These enterprises are likely to exhibit a strong craft-base, being heavily dependent upon skilled labour.

These firms tend to retain union agreements and to be at the capital-intensive end of the industry. Goss continues:

On the other hand, there is a growing sector of the industry concerned with 'instant printing' which can more properly be seen as the industry's 'service wing'. . . . These enterprises have emerged primarily as a result of the simplification and automation of small-scale printing technology and the harnessing of this to electronic/computerized methods of typesetting, thereby eliminating the need for skilled labour.

Employees here generally lack formal training and are rarely unionized.

In view of the differences in markets, products and hence, employers' relative dependency upon skilled workers, Goss demonstrates how these two sectors of the printing industry are characterized by very different employment relations. In the low-skill instant printing sector, there is the widespread use of younger workers who are unable to bargain, or to protect their interests either through collective action or by effective labour legislation. They are highly vulnerable to the commands of their employers and as a result, they are more compelled to comply to autocratic employer stipulations in terms of wages, work and employment conditions and quality of performance. Within the 'manufacturing' sector of printing, on the other hand, such autocratic strategies are inappropriate. Instead, employers are constrained to negotiate effective working relations and more favourable rewards with employees who are in a stronger bargaining position. Because of their bargaining capacity, employees are more indispensable and can better resist proprietorial prerogatives. Under such conditions, the more appropriate owner strategies are those associated with fraternalism (and even paternalism) rather than the autocratic stances of those employed in the lesser skilled instant print sector.

But autocratic employer strategies are not inevitably associated with the employment of unskilled workers. Instead, these can be the development of 'indulgency patterns' and high trust relations between small employers and their staff. In a recent study of the clothing industry, in an attempt to test some of Rainnie's claims about the general tendencies towards autocratic forms of control in low-skill businesses, Ram (1994: 213) collected data in a number of small clothing firms in the West Midlands. In this, he undertook case studies of ethnic enterprises where:

> Asians in the West Midlands [are] pushed into the clothing industry because of the absence of opportunity in mainstream employment rather than the possession of any cultural flair for enterprise. Observing employer after employer frantically attempting to balance the demands of a hostile market, an often chaotic system of production, a far from passive workforce and an indifferent banking system for very little reward leads me to the conclusion that few could have freely chosen such an existence.

According to Ram, the survival of these enterprises is highly dependent upon the use of low-paid female labour operating within the traditional patriarchal structures of Asian society. At the same time, manager–worker relations can only be understood by reference to this culture; for instance, the segregation of male and female workers, deference to older employees, the accommodation within work routines of various rituals and ceremonies, and the centrality of family relations.

Employer–employee relations in these Asian-owned businesses, therefore, are not characterized by autocratic forms of proprietorial control. But neither are they symptomatic of social harmony. Instead, it was ongoing bargaining between employers and employees which, within the context of highly competitive and unpredictable market circumstances, determined work practices, levels of production and the exercise of authority on the shopfloor. In each of the case studies, Ram describes an 'indulgency pattern' whereby employers and employees become interdependent within complex relations of trust, obligation and mutual reciprocity. It is for this reason, he claims, that such small firms are often seen to be inefficiently organized and are criticized for failing to adhere to more 'rational' methods of production. However, as he suggests, attempts to rationalize work processes would break down the indulgency patterns according to which both employers and employees, through mutual reciprocity, achieve their separate goals. To destroy these patterns would be to destroy the business.

Conclusions

In traditional small businesses, there are a variety of employer strategies, each of which shapes the nature of labour relations. But such strategies are themselves determined by a range of external factors which constrain the extent to which proprietors are able to impose their own particular patterns of control. It is rare for employers to manage their businesses in an entirely 'unfettered' autocratic manner, because of the bargaining capacity of their employees. Generally, within the context of personal relations that are face-to-face and highly particularistic, patterns of reciprocity and trust will emerge such that negotiated patterns of work, performance and productivity will become established. Generally, for reasons of employee skill, market capacity and the external threats that face small businesses in often highly competitive circumstances, forms of accommodation emerge between employers and employees which negate the imposition of autocratic forms of control. Instead, modes of paternalism and fraternalism more appropriately describe, albeit crudely, employer–employee relations in the majority of small businesses.

In our discussion, we have focused upon labour relations in small businesses operating within the more traditional manufacturing sector of the economy. This reflects the direction that empirical research has taken and, as a result, there is little information about the nature of employer–employee relations in small enterprises in non-manufacturing sectors. Although there are some studies in retailing and hotel and catering, there are few data on small businesses in those rapidly growing areas of professional services, the media, public relations, advertising, recreation, leisure and entertainment (Curran and Burrows 1987). In small businesses in these sectors, employment relations are likely to be highly variable but also very different from those found in the more traditional sectors of the economy. Often, conventional employer–employee relations do not exist because many such enterprises are organized on the basis of co-ownership or partnership arrangements. In this way, those working in the business also have a stake in its ownership and this, of course, affects the nature of social relations. Further, such businesses often trade on the basis of various intellectual, creative, professional and expert skills which, through processes of mutual adjustment, constitute the trading assets of the business (Handy 1978).

Accordingly, on the basis of personal-based competencies, a rudimentary division of tasks emerges among partners according to which various services are delivered to customers and clients. Charges are made for these services which are used to cover the overall running costs of the business and out of which salaries are paid and profits are shared between the partners. If there is a management process, this is *colleague-based*, with perhaps only a senior partner exercising more explicit forms of managerialism of the kind exercised by professional managers in large organizations rather than the paternalistic, fraternal or autocratic strategies of the owners of more traditional small firms. If managerial control is explicitly exercised by senior partners, it tends to be directed towards 'support staff' – secretaries, administrators, assistants – rather than towards the professional or expert colleagues who constitute the 'operating core' of the partnership. More research needs to be done in these businesses.

Equally, there needs to be more studies of smaller enterprises trading in high-technology products (Keeble and Kelly 1986). What are the characteristics of employer–employee relations in these enterprises, operating as they are in such areas as computer software, electronics, pharmaceuticals and bio-science? In such firms, employees are likely to be university graduates who see themselves as relatively mobile within national and international labour markets and who often prefer a high level of working autonomy. At the same time, they are usually anxious about the exploitation of their intellectual property rights. Further, the employment relationship is particularistic, and protective 'professional cultures' of the kind found in large organizations are unlikely to emerge. In what ways do the contradictions associated with employer–employee relations express themselves in such small businesses when 'professional', 'creative' and 'expert' skills are the source of both intellectual property rights and trading profits? It is issues such as these which need to be placed on the agenda for future research, so that the diversity of practices in labour relations within the small business sector can be more fully documented and comprehensively understood.[2]

The theme of this chapter, then, has been the diversity of small firms and hence of their employment relations. Models which equate such firms with either autocracy or post-Fordist autonomy are far too universalistic. Although the high-skill small firm sector has some features that fit the post-Fordist model, many other parts of the sector do not. They reflect the continuing tensions between centralization and decentralization discussed above, and in many of them, as noted in chapters 17 and 18, issues of low skill and low wages are of growing importance. Diversity and fragmentation, then, constitute continuing tendencies in the small business sector.

Notes

1 The distinctive differences that exist between each of these types of small firm constitute fundamental barriers to their growth. Proprietors are often unable to adjust their interpersonal skills according to the changing social relations associated with business growth.
2 Of course, there are many other relevant issues for research. In terms of employment relations, the interpersonal dynamics within women-owned businesses needs further inquiry. Although there have been comparisons between male and female entrepreneurs (Cromie 1987), there have been few explorations of employment relations in such enterprises (Goffee and Scase 1985; Allen and Truman 1993).

References

Allen, S. and Truman, C. (eds) 1993: *Women in Business*. London: Routledge.

Braverman, H. 1974: *Labor and Monopoly Capital*. New York: Monthly Review Press.

Burrows, R. 1991: The Discourse of the Enterprise Culture and the Restructuring of Britain: A Polemical Contribution. In J. Curran and R. Blackburn (eds), *Paths of Enterprise: The Future of the Small Business*. London: Routledge.

Cromie, S. 1987: Similarities and Differences between Men and Women who Choose Proprietorship. *International Journal of Small Business*, 5, 3, 43–60.

Curran, J. and Burrows, R. 1987: *Enterprise in Britain: A National Profile of Small Business Owners and the Self-Employed*. London: Small Business Research Trust.

Eurostat 1992: *Enterprises in Europe*. DG 23 (Directorate-General for Small and Medium-sized Enterprises, Tourism and Social Economics). Brussels: European Commission.

Fevre, R. 1991: Emerging 'Alternatives' to Full-time and Permanent Employment. In P. Brown and R. Scase (eds), *Poor Work: Disadvantage and* the Division of Labour. Milton Keynes: Open University Press.

Friedman, A. 1977: *Industry and Labour*. London: Macmillan.

Goffee, R. and Scase, R. 1982: Fraternalism and Paternalism as Employer Strategies in Small Firms. In G. Day (ed.), *Diversity and Decomposition in the Labour Market*. Aldershot: Gower.

Goffee, R. and Scase, R. 1985: *Women in Charge: The Experiences of Female Entrepreneurs*. London: George Allen & Unwin.

Goss, D. 1988: Social Harmony and the Small Firm: A Reappraisal. *Sociological Review*, 32, 1, 114–32.

Goss, D. 1991a: *Small Business and Society*. London: Routledge.

Goss, D. 1991b: In Search of Small Firm Industrial Relations. In R. Burrows (ed.), *Deciphering the Enterprise Culture*. London: Routledge.

Handy, C. 1978: *Understanding Organisations*. Harmondsworth: Penguin.

Handy, C. 1984: *The Future of Work*. Oxford: Blackwell.

Hartley, D. 1991: In Search of the Underclass. In P. Brown and R. Scase (eds), *Poor Work: Disadvantage and the Division of Labour*. Milton Keynes: Open University Press.

Harvey, D. 1989: *The Conditions of Postmodernity*. Oxford: Blackwell.

Hoel, B. 1982: Contemporary Clothing Sweatshops. In J. West (ed.), *Work, Women and the Labour Market*. London: Routledge & Kegan Paul.

Johnson, S. 1991: Small Firms and the UK Labour Market: Prospects for the 1990s. In J. Curran and R. Blackburn (eds), *Paths of Enterprise: The Future of the Small Business*. London: Routledge.

Keeble, D. and Kelly, T. 1986: New Firms and High Technology Industry in the United Kingdom: The Case of Computer Electronics. In D. Keeble and E. Wever (eds), *New Firms and Regional Development in Europe*. London: Croom Helm.

Lockwood, D. 1975: Sources of Variation in Working Class Images of Society. In M. Bulmer (ed.), *Working Class Images of Society*. London: Routledge.

Marx, K. 1974: *Capital*, Vol. 1. London: Lawrence & Wishart.

Newby, H. 1977: *The Deferential Worker*. London: Penguin.

Piore, M. and Sabel, C. 1984: *The Second Industrial Divide: Prospects for Prosperity*. New York: Basic Books.

Rainnie, A. 1989: *Industrial Relations in Small Firms*. London: Routledge.

Ram, M. 1994: *Managing to Survive*. Oxford: Blackwell.

Sabel, C. 1982: *Work and Politics*. Cambridge: Cambridge University Press.

Scase, R. 1982: The Petty Bourgeoisie and Modern Capitalism. In A. Giddens and G. Mackenzie (eds), *Social Class and the Division of Labour*. Cambridge: Cambridge University Press.

Scase, R. and Goffee, R. 1982: *The Entrepreneurial Middle Class*. London: Croom Helm.

Scase, R. and Goffee, R. 1987: *The Real World of the Small Business Owner*, 2nd edn. London: Croom Helm.

Wright, E. O. 1978: *Class, Crisis and the State*. London: Verso.

PART IV

Conclusion

20

Assessment: Markets and Managerialism

Paul Edwards

The introductory chapter identified two models of change in industrial relations: flexibility and strategic choice. The former contains a clear set of empirical implications such as the development by management of a strategy of labour flexibility, including the use of different mechanisms for 'core' and 'peripheral' workers. The latter is only a framework that does not say what sorts of choice will be made. As applied to the 1980s and 1990s, however, it generally suggests an increasingly conscious use of choice, rather than a passive acceptance of past practice; an attempt to make choices in the industrial relations field strategic, in the sense that they address fundamental questions of employees' recruitment, motivation and reward while also being explicitly connected to business strategy; and the possibility that appropriate choices can lead to benefits such as improved productivity and competitiveness. Within both models, management is assumed to be the leading actor.

The limited value of both models is readily established. On this basis, it is possible to draw up a balance sheet of change and continuity and thus to indicate how the regulation of employment is developing.

Themes in the Re-regulation of Labour

Transformation or cyclical development?

On the flexibility model, chapter 4 demonstrated the limited degree to which firms have employed the labour utilization methods identified in the model, together with the very traditional rationales underlying such use as there has been. The extent to which firms have deployed a strategic approach to the management of the labour force has been even more restricted. This chapter also returned an essentially negative answer to the question of whether coherent strategic choice has characterized British labour management in the recent past. As chapter 2 shows, a major reason is that the tendency towards short-term responsiveness is deeply rooted in history. Other chapters have taken up the theme with reference to issues such as team working and participation (chapter 12) and training (chapter 17). The evidence on outcomes such as pay bargaining and productivity (chapters 5 and 13) also suggests that a strategic transformation of British industrial relations has not been achieved.

More generally, those who posit such transformations, in Britain or elsewhere, tend to make stark contrasts between different eras. Within managerial thinking, the workplace proceduralism and national-level corporatism of the 1960s and 1970s is contrasted with the human resource management (HRM) of the 1980s and 1990s. As discussed in chapter 3, more analytical work speaks of a shift from 'Fordism' to 'post-Fordism'. The difficulty with both approaches is the unduly sharp distinction between past and present and the presumption that the past was characterized by a few simple principles. There certainly was proceduralism and bureaucracy, but it was the product of the 1970s and not a deeply ingrained aspect of British industrial relations; before that decade, it was informality which was widely seen as the key feature, and weakness, of Britain. And it did not flourish everywhere: as chapter 19 shows, in small firms and in large parts of the service sector it was largely absent. Moreover, as chapter 11 argues, it is wrong to contrast the collectivism of the past with the individualism of the present: the past contained a strong focus on the control of the employee as an individual, while HRM is not the denial of collectivity but an effort to reach a particular blend of collective organization and individual responsibility.

The dynamics of change do not fit well into a linear model of a shift from one self-contained system to another. An alternative, and in some ways preferable, viewpoint is that of cycles. As the work of Barley and Kunda (1992) discussed in chapter 11 suggests, managerial control systems have fluctuated between offering workers autonomy and regulating them tightly. Such fluctuations have been analysed by labour process writers in terms of the two basic strategies, of 'responsible autonomy' and 'direct control', which any management can pursue (Friedman 1977, 1990). This variation reflects inherent tensions in the development of capitalism; for example, that between centralization and decentralization as discussed in chapter 19. Yet a strictly cyclical view implies a mere repetition of previous processes. In fact, any cycle will have differences from its predecessor: recent moves towards individualism are not the same as earlier paternalist systems. As argued in chapter 12, there has been a 're-regulation' of labour. It will be argued here that market definitions have been critical in this new managerial authority.

The nature of 're-regulation'

Four points need emphasis. First, re-regulation involves a *recomposition*, and not simply a reassertion, of managerial authority. It comprises a new combination of elements.

Second, it involves the *interpretation of market forces* by managements. If the market had direct effects on the regulation of labour, there would be no need for elaborate systems of personnel management or for all the new devices of careful recruitment, performance appraisal and communication. The market would decide. Markets do not decide because they are very imperfect mechanisms for determining what goes on inside firms. As shown in chapters 3 and 5, managements develop internal labour markets and pay systems according to their views of how to manage labour. The market can, at most, determine the basic wage necessary to hire workers. How workers are persuaded to turn their capacity for labour into effective effort depends on systems of reward, motivation and discipline. As chapter 19 shows, even in small firms, where the force of the market is apparently most direct, workers have to be persuaded to work in particular ways, 'managerial relations' grow up to interpret 'market relations', and the nature of managerial organization varies between firms in apparently similar market situations.

Third, *how universal are the relevant trends*? To what sort of firms do they apply? One historical lesson is relevant here. At the time of the Donovan report debate focused on one particular case, namely, large manufacturing plants, mainly in the engineering industry, with well-established shop steward organizations. The assumption that such cases typified industrial relations caused many difficulties. More recent discussion underlines the diversity of the time, a diversity which is still plainly evident, as the different worlds of HRM (analysed in chapters 4 and 11, for example) and of low pay and insecurity (see chapters 18 and 19) demonstrate. Indeed, as chapter 19 again emphasizes, even within the apparently homogeneous sector of small firms there are substantial variations, notably between the high-technology sector, in which a sense of team working and 'fraternalism' flourishes, and low-wage and low-skill firms, which rely on autocracy or paternalism.

But the danger of stressing diversity is the implication that there is no underlying process of change and that everything is merely contingent. An underlying dynamic of re-regulation, driven by new market pressures, can be identified. The theoretical implication is the importance of distinguishing different levels of analysis, together with the conditions promoting one set of outcomes rather than another. At the most basic level, a general intensification of competition, itself the product of the restructuring of capitalist economies, has affected many sectors of industry. But, at a more concrete level, the intensity of the resulting pressure has varied, and the ways in which it has affected the regulation of work have been shaped by a set of institutional factors. One feature of this book is the endeavour to indicate the conditions producing one outcome rather than another. Chapter 11 analyses the different 'styles' which firms may adopt and indicates where they may be found. Chapter 12 indicates conditions, including a well-entrenched yet flexible shop steward organization, which encourage large firms to pursue a cooperative strategy of workplace change rather than the more common approach, as analysed in chapter 7, of excluding or marginalizing unions. Chapter 16 points to the different market circumstances of privatized firms as a key factor in their approach to industrial relations. Chapter 19 shows how in small firms various product and labour-market conditions lead firms to develop paternalistic rather than simply autocratic modes of regulation.

One apparently constructive way of dealing with diversity is to identify different types of firm. This would involve indicating the main approaches to labour regulation (sophisticated HRM, paternalism, proceduralism, autocracy, and so on) and establishing how many firms practised each, together with the conditions promoting them. Yet the key problem is that employment practice does not come in neat parcels. As discussed below, firms often draw on the techniques associated with HRM in their own ways: there is no one model of HRM. Indeed, as Marginson et al. (1994) put it, employers' labour policies are characterized by eclecticism. HRM, moreover, often goes along with actions more usually associated with autocracy, such as strict policies on discipline and attendance. It is not a matter of finding some self-contained types but of considering how different approaches may be combined. This has been the approach of several chapters above. Chapter 12, for example, indicates how technical and organizational changes have gone along with new systems of labour management to produce a new regime of labour regulation. This regime can permit a joint approach to decision-making, but more commonly it involves a reassertion of managerial authority.

Before moving to the fourth point, a brief digression on the categorization of styles is required. The reader may wonder whether there is a conflict between the view just given, which, in parallel with the arguments of chapter 4, questions the separateness of styles, and the models of distinct styles presented in chapter 11. It is a matter of emphasis rather than fundamental disagreement. With the benefit of hindsight, the initial model of styles (Purcell and Sisson 1983), which was produced by authors involved with these two chapters, was too simple, as chapter 11 stresses. In particular, it saw styles as self-contained systems rather than identifying analytical dimensions on which various styles could be placed. For the purposes of chapter 4, which asks whether there are discrete models of labour management to be identified with certain sorts of firm, the model of styles offers little analytical leverage. Chapter 11, however, is concerned with the changing balance between two fundamental approaches to the employment relation, individualism and collectivism, and with demonstrating that both characterize past and present approaches: the idea of styles helps to show how one or the other is emphasized and expressed. A style is thus an ideal-typical representation of managerial policy and not an unvarying form of practice; the fact that firms may use 'hard' and 'soft' policies simultaneously is, in the present writer's view, compatible with a model of styles. As the chapter also underlines, a firm may deploy different styles with respect to different parts of its workforce. Finally, the substantive conclusions of chapters 4 and 11, that there has been no human resource management revolution and that managerial authority rather than commitment and consent is the leading element of change, are highly complementary. In short, differing uses of style reflect different questions and not fundamental disagreement about the nature of management practice.

Fourth is the issue of the *balance of outcomes*. How these are interpreted depends on one's analytical, and indeed often political, starting point. Employer and government rhetoric of the 1980s claimed that there was a transformation of attitudes and behaviour. Much research has questioned such a simple model. But there is the danger of erecting an equally simple alternative, of an unrelieved growth of managerial domination. It is true that there have been clear trends towards an intensification of work effort, a widening of earnings differentials, and a weakening of trade unions in particular and collective channels of interest aggregation and representation more generally. Yet technical and organizational change can benefit workers. Indeed, as chapter 7 notes, for many years British unions castigated employers for their lack of technical knowledge and thus found it hard to counter moves to implement far-reaching change. Many employees are likely to have welcomed some changes, to have accepted others as inevitable, and to have been less certain about others. As for outcomes in terms of wages and conditions, chapter 10 underlines the point that, in large parts of the public sector, the pay awards of new review bodies were often comparatively high, though often also at the cost of more pressurized work for those who kept their jobs and job losses for others.

These points may now be developed in more detail. The pressures of markets may be examined by exploring the pattern of change and continuity in the approaches of the state, managements and unions and the effects on workers.

State, Employer and Union Policies

The state

Change has been most dramatic in the approach of the state. During the 1980s, corporatist models and assumptions about the duty of the state to act as a model employer were abandoned. In addition to major alterations to the framework of labour law, the new, and explicitly market-driven, agenda affected areas such as the management of public-sector workers (both directly and through privatization), the extent of protection for the low-paid, and the provision of training. There is no doubt that the post-war consensus was overturned. Yet what of the wider implications?

First, in terms of intentions, it is worth recalling that many of the changes were introduced, not as part of a planned package, but incrementally and sometimes in response to specific issues. As noted in chapters 9 and 16, incrementalism is evident in labour law and in privatization (which did not feature in the Conservatives' 1979 manifesto); labour law also illustrates short-term responses, for example laws to control unofficial strikes in reaction to an apparent wave of such activity. Outcomes have reflected accidents and the force of events as well as intentions. Yet there has also been a strong unifying philosophy: incrementalism was not planned but it reflected some clear assumptions, which in turn rendered certain responses in the face of short-term pressures more likely than others. For example, the action against unofficial strikes reflected the belief that union members are more moderate than leaders. A more reformist approach to a short-term strike problem was highly unlikely.

Second, it is important to distinguish between the effects of the changes on specific institutions and on wider social and economic developments. On the former, even those parts of public service furthest from the market, such as the civil service, have been opened up to commercial regimes. Past assumptions about job security, career paths and responsiveness to change have been ended. Yet two important qualifications run through an assessment of effects (see chapters 9, 10 and 16). First, the extent of change has often been slow and limited. Second, change brings with it new doubts and tensions. Exposing organizations to the market replaces a public service ethos with a more commercial and individualized orientation: how is trust and commitment to be maintained in such an environment? Replacing bureaucracy with the market does not remove the need for negotiation within a complex environment. It replaces one set of norms and signals with another.

On the wider effects of the law, models of a direct impact are too simple. As chapter 6 shows, explanations of declines in union membership in terms of legal changes have problems in identifying the relevant mechanisms and in explaining why, when the legislative climate was favourable, membership did not rise. More generally, as shown in chapter 9, the law has to be interpreted in practice, and quite different interpretations have been made by different groups. And the stated aim of improving labour-market efficiency has not been fulfilled. Perhaps the major role of the law, as the chapter suggests, has been a symbolic one: the law was more in tune with other developments, notably in managerial practice, than was the case with the other main period of restrictive legislation under the Industrial Relations Act. Legal changes were thus connected with the rest of society, even though their role was more to express and symbolize change than to cause it in any direct sense. The issue of symbolic change is taken up further below.

As for wider effects in terms of economic performance, most chapters in this book return a sceptical conclusion. Chapter 8 highlights continuing problems of wage inflation and economic management, chapter 17 weaknesses in training, and chapter 13 Britain's patchy productivity record. Such problems point to the ways in which new approaches underline old issues. Britain has always eschewed not only the managed capitalist economy of a country like Sweden but also the strong links between the state and the private sector which have evolved, albeit in different ways, in Germany or Japan. Many recent developments have heightened this tendency: in the terms introduced in chapter 8, they have pushed Britain away from the corporatist pole.

Employers

Turning to management, the increased self-confidence of managers in promoting change has been a major feature of the 1980s and 1990s. In retrospect, it is this which is the main legacy of the interest in HRM which dominated debates in the 1980s. These debates often turned on whether HRM was 'really' different from personnel management and on the contrast between ideal types of the two, with the terms for HRM (proactive, integrative, organic) being more positive in tone than those for personnel management (short-term, bureaucratic). Such debates tended not to move very far. A related approach was to hold up practice against an ideal of HRM and find it wanting. This was a useful initial step, but it left open the question of what was really happening and indeed whether the ideal was something that firms were even seeking in the first place. It is now possible to be a little more sophisticated.

Research has repeatedly shown that the language of HRM is widely adopted but that it translates into concrete initiatives much more rarely; that there are problems of integrating the 'hard' and 'soft' elements of HRM; that the various components of HRM can be assembled in a huge variety of ways; and that evidence of continuing commitment to HRM principles is limited (Blyton and Turnbull

1992; Storey 1992). Several writers (for example, Ahlstrand 1990) have stressed the symbolism of managerial change. As used here (for a fuller discussion, see Edwards and Whitston 1993: 224–7), to say that change is symbolic does not imply that it is unimportant: symbols are not being contrasted with reality. It means that the change carries certain meanings for the participants through which they make sense of the world, even though it need have no effect on the specific issue that is formally the object of the change. Ahlstrand's example is productivity bargaining at Esso's Fawley refinery; numerous efforts to secure productivity improvements through new agreements on working practices continued to be made, even though there was little evidence of any effect on productivity. The attempts continued to be made because they indicated that managers were doing something: they were a way of making statements both within management and to the workers about the control of work.

HRM has been important symbolically in several respects: establishing the credentials of personnel managers as active parties in the management team, and not mere 'fire fighters' engaged in handling disputes and collective bargaining; developing a wider language within management as to how to regulate labour; and saying to workers that something new is going on. The concrete results may have been small: the limited take-up of advanced HRM techniques; continued reliance on old forms of labour discipline; and little evidence of increased commitment on the part of workers. But the language of HRM has been an important symbol in persuading managers that they can make changes in systems of regulation. This very belief may have had unintended effects, notably a tendency to make frequent changes and to do so without much if any prior consultation, so that many organizations have seemed to be in a permanent state of flux. But its significance cannot be denied.

A key issue regarding managerial authority is, to use a concept introduced in chapter 8, the *articulation* between levels of management. Much of the 1980s was taken up with the debate on decentralization. Within industrial relations, the continuing decline of national collective bargaining analysed in chapter 5 and the growth of individualism discussed in chapter 11 together made the connection between worker and employer more direct. This devolution paralleled efforts in business strategy to reduce bureaucracy and increase the freedom of subsidiaries, often by making their managers responsible in profit and loss terms. Do such developments mean that subordinates' genuine autonomy from corporate control has increased?

Evidence suggests that in many respects such control has remained present, or even increased in intensity. Surveys discussed in chapter 4 indicate the substantial degree to which corporate head offices issue instructions or guidelines to subsidiaries. Head offices are also heavily involved in setting the parameters within which subsidiaries work, even when they are formally decentralized. For example, the Second Company Level Industrial Relations Survey of 1992 found that, in companies where pay bargaining took place at a level below the whole company, two-thirds of head offices were involved in the negotiations (Marginson et al. 1993). The survey also revealed an extensive role for financial control systems. Almost universally, payroll budgets were specifically identified, suggesting the importance of making pay costs visible and open to control. Almost half the firms set budgetary targets for unit labour costs, and very few allowed business unit managers to exceed payroll budgets. In almost half of companies, the negotiation of payroll budgets between subsidiaries and head offices resulted in a change in the budget. Financial control was thus very tight.

An image of autonomy is also inappropriate in relation to the links between the individual worker and the firm. Decentralized systems give a certain freedom to act but also impose clear responsibilities. Payment systems based on performance or merit call for the assessment of individuals against formal criteria. As chapter 11 shows, many such systems have meant in practice an assertion of managerial authority, for it is difficult for individuals to challenge the criteria applied or the fairness with which they are used in each case. In short, market or market-like pressures to perform have become common, but they mean, not the development of independent entrepreneurs, but a more tightly regulated regime within companies.

Unions and workers

Trade unions, it is generally agreed, have been much more passive actors than the state or employers. They have found it difficult to challenge the changes taking place around them. With few exceptions, they have also been unable to identify a distinctive role for collective representation within new patterns of work organization. For example, as chapter 12 shows, quality circles or briefing groups could be set up with union involvement in their planning and execution, but in practice managements have either ignored unions or taken them along as junior partners whose contribution is seen as secondary. The reasons for this state of affairs are rooted in the basis of British unions' bargaining power. As chapters 6 and 7 show, unions were effective in dealing with immediate shopfloor issues, but this depended on favourable economic conditions and managerial toleration (or, more commonly, the abdication of responsibility by managements). When these circumstances changed, unions lacked the organization and tradition to play a strong role as constructive critics of managerial initiatives. Some writers, drawing on the German example, speak of 'productivity coalitions': cooperative groupings of unions and managements at local level which work together to manage workplace change (Turner 1991). There is little evidence of the development of such coalitions in Britain.

In response to a weakened role in bargaining, unions have implemented internal changes. The most dramatic has been a series of mergers, but at least as significant has been a centralization of financial authority within many unions, together with closer control of the use of industrial action. Unions have also been required to alter procedures for electing officials. Articulation of levels within individual unions has thus increased. Articulation between unions and employers directly through collective bargaining and indirectly through national tripartite bodies has decreased.

The effects of these changes on workers have embraced several components, which have impinged differently on different groups. For some, the frequently remarked tendency for real wages to rise meant improved living standards. But, as chapters 3 and 18 underline, this average picture conceals important variations. For other groups, there was experience of unemployment, often on a longterm basis, while the growing inequality of earnings left those at the bottom of the labour market outside the picture of prosperity. Chapter 15 points to continuing discrimination and disadvantage in the labour market.

Looking within the workplace, a distinction between backwardlooking and forward-looking agendas is important. On the former, there is no doubt that many of the traditional demarcations and 'restrictive practices' of the British shopfloor have been removed. This has involved a combination of structural change (fewer workers work in sectors like shipbuilding or the docks where the practices flourished); technical change (new technology has eroded old distinctions and ways of working, dock mechanization again being a clear case); and managerial efforts to re-establish authority. Although it is possible to argue that many of the practices were not as restrictive as they seemed and that they reflected managerial weakness as much as worker militancy, it is also true that they have not really been mourned and that they had their really restrictive side.

But removing a few constraints, which only operated in particular sectors, is not the same as a positive move forward. As chapters 11 and 16 indicate, there have been some clear trends towards a worsening of terms and conditions and an intensification of work effort. Such trends have not been universal in extent or uniform in their effects. To return to the issue of variation raised above, three points can be made. First, market pressures have varied in their intensity. As chapter 16 illustrates, some privatized firms such as gas retained a more dominant position than others and were accordingly able to adopt a less drastic approach to industrial relations than were others. Second, managerial responses have differed, as chapters 4, 11 and 19 variously illustrate. Third, the ability of workers and shop stewards to shape developments has also varied. Chapter 12 highlighted several conditions which promote a cooperative approach to workplace change. They include an existing well-organized representative structure and a willingness by management to use this structure to negotiate change.

The Re-regulation of Labour

How have these various developments come together? In many ways, articulation within organizations has increased: firms have strengthened their financial reporting systems and have been able to coordinate pay deals even with decentralized bargaining; unions have centralized financial control while also making the calling of industrial action a more considered decision than it was in the past. But articulation between them has been reduced, in two ways. First, the peak organizations of employers and unions, the CBI and TUC, have even less power over their members than they did in the 1970s. They do not aggregate the interests of their constituents into an overall policy. Second, links between the organizations of capital and labour have weakened, most notably through the collapse of corporatist institutions at national level but also with the reduced role of unions within the enterprise. This, again, reflects the development of market-like assumptions, with each organization reacting to events and with overarching regulatory frameworks being eschewed.

Where have these developments been moving? Is there an alternative model to that of proceduralism and collective bargaining? The absence of an HRM revolution has led many observers to argue that there is not: in Sisson's (1993) terms, the lack of any coherent alternative model, in particular its absence in the non-union sector, has led to 'Bleak House'. Two developments to this conclusion are required. First, as foregoing chapters have repeatedly stressed, the 1970s were far more differentiated than one model can cover: collective bargaining was never universal, and where it occurred it had a wide range of forms, as the varying role played by shop stewards illustrates most strongly. Second, Bleak House does not mean that there is no dynamic to the system. The present argument is that the recomposition of managerial authority, involving market-related pressures and internal reorganization, is the underlying feature of change. This recomposition necessarily takes different forms in different circumstances. It is not a matter of distinct new models but of the ways in which this recomposition interacts with pressures from elsewhere in the firm, from the state, and from the economic environment.

A popular model in Britain and North America draws from the example of Germany in particular (Turner 1991) to argue that recomposition can be attained through a policy based on trust and commitment. This is based on an integrated approach at all levels of the firm which includes the active involvement of unions in all aspects of change. One might ask why, if the benefits in terms of improved working relationships and thence in productivity are so clear, firms do not adopt this route. One reason is that the evidence of benefits remains patchy (Katz and Keefe 1992). A second is that benefits may flow only in the long term, and thus may be hard to realize in an environment driven by short-term pressures. Third, various conditions need to be in place for them to appear. For example, as chapter 17 shows, the British training regime has made it hard for firms to develop a high-skill strategy even if they want to do so. And chapter 3 demonstrates the openness of the British economy to pressures from the world economy and underlines the failure of models of 'flexible specialization' to acknowledge this fact when alternatives are being discussed.

There are circumstances in Britain under which such a strategy could develop. But these are likely to be rather special conditions, depending on certain market niches and employer and union policies. The preference of the state for market-led solutions is a particular constraint. It should be stressed, moreover, that the German model rests on a statutory requirement to have certain institutions, notably works councils. In the absence of such a requirement, even German employers may not have pursued the cooperative model of change which characterized their approach up to the early 1990s. Britain and the United States offer regimes in which employers' choices are less constrained and in which joint management–union approaches to restructuring are unlikely. As Wells (1993) shows, many of the celebrated American experiments have tended to decay and to be replaced by a more straightforward policy of managerial control.

The prospects for the immediate future are for a continuation of trends observable up to the early 1990s. Industrial relations systems can change direction at certain key junctures, as the US case shows clearly with the rapid implementation of the 'New Deal system', which gave unions substantial legal protection for the first time, in the 1930s and its dismantling in the 1970s. In Britain, turning points have been less dramatic: as chapter 2 shows, apparent shifts have reflected major continuities with the past. But one time of change was the late 1970s and early 1980s, when the post-war consensus first unravelled and was then summarily dismissed by Thatcherism. This period put Britain on a market-led path which in some ways strengthened the pre-existing tendencies of voluntarism. A different approach was conceivable, with workers' alternative plans and an Alternative Economic Strategy receiving much interest in labour circles though proving powerless in the face of a very different Conservative agenda. The 1990s offer less choice. The preferences of employers as well as the Conservative Party for a market-led system are clear, and the ways in which Britain is located in the world economy would be hard to change. The greatest source of change would be the combination of a Labour government and a European Commission keen to introduce European works councils and legislation in areas such as hours of work. Efforts would be made to promote workers' rights and to develop a more interventionist approach to training, and there has been strong commitment to a statutory minimum wage. But there would remain the underlying issues of managing a world of labour relations in which there is disarticulation between parties, in which articulation within them is around the principles of market pressures and meeting individual targets rather than longer-term coordination, and in which the problems of job generation in the context of international competition and demands for labour-market flexibility would loom large. The means of managing this world may change, perhaps considerably, but the implantation of markets and managerialism suggests that a fundamental shift of emphasis would be hard to secure.

References

Ahlstrand, B. 1990: *The Quest for Productivity*. Cambridge: Cambridge University Press.

Barley, S. R. and Kunda, G. 1992: Design and Devotion. *Administrative Science Quarterly*, 37, 3, 363–99.

Blyton, P. and Turnbull, P. (eds) 1992: *Reassessing Human Resource Management*. London: Sage.

Edwards, P. K. and Whitston, C. 1993. *Attending to Work*. Oxford: Blackwell.

Friedman, A. L. 1977: *Industry and Labour*. London: Macmillan.

Friedman, A. L. 1990: Managerial Strategies, Activities, Techniques and Technologies. In D. Knights and H. Willmott (eds), *Labour Process Theory*. London: Macmillan.

Katz, H. C. and Keefe, J. H. 1992: Collective Bargaining and Industrial Relations Outcomes. In D. Lewin, O. S. Mitchell and P. D. Sherer (eds), *Research Frontiers in Industrial Relations and Human Resources*. Madison: Industrial Relations Research Association.

Marginson, P., Armstrong, P., Edwards, P. and Purcell, J. with Hubbard, N. 1993: *The Control of Industrial Relations in Large Companies: An Initial Analysis of the Second Company Level Industrial Relations Survey*. Warwick Papers in Industrial Relations, 45. Coventry: Industrial Relations Research Unit.

Marginson, P., Olson, R. and Tailby, S. 1994: *The Eclecticism of Managerial Policy towards Labour Regulation*. Warwick Papers in Industrial Relations, 47. Coventry: Industrial Relations Research Unit.

Purcell, J. and Sisson, K. 1983: Strategies and Practice in the Management of Industrial Relations. In G. S. Bain (ed.), *Industrial Relations in Britain*. Oxford: Blackwell.

Sisson, K. 1993: In Search of HRM. *British Journal of Industrial Relations*, 31, 2, 201–10.

Storey, J. 1992: *Developments in the Management of Human Resources*. Oxford: Blackwell.

Turner, L. 1991: *Democracy at Work*. Ithaca: Cornell University Press.

Wells, D. F. 1993: Are Strong Unions Compatible with the New Model of Human Resource Management? *Relations Industrielles*, 48, 1, 56–85.

Index

Note: References in **bold** are to figures and tables.